Italy and the East Roman World in the Medieval Mediterranean

Italy and the East Roman World in the Medieval Mediterranean addresses the understudied topic of the Italian peninsula's relationship to the continuation of the Roman Empire in the East, across the early and central Middle Ages.

The East Roman world, commonly known by the ahistorical term "Byzantium", is generally imagined as an Eastern Mediterranean empire, with Italy part of the medieval "West". Across 18 individually authored chapters, an introduction and conclusion, this volume makes a different case: for an East Roman world of which Italy forms a crucial part, and an Italian peninsula which is inextricably connected to—and, indeed, includes—regions ruled from Constantinople. Celebrating a scholar whose work has led this field over several decades, Thomas S. Brown, the chapters focus on the general themes of empire, cities and elites, and explore these from the angles of sources and historiography, archaeology, social, political, and economic history, and more besides. With contributions from established and early career scholars, elucidating particular issues of scholarship as well as general historical developments, the volume provides both immediate contributions and opens space for a new generation of readers and scholars to a growing field.

Thomas J. MacMaster is teaching at Morehouse College, Georgia. His research focusses on the slave trade and human trafficking in the early medieval Mediterranean, the topic of his forthcoming monograph *Slavery and the Making of the Medieval World*. He has also published more generally on the transition from late antiquity to the early Middle Ages.

Nicholas S.M. Matheou is programme manager at the Armenian Institute, London. His research focusses on the social, political and economic history of the medieval Middle East and Mediterranean. He has published on East Roman political thought, has a forthcoming study and translation of an eleventh-century Armenian historian and his current research project focusses on the medieval city of Ani.

Birmingham Byzantine and Ottoman Studies

General Editors
Leslie Brubaker
Rhoads Murphey
John Haldon

Birmingham Byzantine and Ottoman Studies is devoted to the history, culture and archaeology of the Byzantine and Ottoman worlds of the East Mediterranean region from the fifth to the twentieth century. It provides a forum for the publication of research completed by scholars from the Centre for Byzantine, Ottoman and Modern Greek Studies at the University of Birmingham, and those with similar research interests.

Iconophilia
Politics, Religion, Preaching and the Use of Images in Rome, c.680–880
Francesca Dell'Acqua

Well-Preserved Boundaries
Faith and Co-Existence in the Late Ottoman Empire
Gülen Göktürk

An Ottoman Era Town in the Balkans
The Case Study of Kavala
Velika Ivkovska

Italy and the East Roman World in the Medieval Mediterranean
Empire, Cities and Elites 476–1204
Edited by Thomas J. MacMaster and Nicholas S.M. Matheou

Centre for Byzantine, Ottoman and Modern Greek Studies
University of Birmingham

For a full list of titles in this series, please visit https://www.routledge.com/series/BBOS

Italy and the East Roman World in the Medieval Mediterranean

Empire, Cities and Elites 476–1204

Papers in Honour of Thomas S. Brown

Edited by
Thomas J. MacMaster and Nicholas S.M. Matheou

Routledge
Taylor & Francis Group
LONDON AND NEW YORK

First published 2021
by Routledge
2 Park Square, Milton Park, Abingdon, Oxon OX14 4RN

and by Routledge
605 Third Avenue, New York, NY 10158

Routledge is an imprint of the Taylor & Francis Group, an informa business

British Library Cataloguing-in-Publication Data
A catalogue record for this book is available from the British Library

Library of Congress Cataloging-in-Publication Data
Names: MacMaster, Thomas J., 1971- editor, author. | Matheou, Nicholas S. M., editor, author. | Brown, T. S., honouree.
Title: Italy and the East Roman world in the medieval Mediterranean : empire, cities and elites 476-1204 : papers in honour of Thomas S. Brown / edited by Thomas J. MacMaster and Nicholas S.M. Matheou.
Description: New York : Routledge, 2021. |
Series: Birmingham Byzantine and Ottoman studies ; volume 30 |
Includes bibliographical references and index. |
Subjects: LCSH: Italy--History--476-1268. | Italy--Civilization--476-1268. | Byzantine Empire--History--527-1081. | Mediterranean Region--History--476-1517. | Civilization, Medieval.
Classification: LCC DG503 .I79 2021 | DDC 945/.02--dc23
LC record available at https://lccn.loc.gov/2021007437

ISBN: 978-1-138-09131-3 (hbk)
ISBN: 978-1-032-05387-5 (pbk)
ISBN: 978-1-315-10809-4 (ebk)

Typeset in Times
by MPS Limited, Dehradun

Birmingham Byzantine and Ottoman Studies Volume 30

For Tom: our inspiration, teacher, colleague and friend.

Contents

Figures

Contributors

Michael Angold is Professor Emeritus of Byzantine History at the University of Edinburgh. He is currently working on the sermons of the Patriarch Germanos II (1223–1240).

Ross Balzaretti is Professor of Italian History at the University of Nottingham. His recent publications include *Dark Age Liguria: Regional Identity and Local Power, c.400–1020* (2013) and *The Lands of Saint Ambrose: Monks and Society in Early Medieval Milan* (2019). He is currently finishing a new translation of Paul the Deacon's "History of the Lombards" and associated texts to be published as *North Italian Histories 600–900 AD*.

Alessandro Bazzocchi holds a degree in Papyrology, Ph.D. in Roman history, and is an expert on the subject of Modern history, a councillor of the Ravenna Society of Studies, and member of the editorial staff of the scientific journal *Ravenna Studie Ricerce*.

Francesco Borri worked for many years at the Institut für Mittelalterforschung of the Österreichische Akademie der Wissenschaften in Vienna, before joining the Ca' Foscari University of Venice, where he teaches medieval history. His research focusses on the early Middle Ages, aristocratic identities, paganism, and navigation. Among his most recent works: *Alboino: frammenti di un racconto (VI–XI s.)* (2016); "A Placid Island: H.P. Lovecraft's Ibid", *Lovecraft Annual*, 18 (2018), pp. 105–135 and *I Longobardi a Venezia: scritti per Stefano Gasparri*, HAMA, 40 (2020), which he edited together with Irene Barbiera and Annamaria Pazienza.

Enrico Cirelli is assistant professor in Archaeology of medieval Europe at the Department of History and Civilizations, Alma Mater Studiorum—University of Bologna. His main research areas cover late roman and medieval urbanism, fortified settlements and archaeology of productions and material culture. He directs archaeological excavations and surveys in Italy and Croatia, and participates in other international research project in Spain, Albania, Palestine, Jordan, Libya, Tunisia, and Algeria. His book *Ravenna: archeologia di una città* won the Ottone d'Assia and Riccardo Francovich prize (2008).

Roger Collins has held teaching and research posts at the universities of Liverpool, Bristol, and Edinburgh, and has been an Honorary Fellow in the School of History, Classics and Archaeology at the University of Edinburgh since 1998. He has published widely on early medieval Iberia and the Frankish world, and is currently researching for a monograph titled *Eurasia Transformed, 200–1000*.

Brian Croke is an Honorary Associate at the University of Sydney, with a long record of published research on Roman and Byzantine history and historiography, and on modern historiography. He has books forthcoming on *Emperors in Context: Theodosius to Justinian*, *Reading, Writing and Interpreting History c.250–c.650* and *Justinian*. From 1979 to 2017 he enjoyed a career in Catholic education, and Australian education, for which he was honoured by church, state, and the education profession.

James Crow is Professor of Classical Archaeology at the University of Edinburgh, his research focusses on the archaeology of settlement and frontiers. Over 30 years his fieldwork and studies have ranged from Hadrian's Wall in Britain to the Eastern Mediterranean in particular Greece and Turkey from Roman to later medieval times. Recently he has focussed on Byzantine urban and landscape archaeology especially the water supply of Constantinople and on the coastal regions of the Black Sea and the Aegean. He is currently preparing a monograph on his research on the Anastasian Wall outside Istanbul.

Deborah M. Deliyannis is Professor of History at Indiana University. In addition to publishing an edition and English translation of Agnellus of Ravenna's *Liber pontificalis ecclesiae Ravennatis*, she has published *Ravenna in Late Antiquity*, and is a co-author of *Fifty Early Medieval Things: Materials of Culture in Late Antiquity and the Early Middle Ages*.

Eduardo Fabbro received his Ph.D. from the University of Toronto in 2015 and held a Mellon Postdoctoral Scholarship at McGill. He specialized in early medieval Italy, military history, and the work of eighth-century historian Paul the Deacon. He is currently a lecturer at Trent University.

John Haldon is Shelby Cullom Davis'30 Professor of European History Emeritus at Princeton University. He is currently also Director of the Princeton *Climate Change and History Research Initiative* (https://cchri.princeton.edu/) and Executive Director of the *Program in Medieval Studies Environmental History Lab*. His research focusses on the history of the medieval Eastern Roman (Byzantine) empire, in particular in the period from the seventh to the twelfth centuries; on state systems and structures across the European and Islamic worlds from late ancient to early modern times; on the impact of environmental stress on societal resilience in pre-modern social systems; and on the production, distribution, and consumption of resources in the late ancient and medieval world.

Cristina La Rocca is full professor of medieval history at the University of Padua. Her research interests cover various aspects of the early Middle Ages, generally focussed on the Italian case in relation to the broader European context. She has also examined the problem of the city in the early Middle Ages, from a social, topographical and political point of view, and the problem of the "ethnic" interpretation of early medieval burials in nineteenth-century Italian research, from a historiographical point of view. Cristina is the author of a series of works on early medieval wills and on the relationships between genders and the structure of kinship.

Nicole Lopez-Jantzen is an Associate Professor of History at CUNY Borough of Manhattan Community College, where she teaches courses on pre-modern Mediterranean, modern European, and women's history. She has also taught courses on medieval history and early Christianity at Drew University, John Jay College, Fordham University and Queensborough Community College. Dr. Lopez-Jantzen received her doctorate in history from Fordham University in 2012, where she analysed the struggle over Ravenna as part of a larger conflict over authority in the post-Roman West. Her recent research has focussed on race, gender, and sexuality in early medieval Italy. In addition to a forthcoming article on sexuality, her article "Between Empires: Race and Ethnicity in the Early Middle Ages" was recently published in *Literature Compass,* 16.9–10 (2019). She is also the co-chair of BMCC's Women's HerStory Month Committee and on the board of the Society for Medieval Feminist Scholarship.

Thomas J. MacMaster was the last of Tom Brown's Ph.D. advisees to receive his doctorate from the University of Edinburgh. His thesis, "The Transformative impact of the slave trade on the Roman World, 580–720" (2016), serves as the basis of his forthcoming monograph *Slavery and the Making of the Medieval World.* He is currently working on it and the Bloomsbury Cultural History of Slavery and Human-Trafficking in the Pre-Modern World. MacMaster had previously worked under Tom Brown for his 2011 MSc in First Millennium Studies. He looks to Brown as a model for combining scholarship and both academic and pastoral guidance in his own teaching now that he has returned to Georgia.

Nicholas S.M. Matheou began his academic journey as an undergraduate studying under Tom at the University of Edinburgh, and is currently Past & Present Research Fellow at the Institute of Historical Research, School of Advanced Study, University of London. His research focusses on the social, political, and economic history of medieval Anatolia, Upper Mesopotamia and Caucasia; his current research project is titled: *"The Fate of Unjust Cities": Commercial Capitalism, Global History & the Abandoned City of Ani, 900–1400*.

Edward M. Schoolman teaches at the University of Nevada, Reno, where he focusses on the late antique and early medieval Mediterranean. He published a monograph, *Rediscovering Sainthood in Italy: Hagiography and the Late Antique Past in Medieval Ravenna*, in 2016, and is working on new book project on Greek identity; as part of an interdisciplinary team, he has begun to explore the interconnections between history and ecology in Italy.

Patricia Skinner held a Personal Chair in History at Swansea University. Tom Brown's Gentlemen and Officers inspired many of the early pathways that she took in her research career. Her book, *Medieval Amalfi and its Diaspora* (2014) owes much to his inspiring work.

Vera von Falkenhausen is professor emerita of Byzantine History at the Università di Roma-Tor Vergata. She taught at the universities of Pisa, Potenza, and Chieti.

Bryan Ward-Perkins is Emeritus Professor of Late Antique History at the University of Oxford, where he taught from 1982 to 2019. In 2005 he published *The Fall of Rome and the End of Civilization*, a wide-ranging essay arguing that the end of the empire in the West was much more disruptive than commonly depicted in recent scholarship. Since then he has directed two major research projects, both with freely available and searchable databases: *The Last Statues of Antiquity* (with Bert Smith), and *The Cult of Saints in Late Antiquity*.

Preface and acknowledgments

Trimming the preface to this book down to a few simple paragraphs has been far more of a challenge than it should be. This is not because it is difficult to find positive things to say about Tom Brown, whether as a scholar, an educator, or as a human being, rather, it is because it is hard not to say too much. As the present volume's editors began to discuss the idea of honouring Tom, first with a dedicated stream of sessions at the Leeds International Medieval Congress, and later with this volume, we were regularly met with effusive praise for Tom—if we had written all of it down to share here, this would be a very long piece indeed.

Certainly, it is a fairly straightforward task to point to Tom Brown's contribution to both academic and more popular studies of the early medieval world. Even without including his bibliography in this volume, many of the chapters presented clearly reflect that fact and show the esteem in which his work on Byzantine Italy is held by colleagues. Of course, that same bibliography also reflects the many other ways that he has become quietly ubiquitous in early medieval history. Important in this regard was Tom's central role in establishing the journal early medieval Europe, which for nearly three decades now has provided a key forum for the area's development into a thriving field of study—a dramatic contrast to the poor cousin it often seemed to other areas of the discipline in the early 1990s.

At the same time, Tom has also nurtured students at all levels, whether encouraging sub honours students to look deeper into the often neglected areas of the medieval world, both chronologically and regionally, or by helping to build new taught programmes. One of us, Nicholas, took every course Tom offered at an undergraduate level, taking his first steps in the study of medieval Southern Italy, the empire of New Rome, Armenians, and the wider Mediterranean in these tutorials and seminars. Long a centre for both Medieval Studies in general and Byzantine history in particular, Tom's courses ensured that the University of Edinburgh retained an almost unique breadth of coverage at both undergraduate and postgraduate levels, and his teaching provided continuity between a previous cohort of specialists and the current dynamic group teaching and researching this field in the "Athens of the North". Likewise, the other of us, Thomas MacMaster, from his first day as a postgraduate student at Edinburgh learned not just from Tom's immense knowledge or his seemingly endless bibliographies but also a great many practical and non-academic things.

It is probably on these last, non-academic aspects that Tom is most impressive. From the first academic conference Thomas attended as an Edinburgh student to the last, it seemed that someone would always share a personal anecdote not of his scholarship but, more often, tales of his kindness and compassion. For students who experienced personal difficulties, including one of us, Tom displayed greater concern and helpfulness than might be required or expected of someone in his position. His innate human warmth and pastoral care, combined with his careful scholarship and intellectual guidance, has set a model for many of what an academic should aspire towards. This is seen not least in the present editors' own collaboration, a product of Tom telling Thomas to look out for Nicholas at a graduate conference they were both attending, after the latter had left Edinburgh to complete postgraduate studies elsewhere.

On the other hand, we are aware that, despite the importance of his academic output, Tom regretted that the competing demands of teaching, administration and family health issues prevented him from publishing the full fruits of his research during his university career. However we know that Tom has already shown himself to be highly "research active" during retirement and we hope that the papers by friends and colleagues in this volume will inspire further published work in the fields which Tom loves, not least by Tom himself.

It is, then, with extreme pleasure that we have produced this volume in honour of Tom. He has given so much of himself to so many of us, whether as a teacher, mentor, colleague, peer, editor, collaborator, and, sometimes, critic, that it seems the very least that might be done in celebration of all that he has given so many.

Besides Tom, we would also like to thank all the contributors for their willingness to contribute, their patience over the project's completion, and the care they have taken in producing a stunning range of chapters that reflect the depth and breadth of Tom's influence and interests. Each contributor in turn would like to thank Tom for the various ways he has been a crucial part of their life and career, and some contributors have also included more specific thanks in their chapters. We would also like to thank John Smedley, our original series editor at Ashgate before this was taken over by Taylor & Francis, who played a crucial role in the early stages of the project. Likewise, we owe deep thanks to Michael Greenwood for ensuring the project's continuation, and helping bring it now to its completion. Finally, we want to thank the two anonymous reviewers for their diligence in making this volume a firm contribution to scholarship at the highest level, and so an even more fitting tribute to Tom. We are very proud of the result, and hope that it inspires future students and interested readers to immerse themselves in the study of Italy, the empire of New Rome, and the early medieval Mediterranean in all its diversity, just as Tom has for us.

Thomas J. MacMaster & Nicholas S.M. Matheou

Introduction: Italy and the East Roman World, 476–1204

Set in the middle of the Mediterranean, Italy has long had close links with all the shores of this sea—with the eastern Mediterranean, since the time when Aeneas (at least in myth) came from Troy and settled in Latium, and when Greek colonists established "Magna Graecia", founding most of the great cities of southern Italy, including Taranto, Syracuse, Catania and Naples. These links were just as strong at the end of Antiquity and into the early Middle Ages, the period covered by this book, though the direction of travel of people, goods and political power shifted markedly between the beginning of our period and its end.

In 476 the last Roman emperor in Italy was deposed and replaced by a king of Germanic descent, who formally acknowledged the overlordship of the *Augustus* ruling from Constantinople. In a bloody war instigated by the Emperor Justinian, which lasted from 535 until 554, his armies were able to translate this formal overlordship into real domination, and Italy became an outlying province of the Eastern Roman Empire (which, for convenience, is often termed the "Byzantine", although its rulers called it "Roman" right up to its fall in 1453). As we will see from the papers in this volume, in this early period the flow of people, goods and political control was very definitely from East to West, from a dominant Byzantine eastern Mediterranean into Italy. However, by the end of our period, things had changed dramatically: in 1071 the last East Roman stronghold in Italy, Bari, fell to Norman adventurers, who then led aggressive campaigns from southern Italy into Greece. In 1204 came the culmination of this trend, when western "Crusaders", allied with a comparatively new maritime power, Venice, captured and sacked Constantinople itself and set up a "Latin" dynasty of emperors in the East Roman capital: spoils from Constantinople flowed into Venice (where they can still be seen in the Treasury and built into the exterior of S. Marco), while adventurers from Italy and elsewhere flocked eastwards in search of land and office—men like the Venetian Thomas Morosini, the first Latin Patriarch of Constantinople (the subject of Michael Angold's paper in this volume, Chapter 11).

By contrast, in the earlier centuries of our period it was the East Roman empire that was dominant over much of Italy, and, with that domination, the flow of officials, soldiers and others was from East to West, a flow which increased for a different reason in the seventh and eighth centuries, when refugees from the Arab invasions of the Near East, Egypt and North Africa arrived in substantial numbers in Italy: for a considerable period in these centuries, Greek-speaking Easterners even dominated the papacy in Rome. Much of Italy from Rome southwards was bilingual in Greek and Latin, or even primarily Greek speaking. Eastern immigrants, and the impact they had, are the subject of several papers in this volume. Jim Crow (in Chapter 5) tells the story of one of the highest-ranking East Roman officials to be sent to Italy: Smaragdus, who twice served as governor, or "exarch", restored the aqueduct of Ravenna and in 608 dedicated a statue to the emperor Phocas in Rome's forum; while in Chapter 14 Nicholas Matheou sets out the evidence for a substantial and influential group of immigrants in southern Italy: the Armenians of "Longobardia" (modern Puglia), who played a prominent role in the politics of Bari from the late ninth century until the Norman capture of the city. The cultural impact of such settlers from the Eastern Mediterranean was considerable: in Taranto, as Vera von Falkenhausen shows in Chapter 18, Greek liturgy, language and naming-practices were dominant in the medieval city, in part a legacy from the pre-

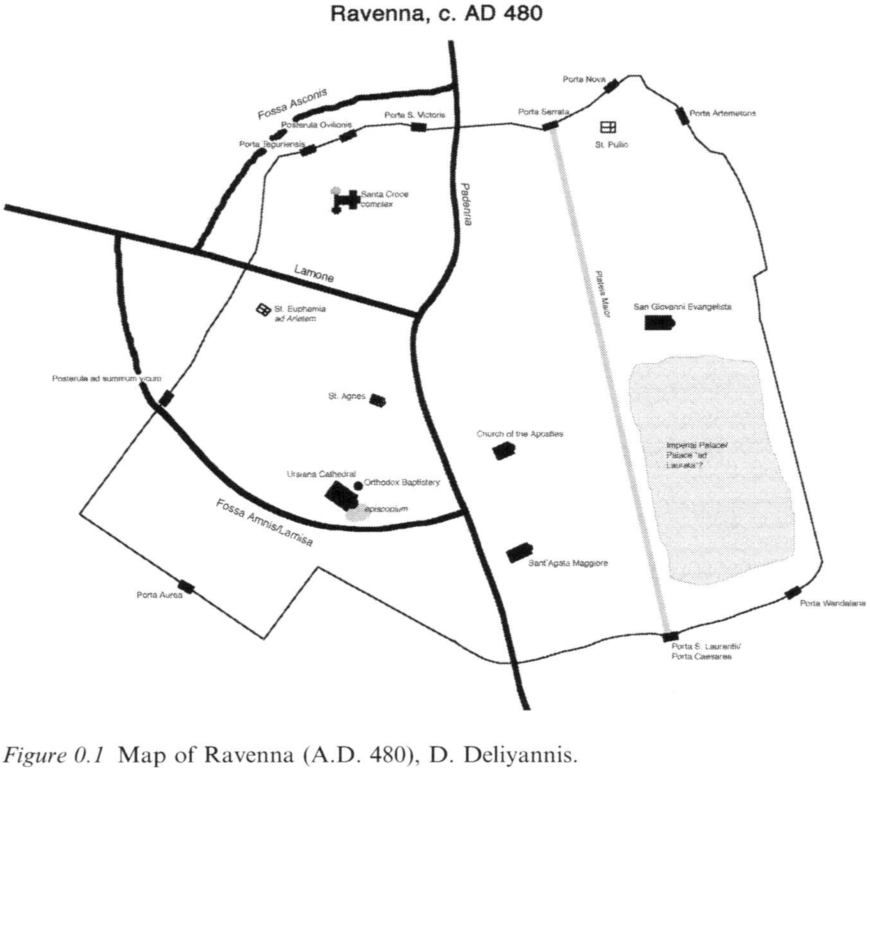

Figure 0.1 Map of Ravenna (A.D. 480), D. Deliyannis.

Roman Greek colonisers, but also the result of centuries of East Roman rule. Until the thirteenth century, the city of Taranto was more Greek than Latin, and so in some ways more closely aligned with the eastern Mediterranean than it was with the North and West.

Goods, as well as people and culture, travelled to Italy in quantity from the eastern Mediterranean, particularly during the fifth and sixth centuries, as shown by the excavations over the last two decades at Ravenna's port of Classe, which have uncovered large quantities of wine and oil amphorae from Asia Minor and the Near East and which are at the heart of Enrico Cirelli's paper (Chapter 9); this trade continued into the eighth and ninth centuries, though on a reduced scale and now following different routes, for instance through Comacchio on the River Po. What is striking from the archaeological evidence is the dominance of the East when it came to sophisticated goods: quality agricultural products, quality manufactured goods, and quality building materials (like the marble columns and liturgical fittings of Ravenna's famous churches) were all Eastern in origin. The reciprocal trade from Italy was in raw materials, of which the best documented, and the saddest, was the trade in slaves, which is the subject of Thomas MacMaster's paper (Chapter 16); it was on this trade that much of the early wealth of Venice and Amalfi was based. The slow growth of Western trading settlements in the eighth, ninth and tenth centuries, is often lauded as the origin of West European prosperity, but

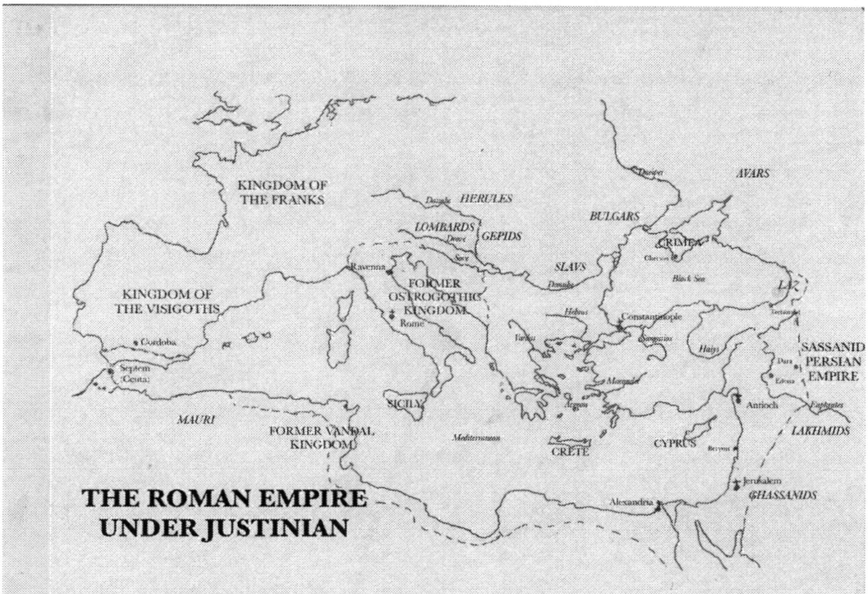

Figure 0.2 Map of the Eastern Roman Empire under Justinian I (A.D. 527–565), redrawn with the kind permission of M. Angold.

it is worth remembering that initially this prosperity was substantially based on human misery.

How the East Roman empire gradually lost control of Italy—between Justinian's final victory in 554, which put the entire peninsula, and its islands, under the rule of Constantinople, and the fall of Bari in 1071—is of course a long and extremely complex story, with several ups and downs in Byzantine power, but two major factors played a role. One was, quite simply, the impact of further invaders. The first of these were the Lombards, who entered Italy in 568, just fourteen years after Justinian's final victory, and rapidly took over much of the Po plain and much of central and southern Italy, though leaving Ravenna and Rome (and other cities, like Naples) in East Roman hands. Ross Balzaretti's paper in this volume (Chapter 17) examines the impact of Lombard conquest on Milan—an impact that was partly negative, causing the city's bishop to flee to Byzantine Genoa, but also positive, since early Lombard kings used Milan, which had been a major imperial residence in the fourth century, to enhance their status. In the very early seventh century, King Agilulf issued grants from the palace of Milan and used the city's Roman circus to proclaim the

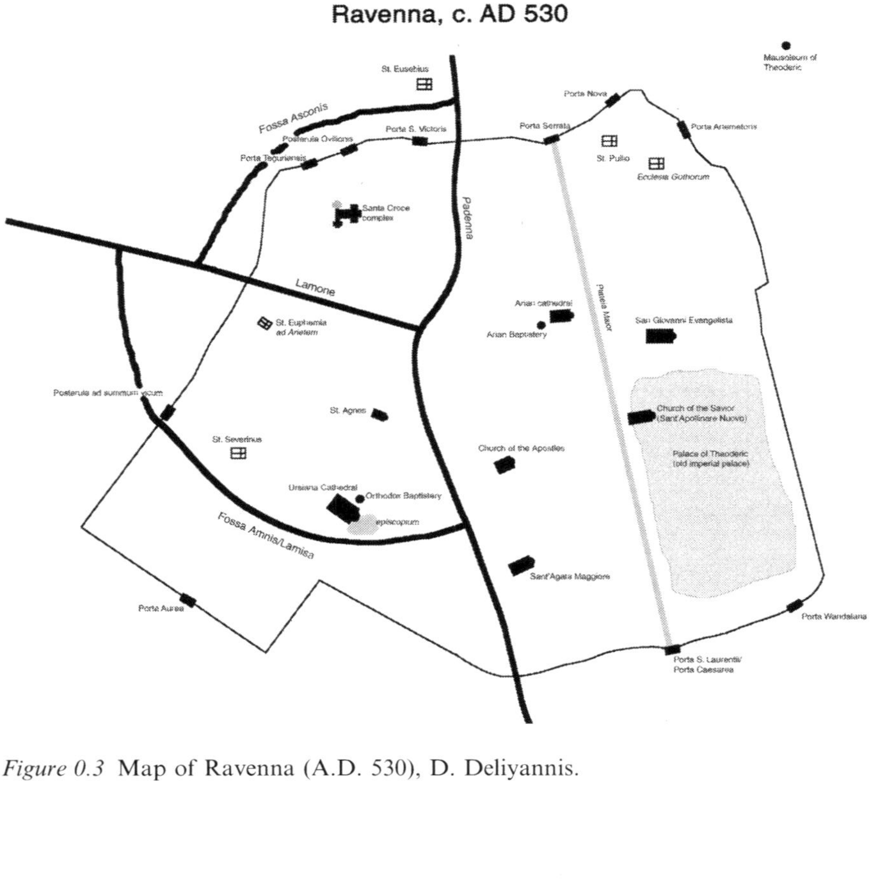

Figure 0.3 Map of Ravenna (A.D. 530), D. Deliyannis.

elevation of his son to joint rule. In doing this, he was explicitly asserting his own authority but also tacitly acknowledging the status of Constantinople by imitating the court ceremonial focussed on the hippodrome of the Byzantine capital.

Despite frequent attempts to dislodge them, the East Romans never succeeded in making much headway against the Lombards; rather, territorial gains tended to be in the opposite direction. In 751 even Ravenna fell to the Lombards, confining Byzantine power at the head of the Adriatic to nominal control of some maritime cities like Venice, and over the Istrian peninsula, though this too was lost at the end of the century to the Franks (as explained in Francesco Borri's paper, Chapter 13). With its fall to the Lombards, Ravenna's political importance through the sixth to the eighth century, as a bridgehead of eastern power in Italy, disappeared for ever, though in both ideology and reality it remained an important city and symbol, contested by Lombards, Franks, an emerging papal monarchy and the archbishops of the city itself (as explored by Nicole Jantzen-Lopez in Chapter 10).

In thinking about the difficult relations between Lombards and East Romans, we instinctively tend to assume that the latter were the more

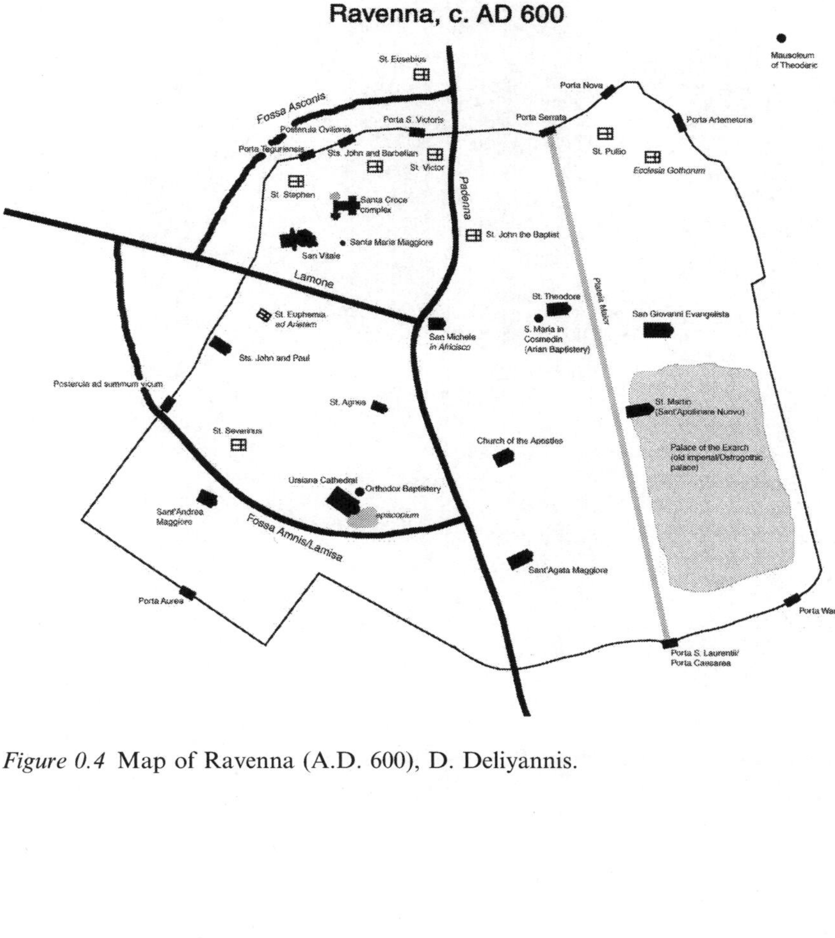

Figure 0.4 Map of Ravenna (A.D. 600), D. Deliyannis.

legitimate and "civilised", because of their direct political descent from the Roman Empire. But, as Eduardo Fabbro's chapter (Chapter 4) makes clear, the Lombard perspective, as exemplified by Paul the Deacon's *History*, was very different—here the Byzantines are presented as the treacherous parties

Figure 0.5 Map of eighth-century Italy, redrawn with the kind permission of T.S. Brown.

in dealings between the two powers. In portraying them in this way, Paul played a part in promulgating the idea, prevalent today, that "Byzantine" can be used as an adjective to describe excessively complex, even deceitful, machinations.

In the late eighth and in the ninth centuries the political map of Italy changed dramatically: firstly, through Frankish invasion, destroying in 776 the Lombard kingdom of the North. This did not immediately impact greatly on East Roman power in Italy, since Ravenna and the exarchate had already fallen to the Lombards, and Constantinople's control was already essentially restricted to Sicily and the far South. But for Northern Italy the Frankish conquest, and the re-creation of a Western empire through Charlemagne's coronation in Rome on Christmas Day 800, definitively broke political links with the East, and established instead North European claims, and often effective control, over Northern and Central Italy. For the East Romans and their hold on Italy, much more significant and much more harmful was the Arab invasion of Sicily, which began in 827 and was largely completed in 902, when Taormina finally fell.

The second factor that gradually reduced East Roman power in Italy was subtler, slower and even more interesting than foreign invasion: the gradual erosion of Constantinople's control over much of Italy through the growth,

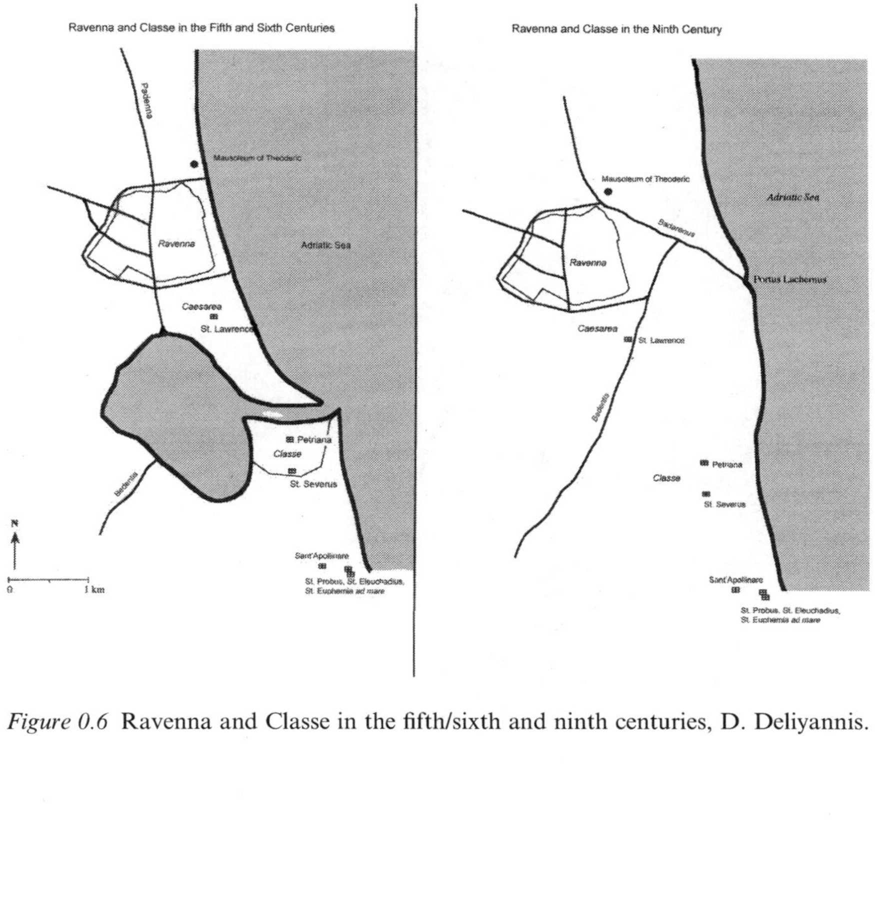

Figure 0.6 Ravenna and Classe in the fifth/sixth and ninth centuries, D. Deliyannis.

within areas of Byzantine control, of local autonomous powers. The most famous and enduring of these were the papal monarchy that asserted itself in the eighth century (and lasted until 1870) and the Venetian Republic with origins in approximately the same period (and finally destroyed by Napoleon in 1797). But these cases were not alone: several Byzantine cities of the South, including Naples and Amalfi, also became effectively independent powers through the eighth to tenth centuries (though here for a much shorter period, being absorbed into a strongly centralised Norman kingdom in the eleventh and twelfth centuries). In none of these cases is there evidence of overwhelming dissatisfaction with East Roman power, such as to lead the cities to suddenly throw off colonial shackles, in the way that African and Asian colonies revolted against European powers in the twentieth century. Rather, helped by dissatisfaction over tax burdens (and occasionally also over religious policy), these cities drifted into independence primarily because the emperor in Constantinople lacked the resources to maintain an effective military force in Italy, so they had to look to their own defence. Rome was an extreme, indeed unique, case of all power eventually flowing into the hands of its bishop, but as Edward Schoolman's chapter

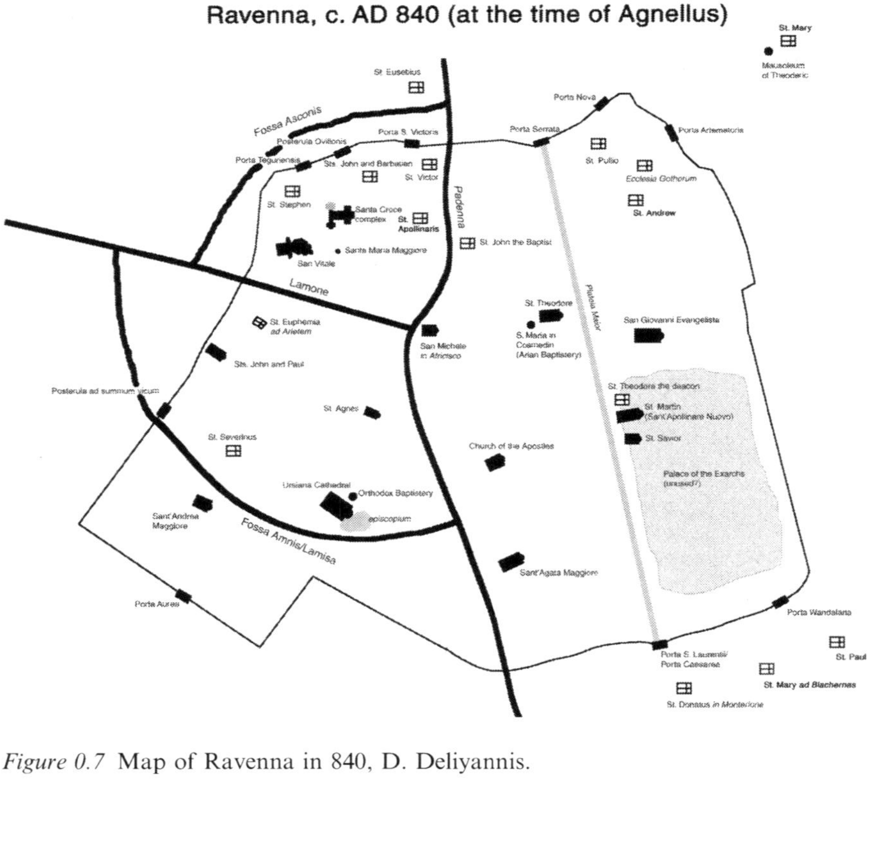

Figure 0.7 Map of Ravenna in 840, D. Deliyannis.

(Chapter 12) shows, an incremental rise in episcopal power can also be documented elsewhere, for instance in Ravenna and Naples. The ever-increasing power of the bishops, as their landed endowment grew through pious donations and as secular power lurched through a series of crises, was not an unequivocal gain, since engagement with worldly affairs often led to conflict with the high ideals of ecclesiastical office (for which see Patricia Skinner's Chapter 16).

Even in regions like Ravenna, where East Roman power remained relatively strong (until falling to invaders), society underwent radical change during this period. In particular, it moved from a typically "Roman" structure, with a full-time salaried army, and a landed aristocracy that never sullied itself with the business of war, to a world that was characteristically "medieval": where high-ranking military men acquired estates and merged with the local landed aristocracy, and where all land-owners (except churchmen) became trained in the arts of war. This transformation was the subject of a remarkable book by Tom Brown, the honorand of our volume, which (with a playful nod to Evelyn Waugh's *Officers and Gentlemen* of 1955) he entitled "Gentlemen and Officers" (British School at Rome 1984). The sub-title "Imperial Administration and Aristocratic Power in Byzantine Italy A.D. 554–800" was necessary to locate his subject matter in place and

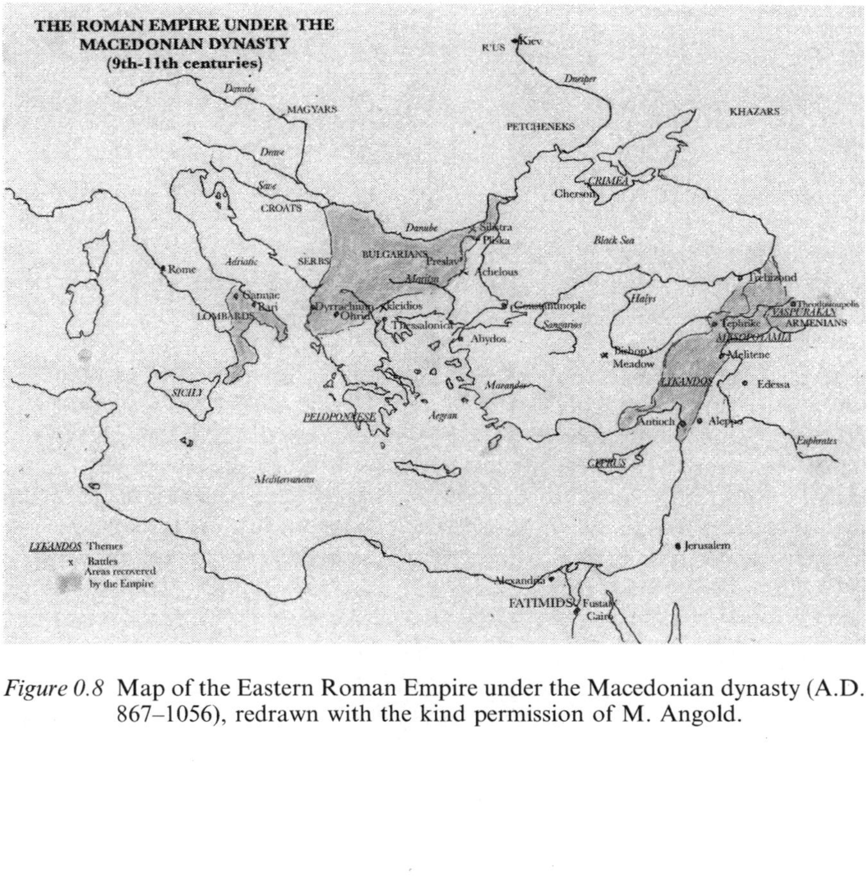

Figure 0.8 Map of the Eastern Roman Empire under the Macedonian dynasty (A.D. 867–1056), redrawn with the kind permission of M. Angold.

time, but its main title perfectly encapsulated his central theme: the merging into a single aristocracy of "Gentlemen" (in other words, land-owners) and "Officers" (in other words, high-ranking military men). This, as John Haldon's broad comparative essay makes clear (in Chapter 8), was a development that happened all over the Byzantine Empire, and was the single most important internal change of the sixth to eighth centuries.

But only in Ravenna can we track this momentous development in any detail, because only in Ravenna, through the remarkable survival of documents in the Archiepiscopal Archive, do we have a run of charters (on papyrus), recording the sale, exchange and lease of rural and urban properties, that is continuous from the sixth century onwards. Elsewhere in Western Europe there is no comparable collection before the eighth century (when charters start to become numerous from Lucca in Tuscany); furthermore, as the papers by Alessandro Bazzocchi and Deborah Deliyannis show (Chapters 6 and 7), the charter evidence of Ravenna is supplemented by a collection of surviving inscriptions, and a record of continuous building patronage, that are probably only exceeded by the evidence from contemporary Rome. In the Byzantine Eastern Mediterranean there is nothing remotely comparable to this level of survival of evidence until many centuries later. The only other area in the whole of Western Eurasia where early documents survive on the scale that they survive in Ravenna, is Egypt, where the dry conditions have ensured the recovery of thousands of papyri from the soil. But the evidence from Egypt, though considerably more extensive even than that of Ravenna, is fairly fragmentary, at least in general, and the documents are of a wide variety of types, making it extremely difficult to detect broad trends within them; furthermore the history of Egypt was radically shaken up by Muslim Arab invasion and settlement in the seventh century. Only in Ravenna can we examine the gradual transformation of late-antique society within a context of essential continuity.

But Ravenna's importance in historical study goes well beyond the exceptional quality and quantity of its evidence: as a city that was both "Italian" and "Byzantine", it played a pivotal role between Western Latin Europe and the Eastern Mediterranean, and its history can illuminate trends in both broad regions. For the East Roman Empire, the gradual militarisation of Ravenna's landed aristocracy and the "landing" of its military, offers uniquely detailed evidence that the emergence of an army rooted in the land (the essence of the "thematic system" throughout the empire), was a slow "bottom-up" development more than the result of decisions from on high. While for the Latin West, the same development, within a region that was always "Roman", shows that the militarisation of society (which occurred all over Western Europe) could happen without the spur of an influx of Germanic warriors. A western militarised aristocracy, and a Byzantine landed army, meet in Ravenna, and are found to be the same thing. It was Tom Brown who brought out this pivotal truth (Figure 0.1–0.8).

Part I

Sources and historiography

1 Cassiodorus and the reluctant *provinciales* of Dalmatia

In presenting both the efficiency of Gothic rulership and the usefulness of bureaucrats for conducting internal and external relationships, Cassiodorus—one of the most important figures of Gothic administration in sixth-century Italy—introduces in his *Variae* the political problem of dealing with the various peripheries of the Gothic kingdom. He shows how aware he was of the different characteristics and attitudes of local identities and élites, and of the different rhetorical discourses that were suitable to include them in the management and the administration of the kingdom as a whole entity. At the same time, in addressing the official correspondence from Ravenna, the centre of the kingdom, to functionaries and military officials settled in those peripheries, Cassiodorus is showing us both the main points of Gothic "correction" to local behaviours and the multiple definitions of the resistance to Gothic rule. Those peripheries were variable during time, including territories beyond Italy that were military conquered or annexed, particularly during the reign of Theodoric (493–526): to the west, a portion of Southern Gallia and the Visigothic kingdom; to the north, Raetia and Noricum, and, to the east, the Illyrian provinces of Pannonia, Savia and Dalmatia, from 508 including the city of Sirmio and therefore the control of Pannonia Sirmiensis. The acquisition of these territories was crucial in defining Theodoric's status as the most successful barbarian king in the West, and in legitimating Gothic power in the former territory of the Western Roman empire, but, at the same time, it was an ephemeral one that revealed the fragility of Gothic domination in these areas: after Theodoric death in 526 and the beginning of Justinian's campaigns in 537, all those territories were finally lost, leaving Gothic identity connected to Italy only. In transforming the official correspondence of the Gothic kings in his *Variae* around 540, Cassiodorus was therefore showing how difficult and how compelling it was for Gothic administration to deal with these different territories and how crucial bureaucracy was in organising and in settling local disorder and disputes, performing its patrimony of rhetorical abilities and administrative solutions.

This chapter will discuss the relevance and the characteristics of Dalmatia and its natural resources and élite in Cassiodorus *Variae,* showing how to dominate Dalmatia and a substantial part of the Illyricum was, at the beginning of the sixth century, a very important practical and symbolic issue that allowed—even for a short time—the definition of the Gothic rulers' special identity not only as military leaders but especially as keepers of justice and laws through its administrative officers. In the *Variae* the territory of Dalmatia was represented as a very problematic and slippery one, a land where the *provinciales* need protection, patronage and control. Detecting Dalmatia's identity in Cassiodorus' *Variae* seems particularly significant, for both the discussed intrinsic characteristics of this crucial sixth-century source and its significance for political communication and languages.[1]

The growing interest in the history of Dalmatia from both early medieval historians and archaeologists has substantially improved our knowledge of this crucial territory of the Late Roman Empire. The material and written evidence point out the special development of this region as a frontier between East and West, a land rich in natural resources and as a place where local lay and ecclesiastical élite were able to experiment the strength of their political support for military leaders and also for the independence of their local ecclesiastical institutions.[2] The jurisdictional and fiscal possession of Dalmatia, especially its coastal part, was a controversial issue: as Jonathan Arnold has recently pointed out, from at least the fifth century this province was contended between the Eastern part of the Roman Empire and the various barbarian leaders in the West, giving birth to an anomalous situation, where political and administrative control was *de facto* assigned to Ravenna, and so was included in the prefecture of Italy, although formally under East Roman sovereignty.[3] The date of late Roman inscriptions in Dalmatia, combining the *indictio* and the consuls' names in the West seems good evidence for the fact that Dalmatia considered itself being a part of the Western Empire.[4]

The control of Dalmatia was crucial for various reasons. First Dalmatia was an important military base for gaining both military and political control: disputed as it was between the two parts of the Empire, from the fifth century it became a territory where military leaders managed to shape their own careers and to organise the base for military support, as in the case of the *magister militum Dalmatiae*, subsequently emperor, Julius Nepos (454–481). The control over this province was therefore considered crucial to dominate the military and royal leadership in the West, as is shown by the continuous effort from the kings in Italy to include its territory under their rule: from Odovacer in 475, followed by Theodoric at the beginning of the sixth century until 535, when Justinian reconquered it to the Eastern Empire. The progress of Theodoric's power between the years 504–507 included in fact one of the few military campaigns promoted by the Gothic ruler and, although this war was conducted without any particular effort, it allowed Theodoric to increase the territory under his rulership in this area. The Illyricum campaign in fact allowed Theodoric to present himself as the protagonist of the most important reconstruction of the territory of the Western empire in the sixth century. In this perspective the control of the Illyricum, followed—after the battle of Vouillé (507)—by the control of Provence, were important tools to display the extent of Theodoric power in the West and to compete against the most powerful and rival barbarian king, Theodoric's brother in law, Clovis king of the Franks.

It is therefore interesting to show how Cassiodorus' *Variae* deals with these peripheries of Theodoric's kingdom, defining their own special character and shaping different attitudes and treatments of its dwellers. As an addition, I would also like to offer to Tom—who has dedicated so many illuminating pages to the theme of Gothic rule in Italy and to the cosmopolitan identity of their capital Ravenna—a little contribution on the particular identity of foreigners in Dalmatia and the didactic and institutional role Ravenna, as the capital of the kingdom, maintained to have towards them.

Both the institutional organisation and the territorial boundaries of Dalmatia in this period have been under scholarly scrutiny: under Gothic rule the province was part of the prefecture of Italy (together with Savia and Noricum Mediterraneum). In the *Variae* until 525/6 the province seems distinct from Savia, although under the government of one *comes*, under whom two civil administrators were acting separately: Epifanius in Dalmatia and Severinus in Savia (both 507/511). After Theodoric's death, in 526, Severinus was appointed to Dalmatia, with Count Osuin, suggesting a unification of the two provinces.[5]

As Stéphane Gioanni has recently stressed, the historical in-between position of Dalmatia was the base for the creation of a certain independence of local élites and local clergy, who were profiting of the distance from Ravenna, also at the level of episcopal power, to claim the power of electing their own representatives.[6] As later revealed by the correspondence of Gregory the Great at the end of the sixth century, local clergy in Dalmatia was trying to avoid the supervision of the church of Rome, as is shown by the conflict between Sabinianus, the bishop of Zadar, and Maximus the bishop of Salona in 597 and 598.[7]

The identity of Dalmatia was certainly connected to the military, to soldiers' capability to defend the surrounding territory, but also to its natural resources: Dalmatia was a rich land and its mineral resources of iron, gold and silver were well known since Marcus Aurelius' times, and their extraction and use was carefully organised by the Roman State:[8] in 507/508 Count Osuin was addressed by Theodoric in a letter where he is admonished to give weapons to the *Salonitani milites* so they could learn how to use them so "they could learn during peace, what they can perform in war".[9] This theme is frequent in Theodoric's letters on fortifications,[10] and the final section of this letter compares soldiers to young calves learning the art of fighting, and is perfectly coherent to the theme of the exercise of learning that must be done since the time of youth in order to become adults.[11] Notably the subject is used by Cassiodorus with increasing frequency after Theodoric's death and the accession to power of young Athalaric in 526.

Dalmatia is also presented at the centre of disorder and disobedience to Roman rule, and conversely as an exemplary region where every effort is made to perform Theodoric's right domination and his will of maintaining order in the name of the Roman law: Ianuarius, the bishop of Salona, was insistently asked by Theodoric to fulfil a debt he had with John who provided him with sixty large jars of oil but was not yet paid;[12] Epiphanius *vir spectabilis* is charged to arrange the petition of a widow for her goods to be settled;[13] in Savia, Fridibadus, probably a *comes*, was in charge in 507/511 for controlling the theft of animals, homicides, thieves and abuses that were oppressing the provincials, the *curiales* and the army;[14] in 526 the count Severinus was sent to Savia to investigate a case of tax evasion and to severely judge all those responsible. On this occasion a detailed list of the various ways this could be performed is presented, picturing the territory as an area of relatively unsubordinated behaviour towards the Gothic administration, largely diffused in different groups of people: local landowners who were oppressing their tenants, local agents who were subtracting the money from the public treasury, local officials who were imposing unjustified amount of taxes to local landholders and *antiqui barbari*—presumably barbarian soldiers settled in the area—who had married local wives and were reluctant to pay taxes for the lands they possessed.[15] Count Simeon was charged to collect the *siliqua* and to investigate on its evasion.[16] The aim of these controls were to export licit behaviour in the Provincia "because we are not looking for gain, but we wish instead to detect the uses of those who are under our rule".[17]

The discourse on Dalmatia became very important and acquired new meaning after Theodoric's death, experimenting with increasing forms of inclusion into the system and increasing forms of gratification. On the one hand, the support for Athalaric's access to royal power was explicitly asked from the Romans "settled in Italia and Dalmatia":[18] in Cassiodorus's hierarchical list they are in the fourth position, just after the emperor Justin, the Roman Senate and the inhabitants of Rome. On the other hand, the officials who were appointed there were of higher rank and well inserted into the network of the region, as in the case of the *illustris* Severinus and the *comes* Osuin,[19] nominated for the second time as governor of Dalmatia in 527, after 20 years from his previous charge.[20] This care for the Dalmatian territory, its resources and its inhabitants, and, on the other side, the necessity of dealing with irregular behaviour in respect to Gothic rules seems therefore a characteristic that Cassiodorus is stressing in presenting and selecting his letters dedicated to this area. In this context, it is interesting to add a new letter in the Dalmatian corpus in the *Variae*, a letter previously attributed to Ravenna,[21] *Variae XII*, 17, addressed to *Iohannes liquatarius Ravennatis* and written by Cassiodorus in the name of the young king Athalaricus. As the letter was inserted by Cassiodorus in the twelfth book of the *Variae*, who collected the letters written when he was acting as

Praetorian Praefect, its date can be defined quite precisely between 533 and 534.[22] The texts reads:

> King Atalaric to John collector of the *siliqua* of Ravenna
>
> Fortification of cities is everyone's certain hope, since foreign people learn in peacetime what they will actually have to fear in wartime. In fact, the population of individual cities is entirely composed by individuals of different origins. Who can tell which people will come to conflict?
>
> And for this reason everyone must be aware of what future enemies would not like to face. Consequently, according to our order you will take care to urge the owners to dig wide chasms of ditches near Mount Caprario and the places surrounding the walls, so that there a such abyss is opened as not to allow any entry. For what reason, o nefarious men, do you search for illegal access, you who are lawfully allowed to enter from the city gates? I do not know what you want to hide you who do not want to enter openly.
>
> Right conscience does not move away from public streets, it rejoices in conversing with travelers and when it joyfully entertains with different people it is not burdened by the boredom of fatigue.
>
> On the other hand, the desire not to be recognised is a friend of crime, and those who keep their path hidden reveal their conscience.
>
> Therefore the ancient tracks are to be brought back to collective use, so that travelers, while trying to save effort, do not have to risk their lives. In fact, it is rightly to be considered an enemy he who strives to violate the defenses of the city.[23]

The letter is addressed to *Iohannes liquatarius Ravennatis*, a public officer charged to collect the *siliquaticum*, here in its abbreviated form, the trade tax introduced by Valentinian III in 444 (1 siliqua or 1/24 per solidus) from both buyer and seller, a tax extended to all sales also of movable property.[24] The tax was applied mainly in Italy and the collection of it is mentioned frequently in Cassiodorus's *Variae* refererring to various Italian cities,[25] and otherwise only to Dalmatia only outside Italy.[26] In particular in *Variae* III, 25 and 26, the count Simeon "well known to us for his loyalty and his devotion" was charged in 510/511 to investigate the phenomenon of the evasion of this tribute in Dalmatia,[27] and to collect the *siliquaticum* for the first, second and third indiction, that is for the years 507–510.[28]

The general contents of the letter deal on the one hand with the reparation of the city wall of an unnamed city: the gaps are in fact used by traders to trespass and so avoid the city gates where the *siliquaticum* was collected; on the other, as a remedy to this abuse, they order the *possessores* (land holders)[29] to rebuild the ruined parts of the city walls and to excavate deep ditches alongside them, especially in the area of the *Caprarius* mountain. Also in Arles, in the *castellum* Verrucas and in Tridentina region,[30] local landlords were given the responsibility of organising and paying for the building and the maintenance of city walls, as stated in Valentinian III's novel X, 3, in 444.[31]

There are two principal reasons to attribute this letter to the context of the city of Salona and not to Ravenna. First a topographical and geographical one. From the letter, it is clear that the city in question is located next to a mountain, called Mons Caprarius: the tax evaders were in fact descending from it into town not trough the official road, but through unofficial paths. From this reason, the *possessores* are invited to dig deep ditches along the city walls. While, of course, no mountain is situated next to Ravenna, located as it is at Eastern end of the Po plain (the nearest modest hill being more than 80 kilometres to the West), at about ten kilometres to the North-West of Salona, the mountain Kozjac (ancient Latin oronim Mons Caprarius) (ca. 800 m.) is situated, and today it's connected to Salona through various pathways.[32] It is also very probable that Mons Caprarius was the ancient name of the mountain: oronims are generally considered by linguistic studies very stable names for natural features, although real interest for mountains was developed only in the late nineteenth century. In one of the first topographical reconstructions of the Roman city of Salona by Francesco Carrara in 1850, the name "Porta Capraria" was imagined for the city gate in the North-Western corner of the city walls, "dal monte che le sta sopracollo"—from the mountain which stands over it.[33]

The second reason is a thematic one: the protagonists of this letter are in fact foreigners that, coming from the North, are trying to evade the trade tax. These enemies of the State are depicted as thieves: they walk in secret, not in the public road and "the will to not be recognised is a friend of crime, and whoever keeps his way hidden reveals his conscience".[34]

The city itself is represented as a liminal place, where many foreigners often gather together and, as Cassiodorus states, it is very difficult to know who between them will be the enemy in the future.[35] So the city walls have a didactic value for the foreigners, because in times of peace they learn what they will fear during war.[36] This description is certainly more suitable to a city located at the frontier of Theodoric's kingdom than to its capital, and the ethnic variety of the inhabitants of Salona is well shown by their epitaphs preserved in the late Roman cemeteries of the city.[37]

Salona was the capital of Dalmatia, and archaeological excavations and the study of the settlement patterns, conducted from the end of the nineteenth century up to recent years by a joint team of French and Croatian archaeologists, has thrown entirely new light on the settlement organisation, its spaces and its relationship to inland territory.[38] Interestingly the description of Salona's dangers is typical of the Dalmatian context. The reluctance of its inhabitants to obey Gothic rules, pay taxes and finally to respect the official tracks of social mobility are connected to Cassiodorus's traditional themes in the *Variae* addressed to Italy: the maintaining of city walls as a responsibility of local landholders and the maintenance of official paths as a way of controlling people's behaviour. *Variae XII,* 17, therefore shows, if the attribution to Salona here proposed is correct,[39] another possible reading of the inclusion of Dalmatia into the Ostrogothic kingdom: the reluctant provincials of Theodoric's time were in fact transformed, in Athalaric's letter, into the protagonists of continuous danger coming down from the paths of a mountain.

The case of the *Variae* concerning Dalmatia is a good example of the ethnographic discourse displayed by Cassiodorus in sketching the variety of resistances, in terms of local marriages, land abuses, reluctance to pay taxes and to observe Gothic rules, and at the same time the difficulties in exporting those rules to a territory far away from Italy that, nonetheless, was strategic for various purposes. The destroyed walls of Salona, through which tax evaders can easily walk into the city, show well the practical and the ideological usefulness of public buildings and their necessity for everyday life, in peace as in wartime.

Notes

1 I have used the MGH standard edition: Cassiodori Senatoris *Variae*, ed. Theodorus Mommsen (Monumenta Germaniae Historica, Auctores Antiquissimi 12), Berlin, Weidmann, 1894. *Variae* have been recently the object of important research after a long neglect: C. Kakridi, *Cassiodors Variae: Literatur und Politik im ostgotischen Italien*, München, De Gruyter, 2005; A. Giardina, *Cassiodoro politico*, Rome, Bretschneider, 2006; S. Bjornlie, *Politics and tradition between Rome, Ravenna and Constantinople: a study of Cassiodorus and the Variae 527–554*, Cambridge, Cambridge University press, 2015. A project on the Italian translation of the *Variae* has been published: Cassiodoro, *Varie*, ed. A. Giardina, G.A. Cecconi, I. Tantillo, Rome, l'Erma di Bretschneider, 2014.

2 See the rich article by Hrvoje Gračanin, *Late Antique Dalmatia and Pannonia in Cassiodorus' Variae*, in "Millennium", 13 (2016), pp. 211–273, and its bibliography; from an archaeological perspective: D. Dzjino, *The rise and fall of the Dalmatian "Big-men": Social structures in Late Antique, Post-Roman and Early Medieval Dalmatia*, in Studia Academica Šumenensia, 1(2014), pp. 131–137.

3 J. Arnold, *Ostrogothic Provinces: Administration and Ideology*, in J. J. Arnold, M.S. Biornlje, K. Sessa (eds.), *A companion to Ostrogothic Italy*, Leiden Boston, Brill, 2016, pp. 75–78; F. Wozniak, "East Rome, Ravenna and Western Illyricum: 454–536" in Historia: Zeitschrift für alte Geschichte, 30.3 (1981), pp. 351–382.

4 As proposed by E. Marin, *La datation indictionnelle en Dalmatie*, in Les temps chrétiens de la fin de l'Antiquité au Moyen Age, IIIe-XIIIe siècles, Paris, CNRS Editions, 1989, pp. 149–162.

5 R. Lizzi Testa, comment to *Variae* 3 7, in Cassiodoro, *Varie*, II, Libri III-V, Rome 2014, p. 209.

6 S. Gioanni, *Entre les nues de l'Adriatique. Réseaux, compétitions et autorité pontificale entre l'Italie et la Dalmatie du Ve au XV siècle*, in L. Jégou, S. Joye, T. Lienhard, J. Schneider (eds.), *Faire lien. Aristocratie, réseaux et échanges*

compétitifs: Mélanges en l'honneur de Régine Le Jan, Paris, Publications de la Sorbonne, 2015, pp. 81–90.

7 S. Gioanni, *Les évêques de Salone (II–VII siècle) d'après l'Historia Salonitana (XIII siècle) de Thomas l'Archidiacre: histoire et hagiographie*, in F. Bougard, M. Sot, Liber, *Gesta, Histoire. Ecrire l'histoire des évêques et des papes de l'Antiquité au XXIe siècle. Actes du colloque international organisé au Centre d'Études Médiévales d'Auxerre les 25, 26 et 27 juin 2007*, Turnhout, Brepols, 2009, pp. 243–263; S. Gioanni, *Entre les nues de l'Adriatique*, pp. 81–84.

8 List of inscriptions attesting *Procuratores metallorum* and *Procuratores argentariarum Pannonicorum et Dalmaticorum* in A.M. Hirt, *Imperial mines and quarries in the Roman World: Organizational Aspects 27BC–AD 235*, Oxford, Oxford University Press 2010, pp. 82–83.

9 *Variae*, I 40: "discat miles in otio, quod perficere possit in bello".

10 C. La Rocca, *Fortificare le città e prevenire i pericoli. Doveri e qualità regie nell'Italia teodericiana*, in *Faire lien.*, pp. 421–428.

11 Examples of animal behavior are included by Cassiodorus as models of natural order: they are discussed by Bjornlie, *Politics and tradition*, pp. 262–279.

12 *Variae* III 7.

13 *Variae* V 24.

14 *Variae* IV 49.

15 *Variae* V 14,15.

16 *Variae* III 25, 26.

17 *Variae* III 25: "quia non tantum lucra quaerimus, quantum mores subiectorum deprehendere festinamus".

18 *Variae* VIII 4.

19 *Variae* V 14, 15: IX, 2; Severinus 4, in A.H.M. Jones, J.R. Martindale, *The Prosopography of the Later Roman Empire, II, A.D. 395–527*, Cambridge, Cambridge University Press, 1980, p. 1001.

20 The first nomination of Osuin in Dalmatia is recorded in *Variae* I 40; III 26 and IV 9, 1 (507/511); the second one in *Variae* IX, 8 e 9 (527), where Osuin is defined: *illustrem comitem Osuin et palatio nostro clarum et provinciis longa conversatione notissimum Dalmatiis decrevimus praesidere.*

21 I.e. by V. Fauvinet—Ranson, *Decor civitatis, decor Italiae: monuments, travaux publics et spectacles au VI. Siècle d'aprés les Variae de Cassiodore*, Bari, Edipuglia, 2006, pp. 190–193.

22 Krautschick, p. 106, Fauvinet Ranson, p. 191.

23 *Iohanni liquatario ravennati Athalaricus rex Munitio civitatum spes est certa cunctorum, quando in pace ab exteris gentibus discitur, quod veraciter in certamine timeatur. Plena est enim diversis generibus homi-num habitatio urbium singularum. Quis novit cum qua gente confligat? ideoque omnes debent agnoscere quod futuris hostibus gratum non sit adire. quapropter ex nostra iussione possessores ammonere curabis, ut iuxta montem Caprarium et loca cir-cumiecta muris fovearum ingentia ora pandantur talisque ibi pateat hiatus, ut nullusibi relinquatur introitus. cur, nefandi homines, perscrutamini accessus inlicitos, qui-bus portarum permittitur licenter ingressus? nescio quid videmini tegere, qui palam non desideratis intrare. Conscientia recta vias publicas tenet, obviorum collocutione gratulatur et cum diversos gratanter inquirit, laboris taedio non gravatur. Amicum estautem crimini velle nesciri et qui vias suas occulit, conscientiam prodit. Proinde inusus generales itinera prisca revocentur, ne, dum compendium laboris quaerunt, vitae dispendia patiantur. ille enim iure habendus est hostis, qui munimina nititur violare civitatis.*

24 R. Delmaire, *Largesses sacrées et res privata. L'Aerarium impérial et son Administration du IVe au VIe Siècle*, Rome, École Française de Rome, 1989 (Collection de l'École française de Rome CXXI), 1989, p. 300; N. Everett, *Lay*

documents and archives in early medieval Spain and Italy, c. 400–700, in W. Brown, M. Costambeys, M. Innes, A. Kosto (eds.), *Documentary culture and the Laity in the Early Middle Ages*, Cambridge, Cambridge University Press, 2013, p. 74.

25 *Var*. II, 4, 12, 30, IV, 19, V, 31.

26 III, 25, 26.

27 Var. III, 26 "Simeonium itaque virum clarissimum, cuius fides olim nobis est cognita vel devotio comprobata, ad ordinationem siliquatici nec non ferrarium ad provinciam Dalmatiam nostra ordinatione (sc. Theodorici regis) direximus".

28 Var. III, 25 "Proinde sinceris animi tui praeclara documenta noscentes siliquatici titulum, quem †fidae† dominicatus iure dederamus, discussionem indictionis primae, secundae vel tertiae per provinciam Dalmaticam ordinatio tibi nostra committit".

29 For a discussion of the different meanings of *possessores* in Cassiodorus's *Variae,* cfr. G.A. Cecconi, *Crisi e trasformazioni del governo municipale in Occidente fra IV e VI secolo,* in J.-U. Krause, C. Witschel (eds.), *Die Stadt in der Spaetantike—Niedergang oder Wandel?*, Stuttgart, Franz Steiner Verlag, 2006, pp. 285–318.

30 Respectively *Variae*, III 44; III 48; V 9.

31 Nov. Val. X, 3.

32 The Roman road system from Salona is analysed by D. Djino, *Illyricum in Roman politics, 229 B.C.–AD 68*, Cambridge, Cambridge University Press, 2010, pp. 171–173.

33 F. Carrara, *Topografia e scavi di Salona*, Trieste 1850, pp. 58–60.

34 *Variae* XII 17, 3: "Amicum est autem crimini velle nesciri et qui vias suas occulit, conscientiam prodit".

35 *Variae* XII 17, 1: "Plena est enim diversis generibus hominum habitatio urbium singularum. Quis novit cum qua gente confligat"?

36 *Variae* XII 17 1: "Munitio civitatum spes est certa cunctorum, quando in pace ab exteris gentibus discitur, quod veraciter in certamine timeatur".

37 N. Gauthier, "Les inscriptions funeraires tardoantiques de Salone", in L. Clemens, H. Merten, C. Schäfer (eds.), *Frühchristliche Grabinschriften im Westen des Römischen Reiches*, Trier 2015, pp. 209–216; N. Gauthier, N. Marin E. Prévot (eds.), *Salona IV. Inscriptions de Salone chrétienne, IVe-VIIe siècles*, voll. 1–2, Rome, Collections de l'Ecole Française de Rome 194.4, 2010.

38 On the archaeological excavations at Salona, see N. Duval, E. Marin (eds.), *Salona: recherches archéologiques franco-croates à Salone. 3: Manastirine: établissement préromain, nécropole et basilique paléochrétienne à Salone*, Rome, Collections de l'Ecole Française de Rome 194/3, 2000. Recent overviews are J. Jelicic-Radonic, *Salona, the urbs orientalis*, in M.Jurkovic, P. Hardwick, S. M. Hordis (eds.), *The town in the Middle Ages*, Turnohout, Brepols, 2006, pp. 43–54; T. Turkovic, N. Marakovic, *Late antique changes in the urban structure of the Dalmatian metropolis: The episcopal complex in Salona*, in P. Diarte Blasco (ed.), *Cities, lands and ports in late antiquity and the early Middle Ages. Archaeologies of change,*, Roma 2017, pp. 39–52, arguing for a continuity of the periphery of the city and for a superimposition of the Episcolal Quarter on a suburban settlement.

39 This identification is not accepted by Gračanin, *Late Antique Dalmatia*, pp. 272–273, claiming that the diffusion in Italy of oronims like Mons Caprarius and that Iohannes "so an official residing in Ravenna and his presumed jurisdiction in a province that administratively did not belong to the praetorian prefecture of Italy (…) when the Ravenna government wanted to have the due arrears of the siliquaticum collected a special commissioner who had been directly instructed by the king was sent to Dalmatia". These two arguments don't seem

conclusive, because the oronim Mons Caprarius is in fact not so common in Italy and because the adjective *Ravennati* is related to Johannes's origins or residence and not to the city where the tax has to be collected and of course Dalmatia since the Illyricum campaign (508) belong to the prefecture of Italy: H. Wolfram, *Geschichte der Goten. Von. den Anfängen bis zur Mitte des sechsten Jahrhunderts Entwurf einer historischen Ethnographie*, Munchen 2009 (1979), p. 301.

2 Procopius of Caesarea in Renaissance Italy

Introduction

This chapter examines the two arrivals of perhaps the most famous East Roman historian, Procopius of Caesarea, in the Italian peninsula, two exemplary encounters between Italy and the East Roman world. The first time was in person from Constantinople in AD 536, as a secretary and legal adviser to the Roman general Belisarius. Nine centuries later, around 1423, he arrived again, this time in a manuscript of his *Gothic War*, a contemporary history that described sixth-century Italy as the battleground between the armies of the Goths and those of emperor Justinian.[1] The rediscovery of Procopius' *Gothic War* in fifteenth-century Italy can be attributed to the humanist scholar Leonardo Bruni (1370–1444) in Florence. Following Bruni, it was Flavio Biondo (1392–1463) in Rome who first used Procopius for sixth-century Italian history while Bruni and others translated and repurposed Procopius' text for their own ends. At a time when the understanding of Italy's past had all but disappeared behind the individual communal power and historiography of Florence and Venice, Milan and Genoa, Naples and Rome, Procopius helped show how Italy had once been a single united polity which might be achievable once more someday. Thanks to Procopius, a lost part of Italian history could now be reclaimed, as the *Gothic War* threw light on long-forgotten aspects of Italian topography, buildings, mythology, and other things. Moreover, for the rhetorically trained Procopius, writing history was a complementary exercise, just as it was for the civic, imperial, and papal officials of fifteenth- and sixteenth-century Italy,[2] men such as Bruni and Biondo, Bartolomeo Scala (1430–1497), and Niccolò Machiavelli (1469–1527). They all rediscovered in Procopius for the first time a new and different perspective on their common Italian past. This chapter explains the rediscovery of Procopius' *Wars* in Italy from the 1420s (Bruni, Biondo), along with its impact on Renaissance historiography and Italian history (Machiavelli, Alberti, Tarcagnota), by first considering: (1) Procopius' personal time in Italy (530s) and what he saw and experienced there and later described in his *Gothic War,* when Italy was once part of a Roman empire ruled from Constantinople; (2) the decline in historical knowledge of sixth-century Italy, as that empire disappeared in subsequent centuries to be replaced by powerful urban communes such as Florence where Procopius first reappeared in the 1420s.

Procopius discovers Italy, 536–540

Not for sixty years had there been a Roman emperor in the west when Procopius from Caesarea in Palestine first set foot on Italian soil in 536. As the secretary and assistant to the general Belisarius, he was part of the Roman army entrusted by the emperor Justinian (reigned 527–565) with restoring Roman authority in Italy. Procopius had earlier accompanied Belisarius on successful military campaigns against the Persians in Mesopotamia and most recently against the Vandals in North Africa. Having resecured Africa in 534, Justinian had now turned his army to Italy. Since the early 490s Italy had been ruled for the Roman emperor at Constantinople by the Gothic army and court, originally under their powerful king Theodoric (to 526) and his successors Athalaric (526–536) and Theodahad (536). After such a long period, during which the Gothic kings had respected and acknowledged the emperor and preserved Roman administrative structures and practices, it was not clear where the loyalties of the aristocracy and the people of Italy might lay when the Roman army sent from the East came into view. As Procopius arrived in Italy in 536, the emperor's forces would soon find how much local support to expect. Belisarius' mandate was not to install a new emperor in the West, neither at Rome nor at the Gothic capital of Ravenna, but to vanquish the Gothic political entity altogether and substitute it with a fully Roman one ruled from Constantinople. If the Gothic king was not prepared to relinquish control of Italy, as entrusted to his family by a previous emperor but now being reclaimed by the current emperor, then he would have to be forced out.[3]

In Procopius' native Caesarea, and likely in the nearby Greek intellectual centre that was Gaza, he had the advantage of the best possible literary and rhetorical education. He was also educated in law that may have involved study in Beirut as well. As a student of Roman law he needed to master Latin. Therefore, Procopius brought to Italy both fluency in Latin and a deep knowledge of Homer, Thucydides, and the classical texts that formed the backbone of a contemporary education including Vergil for Latin. He knew that Italy was still what it had long been under Roman rule, a single political entity with different administrative provinces under a single Roman law.[4] The geographical framework of Procopius' Italy is that of the Roman provinces. Books 5 to 8 of his *Wars* covered the Roman conflict with the Goths in Italy from 536 to 552. Centuries later, their incidental detail on Italian history, geography, people, buildings, administration, mythography, nomenclature, and other contemporary observations was to prove invaluable to Italian scholars when they turned to investigating their sixth-century past. So, what could they discover in Procopius' account?

In mid-536, from Messina in Sicily, Procopius crossed with the Roman army to mainland Italy, noting that it was the place where "the poets place

Scylla and Charybdis".[5] Then they marched through the provinces of Bruttium and Lucania to besiege Naples. Procopius observes that the city's aqueduct "on a high arch of baked bricks" was covered not only up to the wall but beyond it into the city, which is where the Romans finally found an entrance.[6] Being encamped outside Naples also gave Procopius the opportunity to reflect on Mt. Vesuvius whose threatening presence overshadowed the neighbourhood. Still, it is not possible to be sure whether or not he actually climbed the mountain himself to verify his claim that "It is possible to see fire there, if one dares to peer over the edge".[7] Departing Naples, Belisarius left a garrison there and another military guard nearby Cumae. There, Procopius explains, the locals point out the Cave of the Sibyl "where they say her oracular shrine was".[8] Before long, Belisarius was convinced he should take his army straight to Rome so they marched further inland along the Latin way entering the city on 9 December 536, just as the Goths left the city.

Procopius was to spend another three and a half years in Italy as the Gothic war unfolded. His history reflects his journeying through Italy from 536 to mid-540 from Rome (537) to Ravenna (540). Most of the year 537 saw Procopius inside Rome where he was surrounded by classical history and culture. There he records physical observations such as the size of the fourteen aqueducts leading into Rome,[9] the "noteworthy sight of the Mausoleum of Hadrian" with its wonderfully made marble horses,[10] the "altogether incredible sight" of the perfectly preserved ship in which Aeneas reached Italy,[11] as well as the statue and Temple of Janus with its big bronze doors. During the Gothic siege of Rome in 537/538 someone tried to open them as the Romans once used to do in time of war but, as Procopius explains, in Christian times such superstitions were safely ignored.[12] Not ignored was a copy of the statue of Athena from Troy "chiselled in stone in the temple of Fortuna, where it lies before the bronze statue of Athena, which is set up under the open sky in the eastern part of the temple".[13] Procopius observes that the Roman statue resembles Egyptian rather than Greek ones.[14] Christian Rome could not escape his notice. Procopius reserves particular attention to the apostolic sites in Rome associated with Peter and Paul: the gates named after Peter (Porta Aurelia)[15] and Paul (Porta Ostiensis),[16] the original churches on the burial sites of Peter[17] and Paul.[18] Procopius discovered at Rome that Peter was "revered by the Romans and held in awe above all others"[19] and that the Goths respected the apostolic sanctuaries and ensured that they remained unharmed.[20] As a close associate of Belisarius, Procopius most likely met both Pope Silverius and his successor Vigilius. On one occasion, he explains how Belisarius deposed Silverius on a charge of conspiring with the Goths and replaced him with Vigilius[21] who later proved such a handful for the emperor Justinian.

From Rome, Belisarius sent Procopius on a special mission leaving the city with his associates under cover of darkness. Bypassing the Gothic camps, they journeyed South along the Appian Way headed for Terracina.

Procopius provides a first-hand account of the Roman road, impressed by its width[22] and the solidity of the surface where the joined stones "give the appearance when one looks at them, not of being fitted together so much as having grown together" (5.14.10). Near Terracina Procopius saw the rocky mount where Odysseus is said to have met Circe which he declares "untrustworthy information", although he does explain how the terrain might have been construed as the island described by Homer (5.11.2–4). It may also be on this occasion that he continued on the Appian Way as far as Beneventum whose name he explains as related to exposure to severe winds blowing across from Dalmatia. More significantly, he notes that the city was originally built by Diomedes, when driven out of Argos after the capture of Troy. Diomedes left to the city, Procopius goes on, "the tusks of the Kalydonian boar, which his uncle Meleagros had received as a prize from the hunt, and they are still there even up to my time, a remarkable sight and well worth seeing, measuring not less than three spans around and having the shape of a crescent".[23]

When the Roman army left Rome in 538 to pursue the Goths all the way to Ravenna, Procopius was on the move through Italy again. Occasionally he comments on the topography or the literary associations of the places the army encountered along the route, beginning with the narrow rocky pass through Petra Pertusa: "Now this fortress was not devised by man but was made by the nature of the place; for the road passes through an extremely mountainous country at that place".[24] He then notes that below is a river too swift to ford and above is the most precipitously high cliff face so that "the men of ancient times constructed a tunnel at that point and a gate for the place".[25] The Roman army passed through the narrow opening and reached Narni where the general Bessas had earlier encountered strong Gothic defences. Like Petra Pertusa, Narni was naturally protected by a combination of mountain and river.[26] Procopius explains the difficulty of both roads leading to Narni and implies the Romans took the road over the old Roman bridge that he says is "a noteworthy sight for its arches are the highest of any known to us".[27] From Narni, the Romans will have marched via Orvieto where Belisarius stopped to consider how to capture the hilltop town well protected by its topography, as Procopius explains,[28] then across the Apennines to Urbisaglia. There, Procopius records the city's destruction by Alaric in 408 as being so thorough as to leave visible by 538 only "a small remnant of a single gate and of the floor of the adjoining edifice" (6.16). Then the army of Belisarius, which included Procopius, moved on to Fermo where they linked up with the army of Narses recently sent separately to Italy. There they planned the next phase of the war, conscious of the need to relieve Roman-occupied Rimini, which the Goths were then blockading (6.16.1–3). Centuries later, all of this detail on central Italy to be read in Procopius was to prove instructive for scholars and their audiences.

Further on, Procopius reports in detail the Romans' siege of Osimo: it is the capital city of Picenum, about eighty-four stades from the coast, situated on a very high hill with no level approach "and for this reason it is entirely inaccessible for an enemy".[29] The Goths also realised that the Romans could never expect to leave the neighbourhood of Ancona, let alone move on Ravenna, while the Goths occupied Osimo. It was at Osimo that Procopius records his direct engagement in the action when Belisarius accepted his suggestion for using two different trumpets, one leather and one brass, not just two different signals from the same trumpet, in order to ensure clear communication with troops spread out around the base of the mountain leading up to the city.[30] The siege dragged on until, as Procopius tells the story, it was discovered that on the steep slope behind the city there was a cistern replenished from a stream that enabled the inhabitants to keep their water supply topped up. Only when it was obstructed would they come under pressure and surrender.[31] Having captured Osimo and Ancona, Belisarius and the Roman soldiery progressed to Urbino. Procopius describes the city's vulnerable location and how Belisarius sent envoys to negotiate its surrender.[32] Finally, they reached their destination, Ravenna, and began a blockade of the city by land and sea.

"While I watched the entry of the Roman army into Ravenna at that time", Procopius later wrote of events in March 540, "it occurred to me that the outcome of events is not fulfilled by the wisdom of men or any other virtue on their part, but that there is some supernatural power that is ever warping their intentions and leading them in such a way that there will be nothing to hinder that which is being brought to pass".[33] What Procopius meant by this reflection was that the Roman army was numerically far inferior to the Goths yet their enemy happily conceded victory to them. Between Rome and Ravenna, Belisarius' army had met no real opposition. On sizing up the smaller numbers and ordinary physiques of the Roman soldiers, the Gothic women felt duped and accused their husbands of cowardice.[34] During the weeks Procopius spent in and around Ravenna he was able to observe its life and lore. While he makes no comment on any of the city's buildings he does describe what he calls an "amazing phenomenon" that occurs daily, going on to explain how the local tide can be extremely high and create a navigable inlet well away from the coast. So, boats and their cargoes are readied and when the tide comes in they are able to sail out. The phases of the moon, Procopius observes, dictate the strength of the tide.[35]

Around mid-540 Procopius left Ravenna for Constantinople with much to tell and much to write about. Clearly, in Italy, he had been making his own notes of events along the way quite apart from his daily work for Belisarius in managing all the relevant correspondence, files, and paperwork for the general and his close associates. Over the following decade Procopius was able to reflect and write up his account of Belisarius' years in Italy, as well as his earlier wars against the Persians and Vandals. By the time he came to release the manuscript of his history in 551, however, the Italian military success in which he had participated in 540 had completely unravelled. The gap left by Vitiges had been filled by the energetic king Totila who had largely succeeded in 546 in recapturing from the Romans all the forts and towns they had occupied, including Rome. The garrisons left in Italy had clearly been insufficient and lacked strong co-ordinated leadership and resources. Belisarius was sent back to Italy in 545 to confront Totila but returned empty-handed four years later. By the time Procopius' history appeared (Books 1–7), Justinian had resolved on a well-equipped attack on Italy to secure it once and for all, although it wasn't until the following year (552) that his general Narses succeeded in defeating and killing Totila and then his successor Theia. As Procopius completed his history around 553/4 (Book 8), the Roman reconquest of Italy was taking shape. Narses was to remain there holding both civic and military power. Based at Ravenna, he spent years overseeing the military and civil restoration of Italy, including a bridge at Rome that proclaimed the restoration of the "liberty of the city of Rome and the whole of Italy" (*totius Italiae*: CIL 6.1199).

Procopius never journeyed back to Italy himself after leaving with Belisarius' army in 540 but he was kept informed of the protracted war being fought in places he had once known first-hand, interrogated participants doubtless including Belisarius himself, and studied available documentation for the period from 540 to 552. Procopius' account of his experiences in Italy from 536 to 540, and his unparalleled contemporary description of city and country, remained a rich source of information but it was not known in Italy at all. Shortly after the death of Justinian in November 565 the security and unity of Italy was again interrupted by the invasion of the Lombards who captured Verona and Vicenza in quick succession in 568. Procopius had known Lombards in the army of Belisarius and had devoted part of his history to narrating their current relations with the Roman emperor. In the end, so he reports, they proved too volatile for the Romans and Narses sent them home following the defeat of Totila in 552.[36] Now the Lombards were back in Italy to stay. Italy's single united Roman past was definitely over. It could only be traced in those Romans who wrote about Italy as contemporaries. One of these was Procopius.

East and West engaging with Italy's past, *c.*600–1400

Procopius' history offered a detailed treatment of Italian history from the early 530s to the early 550s, two crucial decades in the formation of medieval and Byzantine Italy. In Constantinople, the Roman empire of Justinian had carried on uninterrupted, but diminished, while the works of Procopius continued to be copied and read in the East right down to the thirteenth and fourteenth centuries. Although Byzantine scholars could read about Justinian's wars in Italy, it was not the content of the history that attracted them as much as the verve and style of the narrative. For the Byzantines, Procopius remained a good read.[37] Meanwhile, in Italy itself Procopius' histories and their content were unknown. Instead, even the most scholarly and literary Italians knew little about their own sixth-century past, and it was difficult for them to find out much beyond the traditions that had grown up over the centuries.

Since the time of Procopius, Italy had never been as united, politically and administratively. Rather it was now distinctly fragmented and its history localised with knowledge of the wars of Justinian, let alone of sixth-century Italy more generally, distorted, obscured and largely lost to view. The Lombard conquest of the Byzantine capital of Ravenna in 751, followed by their defeat at the hands of Charlemagne who became not only their king but also emperor of the West in 800, symbolised a decisive rupture between East and West.[38] Meanwhile, it was the papacy at Rome that had come to consolidate itself as the real international power located in Italy. Occasional cultural and political contact between Constantinople and Italy remained but their religious ties frayed further, especially during the period of Byzantine iconoclasm in the eighth and ninth centuries,[39] only to be further exacerbated by the mutual excommunication of East and West in 1054.

One key product of contact between Italy and Byzantium through this period was the influential ninth-century history from the pen of the papal librarian and imperial envoy Anastasius whose *Chronographia Tripertita* was based on his adaptation and translation of three Eastern works, namely Nicephorus, Syncellus, and Theophanes, and written between 871 and 874.[40] While Anastasius opened the eyes of Italian readers to the Byzantine East and the spread of Islam in the seventh and eighth centuries, thereby helping to explain both the Byzantine claims on Southern Italy and Sicily as well as the monastic refugees in Rome from Sicily and Southern Italy threatened by Arab invaders, his history offered virtually nothing about sixth-century Italy. Observant Italian readers would have noticed in Anastasius' history mention of a certain writer of events named "Procopius" because he is cited by Theophanes.[41] Unfortunately, they would not have realised, or even inferred, that Procopius had also written the history of the Gothic war in Italy from 535 to 552, based in part on first-hand knowledge. It was not so much that Anastasius was not translating Theophanes completely at that point but that Theophanes himself only had access to, or only used, the first tetrad of Procopius' *Wars* (Persians and Vandals) and not the second tetrad (Goths). Anastasius may have seen or even read in Constantinople a manuscript of Procopius' *Wars* covering the Gothic war although there is no trace of any such knowledge, either here or in his many other literary works.

Some knowledge of the Roman emperor's war against the Goths in Italy could be found, however, in one of the most popular histories of the entire Middle Ages even in Italy, namely what was usually called the *Historia Romana*. This long work took various manuscript forms but basically consisted of the fourth-century history of Eutropius, which was supplemented and extended to the time of Justinian by Paul the Deacon writing his *Roman History c.*770 at Benevento. Paul had been a monk at Monte Cassino and spent time at the court of Charlemagne at Aachen. In recounting

Justinian's war against the Goths Paul had relied mainly on two earlier sources of information. The first was the *Lives of the Popes* (*Liber Pontificalis*) and the other the histories (*Romana*, *Getica*) of Jordanes, writing in Latin in Constantinople at the same time as Procopius although he never visited Italy himself.[42] Around the turn of the eleventh century, Paul's popular work was itself extended by Landolf also probably writing in Benevento, a place Procopius had visited and where Lombard influence lingered longest. Landolf's *Historia Romana* consisted essentially of supplementing and continuing Paul the Deacon's *Historia Romana* to around 813 by deploying extracts from Paul's own *History of the Lombards* (written 790s) but mainly otherwise drawing from the *Chronographia Tripertita* of Anastasius. Although Landolf did not use Procopius directly as a source, he did copy from Anastasius the sections on the wars in Persia and Africa that were based on Procopius. Moreover, he retained Anastasius' translation of Theophanes' original indication of his source—"Procopius harum rerum conscriptor".[43] Most extant manuscripts provide the works of all three writers (Eutropius, Paul, Landolf) as a connected whole entitled *Historia Romana*.[44]

"The basic problem of Italian history", as an eminent Edinburgh historian once put it, "is that before the 19th century there is no Italian history, at least not in the sense that we talk of English or French history".[45] Italy made no political or historiographical sense, so even a recent and comprehensive chapter on national histories in the Middle Ages can afford to omit Italy entirely.[46] Much the same could be said of Sicily by the twelfth century.[47] From the ninth to the fourteenth centuries, most historical works produced in Italy were naturally local. The horizons of the present dictated the horizons of the past. Although by 1050 the elites of northern Italian cities functioned inside a larger kingdom of Italy, a century later the same elites were managing their governance locally. By 1150, the commune was the featured political locale, not Italy as a whole[48] although there were occasional attempts to enlarge the historiographical vision. The most influential was the chronicle of popes and emperors compiled in the 1270s by the Polish Dominican, Martin of Opova that became very popular in its time. Among Martin's few entries on sixth-century Italy he records the Gothic war of Justinian, but in earlier recounting the invasion of Attila in Italy he confuses Attila and the sixth-century Gothic king Totila.[49]

The Italian cities that experienced the Gothic war as part of their sixth-century history, that is, many of the places described by Procopius, scarcely mention it in their various local histories. The one notable exception, however, was Florence. Yet, even there, the tradition had become confused and garbled by the thirteenth century. The *Chronica de origine civitatis* from the late twelfth/early thirteenth century narrates events dated to the mid-fifth century in which a certain barbarian chief named Totila, the "scourge of God" captured Florence and killed 20,000 of its nobility, then burnt and razed the city which was rebuilt shortly after by the Romans.[50] The *chronica*is utilised in the *Gesta Florentinorum* of the local judge Sanzanone that ends suddenly in 1231. Again, Sanzanone's understanding of fifth- and sixth-century Florence and Italy was very limited. So too, this tradition was well known to Dante who cited as an example of a scholarly construction the analogy of the French king Charles as being the "second Totila".[51] This is a reference to Charles of Valois's capture of Florence in 1301 and the earlier destruction of Florence by Totila in 542, at least according to the *chronica*. Between them, Sanzanone and the Gesta, or perhaps their sources for early Florentine history, provide the material copied by many others.[52]

All these documents provide material used by the Florentine merchant chronicler Giovanni Villani in the early fourteenth century.[53] In successive chapters of his popular vernacular chronicle Villani explains how the Gothic king Totila treacherously captured then destroyed Florence in 450,[54] which is why he came to be called the "scourge of God".[55] Later, the Goths under Theodoric arrived in Italy.[56] They were Arian heretics so eventually they failed and the Romans summoned help from Constantinople to defeat them. Belisarius came, then Narses, and drove out the Goths.[57] Villani also adds that Charlemagne rebuilt Florence as a Roman and imperial city in response to a request from the locals.[58] While faithfully reporting all this, Villani appears conscious of the loss of local records in Totila's burning of the city in 450[59] and having to depend on a document called "the ancient deeds of the Goths".[60]

In the Florentine tradition Totila and Attila had clearly become fused and interchanged over time, barbarian destruction of the city was considered total and it remained in ruins until Charlemagne could come to restore it centuries later.[61] By the early fifteenth century, therefore, an unresolved question for Renaissance Florence was whether the city had once been destroyed by the Hunnic king Attila (fifth century), or by the Gothic king Totila (sixth century). Next there was the matter of which of them is properly labelled "scourge of God", then whether or not Charlemagne rebuilt Florence, as the tradition would have it. It was only with the rediscovery of Procopius that fact could finally supplant tradition.

Procopius returns to Italy, 1420s to 1440s

Manuscripts of Procopius' works never reached the West after the sixth century, not even in the Greek-speaking parts of Southern Italy and Sicily. At least there is no trace of them. To understand Procopius required both a knowledge of Greek and a disposition to appreciate the author's content. The study of Greek in Renaissance Italy really only began with the employment in Florence in 1397 of the scholar and teacher Manuel Chrysoloras from Constantinople. Among a growing band of local humanists, and with Florence as an increasing attraction for ambitious scholars from other places, Chrysoloras found some keen and willing students. Among them was Paolo Vergerio (1369–1444) who later became a renowned teacher at Padua where he once pointed out that only the Greek historians could restore to Italians so much of their lost history.[62] Polybius was probably one Greek historian that Vergerio had in mind here, but it is possible Chrysoloras had alerted his students to later historians such as Procopius as well. It was another of Chrysoloras' students, Leonardo Bruni from Arezzo, who was actually responsible for the rediscovery of Polybius in Italy and in 1422 used the incomplete manuscript of his history to produce a Latin history of the first Punic war,[63] which turned out be a "runaway success".[64] Bruni's main historiographical achievement, however, became his *History of Florence*.

In the first volume of his history, Bruni deliberately set out to attack what he considered "fictitious legends", the kind of material repeated about the Goths in Villani and the Florentine tradition. So, he situates the Etruscans in advance of the Romans before going on to claim that veterans of the army of Sulla founded Florence during the free Roman Republic while the rule of emperors was a tyranny that led to its decline.[65] Bruni uses local Florentine monuments and customs to critique the traditional historical accounts, noting, for example, that 8 October each year was celebrated as the Roman victory over the Goths of Radagaisus in 406 and that there was a commemorative inscription on a Florentine temple (church). Bruni claims, however, that his "own more diligent researches" point to the year but not the exact day.[66] As for the sack of Rome by the Goths in 410, he claims that "it shames me to write".[67] Bruni's comparative researches also cleared up the confusion around Attila and Totila, noting that "I am convinced therefore that a confusion of names has led some authors erroneously to mistake Totila for Attila".[68] As he explained, Attila did not destroy Florence in the early 450s as some claim because "he was never in the neighbourhood". Likewise, Totila was an Italian-born Gothic leader defeated by the Roman general Narses a century later in 552, again emphasising that "we should like to note this because many persons, misled by vulgar traditions, have held quite different views about him".[69] Even so, Bruni does not correctly attribute the "scourge of God" epithet to Attila but still to Totila, noting that "some called [him] the 'scourge of God' because of the savagery with which he inflicted carnage".[70] As for Charlemagne's rebuilding of Florence, Bruni argues that because it was never actually destroyed by Totila he could hardly be said to have rebuilt it. Rather, Charlemagne simply refounded Florence.[71] Bruni also adds that with the papal coronation of Charlemagne as Roman emperor in 800 "was born the division of the Roman Empire which still exists today with some arrogating to themselves the title of Roman emperor in Greece, others in Gaul and Germany".[72] In carrying on the story, Bruni remarks that eventually the Roman emperors following Charlemagne were located in Germany while the Italian cities became free and only nominally acknowledged any imperial hegemony.[73] Then they grew larger and more independent, competitive for the support of popes or emperors.[74] Either Bruni wrote Book 1 of his

Florentine History around 1420 without knowledge of Procopius' *Wars*, or he came back to revise it after 1425, on discovering Procopius. The latter is quite possible given the *Florentine History*'s iterative construction over many years.

In any event, Bruni's history proved popular locally, so popular in fact that it was claimed that you could not walk anywhere in the city without finding someone copying it.[75] While Florence had already become a centre for the rediscovery and collection of Latin manuscripts of Roman authors, Bruni was no less interested in discovering and making use of Greek manuscripts too. Hence, in 1419, Giovanni Aurispa (1376–1459) was highly appreciated by Bruni and others when he arrived in Florence with Greek manuscripts he had purchased in Constantinople, especially manuscripts of Christian and patristic writers.[76] Following a period in Constantinople, including as tutor to the son of the current emperor Manuel II (ruled 1391–1425), Aurispa returned to Venice in 1423 with a substantial cache of 238 Greek manuscripts.[77] Back in Florence in 1424 Aurispa made available to local scholars such as Bruni many of his manuscripts, this time definitely including one of the histories of Procopius that is now in the Laurentian library at Florence.[78] The Procopius manuscript, recorded by Aurispa as "On the deeds of Belisarius and Justinian in Italy" had actually been gifted to Aurispa by the emperor Manuel himself.[79] Bruni recognised it and read it. Procopius was now in Italy once more.

There is no trace of Bruni, or anyone else, making any use of the Procopius manuscript at Florence between its rediscovery in *c.*1424 and 1440. Meanwhile, it is possible that another manuscript of Procopius had appeared in Florence during the church council held there in the mid-1430s. A large contingent from Constantinople and the East attended the council and they brought many Greek manuscripts with them.[80] At least one of the Greek bishops, later a Roman cardinal, Basil Bessarion (1403–1472), had a copy of Procopius in his library, which Bruni may have seen at that stage. Still, it was soon after the Council that Bruni resolved to write a new history of the Italian war of Justinian (*de bello Italico*). This ambition was only made possible by the rediscovery of Procopius' account of the sixth-century Gothic war in a local Florentine manuscript. What Bruni did was more or less translate and paraphrase Procopius but without ever mentioning him. Instead, his preface just said that he constructed the history "from the commentaries of the Greeks". Whether this was a deliberate attempt to conceal the little-known Procopius as his source of information, as often thought and even remarked at the time, is questionable. At least Bruni was quick to explain that he was only now doing for Procopius what he had earlier done for Polybius, namely, utilise his account but eliminating what he considered extraneous matter such as digressions and long speeches.[81] Bruni was making history popular and he advocating strongly for history.[82]

There are three extant letters in which Bruni explains himself in relation to his use of Procopius in the *de bello gothico*. The first (dated 31 August 1441) is to Cyriac of Ancona to say that that "This work is not a translation, but a work which I myself have compiled, just as Livy drew material from Valerius Antias or Polybius and ordered it according to his own judgment".[83] That is why Bruni considers his new work justly called a "history" and not merely a "translation" of Procopius. The second letter is to Giovanni Tortelli (1400–1466), where Bruni expands: "I have written them not as a translator but as a creator and author. If I were to write on the present war [Charles V's troops in Italy] I would hear of events from others, but the plan and arrangement and the words would be my own, and they would be carefully set down according to my own judgment. I have taken only the events from Procopius in just this way and left behind everything else (i.e., digressions, speeches) since his only virtue is that he was present during this war: in every way he is a contemptible writer".[84] The third letter of Bruni (dated 23 August 1443) is to Francesco Barbaro. Here again Bruni is critical of Procopius' style and imitation of Thucydides. The acknowledged value of Procopius to Bruni was that he was essentially a reliable eyewitness of events in Italy in the 530s.

Like his previous histories, especially his history of Florence itself, Bruni's new *Italian War* quickly gained popularity when it appeared in 1441. The Florentine scribes were busy once more. For a long time later Bruni's history remained popular and controversial, in both its original Latin as one of the first printed books in Italy (Foligno, 1470) and in Italian translation (1456, printed Florence 1526). Bruni used the very manuscript brought to Florence by Aurispa, which had a lacuna covering the death of the Gothic king Totila in 552,[85] but left space for it to be filled in from some other manuscript at a later date.[86] Bruni was fully aware of this gap in the manuscript.[87] Leaving aside Bruni's literary method, here for the first time was a new insight into sixth-century Italy, although it had come from the East.

Bruni was known in Florence to Flavio Biondo (1393–1463) and may have introduced Biondo to Procopius. Not long after, but now in Rome, Biondo was exploiting Procopius as a source of information for an earlier part of the history he had already written. His *Historiae ab inclinatione Romani imperii decades* (sometimes called just *Decades* although the author always called it *Historiae*) was completed by 1443 with the later books written first.[88] It was structured on tracing the decline ("inclination") of Italy and the Roman world from the Gothic sack of Rome in 410 marking years from that point as Livy had done for years from the foundation of Rome. Jacob Burkhardt (1818–1897) had a high opinion of Biondo's *Historiae* considering that "this book alone would entitle us to say that it was the study of antiquity which made the study of the Middle Ages possible, by first training the mind to habits of impartial historical criticism".[89] He particularly noted the need for closer investigation of Biondo's sources of information as a future task, first taken up by Buchholz (1891). The relevant sources for the sixth century were those already known: the *Liber Pontificalis*, Jordanes, Paul the Deacon, and Agnellus of Ravenna, as well as Anastasius for Eastern history.

Given Biondo's aim to provide a critical and comparative approach to the available material he also needed access to Procopius.[90] Unlike Bruni, however, he was not able to read Procopius' original Greek so he had to have a working translation made for his purposes that involved writing a new history of the Roman world from the fifth century onwards. A translation was commissioned, although the identity of the translator and the manuscript used remain unknown.[91] It is at least likely that since Biondo was working in Rome at the time he used the manuscript that had already come into the new Vatican library (*Vat. Gr.* 152).[92] A detailed textual study of the relevant chapters of the *Historiae* may be able to provide more certainty to this conjecture.

While making earlier reference to Procopius, Biondo provides his overall critical assessment of the Roman historian's value at the commencement of Book 4. There he notes that Procopius can be both a help and a hindrance in narrating the Gothic war,[93] before providing details about the historian to an audience mainly encountering Procopius for the first time: he hailed from Caesarea in Palestine but was a medical doctor (mistaken but often repeated) attached to general Belisarius. His skills were versatile but, above all, he wrote histories. At that point, Biondo explains two important facts: (1) he is using Procopius because none of the earlier Latin writers covering Justinian's reign have done so, although he requires a translation to be made; (2) he realises that Bruni whom he labels "a most distinguished writer of our age" had just recently used nothing more than Procopius in preparing his *de bello italico* but without once acknowledging his source. In reality, in his own history Biondo himself used both his translation of Procopius and the work of Bruni.[94] Returning to Procopius, Biondo applied his critical skills to the historian's text thereby testing the accuracy of the sixth-century account. From Forlí in the Romagna, Biondo had a good first-hand knowledge of the geography around Ravenna. This leads him to query Procopius' account of the tidal water flow around Ravenna.[95] In asserting that in his day no such watercourse divided Ravenna because it was twelve miles from the city Biondo is slightly reticent, uncertain whether his translation may be letting him down at this point. In any event, Biondo is suspicious of Procopius' information on the Italian war and from time to time challenges his information.[96]

While Biondo's work was complex and novel, it was not immediately popular, at least nowhere near as popular as the works of Bruni were. On recording Biondo's death (4 June 1463), the humanist Pope Pius II (previously Aeneas Silvius Piccolomini) claimed that a literary reputation awaited anyone who could make Biondo's history more stylish and readable.[97] In the end it was Pius himself who produced a more coherent and summary version of the whole work.[98] In doing so he numbered the books sequentially (Books 1–20), largely omitted Biondo's detailed discussion of certain events and sources such as the elaboration at the commencement of Book 3. Accordingly, Biondo's detailed explanation of his use of Procopius at the beginning of Book 4 was overlooked by Pius II, along with all citations from Procopius, while the various explanations for the victories of Totila elides the personal opinion of Biondo. The *Historiae* of Biondo was never itself translated into Italian, but Pius II's truncated version was translated a century later (1553), thereby making the general content of Biondo's history more accessible although it still could not save the *Historiae* from "fairly swift oblivion".[99]

The combined efforts of Bruni at Florence and Biondo at Rome so close together in the early 1440s suddenly brought Procopius to the notice of humanist scholars but those capable of reading a Greek manuscript were still very few. Direct access to Procopius therefore required a full translation. Giovanni Tortelli, well known to both Bruni and Biondo, was entrusted with responsibility for Procopius as part of Pope Nicholas V's great translation project. He arranged to have what was probably the Vatican manuscript (*Vat.Gr.*152) sent to Lianoro Lianori (1425–1477) at Ferrara who prepared a sample translation of part of Procopius in September 1449 but, for reasons unknown, he never actually completed the Procopius.[100] It was to take more than half a century to make up for this lost opportunity when in 1506 there appeared the first translation of part of Procopius *Gothic War*, which had been completed in manuscript in the 1480s. This was by Christopher Persona (1416–1486) and published posthumously in Rome. He had probably used the same Vatican manuscript as Biondo and the abortive translation of Lianori. Besides the Gothic wars, the Vatican manuscript also included the Persian and Vandal wars written by Procopius. These were soon translated by Raphael Maffei (1451–1522) and published in 1509.

Before the availability of Procopius' *Wars* in translation, other scholars such as Bartolomeo Scala (1430–1497) were able to take advantage of its new contents. Procopius was definitely consulted by Scala, another Florentine chancellor who set about yet another *History of Florence* in the 1490s. He uses not only Bruni and Biondo but also cites Procopius directly for the siege of Florence by Totila in 542.[101] Even so, he too still labels Totila as the "scourge of God".[102] That particular misattribution proved hard to shift, especially in the continuing chronicle tradition at Florence. Sozomen of Pistoia (1387–1458), younger than Bruni but inspired to learn Greek at Florence not long after, produced a chronicle to his own times. Although it covered the fifth and sixth century, it is unclear whether Sozomen used Procopius directly but he certainly followed Bruni and Villani.[103] Whether inspired by his Florentine teacher Sozomen or not, Matteo Palmieri (1406–1475) wrote a famous work *de temporibus* in 1448 for which his researches were much admired.[104] He noted that the Romans had rescued Florence from the Goths but four years later Totila so devastated the city that he won the nickname "Scourge of God" ("flagellum Dei").[105] Likewise, Bartolomeo Platina (1421–1481), humanist and Vatican librarian, was probably continuing to rely on Martin of Troppau, rather than Procopius, when in 1475 he still labelled Totila as the "scourge of God".[106]

Finally, at this time (1472/1473), another educated official at the papal curia, Nicholas of Modruš (1427–1480), also wrote an unpublished Gothic history (*de bellis Gothicis*) that survives in two incomplete manuscripts.[107] Although educated in humanist skills and outlook at Venice, Nicholas was actually a Slavic speaker from Venetian Dalmatia who became bishop of Dalmatian Modruš. He deployed his Venetian learning for local political purposes. For instance, his Gothic history portrayed the Goths not so much as part of the history of Italy, but as the background to the formation of his native Illyrian homeland, where Totila's putative brother Ostroilo is claimed as the founder of the Croat-Dalmatian kingdom. Nicholas had served as papal envoy in Hungary for a number of years, then at the papal court where he wrote his history at precisely the time he was involved in a papal naval expedition against the Ottoman Turks in 1473. Only very recently has his history been brought to light, dated, and interpreted.[108] Nicholas does make frequent reference to Procopius *Gothic History* in his own history, although the latter part of his history covering the period, when he might have used Procopius more extensively, is missing.[109] In any event, with his limited Greek it seems unlikely that he consulted an original Greek manuscript of Procopius, even though by now there was one available to him in the Vatican library.[110] Instead, he chose to rely for his facts on the previous works of Bruni and Biondo. Such diligent scholars as Sozomen, Palmieri, and Platina, as well as Nicholas of Modruš, are likely to have been familiar with Procopius only through the works of Bruni and Biondo. Even so, Procopius' influence on Renaissance scholars remained tenuous at this stage.

Italy rediscovered through Procopius, 1420s–1527

Bruni had read and used Procopius from an original Greek manuscript while Biondo had to rely on a translation. Other scholars eventually had access to other Procopian manuscripts that had reached Italy from the East. Yet, as noted above, all the evident users of Procopius in fifteenth- and early sixteenth-century Italy relied on translations, first in Latin then Italian. Separately, Bruni's *de bello Italico* enjoyed widespread popularity in both its original Latin and in Italian translations. With the advent of printing from the 1460s Bruni's history based on Procopius appeared in a more permanent and circulated form.[111] What was predominantly of interest in fifteenth- and sixteenth-century Italy were the books of Procopius' sixth-century Gothic war in Italy. Almost no use was made of Maffei's translation of the Persian and Vandal Wars (1509). Moreover, what was especially interesting about Procopius' account of Italy was the insight it provided to sixth-century Italian geography and topography. It proved valuable first to Biondo who developed for his *Italia Illustrata* (1453) the model of a clear regional format, with use of classical texts as sources of information on Italian places and events. Biondo had earlier produced a local topographical work (*Roma Instaurata* 1444–1448), and later a major work on Roman life and customs

(*Roma Triumphans,* 1479). Although he never cites Procopius directly in these works, in the *Italia Illustrata,* which covers the whole of Italy in a unified way, he does refer back to sections of his *Historiae/Decades* for which Procopius had been the ultimate source presumably relying on his translation.[112] Indeed, Biondo's critical approach to texts like Procopius in his topographical works was a key development in historiographical practice.[113]

Over time, others took up Biondo's model. Lorenzo Abstemio (1440–1508), for example, came to the court of Duke Montefeltro at Urbino later in life as librarian. In the entry on Urbino in his unpublished *de totius orbis civitatibus* he used Procopius to cover the Roman siege of the city in 538. Whether or not he had access to a manuscript of the original Greek in the ducal library, or had to rely on the Latin translation of Persona (1506) is not determined.[114] Then there was the dense and detailed *Descrittione di tutta italia* of Leandro Alberti (1479–1552), for example, first appeared in Italian (1550) and only posthumously in Latin (1567). It was dedicated to Catherine de Medici. Although, earlier, a Dominican priest based in Bologna, named Alberti (1525–1528), had a rare opportunity himself to travel by accompanying his provincial visiting all the Dominican houses throughout Italy and Sicily. He followed closely the format and content of Biondo but undertook independent research including on Procopius' *Wars.*[115] He found in Procopius' description of Italian places he knew and noted in the 530s to 550s a unique pointer to sixth-century topography and chorography. In fact, Alberti cites the historian a total of fifty-seven times in the course of his work when discussing places such as coastal Tuscany,[116] Orvieto,[117] Umbria, Spoleto and Assisi,[118] Narni,[119] Rusciane,[120] Osimo,[121] and Pesaro.[122] At times, the first-hand experience and record of Procopius enabled Alberti to correct Biondo and others.[123]

By Alberti's time, Biondo's *Italia Illustrata* had only recently been translated into Italian when all his major works appeared close together: *Roma Ristaurata et Italia Illustrata* (1542), *Roma Triumphans* (1543) along with Pius II's version of his *Historiae/Decades* (1547). They were all published by Michele Tramezzino at Venice with the translations undertaken by Lucio Fauno. It is now clear that, for whatever motive, Giuseppe Tarcagnota (1490–1556) used "Lucio Fauno" as a pseudonym.[124] Besides the translations, Tarcagnota also produced original works of his own, researching and writing along the tracks laid down by Biondo a century earlier. Of particular interest are his *Antiquities of Rome* published under the name of Lucio Fauno originally in Latin (1549) then in Italian (1552),[125] and his smaller work on Naples published under his real name (Tarcagnota 1566). Although to date modern scholars appear to have totally ignored these works, Tarcagnota demonstrates his reliance on Procopius for key information in both cases. In the *Antiquities of Rome* he used Procopius for different gates of the city and for the Mausoleum of Hadrian,[126] while in the *Naples* he explains that the eyewitness account of Procopius shows that

Naples was not sacked or burnt in the 530s.[127] Yet another work of Tarcagnota, again never studied so it would appear, is his very detailed *World Histories*. For the sixth century he may have modelled himself on Biondo's *Historiae/Decades*. Certainly, he did use Biondo, but Procopius is also cited extensively.[128] The *Wars* of Procopius, that is to say, the books covering the Gothic war (Books 5–8) in Persona's Latin translation (1506) were now an essential and available source of information for sixth-century Italy and used for both historical and topographical purposes. In some cases the need was as narrow as an individual town or region such as Adami on Fermo,[129] various historians on Genoa[130] and Pellini on Perugia.[131] So too Procopius' *Wars* was also used as required by other historians at the time such as Pigna[132] and Summonte,[133] as well as by more antiquarian scholars such as Onofrio Panvinio (1530–1568).[134] While the understanding of Italy as a coherent geographical whole was already made visible in both Biondo's *Histories* and his *Italia Illustrata* in the 1440s, it was made clearer still for the sixth century by Procopius' *Gothic War* which had begun to be consulted and exploited more widely.

By the mid-sixteenth century the writing of history in Italy had taken a decisive turn away from the humanist example of Bruni with its focus on form, style, and eloquence. In addition, the political background had also been complicated by the death of Lorenzo Medici in 1492 and the 1494 invasion of Italy by the French king Charles VIII in the course of asserting his claim to the throne of Naples. The French invasion's physical impact may have been small, but its psychological impact was large as it came to destabilise the city-states of Northern Italy and create a new sense of Italian unity.[135] Doubtless many among the new generation of humanists and officials found some precedent in Procopius's account of Belisarius' invasion of Italy in 536 and his eventual capture of Rome and Ravenna. Niccolò Machiavelli, who was familiar with the *Wars* of Procopius, may have been one of them.

In politically enforced retirement on his Tuscan farm by 1513 and at work on his *Prince*, Machiavelli wrote regularly to his friend Francesco Vettori, then Florence's envoy in Rome. Vettori returned the favour on 23 November 1513.[136] In outlining his routine to Machiavelli the ambassador explained that when finished riding outside the city he would return home for the evening where, so he comments, "I have arranged to get quite a few histories, especially of the Romans: for instance, Livy with the epitome of Lucius Florus, Sallust, Plutarch, Appianus Alexandrinus, Cornelius Tacitus, Suetonius, Lampridius, and Spartianus, and those others who write about the emperors—Herodian, Ammianus Marcellinus, and Procopius".[137] In other words, Vettori presumably had copies to read of the first printed versions of Procopius, namely the recent translations of Persona (1506) and Maffei (1509). Vettori's reading of Procopius would have made sense to Machiavelli because he too knew the Procopian translations of Persona (Gothic war) and Maffei (Persian and Vandal wars), or soon would be as he moved from working on the *Prince* to his *Discourses on Livy* (1518), even though neither appeared in his lifetime. At one point in the *Discourses* Machiavelli discusses the movements of nations over time and what drives them from one place to another. Along the way, he quotes Procopius's account of seeing in Africa an inscription that reinforces the belief that the Moors were originally Syrian but fled to Africa in fear of the Hebrews.[138] Drawing on Procopius *Wars*,[139] he says:

> And since I have said above that nations such as those I have been describing, are often driven by wars from their ancestral homes, and forced to seek a new country elsewhere, I shall cite the instance of the Maurusians, a people who anciently dwelt in Syria, but hearing of the inroad of the Hebrews, and thinking themselves unable to resist them, chose rather to seek safety in flight than to perish with their country in a vain effort to defend it. For which reason, removing with their families, they went to Africa, where, after driving out the native inhabitants, they took up their abode; and although they could not defend their own country, were able to possess themselves of a country belonging to others.

Machiavelli then goes on to add, from Procopius:

> And Procopius, who writes the history of the war which Belisarius conducted against those Vandals who seized on Africa, relates, that on certain pillars standing in places where the Maurusians once dwelt, he had read inscriptions in these words: "We Maurusians who fled before Joshua, the robber, the son of Nun;"[1] giving us to know the cause of their quitting Syria. Be this as it may, nations thus driven forth by a supreme necessity, are, if they be in great number, in the highest degree dangerous, and cannot be successfully withstood except by a people who excel in arms.

Back in favour and back in Florence by the early 520s, Machiavelli was commissioned by the Medici to write a *History of Florence*. However, he clearly felt the need in his beginning chapters to move beyond previous historians of Florence such as Bruni, not least by situating his story within the history of Italy.[140] He therefore began in post-Roman times by treating the various successive invasions and occupations of Roman Italy.[141] Like the Moors he had encountered in the *Discourses* only a couple of years previously, Machiavelli now saw how so many different nations had occupied and reshaped Italy.[142] Part of this account is the war of Justinian to reclaim Italy that was fought through Belisarius, then Narses.[143] At this point, he was doubtless drawing on his earlier reading of Procopius, which had helped shape his understanding of Italy as a unified geographical entity with a coherent past, as distinct from its present constituent communes and towns.

By the time Machiavelli died in 1527, the forces of Holy Roman Emperor Charles V had defeated the French and captured their King (Francis I). Now they were marching on Rome itself, which they duly sacked. This spiritual blow will have sparked interest in previous captures of the city by Alaric in 410, but especially those by Belisarius (547) and Totila (546, 550) described by Procopius, and may well lie behind Giorgio Vasari's exaggerated picture of Totila's impact on Rome.[144] It was left to Machiavelli's younger friend Francesco Guicciardini to consider the political and historical implications of these events with their common friend Vettori. More significantly, Guicciardini was stimulated to undertake a large-scale history of Italy covering events from 1494 to the recent sack of Rome.

On display in Guicciardini's history is the Florentine's analysis of the complex European problem that the history of Italy had now become.[145] Italy was no longer in charge of its destiny. Whether or not Guicciardini found value in Procopius, as Machiavelli and Vettori had done, is unknown. Florentines still believed, according to Guicciardini, that Totila had destroyed Florence only for Charlemagne to rebuild it centuries later. Hence the prestige still enjoyed by the French at Florence at the time of their invasion in 1494,[146] but it was a risky position to take a century after the rediscovery of Procopius by Bruni and previous humanist histories from Biondo to Scala. So, Vasari had to be counselled out of depicting Charlemagne's rebuilding of Florence as part of his decoration of the Palazzo Vecchio.[147]

Since Procopius' *Buildings* did not include a chapter on Italy among its six books the work was not of prime interest to those writing about Italian history and geography. However, its focus on the art and architecture of an imperial capital (Constantinople) suggested new insights and provided new examples for Italian scholars concerned with the antiquities of the original imperial capital, Rome itself. For example, in his 1564 dialogue on historical or scriptural errors and abuses in sacred paintings, such as Michelangelo's *Last Judgment* in the Sistine Chapel, Giovanni Gilio (d.1584) made use of Procopius' account of the mosaic representation of Justinian's triumphs over both Vandals and Goths in the portico of the imperial palace.[148] They were identified as an accurate historical representation.[149] Benedetto Egio at Rome saw the importance of translating Procopius' *Buildings* into Italian (1547), as he had already done for the Gothic War (1544–1547) and Persian War (1547), followed by Paul the Deacon's *History of the Lombards* (1548). All these volumes were published at Venice by Tramezzino when engaged with Tarcagnota's original topographical works and translations of Biondo.

Conclusion

In 540, Procopius sailed away from Ravenna to Constantinople, never to return. Instead, his preoccupation became the history of recent Roman wars including the Italian wars of the 530s to the 550s in which the imperial capital sought to reclaim Italy as part of a united Roman realm. Although his histories gained immediate popularity in Constantinople and the East, and remained familiar to successive generations of Byzantine scribes and scholars for centuries thereafter, there is no evidence they ever reached Italy. When they finally did so in the 1420s they enabled the emerging humanist historiographical culture, especially at Florence but also at Venice, Rome, Ferrara, and Padua, to see close-up a phase of Italian history which was otherwise lost by then. Above all, Procopius' first-hand knowledge of part of sixth-century Italy contributed to the new quest of Renaissance Italian scholars, such as Biondo in his *Italia Illustrata* and Alberti in his *Descrittione,* to understand better the topography and geography of an Italy that was once an administrative and cultural unity. Such a reality was not evident from their own lived experience, nor from their familiarity with the works of Sallust, Livy, and more recently Tacitus. Procopius shed light on the early history of places such as Florence, which was now so central to Italian history but not so important in Roman times, even in the sixth century. Yet, at the same time, Procopius also improved fifteenth- and sixteenth-century understanding of the continuously inhabited cities of Rome, Naples, and Ravenna.

In modern times it is Tom Brown who has done more than anyone to illuminate Italian history and the history of its relations with the East through the story of Ravenna itself. From his seminal *Gentlemen and Officers* (1984) all the way to "Ottonian Ravenna" (2015), Tom has probed, developed, and expanded our understanding of the role of the Byzantine empire and culture in Italy. It is therefore a pleasure to dedicate to him a contribution which scarcely mentions Ravenna, but which links Procopius the Easterner who knew Ravenna in 540 to the Procopius whose knowledge of sixth-century Ravenna was rediscovered from the East, and readily utilised, in Italy nearly a millennium later. The use of Procopius' *Gothic War* in Italy after the 1420s constitutes an instructive episode in Renaissance historiography.

Notes

1 A. Momigliano, "Polybius' Reappearance in Western Europe", in *Polybe—Entretiens sur l'antiquité classique* 20. (Vandoeuvres-Geneva 1974), 347–372 = *Essays in Ancient and ModernHistoriography.* (Oxford: Blackwell, 1977), 79–98, traces the same set of circumstances to explain the rediscovery of the person and histories of Polybius in Italy.

2 E. Cochrane, "The Profession of the Historian in the Italian Renaissance", *Journal of Social History 15,* 1981, 69; D. Kelley, *Renaissance Humanism.* (Boston, 1991), 23.

3 Among several modern accounts of the period most valuable remain C. Wickham, *Early Medieval Italy Cultural Power and Local Society 400–1000.* (London, 1981) and P. Heather, *The Goths.* (London, 1998). Still worth reading is the multi-volume *Italy and her Invaders* (1880–1899) of Thomas Hodgkin (1831–1913) in conjunction with the critical appreciation of its importance by T.

S. Brown, "Gibbon, Hodgkin and the invaders of Italy", in R. McKitterick and R. Quinault (eds.), *Edward Gibbon and Empire.* (Cambridge, 1997), 148–152. The status of Procopius' Italy, as viewed from Constantinople, and the memory of empire in the West, are variously covered in recent research: J. Arnold, *Theodoric and the Roman Imperial Restoration.* (Cambridge, 2014); M. Shane Bjornlie, *Politics and Tradition Between Rome, Ravenna and Constantinople* (Cambridge, 2015); and M. Kruse, *The Politics of Roman Memory.* (Philadelphia, 2019).

4 Essential background on Procopius: A. Cameron, *Procopius and the Sixth Century.* (London, 1985), 188–206 and C. Whately, *Battles and Generals. Combat, Culture and Didacticism in Procopius' Wars.* (Leiden, 2016), 38–67. The text of Procopius' *Gothic War* is available in J. Haury (ed.), *Procopii Caesariensis Opera Omnia*, Vols. 1 and 2 (*Bella*), rev. G. Wirth 1962–1963. (Leipzig, 1905) and the translation in A. Kaldellis, *Prokopios. The Wars of Justinian.* (Indianapolis, 2014).

5 Procopius, *Wars*, 5.8.1

6 Procopius, *Wars*, 5.10.13.

7 Procopius, *Wars,* 6.5.24. Details in M. Henry, "Procope en Italie: les notices sur le Vésuve", *Historia* (2008), 57: 317–326, although the case made for Procopius' direct observation of Vesuvius in 552/553 is not compelling. If he were part of Narses' expedition, as he had been with Belisarius from 536 to 540, he would surely have mentioned the fact because it would have added to the credibility of his history rather than have to resort to guesses as to why Narses was appointed (*Wars* 8.22.11–19). There are no other indications of personal autopsy in this part of his narrative (8.21.1ff), while the whole of *Wars* 8 is distinctly more bookish and indirect than *Wars* 1–7 (cf. Whately 2016, 197–218).

8 Procopius, *Wars*, 5.14.3.

9 Procopius, *Wars*, 5.19.13.

10 Procopius, *Wars*, 5.22.12–14.

11 Procopius, *Wars*, 8.22.7–16.

12 Procopius, *Wars*, 5.25.18–24.

13 Procopius, *Wars*, 5.15.11.

14 Procopius, *Wars*, 5.15.13.

15 Procopius, *Wars*, 5.19.4.

16 Procopius, *Wars*, 6.4.3, 7.36.7, 10.

17 Procopius, *Wars*, 5.22.21, 6.9.17, 7.20.22, 7.36.17.

18 Procopius, *Wars*, 6.4.9.

19 Procopius, *Wars*, 5.23.5.

20 Procopius, *Wars*, 6.4.10.

21 Procopius, *Wars*, 5.25.13.

22 Procopius, *Wars*, 5.14.7.

23 Procopius, *Wars,* 5.15.8. Details in L. Miletti, "Rediscovering Myths in the Renaissance: The Calydonian Boar and the Reception of Procopius' Gothic War in Benevento", *Greek, Roman and Byzantine Studies* (2015), 55: 788–811, although Miletti's arguments are extremely tenuous at best, namely that (1) the appearance of a boar on the coat of arms of Benevento in 1489 can only have come from a studious reading of Procopius *Wars* (p. 798) and (2) that in Rome the scholarly Francesco Settala "became conversant" with Persona's private manuscript translation of Procopius and later "decided to divulge it" locally at Benevento (p. 803) years before it was printed (1506). The first mention of Procopius by a local writer was in 1754 (p. 808).

24 Procopius, *Wars*, 6.12.10.

25 Procopius, *Wars*, 6.12.11–13.

26 Procopius, *Wars*, 5.17.5–10.
27 Procopius, *Wars*, 5.17.11.
28 Procopius, *Wars*, 6.20.5–11.
29 Procopius, *Wars*, 6.23.1–7.
30 Procopius, *Wars*, 23.23–9.
31 Procopius, *Wars*, 6.27.1–2.
32 Procopius, *Wars*, 6.19.3.
33 Procopius, *Wars*, 6.30.32.
34 Procopius, *Wars*, 6.30.33–34.
35 Procopius, *Wars*, 5.1.19–23.
36 Procopius, *Wars*, 8.33.2.
37 B. Croke, "Procopius, from Manuscripts to Books: 1400–1850", in G. Greatrex (ed.), *Work on Procopius outside the English-speaking World: A Survey* (2019), *Histos.* Supplementary Volumes 9, 1–173, at https://research.ncl.ac.uk/histos/documents/SV09.01.CrokeProcopiusFromManuscriptstoBooks.pdf, 5–12.
38 Wickham 1981.
39 T. S. Brown, "Culture and Society in Ottonian Ravenna: imperial renewal or new beginnings?" in J. Herrin and J. Nelson (eds.), *Ravenna, its role in earlier medieval change and exchange.* (London, 2015), 335–344.
40 For Anastasius' education and career: B. Neil, *Seventh Century Popes and Martyrs. The Political Hagiography of Anastasius Bibliothecarius* .(Turnhout, 2006), 11–34, and for date, context, influence, manuscripts, and other details: B. Neil, Theophanes Confessor on the Arab Conquest: the Latin Version by Anastasius Bibliothecarius' in M. Jankowiak and F. Montinaro (eds.), *Studies in Theophanes*, Travaux et Mémoires 19. (Paris, 2015), 149–157, noting (p. 154) that Anastasius includes only about half of Theophanes' original Greek text for the reign of Justinian, that is, the years covered by Procopius.
41 C. De Boor (ed.), *Theophanis Chronographia*, vol. 2. (Leipzig, 1885), 135.1: "Procopius, harum rerum conscriptor"; 135.16: "Procopius".
42 W. Goffart, *The Narrators of Barbarian History (A.D 550–800).* (Princeton, 1988), 347–370.
43 Landolfus Sagax, *Historia Romana*, ed. H Droysen, MGH. AA. 2. (Berlin, 1878), 370 (l. 12).
44 L. B. Mortensen, "The Diffusion of Roman Histories in the Middle ages; a list of Orosius, Eutropius, Paulus Diaconus and Landolfus Sagax manuscripts", *Filologia Mediolatina* (1999–2000), 6–7: 103–200.
45 D. Hay *The Italian Renaissance in its Historical Background.* 2nd edition. (Cambridge, 1966), 29.
46 E.g. N. Kersken, "High and Late Medieval National Historiography", in D. Delyannis (ed.), *Historiography in the Middle Ages.* (Leiden. 2012), 181–215. By contrast, relevant Italian works are covered in A. Vasina, "Medieval Urban Historiography in Western Europe (1100–1500)", in D. Delyannis (ed.), *Historiography in the Middle Ages.* (Leiden, 2012), 317–352, at 325–341.
47 T. S. Brown, "The Political Use of the Past in Norman Sicily", in P. Magdalino (ed.), *The Uses of the Past in Twelfth Century Europe.* (London, 1992), 191–210
48 C. Wickham, *Sleepwalking into a New World. The emergence of Italian City Communes in the Twelfth Century.* (Princeton, 2014), 6.
49 A modern edition of Martin's *Chronicon Pontificum et Imperatorum* by Anna-Dorothee van den Brincken is available at http://www.mgh.de/ext/epub/mt/.
50 O. Hartwig (ed.), *Quellen und Forschungen zur ältesten Geschichte der Stadt Florenz.* (Marburg, 1875), 58–59.
51 Dante, *de vulgari eloquentia* 1.6.

52 Cf. J. Thompson, *A History of Historical Writing,* vol. 1. (New York, 1942), 475: "The archives of Florence abound with manuscripts of other early anonymous chroniclers, their accounts being more or less copied from one another or from a common original, so that little confidence can be attached to them".
53 L. Green, *Chronicle into History.* (Cambridge, 1972), 15, 156.
54 Villani, *Chronicle,* 3.1.
55 Villani, *Chronicle,* 3.3, cf. 1.1.
56 Villani, *Chronicle,* 3.5.
57 Villani, *Chronicle*, 3.6.
58 Villani, *Chronicle*, 3.21.
59 Villani, *Chronicle*, 1.1.
60 Villani, *Chronicle*, 3.6.
61 The many tangled threads of this tradition are picked apart in detail by T. Meissen, "Attila, Totila e Carlo Magno fra Dante, Villani, Boccaccio e Malispini: per la genesi di due leggende erudite", *Archivio Storico Italiano* 132 (1994), 561–639.
62 P. Vergerio, *De ingenuis moribus et liberalibus adulescentiae studiis liber* 39 (ed. and trans. C. Kallendorf), *Humanist Educational Treatises.* (Cambridge, MA, 2002), 46–47 with D. Geanakoplos, *Constantinople and the West.* (Madison, 1989), 45–46.
63 G. Ianziti, *Writing History in Renaissance Italy.* (Cambridge, MA, 2012), 14–16, 63–98.
64 Ibid, 62.
65 L. Bruni, *History of the Florentine People*, ed. and trans., J. Hankins, vol. 1. (Cambridge, MA, 2001), 1.38–40.
66 Ibid, 1.48.
67 Ibid, 1.52.
68 Ibid, 1.76
69 Ibid, 1.63.
70 Ibid, 1.55–58.
71 Ibid, 1.77.
72 Ibid, 1.69.
73 Ibid, 1.74–5.
74 Ibid, 1.79–83.
75 M. Davies, "Humanism in Script and Print", in J. Kraye (ed.), *Cambridge Companion to Renaissance Humanism.* (Cambridge, 2015), 47–62, at 53.
76 E. Bigi, "Aurispa, Giovanni", *Dizionario Biografico degli Italiani* 4 (1962) at http://www.treccani.it/enciclopedia/giovanni-aurispa_(Dizionario-Biografico)
77 R. Sabbadini, *Le scoperte dei codici latini e greci ne'secoli XIV e XV*, rp.1996. (Florence, 1905), 46–47; N. Wilson, *From Byzantium to Italy. Greek Studies in the Italian Renaissance.* (Baltimore, 1992), 25.
78 *Laur.Plut.*69.8; A. M. Bandini, *Catalogus codicum manuscriptorum Bibliothecae Mediceae Laurentianae*, vol. 2. (Florence, 1768), cols 627–628. The manuscript is clearly titled, in red ink, the history of the Gothic wars of Procopius of Caesarea. It is now available online at: http://mss.bmlonline.it/s.aspx?Id=AWOIt8GII1A4r7GxMMY5&c=Procopius%20De%20gothicis%20bellis#/oro/17.
79 P. Schreiner, "Giovanni Aurispa in Konstantinopel. Schicksale griechischer Handschriften im 15. Jahrhundert", J. Helmrath/H. Müller (eds.), *Studien zum 15. Jahrhundert. Festschrift Erich Meuthen.* (Munich, 1994), 623–633, at 626, with Sabbadini, *Carteggio di Giovanni Aurispa.* (Rome, 1931), 11 (lines 16–17: "Gentilium quidem auctorum ipse rex mihi volumina duo dono dedit: Procopius, De gestis Bellisarii aut Iustiniani in Italia…".) and Franceschini (1976), 73.

80 D. Geanakoplos, *Constantinople and the West.* (Madison, 1989), 243.
81 G. Ianziti "Bruni on Writing History", *Renaissance Quarterly* 51 (1991): 381–391.
82 L. Bruni, "The Study of Literature" in C. Kallendorf (ed. and trans.), *Humanist Educational Treatises.* (Cambridge, MA. 2002), 92–125.
83 Bruni, *Epistolae*, 9.5 (*Leonardi Arretini Epistularum*, ed. L. Mehus. (Florence, 1741), part 2, 149–150, cf. P. Botley, *Latin Translation in the Renaissance. The Theory and Practice of Leonardo Bruni, Giannozzo Manetti and Erasmus.* (Cambridge, 2004), 32; Ianziti (2012) 18, 279–300.
84 Bruni, *Epistolae*, 9.9 (ed. Mehus, 1741), part 2, 156–157, with Botley (2004) 33 and Ianziti (2012) 19.
85 Procopius, *Wars* 8.32.27–8.
86 *Laur.Plut.* 69.8, fols.267v–268r.
87 Explained in E. Fryde, *Humanism and Renaissance Historiography.* (London, 1983), 84–87, cf. J. Haury, "Über Prokophandschriften", *Sitzungsberichte der k. Bayer. Akademie der Wissenschaften zu München 1895* (Munich, 1896), 132–137. The lacuna in Bruni's manuscript (Haury (1905), vol. II, 642.24 to 662.19 = *Wars* 8.29.2–33.5) originated in Constantinople and is manifest in several other manuscripts covering *Wars* Book 8 (*Basileensis graecus D IV* 6 (Haury's "k", vol. 1, XLIX–L), *Monac.graec.*87 (Haury's "n", vol. I, L), *Matritensis regius* 38 (Haury's "gamma", vol.1, LII).
88 The best introductory guide to the *Historiae* remains D. Hay, "Flavio Biondo and the Middle Ages", *Proceedings of the British Academy* 45 (1960), 97–128, complemented by the singular interpretation of Biondo's construction of the "translatio imperii" in J. Pocock, *Barbarism and Religion,* vol. 3: *The First Decline and Fall.* (Cambridge, 2003), 179–202.
89 J. Burkhardt, *Civilisation of the Renaissance in Italy.* (London, 1990), 161.
90 N. Pellegrino, "From the Roman Empire to Christian Imperialism: The Work of Flavio Biondo", in S. Dale, A. Williams Lewin, D. J. Osheim, *Chronicling History. Chroniclers and Historians in Medieval and Renaissance Italy.* (University Park, PA, 2007), 273–298, at 288.
91 Ianziti (2012) 281, n.14; L. Delle Donne, "Le fasi redazionali e le concezioni della storia nelle decadi di Biondo: tra storia particolare e generale, tra antica e moderna Roma" in A. Mazzocco and M. Laureys (eds.), *A New Sense of the Past: The Scholarship of Biondo Flavio (1392–1463).* (Leuven, 2016), 55–88.
92 Haury (1896) 137, 158–159 (suggesting possibility of *Vat.Gr.*152).
93 F. Biondo, *Blondi Flavii Forliviensis Historiarum ab inclinatione Romanorum decades* (Basel, 1531), *Historiae/Decades* 1.4: "partim multum adiuvabit, partim non levia alicubi afferent impedimenta", with Ianziti (2012) 20–21.
94 Originally explained in P. Buchholz, *Die Quellen der Historiarum Decades des Flavius Blondus.* (Leipzig/ Naumberg, 1891), 33–38, cf. Hay (1960) 50; Pocock (2003) 192.
95 Procopius, *Wars*, 5.1.18.
96 Fryde (1983) 21 for some of these issues, cf. Ianziti (1998) 385–386.
97 Pius II, *Commentarii rerum memorabilium.* (Frankfurt, 1614), 310.
98 Pius II, *Abbreuiatio Pii Pont. Max. supra decades Blondi ab inclinatione imperii vsque ad tempora Ioannis vicesimi tertii Pont. Max.* (Venice, 1484).
99 D. Hay, *Annalists and Historians, Western Historiography from the VIIIth to the XVIIIth Century.* (London, 1977), 102.
100 Fryde (1983) 27; F. Bachelli (2005), "Lianori, Lianoro", *Dizionario Biografico degli Italiani* 65, at http://www.treccani.it/enciclopedia/lianoro-lianori_(Dizionario-Biografico)/.
101 *Wars* 7.5.1; B. Scala, *De Historia Florentinorum.* (Florence, 1677) 28–35 (Book

I), 43–44 (Book II), with D. Wilcox, *The Development of Florentine Humanist Historiography in the Fifteenth Century*. (Cambridge, MA./1969) 182–194.

102 Scala 1677, 28.

103 G. Zaccagnini (ed.), *Sozomeni Pistoriensis Presbyteri Chronicon UIniversale* (Rerum Scriptores italicarum, 2nd series, 16.1) (Città di Castello, 1908), xxvii.

104 Vespasiano, *Renaissance Princes, Popes and Prelates. The Vespasiano Memoirs*. (New York, 1963), 417.

105 Palmerius, *Matthei Palmerii: Liber de Temporibus*, ed. G. Scaramella (*Rerum Scriptores italicarum* 26.1) (Città di Castello, 1906) 56 (ad 544), 57 (ad 548).

106 B. Platina, *Opus de vitis ac gestis summorum pontificum*. (Venice, 1562), 69.

107 The manuscripts of Nicholas' *De bello gothico* are (1) *Corsinius* 43.E.3 (127A), Biblioteca dell'Accademia nazionale dei Lincei e Corsiniana, Rome, fols, 1r–60v (the autograph dating to 1473), and (2) *Vat.Lat.* 6029, fols. 1–110v (accessible at https://digi.vatk.or.was.sep.lib.it/view/MSS_Vat.lat.6029, and described in detail in Špoljarić (2013), 505–506), written by another scribe a year later with some corrections by Nicholas. A collation of these manuscripts, pending an edition, is that of L. Špoljarić, *Nicolas of Modrus, "The Glory of Illyria": Humanist Patriotism and Self-Fashioning in Renaissance Rome* (Ph.D. Dissertation: Central European University, Budapest, 2013), 290–414.

108 L. Špoljarić 2013, 2019.

109 L. Špoljarić, "Nicholas of Modruš and His De Bellis Gothorum: Politics and National History in the Fifteenth-Century Adriatic", *Renaissance Quarterly* 72 (2019), 457–469.

110 Nicholas cites Procopius at the following points: *Vat.Lat.* 6029, fols. 68v ("refer[t] Procopius"), 77v ("ut Procopius testator"), 78r ("Procopius Cesariensis Bellisarii medicus cuius testimonio frequenter utimur"), 91r ("ut Procopius vult"), 91v ("a Procopio memorantur"), 106v ("Procopius Neapoli conscripserat").

111 Croke 2019, 13–30.

112 *Italia Illustrata,* quoted by F. Biondo, *Italy Illuminated*, ed. and trans., J. White, Vol. 1: Books I–IV (Cambridge, MA. 2005)at 1.24 (68–69): Narses at Luca; 2.28 (162–163): appointment of Pope Silverius; 3.3 (242–243): Pesaro destroyed by Totila and rebuilt by Belisarius; 3.4 (224–225): Belisarius gains Urbino; 3.15 (260–261): defence of Ancona lifted by Narses; 4.7 (284–285): Goths besiege Rimini; and F. Biondo, *Italy Illuminated,* ed. and trans., J. White, Vol. 2: Books V–VIII. (Cambridge, MA. 2016) at 5.7 (10–11): Narses defeats Totila; 5.39 (60–61): Milan surrenders to Goths; 6.40 (149–149): Totila's father at Treviso; 7.57 (262–263): Benevento destroyed by Totila.

113 P. Burke, *The Renaissance Sense of the Past*. (London, 1969), 25–31.

114 See D. Mutini, "Lorenzo Abstemio", *DBI* 4 (1962), 161–162, and M. Stocchi, *Pagine di storia dell'umanismo italiano*. (Milan, 2014), 141, 266. The unpublished work is contained in two Vatican library manuscripts: Urb.lat. 294 and 295.

115 D. Hay, "The Italian View of Renaissance Italy", in *Florilegium Historiale: Essays presented to Wallace Ferguson,* eds. J. Rowe and W. Stockdale. (Toronto, 1971), 10–13.

116 G. Petrella, *L'officina del geografo: la "Descrittione di tutta Italia" di Leandro Alberti e gli studi geografico-antiquari tra Quattro e Cinquecent*. (Milan, 2004) p. 34v; Procopius, *Wars* 5.26.5.

117 Alberti, *Descrittione,* 56r; Procopius, *Wars*, 2.11.

118 Alberti, *Descrittione,* 80v; Procopius, *Wars*, 7.12.11.

119 Alberti, *Descrittione,* 91v; Procopius, *Wars*, 5.16.6–11.

120 Alberti, *Descrittione*, 201v; Procopius, *Wars*, 7.28.8.

121 Alberti, *Descrittione*, 253v; Procopius, *Wars*, 8.23.40.

122 Alberti, *Descrittione,* 287v; Procopius, *Wars*, 7.11.32–3.

123 Petrella 2004, 84.
124 G. Tallini, "Nuove coordinate biografiche per Giovanni Tarcagnota (1508–1566)", *Italianistica* 42 (2013), 25–55; L. A. Rosa, "Fauno, Lucio", in *Dizionario Biografico Italiano* 45 (1995), at http://www.treccani.it/enciclopedia/lucio-fauno_(Dizionario-Biografico)/.
125 The Italian edition claims to be revised, corrected, and supplemented in places with a compendium at the end designed to show what is covered in each of the five books.
126 L. Fauno, *Delle antichità della città di Roma*. (Venice, 1552), 12 (1.8: Goths discovered at Pincian Gate); (5.11 marble section of Mausoleum of Hadrian); (5.20: Pancratian Gate).
127 G. Tarcagnota, *Del sito, et lodi della citta di Napoli: con vna breve historia de gli re svoi, e delle cose piu degue altroue ne' medesimi tempi auenute*. (Naples, 1566), 45 (Book II).
128 G. Tarcagnota, *Delle historie del mondo di M. Giovanni Tarcagnota. Parte Seconda*. (Venice, 1583), 240–272 (Book 7). Procopius is referred to as a "doctor in Belisarius' army" (pp. 242, 271), and cited on other occasions (pp. 243, 244, 246, 248, 249, 250).
129 E. Cochrane, *Historians and Historiography in the Italian Renaissance*. (Chicago, 1981), 218.
130 Ibid, 246.
131 Ibid, 286.
132 Ibid, 263.
133 Ibid, 287.
134 Panvinio deployed Procopius in several of his works, most notably his posthumous *Republicae Romanae Commentariorum libri tres* (Paris 1588) where he cites the historian on pages 41, 48, 49, 50, 63, 87, 102, 109, 110, 111, 113, 114, 116.
135 D. Hay, 1966, 178.
136 C. Celenza, *Machiavelli. A Portrait*. (Cambridge, MA, 2015), 57–64.
137 J. Najemy, *Between Friends: Discourses of Power and Desire in the Machiavelli-Vettori Letters of 1513–1515*. (Princeton, 1993), 216–217.
138 Macchiavelli, *Discourses* 2.8.
139 Procopius, *Wars*, 4.10.13–27.
140 A. M. Cabrini, "Machiavelli's Florentine Histories", in J. Najemy (ed.), *The Cambridge Companion to Machiavelli*. (Cambridge, 2010), 135.
141 *History of Florence* 1. 2–5.
142 J. Najemy, "Machiavelli between East and West", in D. Ramada Curto, E. R. Dursteler, J. Kirshner and F. Trivellato (eds.), *From Florence to the Mediterranean and Beyond. Essays in Honour of Anthony Molho*. (Florence, 2009), 127–145, at 139–140.
143 *History of Florence* 1.6–7.
144 G. Vasari, *Lives of the Artists*. tr. G. Bull. (London, 1965), 37.
145 F. Gilbert, *Machiavelli and Guicciardini. Politics and History in Sixteenth Century Florence*. (Princeton, 1965), 294–295; Hay (1966) 40–41.
146 *History of Italy*, Book 1, p. 35.
147 N. Rubinstein "Vasari's Painting of the Foundation of Florence in the Palazzo Vecchio", *Essays in the History of Architecture presented to Rudolf Wittkower*, vol. 1. (London, 1967), 64–73, at 67.
148 Procopius, *Buildings* 1.10.15–19.
149 Gilio, *Due dialogi di M. Giovanni Andrea Gilio da Fabriano*. (Camerino, 1564), 118; M. Di Monte, "Gilio, Giovanni Andrea", *Dizionario Biografico degli Italiani* 54 (2000) at http://www.treccani.it/enciclopedia/giovanni-andrea-gilio_%28Dizionario-Biografico%29/

3 Ambrosio de Morales and the *Codex Vetustissimus Ovetensis*

Roger Collins

Very few examples of diplomatic correspondence have survived from the early medieval West, though narrative sources indicate something of the importance of such communications between rulers.[1] Perhaps the best known are the letters from the Frankish court of Childebert II (574–596) and his mother Brunechildis, preserved in the collection now called the *Epistolae Austrasicae*.[2] Equally interesting are another sequence of letters from Spain in the reigns of the Visigothic kings Gundemar (610–611/12) and Sisebut (611/12–620), which include the evidence for an attempted grand alliance against the Austrasian king Theuderic II (596–612), the diplomatic correspondence between Sisebut and the Byzantine patrician Caesarius, governor of the imperial enclave in the south-west of the Iberian Peninsula, and the only known letter from a Visigothic monarch (Sisebut) to a Lombard king (Adaluald).[3]

These are not the only items in this collection, which also contains other letters to and from King Sisebut, a group of seven letters to various recipients sent by a Count Bulgar, probably from a frontier district in the province of *Narbonnensis* in the reign of King Gundemar (610–611/12), a letter addressed to King Reccared (the first or the second of that name?) by a monk called Tarra, and a criticism of an official named Froga by Bishop Aurasius for his patronage of the Jews. Random they may seem, though close in date where this can be ascertained, but they represent the kind of royal, official, ecclesiastical and other correspondence that must have once existed in profusion, and which was probably never intended for long-term preservation in carefully edited literary letter collections.

Nor are the letters alone in this chance survival. In the middle of the collection, and transmitted uniquely with it, is to be found the *Vita Desiderii*, the life of the southern Gallic bishop, Desiderius of Vienne, who was murdered, apparently on the orders of the Austrasian Frankish king Theuderic II (598–613), for criticising the morality of the royal house. Extraordinarily, this work of hagiography is said to have been written by the contemporary Visigothic king Sisebut.[4] Arguments about his authorship and intentions need to take account of the context in which the text is found.

The same is true of another body of texts preserved uniquely in the same manuscript that contains the letter collection and the *Vita Desiderii.* This is a collection of *formulae* or model documents that can easily be shown to derive from authentic documents that have been lightly edited, so as to remove specific details of names, dates, and places. However, this process was so incompletely carried out as to leave traces of all three, sufficient to suggest that some of the texts may date in whole or part from the reign of Sisebut, already so well attested to in the letter collection, and may have some association with Córdoba.[5]

Although there are copious survivals of charters from the Christian kingdoms in the north of Spain from the centuries following the Arab conquest of 711, it used to be thought that only five such documents survived from the Visigothic period itself, and all were fragmentary.[6] However, four complete and authentic sixth-century charters were recently found in the form of later copies. Two of them are episcopal and the other two royal, one having been issued by Leovigild in 576/7 and the other by Reccared in 586.[7] These can be supplemented by other documents, none complete, found scratched on slate in various parts of the centre of the peninsula; some, though not all, of this same period.[8] But overall, the preservation rate of Visigothic charters has been slight, not least in comparison with Frankish ones. So, the existence of an additional forty-five such documents of several different kinds, albeit with some information removed, is a significant addition to the evidence available for the study of legal, social and literary features of seventh-century Spain.

All these texts—the letters, the *Vita* and the *formulae*—have been well edited, and more than once.[9] Their evidence has often been drawn upon, usually via the modern editions, for which all those studying this period are appropriately grateful. However, important as these texts are, both individually and collectively, they form part of a larger whole: the complete contents of the manuscript in which, uniquely, they have been preserved, and which includes items that have never been edited. To take account of the full context of their survival and to ask how it was achieved is a necessary part of evaluating their evidence. The process was, as often the case, a complex one, with different chronological and compositional stages. But the fundamental questions remain: when and how were these texts brought together, and for what purpose? In other words, the significance of what is now the sole manuscript to contain them may be greater than just the sum of its parts. Its existence ultimately depended upon a single extraordinary event.

Few visitors to the tenth-century Umayyad palace city of *Medina al-Zahra* (Medina Azahara), five miles west of Córdoba, take much notice of the former monastery of San Jerónimo del Valparaíso, once owned by the austere Spanish order of the Jeronimites, which stands a few hundred yards north-east of the modern entry to the site.[10] Here, one day in 1535, a monk, D. Gerónimo de Andujar, was passing through the corridor on the ground floor, in which the cells of the novices were located, when he heard moans coming from behind one of the doors.[11] On entering, he found a pool of blood on the floor and the occupant of the cell, a twenty-two-year-old novice and former student of the University of Salamanca, by the name of Ambrosio de Morales (d. 1591), rapidly bleeding to death. This was the result of his having just completely castrated himself, in an ill-advised bid to free himself of carnal temptation. Fortunately, D. Gerónimo proved resourceful, surprising as the steps he took may seem to us. He immediately set fire to a felt hat, and then applied the warm ashes to the novice's still bleeding wound, causing the blood to coagulate, and thereby saving his life.[12]

It did not, however, save his career as a Jeronimite, for his self-mutilation automatically excluded him from the order, and, once recovered, Morales was obliged to leave the monastery. His family connections gained him a new career, first as a student and then as the Professor of Rhetoric in the University of Alcalá de Henares, where his father had once been Professor of Moral and Metaphysical Philosophy.[13] Here he acquired a number of prestigious pupils, including King Philip II's half-brother D. Juan de Austria, and several of them would rise to prominent positions in the church, securing him important patronage for his own scholarly advancement. In 1560, a chance conversation with some Italian diplomats at the royal court in Toledo led him to take up the writing of history, both of his native city of Córdoba and of the Spanish kingdoms more generally.[14] He applied for and obtained the unpaid post of *Chronista Real* in 1563.

His main intention in so doing was to continue the long-stalled *Coronica general* or general history of Spain of Florián Ocampo (c. 1499–1558), which, although five volumes in length, had not gone beyond the entirely legendary prehistory of the Iberian Peninsula prior to the Punic Wars. While able to write much of the ensuing Roman history of Spain on the basis of the easily available printed editions of classical literary sources, Morales needed more information in order to take his work on into the Visigothic period and beyond the Arab conquest of 711. He was also increasingly aware of the value of other types of evidence, including archaeological remains, inscriptions, and coins.[15]

Between completing the Roman sections of his history and starting work on the post-Roman periods, Morales made a visit to the north of Spain in 1572, on behalf of king Philip II. He was tasked with recording the holdings of manuscripts, relics, and royal burials in the various churches that he visited.[16] The results of this journey were remarkable, particularly for the account he gave of the manuscripts he saw in Visigothic script, not least in the library of the cathedral of Oviedo in the Asturias. The subsequent loss of almost all of these codices before the end of the eighteenth century means that Morales' account of them, brief as it is, contains almost all we know of their contents.[17] No other scholar was able to describe the manuscripts in greater detail before their disappearance.

It has to be recognised that the speed with which Morales was required to carry out his inspection and the distances to be covered limited his ability to make much use of what he found in these manuscripts in the north for his own historical purposes. However, he already had access to an important collection of texts relating to the Visigothic and later periods, thanks to a manuscript that he had previously been loaned by Pedro Ponce de León, Bishop of Plasencia and Inquisitor General of Castille (d. 1573). This the bishop himself had borrowed from the cathedral of Oviedo in the Asturias in 1557, and which he never returned.[18] The manuscript, which Morales called the *Codex Vetustissimus Ovetensis*, the "oldest manuscript of Oviedo" (henceforth CVO), contained a number of texts of Visigothic origin that are the focus of this enquiry, and Morales made explicit reference to some of them in the two parts of his history that he devoted to that period.[19] He may not have kept the manuscript long, as it was clearly returned to Bishop Ponce de León prior to his death in January 1573.[20] But before doing so, Morales had a copy made by professional notaries, almost certainly in Alcalá. It was thanks to this that the contents of the original manuscript, which itself is never heard of again after 1573, came to be preserved.[21]

The copy made for Morales survives as MS Madrid, Biblioteca Nacional Española 1346 (henceforth M). It came into the national collection from *la primitive Biblioteca de Felipe V*, the library of King Philip V (1700–1746), in 1836.[22] This royal library had been created as a result of the king's own book-collecting enthusiasm, and it was initially formed from a combination of books he himself had brought from France, together with a large number of items confiscated from those on the losing side in the civil war over the Spanish Succession. Prominent amongst these was the Archbishop of Valencia, whose library was seized in 1710.[23]

This is a likely route for the transmission of Morales' copy of CVO after his death in 1591, as it includes marginal notes in the hand of Juan Bautista Pérez Rubert, Bishop of Segorbe (d. 1597), probably the most learned and critical of scholars of early Spanish historiography of the time.[24] A native of Valencia, he had been a canon of Toledo Cathedral prior to his reluctant acceptance of elevation to the diocese of Segorbe, a suffragan see of Valencia, which lies immediately to the south of it.[25] How he came to have borrowed or to possess Morales's manuscript is unknown, but one definite possibility is that it accompanied him to Segorbe in 1591, before coming into the hands of Philip V a little over a century later.

The manuscript itself contains textual items copied from several other sources, not just the CVO. Mostly these come from another identifiable manuscript that Morales had available to him in Alcalá, known as *el Códice de Batres*, but some texts were taken from other exemplars that cannot now be identified.[26] So, to recover the contents of CVO, it is first necessary to separate them out from the items in M that came from other sources.

This presents few problems, though Morales himself left a false clue in the form of a list of contents in his own hand, and which he headed *Codex Vetustissimus Ovetensis*.[27] However, this only includes the first seven items, plus the introductory designs and diagrams; in all, the materials that fill folios 1 to 42v of the manuscript. Fortunately, after the notaries he employed had copied the texts, he added headings and marginal notes throughout, including references to the manuscripts from which each particular item had been taken.

The components of the CVO, as deduced from its sixteenth-century copy, are as follows (titles, where given, are from Morales):

1. Two genealogical tables, depicting the descent of the first kings of the Asturias from the Visigothic royal dynasty of Chindasuinth via a Duke Theofred; said to have been written by Bishop Pelayo of Oviedo (1098/1101–1130) *propria manu* (ff. 1–4).
2. *Notitia sedium Hispaniae episcopalium* (f. 7): a list of the metropolitan sees and their suffragans.[28]
3. The *Liber Itacii* (ff. 7–11v).[29] This is a lengthy listing of churches attached to the various episcopal sees of Galicia. While the author's name, Itacius, is reminiscent of the fifth-century chronicler Hydatius, Bishop Pelayo of Oviedo, who concocted this text, may actually have borrowed it from a the name on a tomb in his cathedral.[30]
4. The Chronicle of Alfonso III, in its *ad Sebastianum* version (ff. 11v–17v).[31]
5. *"Vulsae Chronica (Gothorum)"* (f. 18 r/v).[32]
6. *Templi Compostellani instaurato {incerto autore}* (ff. 19r–20r).[33]
7. A letter of Gregory the Great to King Reccared (ff. 20v–21).[34]
8. The *Historia Wambae* of Julian of Toledo, in all its parts (ff. 23–42v).[35]
9. A collection of early to mid-seventh-century letters but also including the *Vita Desiderii* attributed to the Visigothic king Sisebut (ff. 43r–69).[36]
10. A collection of *formulae* used in the composition of various types of legal document (ff. 75r–90).[37]
11. *Rescriptum Gregorii ad Leandrum (His)Palensem Episcopum*: A section of a letter of Pope Gregory the Great to Leander of Seville, combined with part of one to King Reccared (ff. 90r–92r).[38]
12. *Notas ob eruditione infantum editas ut fertur a Seneca Cordubense poeta* (ff. 93r–98r): a table of shorthand notations, which according to Isidore of Seville was systematised by the Roman author Seneca.[39]

It is thus easy to deduce that of the 252 folios of which the manuscript is comprised, only the first ninety-six of them are copied from the CVO. This suggests the exemplar was a relatively small manuscript, especially as eight of those ninety-six folios are blank. So, it may be wondered if the copy is partial rather than complete, and that some items in the original were not included.

A comparison may help resolve this query. M also includes several texts taken from another manuscript that Morales is known to have used, and which was available to him in the University of Alcala. Unlike the CVO, this has survived, and is now MS Madrid BNE 1513. It is described by Morales as *el libro antiguo de la libreria de Alcala de Henares*, and is also known as the *Códice de Batres*, after the residence of the poet Garcilaso de la Vega (1503–1536), one of its former owners.[40] Of late twelfth or early thirteenth century date, it contains Bishop Pelayo of Oviedo's compilation of chronicles, which he made in the 1130s and various other related works. The texts taken from it are contained on folios 97 to 181 of M, and by comparing the two, it is possible to say that everything found in MS Madrid BN 1513 is indeed copied in M, and that the latter is, therefore, a full record of its exemplar. This in turn might suggest that M's record of the contents of the CVO is similarly complete.

However, there are strong grounds to doubt this. Included in the second part of the manuscript, where the contents are mainly copied from the *Códice de Batres*, is a list in Spanish and Latin in the hand of the notary who wrote this section, but above which Morales himself has written *Liber Vetustissimus Ovetensis ecclesiae,* and to which he has made corrections.[41] Most of what is contained in the list corresponds to texts found in the copy, and it has been marked by Morales as belonging to CVO. However, there are other items that do not, and there are some differences in their ordering. These are as follows:

1. *Genealogias de Sagrada escritura hasta Nuestra Señora y Santa Ana* are placed after the genealogical tables linking the Visigothic and Asturian kings. No such text appears in M.
2. Two papal letters, said to have been sent to Spain from Rome in 493 (Era 531), follow the *Liber Itacii.* These are not copied in M.
3. They are followed by an *Antiquum Privilegium Archipresulatus obetensis ecclesiae,* also not to be found copied in M, and which is said to have been granted by a council in 673 (Era 711). The document describes how the Ark (of the Covenant) "together with many holy relics" was translated from Jerusalem to Oviedo.
4. Next comes the *Choronica Regum Gotorum a Beato Isidoro Hispalensis Episcopo ab Atanarico Rege Gotorum primo usque ad Chatolicum Regem Vambanum scripta*; which is similarly not copied in M. It is followed by the *Choronica Regum Uulse Gotorum* that does appear in M, as does the next item, the *historia de los Reyes de Castilla de Sebastian Obispo de Salamanca* (i.e., the Chronicle of Alfonso III in the *ad Sebastianum* version).
5. According to the notary's list, *sigue tras esta una historia de la origen de los Reyes de Francia de un Obispo Gregorio*, but this has been crossed out by Morales, leaving it uncertain as to whether or not this text, which is copied in M, but as the penultimate item in the manuscript (ff. 186r–214r), was or was not an original component of CVO. However, as this text definitely does appear in MS Madrid, BNE 1513, ff. 72v–101v, it is likely the notary had made a mistake including it here.[42] Morales

also inserts over his crossing out of this item: *luego fundacion de la iglesia de Santiago*, in other words the spurious charter of Alfonso III, which has a quite different location in the copy.

6. The Tironian notes, here described as *indices de abreviatura de la esfatura Gotica*, and the *formulae* come next, but in reverse order to that found in M, and between them appears *Unos tradaditos de las siete Artes liberales*, which is not copied in M.
7. After the collection of letters, of which a few details of specific items are mentioned here, there comes the *Corographia Isidori Iunioris* and finally *Genealogia totius Bibliothecae ex omnibus libris veteris novique testamenti*.[43] These two final items are entered in Morales's hand, not that of the notary.

From the evidence of this list, it is clear that most of the contents of the CVO that has not been copied into M comes from the compilations of Bishop Pelayo of Oviedo (1098/1101–1130). Long notorious for his forging of texts, his purposes in so doing were twofold: to establish the independence of the see of Oviedo from any form of metropolitan authority, and to provide a history that explained the presence in Oviedo of a significant collection of relics, including the Ark of the Covenant. The explain the presence of the latter, he devised a quite spurious set of narratives and documents intended to authenticate a story of how the Ark and various early Christian relics accompanying it were taken from Jerusalem to Spain at the time of the Arab conquest, and then were transferred from Toledo, ultimately to Oviedo, when the Visigothic kingdom in turn succumbed to the Muslims.

As well as wholescale invention, most notably in the *Liber Testamentorum* or cartulary of Oviedo, most of whose royal and papal charters he forged, Bishop Pelayo took advantage of his compiling of historical collections to interpolate spurious material into authentic texts, where it served his purposes. Thus, for example, in the table of episcopal sees copied from CVO into M, he inserted the explicit claim into the text that neither the see of Oviedo, nor that of León, belonged to any of the metropolitan provinces of the Spanish church.[44] As the list he used was of Visigothic date, the actual omission of these two dioceses from any of the metropolitan provinces is due to the fact that neither town was the seat of a bishopric in that period.[45] Similarly, he interpolated passages into the quite authentic early tenth century *ad Sebastianum* version of the Chronicle of Alfonso III to help authenticate his interpretations of the history of his see.[46] Anything that furthered his purposes might be used, and this included promoting the view of the Asturian kings—and thus their Castillian successors of his day—as the lineal descendants of a late seventh-century dynasty of Visigothic kings, whose own interrelationships he also had to manipulate.[47]

Bishop Pelayo is credited with compiling at least two distinct collections of historical texts, of which CVO contained the only known example of the first one, now preserved solely via M.[48] The presence of texts of explicit or deduced Visigothic date within it raises various questions, including the integrity of their contents, the reason for their presence, and the date at which the collection was formed. To extend the enquiry back from sixteenth-century M to the seventh century, in which these texts were written (or so it is being assumed), it is necessary to pass through this Pelagian phase in their transmission.

The easiest question, perhaps surprisingly, is that of the danger of interpolation or outright forgery. The prevalence of such practices in so many texts with which Pelayo is associated might raise doubts on the integrity of the apparently seventh-century items in the CVO. However, as a forger, he was never very subtle. His particular interests and purposes are always quite obvious, and his interventions easily detected. Even in the case of the collection of *formulae* there is no evidence at all either of his altering the texts, or even of using them to add verisimilitude or even just some literary polish to his own fabricated charters in the *Liber Testamentorum*. The latter are, on the contrary, all very simple and direct in their structure and formal characteristics.[49] So, without discussing every component of CVO as preserved in M in detail, it can be said that the texts that were composed or interpolated by Pelayo can be quickly detected, and none of the ones of Visigothic origin fall into that category.

Why Pelayo's collection of historical texts that he put together to justify his claims for his see should include items which did not directly serve his ideological purposes can only be a matter for conjecture. But it may well be that they served as a form of camouflage, providing a body of authentic and useful works in the midst of which the ones he had doctored could be all the better concealed. This is not to deny, though, that he may have had genuine scholarly interests, and that he also saw practical value in some of the early texts he included.

The question of the dating of Bishop Pelayo's compilations is more complicated. Simply put, it is believed that while his first collection is represented only by the sixteenth-century M, copying the lost CVO, a second collection is better preserved, in that it survives in a handful of manuscripts of medieval date, including the previously mentioned *Códice de Batres*, MS Madrid, BNE 1513. It can be seen by comparison of contents of the two that almost all the items of Visigothic origin found in the first collection have been omitted from the second. On the other hand, the latter contains a more fully elaborated sequence of chronicles, each ascribed to a different episcopal author, together creating an unbroken if uneven narrative history that extends from Creation to the reign of Alfonso VII of Castille (1126–1157).

The problem in accepting the existence of just two versions lies in Morales's testimony as to what he saw on his visit to Oviedo in 1572. He recorded the presence in the cathedral library of four codices that either contained texts put together by Bishop Pelayo or which included the same combination of an elaborate cross design and an ownership acrostic in the opening folios that was copied from CVO into M. In other words, these four manuscripts and CVO had features that linked all of them to Bishop Pelayo.

The four books described by Morales which either contained an initial folio depicting the "Cross of the Angels", or which he says were compiled by Bishop Pelagius of Oviedo are as follows:

1. *Another book has at the beginning a portrait of the Cross of the Angels, and in the ordinary figure it says: "I am Prince Alfonso". It contains St. Gregory's brief exposition of the entire New Testament. It is a famous book and highly esteemed though it has not yet been printed.*
2. *A book that Bishop Pelagius of Oviedo compiled in the time of Alfonso VI, the conqueror of Toledo, and to whom he gave this book and in it there are written things by the Bishop himself. It contains the oldest stories of Spain: Bishop Sebastian of Salamanca: Bishop Sampiro of Astorga: Pelagius himself, and others. There are also others that the Gothic King Sisebut wrote and other things from that time. A rare book.*
3. *The Ecclesiastical histories of Eusebius and Rufinus. It has at the beginning the Cross of the Angels, and, in the figure, it says: "I am Prince Alfonso". There at the beginning, it was written that it had been written seven hundred years ago. But he did not indicate how he could confirm it.*
4. *A book of many stories together, where everything is found in the other Pelagius book: a famous and rare codex.*[50]

The first and third of these explicitly contained what is described as a depiction of the "Cross of the Angels" in the opening folio, and the fourth may do so too, as it is said to consist of all that was in the other collection of historical texts. The actual *Cruz de los Angeles* is the equal-armed gold cross, decorated with semi-precious stones and antique seals, preserved in the Camera Sancta or treasury of Oviedo Cathedral. According to the inscription extending over all four arms on the reverse, it was donated to the cathedral church of San Salvador by King Alfonso II (791–842) in 808.[51] The manuscripts in question also contain the acrostic inscription ADEFONSI PRINCIPIS SVM. Both the cross and the acrostic, which covers the entire recto of the second folio, also appear in M, and it may be assumed its versions of both are very similar to those that would once have been found in the two Oviedo manuscripts.[52]

It has to be asked: which King Alfonso is being indicated? Morales states that one of these manuscripts (number two) was explicitly a gift from Bishop Pelagius to King Alfonso VI, "he who captured Toledo", and who ruled Castille from 1072 to 1109. If so, then it is likely that all four books belonged to him, and that the Cross of the Angels and acrostic ADEFONSI PRINCIPIS SVM are marks of his ownership. However, Morales records that the manuscript in question contained the chronicles both of Sampiro and of Bishop Pelayo himself. As the latter concluded with its account of the death and burial of Alfonso VI in 1109, it must be thought rather unlikely that a manuscript containing it was presented to the king by its author.[53] So, if the manuscript Morales described was given to a King Alfonso, or, more probably, was a copy of such a presentational codex (as the original may be assumed to have entered the royal library), then the recipient must have been Alfonso VII (1126–1157). So, it is likely that all four books were written for him rather than his grandfather. This also implies that, paradoxically, the *Codex Vetustissimus Ovetensis* was probably amongst the least old of the Oviedo manuscripts *en letra gothica*, and that it belongs to the final phase of the use of Visigothic script in northern Spain.[54]

Morales also stated that the two manuscripts which contain historical texts combined the chronicles of Sampiro and Pelayo himself with writings by King Sisebut and by others of his time. It would be unreasonable to think these were not some if not all of the items of Visigothic date found in CVO.

As already mentioned, Morales was unable to carry out any close textual study of the codices he inspected in Oviedo in 1572. Nor were his judgments on dating and authorship always reliable. For example, he learnedly, but mistakenly, defended the authenticity of the spurious *Voto de Santiago*, an extraordinarily generous charter of financial rights supposedly given to the cathedral of Santiago de Compostela by King Ramiro I (842–850) of the Asturias as a thank-offering for a (non-existent) victory over the Muslims of al-Andalus.[55] So, it could be suggested that his notes on the manuscripts were confused, and that Sampiro and the writings ascribed to King Sisebut did not coexist in two of the codices he saw in Oviedo, but in just one. However, this seems unlikely. Thus, it may be there was indeed yet another version of Pelayo's compilation that combined features of the other two more fully documented ones, but which does not now survive in any manuscript.

It is time to pass beyond the formation of Bishop Pelayo's historical collections, in however many versions may once have existed. When the works either wholly confected or interpolated by him are filtered out, what is left is a collection of texts that at first sight seem very different in genre but are surprisingly similar in both date and purpose. Adding items listed by Morales's notary as being in the CVO but not in the copy, M, the content that is free of interference from Bishop Pelayo consists of the following:

1. The Chronica Regum Visigothorum (Morales's Chronica Wulsae).
2. Julian of Toledo's Historia Wambae.
3. The letter collection and Vita Desiderii.
4. The collection of *formulae*.
5. The table of Tironian notes ascribed to Seneca.
6. The group of short treatises on the Seven Liberal Arts.
7. The Biblical genealogies.
8. The "Corographia" Isidori Iunioris, from the time of Athanaric to that of Wamba.

9. To these might be added the peculiarly restructured letters of Pope Gregory the Great to Leander of Seville and to King Reccared, which are related to the Hispana, the seventh-century Spanish canon law collection.

The identity or character of most of these texts can easily understood, but the "*Corographia*" of Isidore Junior requires an explanation. Fortunately, Morales's notary provides both the opening and the concluding phrases of the work. The former makes it clear that what is being referred to is Isidore's *De Origine Gothorum*, the second and longer version of what is usually called his History of the Goths, Vandals, and Sueves.[56] Isidore's own work only extended as far as the year 625, in the reign of Suinthila (620–631), while the closing phrase quoted by the notary shows the text in the CVO version referred to the beginning of the joint rule of Chindasuinth and Reccesuinth in 649. The discrepancy between this and the statement that it actually ended in the reign of Wamba (672–680) may be due to a concluding computation of years compiled at that time, which extends to the end of Reccesuinth's reign in 672.[57] Indeed, it is likely that the whole post-Isidoran section was little more than a regnal list, but it is regrettable that it was not copied into M, as no other trace of it has survived.[58] Even though Pelayo included Isidore's Gothic history in a version of his historical compilation, to be found in the *Códice de Batres* and elsewhere, this did not include any extension of the text beyond the mid 620s, other than for a continuation of the list of Byzantine emperors until the fifth year of the reign of Tiberius III (= 702/3).[59]

If not apparent from the titles alone, most of these texts can be shown to have educational or instructional purposes. This has been argued elsewhere in the case of the *Historia Wambae* and the letter collection.[60] The list of shorthand notations, or Tironian notes, and the lost *trataditos de las Siete Artes liberales* obviously fall into such a category, leaving only the *formulae* in need of an explanation.

The collection of these legal texts appears without an overall heading, and it consists of forty-five items.[61] Almost all of them have titles, indicating the nature of the text, added by another hand to that of the original notary who copied them, and not that of Morales either. Numbers one to six are *cartulae libertatis;* seven to ten are deeds of gift or foundation; eleven to thirteen are documents of sale; including of a slave (no. 11); fourteen to twenty are dowries; twenty-one, twenty-two, twenty-five, and twenty-six are wills; twenty-three and twenty-four are deeds of gifts between husband and wife; twenty-seven and twenty-eight are commutations; twenty-nine to thirty-one are gifts; thirty-two is a *cartula obiurgationis;* thirty-three is a division of inheritance; thirty-four is an emancipation; thirty-six and thirty-seven are both *precaria*; and the final seven relate to various judicial processes.

Although most of the specific details of names, places, and dates have been removed from the texts, it is clear that this is no formulary in the classic sense.[62]

There are too many examples of certain types of document, such as manumissions of slaves, while others could never have been used as model texts. For example, document no. 20 is a ninety-nine-line Hexameter poem recording the wedding gift of a senator of Gothic origin to his new wife. This is referred to as something that in Gothic antiquity (*vetustas Getica*) would have been called a *morgengeba*, and it is explicitly dated to the third year of the reign of King Sisebut (613/614).[63] Other documents are almost as restricted in their wider utility; thus, for example, document no. 9 is explicitly intended for the foundation of a monastery by a king.[64]

The texts themselves, as well as being generally deprived of their specific details, are not complete. In a few cases there are obvious *lacunae*, with documents beginning mid-sentence; something that may be explained by loss in the original or damage to a subsequent copy that became the exemplar for CVO.[65] But more widely, what are preserved are introductory or closing *formulae* rather than complete documents. For all these reasons, it is safe to say that this collection is not intended to be one of model texts for notarial use. Instead, it would be better to argue that these documents, abbreviated in the way they have been, were preserved for literary rather than legal or scribal training.

The few clues that come from chance details that in most cases have been removed from the documents provide us with Córdoba as the only place name and the reign of Sisebut (611/12–620) as the sole chronological indicator, and these have been applied, tentatively, to the collection as a whole. Taken with the group of letters in the epistolary compilation preserved in CVO that come from the same period (though with no references to Córdoba), it is not unreasonable to suspect that some of the letter collection and the *formulae* were already combined at any early date, possibly before the letter collection was expanded into its current and fullest form, probably in Toledo in the middle of the seventh century. As for the other components, the *Historia Wambae* dates from the reign of Wamba (672–680), and it was composed in Toledo. From the same period, and possibly the same location too, must come the version of Isidore's *De Origine Gothorum* with continuations. The *Chronica Regum Visigothorum* (Morales's *Coronica Wulsae*), which records late seventh-century ceremonies of royal unction in Toledo, is another product of the capital, and in this version must date to the period between 701 and 710/711. The treatises on the liberal arts, which have not survived, and the table of Tironian shorthand notes ascribed to Seneca, which has been preserved, cannot be precisely dated or located, but both would fit well with the kind of literary interests being pursued in various centres in seventh-century Spain, not least in Toledo.[66]

By way of a provisional conclusion, it looks as if a collection of texts of primarily educational or instructional purpose, put together in the later seventh or very early eighth century, probably in Toledo, originated as a corpus before being incorporated as a distinct component of one or more versions of Bishop Pelayo's historical compilation in the twelfth century. Included within that late seventh collection are items, notably a group of the letters and the *Vita Desiderii*, that come from earlier in the seventh century, and with some links to both Córdoba and Toledo. Their presence hints at previous phases in the formation of this corpus that can be barely glimpsed now.[67]

As a final speculation, it should be noticed that there is evidence for the circulation of at least some of this late seventh century set of texts independent of its survival via Pelayo of Oviedo and from periods prior to the formation of his collections. In preparing his edition of the *formulae*, Juan Gil compared their texts with a wide range of documentary records from northern Spain from the Arab conquest of 711 to as late as the eleventh century. Although several of the categories of text contained in the formula collection did not have equivalents in these later periods, others, such as basic deeds of gift, exchange, bequest, and foundation, did. While the majority of the surviving documents in these classes are relatively simple in their literary character, others included textual passages that are close to those found preserved in the collection in CVO, copied in M.[68]

Interestingly, such examples of textual parallels with the *formulae* found in M occur in a variety of Asturian, Galician, Leonese and Castillian charter collections and cartularies, but always in short chronological periods. Thus, the instances of this in the *Becerro* or cartulary of Sahagún are found in documents of 1069, 1071, and 1073.[69] The examples from Oviedo date from 951 and 953, and those from Valpuesta from 894, 900 and 919.[70] As some of the textual parallels in both the *formulae* and the charters are clearly archaic, as in references to granting Roman citizenship, or anachronistic, as in some citations of *Lex Aquila*, it is hard not to believe that the monastic scribes had to hand a collection like the one that Pelayo included in CVO, when drawing up their documents.[71] It also seems most likely that the purpose of the borrowing was literary embellishment or a desire to enhance the authoritative feel if not sense of their documents. While it could not be claimed that the whole collection of Visigothic period texts in which the *formulae* appear in CVO might be found in manuscripts, say in León c. 870, Valpuesta c. 895, Oviedo c. 950, Sobrado c. 960, and so on, the closeness of the textual borrowings and the inherent strangeness of seventh century or earlier legal phraseology reappearing intermittently in tenth- and eleventh-century northern Spain suggests that this formula collection, or others of similar character, were circulating at that time.[72] And it may be the rest of the Visigothic compilation found in CVO/M accompanied it. While only a partial sixteenth-century copy, M has preserved enough of CVO to lead its readers back through a variety of compositional and compilatory processes in the twelfth century and the seventh to recapture yet more of the literary world of Spain in the Visigothic period.

The ultimate fate of CVO may be deduced from the role it had to play as the exemplar for a section of another manuscript, also of later sixteenth-century date and associated with Ambrosio de Morales. This is MS El Escorial b. III. 14 (henceforth E). Its compositional history and purposes are, however, much less obvious than is the case with M, and it has been subjected to rather less scholarly scrutiny. 230 folios in length, and the work of several scribal hands, its contents are more eclectic.[73] Like M it is copied from earlier manuscripts, several of which have since been lost, but there is less thematic unity in its choice of contents. While most of BNE 1364 derives from versions of the historiographical collection of Bishop Pelayo of Oviedo, no such predominant connection can be seen in the Escorial manuscript.

It commences with a list of its contents in what very clearly Ambrosio de Morales' distinctive script, but the notes throughout the codex assigning items of the contents to particular exemplars are not by him. His contribution, other than for the initial listing is confined to two brief notes. There is also one marginal note in the equally distinctive but very different handwriting of Juan Bautista Pérez.[74]

The exemplars are described in virtually identical fashion each time they are referred to, and consist of the following:

1. "A book written in Gothic letters on parchment, which is entitled decrees of the canons of the Roman pontiffs and is preserved in the church of Oviedo".[75]
2. "The oldest codex in parchment folios written in Gothic letters which is preserved in the church of Oviedo".[76]
3. "The codex in Gothic letters written on parchment which is called the book of Homilies collected from various teachers. This book is preserved in the monastery of Saint Emiliano de la Cogolla of the Order of Saint Benedict".[77]
4. "The little book written on parchment which is preserved in the library of the church of Salamanca".[78]

The suspicion that the second of these is CVO is confirmed by the items of contents ascribed to it in the Escorial manuscript: (1) "the ancient privilege of the archbishopric of Oviedo", and (2) the Visigothic letter collection and Sisebut's *Vita Desiderii*, though here in an order slightly different to that found in M.[79]

The group of four manuscripts thus copied appears geographically eclectic, extending from Salamanca to San Millán de la Cogolla in the Rioja, via Oviedo. However, at least two of them and probably all four were no longer to be found in the libraries referred to in the notes in E. CVO was not returned to Oviedo after its loan to Bishop Ponce de León, and the other manuscript given an Oviedo provenance in these notes, the *Decreta canonum presulum Romanorum,* was not amongst the codices in Visigothic script that Morales listed in the course of his journey there in 1572. The manuscript from San Millán was definitely not to be found in that monastery's library.

Instead, a catalogue of the holdings of the library of El Escorial shows that it had become part of its book collection by 1576 at the latest.[80] Nothing so specific was known about the "little book" from Salamanca, but no later trace of it has been found there. All four manuscripts are no longer extant.

One of them was definitely in the library of El Escorial by 1576, and all or many of Bishop Ponce de León's books were acquired by the monastery after his death in 1573, irrespective of how he himself had come by them.[81] So, it is an at least reasonable hypothesis that the other two manuscripts were similarly located by about the same time, and that it was in El Escorial that E was compiled. This is confirmed by mention in E of yet another manuscript, MS El Escorial & I. 14, which includes a very small part of the Visigothic letter collection.[82] According to two notes in E, it served as the joint exemplar for E, alongside CVO, for the section of text they have in common.[83] This is also confirmed by an unnoticed correction. At the very end of the letter collection in E, the scribe began to write the heading of another epistle: *Clementissimi atque gloriosissimi domini nostri Recesuinti Regis.* This is the opening of the letter from Fructuosus of Braga to Recesuinth that is the last item in the letter collection in MS El Escorial &. I. 14, but which does not form part of it in CVO. The assumption must be that the scribe was following the former, but then discovered that this particular item did not appear in his other exemplar, and so crossed out the heading, before moving on to copy an entirely separate work, the *Mors testamentumque Alexandri Magni.*[84]

That this manuscript, unquestionably belonging to the Escorial library, was being used for its portion of the Visigothic letter collection, in conjunction with the testimony of CVO, establishes that it was there that E was compiled, and further supports the view that the other four exemplars, including CVO, were similarly housed in the monastery by the late 1570s. It is therefore not difficult to guess that their eventual fate was to be destroyed in the great fire that caused so much loss there in 1671. Hence, it is only the copies made in the late sixteenth century, and in particular MS BNE 1346 (M), that preserve what may be known of the contents of CVO.

While the degree of loss of original evidence for the Visigothic period in Spanish history is far from being unique in the field of early medieval history, it has to be recognised that many key texts only survive thanks to the work of sixteenth- and seventeenth-century antiquaries, as well as the taste for fabrication of a twelfth-century bishop. Behind the seeming assurance of modern critical editions there often lie complex and compromised lines of transmission that need to be understood if sense is properly to be made of this evidence. Understanding of the contexts in which such texts first appear, however late in date, can help in interpreting their nature and purpose, as, for example, in the case of the *Formulae visigoticae*, which are not what they are often said to be. Such investigations as this briefly sketched here are also vital for the better understanding of other early medieval societies, such as that of Byzantine Italy, so well illuminated by the work of Tom Brown.

Notes

1 This is a period whose understanding has been much enhanced by the research and teaching of Tom Brown over many years, and it is a particular pleasure to have the opportunity of acknowledging that here. See Andrew Gillett, *Envoys and Political Communication in the Late Antique West, 411–533* (Cambridge, 2003); for the late 6th century see Roger Collins, "Gregory of Tours and Spain", in Alexander Callender Murray (ed.), *A Companion to Gregory of Tours* (Leiden, 2016), 498–515.

2 Elena Malaspina (ed.), *Il "Liber epistolarum" de la cancelleria austrasica (sec. V–VI)* (Rome, 2001), with substantial introduction and notes; also see Gillett, *Envoys*, 267–269. See the important and suggestive study: Graham Barrett and George Woudhuysen, "Assembling the *Austrasian Letters* at Trier and Lorsch", *Early Medieval Europe*, 24 (2016), 3–57, which rightly contests the identification of this corpus as that of a formulary or set of model texts.

3 For these reigns see Roger Collins, *Visigothic Spain, 409–711* (Maldon MA and Oxford, 2004), 74–77, and 77 n. 36 for their re-dating. On the letters see in general Salvador Iranzu Abellán, "La transmisión de la producción epistolar hispana de la Antigüedad tardía y de época visigoda", in Thomas Deswarte and Klaus Hebers (ed.), *Frühmittelalterliche Briefe/La letter au haut Môyen Age* (Cologne–Weimar–Vienna, 2108), 255–267, at 263–266.

4 Jacques Fontaine, "King Sisebut's *Vita Desiderii* and the Political Function of Visigothic Hagiography", in Edward James (ed.), *Visigothic Spain: New Approaches* (Oxford, 1981), 93–129.

5 Carmen Codoñer (ed.), *La Hispania Visigótica y Mozarabe. Dos épocas en su literatura* (Salamanca, 2010), 100–103, 191–196.

6 Madrid, Archivo Histórico Nacional, Sección de Códices, 1452; see Angel Canellas Lopez (ed.), *Diplomática hispano-visigoda* (Zaragoza, 1979), items 119a, 178, 192, 229.

7 Guillermo Tomás-Faci and José Carlos Martín-Iglesias, "Cuatro documentos inéditos del monasterio visigodo de San Martín de Asán (522–586)", *Mittellateinisches Jahrbuch* 52 (2017), 261–286.

8 Isabel Velázquez Soriano (ed.), *Documentos de época visigoda escritos en pizarra (siglos VI–VIII)*, 2 vols. (Turnhout, 2000).

9 Juan Gil, *Miscellanea Wisigothica* (Seville, 1975) is the best critical edition of all three. An *Editio Altera*, published in Seville in 1991, is merely an exact reprint.

10 On the Jeronimites see J.R.L. Highfield, "The Jeronimites in Spain, their Patrons and Success, 1373–1516", *Journal of Ecclesiastical History*, 34 (1983), 513–533.

11 E. Flórez (ed.), *Relación del Viage de Ambrosio de Morales Chronista de S.M. El Rey D. Phelipe II a los Reynos de León Galicia y Principado de Asturias El Año de MDLXXII* (Madrid, 1765), V–VI, quoting "el libro antiguo" and documents from the monastery. Unfortunately, the precise dating was not recorded. See also Sebastián Sánchez Madrid, *Arqueología y humanism: Ambrosio de Morales* (Córdoba, 2002), 52–54.

12 Flórez, VII; I am very grateful to Dr. Edward Duvall F.R.C.Path. for explaining how this would create a "coagulatory cascade", thereby staunching the flow of blood.

13 Enrique Redel y Aguilar, *Ambrosio de Morales: estudio biografico* (Córdoba, 1909), 78–89.

14 This is examined more fully in Roger Collins, "Ambrosio de Morales, Bishop Pelayo of Oviedo, and the Lost Manuscripts of Visigothic Spain", in Carmen Codoñer and Paulo Farmhouse Alberto (eds.), *Wisigothica, After M.C. Díaz y Díaz* (Florence, 2014), 609–632.

15 Sánchez Madrid, *Arqueología y humanismo*, 89–133.

16 Collins, "Ambrosio de Morales", 610–618. His report, submitted to the king on his return, was not published until 1756: see note 6.

17 Collins, "Ambrosio de Morales", 630–632. One of the MSS from Oviedo perished in the fire in the library of El Escorial, but the fate of those that remained in the cathedral library of Oviedo is entirely unknown.

18 Luís Vázquez de Parga, *La División de Wamba* (Madrid, 1943), 61 n.1, citing a note in MS Madrid BNE 12121, though this is the press mark now assigned to a mid-seventeenth-century Italian-Persian dictionary.The manuscript features in the list of his books made after the bishop's death: Georges Cirot, *De codicibus aliquot ad historiam Hispaniae antiquae pertinentibus olimque ab Ambrosio de Morales adhibitis* (Bordeaux, 1924), 99.

19 *Los Otros Dos Libros Undecimo y Duodecimo de la Coronica General de España que continua Ambrosio de Morales natural de Cordova, Coronista del Rey Catholico neustro señor don Philipe segundo deste nombre, y cathedratico de Rethorica en la Universidad de Alcala de Henares* (Alcalá de Henares, 1578), ff. 107v–108, 112 r/v.

20 The manuscript features in the list of his books made after the bishop's death: Georges Cirot, *De codicibus aliquot ad historiam Hispaniae antiquae pertinentibus olimque ab Ambrosio de Morales adhibitis* (Bordeaux, 1924), 99.

21 There is an eighteenth-century copy of parts of MS Madrid, BNE 1346 in the same library: BNE 18735/19, not including the *formulae*.

22 MS Madrid, BNE 136, guard folio 3. See Juan Gualberto López-Valdemoro de Quesada, Conde de las Navas, *Catálogo de la Real Biblioteca*, vol. II, pt. 1 (Madrid, 1910) for the history of the royal collection.

23 Henry Kamen, *Philip V of Spain: The King Who Reigned Twice* (New Haven and London, 2001), 99.

24 E.g. MS Madrid, BNE 1346, ff. 11v, 14 r/v, 18v, 23v, 25, 36, 118v, 146. On Bishop Pérez and his manuscripts see Joaquin Lorenzo Villanueva, *Viage literario a las Iglesias de España*, vol. III (Madrid, 1804), Cartas XXIV–XXVI, 148–219; see also José Godoy Alcántara, *Historia crítica de los falsos cronicones* (Madrid, 1868), 34–43. Bishop Pérez included some textual items, seemingly taken directly from CVO, in a compilation he made, of which copies survive in MSS Madrid, BNE 590 (early seventeenth century) and 13085 (eighteenth century).

25 MS Madrid, BNE 18, 692: letter from Bishop Pérez to Juan Vázquez del Marmol, *Corrector de los libros por su Magestad*, Toledo 2 August 1591.

26 This is now MS Madrid, BNE 1513.

27 MS Madrid, BNE 1346, guard folio 5. There is a full list of contents in an eighteenth-century hand on guard folio 4.

28 No heading in the manuscript, but this is normally regarded as a version of the *Divisio Wambae*: see Luís Vázquez de Parga, *La División de Wamba* (Madrid, 1943), 59–93.

29 Headed: *Liber de nominibus suevorum, et ewandalorum, Alanorum et Gotorum ab era ccv. Vocatus est liber iste Itacium ab illo qui eum nomen accepit*. This is an idiosyncratic extended form of the *Divisio Wambae*; ed. Vázquez de Parga, *La División de Wamba*, 97–103. Deriving its historical information from the second and longer version of Isidore's *Historia Gotorum* it incorporates a list of the dioceses of Galicia and the churches (parishes?) attached to each of them, supposedly formulated at a council held in Braga in 467 under the Suevic king "Theoderic" (*recte* Theodemir).

30 Natalia Rodríguez Suárez, *Ambrosio de Morales y la Epigrafía Medieval* (León, 2009), no. 29, 121–122. The tomb is now in the chapel of Alfonso II.

31 Ed. Juan Gil,

32 A marginal note by Juan Bautista Pérez (See note 18) indicates that this title in the manuscript, added by Morales, is the result of a misreading, and should be *Chronica Wisegothorum*. It is actually an early eighth century regnal list of Gothic

kings from Athanaric to Wittiza: ed. Karl Zeumer, *Leges Visigothorum*, MGH *Legum, Sectio* I, tom. I, 457–461.

33 The title is that given by Ambrosio de Morales in a marginal note, with *incerto Auctore* subsequently crossed out. The text is a forged charter of King Alfonso III of the Asturias (866–910) for the church of Santiago.

34 No heading; the text is Greg. Reg. IX. 229, but only the final section, which in the collection of Gregorian epistles in the *Hispana* collection is treated as a separate letter: Dag Norberg (ed.), *S. Gregorii Magni Registrum Epistularum*, vol. 2, CCSL vol. CXLA (1982), 810–811. Following this, the bottom half of f. 21 of MS 1346 and all of ff. 21v and 22 r/v are blank.

35 Ed. Wilhelm Levison, *Sancti Ivliani Toletanae Sedis Episcopi Historia Wambae*, CCSL vol. CXV (Turnhout, 1976), 214–255, reprinting the MGH edition (SRM vol. VL, 486–535).

36 No heading for the collection as a whole, which starts with Isidore's epistle to Helladius of Toledo. For the best edition see Juan Gil, *Miscellanea Wisigothica* (Seville, 1972), 3–49. This collection is discussed in detail in Collins, "Ambrosio de Morales", 618–626. Ff. 69v–74v blank.

37 No heading. An unknown hand has written Formula at the top of f. 75r, and Morales has written Ex vetustissimo Ovetensi. For the best edition see Gil, *Miscellanea Wisigothica*, 70–112; see also Karl Zeumer, *Formulae Visigothicae*, in *Formulae Merowingici et Karolini aevi* (MGH).

38 Greg. Reg. I. 41, but only ll 1–45 out of 64 in the CCSL edition, followed by Reg. IX. 229, from l. 64 to l. 135 (ll. 136–159 appear as item 7); all in a much-corrupted text, similar in many but not all instances to the principal Hispana text form.

39 *Etymologiae* I. xxii. 2, ed. W.M. Lindsay, *Isidori Hispalensis Episcopi Etymologiarum sive Originum Libri XX* (Oxford, 1911); Oskar Lehmann, *Quaestiones de notis Tironis et Senecae* (diss., 1869). Ff. 92v and 96v are blank.

40 *Inventario general de los manuscritos de la Biblioteca Nacional*, vol. 4 (Madrid, 1958), 401–404. See also Galván Freile, "El Ms. 1513 de la Biblioteca Nacional de Madrid: primeros pasos en la miniature gótica hispana", *Anuario de Estudios Medievales*, 27 (1997), 479–497.

41 MS Madrid, BNE 1346, f. 116r/v.

42 MS Madrid, BNE 1513, ff. 72v–101v. That it appears in M in the section otherwise copied from this manuscript strengthens the view that the notary had just made a mistake and that this text had not been a component of the CVO.

43 Added by Morales, this may just be a duplication of the *Genealogias de Sagrada escritura* included by the notary after the royal genealogies at the start of the compilation of texts.

44 MS Madrid, BNE 1346, f. 7r.

45 See Luís A. García Moreno, *Prosopografía del Reino Visigodo de Toledo* (Salamanca, 1974) for a reconstruction of the dioceses and their incumbents.

46 Juan Gil Fernández, José L. Moralejo and Juan Ignacio Ruíz de la Peña, *Crónicas Asturianas* (Oviedo, 1985), 48–49 on the *interpolaciones locales unas y peagianas otras*. The version of this text in the Códice de Batres, MS Madrid, BNE 1513, is *mas interpolada todavía con relatos maravillosas*.

47 This was a process already well established in the Asturias, since at least the composition of the authentic *ad Sebastianum* text of the Chronicle of Alfonso III, where the first Asturian king, Pelagius is described as the son of a Duke Fafila *ex semine regio:* ed. Gil, *Crónicas asturianas*, 123. See Thomas Deswarte, *De la destruction à la restauration. L'idéologie du royaume d'Oviedo-León (VIIIe–XIe siècles* (Turnhout, 2003), pt. I.

48 Two manuscripts seen but only briefly described by Morales during his visit to Oviedo in 1572 also seem to have contained this collection. Like the other

manuscripts *en letra gothica* that he saw there, they had been lost by the later eighteenth century.

49 Francisco Javier Fernández Conde, *El Libro de los Testamentos de la Catedral de Oviedo* (Rome, 1971), 367–372.

50 *Relacion del Viage de Ambrosio de Morales Chronista de S.M. El Rey D. Phelipe II a los Reynos de León Galicia y Principado de Asturias el Año de MDLXXII* (Madrid, 1765), 96–97: 1. Otro Libro tiene al principio el retrato de la Cruz de los Angeles, y en la cifra ordinaria dice: Adefonsi Principis sum. Contiene exposicion breve de S. Gregorio sobre todo el Testamento Nuevo. Es insigne libro y de mucha estima, por no andar aun impreso. 2. Un Libro que recopiló el Obispo Pelagio de Oviedo en tiempo del Rey D. Alonso el Sexto, que ganó à Toledo, à quien el dió este libro y en el hay escritas cosas de mano del mismo Obispo. Contiene las Historias mas antiguas de España: de Sebastiano Obispo de Salamanca: de Sampiro Obispo de Astorga: y del mismo Pelagio, y otra. Estan alli tambien otras que escribió el Rey Sisebuto de los Godos, y otras cosas de aquel tiempo. Libro raro. 3. Historia Eclesiastica Eusebii, et Ruffini. Tiene al principio la Cruz de los Angeles, y en la cifra dice: Adefonsi Principis sum. Alli escribió uno al principio que habia setecientos años que se escribió. Mas no tubo por donde lo pudiese afirmar. 4. Un Libro de muchas Historias juntas, donde está todo lo que en el otro libro de Pelagio: Codice insigne y raro

51 César Garcíavde Castro Valdés, *Signum Salutatis. Cruces de orfebrería de los Siglos V al XII* (Oviedo, 2008), 120–127, with prior bibliography. On Morales and the inscription see Natalía Rodríguez Suárez, *Ambrosio de Morales y la Epigrafía Medieval* (León, 2009), item 37, 132–134.

52 The design of the cross in MS BNE 1346 is markedly different in detail from the extant Cruz de los Angeles, in respect to the placing of the decoration on the arms, the existence of pendant alpha and omega letters, and the lack of a central roundel. So, it is not modelled directly on the Oviedan cross.

53 B. Sánchez Alonso (ed.), *Crónica del Obispo Don Pelayo* (Madrid, 1924), 12–15. Potentially, there could have been an earlier version of the chronicle that concluded at some other date, but the facts that the work is extremely brief and that no trace has ever been found of any such alternative text form would argue against such an hypothesis.

54 It continued for a few decades after the formal condemnation of the Visigothic liturgy at the Council of Burgos. See Roger Collins, "Continuity and Loss in Medieval Spanish Culture: The Evidence of MS Silos, Archivo Monástico 4", in Roger Collins and Anthony Goodman (ed.), *Medieval Spain: Culture, Conflict and Coexistence* (Basingstoke, 2002), 1–22.

55 "Información de Derecho por averiguación de Historia, en el punto de si hizo el Voto y dió el privilegio a la Santa Iglesia de Santiago el Rey Don Ramiro el I. ó el II.", in Francisco Valerio Cifuentes (ed.), *Opúsculos castellanos de Ambrosio de Morales cuyos originales se conservan inéditos en la Real Biblioteca del Monasterio del Escoria*l, vol. 1 (Madrid, 1793), 431–468.

56 The opening quoted runs: *Gotorum antiquissimam esse gentem*. Cf. Cristóbal Rodríguez Alonso (ed.), *Las Historias de los Godos, Vándalos y Suevos de Isidoro de Sevilla* (León, 1975), 172.

57 *Huius filius Recisuinetus in consortio Regni assumptus est. Computatis igitur Gotorum Regum Temporibus.* MS Madrid, BNE 1346, f. 116. The title quoted indicates the work extended *usque ad Chatolicum Regem Vambanum.*

58 Teodor Mommsen, *MGH Auctores Antiquissimi,* vol. XI (Berlin, 1894), 262–264 on the testimony of MSS associated with Bishop Pelayo on the *Historia Gothorum/De Origine Gothorum* of Isidore.

59 Cf. MS Madrid, BNE 9549.

60 Roger Collins, "Julian of Toledo and the Education of Kings in Late Seventh-Century Spain, in *eodem, Law, Culture and Regionalism in Early Medieval Spain* (Variorum CS 356, 1992), item III.
61 The eleven and a half folio sides left blank between it and the preceding letter collection may have been intended for copying the treatises on the Liberal Arts had Morales wanted them.
62 Although it is still described as such, most recently in Barrett and Woudhuysen, "Assembling the Austrasian Letters", 19, and in the entirely ill-grounded Edorta Córcoles Olaitz, "About the Origin of the *Formulae Wisigothicae*", *Anuario da Facultade de Dereito da Universidade de Coruña*, vol. 12, (2008), 199–221.
63 Ed. Gil, *Miscellanea Wisigothica*, 90–94. Morales's notary praises it as *verso no muy malo*: MS Madrid, BNE 1346 f. 116v. The reference to *morgengaba* is a bit of antiquarianism and not evidence of "Germanic" survivals.
64 Ed. Gil, *Miscellanea Wisigothica*, 82–85.
65 Obviously lacunose are docs. 7, 11 and 35, which begin in mid-sentence. But the losses must predate CVO, as the texts copied in M treat these documents as complete. Gaps of one or of two lines are left between some of the documents—nos. 1 and 2, 8 and 9, 9 and 10, 14 and 15, 17 and 18, and generally thereafter, but not in the case of nos. 7 and 11.
66 E.g. W.M. Lindsay (ed.), *Julian of Toledo, "de Vitiis et Figuris"* (London etc. 1922); María A.H. Maestre Yenes (ed.), *Ars Iuliani Toletani Episcopi* (Toledo, 1973); Manuela Vendrell Peñaranda, "Estudio del Códice de Azagra, Biblioteca Nacional de Madrid, Ms 10029", *Revista de Archivos, Bibliotecas y Museos*, 82 (1979), 655–706.
67 Collins, "Ambrosio de Morales", 617–625 for suggestions about the formation of the letter collection.
68 In particular formulae numbers 1 to 9 and 21 to 23: Gil (ed.), *Miscellanea Wisigothica*, 71–84 and 94–96. Other textual similarities are either very brief or general. A parallel to item number 10 comes from a suspect charter; 82. Yet more parallels may be found. For a fuller consideration of this issue, see Miguel Calleja Puerta, "Ecos de las *formulas visigóticas* en la documentación altomedieval astur-leonesa": http://elec.enc.sorbonne.fr/cid2012/part4.
69 Marta Herrero de la Fuente (ed.), *Colección diplomática del monasterio de Sahagún (857–1230)*, vol. II (1000–1073) (León, 1988).
70 Santos García Larragueta, *Colección de documentos de la Catedral de Oviedo* (Oviedo, 1962), docs. 55 and 57; María Desamparados Pérez Soler (ed.), *Cartulario de Valpuesta* (Valencia, 1970), docs. 5, 7 and 10; on dating no. 5 see Antonio C. Floriano (ed.), *Diplomática Española del period astur*, vol. II (Oviedo, 1951), doc. 162.
71 Gil, *Miscellanea Wisigothica*, formulae nos. 2, 6, and 7, with their notes, for examples of these features in both the formulae and in actual charters of the ninth and tenth centuries.
72 Emilio Saéz (ed.), *Colección documental de la Catedral de León (775–1230)*, vol. I (775–952) (León, 1987), docs. 5 and 6.
73 Álvaro Cancela has identified eight or possibly nine different scribal hands involved in copying the texts, each perhaps responsible for a separate quire.
74 f. 87r and 89r; f. 89r respectively. Pérez silently corrects Morales' assigning this text to Lucas of Tuy, by noting it came from Isidore's *De viris illustribus.*
75 *Extractum fuit ex libro literis gothicis conscripto in membranis qui nuncupatur decreta canonum presulum Romanorum et aservatur in eclesia ovetensi*: f1r, and cf. f. 41r
76 *Ex vetustissimo foliorum membraneorum codice literis gothicis conscriptorum qui in bibliotheca ecclesiae ovetensis aservatur*: f. 9 r, f. 104r and f. 114r

77 *Hic tractatus fuit extractus ex codice literis gothicis conscript in membranis nuncupato liber Homiliarum ex diversis doctoribus collectarum. Qui asservatur in monasterio Divi Emiliani de la Cogollam ordinis Sancti Benedicti*: f. 19r
78 *Haec transcript sunt ex libello vetusto in membranis conscript qui aservatur in bibliotheca ecclesiae Salmantinae*: f. 152v and cf. f. 156v.
79 Collins, "Ambrosio de Morales and the Lost Manuscripts", 619–623.
80 Manuel C. Díaz y Díaz, *Códices visigóticos en la monarquia leonesa* (León, 1983), 273, n. 273, citing G. de Andrés, *Documentos para la historia del monasterio de San Lorenzo de El Escoria*l, VII (Madrid, 1964), 105. Díaz y Díaz, *ibid.* 270–278 for the important argument that this Homiliary and not the only extant medieval manuscript of *De Habitu Clericorum* was the exemplar for E.
81 Guillermo Antolín, *Catalogo de los códices latinos de la Real Biblioteca del Escoria*l, vol. V (Madrid, 1923), 104–126.
82 Antolín, *Catálogo*, vol. IV (Madrid, 1911), 364–369; Díaz y Díaz, *Códices visigóticos*, 79, n. 78, assigning it to the ninth century had an origin in al-Andalus.
83 MS El Escorial b. III. 14, ff. 132v and 140v.
84 MS El Escorial b. III. 14, f. 149r. The heading of the *Mors testamentumque* is added as a marginal note in another hand.

4 Constructing the enemy: Byzantium in Paul the Deacon

According to Paul the Deacon, after the Avars had ravaged Friuli (in *c.* 610), the Patrician Gregory approached the Friulian Duke Taso with talks of friendship (*HL* 4.37). The patrician invited him to come to Oderzo with an offer to cut his beard, thus adopting him as a son according to the tradition. Taso, fearing no ill will, headed to meet Gregory, accompanied by his brother and a few selected young men. As soon as they were inside the city, Gregory ordered the gates shut and his men turned on the Lombards. Once all the Lombards were dead, narrates Paul, "[Gregory,] the perjurer he was, on account of the oath he swore, ordered Taso's head to be brought to him, and, as promised, he shaved him".[1] Gregory's betrayal is commonplace when it comes to the Byzantines in Paul's *Historia Langobardorum* (*HL*). From Narses' betrayal by the Byzantine court to the outbreak of Iconoclasm, the *HL* is populated by a series of stories of duplicities, deceit, and backstabbing on the part of the imperial forces in Italy. Throughout the work, Paul strives to show that the Byzantines were deceitful and that treason lurked behind every friendly smile. In a sense, the *HL* is a long rant, aimed at dissuading readers from close association with the eastern empire.

Although this aggressive posture towards the empire is one of the most explicit statements in the *HL*, it has hardly played a part in the debate on the purpose and composition of the book.[2] This silence is possibly due to the fact that Paul's take on Byzantium contributes little to the most pressing debate around the *HL*, namely, to whom it was written and who sponsored it. At the surface, a slanderous history of the empire would please both likely audiences, namely, the Beneventans (for Grimoald III, d. 806) or the Carolingians (for Pippin, d. 810).[3] Both had reasons to dislike the Byzantines: if on one side, Charlemagne's relationships with the eastern empire were complicated, on the other, the imperial enclaves in Italy had always prevented the Lombards from unifying the peninsula. Paul's anti-Byzantine stance thus fits the arguments for both sides, and, consequently, has had little bearing on resolving the issue. On a closer look, Paul's clear stance against negotiations with Byzantium fits into a specific context linking Charlemagne, the Beneventan heir Grimoald III, and the destinies of post-conquest southern Italy. By the late 780s, Charlemagne was set to co-opt the Beneventans, impose a dependent status, and use them against an incoming Byzantine invasion. In this context, a libel against the Byzantines, targeted at Grimoald III, could be a fundamental tool to foster Carolingian policy in southern Italy. This chapter argues that Paul produced the *HL* for Grimoald III, on Carolingian commission, to enlist the young prince to support the Frankish agenda for the peninsula, and more specifically, to revert his mother's alliance with Constantinople and fight off the Byzantine-sponsored return of the dethroned Lombard King Adelchis.

The compositions of the *Historia Langobardorum*

The composition of the *HL* has received a good amount of scholarly attention in the last decades.[4] There is much consensus on many details of Paul's life and his work on the *HL*, but some key points remain controversial. For instance, most scholars agree that *HL* was the continuation Paul had promised for the *Historia Romana* (*HR praef.* and 16.23), a work Paul finished between the late 760s and the early 770s.[5] The *HR* was dedicated to Adalperga, the daughter of King Desiderius (756–774) and wife of Arichis, Duke of Benevento. The book consists of a history of Italy based on Eutropius's text, which Paul expanded by adding elements from ecclesiastical history, which Adalperga had allegedly complained Eutropius lacked, and by extending the narrative until Justinian.[6] The *HL*, after presenting the origins of the Lombards in book i, resumes the narrative from the *HR* with Justinian and continues the work up to Liutprand's death (744).[7] There is nonetheless a noticeable change in style: while the *HR* reads like a chronicle, with its concise prose and (relatively) precise dating, the *HL* incorporates more extensive anecdotes and moral stories, resembling Frankish works of history such as Gregory of Tours (which Paul used extensively) and Fredegar (which he might have known).[8] Manuscript evidence suggests the *HL* was well received, especially in Carolingian learned circles, and ninth- and tenth-century copies are plentiful in Gaul and in (the then Carolingian) northern Italy.[9]

Scholars also mostly agree on the *termini* of the composition. Although Paul might have already started gathering information for his continuation of the *HR* by the early 770s,[10] he certainly only completed the work after the mid 780s, maybe as late as 796. The *terminus post quem* is set by the Carolingian conquest of 774, to which Paul hints at (*HL* 5.6), and by the *Gesta Episcoporum Mettiensium*, a work to which he refers in the *HL* (*HL* 6.16), that was finished in 784.[11] A composition after 784—during or after Paul's sojourn in Francia—also accounts for the Carolingian stylistic influence in the work, as well as for some of the sources Paul used, which were more likely to be available in Francia than in Italy.[12] The *terminus ante quem* has traditionally been Charlemagne's imperial coronation (800), a significant event to which Paul does not refer. More recently, Walter Pohl has suggested a more precise dating based on Paul's treatment of the Avars, destroyed by Charlemagne in 796, whom Paul still considers an ongoing threat (*HL* 1.27).[13] Therefore, it is generally accepted that Paul stopped working on the *HL* at some point after 784 and before 796—either because he considered the work finished or because he died (see below).

The intended audience and purpose of the work remain a matter of debate. Different from the *HR*, the *HL* has neither preface nor dedicatory, nor any other direct evidence to contextualise its composition. This bibliographical silence is vexing for the modern scholar, to whom the *HL* remains a fundamental source for Italy under the Lombards and, consequently, much ink has been spilt on the possible context of production. Traditionally, the *HL* was seen as a monument to the (recently) lost Lombard kingdom—not too politically engaged lest it would incur the anger of the conquerors.[14] Even though this reading still has some currency in recent scholarship, it has mostly been dismissed on account of the *HL*'s often positive take on the Franks, and especially Paul's hint that the Carolingian conquest was divinely ordained (*HL* 5.6).[15] To counter this traditional narrative, scholars have suggested two different contexts of composition; the first argues that Paul wrote to Grimoald III, and thus proposing a "Beneventan conception", the second defends a "Carolingian conception", which suggests the text was composed under Charlemagne's sponsorship.

Karl Krügger was the first to extensively defend the idea that the significant role played by King Grimoald I (*c.* 662–71) in the *HL* suggests that Paul was writing to Grimoald III, the Duke of Benevento (788–806).[16] Goffart, the most prominent supporter of the "Beneventan conception", has thoroughly examined the text, and concluded that Paul's emphasis on Beneventan history, the disproportional attention and good press given to Grimoald I, and the constant display of models of kingship suggest that Paul was writing to inform and educate the Beneventan ruler. Thus, Goffart assumes that, after returning to Monte Cassino, which he speculates happened around 785, Paul resumed both his patronage under the ducal family and the project he started with the *HR*.[17] Paul would have worked on the *HL* until he died, possibly around 799,[18] leaving his final work behind, still incomplete.[19] An unfinished work would account for the lack of a dedicatory and preface, and also the progressively sloppier style some scholars notice on book vi.[20] Additionally, Goffart, relying on his breakdown of the internal structure of the work, argues that Paul would have envisioned eight books, instead of the six he completed.[21]

Unconvinced by Goffart's "Beneventan conception", Rosemond McKitterick argued instead that the context of production for the *HL* was not the Beneventan south but the Carolingian court in the north.[22] She suggests that Paul's pro-Carolingian stance went beyond his positive take on Charlemagne and that he was writing for a Carolingian audience in northern Italy, "conceivably at the specific request of [Charlemagne] the Frankish ruler who had asked him to write so much else".[23] In her reading, Paul presented all Lombard kings as wanting in comparison to Charles. Thus,

Paul adapted the Carolingian narrative of the *rois fainéants* to the Lombard Cunincpert and Perctarit, justifying thus Carolingian succession not only over the Merovingian kings but also over their Lombard counterparts. The *HL* would have been closely connected to the Frankish Royal Annals (*Annales Regnum Francorum*), which are similar in perspective and whose author arguably frequented the same circles as Paul.[24] For McKitterick, Paul strove to show the links of friendship between Carolingians and Lombards and to reinforce the rights of the northern kingdom, now under Charlemagne, over the southern duchies. For that reason, the argument goes, Paul strategically ended the book before the repeated Frankish invasions of Italy in the eighth century, when the Lombard-Frankish relationship had turned sour.[25] More strikingly, she looks at the textual history of the *HL*, showing beyond reasonable doubt a clear pattern of dissemination that points mostly to northern Italy and Gaul, rather than to southern Italy, and thus Carolingian and not Beneventan.[26] To make sense of this evidence, Mckitterick suggests the *HL* was an *admonitio* for the Franks in Italy, composed in the mid-780s. The book was then a compilation of Lombard history in Frankish lines, possibly intended to provide an "informative history for the instruction of the young Frankish ruler Pippin of Italy and his Franco-Lombard entourage".[27]

In more recent years, the two arguments have come to a stalemate. Most scholars tend to acknowledge the diplomatic solution produced by Walter Pohl, who suggested that the *HL* is essentially polysemic and, thus, it is impossible to single out one distinct reason behind its composition.[28] Pohl is undoubtedly correct to suggest that the *HL* contains a great variety of topics, which attests not only for the breadth of Paul's interests but also for his varied political and social allegiances, such as his Lombard (and aristocratic) background, his ecclesiastical training, and his condition as a foreign scholar in the pay of the Frankish court. This polysemy, however, does not necessarily refute Goffart's or McKitterick's arguments: a political motivation (or rather motivator) does not reduce the *HL* to a simple pamphlet, aimed uniquely at political propaganda, nor suggests that Paul was unable to incorporate material unrelated to the political thrust behind the text. Nor, indeed, that his selection of material was not, here and there, influenced by different reasons, such as stories he found in his sources and believed he should report, or random snippets he thought to be amusing, entertaining, or in some way worth incorporating in the text, even if not germane to his central argument.

Furthermore, the polysemic nature of the text does not dismiss the evidence for sponsorship compiled by McKitterick and Goffart. Indeed, what we know of Paul's other works, suggest that he wrote usually on commission.[29] Given the historical context and the contents of the *HL*, this commission could only come from two possible sponsors: either the Beneventan government, to whom Paul wrote the *HR* in 773, or the Carolingian court, which sponsored, amongst other works, the *Gesta Episcoporum*

*Mettiensium*finished in 784. Since the two powers remained antagonistic for most of Paul's life, scholars have usually taken for granted Paul was writing either for one or the other. A Carolingian sponsor fits better Paul's post 774 engagements, as well as the balance of power in late eighth-century Italy. Although Benevento survived the Carolingian conquest of 774, as well as numerous Carolingian incursions after that, it is hard to picture the battle-scarred duchy as an especially prosperous patron of arts in the period. McKitterick's survey of the textual tradition also points to a Carolingian context and convincingly rules out a southern Italian composition. Likewise, McKitterick has convincingly shown that the style of the *HL* (which clearly contrasts with the *HR*) and the sources incorporated into the text all suggest a significant level of dialogue with the Carolingian historiographical tradition.[30]

The solution McKitterick advanced, such that Charlemagne sponsored a work targeted at Pippin and the Carolingian court in northern Italy, is nonetheless problematic. First, as Coumert has rightly remarked, had the *HL* been present at the Pavian court in the early eighth century, the author of the *Origo gentis Langobardorum codicis Gothanis* would have made use of it.[31] The text, a continuation of the *Origo* up to Pippin, can be firmly placed in the Carolingian court, and dated between 807 and 810. The anonymous author, who was very interested in rescuing the religious history of the Lombards after the confrontation with the Pope, would have found much of interest in Paul's *HL*.[32] Second, the emphasis Paul puts on Grimoald I's career and on Benevento makes the connection with Grimoald III's position hard to dismiss, as Goffart has strongly demonstrated. McKitterick's suggestion that this attention was solely due to Paul's "loyalty being no doubt somewhat torn"[33] fails to explain why he was so keen to highlight the feats of the namesake of the heir to the one Italian power still resisting the Franks.[34] Such open support of an enemy would cross the line between torn loyalties and treason. Paul's emphasis becomes even more remarkable if one considers Grimoald I does not seem to have been especially well known, given how little information about the king survived. The prominence of Grimoald I's story and the similarities with Grimoald III can hardly be coincidental, even if Paul did not portray the king as the hero Goffart suggests.[35]

Goffart's reading, however, is also not unproblematic. If the internal evidence points strongly to Grimoald III as the intended audience, to assume that he (or the Beneventan government) commissioned the work remains speculative. There is little in the text suggesting an independent Beneventan agenda or the kind of anti-Carolingian sentiment that would be expected from the post-791 Beneventan court. On the contrary, the *HL* not only establishes the Carolingian conquest as a divinely ordained victory (*HL* 5.3), but also concludes by praising the wisdom of maintaining good terms with the Franks (*HL* 6.58).

In sum, the evidence is divided between the two possible but seemingly mutually exclusive explanations, with the internal evidence supporting the

"Beneventan conception", while the style and the external evidence all point to a Carolingian background. This impasse, however, is not necessary. Both Goffart and McKitterick operate on the assumption of an uncomplicated connection between sponsorship and targeted audience. The former, based on the evidence for Grimoald III as the intended audience, speculates that the Beneventan court sponsored the work; the latter, relying on the evidence for a Carolingian sponsorship, conjectures a Carolingian audience. Leaving aside the interpretations, the evidence supporting the two arguments suggests Grimoald III as audience *and* the Carolingian court as the sponsor. A "Carolingian conception", under the direction of Charlemagne, but targeted at Grimoald III, solves the stalemate. On one side, it accounts for the Carolingian influences in style, tone, and the distribution of the manuscripts; on the other, it explains the clear and direct references to Grimoald. The remaining question is this: is there evidence to suggest Charlemagne commissioned Paul to produce a Lombard history for Grimoald III?

The Byzantine history in the *HL* suggests precisely so. Goffart has already noticed the similarities between the *HL*'s account of Grimoald I's victory over the Byzantines and Grimoald III's first acts as a ruler in 788.[36] Goffart believed this similarity was intended to connect Grimoald III to Grimoald I. For him, Paul was working on the *HL* by the late 790s from Benevento (or Monte Cassino), where Grimoald III had been ruling since 788, and thus Paul included references to the first years of Grimoald's reign. This praise included, for instance, the description of Grimoald I's defeat of Constans II's invasion, which "did not too inaccurately reflect the first months of the current prince", referring namely to Grimoald III's victory in 788. It is possible, however, that here the *HL* was intended to be programmatic and not eulogistic. The Byzantine invasion of 788 was long on the make and was undoubtedly on the radar at least since 776.[37] What if, instead of indirect praising the well-established ruler's past in the 790s, Paul was writing before 788 and showing Grimoald I's victories to instruct the young Beneventan prince on how he should behave against the much-anticipated Byzantine invasion? When Charlemagne released Grimaold III from his exile and set him a duke in Benevento, he expected him to fight off the incoming Byzantine invasion. If we read the *HL* as programmatic, Grimoald I's story, and indeed much of what Paul wrote about the Byzantines, fits the political intentions Charlemagne had when he allowed Grimoald III to return to Italy.

A tale of two exiles

It is likely that, in 787, both Paul and Grimoald found themselves in Charlemagne's court. The exact date Paul joined the Carolingian court is unknown, but it has been suggested that he was hired by Charlemagne when the king visited Italy in 780–81.[38] On that trip, Charles had met with a

Byzantine embassy and arranged the marriage of his daughter Rotrud to (the future) Constantine VI.[39] Since Charles needed someone to teach his daughter Greek, he arguably hired Paul as a tutor, whom he also commissioned to compile a royal Homiliary.[40] Afterwards, Paul remained attached to the royal court, working on commission. In 783, he was allowed to plead for his brother Arichis, who was involved in a rebellion against the Franks in 776. The request, in the form of a beautiful poem composed to Charlemagne, is one of Paul's most beautiful works.[41] He was then hired to write a history of the bishops of Metz, which he finished in 784,[42] as well as several epitaphs for prominent figures, most of them connected to the royal family.[43] "Unless I earn my living with letters", Paul told his friend Peter, "I have nothing to give".[44] Paul's life in court was certainly not terrible: he had remarkable resources at his disposal, a community of scholars, and access to a diversity of books unavailable in Italy. Nonetheless, he missed his native Italy. In a letter to the abbot of Monte Cassino, he lamented, not without some dramatic exaggeration, that although everyone treated him well, the court was to him a prison. And he added that, whenever the memory of home and his time in Monte Cassino came to mind, he bemoaned: "I hesitate, I am astounded, I become limp, and amongst drawn breaths deep in my chest, I cannot hold back the tears".[45]

During his time in Francia, it is tempting to see Paul working on the promised continuation of the *HR*, now using the resources at his disposal at the Carolingian court. Much of the material in the *HL* that follows the *HR* in form and style was readily available in Italy, such as the *Liber Pontificalis* and Bede's *Chronica maiora*, and it is not unlikely that Paul had already brought this material from Italy. This material can be easily spotted in the connection between the end of the *HR* and book ii of the *HL,* from the triumph of Narses and Justinian in Italy in *HR* 16.23 (recapitulated in *HL* 1.25) to the description of Justinian's reign and Narses' fate in *HL* 2.1–5, and to the (usually) short chronicle entries on the emperors up to Leo III (717–41).[46] It seems unlikely that back in 773 Paul intended this continuation to be a "history of the Lombards", especially considering that the focus of the *HR* was Italy, and not her many invaders.[47] Nonetheless, if he indeed intended to do so, he had at his disposal the *Origo gentis Langobardorum*, which he had already used in the *HR* (*HR* 16.20).

Although Paul may have compiled much of the material he would use in the *HL* while still in Italy, he also found useful sources in Francia. For instance, Paul possibly used Gregory's *Historiae* to expand the entries on emperors such as Justin II and Tiberius II.[48] Some sections of the *HL* depend on material Paul could only have found in Francia. For example, he relied heavily on Gregory of Tours' *Histories* for books ii and iii, and also Fredegar, whom Paul used for a few of the stories in books i and iv.[49] Additionally, there are a few topics that probably only came to Paul's attention while in Francia, such as the overall negative view of the Lombards' Christianity, which he strove to contest in parts of the *HL*.[50]

One can only speculate when Paul returned definitely to his native land.[51] While some suggest Paul returned to Italy bringing a request from Charlemagne to pope Hadrian in 785, and was around to greet Charles in Monte Cassino when he visited the monastery in 786/7,[52] others defend that Paul returned with Charles in his 786/7 trip.[53] There is no conclusive evidence for either date. Scholars have relied on a *terminus ante quem* based on the epitaph Paul wrote to the Beneventan duke Arichis, who died on August 787, suggesting Paul was in Benevento for the funeral.[54] The evidence for the epitaph, however, is indirect and it is not impossible that Paul wrote it while still in Francia.[55] Indeed, Paul might have composed the epitaph to the grieving Grimoald III, whom he mentioned in the poem. The verses, although suitable for the occasion, were not necessarily set to stone at the funeral, if they ever were.[56] Goffart has rightly claimed "there is no positive reason for locating Paul in Francia after 784".[57] There is also, however, no positive reason for locating him back in Italy. Indeed, the sources are simply not there to reconstruct Paul's life events after 784.[58] One can only state with some certainty that Paul was buried in Benevento, where he had retreated after returning from Francia.[59] When he finally came back to the monastery is impossible to know.

Grimoald III's exile in Francia was shorter and less voluntary: the young prince came in 787 as a hostage, a gage of his father Arichis' good faith. After 774, the Beneventan duke Arichis managed not only to prevent the capture of his duchy but also used the debacle of the northern kingdom to expand his independence.[60] Soon after the Carolingian conquest of the north, Beneventan official documentation started depicting him no longer as a simple *dux*, but as a *princeps*, claiming Benevento was no longer part of a kingdom but a kingdom of its own.[61] The situation of the other Lombard duchies was not as favourable. In 776, Hordgaud of Friuli rose against the Carolingian domination in a vast conspiracy, possibly supported by many Lombard dukes, such as Hildebrand of Spoleto, Arichis of Benevento, and Reginbald of Chiusi[62]—that was the rebellion in which Paul's brother was involved. The conspirators plotted to use Byzantine help to expel the Carolingians and bring back Adelchis, the fugitive heir to the Lombard throne.[63] Charlemagne moved fast, and before the conspirators could coordinate any action, he crushed the northern duchies and re-staffed them with more reliable Frankish personnel.[64] Despite the defeat of the rebellion, the plan to side with the Byzantine Empire, especially in connection with a planned return of Adelchis and the restoration of the Lombard monarchy, was not abandoned by the Lombard elites and remained a significant concern for the Carolingian policymakers until the 810s.[65]

The southern dukes in Spoleto and Benevento were not implicated, and it is likely that Charles had diplomatically defused them beforehand.[66] In 779, Hildebrand of Spoleto crossed the Alps to make a formal submission to Charles, which, at that point, did not imply an actual change of status, but rather replacing papal control with Frankish supervision.[67] Arichis, however, remained free to pursue his independent policy in southern Italy (to the chagrin of the pope) and maintained good reports with the Byzantine government, with whom he cooperated actively in the late 770s.[68] Charles countered Arichis diplomatically, making overtures to Byzantium, namely the marriage between Rotrud and Constantine mentioned above, and building connections with the two major monasteries in the region, Monte Cassino and San Vincenzo al Volturno.[69] Frankish diplomacy failed, however, to deter Arichis, who maintained his staunchly independent attitude, now by attacking Amalfi.[70] It was only in 787 that Charles reversed his moderate policy and, returning to Italy he turned the Frankish military might against the recalcitrant duke.[71] Arichis tried negotiating, offering Roduald, his older son, as a hostage, but Charles ignored his offer and marched on towards Benevento. Arichis retreated into the fortified city of Salerno, and as the Frankish troops approached, he made a final offer: he was willing to surrender both his sons, Roduald and Grimoald as hostages, together with much wealth. That Charles accepted, "not to devastate that land, and empty the bishoprics and the monasteries", disingenuously claims the Royal Frankish Annals.[72]

It seems clear that Charlemagne never intended to annex Benevento, and even after he successfully established Grimoald III there in 788, he did not count it as part of the kingdom.[73] The duchy was too remote from the Frankish mainland, and to get around its intricate mountainous geography would require the Franks to control the sea, then firmly in Byzantine hands.[74] For that reason, fighting Benevento and the Empire at the same time would be a logistic nightmare, hence Charles' adamant resistance to a Byzantium-Benevento alliance. Initially, Charles had promised to let the pope control Benevento, so that Rome would take care of southern Italy.[75] The realities of Italian politics convinced him otherwise, and he settled at defusing the military threat posed by the duchy while maintaining it as a buffer zone between the Carolingian dependent papal lands and the Byzantine enclaves in Sicily and Calabria. To do so, Charles had to preserve the integrity of Benevento, and find a reliable and locally acceptable name to command it. It is tempting to suggest that, from the start of the 787 campaign, Charles envisioned to replace the troublemaker Arichis with the more pliable teenager Grimoald. When offered both heirs as hostages, Charles openly refused to take Arichis' older son Roduald (who would have been twenty-five in 787),[76] separating him instead from Grimoald, whom he took to Francia. It is possible Charles believed that, during the time Grimoald spent in court, the teenager could receive a proper Frankish education, which would make an ally out of him (an effort that would be wasted on the already grown-up Roduald).[77] An effective "Frankization" of Grimoald would be especially necessary since the relationship with Byzantium had recently turned sour, and Charles was about to break the betrothal between his daughter and Constantine.[78] If Charles was able to bring Grimoald over to his side, he could defuse Benevento as a threat, and build it up as a buffer zone against the Byzantines.

Fortunately, Charles happened to have at the royal court not only a Lombard scholar but also one who had been close to Grimoald's mother (and possibly even Grimoald): Paul the Deacon.[79] There is no direct attestation of Paul working as a tutor to Grimoald, but there is some interesting indirect evidence in the *HL* that suggests that the text relied on the main connection between the two, namely, the experience of being removed from their homeland. Exiles are central figures in the *HL*. In book iv, Paul describes the invasion of his ancestral home (*HL* 4.37), when the Avars crossed the border into Friuli. The Friulian Duke Gisulf[80] died in battle but his four sons (Taso, Cacco, Roduald, and the infant Grimoald) managed to escape into exile. At this point, Paul stops the story, saying that "[t]he moment now requires that, leaving aside the general narrative, I recount something private about me, the one who writes this book, and about my genealogy".[81] He then tells the story of his *abavus*, Leupchis, who came to Italy from Pannonia with the Lombards, lived a long life and left five children: those, however, were taken into captivity in that same raid and dragged into the Avar homeland. There they endured the misery of captivity, until, when coming of age, one of them, Lopichis, "inspired, we believe, by the Author of Mercy", cast off the yoke of servitude and left in search for Italy to find back "the rights of freedom". Lopichis returned home, where he met his friends and family, rebuilt his house and found a wife. The property of his father, however, he never received back. "This man", concludes Paul, "was my great-grandfather, and he fathered my grandfather Arichis, and Arichis, my father Warnefrit, and Warnefrit, from Theodolinda, his wife, fathered me, Paul, and my brother Arichis, who was named after my grandfather".[82]

Paul is not famous for his personal anecdotes, and he is seldom present in his own stories.[83] This little tale, however, established his kinship with his intended reader: not unlike Grimoald's namesake and Paul's great-grandfather, Paul, the grammarian, and Grimoald, the young Beneventan heir, were both Lombards exiled by an invasion, in their case, the Carolingian invasion of Italy of 774. The Lombard diaspora after the Avar invasion is not the only exile story in the *HL*. Indeed, there is a significant number of them in the *HL*, suggesting Paul invested much in this connection. The long list starts with the very origin of the Lombards, whom the lack of food forced to leave their Scandinavian homeland to seek new homes (*HL* 1.2–3).[84] Exile is also part of a tale involving Alboin, who had to feast and fight at his enemies' den—and received from them his weapons—to be granted the right to sit at his father's table (*HL* 1.23–24). It is the story of Grimoald I, who was first exiled by the Avars, then, returning to Friuli, he left it to Benevento (4.39), and then departed Benevento to rule in the north (*HL* 4.51). It is the story of Perctarit (*HL* 5.33), of Cunincpert (*HL* 5.39), and of Ansprand, Liutprand's father (*HL* 6.21), all banished at some point in their lives. In many ways, Paul's *HL* is a story of successful exiles, of people that for one reason or another were sent away (especially from Italy) only to return in victory. More than a random occurrence, these stories arguably point to a connection between Paul and the young Beneventan heir and to their shared exile in Francia. Paul was well aware of the condition of Grimoald, whom once he called "an exile, [whom] hard Gaul holds",[85] and the emphasis on exiles on the *HL* suggests he used the connection as a way to reach out for the Beneventan prince.

Of Grimoald and Greeks: the programmatic *Historia Langobardorum*

If Charlemagne indeed brought Grimoald and Paul together as part of the "Frankization" process necessary to send Grimoald to rule Benevento, as suggested here, it is then likely that he commissioned Paul to write an account of Lombard history. Such work would educate the young hostage on his people's past, with emphasis on the submission of Benevento to the king in Pavia (which after 774 meant the Carolingian power across the Alps). Paul had planned for a continuation to the *HR* at least since 773, and he might have been working on incorporating the new sources he found in Francia into it. Given that Grimoald was only fourteen, and that his brother stood before him in the succession line, time was initially not a major constraint. In any case, the work, as part of Grimoald's education, had to be completed before the young man was sent back to Italy to replace his brother as duke of Benevento. This timeline changed dramatically by the end of the summer 787, when Grimoald's older brother Roduald died in July, soon followed by his father.[86] At this point, as we suggested above, Paul wrote for Grimoald an epitaph to his father, in which he describes his mother Adelperga as "formerly happy, now the most miserable wife (*miserrissima uxor*)", who saw the death of the husband over the funeral of her son, while her other son was exiled in Gaul.[87] All of a sudden, the exiled teenager had become the legitimate Duke of Benevento, and the plan to send him back properly "frankified" had to be rushed.

This sense of hurry was certainly magnified when the *miserrissima uxor*, now in command of Benevento, raised the pressure on Charlemagne to return Grimoald.[88] The widow, however, also resumed her husband's former policy of rapprochement with Byzantium and allegedly entered secret cooperation to restitute the Lombard monarchy.[89] In a series of letters to Charlemagne, Pope Adrian warned the king about Byzantine envoys in southern Italy negotiating a combined action against him and the local Frankish government.[90] Adelchis, the pope added, was already in Calabria,[91] and the Beneventans were only waiting for Grimoald for a call to arms.[92] Suspicious of Adrian's ongoing slandering of Benevento, Charles sent a mission to confirm the story and check whether Benevento had indeed broken faith with him. In their report (dated January 22, 788), his *missi* not only confirmed Adelperga's rebellion, but also described how the

Beneventans tried to keep them hostage until the Franks returned Grimoald, and how they had to fight their way out.[93] Adelperga's rebellion could not have come at a worse time, when Charles was busy dealing with the Bavarian Duke Tassilo.[94] Although the duke had recently submitted to Charles, there was growing suspicions that he was trying to ally with the Avars against the Carolingians.[95] Whether those rumours were true or not, Charles knew by the autumn of 787 that the situation in Bavaria could require further military action. If Tassilo could indeed bring in Avar support, and if Adelperga's negotiations with Byzantium could deliver an imperial army commanded by Adelchis, that could result in a general conflagration in Italy and the Alpine zone. Such a scenario would put at risk not only the Carolingian-controlled kingdom in northern Italy but also two decades of Carolingian policy in the region.[96]

Charles's solution was to defuse the situation in Benevento by agreeing to Adelperga's demands and reinstating Grimoald as duke (but not as prince), so that he could concentrate his efforts in crushing Tassilo before the Bavarians could link up with the Avars.[97] For Charles's plan to work, Grimoald would have to play along. He needed his recent hostage not only to reverse his mother's policy, taking Benevento back into Carolingian control; more than that, Grimoald would have to actively fight off the incoming Byzantine attack (which would probably include his own uncle and former Lombard king Adelchis).[98] To guarantee his loyalty, Charles required that Grimoald swore an oath and that the Lombards shaved their chins—probably as a sign of submission—and, once in possession of his duchy, that Grimoald kept Charles' name on the coins and charters.[99] But more than the oath of the prince, Charles would have to rely on the training Grimoald received in Francia, and on how effective this training was to align the prince with the Franks. It was a tall order, and it shows how much Charles trusted the education Grimoald received at the court and, if our reading of the *HL* is correct, how much the king believed in Paul the Deacon. In May 788, Grimoald agreed to Charles's terms and was sent off to Benevento.[100] With Benevento and the incoming Byzantine attack thus settled, Charles could safely allocate Frankish military resources to Bavaria.[101]

Paul's "six books against the Greeks": Grimoald's Tale

Paul also modifies Fredegar to connect the stories with the long narrative about Grimoald I, a part of the *HL* we could call "Grimoald's Tale".[102] The story of Grimoald I, duke of Benevento (*c.* 647–62) and king of the Lombards (662–71), stands almost as a narrative of its own, and is certainly the longest tale Paul told in the *HL*, carrying on from the foundation of Friuli by Grimoald's father Gisulf in book ii up to Grimoald's death in book v. One should keep in mind that the historical Grimoald I is a nightmare for scholars of Lombard Italy: apart from the king's brief contributions to the

Lombard laws[103] and a snippet in the *Origo gentis Langobardorum* (which might as well be a post-*HL* interpolation),[104] no source before Paul mentions him. Even for Constans II's Italian campaign, one of the highlights of Grimoald's reign in the *HL*, which is well attested in the *LP*, there is no mention of Grimoald's involvement.[105] Paul, on the other hand, dedicated a very significant slice of the *HL* to him, packing it with events the modern scholar has no chance to confirm.[106] Paul might have consulted sources now lost to us, but in the present state of the documentation, it is impossible to tell fact from fiction.

A particularity of "Grimoald's Tale" is that in it—and only in it—Paul uses *Greci* to refer to the Byzantines.[107] The pejorative use of "*Greci*" had a long history in the Latin west, and Paul was not starting a new trend with the *HL*.[108] Paul had already used the term pejoratively, as we see in his use of "pergraecare", which he glosses in a commentary on Festus as "epulis et potationibus inseruire", that is, "to surrender to food and drinks" in a decadent way.[109] Paul relied on a similar expression in the *HR*, in which he pictured the Gothic king Theodoric being reproached by his people for "Graecorum epulis superflueret", indulging in Greek banquets.[110] More generally in Latin literature, the pejorative use of "*Greci*" gained new currency at the end of the eighth century, starting with the conflicts between the popes and Constantinople, and later on spreading through Carolingian literature.[111] These precedents notwithstanding, Paul's consistent use of "*Greci*" in the chapters related to Grimoald I stands out from his common usage and supports the idea that this section of the work is a later composition and served as propaganda against the Byzantines, thus aimed directly at Grimoald III.

Grimoald I is first mentioned in the story of the Avar invasion that destroyed Friuli (*HL* 4.37–38). Paul used the invasion and its aftermath to pack several of his main themes, some of which we mentioned before, such as the good fortune of exiles and the unreliability of Byzantine friendship. Paul also used the invasion to introduce another topic relating to Grimoald III: the threat of women in power, a warning arguably referring to Grimoald III's mother, Adalperga. Paul exposes this theme with the story of Romilda, Grimoald I's mother. After the death of her valiant husband Gisulf, she and the rest of the Lombards sought refuge behind the walls of the cities. However, Romilda lusted for the Avar commander, and thus the "nefarious whore" (*meretrix nefaria*), as Paul calls her, surrendered her people to the Avars, opening the gates of Cividale. "The Avars" recounts Paul "killed by the sword all Lombards who had already come to age, and condemned to the yoke of slavery the women and children".[112] Romilda, the "cruel betrayer of the nation" (*dira proditrix patriae*), did not get her reward: instead, the Avar king, who pretended to accept her as a wife, handed her to be raped and murdered. The parallels with Adalperga, Grimoald III's mother, are evident. After the death of her husband (Arichis), Adalperga was negotiating with the enemies of the Lombards, the Byzantines, and, as Romilda before her, she was bound to be betrayed and to bring ruin to them all. The similarities were hard to miss for the contemporaries, and so was the harsh treatment Paul reserved for his former sponsor.

The second part of "Grimoald's Tale" contains stories of Grimoald as a duke. Paul first describes how Grimaold and his brother Roduald left Friuli for Benevento in a voluntary exile. After the death of Taso and Cacco, their uncle Grasulf assumes the duchy, and their younger brothers, Grimoald and Roduald (also the name of Grimoald III's older brother), finding it unacceptable to live under him, left to seek fame and glory in Benevento. There, Arichis, who used to tutor Gisulf's sons in Cividale, received them kindly (*HL* 4.39). After the death of Arichis's son Aio, first Roduald and then Grimoald ruled Benevento (*HL* 4.43–44). Paul reports a single event from Grimoald I's time as a duke:

> Since he was very warlike (*bellicosissimus*) and always noble, when the Greeks came (*venientibus Grecis*) at that time to plunder the sanctuary of the holy archangel [Michael] in Monte Gargano, Grimoald, coming upon them with an army, stroke them down with extreme slaughter.[113]

However short, this story ranks among Paul's most well-crafted pieces of propaganda.[114] It remits to a well-known hagiographic text, the *Liber de apparitione sancti Michaelis in monte Gargano*, probably composed by the end of the seventh century.[115] In the *Liber*, the Neapolitans, there described as pagans, attacked the Christian Beneventans and Sepontians.[116] In preparation for the battle, while the pagans celebrated their public games (*ludis scenicis*) to guarantee the support of their false gods, the Christians came to Gargano to ask for help from Saint Michael. Saint Michael appeared in a vision, promising help on the day of the battle. Confident on the saint's help, the Beneventans and Sapontians marched against the Neapolitans and, when the lines first met, Mount Gargano erupted, raining fire on the enemies of Saint Michael. The Neapolitans ran away, with their enemies chasing them and slaughtering them until they reached the walls of their city. Those who survived were soon to find out that almost six hundreds of them were fulminated by lightning; they immediately converted to Christianity.[117] Retelling the story, however, Paul connects the attackers with the *Greci* and the victorious defender with Grimoald. In a single stroke, he not only associated the Byzantine with the "pagans Neapolitans" but ultimately connected Grimoald (and Benevento) with the divine support of Saint Michael.

The next chapter in Grimoald's story is his rise to kingship. Paul describes how Grimoald conquered the northern kingdom, which had split in a Merovingian-style division, introducing his Lombard version of the *rois fainéants*.[118] The story carries a few lessons on how to treat defeated enemies, and how to reward loyalty, in the general style of royal *specula* (*HL* 5.1–4). Later on, Grimoald defeats a Frankish invasion using his wits, and getting the Frankish army drunk before his attack (*HL* 5.5). All that sets the scene to the highpoint of the story: Constans II, desiring to snatch Italy out of the hand of the Lombards, travelled by sea and landed in Taranto. The emperor moved north taking all the Beneventan cities until he finally came to Benevento itself, which he energetically sieged (*HL* 5.7). Romuald, Grimoald's son and duke of Benevento, sent his tutor Sesuald north to warn the king of the attack and held the city while he waited for reinforcements. On his way south, Grimoald sent Sesuald before him to inform Romuald of his movements, but the *Greci* captured him on the way (*HL* 5.7). While the *Greci* negotiated a truce, they sent Sesuald to talk to Romuald, constraining him not to reveal the whereabouts of Grimoald and the likelihood the siege would be broken. Sesuald, however, told the truth, and asked Romuald to take care of his family, since "this perfidious people will not allow me to live".[119] The emperor then had his head cut off and catapulted it into the city but desisted from further sieging Benevento, retreating to Capua (*HL* 5.8–9).

Paul, however, did not ascribe the actual military victory to Grimoald I. When the two armies finally joined battle, it was Romuald who led the Lombards, defeating the *Grecus* commander Saburrus. Grimoald wanted to lead the army, but Romuald assured his father there was no need to: he asked for only a part of the army and, trusting God, promised to bring the king glory (*HL* 5.10). During the battle, an exceptionally strong Lombard called Amalongus struck a little Greek man (*Greculus*), raising him up on the air with his spear. Paul concludes:

> The *Grecus* army, having seen that, was instantly terrified with a great fear, and turned into a rout, and struck down by the utmost disaster, escaping death, they surrendered victory to Romuald and the Lombards.[120]

Constans II, when he realised he could accomplish nothing against the Lombards, turned against his own, plundering the churches in Rome. Moving his capital to Sicily, the emperor oppressed the population until they killed him in his bath.[121] The *Greci* were thus defeated not by the king of the Lombards, but by his son, the duke of Benevento, who, supported by God, fought for the glory of his king. Contrasting the two Byzantine invasions, it is clear that Paul chose to highlight the divine support behind the dukes of Benevento, Grimoald as a duke in Gargano and Romuald; he was unwilling to extend it to Grimoald as a king.

The next (and final) part of Grimoald's reign is a combination of praiseworthy actions in Benevento and cruelty in the north. After rescuing the Beneventans and their provinces from the *Greci*, Grimoald I returned to Pavia.[122] The rest of his rule, Grimoald I spent fighting the Romans, whom he despised with "an extraordinary hate" (*non mediocre odio*) (*HL* 5.27–28). Paul describes Grimoald I attacking during Easter one of the cities, Forum Populi (Forlimpopoli, on the Via Emilia, close to Forlì), and killing people out of the baptismal font (*HL* 5.27)—an especially wicked act.[123] Grimoald also went after all the Lombards who rebelled against him while he was away fighting Constans, especially Lupus of Friuli. To put down the duke without causing a civil war, Grimoald I invited the Avars in, who indeed cast out the duke (who sought refuge amongst the Slavs and was eventually killed by the Friulians), but also caused havoc in Friuli—ironically, king Grimoald produces a tragedy in Friuli akin to the one that set his early life in motion. To get rid of them, the king had to pull another of his military tricks, convincing the Avars his troops were much more numerous than they actually were (*HL* 5.18–21).[124] The only positive act Paul includes has again to do with Benevento, where Grimoald successfully settles a group of Bulgarians (*HL* 5.29). Finally, instead of a restful repose, Grimoald died poisoned by his doctors while treating a hunting wound (*HL* 5.33).

Overall, Paul's Grimoald is a good ruler. He is, nonetheless, somewhat unfit to be king. He was tricked into taking the kingship in the first place (*HL* 4.51), he handled Perctarit's situation poorly (and was only prevented from sinning by a miracle) (*HL* 5.1–4), and was unable to control his emotions towards the Romans (*HL* 5.27–28). More significantly, Paul does not describe the victories Grimoald achieved as king as granted by God. As duke, Grimoald conquered with the help of God; as king, he could only triumph by deceit.[125] Compared to the stories of Grimoald as a duke, Paul's take on him as a king make it clear how his reach for the throne, albeit successful, had exposed him to anger and sin. Grimoald I is not a hero, nor was he presented to be a model for Grimoald III to follow: with his story, Paul showed not only what he (and Charlemagne) expected Grimoald III to do, but also what *not* to do. He should be skeptical of the Byzantines and fight off the incoming invasion, but he should stay away from the kingship.[126]

Conclusion

The argument advanced here is that the *HL*, as Rosemond McKitterick has strongly suggested, was produced under Carolingian sponsorship, possibly by Charlemagne's request. Its targeted audience, however, was not Pippin or the Carolingian court in northern Italy, but instead, as Walter Goffart established, Grimoald III, whom Charlemagne expected to follow Frankish policy once reinstated in Benevento in 788. This policy was to reverse current diplomatic thrust in Benevento to combine forces with Constantinople, and use Byzantine resources to resist the Carolingian infiltration in the south, eventually restoring the kingdom in the north under Adelchis, heir to the deposed King Desiderius. More immediately, the Carolingians needed Grimoald III to mobilise the forces in Benevento to fight off (and not for) the incoming Byzantine invasion. Afterwards, Charles wanted Grimoald to remain quiet in Benevento and put aside any grandiose plan he could have for Italy. Charles was undoubtedly aware that, with Adelchis killed or exiled, Grimoald III would be the heir to Desiderius, his maternal grandfather, and it was important that the young duke was discouraged to act upon this claim. To achieve this political reorientation, Charles used all the resources available to him. He drew charters limiting the ducal powers and bound Grimoald to himself by oaths.[127] The strength of those mechanisms, however, depended on the continuous threat of Carolingian retaliation, and that would require a regular military presence in the south Charles could not (or did not want to) maintain.

Thus Charles relied on a more subtle mechanism, educating Grimoald on the examples of the Lombard past. The *HL*, with its collection of stories of brave Lombard dukes and treacherous Byzantine governors, could provide the necessary ideological training to bend Grimoald willingly to the role Charlemagne expected of him. Read as a political agenda, the *HL* aimed to bring Grimoald III clear guidelines for his future as duke of Benevento. The way Paul treats Byzantine history in "Grimoald's Tale", and in other passages related to dealings between Lombards and exarchs, discourages the reader from the current Beneventan policy of advocating the Byzantines as a solution to counter the Carolingian conquest. Pedagogically, Paul deploys a large number of anecdotes that admonish his reader to the dangers of association with the Byzantines, highlighting how historically the Lombards always lost from such arrangements. Grimoald I's story, and especially the emphasis on his role as the defender of Benevento against the Byzantines, set the example for a strong anti-Byzantine duchy. Paul was nonetheless careful to discourage Grimoald III of any larger project to restore the Lombard throne in the north. He makes it clear that kingship was a burden to Grimoald and that both his involvement with court politics in Pavia and his dealings with "royal affairs" (such as the repression of the rebel duke Lupus and the Roman cities) led the king astray from his righteous path.

As a corollary, the date of composition of the *HL* can be arguably stated as between 787, when Grimoald was brought to court, and 788, when he left for Benevento. This timeframe assumes that Paul worked on the material used in the *HL* beforehand, most likely as the promised continuation to the *HR*, and that once Charlemagne commissioned a text to educate the young Grimoald on his native land (and on how to best rule it, according to the Franks), Paul had already a draft from which he could work. This limited timeframe, and especially the rush produced by the need to expediently return Grimoald, also account for the nature of book vi, and the apparently unfinished elements in the text.

Afterword: Grimoald and the *Historia Langobardorum*

Grimoald was sent back to Benevento in May 788, and later on that year the Byzantine invasion landed in southern Italy. A combined force of Grimoald's Beneventans and Spoletans troops, together with a Frankish detachment, fought them off valiantly.[128] It is not certain if Adelchis was present. Grimoald lived up to Charles's expectations, and Franks had a free hand to terminate Tassilo with extreme prejudice (788), and eventually exterminate the Avars (793).[129] Grimoald kept his head down, printed Charles's name on his coins and his charters. In 791, however, Grimoald reverted this policy and once again tried free Benevento from the Carolingian influence. The extent of his success is hard to grasp, but the fact that the *Frankish Royal Annals* turn silent on southern Italy points to the collapse of Carolingian control and (at least limited) success of the Beneventan rebellion. Grimoald was finally brought back to heel in 812 when the Carolingians imposed a heavy tribute on Benevento.[130] As for the *HL*, its reception in Benevento was bleak, or at least the surviving manuscripts seem to show. The only surviving early manuscript that can be traced back to southern Italy is the Assisi palimpsest, whose state precludes much speculation, but whose origin might be connected to Grimoald's copy.[131]

Notes

1 *HL* 4.38: Gregorius vero patricius, proter iusiurandum quod dederat, caput Tasonis sibi deferri iubens, eius barbam, sicut promiserat, periurus abscidit.

2 Paul's bitter tone towards the Empire has already be noticed by B. Luiselli, "La società longobardica del secolo VIII e Paolo Diacono storiografo tra romanizzazione e nazionalismo longobardico", in A. Bruzzone and M.L. Fele (eds.), *Romanobarbarica: scritti scelti* (Florence, 2017), 567–599, 596; originally printed in B. Luiselli, "La società longobardica del secolo VIII e Paolo Diacono storiografo tra romanizzazione e nazionalismo longobardico", *Paolo Diacono, Storia dei Longobardi* (Milano, 1991), 5–48; also by W. Pohl, "Paolo Diacono e la construzione dell'identità longobarda", in P. Chiesa (ed.), *Paolo Diacono, uno scrittore fra tradizione longobarda e rinnovamento carolingio* (Udine, 2000), 413–426, 421; and more recently, W. Pohl, "Creating Cultural Resources for Carolingian Rule: Historians of the Christian Empire", in R. McKitterick, S. Meeder and C. Gantner (eds.), (Cambridge, 2015), 15–33; A. Plassmann, *Origo gentis: Identitäts- und Legitimitätsstiftung in früh- und hochmittelalterlichen Herkunftserzählungen* (Berlin, 2006), 194–195.

3 The main defenders of these theories are, respectively, W. Goffart, *The Narrators of Barbarian History (A.D. 550–800): Jordanes, Gregory of Tours, Bede, and Paul the Deacon* (Princeton, 1988); and R. McKitterick, "Paul the Deacon and the Franks", *Early Medieval Europe* 8 (1999), 319–339; R. McKitterick, "Paolo Diacono e i Franchi: il contesto storico e culturale", in P. Chiesa (ed.), *Paolo Diacono: Uno scrittore fra tradizione longobarda e rinnovamento carolingio* (Udine, 2000), 9–28; R. McKitterick, *History and Memory in the Carolingian World* (Cambridge, 2004). See n. 4 for a full bibliography.

4 The bibliography on Paul the Deacon, and especially on the composition of the *HL* is extensive. See, especially, K.H. Krüger, "Zur 'beneventanischen' Konzeption der Langobardengeschichte des Paulus Diaconus", *Frühmittelalterliche Studien* 15 (1981), 18–35; K. Gardiner, "Paul the Deacon and Secundus of Trent", in B. Croke and A.M. Emmett (eds.), *History and Historians in Late Antiquity* (Sydney, 1983), 147–153; Goffart, *Narrators* 329–431; D.A. Bullough, "Ethnic History and the Carolingians: an Alternative Reading of Paul the Deacon's *Historia Langobardorum*", in D.A. Bullough (ed.), *Carolingian Renewal: Sources and Heritage* (Manchester 1991), 97–122; W. Pohl, "Paulus Diaconus und die 'Historia Langobardorum': Text und

Tradition", in A. Scharer and G. Scheibelreiter (eds.), *Historiographie im frühen Mittelalter* (Vienna, 1994), 375–405; and more recently, Pohl, "Cultural Resources"; McKitterick, "Paul the Deacon"; (slightly modified in McKitterick, "Paolo Diacono"; and McKitterick, *History and Memory*); L. Capo, "Paolo Diacono e il mondo franco: l'incontro di due esperienze storiografiche", in P. Chiesa (ed.), *Paolo Diacono: uno scrittore fra tradizione longobarda e rinnovamento carolingio (atti del Convegno internazionale di studi, Cividale del Friuli, Udine, 6–9 maggio 1999)* (Udine, 2000), 39–74; P. Chiesa, "Caratteristiche della trasmissione dell'*Historia Langobardorum*", *Paolo Diacono e il Friuli altomedievale (secc. VI-X): atti del XIV Congresso internazionale di studi sull'alto Medioevo, Cividale del Friuli - Bottenico di Moimacco, 24–29 settembre 1999* (Spoleto, 2001), 45–66; L. Pani, "Aspetti della tradizione manoscritta dell'*Historia Langobardorum*", in P. Chiesa (ed.), *Paolo Diacono: uno scrittore fra tradizione longobarda e rinnovamento carolingio* (Udine, 2000), 367–412; Plassmann, *Origo gentis*, 191–242; M. Coumert, *Origines des peuples: les récits du Haut Moyen Âge occidental (550–850)* (Paris, 2007), 215–240; S. Ghosh, *Writing the Barbarian Past: Studies in Early Medieval Historical Narrative* (Leiden, 2015), 117–119.

5 See Goffart, *Narrators* 378; G. Zanella, "La legittimazione del potere regale nella 'Storie' di Gregorio di Tours e Paolo Diacono", *Studi Medievali* 31 (1990), 55–84, 71; the idea that the *HL* continued the *HR* can be traced back to T. Mommsen, "Die Quellen der Langobardengeschichte des Paulus Diaconus", *Neues Archiv* 5 (1880), 51–103, 76–84. For the dating, see Goffart, *Narrators* 337.

6 For the *Historia Romana,* see E. Sestan, "Qualche aspetto della personalità di Paolo Diacono nelle sua 'Historia Romana'", in E. Sestan (ed.), *Italia medievale* (Napoli, 1966), 50–75; Goffart, *Narrators*; L.B. Mortensen, "Impero Romano, *Historia Romana, Historia Langobardorum*", in P. Chiesa (ed.), *Paolo Diacono: uno scrittore fra tradizione longobarda e rinnovamento carolingio: atti del Convegno internazionale di studi, Cividale del Friuli, Udine, 6–9 maggio 1999* (Udine, 2000), 355–366; M. Maskarinec, "Who Were the Romans? Shifting Scripts of Romanness in Early Medieval Italy", in W. Pohl and G. Heydemann (eds.), *Post-Roman Transitions: Christian and Barbarian Identities in the Early Medieval West* (Turnhout, 2013), 297–363; Pohl, "Cultural Resources", 22–26.

7 Goffart, *Narrators* 378.

8 On Paul's use of Fredegar, see n. 110.

9 McKitterick, "Paul the Deacon", 334–337.

10 On the idea that Paul was long preparing the material for the *HL*, see Goffart, *Narrators* 340.

11 For the dating of the *Gesta*, see W. Goffart, "Paul the Deacon's 'Gesta Episcoporum Mettensium' and the Early Design of Charlemagne's Succession", *Traditio* 42 (1986), 59–93, 63–64, n. 22; M. Sot, "Le *Liber de episcopis Mettensibus* dans l'histoire du genre *Gesta episcoporum*", in P. Chiesa (ed.), *Paolo Diacono: Uno scrittore fra tradizione longobarda e rinnovamento carolingio* (Udine, 2000), 527–550; D. Kempf, "Paul the Deacon's *Liber de episcopis Mettensibus* and the Role of Metz in the Carolingian Realm", *Journal of Medieval History* 30 (2004), 279–299; see also Goffart, *Narrators* 373–378.

12 McKitterick, "Paul the Deacon", 331–332; Coumert, *Origines*, 220–221.

13 Pohl, "Paulus Diaconus", 376; see also Pohl, "Paolo Diacono", 413.

14 For the traditional view, see esp. Sestan, "Qualche aspetto"; G. Vinay, "Un mito per sopravivere: l'*Historia Langobardorum* di Paolo Diacono", *Alto medioevo latino* (Napoli, 1978), 125–149; R. Morghen, "La civiltà dei Longobardi nella *Historia Langobardorum* di Paolo Diacono", *Tradizione religiosa nella*

civiltà dell'Occidente cristiano: saggi di storia e di storiografia (Roma, 1979), 53–68; Bullough, "Ethnic History"; L.B. Mortensen, *Civiliserede barbarer: historikeren Paulus Diaconus og hans forgængere* (København, 1991), 67–85; Luiselli, "Società longobardica", 595–596; S.M. Cingolani, *Le storie dei Longobardi: dall'origine a Paolo Diacono* (Roma, 1995); Capo, "Paolo Diacono". Claudio Leonardi, although incorporating new elements, still reads the *HL* as a monument to the Lombard past, see C. Leonardi, "La figura di Paolo Diacono", *Paolo Diacono e il Friuli altomedievale (secc. VI–X)* (Spoleto, 2001), 13–24.

15 See Coumert, *Origines*, 217. For the Carolingian victory as divine judgment, see E. Sestan, "La storiografia dell'Italia longobarda: Paolo Diacono", *Settimane di Studio del Centro italiano sull'alto medioevo* 17 (1970), 357–386, 371.

16 See Krüger, "Zur beneventanischen Konzeption". Krüger follows, in broad strokes, Pier S. Leicht, who saw Adalperga as the motivator of Paul's picture of Grimoald I for her son, and Karl Hauck, who suggested Benevento as the place where Paul worked on his "... berühmtestes Werk, die Geschichte seines Volkes ..." See, respectively, P.S. Leicht, "Paolo Diacono e gli altri scrittori delle vicende d'Italia nell'èta carolingia", *Atti del 2°Congresso internazionale di studi sull'alto medioevo* (1953), 57–74; K. Hauck, "Mittellateinische Literatur", in W. Stammler (ed.), *Deutsche Philologie im Aufriss. Unter Mitarbeit zahlreicher Fachgelehrter* ([Berlin], 1966), 2555–624, 2574. For the central importance of Grimoald I in the *HL*, see also H. Rogan, *Paulus Diaconus—laudator temporis acti: Königsdarstellung und Aufbauprinzip der Buchschlüsse als Antwort auf die Frage nach dem von Paulus intendierten Ende der Historia Langobardorum* 1. Aufl. edn (Graz, 1993), 263–301.

17 Goffart, *Narrators* 344–347; 79–81.

18 A 799 death is possible but fully speculative; see Ibid. 346; McKitterick, "Paul the Deacon", 324; Pohl, "Paolo Diacono", 413–414.

19 Also defending an incomplete work: R. Morghen, "La civiltà dei Longobardi nella 'Historia Langobardorum' di Paolo Diacono", *La civiltà dei Longobardi in Europa: Atti del Convegno internazionale sul tema* (Rome, 1974), 9–23; Krüger, "Zur beneventanischen Konzeption", 18; Goffart, *Narrators* 344; O. Capitani, "Paolo Diacono e la storiografia altomedievale", *Paolo Diacono e il Friuli altomedievale (secc. VI–X)* (Spoleto, 2001), 25–44, 31–38; cf. C. Leonardi, "La figura di Paolo Diacono", ibid., 13–24, 17; 23.

20 See esp. Morghen, "La civiltà"; Krüger, "Zur beneventanischen Konzeption", 18; Goffart, *Narrators* 344; 78–82.

21 Goffart, *Narrators* 379–380; also, Plassmann, *Origo gentis*, 199.

22 McKitterick, "Paul the Deacon", 326. This point had already been raised by Helmut Rogan; McKitterick makes no reference to his work. See Rogan, *Paulus Diaconus*, 27–29. More recently, Claudio Leonardi followed McKitterick, albeit not enthusiastically, see Leonardi, "La figura", 15–16.

23 McKitterick, "Paul the Deacon", 327.

24 Ibid. 331–34.

25 Ibid. 327–331.

26 Ibid. 334–337 See, however, Paolo Chiesa's suggestion that a southern tradition might have existed, but was lost due to accident, see P. Chiesa, "Caratteristiche della transmissione dell'*Historia Langobardorum*", *Paolo Diacono e il Friuli altomedievale (secc. VI–X)* (Spoleto, 2001), 45–66, 61–66; followed by C. Heath, *The Narrative Worlds of Paul the Deacon: Between Empires and Identities in Lombard Italy* (2017), 115–116.

27 McKitterick, "Paul the Deacon", 338.

28 An idea put forward in Pohl, "Paulus Diaconus", 388; followed by Plassmann,

Origo gentis, 196; Coumert, *Origines*, 219; M.T. Kretschmer, *Rewriting Roman History in the Middle Ages: the "Historia Romana" and the Manuscript Bamberg, Hist. 3* (Leiden, 2007), 7–9; A.J. Stoclet, *Fils du Martel: la naissance, l'éducation et la jeunesse de Pépin, dit "Le Bref" (v. 714–v. 741)* (Turnhout, 2013), 183–185. More skeptically, Heath, *Narrative Worlds*, 109.

29 *Contra* Lidia Capo, who believed the *HL* was an exception, "scritta e pensata secondo il proprio gusto e le proprie ragioni ..." see L. Capo, *Paolo Diacono: Storia dei Longobardi* 7. edn (Milano, 1992), XXVIII.

30 McKitterick, "Paul the Deacon", 327; see also Leonardi, "La figura", 15–16.

31 Coumert, *Origines*, 219.

32 For the *Origo codicis Gothanis,* see L.A. Berto, "Remembering Old and New Rulers: Lombards and Carolingians in Carolingian Itlalian Memory", *The medieval History Journal* 13 (2010), 13–53, 28–29; 32–35; E. Fabbro, "The Charlemagne and the Lombard Kingdom that Was: the Lombard Christian Past in Post-Conquest Italian Historiography", *Journal of the Canadian Historical Association* 25 (2015), 1–26, 13–16.

33 McKitterick, "Paul the Deacon", 326.

34 For the political interactions between Francia and Benevento, see n. 62.

35 For instance, Goffart, *Narrators* 399.

36 Ibid.346 Grimoald I's victory against the Byzantines: *HL* 5.6–10 (see also *HL* 4.46); compare with Grimoald III's victory: *ARF* and *Ann. qui dic. Ein.* s.a. 788; see also Alcuin, *Ep.* 7 (MGH *Epp.* 4, 32), Grimoald's epitaph (*Chr. Sal.* c.29), Poeta Saxoni Ann. II, vv. 380–426 (MGH *Poetae Latini*, 4.1, 28–29).

37 Already mentioned by Pope Adrian in *Cod. Car.* 57 (end of 775).

38 See Goffart, *Narrators* 341. But maybe as late as 782/3, see Ibid. 341, n. 45.

39 *Annales Mosellani*, s.a. 78. On the visit, see O. Bertolini, "Carlomagno e Benevento", in W. Braunfels (ed.), *Karl der Grosse: Lebenswerk und Nachleben* (Düsseldorf, 1966), 609–671, 624–625; R. Collins, *Charlemagne* (Toronto, 1998), 69–670; G. Minois, *Charlemagne* (Paris, 2010), 211–218.

40 See Goffart, *Narrators* 345–346. Commission of the Homiliary, MGH *Capitularia* I, no. 30, 80–81.

41 For Paul's poems, see K. Neff, *Die Gedichte des Paulus Diaconus: kritische und erklärende Ausgabe* (München, 1908). Here, Neff, 11.

42 Bertolini, "Carlomagno", 624–625; Collins, *Charlemagne*, 68. See n. 11.

43 Neff, 24–29.

44 Neff, 13, l.21: "Vitam litteris ni emam, nihil est, quod tribuam".

45 Letter to Theodemar, MGH *Epp.* IV, 506–508, 507. "hereo, stupeo, langueo, nec inter imo pectore tracta suspiria retinere lacrimas possum".

46 In the *HL*, Paul continued his alternation of good, Church-loving emperors and bad emperors he started at the last book of the *HR*, see *HL* 3.11, 3.12, 4.26, 4.36, 4.49, 5.11–13, 5.30 and 6.4, 6.11, 6.13 together with 6.27–32 and 6.34, 6.49). This smooth transition between the *HR* and the *HL* was already noticed during the middle ages: an anonymous thirteenth-century compiler (Ms. Berolinensis Lat. IV, 4) selected the relevant passages from the *HL* and added them to the *HR* as book XVII; an edition is available on *MGH AA* 2, 396–405. On Paul's general take on Eastern history, see Pohl, "Cultural Resources", 26–31.

47 Goffart, *Narrators* 353; see also Maskarinec, "Romans", 299–314.

48 Pohl, "Cultural Resources", 28–29. On Paul's use of Gregory, see also D. Bianchi, "Da Gregorio di Tours a Paolo Diacono", *Aevum* 35 (1961), 150–66.

49 See n. 110.

50 See Fabbro, "Charlemagne".

51 For the debate on Paul's return date, see Goffart, *Narrators* 342, n. 49; and more recently, Heath, *Narrative Worlds*, 32–33.

52 A return in 785 is based on Charlemagne's commission of a *Sacramentarium* to Pope Hadrian, which the king would have entrusted Paul in the beginning of 785; nothing suggests Paul carried the commission on his way back home. Supporting a 785 return, E. Menghini, "Dello stato presente degli studi intorno alla vita di Paolo Diacono", *Bolletino della Società pavese di storia patria* 4 (1904), 15–100; 231–285; 313–362, 349–355; Kempf, "Paul the Deacon", 281 and n. 5. For Charlemagne's request, see *Cod. Car.* 89, MGH *Epp.*, III, 626 and, for the date, C. Vogel, "La réforme liturgique sous Charlemagne", in B. Bischoff (ed.), *Karl der Grosse* (Düsseldorf, 1965), 217–232, 224–225. An early date would fit the narrative that Paul was already in Monte Cassino when Charlemagne visited the monastery in 786/87 (*Ann. Laur.*, s.a. 786, MGH *SS* 1, 33; Pauli *Cont. Romana*, s.a. 787, MGH, *SS. rer. Lang.*, 202); although the visit is well established, the only source for the encounter between Charles and Paul is a brief and probably significantly embellished biography of Paul the Deacon in the eleventh-century work Leo Marsicanus and Peter Diaconus, *Chronicon Cassinensis*, 1.15 (MGH, SS 34, 51–55); no precise date is given for the meeting.

53 See, for example, F. Dahn, *Paulus Diaconus* (Leipzig, 1876), 55–56; McKitterick, "Paul the Deacon", 324; less explicitly, D.A. Bullough, *The Age of Charlemagne* (New York, 1966), 60–61. There is no solid evidence directly connecting Paul and Charlemagne's trip.

54 *Chron. Sal.c.* 21. For the epitaph, Neff, 35.

55 Already suggested by G. Grion, *Della Vita di Paolo Diacono, storico dei Longobardi* (Udine, 1899), 36. Menghini dismissed Gion's suggestion arguing that the praise for Arichis would not be acceptable for someone living in Charlemagne's court, Menghini, "Stato presente", 351–52. By 787, however, the mood between Charlemagne and Grimoald III was no longer antagonistic but conciliatory, culminating with the restitution of Grimoald to Benevento in 788.

56 Although the poem was certainly intended as an epitaph ("Lugentum lacrimis populorum roscida tellus/Principis haec magni nobile corpus habet"), it is however possible that it was never actually set to stone. Notice how the *Chron. Sal.* (c.20), the only source for the poem, presents the text: "nunc quae a diacono Paulo, eleganti viro, prolata sunt, minime omittamus, set huic ystoriae enucleatim inserere faciam". Compare with a tombstone that the author claims he actually saw: "Item alios versus, quae super tumulum Romoald, filii Arichis, repperibimus".

57 Goffart, *Narrators* 342.

58 A point Goffart clearly acknowledged, see Ibid. 342–343.

59 *Epytaphyum Pauli Diaconi*, MGH *SS. rer. Lang.*, 23–24.

60 For Beneventan resistance and Charlemagne's policy in southern Italy, Bertolini's work is still fundamental: Bertolini, "Carlomagno"; see also H. Belting, "Studien zum beneventanischen Hof im 8. Jahrhundert", *Dumbarton Oaks Papers* 16 (1962), 143–193; S. Gasparri, "Il ducato e il principato di Benevento", in G. Galasso and R. Romeo (eds.), *Storia del Mezzogiorno, II, Il Medioevo, 1* (Napoli, 1988), 83–146; G. Albertoni, *L'Italia carolingia* (Roma, 1997), 11–32; G. Tabacco, "L'avvento dei Carolingi nel regno dei Longobardi", in S. Gasparri (ed.), *Il regno dei Longobardi in Italia: archeologia, società, istituzioni* (Spoleto, 2004), 443–479. More generally, on the Carolingian rule of Italy, see C. Wickham, *Early Medieval Italy: Central Power and Local Society 400–1000* (London, 1981), 47–55; P. Delogu, "Lombard and Carolingian Italy", in R. McKitterick (ed.), *The New Cambridge Medieval History, Vol. II c. 700–c. 900* (Cambridge, 1996), 290–319, 300–310; Collins, *Charlemagne*, 58–76; R.

McKitterick, *Charlemagne: the Formation of a European Identity* (Cambridge, 2008); Minois, *Charlemagne*, 181–87; 211–52; J.R. Davis, *Charlemagne's Practice of Empire* (Cambridge, 2015).

61 Belting, "Studien", 146; Bertolini, "Carlomagno", 616.

62 Or so suggested Pope Adrian, *Cod. Car.* 57, who might have exaggerated the extent of the rebellion to convince Charles, sees Collins, *Charlemagne*, 63, n. 28.

63 *Cod. Car.* 57. The extensive epistolary material produced by the papal court in the 770s and 780s, and preserved in the *Codex Carolinus*, is the essential source for southern Italian events in the period. Pope Adrian I, however, had much at stake in southern Italy, which Charlemagne originally promised would be fully transferred to the pope, and his reports to Charlemagne, especially his accusations against Benevento, should always be taken with a grain of salt. His partisanship notwithstanding, much of the information he provided was reliable (compare, e.g. *Cod. Car.* 82 and *Cod. Car.* App. 2.).

64 *ARF* and *ARF (rev.)* s.a. 776.

65 Bertolini, "Carlomagno", passim.

66 Diplomatic mission to the south: *Cod. Car.* 55.

67 *ARF* s.a. 779. Hildebrand's realignment with the Carolingians can be traced back to 775; see G.V.B. West, "Charlemagne's Involvement in Central and Southern Italy: Power and the Limits of Authority", *Early Medieval Europe* 8 (1999), 341–367, 343–350.

68 *Cod. Car.* 64; see Bertolini, "Carlomagno", here, 621–622.

69 For the Byzantine, *Annales Mosellani*, s.a. 781; Collins, *Charlemagne*, 69. For the monasteries, see West, "Charlemagne's Involvement", 350–361.

70 *Cod. Car.* 78.

71 On the intentions of Charles visit in 787, see Bertolini, "Carlomagno", 624–625; Collins, *Charlemagne*, 68.

72 ARF s.a. 787.

73 The main indication is that Charles had Grimoald swore the oath to him, and not Pippin, the Carolingian king of Italy; see Bertolini, "Carlomagno", 633; Collins, *Charlemagne*, 70–71.

74 Bertolini, "Carlomagno", 649.

75 For the territorial claims of the papacy, see Ibid.607–616; T.F.X. Noble, *The Republic of St. Peter: the Birth of the Papal State, 680–825* (Philadelphia, 1984), 132–83.

76 Roduald was born in 761/62 (*Chron. Sal.c.* 21), while Grimoald was born before Paul finished the *HR* (where he is not mentioned), which is generally accepted to be finished before the fall of the Lombard kingdom in 774, normally dated to *c.* 770.

77 *Contra* West, who suggests the presence of Grimoald at the court was "by chance"; see West, "Charlemagne's Involvement", 357.

78 Bertolini, "Carlomagno", 634; Collins, *Charlemagne*, 72.

79 That Paul had perchance a role as intermediary between Charles and Arichis has already been suggested in Gasparri, "Il ducato", 110–111; and later in B.M. Kreutz, *Before the Normans: Southern Italy in the Ninth and Tenth Centuries* (Philadelphia, 1991), 7.

80 Modern scholarship tends to read two different Gisulf's in Paul's early Friulian history, given the chronological problems in Paul, suggesting that Gisulf I became duke in 568 (*HL* 2.9) and Gisulf II, his son, was the one killed by the Avars in 612 (who had an infant son, Grimoald). This historiographical slight of hand is only necessary if one assumes Paul's chronology was solid.

81 "Exigit vero nunc locus, postposita generali historia, pauca etiam privatim de mea, qui haec scribe, genealogia retexere" It has been suggested that Paul added

this section of *HL* 4.37 later, since it is not introduced in the heading of the chapter, see Chiesa, "Caratteristiche", 52 and n. 19.

82 *HL* 4.37 "Iste, (...), extitit meus proavus. Hic etenim genuit avum meum Arichis, Arichis vero patrem meum Warnefrit, Warnefrit autem ex Theudelinda coniuge genuit me, Paulum, meumque germanus Arichis, qui nostrum avum cognomina retulit".

83 Rogan, *Paulus Diaconus*, 25–26.

84 Compare with *Origo,c.* 1.

85 Neff, 35, ll. 39; 43–44.

86 *Chron. Sal.c.* 20–21.

87 Neff, 35, ll. 39; 43–44.

88 *Cod. Car.* 80, *Cod. Car.* App. 2. See Bertolini, "Carlomagno", 646; Noble, *Republic*, 178–179.

89 Goffart, *Narrators* 353.

90 *Cod. Car.* 80; 82.

91 *Cod. Car.* 80.

92 *Cod. Car.* 88.

93 *Cod. Car.* App. 2; cf. *Cod. Car.* 82.

94 *ARF* s.a. 787.

95 *ARF* s.a. 788; Einhard, *Vita Caroli, c.* 11. Collins is skeptical of Avar involvement, especially given precedents of false accusations of foreign alliances to justify attacks (e.g. Eudo of Aquitaine, Maurontus of Provence), see Collins, *Charlemagne*, 72; see also Bertolini, "Carlomagno", 646.; the Avars, however, did invade Bavaria shortly after Tassilo was removed from office, *ARF* s.a. 788.

96 Collins, *Charlemagne*, 89.

97 Bertolini, "Carlomagno", 648–649.

98 Cf. Albertoni, *Italia carolingia*, 26, who suggests Grimoald opposed Adelchis because he saw him as a threat to his position.

99 Erch. *Historia*, *c.* 4. Pope Adrian loudly disagreed with that plan: *Cod. Car.* 82.

100 Erch. *Historia*, *c.* 4; Chr. Sal. *c.* 23–25.

101 Confident Grimoald would face the Byzantines, Charles was able to move the northern Italian army under Pippin to threaten Tassilo's southern flank: *ARF* s.a. 787.

102 Rogan, *Paulus Diaconus*, 263–301.

103 *LLGrim.* in *MGH LL* 4, 91–95. There are also two inscriptions in the grotto of Monte S. Angelo, one referring to Roduald, the other to *pater eius*, which possibly refer to Grimoald; they inform nothing about the political situation of the mid-seventh century. The inscriptions are available in C. Carletti, "Iscrizioni murali", in C. Carletti and G. Otranto (eds.), *Il Santuario di S. Michele sul Gargano dal VI al IX secolo: contributo alla storia della Langobardia meridionale: atti del Convegno tenuto a Monte Sant'Angelo il 9–10 dicembre 1978* (Bari, 1980), 1–79, 90–91, no. 82 and 64–65 no. 44, respectively.

104 *Origo*, *c.* 7.

105 *LP*, Vita Vitaliani, 78.2–4.

106 The entire story, from Friuli to Benevento, from duke to king, takes about 20 pages of text out of 93 of the MGH edition.

107 There are, however, two exceptions: in *HL* 2.5, copied straight from *LP Vita Iohannis*, 63.3, Paul preserved the *Greci* from the original; and in *HL* 3.15 he refers to Maurice as "ex Grecorum genere". Derivates of *Grecus* are used elsewhere in the work exclusively for the language.

108 See C. Wickham, "Ninth-Century Byzantium through Western Eyes", in L. Brubaker (ed.), *Byzantium in the Ninth Century: Dead or Alive? Papers from the thirtieth Spring Symposium of Byzantine studies, Birmingham, March*

1996(Aldershot, 1998), 245–256; C. Gantner, "The Label 'Greek' as Part of the Papal Diplimatical Repertoire in the Eighth Century", in W. Pohl and G. Heydemann (eds.), *Strategies of Identification: Ethnicity and Religion in Early Medieval Europe* (Turnhout, 2013), 303–349; Maskarinec, "Romans", 326–328.

109 *Excerpta ex libris Pompei Festi de significatione uerborum*, LLT-B, 235.

110 *HR*, 15.14.

111 See n. 124.

112 *HL* 4.43: "Avares vero omnes Langobardos qui iam in virili aetate erant gladio perimunt, mulieres vero et parvulus captivitatis iugo addicunt".

113 *HL* 4.46: "Qui, dum esset vir belicosissimus et ubique insignis, venientibus eo tempore Grecis, ut oraculum sancti archangeli in monte Gargano situm depreadarent, Grimuald super eos cum exercitu veniens, ultima eos caede prostravit".

114 As Gasparri has already remarked, there is no further evidence for this Byzantine invasion, see S. Gasparri, *I duchi longobardi* (Rome, 1978), 89, n. 231; N. Everett, "The *Liber de apparitione S. Michaelis in Monte Gargano* and the Hagiography of Dispossession", *Analecta Bollandiana* 120 (2002), 364–391, 373–374 and n. 30.

115 *Liber de apparitione sancti Michaelis in monte Gargano*, in *MGH SS. rer. Lang.*, 540–545. See Everett, "Liber de apparitione".

116 *Liber de apparitione*, *c.* 3.

117 *Liber de apparitionec.* 3.

118 *HL* 4.51, see Stoclet, *Fils du Martel*, 179–209.

119 *HL* 5.8: "quia gens ista perfida me vivere non sinebit".

120 *HL* 5.10: "Quod cernens Grecorum exercitus, mox immense pavore perterritus in fugam convertitur, ultimaque pernicie caesus, sibi fugiens mortem, Romualdo et Lanogbardis victoria peperit".

121 *HL* 5.11, cf. *LP*, Vita Vitaliani, 78.2–4.

122 *HL* 5.16.

123 Paul found an attack during Easter highly condemnable: he presents an attack during Easter festivities as the cause of Stilicho's defeat against Alaric (*HR* 12.13); likewise he altered the date of the Lombard invasion of Italy from Easter (*Origo,* c.5) to the day after (*HL* 2.7); see E. Fabbro, "'*Capitur urbs quae totum cepit orbem':* the Fates of the Sack of Rome (410) in Early Medieval Historiography", *The Medieval Chronicle* 10 (2015), 29–67, 61–63.

124 Against Goffart's positive picture of Grimoald I, Pohl has already pointed out this track record of "evil" deeds; see Pohl, "Paulus Diaconus", 386–387.

125 Compare *HL* 4.46 and 5.10 to *HL* 5.5 and 5.21.

126 At the same time, Paul makes a strong argument for importance of kingship over dukes: compare especially *HL* 2.32 and 3.16 (modelled after 1 Sam 8.11–17), but see also *HL* 1.14, 1.20, and 1.27.

127 Erch. *Historia*, *c.* 4.

128 *ARF* and *Ann. qui dic. Ein.* s.a. 788; see also Alcuin, *Ep.* 7 (MGH *Epp.* 4, 32), Grimoald's epitaph (*Chr. Sal.c.* 29), Poeta Saxoni Ann. II, vv. 380–426 (MGH *Poetae Latini*, 4.1, 28–29); see Goffart, *Narrators* (McKitterick, "Paul the Deacon", 329).

129 On Charles campaigns against the Bavarians and the Avars, see Bertolini, "Carlomagno", 653–654.

130 See Collins, *Charlemagne*, 77–101.

131 R. Morghen, "Il palinsesto assisiense della *Historia Langobardorum* di Paolo Diacono", *Bulletino dell'Istituto Storico Italiano* 38 (1918), 7–23; Pohl, "Paulus Diaconus", 390–391, n. 91; Pani, "Aspetti", 388, n. 56; 404.

Part II

The Exarchate of Ravenna

5 Travels of an exarch: Smaragdus and the Anastasian Walls

Let's start with a question or riddle, the first part of which Tom Brown could answer with ease, but the second part may be new to him. For panellists on an afternoon radio quiz show the question might be framed: "Who links the Roman Forum, Ravenna and the Black Sea, but unexpectedly underwent a sex-change in a Constantinopolitan monastery?"

The answer to the question begins at the northern end of the Anastasian Wall or the Long Wall of Thrace. Located 66 km west of Constantinople, the wall starts in the south from the shallow waters of the Sea of Marmara and follows high north-south ridges across the Thracian peninsula to the mudstone cliffs of Evcik, overlooking the waters of the Black Sea (Figure 5.1). Altogether it is 57 km in length, equivalent to the Antonine Wall in Scotland. In the southern third of its course the wall survives only as a low mound or as the straight alignment of a country road, but to the north it passes through dense forest and continues to the coastal cliffs, well preserved in many places and still standing up to 4 metres in height. Along with the wall itself, which probably rose to a height of 9–10 metres, there were regular towers at intervals of about 120 metres, and regular small forts with passages through the wall, these are called by their Turkish name as *bedestens*. West of the sandy cove at Evcik, the line of the wall takes the high ground and then turns at right angles and follows the cliff face and then another turn to the north where the broken core is exposed in the cliff face high above the beach. Set back from this end is a ruined building, approximately square with apses at the east end and a collapsed dome filling the interior. The church can be identified from a late compendium of seven wonders, as the church of St George.[1] The building was surveyed in 1996 and was seen to have at least three phases (Figure 5.2).[2] First a square domed structure with the main entrance at the west end, and a door and window in the south side. It was constructed of small irregular blocks with some re-use of larger squared stones. A narthex was added to the west with apses at either end to the north and south. The northern apse was carefully built with articulated brickwork and niches typical of the eleventh and twelfth centuries' work at Constantinople and Messembria. In the final phase the north and east end of the church was clad with large sandstone

Figure 5.1 Evcik, the north end of the Anastasian Wall is visible with the remains of the church of St George to the right. (Para-glider photograph by Gökhan Cağlayan with permission.)

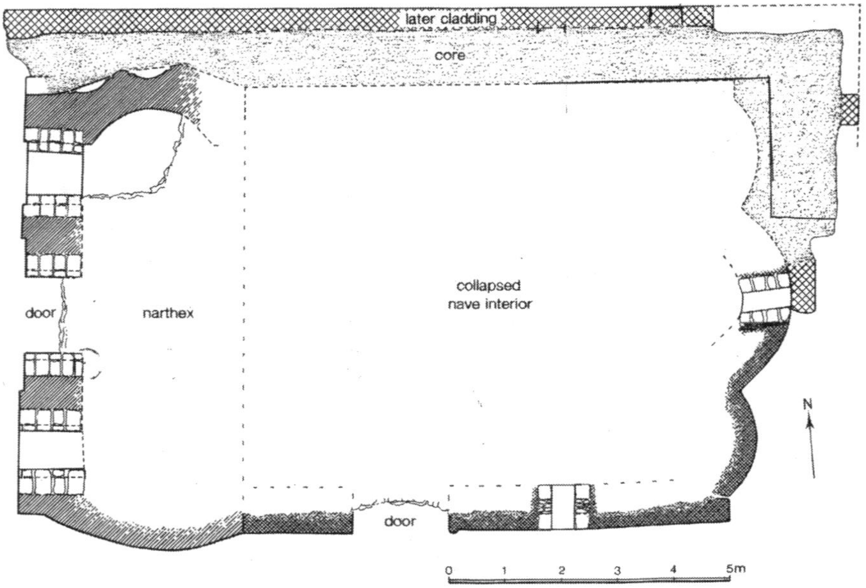

Figure 5.2 Plan of the church at Evcik (1995).

blocks derived from the Anastasian Wall, the closest ruins of which were located only 10 metres from the church. Illegal excavation by *defineciler* (treasure hunters) in the winter of 1994–1995 showed that nearly 2 metres of the building were concealed by a combination of subsidence and wind-blown sand. In 2002 Dr Alessandra Ricci of Koç University who was co-director of the Anastasian Wall Project until 1999, visited Evcik with a party of students from the Italian Lise in Istanbul. She was able to observe further more intrusive and destructive interventions by *defineciler* who had dug a deep pit revealing the opening of a cistern at the west end below the narthex, and had torn down the eastern end of the south wall. Amongst the disturbed stones was a large rectangular block, recently broken into two pieces (Figure 5.3). On the face that had been placed into the wall was an inscription. Concerned about the possible return of the *defineciler* Dr Ricci immediately informed the local Jandarma Karakol at Karacaköy. They took the stones to the town and it was then conveyed to Istanbul Archaeological Museums.

We were able to send photographs of the inscription taken by Dr Ricci to Professor Cyril Mango so that the text could be included within his corpus of dated Byzantine inscriptions, currently in preparation with the assistance Dr Anne McCabe. Professor Mango kindly read the text and has provided a translation and comments. We understand that the staff of Istanbul Archaeology Museums is currently undertaking a more detailed study of the

Figure 5.3 Photograph of the inscription after damage by treasure hunters at the south-east angle of the church (Dr Alessandra Ricci with permission).

inscription; however, given the significance of the text, we are able to present a preliminary reading here.

The inscription is carved onto a large roughly squared building block, one of the standard building modules for the construction of the Anastasian Wall. The block is approximately 110 by 40 cm in length and breadth, and the text is carved onto a rectangular panel flanked by two triangles, creating an ansate panel, which is set forward by a clear drafted margin around the edges of the block, much of which has been broken away (Figure 5.4).

Professor Mango read the Greek text as follows:

> X Ἀνένεοθι ἐπί Ἡράκ- | λιου το θεοστεφ- | ούς ἱμον δεσποτου κ- | ε Ζμαράγδου του ἐν- | δοξότατου κε πᾰνύφιμου πατρίκιου

On line 7 on the left edge of the stone are the letters Λ΄Δ Θ: the meaning of these is unclear. He provides the following translation:

> "Renewed under Heraclius, our lord crowned by God, and Smaragdus the most glorious and most renowned patrician".

This text is the only inscription to survive from the Anastasian Wall. Brick stamps have been recorded, especially in the southern sector and all indicate construction at the beginning of the sixth century. Two middle-Byzantine inscriptions from the region were mistakenly associated with the Anastasian Wall,[3] but otherwise nothing is recorded. The involvement of Emperor Heraclius (610–641) is clear from the text although no reconstruction is attested in the surviving historical sources for his reign. The reconstruction was undertaken under the supervision of the "renowned patrician" Smaragdus, and he is the main subject of this chapter since some notion of his chronology may enable us to get a better idea when the works were

Figure 5.4 Photograph of the inscription (Dr Alessandra Ricci with permission).

carried out during the 31 years of Heraclius' rule. Therefore, before considering the possible historical context and nature of any buildings works we need to consider Smaragdus and his known career.

Smaragdus is an unusual name, meaning emerald, and only two named individuals are recorded in the last volume of the Prosopography of the Late Roman Empire. Its use as a given name probably derives from one of a group of fictional martyrs of the time of Diocletian, including Largus, Smaragdus and Hyacinthus.[4] There was also a female form, Smaragda, who will make also an appearance, and the female version is still current in Modern Greek, as is Esmerelda in Spanish. The individual identified in *PLRE* as Smaragdus 2[5] is well known from Byzantine Italy where he is known to have dedicated a statue to Phocas in the Roman forum, the last imperial statue in Roman history. It was erected on 1 August 608, two years before Heraclius' successful overthrow of Phocas and probably the last occasion that Smaragdus was securely attested in Italy. The inscription describes him as *ex praeposito sacri Palatii ac patricius et exarchus Italiae*, "former prefect of the imperial bedchamber, patrician and exarch of Italy".[6] His earlier career is well documented. He was twice exarch of Italy: from 584/585 to 589/590 under Maurice (at which time he already had the title *patricius)* and from 603 to 608 under Phocas.[7] He was active and successful in furthering imperial and Byzantine religious interests with the papacy and the Lombards during Maurice's campaigns in the east, and during the troubled years after Phocas' seizure of power. As commander in Italy he fortified Ferrara and Argenta and in Ravenna he is recorded as having restored the water supply under an emperor with the honorific of *Gepidicus*, a title known to have been used by Maurice.[8] As the inscription from the Roman Forum suggests Smaragdus held other offices as *praepositus sacri cubicula* and elsewhere he is attested as *cartularius sacri palatii*, both offices of the imperial household almost invariably filled by eunuchs.[9] Since the time of Narses, eunuch commanders and viceroys had an impressive record in Italy that challenges conventional stereotypes of imperial eunuchs. It is a measure of Smaragdus' competence and loyalty to imperial office that, as the Evcik inscription is able to demonstrate, he weathered two military coups to hold the highest commands under at least three successive emperors.

A further moment in the career is a reference in the *Patria,* a "found history" of Constantinople compiled in the tenth century. In the section of book 3 concerned with monastic foundations in the City, it is written: "*Ta Smaragdes* with the bath was built by patrician and general Smaragdos in the time of Tiberius the Thracian, because his house was there".[10] As Albrecht Berger has observed, the text refers to the monastery in the feminine thus it is "of Smaragda", a lady patron otherwise unknown which the compilers of the *Patria* combined with a reference to Smaragdos, a *patrikios* and *strategos*. Berger draws attention to a similar gender shift in the name of the monastery of *Ta Paulinou* that the Patria attributes to the fifth-century *magistros* Paulinos and then elaborates with an anecdote from Malalas' Chronicle about Paulinos and the empress Eudokia. In practice the founder of *Ta Paulinou* was a noble lady Paulina in the later fifth century.[11] Despite the confusion about gender of the monastic founder where does it leave the reference to the bath, the town house, and Tiberius the Thracian? The emperor Tiberius Constantine, the father-in-law of Maurice, died in 582, only two years before Smaragdus first emerges in texts, and 26 years before he is securely last attested in the Roman Forum. Thus it is quite possible that by the very end of Tiberius' reign as a member of the imperial household, he already held the rank of patrician, although whether the title of *strategos* can be accepted under Tiberius might be questioned as it is unattested elsewhere.

We now need to turn to the last recorded achievements of Smaragdus' career and to consider when he was called upon the direct the construction of what sixth-century sources refer to as "the Wall of Constantinople".[12] His involvement also raises the issue of how long we might expect a senior career to last, although as we have observed he was able to weather two violent regime changes, albeit from the distance of Ravenna, and serve three and perhaps four emperors. For a comparable career spanning several decades Justinian's great commander Belisarius began his military successes in 527 at Dara and his final victory against the Kutrigurs in 559, 32 years later.[13] Similarly for Smaragdus if we start at the secure date of 584/5 when he was first attested as exarch and patrician, and set aside a slightly earlier Tiberius Constantine reference, a similar period brings us to 615, well into Heraclius' reign. Indeed some authorities suggest he was still exarch in Ravenna until at least 611.[14]

In 559 the defences of the Long Wall had failed the capital and the Kutrigurs were able to penetrate as far as the city's walls. As noted earlier, Belisarius quickly mustered a defence force that was able to turn back the Kutrigurs and gain his last triumph. But such a narrow escape called for positive imperial action and in the same year the emperor Justinian made a rare journey from the capital to the nearby walled town of Selymbria (Silivri), close to the southern end of the wall to oversee the restoration of the linear works, recently damaged by the earthquake of 557/558. Justinian remained for over three months and returned in triumph to the city.[15] The restoration ensured the security of the city from barbarian attacks until the close of the century. In 583 the Avar Khagan had invaded Moesia and had captured the city of Anchialus on the Pontic coast. Roman envoys reported that "The Khagan did not act moderately in his crimes, but even added more wilful threats that he would destroy the Long Walls, as they are called".[16] In practice the walls ensured the security of the capital's inner hinterland and as late as 598/600 the emperor Maurice led troops and circus factions from the city up to the walls as the defeated troops of Comentiolus retreated after the latter's defeat in Moesia by the Avars, but the defences remained secure.[17]

Theophanes recalls how news of the arrival of Heraclius' fleet in the Dardanelles against Phocas prompted the dispatch of, "the *magister*

Domentziolos (Phocas' brother), to guard the Long Wall; and when the *magister* learned that Herakleios had reached Abydos, he abandoned the walls and fled to Constantinople". The wall was clearly no security against a seaborne approach to the city.[18] So what was the occasion for Heraclius' restoration, overseen by "the most glorious and most renowned patrician Smaragdus"? Miracle 5 of Saint Demetrius of Thessalonica reports that "We have previously spoken of the Sklaveni, that is to say of Chatzon, and of the Avars, how they devastated almost all of Illyricum, namely the two Pannonias, the two Dacias, Dardania, Mysia, Prevalitana, Rhodope, as far as Thrace and the region of the Long Wall towards Byzantium: all the populations were deported to the country near to Pannonia on the Danube in the district of Sirmium, where they were installed as subjects by the Khagan".[19] Lemerle in his commentary associates this account with the so-called Avar Surprise, when Heraclius was ambushed near the Long Wall by the Avars and only narrowly escaped to Constantinople. The date of the event remains contested, Lemerle and others prefer 617/619 following Theophanes' chronology, whereas much recent scholarship accepts the Chronicon Pascale and dates the events to 5 June 623, which followed Heraclius' successful return from fighting against the Sassanians.[20] The events outlined in the miracle attest to extensive raids by the Sklaveni across the Balkans, and up to the Long Wall, and complement the events of 623, although it is possible that they reflect an earlier incursion in Heraclius' reign.[21] Without rehearsing the differing accounts of the "Avar Surprise" in detail, certain specific aspects of the historical accounts may help to establish the chronology of the Smaragdus inscription and help to explain its circumstances and location.

As stated in the introduction the inscription was discovered at Evcik at the very northern end of the Anastasian Wall, and although it was found in a secondary location, given its size it will have come from a location very close to the find spot. The northern sector of the wall is today very densely wooded, a managed forest of oak and hazel mainly used for the charcoal production.[22] In the early twentieth century, military reports described this forest as too dense to allow the passage of a modern army. The antiquity of the forest is attested in medieval sources as the mountains of the Propontis were used for siege engines in campaigns against the Cumans.[23] From the written sources it is clear that Heraclius was due to meet the un-named Avar Khagan at Heracleia for chariot-races in the hippodrome of the city, traces of which still survive.[24] Heraclius himself was based in Selymbria and was accompanied from the city by members of the circus factions and a throng of shopkeepers and others who came to join in the games that were seen as part of the events in preparation for a negotiated peace treaty. At the same time, according to Nikephoros' *Short Chronicle*, the Khagan treacherously selected troops who were sent "to the overgrown and wooded heights overlooking the so-called Long Wall and scattered them secretly in the bushy hills that are there so that, taking the emperor in the rear, they might encircle him and make him an easy prey of them and his retinue".[25] The course of the main roads running through the Long Wall to the west are not known with any certainty, but today along the southern edge of the forest is the prominent scarp along which runs the main railway line from Istanbul-Sofia, once the track of the Orient Express.[26] It seems likely that this was always the division between the wildwood forest and the arable lands extending towards the coast. One ancient road led along the coast, and other headed inland to form the so-called Heere Strasse, the main military road linking Constantinople with Serdica (Sofia) and Singidunum (Belgrade) on the Danube.[27] If there were to have been an ambush from the "bushy heights" it would seem that this must have targeted the upper road and the point where it crossed the Long Wall. One scenario is that the emperor travelled up within the line of the wall or a track parallel from Selymbria up to the upper road where he was to meet with the host of circus factions and others from Constantinople. To launch their raid from the heights and capture so many, the Avars must have already penetrated the Long Wall to the north, although the Khagan chose to remain outside, probably so he could avoid being trapped himself in case his ambush backfired. Heraclius by hiding the imperial regalia was able to escape amongst the crowd although according to the sources many thousands were captured and the Avars penetrated close to the Theodosian Wall as well as laying waste villages and fields close to the city. Through a combination of poor maintenance and garrisoning the barrier wall had failed for the first time since 559. Significantly from Nikephoros' account it was the wall through the forest that had allowed the select Avar band to ambush the emperor and it is not surprising that any restoration extended along the whole length of the wall to include the northern end where the Smaragdus inscription was found.

Heraclius' aim was to secure a treaty in the Balkans to ensure security for his deep strike against the Sassanians in the heartlands of their empire. The disaster at the Long Wall meant he had to pay off the Avars with 200,000 *solidi* in order to redeem the captured citizens. It is in this context that we may best situate the construction recorded by the Evcik inscription. Twelve years after his last appearance in our sources as exarch in 611, Smaragdus is still likely to have been younger (or no older) than Justinian was when he oversaw the works in 559. A comparison can be made with Longinus former prefect of Constantinople who under Justinian had completed the works on the Basilica Cistern, but as ex-consul and prefect he is reported to have restored bridges along the aqueducts in the same region of Thrace.[28] On the wall itself there are traces of reconstruction and repair evident from the wall curtain, although the significant reconstruction noted in a tower close to Dervş Kapı, towards the centre of the wall, is more likely to belong to the restoration late in Justinian's reign after the Kutrigur incursion of 559.[29] Closer to Evcik at the Büyük Bedesten traces of a major outer earth bank covered the approaches to the fort from the west, certainly an indication of later defensive work and a rare example of a Byzantine military earthwork.[30]

But subsides and walls could not provide for the security of Constantinople and three years later the Khagan returned with a great army of Avars and Slavs and siege equipment to begin the city's first great siege. It was the first occasion that the walls of Theodosius were properly tested and they were able to repulse a well-equipped hostile army; massive military architecture and the blessing of the city's patron, the Theotokos, ensured the city's security with rare exceptions until 1453.[31] The Anastasian Wall does not figure in the detailed accounts of the Avar siege of 626 and faced by a great assault could no longer serve as the city's outer bulwark. There is no evidence to suggest that the Anastasian Wall continued to be maintained or garrisoned after the inner walls of the city were repaired.

Smaragdus' lapidary trail has lead us from the last imperial statue and inscription in the Roman forum, to the maintenance of the water supply of the imperial city of Ravenna to the final restoration of the Anastasian Wall; a monument Edward Gibbon termed the Last Frontier.[32] In his role as exarch he showed himself an effective imperial representative. Like most imperial officials in Italy he came from the eastern part of the empire, although as a eunuch he is likely to have originated from outside of the empire.[33] But unlike Narses and other Armenians, his name does not assist us. One might consider that as an exotic name it was given to him as a young man to recognise his special qualities, but that may be modern speculation. He certainly succeeded and as far as the new emperor was concerned he must have been familiar as a close colleague from the west since the elder Heraclius was exarch in Carthage at the same time as Smaragdus held office in Ravenna. Their acquaintance as well as their possible common Armenian or eastern origin might explain how Smaragdus, once returned to Constantinople, was set the task to restore the Anastasian Wall, as the emperor himself set off to rescue his empire in the east. Heraclius has been characterised as the last Roman,[34] but Smaragdus may be more deserving. His deeds ticked all the boxes of imperial evergetism in both east and west: public statues, urban fortifications and water infrastructure and, lastly, the final restoration of a frontier in Roman guise.[35]

But times had moved on, and eastern Rome in the early seventh century had ceased to be a territorial empire defined by set borders. The empire still possessed a great, populous and securely defended hub reaching out through sea and land routes to territories from the Caucasus to the Balearic Islands. Despite the restoration of the Anastasian Wall it was not to figure in any further military events. Like much else of late antique Byzantium it was not forgotten and is described in the fifteenth century by the humanist Manuel Chrysoloras in his comparison of Old and New Rome, who wrote "Thus the walls remain, not only as evidence of the power of those who built them, but also as testimony of the prudence and foresight for the future"[36] Indeed in 655 the regions just to the west of the wall close to Bizye (Vize) were deemed places where "the Roman empire does not extend even by one step":[37] a profound indictment of the previous century's ambitions. What mattered for the maintenance and long-term survival of the eastern Roman empire was the security of centres of administration and urban life such as Syracuse and especially Ravenna, which were to endure for two centuries more.

Notes

1 K. Brodersen, *Die sieben Weltwunder: Legendäre Kunst-und Bauwerke der Antike* (Munich, 1996); for the structure and location of the wall, see J. Crow and A. Ricci, "Investigating the hinterland of Constantinople: interim report on the Anastasian Long Wall", *Journal of Roman Archaeology*, 10 (1997), 235–262.
2 J. Crow, and A. Ricci, "Anastasian Wall Project 1995", *Bulletin of British Byzantine Studies*, 22 (1996), 30–34.
3 Two inscriptions from Çorlu (Tzourolos) have been mistakenly associated with the Anastasian Wall, see discussion in C. Asdracha, "Inscriptions Byzantines de la Thrace Oriental (VIIIe–XIe siècles) présentation et commentaire historique" *Archaiologikon Deltion,* 44–46 (1989–1991/1996), 239–334.
4 S. Tougher, *The Eunuch in Byzantine History and Society*, Routledge, (Abingdon, 2008) 73, n. 64.
5 *The Prosopography of the Late Roman Empire* III, Smaragdus 2; T. S. Brown, *Gentlemen and Officers: Imperial Administration and Aristocratic Power in Byzantine Italy AD 554–800,* (London, 1984), 276.
6 *Corpus Inscriptionum Latinorum* VI, 1200; http://laststatues.classics.ox.ac.uk/database, LSA-1313 (C. Machado) (accessed 17/9/16); Brown, *Gentlemen and Officers*, 149.
7 See Brown, *Gentlemen and Officers.*
8 Brown, *Gentlemen and Officers*, 44, n. 12; for Theodoric's maintaintence of the water supply nearly a century before see Y. Marano, "Watered…with the Life-giving Wave: Aqueducts and Water Management in Ostrogothic Italy", in P. Erdkamp, K. Verboven, and A. Zuiderhoek, *Ownership and exploitation of land and natural resources in the Roman world*, Oxford Studies in the Roman Economy, (Oxford, 2015), 154–156, Fig. 9.1.
9 A. H. M. Jones, *The Later Roman Empire, 284–602, A Social and Economic History*, (Oxford, 1964), 566–570; R. Guilland, *Recherches sur les institutions byzantines* (Berlin-Amsterdam, 1967), I, 335, 359.
10 In *Scriptores originum Constantinopolitanarum*, ed. T. Preger, *Patria* 3,197; A. Berger (trans.), *Accounts of Medieval Constantinople, the Patria*, (Harvard, 2013), 218–219, 322–323, n. 199.
11 *Patria* 3,146, Berger, *Patria*, 200–201, 319, n. 150.
12 Malalas, *Chronographia*, ed. L. Dindorf (*CSHB*), (Bonn, 1831) 18. 129, uses this term in the context of the earthquake damage to the walls at the time of the disastrous attack of the Kutrigurs, note that Theophanes, *Chronographia*, ed. C. de Boor, (Leipzig, 1883), AM 6051, largely quoting the same source amends this term to "Anastasian Wall", although later in the same passage reverts to Malalas' subsequent use of "Long Wall".
13 N. Sarantis, *Justinian's Balkan Wars, Campaigning, Diplomacy and Development in Illyricum, Thrace and the Northern world AD 527–565*, (Prenton, 2016).
14 Guilland, *Recherches*, I, 335.
15 Theophanes, *Chronographia*, AM 6051; C. Mango and R. Scott, (trans.) *The Chronicle of Theophanes Confessor: Byzantine and near eastern history AD 284–813* (Oxford, 1997), 342.
16 Theophylact Simocatta, *Historiae*, ed. C. de Boor, rev. P. Wirth, (Stuttgart, 1972), 1.4.7; M. and M. Whitby, *The History of Theophylact Simocatta, An English translation with introduction and notes.* (Oxford, 1986), 26–27.

17 For a comprehensive new discussion of the barbarian raids and the Roman response throughout the sixth century see, Sarantis, *Justinian's Balkan Wars*, esp. 375–386; a more detailed history of the Long Wall is in preparation in Crow, forthcoming.
18 Theophanes, *Chronographia*, AM 6102 (AD609/10); Mango and Scott *Theophanes*, 428; note that W. Kaegi, *Heraclius, Emperor of Byzantium*, (Cambridge, 2003), 48–49, mistakes the Long Wall for the Theodosian Land Walls in his account of Heraclius' advance on the city.
19 *Miracula Sancti Demetrii, PG*, 116, cols. 1202–1324; P. Lemerle, *Les Plus Anciennes Recueils des miracles de saint Démetrius*, (Paris, 1979), Miracle 5, 284 (p. 222, 228); see F. Curta, *Southeastern Europe in the Middle Ages, 500–1250*, (Cambridge, 2006), 70–72.
20 *Chronicon Pascale*, ed. L. Dindorf, (CSHB), (Bonn, 1832); See M. and M. Whitby, *Chronicon Pascale 284–628 AD, Liverpool Texts for Historians 7*, Liverpool 1989, 165, and a discussion of the chronology in appendix 4, 203–205; Mango and Scott, *The Chronicle of Theophanes*, 434; Kaegi, *Heraclius*, 118–121.
21 F. Curta, *The Making of the Slavs, history and archaeology of the Lower Danube region, ca. 500–700*, (Cambridge, 2001), 114, draws attention to the reduction of troops in the Balkans to face the Sassanian invasions in Asia Minor.
22 J. Crow, J. Bardill, and R. Bayliss, *The Water Supply of Byzantine Constantinople*, (London, 2008), 4–5.
23 See, J. Crow, "The Long Walls of Thrace", in C. Mango and G. Dagron (eds.), *Constantinople and Its Hinterland*, Society for the Promotion of Byzantine Studies 3, (Aldershot, 1995), 116–117, for the early-twentieth century description; see C. Morrisson, "Trading in Wood in Byzantium: Exchange and Regulations", in P. Magdalino and N. Necipioğlu (eds.) *Trade in Byzantium, Papers from the Third International Sevgi Gönül Byzantine Studies Symposium*, (Istanbul, 2016), 105–128, esp. 112 for medieval references to the timber resources of south Thrace and the Stranza Mountains (Istranca Dağlar).
24 N. Asgari, "Perinthos (Marmara Ereglisi) Arastirmalari, II', *XI Turk Tarihi Kongress,* (1994), 343–350, figs 93–109.
25 Nikephoros, *Historia Brevis*, ed. C. de Boor (Leipzig, 1880), 10; *Nikephoros Patriarch of Constantinople, Short History*, C. Mango, Text translation, and commentary, Dumbarton Oaks Texts 10, (Washington D.C. 1990), 53, 178–179.
26 For the topography and landscape of the region see, J. Crow and S. Turner, "Silivri and the Thracian hinterland of Istanbul: an historic landscape", *Anatolian Studies,* 59 (2009), 167–181, Fig. 2.
27 For a discussion of the written sources for communications; see A. Külzer, "The Byzantine Road System in Eastern Thrace: Some Remarks", *Byzantinische Forschungen,* 30 (2011), 179–201 and a detailed discussion of the road network communications will appear in Crow forthcoming, chapter 2.
28 Crow, Bardill and Bayliss, *Water Supply*, 18; J. Crow, "Ruling the waters: managing the water supply of Constantinople, AD 330–1204", *Water History*, 4 (2012), 35–55, esp.47–48.
29 Crow and Ricci, "Investigating the hinterland", 248, Fig. 8.
30 See the earthwork enclosure at Caričin Grad, V. Ivanišević, "Caričin Grad (Justiniana Prima): A New-Discovered City for a 'New' Society", 46, Fig. 2.
31 J. Howard Johnston, "The Siege of Constantinople in 626", in C. Mango and G. Dagron (eds.), *Constantinople and Its Hinterland*, Society for the Promotion of Byzantine Studies 3, (Aldershot, 1995), 131–142; the Blachernae wall—the Pteron—was constructed in the following year, *Chronicon Pascale AD 627*; Whitby and Whitby, *Chronicon Pascale*, 181, n. 481.

32 See Crow, "Long Walls", 120–121; Crow and Ricci, "Investigating the hinterland", 259.
33 Brown, *Gentlemen and Officers*, 50–51; Tougher, *Eunuch in Byzantine History*.
34 Kaegi, *Heraclius*, 1–4.
35 At this period in the eastern provinces of the empire imperial agency was more often executed by bishops, see, D. Feissel, "Jean de Soloi, un évêque chypriote au milieu du VIIe siècle", in C. Zuckerman (ed.), *Constructing the seventh century, Travaux et mémoires* 17 (2013), 219–236.
36 C. Smith, *Architecture in the culture of Early Humanism, Ethics, Aesthetics and Eloquence*, 1400–1470, (Oxford, 1992).
37 M. Jankowiak, "Notitia 1 and the impact of the Arab invasions on Asia Minor", *Millennium* 10 (2013), 435–462.

6 Remarks on the sociocultural and religious history of early Byzantine Ravenna in the light of epigraphic and archival evidence

There are three contributions in particular which show research methods applied to medieval history sketched out and then developed by Thomas Brown: the monograph *Gentlemen and Officers. Imperial Administration and Aristocratic Power in Byzantine Italy A. D. 554–800*, London 1984, and two articles closely related, in many respects, to Ravenna: "L'aristocrazia di Ravenna da Giustiniano a Carlo Magno", appearing in 1986 in *Felix Ravenna. Rivista di antichità cristiane, ravennati e bizantine*, 91–98, and "Everyday Life in Ravenna under Theoderic. An Example of his 'Tolerance' and 'Prosperity'?", in *Teoderico il Grande e i Goti d'Italia. Atti del 13. Congresso internazionale di studi sull'alto Medioevo, Milano, 2–6 novembre 1992*, Spoleto 1993, 77–100. The latter work is based on an academic conference paper given in Ravenna. In these articles the author emphasised the importance of the archival and literary evidence for early medieval Ravenna "unica città occidentale che abbia lasciato un'imponente e continua testimonianza dell'evidenza letteraria e documentaria, dalla tarda antichità in poi".[1] Stressing therefore the uniqueness in medieval history of the case study of Ravenna, he encouraged those readers who are, like him, active scholars in the field of late Roman and Byzantine history to reap such the wealthy harvest of data in order to shed light on a crucial period of European and Italian history: "Inoltre occorre sottolineare il valore particolare di Ravenna come caso modello. La Romagna è l'unica zona in Italia dov'è possibile tracciare le origini e le caratteristiche dell'élite dominante con qualche precisione attraverso il periodo travagliato che va dalla caduta dell'Impero Romano al sorgere dei Comuni".[2] As concerns the important issues faced by Brown in the aforesaid contributions, one cannot deny that in the last twenty years perception has increased of the importance of epigraphy and other kinds of primary sources as a tool for the study of Byzantine society.[3] This achievement is probably due to the different evaluation historians developed through time of the Byzantine period, which previously had been sucked into hard-to-die misreading of the late Roman Empire as synonymous with cultural and social decay, announcing medieval "dark ages", which have left a long-lasting legacy in the field of historiography.[4]

The purpose of the present chapter is therefore to outline the evolution of the society of Ravenna between the Roman and the early Byzantine periods, enhancing in particular the documentary evidence. The chapter will briefly describe the society of Ravenna under the Roman Empire to focus then on the Byzantine period. To achieve this aim data obtained from the inscriptions will be used, in addition to those provided by literary sources, papyrological sources and the iconography of late Roman and Byzantine monuments of Ravenna. Among all the sources listed above, epigraphic ones are particularly valuable for the aim pursued by the present contribution. In many ways in fact the epigraphy of the early Byzantine period differs from that of the previous Roman period, not only in its contents, but also in its use.[5] The latter in particular is important because it is the indicator of changes of a social, political, cultural and religious nature that shed light on various aspects of the society of Ravenna in the Byzantine age.

The large number of inscriptions that are stored in Ravenna provides a detailed picture of the society of an important Roman center. Through the epigraphic evidence of Ravenna. it is therefore possible to perceive the social, political and cultural changes that occurred in one of the main cities of the Mediterranean between the Roman and the Byzantine periods. These changes reflect the general trends of the period and the case study of Ravenna is significant because it was a rich city, populous and on the rise from kate antiquity to the Middle Ages.[6] Between the first and the fifth centuries the administrative order of Ravenna looked extremely unusual for Italy. In Ravenna, due to the presence of the fleet and of its prefect, people perceived the central Roman power permanently and in a direct way.[7] Only in Miseno (located at the extreme offshoot of the Gulf of Naples), and in Rome, was there a structure similar to that of Ravenna.[8] By virtue of the massive military presence, Ravenna then resembled a provincial border city.[9] The admiral of the navy (*praefectus classis*), did not only command the army, but was also involved in the civic administration of Italy.[10] The demand for consumer goods from the base of the fleet influenced deeply the epigraphy of Ravenna.[11] About 600 individuals out of 1,300 recorded in the inscriptions (783 pieces in total) are soldiers of the fleet or dwellers of the base.[12] The occurrences of inscriptions of Ravenna of high standing officers and of members of the Roman Senate are on the contrary very rare.[13] Apart from some large funerary monuments, embellished with vivid portraits of the dead, and other smaller architectural types that cease within the first century, almost all the inscriptions were carved on small-sized steles dated for the most part to the second century.[14] The texts engraved on them present a high degree of uniformity. This feature depends on the fact that inscriptions were strongly influenced, if not based, on the registers that contained the service records of the soldiers and were kept in the archive of the fleet (*tabularium classis*).[15] The inscriptions of the civilians employ the same formulas of the military ones, use often terms and expressions typical of military jargon (*sermo castrensis*) and the dead often bear soldiers' nicknames (*cognomina*).[16]

People recorded on the inscriptions were probably for the most craftsmen, traders and ship owners in business with the army for supplies. The number of artisans of iron and wood (*fabrii*) of Ravenna that one draws from the inscriptions is the highest known in the territory of the empire.[17]

The epigraphy of Ravenna thus attests a rather complex social structure in which prevails a flourishing middle class within which literacy seems quite common.[18] At the same time, one remains impressed by the multicultural character of the society of Ravenna. The highest number of marines and foreigners in general came from the eastern provinces of the Empire, some soldiers even from a city of the south-eastern coast of the Black Sea.[19] The strict observance of such a mixed community to the Roman administrative practices testifies to its high level of integration in the local society. The mixed character of the society of Ravenna under the Roman Empire is reflected also in the wide range of stone materials employed by marble carvers.[20] This was in fact not just a matter of taste but also of different economic possibilities. The craft class in the service of the army and the military class undoubtedly characterise Ravenna until the end of the Roman rule. It is significant, in fact, that two out of the three latest inscriptions of the Roman period concern a *praefectus fabricae armorum*, an equestrian superintendent of the arsenal and of the armaments of the fleet and a long list of iron and wood craftsmen, which was discovered near the base.[21] The third, dated to the fifth century, mentions a former *praefectus annonae Africae provinciae*, the officer responsible for the supply of corn and oil of Rome and Ravenna.[22] This is therefore another document that reaffirms the importance of the navy and of the harbour of Ravenna.

The Byzantine period

The society that emerges from the epigraphic evidence of the Byzantine period looks instead profoundly changed. At the same time is evident that the epigraphy of this period is conceived for different purposes and needs. Most of this evidence is stored in the city's Museo Archivescovile, with the remaining part preserved in the Museo Nazionale and the paleo-Christian buildings of Ravenna bearing mosaic inscriptions, except for documents rescued from the graveyards surrounding the aforesaid buildings and carved upon funerary monuments placed inside them, in particular sarcophagi and funerary marble slabs.[23] Among these collections one in particular is nothing short of rare: it concerns a late-antique graveyard dug up by the narthex of the fifth-century church of Sant'Agata Maggiore (Figures 6.1 and 6.2).[24] It includes thirty-nine inscriptions dating to the fifth and sixth centuries approximately and still unpublished. The largest collection of Byzantine inscriptions is stored in the Museo Arcivescovile di Ravenna. It amounts to twenty-two inscriptions out of ninety pieces in total, ranging from the fifth to the ninth centuries and representing a quarter of the whole exhibition, or roughly 3% of Ravenna's overall epigraphic evidence.[25]

Figure 6.1 Funerary inscription of *Martinus, vir clarissimus praefectus* and his wife *Proseria Publi filia.*

Figure 6.2 The epitaph of *Victorinus vir reuerendus diaconus.*

The epigraphic evidence of the Byzantine period can be divided into three main groups: inscriptions of bishops, inscriptions concerning the officers of the Church and of the exarchate and records of persons presumably of high social standing. In the Byzantine period the military records that were so common previously almost completely disappeared. While the inscriptions of the

Roman period come almost all from the cemeteries of the suburbs of Ravenna and were discovered *in situ*, those of the Byzantine period were largely removed from their original site.[26] In this regard the small necropolis of the aforementioned church of Sant'Agata, which probably in the Byzantine period was not yet included within the city walls, is a lucky exception. Even interior spaces of religious buildings, however, began to attract many who desired to rest near the remains of holy bishops (*ad sanctos*) in order to increase their chances of gaining eternal life.[27] This practice is documented in the churches of San Vitale, Sant'Apollinare Nuovo and Sant'Apollinare in Classe by a few inscriptions, among which stands the one engraved on the sarcophagus of the archbishop Theodorus, who bears the title of *vir beatus*.[28]

The whole set of the Byzantine inscriptions of Ravenna was carved on Proconnesian marble and, to a lesser extent, on other qualities of marble extracted from African or Greek quarries. The choice of these materials did not depend solely on their relative cost effectiveness.[29] They are in fact shiny and white stones, or are ones that generate elegant chiaroscuro effects that increase their monumental and aesthetic effect. In the Byzantine period epigraphy, in short, becomes a means of celebrating the new ruling elite, that is to say the imperial officers and the clergy.[30] During this period, on the contrary, the members of the city council (*ordo decurionum*), no longer raise inscriptions in public spaces.[31] Municipal officials appear only in the papyri, a written medium designed for the private communication, not for the public one.[32] Byzantine epigraphy cuts off all links with institutions and civic values. The inscriptions of bishops and notables express just poetic and religious contents.

Only some inscriptions of the sixth to seventh centuries relating to public improvements are an exception in this sense, even though they no longer mention the members of the city council, but king Theodoric and his court under the Gothic rule and, after the Byzantine reconquest of Italy, the exarchs.[33] The epigraphy of the Byzantine period actually abandons public spaces to move inside the religious buildings.[34] Here it serves as a support to the liturgy and to the visual message of the mosaics. In this regard the most striking example is attested by the mosaic cycle and the inscriptions of the Neonian Baptistery, the main documentary evidence on the rite of baptism in antiquity. The building reveals in fact an amazing interpenetration between iconographic message and inscribed text. In its third band of mosaic, in particular, Heaven is represented as a place of liberation and salvation, where both lush flora of the garden and empty seats symbolise the destination of new life to which men are reborn embracing the faith through baptism, so that it is possible to speak of a true symbiosis between image and related epigraphic message that reads: *In loco Pascuae ibi me conlocavit*.[35] The expression *locum Pascuae* of the inscription represents a metaphor that refers to the image of Heaven depicted in the mosaic. The teaching of the doctrine and the political propaganda are also the purposes of the monogram, a particular kind of inscription which appears starting from the Byzantine period and which consists of two or more letters linked together in order to shorten a word. The case of monograms shows that during the Byzantine period the epigraphic habit was increasingly influenced by writing on papyrus and parchment. In the first place monograms were used in fact to sign official documents.[36] Many sarcophagi of Ravenna bear the monogram formed by the two Greek letters Ch and R, which indicate the Greek word Christos. The presence of the monogram meaning Christ firstly declares the orthodoxy of the deceased person who was buried inside the sarcophagus, then attests her observance of the religion of the dominant regime.[37] Monograms appear in addition on the pulvinos of the pillars of the extant Byzantine churches of Ravenna, where they point out the bishop who promoted their construction. These premises already show that the most innovative feature of the Byzantine period is the wide range of levels and kinds of messages that, both through epigraphy and iconography, public buildings and monuments in general express, anticipating in many respects a feature that would have become regular in the course of the ninth to eleventh centuries.[38]

However, the evolution of the epigraphy of this period is very complex and part of it is not yet understood. Thus if there are valid hypotheses for the loosening of certain abbreviations that are read on the mosaics and on the sarcophagi, we still completely miss the meaning of certain letters depicted on the robes of the characters of the mosaics.[39] The dazzling splendour of the mosaics and of gorgeous Byzantine artefacts can then easily hide from the view of the observer the presence of the inscriptions. But it is not said that even in the case of these artistic masterpieces the inscriptions are of secondary importance. Evangelists represented in the mosaic of San Vitale, for instance, appear to write on papyri while at their feet lay boxes (*capsae*) with plenty of *rotuli*. Remarkably, Saint Matthew employs Aramaic letters. This implies that the authors of the mosaic wanted to refernce Eusebius' *Historia ecclesiastica,* in which the bishop indicates that Matthew wrote his gospel in Aramaic: *Matthaeus patrio sermone conscribens* (*Hist. Ecc.* III, 24).[40] By doing so, the authors of the mosaic cycle of San Vitale sought to emphasise the important role held by sacred codices in both cult and preaching.

In the frontal panel of the ivory seat of the archbishop Maximian are carved the images of Saint John the Baptist and the four evangelists and thus, once again, this device attests first of all the primary function of the bishop, to teach doctrine.[41] Images of the life of Joseph the Hebrew on the sides of the seat and episodes of the nativity and public life of Jesus carved on both backrest sides perform the same function. However, it is only thanks to the presence of a very brief inscription, the monogram placed at the front of the seat, that we can assign it to Maximian.[42] Moreover, the meaning of part of the scenes carved on the seat would not be fully understood if the monogram of Maximian was not present and if we failed to consider the position occupied by the latter in the seat. The scenes of Joseph on the seat of Maximian imply in fact a political meaning. The ivory seat links the mission of the bishop to the spiritual and temporal one carried out by patriarch Joseph, as emerges from a passage of Cassiodorus' *Formula praefecturae praetorio* of 511 in which the Roman senator marks the wise administration and distribution of public revenues by Joseph, in his capacity of Pharaoh's governor, as the model which the imperial magistrate has to aim at.[43] The supply of markets and the defence of the cities of the empire, as well as the right to exercise jurisdiction conducting trials, were among the various duties previously held by both town councils and magistrates that bishops had taken over, sharing them with praetorian prefects and other imperial officers.[44] But Joseph is also the magistrate who serves faithfully his king without aiming to usurp the throne, as Maximian did immediately after the conclusion of the Gothic war when, in the absence of both Vigilius and Datius, respectively, from the sees of Rome and Milan, the Istrian prelate acted as primate of Italy.[45] The positioning of the monogram of the archbishop Maximian above the aforesaid portrait of Saint John the Baptist is a "non-verbal equivalent" of the message inscribed in Agnellus' *pyrgos* placed in the cathedral of Ravenna—*servus Christi*—matching also the way Maximian styles himself in an Istrian document.[46] Since John the Baptist was the one who publicly recognised Jesus as the Messiah, refusing to claim this role for himself, by putting his monogram above image of Jesus' cousin Maximian reasserted his loyalty to the emperor. Finally epigraphy is useful to those who try to establish where the seat was been produced.[47] It is actually highly probable that the chair, even though commissioned and planned by Maximian in Constantinople, had been made by eastern craftsmen, as also may be inferred by Greek characters with the function of numerals inscribed in each scene panel to show their positioning sequence.[48]

Therefore, during the Byzantine period, the joint use of epigraphy and mosaic iconography could perform unexpected functions. A modern observer in fact would perhaps not expect that inscriptions and mosaics could even secure important imperial grants, as if they had been a document deposited with an archive. Also in this respect it seems that Ravenna's evidence anticipates what would have been common practice several centuries later in Greek-speaking provinces of the Byzantine empire, such as continental Greece. The scene on the extreme left of the lowest row of mosaic of Sant'Apollinare in Classe church represents emperor Constantine IV Pogonatus who grants privileges to archbishop Reparatus (671–677).[49] Flanking the sovereign, dressed like Justinian in San Vitale, are his younger brothers Heraclius and Tiberius, while on Constantine's left a prominent figure, probably archbishop Maurus, puts a hand on the shoulder of Reparatus, the recipient of a *rotulus* upon which reads *priuilegia*; under the scene is a commemorative inscription.[50]

Even though repeatedly repaired and restored, the mosaic, commissioned by archbishop Reparatus, still represents a valuable document, closely resembling, in many respects, and probably serving the same function of paintings such as those in Panagia Peribleptos monastery (in Mystras, near Sparta), which depicted the castles and towns granted to the monks by emperor Romanos III, and were surrounded by an inscription that attested the imperial donation.[51] The inscriptions of the Byzantine period comprise together also something like a small *dossier* about the administrative hierarchy of the capital of the exarchate. However we would not know what functions performed the imperial and ecclesiastical officers of these funerary records, if we did not have literary and documentary evidence contemporary to them. Sources like the correspondence between Marinianus, a bishop of Ravenna of the seventh century, and Gregory the Great allows a thorough insight into both administrative and religious functions performed in particular by bishops and clergy of Ravenna's see between the late sixth and the early seventh centuries.[52] The papyri of Ravenna instead shed light on the functions performed by the officers of the exarchate. So we learn that the clergy of Ravenna also assisted the Byzantine officers in their tasks of government in other parts of Italy, while in Ravenna the function that most involved the officers of the exarchate was the management of the complex Byzantine tax system.[53]

In conclusion, the epigraphy testifies to the substantial changes occurred in the society of Ravenna in the Byzantine period. In the fourth century, the epigraphic documents testifying the prosperous middle class of the Ravenna society under the Roman Empire have completely disappeared. It seems that this phenomenon is somehow connected to the suppression of the fleet of Ravenna. In fact the surviving inscriptions related to the fleet do not go beyond the second half of the third century. At the same time not a single inscription of the magistrates nor of the members of the local senate have come to us. The memory of the *curiales* and of the flourishing merchant class of Ravenna survives only in the papyri. The only exception in this regard is the inscription of a marble carver or dealer (*marmorarius*) discovered in the necropolis of the church of Sant'Agata (Figure 6.3). Regarding the epigraphy of Ravenna during the Byzantine period, what remains difficult to explain is the almost total lack of inscriptions of the fourth to fifth centuries. The scholars agree that the number of inscriptions of Ravenna of this period is much lower than what would be expected in a city that from the fifth century permanently hosted the western imperial court. Perhaps the phenomenon may have depended on the re-employment of late antique stone materials, reused again and again during the middle ages.

However, the profound social and cultural changes that occurred in late antiquity could have also been influential along with the increasingly massive presence of a German ethnic element (which accelerated the disintegration of society and the values of which epigraphy was an expression). In particular, the disappearance of the inscriptions of the members of the city council and of the local public officers depended probably on the loss of political power of collegial bodies and civic magistrates in late antiquity. Besides this, the phenomenon could also reflect a change in mentality

Figure 6.3 The inscription of a *marmorarius* discovered by the church of Sant'Agata.

induced by the new recipients of inscriptions in late antiquity. Since in fact the inscriptions were addressed to the whole community those who transmitted a message knew that it would be read by people who shared their own culture and own values. In other words, the authors of the message "counted on their world still continuing in existence for a long time to come, so as to make permanent memorials worthwhile". Little by little these factors came less, especially under the domination of the Goths, between the fifth and the sixth centuries, pushing the notables not to run after epigraphy to transmit the memory of their civic career. In the Byzantine period only the officers of the exarchate and the clergy recur to epigraphy. The inscriptions of this period however seem to play the function of status symbol of the new ruling class and serve to celebrate its social prestige. The increased use of Latin in verse expresses the refined culture of the clients of the inscriptions and marks their distance from the rest of the society. Within the latter social mobility now seems to enjoy little space. Another significant difference of Byzantine epigraphy compared to that of the previous Roman imperial period consists in the wide range of levels and kinds of messages that it expresses together with iconography. In the case of the ivory seat of Maximian the monogram of the bishop not only serves to indicate the owner of the artefact, but also to communicate, with the support of images carved on it, political contents. Similarly the representations of the nativity and of the public life of Christ, like those on the story of Joseph the Jew, can be understood even only with regard to their religious content, without interpreting them in relation to the scenes of the evangelists and of John the Baptist and to the monogram of Maximian at the front of the seat. It can also be reasonably assumed that this variety of contents expressed by epigraphy and representations carved on the artifacts corresponded to different recipients for social and cultural extraction. Finally, two inscriptions attest to the new custom born in the Byzantine period to grant spaces for the burial of officials in the interior of the churches. These concessions probably were due to several reasons. In one case the deceased (the imperial officer *Principius*) got to be buried inside the church probably thanks to the human and work relationships that he had with the clergy.

Often, as is proved in the case of later examples, the burial inside a church envisaged also the setting up of a dedicated space inside the building, such as a chapel, if the funerary monument holder could afford it, and the periodical or daily recitation of services or recitation of prayers for the soul of the dead.[54] Something similar might thus explain the presence of the sarcophagus of Isacius inside the church of San Vitale, whose inscription (the second document in question) narrating the owner's career may possibly have been read to commemorate him, as attested in later periods both in Italy and in other Mediterranean provinces, and especially because the text briefly exposes the officer's career.[55]

Notes

1 T. S. Brown, *L'aristocrazia di Ravenna, cit.*, 91.
2 *Ibid.*, 97–98.
3 A. Rhoby, *A Short History of Byzantine Epigraphy*, in *Inscriptions in Byzantium and Beyond. Methods—Projects and Case Studies*, (Wien) 2015, 27.
4 B. S. Bachrach, *Early Medieval Military Demography: Some Observations on the Methods of Hans Delbrück*, in *The Circle of War in the Middle Ages. Essays on Medieval Military and Naval History*, (Woodbridge 1999), 4 ff.; F. Harley, *Christianity and the Transformation of Classical Art*, in *A Companion to Late Antiquity*, (Chichester 2009), 306–326, particularly 314 ff.
5 A. Donati, *L'epigrafia a Ravenna*, in *Museo Nazionale di Ravenna, Porta Aurea, Palladio e il monastero benedettino di San Vitale*, (Venezia 2015), 176.
6 Zos. V, 34, 3–7; VI, 8, 1–3; E. Rickman, *Portus in Perspective*, in *"Roman Ostia" Revisited. Archaeological and Historical Papers in Memory of Russell Meiggs*, (London—Ostia) 1996, 281–292; L. De Ligt, *The Population of Cisalpine Gaul in the Time of Augustus*, in *People, Land and Politics. Demographic Developments and the Transformation of Roman Italy, 300 BC–AD 14*, (Leiden) 2008, 149, 156 ss.
7 A. Bazzocchi, *Flotta, economia e organizzazione amministrativa a Ravenna e a Faenza nei secoli IV–VI d.C.*, *Felix Ravenna* 61–64, (2005–2008), 93–140.
8 A. Parma, *Nuovi dati su società cittadina e classiari a* Misenum*: prime note, Colonie e municipi nell'era digitale. Documentazione epigrafica per la conoscenza delle città antiche. Atti del Convegno di studi (Macerata, 10–12 dicembre 2015)*, (Roma) 2017, 459–472.
9 R. Chevallier, *Navigations et ports antiques. Esquisse d'une problematique*, in *Atti del convegno internazionale di studi sulle antichità di Classe: Ravenna, 14–17 ottobre 1967*, Ravenna (1968), 244; G. Susini, *Le officine lapidarie romane di Ravenna*, *CCARB* XII, (1965), 548; Id., *Miseno e Ravenna; parallelo critico delle fonti*, *CCARB* XIV, (1967), 376; Id., *La questione della civitas Classis*, in *Atti del*

convegno internazionale di studi, cit., 343–345. G. Bermond Montanari, *Recenti rinvenimenti archeologici d'età romana nella zona di Classe, ibidem*, 356–357.

10 CIL II, 6278 = ILS 5163; CIL III, 7106 = ILS 9340; G. Gregori, *Epigrafia anfiteatrale dell'Occidente romano. Regiones Italiae VI–XI*, II, (Roma 1989), 107; M. Carter, *Gladiatorial Ranking and the "SC de Pretiis Gladiatorum Minuendis" (CIL II 6278 = ILS 5163)*, *Phoenix* 57, (2003), 83–114.

11 A. Donati, *Scrittura, società e cultura*, in *Storia di Ravenna. L'evo antico*, I, (Venezia 1990), 469–480.

12 CIL XI, *Indices*; Giacomini, *Anagrafe dei classiari*, in *Storia di Ravenna*, cit., 321–362; A. Donati, *L'epigrafia a Ravenna*, cit., 175.

13 G. Susini, "*Mandato di comparizione per un duoviro ravennate*", *Epigraphica* 61, (1999), 229–230; A. Bazzocchi, Sextus Urgulanius: IIvir Rauennae vel Rauricae? *L'ordinamento amministrativo di Ravenna in età romana, Libro Aperto* 83, suppl. 1, (2016), 21–25.

14 G. A. Mansuelli, *Le stele romane del territorio ravennate e del Basso Po*, (Ravenna 1967); A. Donati, *L'epigrafia a Ravenna*, cit., 173–177.

15 On the *tabularii* and *librarii classis* cf. CIL XI, 17, 373 = XVI, 154; *TLL* III, c. 1293; M. Roxan—Holder, *Roman military Diplomas* IV, (London 2003), 380.

16 CIL XI, 92, 135, 209; A. Łoś, *Quand et pourquoi a-t-on envoyé les prétoriens à Pompei?*, in *Nunc de Suebis dicendum est. Studia archaeologica et historica Giorgio Kolendo ab amicis et discipulis dicata*, (Warszawa 1995), 165–166; F. Cenerini, *Il territorio delle Ville Unite: le fonti epigrafiche di epoca romana*, in...*In agro decimano. Per un catalogo del patrimonio storico archeologico del territorio a sud di Ravenna*, (Ravenna 2000), 49.

17 CIL XI, introd., 6; J. Waltzing, *Étude historique sur les corporations professionelles chez les romains. Depuis les origines jusqu'à la chute de l'Empire d'Occident*, I, (Louvain 1895), 359, 473.

18 A. Donati, *Scrittura, società*, cit., *passim*.

19 CIL XI, 52; A. Donati, *L'epigrafia a Ravenna*, cit., 175.

20 G. A. Mansuelli, *Le stele romane del territorio ravennate*, cit., *passim*.

21 CIL XI, 9; AE 1977, 265.

22 CIL XI, 323.

23 For a recent and complete catalogue of Ravenna's Roman and Byzantine heritage cf. M. David, *Eternal Ravenna. From the Etruscans to the Venetians* (Washington D.C. 2013).

24 G. Gardini, *Lo scavo del quadriportico della basilica di Sant'Agata Maggiore. Spunti dal carteggio Ricci-Monumenti presso la Biblioteca Classense di Ravenna*, in *Incontro di studio sul tema Studiare Ravenna a Ravenna. Atti della 1. giornata di studi dedicata alla memoria di Luigi Maria Malkowski. Ravenna, 4 dicembre 2010*, (Ravenna 2012), 71–82. Among the most important documents rescued from the necropolis are a huge marble slab bearing the funerary inscription of *Martinus, vir clarissimus praefectus* and his wife *Proseria Publi filia* (Figure 6.1); they were buried respectively in A.D. 541 (under the consulate of the *vir clarissimus Basilius Iunior*) and in December A.D. 508, the latter (during the first indiction of the reign of emperor Justin) Martinus may have been one of the first officers to hold the charge of *praefectus per Italiam*, who replaced the praetorian prefect soon after the fall of the Gothic power in Italy, cf. D. Mauskopf Deliyannis, *Ravenna, cit.*, 252 for the dating of the consular couple; J. O. Tjäder, *Ravenna ai tempi dell'arcivescovo, cit.*, 3–4; A. Laniado, *Le christianisme et l'évolution des institutions municipales du Bas-Empire: l'exemple du* defensor civitatis, in *Die Stadt in der Spätantike, cit.*, 324, note 35. Then comes the epitaph of *Victorinus vir reuerendus diaconus* (Figure 6.2).

25 Ravenna's overall epigraphic evidence can be quickly and easily checked out by

visiting Manfred Clauss' online epigraphic database Epigraphische-Datenbank Clauss-Slaby: http://www.manfredclauss.de/.

26 CIL XI, introd., *passim*.

27 G. Tabacco, *Il cristianesimo latino altomedievale*, in *Storia del cristianesimo. Il Medioevo* (Roma and Bari 1997), 49, 58.

28 E. Schoolman, *Reassessing the sarcophagi of Ravenna*, *Dumbarton Oaks Papers*, 67 (2013), 64. The other texts concern two Byzantine officials: the exarch Isacius, a well-known historical figure, a former tax collector named *Principius*, who had to be originally buried in the church of Sant'Apollinare Nuovo, as can be inferred by the *incipit* of the text: *Hanc arcam iubante Sancto Martino*. The official was probably involved in managing properties belonging to the church of Saint Martin, where he might have requested to be buried cf. Tjäd. I, 2, l. 1 (A.D. 565–570); I, 8, l. 15 (A.D. 564); II, 34, *passim* (A.D. 551); *CIL* XI, 16; CIG IV, 9869; S. Cosentino, *L'iscrizione ravennate dell'esarco Isacio e le guerre di Rotari*, *Atti e Memorie della Deputazione di Storia Patria per le Antiche Province Modenesi* 15 (1993), 23–43.

29 Y. A. Marano, *The circulation of marble in the Adriatic Sea at the time of Justinian*, in *Ravenna its role in earlier medieval change and exchange*, (London 2016), 111–114.

30 *Ibid.*, 111.

31 A. Bazzocchi, *Flotta, economia e organizzazione*, cit., 126–127.

32 *Ibid.*

33 CIL XI, 11, 263, 268; AE 1941, 94, 2006, 442.

34 A. Bazzocchi, *Flotta, economia e organizzazione*, cit., 125–126.

35 *CIL* XI, 257= *ILCV* 2409; G. Montanari, *Ravenna. L'iconologia. Saggi di interpretazione culturale e religiosa dei cicli musivi, (Ravenna 2002)*, 110.

36 I. H. Garipzanov, *The Symbolic Language of Authority in the Carolingian World (c. 751–877)*, (Leiden 2008), 165, 176, 191 and note 135.

37 C. Pietri, *Les aristocraties de Ravenne (V^e^– VI^e^s.)*, *Studi Romagnoli* 34, (1983), 662–663.

38 I. Toth, *Epigraphic Traditions in Eleventh-Century Byzantium*, in *Inscriptions in Byzantium and Beyond. Methods - Projects and Case Studies*, (Wien) 2015, 203; A. Rhoby, *Byzantinische Kirchen als Orte der Interaktion von Wort, Bild und Betrachter—Inschriften im sakrale Kontext*, in *Öffentlichkeit—Monument—Text.* XIV Congressus Internationalis Epigraphiae Greceae et Latinae 27.–31. Augusti MMXII. *Akten*, (Berlin and Boston 2004), 650–651.

39 G. Tabacco, *Le ideologie politiche*, *cit.*, 68; G. Montanari, *Ravenna. L'iconologia*, *cit.*, 141. About the possible meanings of the letters on the clothes of the characters of the mosaics of Ravenna is very interesting a passage of Boethius' *De consolatione Philosophiae* in which we read that the personification of Philosophy wears a robe on which two Greek letters are embroidered: P and Q, pravxi~ and qewriva, which represent the two main branches of Philosophy, cf. Severino Boezio, *La consolazione della filosofia*, a cura di C. Moreschini, (Novara 2013), I, 4–5; 102, note 3.

40 G. Montanari, *Ravenna. L'iconologia*, *cit.*, 95, 119.

41 *Ibid.*, 120.

42 This monogram is a shortened form for the two Greek words ejpivskopo~ Maximiavno~, cf. F. W. Volbach, *Elfenbainenarbeiten der Spätantike*, *cit.*, 93 (in this earlier work Volbach referred that the monogram is written instead in Latin: «Unter dem Sitz, auf der Vorderseite zwischen Ranke mit 2 Pfauen das lateinische Monogram des Bishofs Maximianus vom Ravenna»); Id., *Avori di scuola ravennate nel V e VI secolo*, (Ravenna 1977), 38, 43, 45; G. Montanari, *Ravenna. L'iconologia*, *cit.*, 43.

43 *Ibid.*, 144.

44 T. S. Brown, *The Church of Ravenna and the Imperial Administration in the Seventh Century*, *English Historical Review* 94, (1979), 2; Id., *Gentlemen and Officers*, *cit.*, 176–177; G. Montanari, *Ravenna. L'iconologia*, *cit.*, 145.

45 *Ibid.*, 39–40.

46 *Ibid.*, 43, note 105; I. Toth, *Epigraphic Traditions in Eleventh*, *cit.*, 204, *passim*. Quite similar interrelation between iconography and engraved text recurs in the sarcophagus of exarch Isacius, whose inscribed message is spread along the barrel lid in order to set the most significant words in correspondence with the arms of the central cross carved upon the same hood, cf. CIG IV, 9869; F. Fiori, *NIKA H TYXE. Scritture epigrafiche e ideologia politica nell'Italia bizantina*, in *Lettere come simboli. Aspetti ideologici della scrittura tra passato e presente*, (Udine 2012), 74.

47 F. W. Volbach, *Elfenbainenarbeiten der Spätantike*, *cit.*, 93 (in this earlier work Volbach referred that the monogram is written instead in Latin: «Unter dem Sitz, auf der Vorderseite zwischen Ranke mit 2 Pfauen das lateinische Monogram des Bishofs Maximianus vom Ravenna»); Id., *Avori di scuola ravennate nel V e VI secolo*, (Ravenna 1977), 38, 43, 45; G. Montanari, *Ravenna. L'iconologia*, *cit.*, 43.

48 F. W. Volbach, *Elfenbainenarbeiten der Spätantike*, *cit.*, 24; F. W. Deichmann, *Archeologia cristiana*, (Roma 1993), 256; A. Rhoby, *Inscriptions and Manuscripts in Byzantium: A Fruitful Symbiosis?*, in *Scrittura epigrafica e scrittura libraria: fra Oriente e Occidente*, (Cassino 2015), 20.

49 An inscription is placed above emperor's portrait: *Constantinus maior imperator* [*pater Constantini*] / [*H*]*eraclii et Tiberii imperator*[*um*]; at the base of the mosaic scene reads the inscription mentioned also by Agnellus: *Is igitur socius meritis Reparatus ut esset, Aula novos abitus fecit flagrans per aevum*, cf. *CIL* XI, 293c; T. S. Brown, *The Church of Ravenna*, *cit.*, 22.

50 *Ibid.*, 21–23; S. Pasi, *Il quadro storico di Sant'Apollinare in Classe: una lettura attraverso la storia dei restauri*, *Studi Romagnoli* 62, (2011), 84, 87.

51 C. Rizzardi, *I mosaici dell'arco trionfale di Sant'Apollinare in Classe: precisazioni iconografiche cronologiche e stilistiche*, *Corsi di Cultura sull'Arte Ravennate e Bizantina* 32, (1985), 405, 429; S. Pasi, *Il quadro storico di Sant'Apollinare in Classe*, *cit.*, 83–85; I. Toth, *Epigraphic Traditions in Eleventh*, *cit.*, 210.

52 A. Cacciari, *Mariniano*, *Dizionario Biografico degli Italiani*, vol. LXX, (Rome 2008), 489.

53 Tjäd. I, 2, l. 1 (A.D. 565–570); I, 8, l. 15 (A.D. 564); II, 34, *passim* (A.D. 551); II, 47–48; M. Tagliaferri, *L'arcivescovo Mariniano di Ravenna e l'elezione di Massimo di Salona (592–599)*, in *La Chiesa metropolitana ravennate e i suoi rapporti con la costa adriatica orientale*, (Bologna 2005), 76–77; A. Cacciari, *Mariniano*, *Dizionario Biografico*, cit., 489–491.

54 G. Tabacco, *Il cristianesimo latino altomedievale*, *cit.*, 58; I. Toth, *Epigraphic Traditions in Eleventh*, *cit.*, 212.

55 O. Bertolini, *Il Patrizio Isacio esarca d'Italia (625–643)*, in *Atti del 2° Congresso Internazionale di Studi sull'alto Medioevo. Grado—Aquileia—Gorizia—Cividale—Udine, 7–11 settembre 1952*, (Spoleto 1953), 118–119: S. Cosentino, *L'iscrizione ravennate*, cit., 23 ss.; I. Toth, *Epigraphic Traditions in Eleventh*, *cit.*, 212.

7 Exarchs and others: secular patrons of churches in the sixth to eighth centuries

In the early fourth century, Roman civic values and the requirements of Christian congregations fused to make the construction and decoration of churches a civic and pious act. When the emperor Constantine I gave money and properties to build and endow monumental churches in Rome, Constantinople, Jerusalem, and elsewhere, he set a precedent that was imitated by thousands of Christians, both rich and not-so-rich, which has continued down to the present. In Constantine's Roman empire, patronage of public buildings was a cultural and civic expectation, and pious Christians' patronage of churches came to be documented, commemorated, and praised in typically Roman ways, with overlays of Christian religious meaning.[1] From the beginning, it is clear that patrons of churches expected that their donations would be publicly commemorated, to the benefit of themselves and their families.[2]

Donation can be commemorated in a variety of written, oral, and visual ways. When someone decides to build a church, money and/or property is given to pay for the construction and decoration, and the church might be endowed with properties to support it. Especially in the latter case, charters of donation are drawn up to confirm the gift of property and its conditions. When the church is built, the donors might be commemorated with an inscription, in stone or paint or mosaic, or with a picture (or both) within the building. A dedication ceremony takes place, presided over by the bishop, perhaps with a specially composed sermon. Someone might describe the ceremony, or the building, in a letter to a friend. Some forms of commemoration must have taken place primarily through local oral memory, because the founder was buried in the church, and/or was perhaps named in the liturgy, about which much less evidence survives before the mid-eighth century.[3] And finally, someone might write a text—either about the individual donor, or about his/her city or country, or about a saint associated with the church—that mentions the patron; such a text could be written centuries later, perhaps on the basis of an inscription or picture. All these types of commemoration have their origins in late antiquity, and continued to be used into the Middle Ages to document church construction.

Each genre of text records the donations in a different way; the very language indicates different aims, conventions, and audiences. Inscriptions and narrative sources do not simply enumerate the facts of benefaction, but do so in such a way as to praise it lavishly, and to draw explicit or implicit comparisons between the patrons and people of the past. On the other hand, documents and laws about church foundation have a different kind of rhetoric; in those sources, which are just as formulaic as the other types, the point of the text is to affirm the gift and secure some tangible property right, either to the donor or to the church, even while couched in terms of the donor's piety. Moreover, while these various types of text provide us with invaluable information about the social and cultural contexts of church-building, some have survived better than others. In most cases, we have only one text for any given building, and the conclusions that can be drawn are quite dependent on which type of text it is.[4] For the period before 800 we have only one case, that of Valila the Goth, in which three different types of text about the same individual/building survive, and, as we will see, each text presents Valila's benefactions differently. How, then, are we to interpret the social and cultural meaning of church donation in this period?

Secular patronage of churches has been examined by various scholars in recent decades and is usually described as an act undertaken for social or political aims: to impress fellow members of the elite, to protect property, or to lay claim to a territory and its people.[5] In 1986, Ian Wood discussed "the audience of architecture in post-Roman Gaul" for the period before 600, and concluded that church-building was imbued with the values of the secular Roman aristocracy, as a vehicle for the display of wealth and taste, and thus for social competition. He based his conclusions on texts such as letters and sermons about church-building, as well as poetic dedicatory inscriptions, all of which lavish praise on the buildings and their founders. By contrast, Susan Wood's 2006 book *The Proprietary Church in the Medieval West* focused on the period after 600, and demonstrated that churches were property over which elite members of society were mostly concerned to exercise dominion.[6] Her conclusions, too, were conditioned by the types of sources on which she focused, namely documents of donation and ecclesiastical law. More recently, scholars are examining the spatial distribution of privately funded churches, placing them in landscapes dominated by the lords who were their patrons. Asserting political authority must be hypothesized, however, because the texts themselves do not say that this is why churches were built; instead, surviving texts speak of the charitable, spiritual, and salvific aims of the donors.[7]

Thus, interpretation of secular church-building depends on the type of sources that survive. Both Ian Wood and Susan Wood use the material that survives in greatest numbers from each historical period: letters, sermons, and poetic inscriptions from the period 400–600, and documents and ecclesiastical law for the period 600–800. It is certainly the case that, after 600, letters, inscriptions, poems, and narrative sources become less common, until they are revived in the Carolingian period. Moreover, the literary texts that do survive tend to describe patronage only by bishops and rulers; ordinary secular people drop out of those categories of commemoration, even though, according to surviving documents as well as laws, they were still founding churches.[8] In addition, from the material evidence we can see that most of the large churches of the post-Roman period date to before 600, with smaller chapels built after that date; we do not know whether this reflects economic and social factors, or simply the fact that, by 600, most towns were already filled with large, splendid churches.

These facts raise several questions about church-building in the period 600–800. Were the churches mentioned in foundation documents after 600 small and mean? If you build a small chapel, are you unable to praise it lavishly? Were only rulers and bishops using church-building to establish certain types of authority in this period? Was the practice of writing in praise of church-building being replaced by liturgical commemoration, and does this imply a transition to a more oral culture? Does the shift in the surviving texts imply different ideas about the social meaning of secular church-building? Or does it rather reflect changes in the ways the elite presented themselves, or in literacy practice,[9] and did this change impact ideas about church-building? In other words, was there still a secular "audience of architecture" for the later period, 600–800?

Here we will briefly look at each of three late antique textual commemorative types from Italy and France—charters, inscriptions, and narratives—to consider not only what we learn about builders, but also what kind of message each of these forms of commemoration conveys. I will suggest that there is still evidence for late antique forms of commemoration of secular donors after 600, and thus still a desire for tangible, visible commemoration; we can see this in Ravenna, for which Tom Brown's research provides an invaluable starting point. But this evidence is relatively rare, or at least its surviving traces are. This may indicate a shift in ideological expectations among the secular elite in the period 600–800, but I will argue that it may also indicate the use of less permanent media, such as paint instead of stone inscriptions, and that there was indeed still a secular "audience of architecture" at this time.

Before 600

When churches became a type of public work that could be funded by individuals, the Roman tradition of commemorating donors with inscriptions was adopted; in churches from the fourth and fifth centuries, we can see increasing commemoration of lay donors through inscriptions or portraits.[10] The inscriptions that survive are found either in floor mosaics or inscribed in stone. In the fourth-century floor mosaics in the basilica at Aquileia, individuals are commemorated by the number of square feet of mosaic they funded; such inscriptions are also known from North Africa, from sixth-century Israel, and from Ravenna, where fragments of the original sixth-century floor mosaics in Sant'Apollinare in Classe mention the donors Gaudentia and Felix.[11] Other types of inscriptions provide lists of individuals, or even groups, who funded churches; for example, in Narbonne, in the mid-fifth century, Bishop Rusticus inscribed, on the lintel of the cathedral, that its reconstruction was supported by the praetorian prefect Marcellus as well as by various bishops, who are listed by the amount of their contributions in *solidi*,[12] while a second lintel from Narbonne ten years later also lists, by *solidi*, the donors, who included a priest, a deacon, a *vir illustris*, a *vir clarissimus*, and a *comitissa*.[13] And finally, among the very few surviving dedicatory inscriptions from Gaul, we have one that describes a basilica in Vienne founded by Flavius Lacanius *vir consularis* in the late fifth or early sixth century.[14]

In addition to these rather prosaic enumerations of donations, dedicatory poems were known in Rome at least from the time of Pope Damasus (r. 366–384), and their form was widely imitated throughout the empire by the early fifth century.[15] Many of these are known only because they were later copied into texts ranging from biographies to epitomes, and they therefore tend to focus on the famous donors of the past, especially bishops—Bishop Ambrose of Milan, for example, or Bishop Neon of Ravenna—thus, there were probably more, commemorating secular donors, that did not survive.[16] Even so, we do have some poems about non-episcopal donors; one of the inscriptions in San Nazaro, Milan, commemorated Serena, the wife of Stilicho, for installing the marble floor. In the dedicatory poem in Santa Sabina at Rome (422–432), the donor is listed as the "priest Peter", an otherwise unknown individual, and there are twelve others that name secular individuals, as Julia Hillner has cataloged.[17]

Elaborate dedicatory poems were written by most of the famous authors of the day, and these are often preserved in their collected works.[18] From the 390s to 600, intellectuals were linked to each other through these very letters and poems.[19] Many of the authors were bishops (or eventually became bishops), and many of the recipients of the letters were likewise bishops, thus most of the patrons praised in these texts are bishops. Nevertheless, all of the authors mention at least a few secular donors. Sidonius Apollinaris, in the 470s,[20] apologizes that he cannot attend the dedication of a baptistery built by one Elaphius in his *castellum*, and in another letter he praises Simplicius who, before he was named a bishop, "built for you a church alone out of his own slender resources, when he was still a young soldier, yet a son and father of a family".[21] Other examples before the year 600 can be found in the writings of Avitus of Vienne, Ennodius of Pavia, and Venantius Fortunatus.[22]

Ravenna provides evidence of many inscriptions, largely because the ninth-century historian Agnellus copied them into his history of the bishops of Ravenna. All have something to do with a bishop, but several from the 540s and 550s state that Santa Maria Maggiore,[23] San Vitale,[24] and

Sant'Apollinare in Classe[25] were funded by Julian the *argentarius* (banker).[26] Agnellus paraphrases Julian's epitaph in San Vitale, which says that he spent 26,000 *solidi* on the building.[27] Julian and another secular leader, Bacauda, built a church to St. Michael the archangel.[28] Julian the *argentarius* was clearly advertising himself through his inscriptions as the wealthiest of Ravenna's inhabitants in this period.[29] But he was not the only secular individual funding construction: another inscription recorded by Agnellus is a lengthy poem describing the gift of relics from Pope Gregory I to Archbishop John II, and the latter's construction of a chapel, but then the last two lines name "Fortunate Smaragdus, inspired forever by these merits, whose wealth participated in this foundation".[30] Smaragdus is also listed on a surviving fragment of a stone inscription commemorating the restoration of Ravenna's aqueduct; he was, in fact, the Byzantine governor of Ravenna at the time.[31]

One of the notable aspects of these dedicatory poems and the letters in which they are often found is that they include praise for the elaborate decoration of the church, usually including mention of brilliantly shining marble, mosaics, gold, and gems.[32] The beauty of the church, as a building worthy of God, modeled on the biblical Temple of Solomon, becomes a topos, and is also found in narrative texts (see later). Indeed in many cases we have no idea what these buildings actually looked like, but the donor is nevertheless praised for funding such beauty.

While numerous inscriptions and poems survive from before 600, the same cannot be said of documents.[33] We know that people were founding churches, since church canons often contain laws that churches must be dedicated by the bishop in whose jurisdiction they are located—implying that people other than bishops are building churches.[34] Papal letters address this issue also, notably some by Gelasius and Gregory the Great; they too are chiefly concerned with stating who should dedicate these churches, and also restricting the right of burial and baptism in them.[35] The few donation documents that survive, as we will see later, express a preoccupation with legal rights: who has control of the property being donated, who has authority over the church and its property. Indeed, the impression one gets from these sources is not piety, but hostility and suspicion towards the motives of church-founders and managers.

A third type of source that contains information about donors is the narrative text. Christian historical writing borrowed much from classical and biblical narratives, including the topos that rulers should patronize public works. In texts such as Gregory of Tour's *Books of Histories*, kings and bishops are constantly building churches, but other people occasionally build something also: the wife of Bishop Namatius of Clermont builds a church to St. Stephen, Duke Victorius the Visigoth builds churches, and Duke Chrodinus endows monasteries.[36] How did an author such as Gregory know that these people had founded churches? Did he see inscriptions, or documents? Was he relying on oral tradition? Whatever the case, mention in a narrative text shows us that the memory of the founders had remained alive.

Civic evergetism was a topos in Roman biography, and the first biography of a Christian emperor, Eusebius' *Life of Constantine*, praises its subject effusively for his construction of splendid churches. Churches benefit the community, and the person who funds them demonstrates his wealth and authority in a public way. However, secular biographies were almost non-existent in the late antique West, being replaced by lives of saints, and in the fourth through sixth centuries, most saints were bishops, and most hagiographies ostentatiously do NOT mention church-building by their subjects. Where we see evidence of construction, it comes through in other ways, especially in accounts of lay patrons building churches for saints and martyrs. The early sixth-century *gesta martyrum* from Rome, for example, lists many lay people as founders of shrines.[37] Likewise, in Gregory of Tours' *Gloria martyrum* there are several churches built by "the people", including one built by Alcima and Placidina, sister and wife of a bishop.[38] These locally oriented narratives honour the individuals who provided for the veneration of local saints: in other words, saints and the people who knew them.

A different type of biographical text is the Roman *Liber pontificalis*, first composed at Rome in the second decade of the sixth century. The *Liber pontificalis* tells us that the so-called titular churches were founded in the late fourth and early fifth centuries by secular individuals, both men and women, after whom they may have been named. However, the authors of the *Liber pontificalis* concentrated on popes, and as I have demonstrated elsewhere, secular donors were for the most part written out of the text. This can be seen in the case of the church of St. Martin, where in the Laurentian fragment of the biography of Pope Symmachus, it says the illustrious Palatinus was the founder and donor,[39] but in the first version of the *Liber pontificalis*, Symmachus gets all the credit for this church.[40] Throughout the text, the popes are described as builders in the Solomonic tradition, and the language used to describe the churches emphasizes their splendid appearance and their gold and silver treasures, using language derived from the description of the Temple in the Books of Kings.[41]

As stated earlier, in most cases we have only one text in any genre about any given church. There is only one individual for whom all three types of commemoration for his church-building survive: Valila, a high-ranking member of the imperial administration at Rome in the 470s.[42] The first text is the only document of donation to survive from fifth-century Italy; known as the *Charta Cornutiana*, it states that Valila has endowed a church near Tivoli with properties, explains that the income is to provide lights and repairs to the fabric, specifies precisely which estates and which localities are meant, and lists silver vessels, fabric hangings, and books which are also being donated and should not be alienated.[43] The reason provided is "so that our service might earn divine forgiveness",[44] an early example of the concept that giving away wealth in this fashion is a pious act done to obtain a benefit from God. The second text is a ten-line poetic inscription that describes how Valila converted Junius Bassus' basilica in the city of Rome into the church of Sant'Andrea Catabarbara:[45]

> Valila's wish was to consecrate his estates to benefit you, Christ; To you this testator has dedicated his resources. Pope Simplicius, by making the adjustments for heavenly rites, Rendered these things truly in your service. And because we lack the house (threshold), He arranged for these things [to be] in the name of the apostolic martyr, Andrew. This church, as your heir, takes possession of its lawful title (*titulus iustus*) and, being your successor, it [the church] places mystical laws in the house. Come, devout people, and learn from this transaction, to seek the heavenly kingdom with earthly wealth (*census*).

Valila is listed as the pious donor who hoped to gain a place in heaven by donating his wealth to the Church, while Pope Simplicius (468–483) is named as the one who dedicated it. Finally, the third text is the Roman *Liber pontificalis*' Life of Simplicius, which states only that the pope dedicated this church, while Valila is not mentioned at all![46]

The example of Valila shows a secular individual who (a) gave a large amount of money, property, and moveables to found and support churches as an act of piety; (b) enlisted his local bishop as the manager and dedicator of his churches; (c) was publicly commemorated in those churches as the benefactor, in a poetic style designed to show elite status and taste; and (d) was then written out of a narrative in which his church served to aggrandize the bishop. If we had had only one of these texts, we might not have known why Valila was making a gift of large amounts of wealth; or that, despite a barbarian-sounding name, he still participated in elite poetic traditions; or that he even existed at all!

Thus, by the year 600, there had developed a variety of different ways to praise secular individuals who donated money to build and decorate churches. In inscriptions, letters, and narrative accounts, the donation is praised as an expression of taste or civic virtue; in documents, by contrast, donation is an act of piety, literally a personal contract between the donor and God.

After 600

Once we get past the year 600, the number of surviving inscriptions decreases dramatically, and so do the number of letters. And, following a trend already seen in the *Liber pontificalis*, the horizons of narrative texts shrink, to focus on bishops and kings. At the same time, the number of surviving documents increases, showing us that while large, public church foundations decline, donation and decoration continues by elite and non-elites alike.

Narrative texts at our disposal shrink their focus to kings and bishops. In the *Liber pontificalis*, after 600, almost all the patronage is attributed to the popes alone. Paul the Deacon's *History of the Lombards* carefully records construction by kings and queens, and the odd monk; in only one case does someone else build a church: Theuderata the wife of Duke Romuald of Benevento.[47] Fredegar too lists construction activity only for a couple of kings. Seventh- and eighth-century hagiography shifts quite dramatically from earlier models, particularly in the attribution of church patronage to saints. Indeed, in some cases lists of benefactions made by the saints gets very detailed: a list of endowments, in the case of the late seventh-century St. Balthild, or description of the splendid style of churches in, as in the case of the late eighth-century Life of St. Desiderius of Cahors.[48] Even the *passio* of the martyred Bishop Leudegar says that he gave precious objects, decorated the baptistery, embellished the tomb of St. Symphorian, gave new pavements, an atrium, etc., etc.![49] Links between these *vitae* and documents of endowment or inscriptions seem likely. Yet, these saints are still all bishops and/or royalty. Only in the *vita* of St. Praejectus do we find lay church donors: Count Genesius, who builds a monastery at Praejectus' request, and the lady Caesaria, who bequeaths land on which Praejectus builds another monastery.[50]

What about inscriptions and letters? In the 630s or 640s, Desiderius of Cahors mentions church construction in a few letters, and in one of them even invites his fellow-bishop Paul of Verdun to the dedication ceremony of a church, and tells him that several other bishops are also invited, which sounds like the ceremonies that we know from the fifth and sixth centuries.[51] But there is no mention of any other secular donors other than kings.[52] Some examples of inscriptions and images do survive in Rome. Theodotus, a *dux* and *primicerius sanctae sedis apostolicae* in Rome, in 755 dedicated a *diaconia* at S. Angelo in Pescheria and set up an inscription listing the saints whose relics were included, which concludes that he built it *pro intercessionem animae sua[e] et remedium omnium peccatorum*.[53] Theodotus is further commemorated in a surviving fresco and inscription in the church of Santa Maria Antiqua, which states that the chapel of Saints Julitta and Quiricus was built by him, and includes a picture of him offering the church-building to Christ, as well as portraits of his family.[54] Another late eighth-century *dux*, Eustathius, together with Georgius *gloriosissimus* set up an inscription in Santa Maria in Cosmedin, enumerating specific properties donated to the diaconia.[55] Outside of Rome, surviving inscriptions are thin on the ground, except for a few reliquaries,[56] although the *vita* of Desiderius of Cahors says that the objects he donated to his churches contained inscriptions with his name on them.[57] It is only in the late eighth century that the Carolingian revival of late antique forms results in the composition of poetic inscriptions by authors such as Paul the Deacon, Hrabanus Maurus, Alcuin, and others.[58]

However, survival of documents describing church-building and endowments improves markedly in the period after 600. Indeed, both from Italy and from Francia (and even from England), increasing numbers of foundation documents, charters of donations, and testaments show the impulse to give money to the Church did not abate, and that new *formulae* were being devised to explain and justify such generosity. These *formulae* have nothing to do with the splendor or beauty of the building, but are instead focused on the soul of the donor.

Church-building and decoration shares similarities with gifts (mainly of property) given to the church, especially to monasteries, as traced by many historians and sociologists since the 1970s.[59] As these scholars have shown, such gifts, including church-building, were made with the expectation that the clerical beneficiaries would provide prayers, locations for burial, and *memoria* for the donors, leading to their salvation. Most studies trace a transformation, beginning around the year 1050, in the way gifts to the church were made and understood, engaging with the question of how monasteries, entities supposedly devoted to poverty, could accumulate vast amounts of property and wealth. However, Philippe Jobert traced another transformation in the way that the meaning of such gifts were expressed in documents, which can first be seen shortly after the year 600, when we start to see references in documents to the benefits of church donation for the donor's soul. Such statements in documents are first found in documents of donation at the beginning of the seventh century, in Ravenna and in Francia, and become ever more frequent during the course of the century. In three papyrus documents from Ravenna, which date to between 600 and 625, we see the some of the earliest uses of the phrase *pro remedio animae meae* specifically in relation to donations made to churches.[60] There are also several Frankish testaments which use the phrase *pro remedio animae* or *pro salute animae*, for example the testament of Ermintrude, which is dated to c. 576–637, in which the phrase *pro remedium animae meae* is found several times in the context of her bequests to churches.[61]

Four documents in the Formulary of Marculf (late seventh century) provide examples of charters of foundation or donation to churches; these contain elaborate prologues, complete with Gospel references to charity as a way of freeing oneself of sin (especially Luke 11:41, "But give that which is within as charity, and then all things are clean for you, to justify the donation".[62] Of course, the Gospels do not mention the founding of churches at all, only charity toward the poor.[63] In these *formulae*, we see the practical application of the idea that church patronage counts as *eleemosyna*: In an example in which a monastery is founded to house some paupers, "I also give… what may help [to provide for] the lights of this oratory and the support, sustenance, and provision of food and clothing for these paupers"—the money for lights and the food for the poor are made equivalent.[64] On the one hand, the appeals are to Christ's call for charity—"for fear of God and for love of the poor of Christ"—but at the same time we also see a care *pro salutem animae*, and references to the salvation of the donor's soul and the remission of his/her sins.[65]

By the early eighth century, these phrases are widespread from Italy to England. Much has been made, for example, of the testament of the lay aristocrat Abbo of Provence, dating to 739, which explicitly states that some of his many donations are "for the salvation of our soul".[66] But slightly earlier, from AD 712, there is a remarkably developed statement of this concept in a charter of donation by one Ansbaldus/Ansbertus, which says:[67]

> While each person seems to abide in the present age, he ought to think to what extent he can obtain the consolation of his soul through charity to holy places or subsidies for prayers, as God says: "Give charity, and behold all things are clean for you" (Luke 11:41). And again, "Just as water extinguishes a fire, so charity extinguishes sin." (cf. Eccles. 3:30). Wherefore I Ansbertus, son of the late Willibald, give for the healing of my soul, and for the recompense of eternal salvation.

By the late eighth century, the *Formulae Salicae Merkelianae* includes the phrase *pro remedio animae meae* twice in the formula for a charter of donation to a church.[68] Lombard charters from the early eighth century use the same references to charity (*eleemosyna*), the redemption of the soul (*pro remedio animae meae*), or to the forgiveness of sins (*pro mea peccata*) when dealing with donations to churches, which are almost all rural chapels and monasteries.[69] We likewise find the same phrases in charters from Anglo-Saxon England in the same period,[70] and, as was seen above, Theodotus' inscription in Rome includes the same phrase.

Donation to a church has thus become explicitly identified as a form of charity, conferring the same benefits. It is surely not a coincidence that seventh-century sacramentaries and missals include special masses that are to be performed in honour of a specific person; the liturgical commemoration of donors seems to be part of the trend we see in the documents.[71] Indeed, these documents often survive in cartularies, books whose very purpose was to preserve the names of donors so that they could be prayed for (and also as evidence of landholding).[72] The text of the documents testify to the fact that endowing a church is intended to store up treasure in heaven for the donor, as well as to safeguard or endow property for a clerical family member. We thus assume that founders were commemorated liturgically in their churches, but the explicit *quid pro quo* is not usually expressed in the eighth-century charters.

In order to really understand what donation means for secular people between 600 and 800, we need a case study, like that of Valila, which can show us several of these practices side by side. Ravenna stands as one of the few cities with some tangible evidence for church building in these centuries, alongside some inscriptions, some documents, and a narrative history written in the 830s. However, even the evidence from Ravenna is ambiguous. After the end of the sixth century, Ravenna's building boom came to an end. Neither in inscriptions nor in texts are the bishops and the exarchs after 600 credited with sponsoring large-scale construction. Indeed, we know from material remains that in this period only one large church was built in Ravenna, dedicated to the Savior and located next to the entrance to the palace. Remarkably, we do not know exactly when it was built, or by whom. Presumably Agnellus did not see any inscriptions, or perhaps he did not wish to name the founder, who might have been anyone from an exarch to the Lombard king Aistulf.[73]

Church construction activity did not entirely disappear in Ravenna, however. Instead, as in the documents from Lombard Italy, we see a pattern of continuous, if small-scale, construction and/or decoration. In most cases, these are small chapels (*monasteria*), and only in three cases do we have explicit evidence for the patron. Agnellus tells us that the exarch Theodore (c. 678–687) together with Archbishop Theodore (677–691) converted a synagogue into an *ecclesia* in honour of St. Paul. Agnellus says also that the same exarch Theodore built a *monasterium* next to Sant'Apollinare Nuovo, in honour of St. Theodore the Deacon. Exarch Theodore was not buried in either of these structures, but rather he and his wife were buried in another *monasterium* dedicated to St. Mary *ad Blachernae*; which Agnellus knows because he was its priest. Theodore is also said to have made three gold chalices and a precious altarcloth for Ravenna's church; Agnellus says that these items still existed in his day, which implies that they had inscriptions naming Theodore as the donor.[74] Thus, Exarch Theodore seems to have been quite an active patron in Ravenna, even though we know of his activity only through a text written 150 years later.

There are also a few surviving inscriptions showing that people were donating objects to existing churches, and/or paying for church restoration.[75] In the late seventh century, a bronze cross was placed at the summit of the Orthodox Baptistery, with an inscription commemorating its patrons Felix and Stephen.[76] A *ciborium* for the church of St. Eleuchadius, now in Sant'Apollinare in Classe, was donated by a priest named Peter during the reign of Archbishop Valerius (c. AD 789–810) and commemorated with an inscription.[77] Agnellus provides a list of objects donated by his ancestor Iohannicis to a church, perhaps taken from a document or from inscriptions on the objects themselves.[78] These faint hints tell us that secular patronage continued in this time, and that inscriptions likewise continued to be thought appropriate to commemorate such donations.

But were these the only inscriptions produced in Ravenna at this time? The lack of inscriptions is often taken as evidence of the "decline of the epigraphic habit" after the fifth century.[79] But while there was certainly a decline in the production of stone-cut inscriptions, it is possible that there was also a shift from carved to painted inscriptions.[80] We can see this in the evidence from Agnellus, who records a total of twenty-nine inscriptions, mainly church dedications or epitaphs. Of these, only one of the epitaphs has survived: the stone-cut epitaph of Archbishop Agnellus, who died in 570, and this is the only one that Agnellus specifically says was cut in stone.[81] However, Agnellus also reports six other epitaphs, fairly evenly spaced throughout the seventh and eighth centuries.[82] One is reported as being destroyed (*deletum*), and he says of another "I could not see it clearly".[83] Given the lack of stone fragments for most of these epitaphs, it seems likely that they were painted on the walls above the tombs. Agnellus, of course, is reporting only epitaphs of bishops, but it is possible that other people also had epitaphs painted on or above their tombs; we might also think of the famous epitaph of Droctulf from around the year 600, reported by Paul the Deacon and in various syllogae, but also now lost. Agnellus records a few other inscriptions commemorating church construction or repair by bishops, none of which survive.[84] Finally, one other Ravennate stone inscription, which survives in Sant'Apollinare in Classe, also commemorates not a secular person but a bishop. This is literally an inscribed document recording a donation of property to the church by Archbishop John V in the year 731. We do not know why this one Ravennate donation was memorialized in stone, although, as we have seen, similar examples are known from Rome and other places in Italy.[85] Certainly the practice turned a private transaction into a public memorial.

Although surviving only on papyrus rather than in stone, there are a few documents that note donations to churches at Ravenna from 600 into the eighth century. Donors include Martinus *vir honestus* and his wife Aurilia (c. 600), the freedwoman Sisivera (c. 600), the subdeacon Deusdedit (625), the soldier Paulacis (639), Stephanus *magnificus illustrius grecus* (seventh century), John the *primicerius* of the *numerus Ravennas* and his wife Stefania (c. 700), and Gaudiosus *defensor* of the church of Ravenna (eighth century).[86] As noted earlier, three of these (Martinus, Sisivera, and Desudedit) say that the donation is "pro oblatione et remedio anime meae" or some variant thereof.[87] They are thus similar to the others being produced elsewhere in Italy and Europe at the same time.[88]

If we only had Ravenna's documents, we might assume that the primary form of commemoration desired by pious secular donors in the seventh and eighth centuries was liturgical, or even simply the merit that would be accrued in heaven. However, the surviving objects, inscriptions, and narrative records from Ravenna show us that people did expect their donations to be publicly visible, that in fact they were publicly visible, and that an author like Agnellus generated his picture of the past in part by noting which people had contributed to the beautification of the churches of his city. It seems that the expectation of an "audience of architecture" still existed in these later centuries, even if the media in which the generosity was displayed was less permanent, and the language in which appreciation was expressed had shifted from a late Roman visual vocabulary to an early medieval spiritual one.

Notes

1 Y. Duval and L. Pietri, "Évergétisme et épigraphie dans l'Occident chrétien (IVe-VIe s.)", in *Actes du Xe Congrès international d'épigraphie grecque et latine (Nîmes, 1992)* (Paris, 1997), 371–396.

2 Bowes, *Private Worship*, 65–71.

3 M. McLaughlin, *Consorting with Saints: Prayer for the Dead In Early Medieval France* (Ithaca, 1994), esp. 90–101, notes that *libri memoriales* (books listing people to be commemorated during the liturgy) began to be produced in the mid-eighth century, and that the process of commemorating important members of an ecclesiastical community only became common in the ninth century. Many other studies focus on funerals and prayers for the dead who were buried in a church: A. Angenendt, "Missa specialis. Zugleich ein Beitrag zur Entstehung der Privatmessen", *Frühmittelalterliche Studien*, 17 (1983),153–221; P. Geary, "Exchange and Interaction between the Living and the Dead in Early Medieval Society", in *idem*, *Living with the Dead in the Middle Ages* (Ithaca, NY, 1994), 77–92; F. Paxton, *Christianizing Death: The Creation of a Ritual Process in Early Medieval Europe* (Ithaca, NY, 1996); and the articles in F. Bougard, C. La Rocca and R. Le Jan (eds.), *Sauver son âme et se perpétuer: transmission du patrimoine et mémoire au haut Moyen Âge* (Rome, 2005).

4 Indeed, for most churches we have no texts at all; there are far more churches known from archaeology or surviving remains, especially in the countryside, than we know about their donors. For the fourth and fifth centuries, see K. Bowes, *Private Worship, Public Values, and Religious Change in Late Antiquity* (Cambridge, 2008), esp. 129–188. As Bowes points out, both in cities and in the countryside, we know that churches and chapels were built in private houses, and we must assume that these were being paid for by private individuals also, although, except in the case of famous authors such as Paulinus of Nola, we don't have direct evidence of this. For the sixth to ninth centuries, see S. Wood, *The Proprietary Church in the Medieval West* (Oxford, 2006), 66–91.

5 From B. Ward-Perkins, *From Classical Antiquity to the Middle Ages: Urban Public Building in Northern and Central Italy, A. D. 300–850* (Oxford, 1984), to J. Sanchez-Pardo and M. Shapland (eds.), *Churches and Social Power in Early Medieval Europe: Integrating Archaeological and Historical Approaches* (Turnhout, 2015).

6 I.N. Wood, "The Audience of Architecture in Post-Roman Gaul", in L.A.S. Butler (ed.), *The Anglo-Saxon Church: Papers on History, Architecture and Archaeology in Honour of Dr. H. M. Taylor* (London 1986), 74–79; Wood, *The Proprietary Church.*

7 Duval and Pietri, "Évergétisme et épigraphie".

8 This chapter was inspired by Tom Brown's work on secular individuals in early medieval Italy, particularly in his book *Gentlemen and Officers. Imperial Administration and Aristocratic Power in Byzantine Italy A. D. 554–800* (Hertford, 1984).

9 See, e.g., S. Ghosh, *Writing the Barbarian Past: Studies in Early Medieval Historical Narrative* (Leiden, 2016), esp. 36–38.

10 J.-P. Caillet, *L'évergétisme monumental chrétien en Italie et à ses marges, d'après l'épigraphie des pavements de mosaïque (IVe-VIIe s.)* (Rome, 1993); *idem*, "Affirmation de l'autorité de l'évêque dans les sanctuaires paléochrétiens du Haut Adriatique: De l'inscription à l'image", *Deltion tes Christianikes Archaiologikes Hetaireias, s. 4*, 24 (2003), 21–30, at 21–24; E. Kleinbauer, "Orants as Donors", in O. Feld (ed.), *Studien zur spätantiken und byzantinischen Kunst Friedrich Wilhelm Deichmann gewidmet*, 3 vols (Bonn, 1986), III, 89–94; and A.M. Yasin, *Saints and Church Spaces in the Late Antique Mediterranean: Architecture, Cult,*

and Community (Cambridge, 2009). Other possible depictions of donors are in a small shrine discovered under the church of Ss. Giovanni and Paolo in Rome, dating from the end of the fourth century, has frescoes that may depict donors (Bowes, *Private Worship,* 88–90).

11 Caillet, *L'évergétisme monumental.* There are other mosaic inscriptions from the fifth or sixth century in the current crypt of San Francesco at Ravenna: "[Is]te locus s(an)c(t)i complectitur [ossa Neonis] / [h]uius cana fides altum per saicula [caleum? nomen?] / possidet (et) totos gaudet secura p[er annos]".

12 E.F. Le Brant, *Inscriptions chrétiennes de la Gaule antérieures au VIIIe siècle*, vol. 2 (Paris, 1865), 617: "Marcellus, Galliarum praefectus, Dei cultor, prece exegit episcopum hoc onus sucipere, impendia necessarie repromittens quae per biennium administrationis suae praebuit artificibus mercedem solidorum DC, ad operas et caetera solidorum ID".

13 Wood, "Audience of Architecture", 77; H.I. Marrou, "Le dossier épigraphique de l'évêque Rusticus de Narbonne", *Rivista di Archeologia Cristiana*, 46 (1970), 331–349; and O. Ginouvez, "Le site de Saint-Félix à Narbonne: une église d'origine paléochrétienne et son environnement funéraire (Ve-XVIe siècle)", *Archéologie du Midi médiéval*, 17 (1999), 25–46. Marrou, who publishes the inscriptions, notes that *comitissa* is not a term known until the eighth century, and suggests that perhaps part of this list of donors was added later. Yet another Narbonne inscription, from 450, tells that the priest Othia built and dedicated a church to Sts. Vincent, Agnes, and Eulalia (Marrou, "Le dossier", 346: "+Othia pr(es)b(yter) anno xxxiii / pr(es)b(ytera)t(us) sui baselic(am) ex voto / suo in hon (ore) s(an)ct(orum) mart(yrum) Vincenti / Agnetis et Eulaliae con(s)tr(uxit) et d (e)d(i)c(avit) / Va[le]ntiniano VII et A<vien>o cons(ulibus)"..) An inscription from Numidia names several communities that contributed to a church in the area (Bowes, *Private Worship*, 66; H. Graillot and S. Gsell, *Ruines Romaines au nord de l'aurès* [P. Cuggiani, 1894], 92–93: "Venusianenses initiaverunt, [M?] ucrionenses columnas V dederunt, Cuzabetenses dederunt columnas VI, omnes apsida straverunt, plus Cuzabete(n)ses ornaverunt, rogatus presbiter et Emilius Sacon edificaverunt".)

14 E.F. Le Blant, *Inscriptions chrétiennes*, vol. 2, #405: "Ex voto Flavius Lacanius vir consularis cum suis fecit de proprio basilicam secretaria atque porticum", probably dates to the mid-sixth century (A.H.M. Jones et al., *The Prosopography of the Later Roman Empire*, vol. 2 [Cambridge, 1971], 652). The inscription from Lyon, of unknown date, says, "Templi factores fuerant Fredaldus et uxor Marturis" (Le Blant, *Inscriptions chrétiennes*, vol. 1, #42).

15 Inscriptions preserved in the Greek Anthology attest to the same trends in Constantinople in the fourth and fifth centuries: praetorian prefects, consuls, and the like, and their wives, are identified in later texts as the sponsors of many churches. Bowes, *Private Worship*, 106–123, who lists the following inscriptions from the Greek Anthology: 4–7, 10, 12, 14–17.

16 Agnellus of Ravenna, *Liber pontificalis ecclesiae Ravennatis* (=*LPR*), ed. D.M. Deliyannis (Turnhout, 2006), ch. 28. The first line of this poem is a direct copy of one that had been placed in San Pietro in Vincoli by Pope Sixtus III (432–440), see G.B. de Rossi, *Inscriptiones Christianae urbis Romae septimo saeculo antiquiores*, vol. 2.1 (Rome, 1888), 110.

17 de Rossi, *Inscriptiones Christianae*, 111; about this inscription, see E. Thunø, "Looking at Letters: "Living Writing" in S. Sabina in Rome", *Marburger Jahrbuch für Kunstwissenschaft*, 34 (2007), 19–41. Julia Hillner has examined the evidence in Rome for lay patronage, and counts twelve examples in the fourth and fifth centuries, ten of which we know from inscriptions; eight of these represented decoration of an existing church: J. Hillner, "Families, Patronage, and

the Titular Churches of Rome, c. 300-c. 600", in K. Cooper and J. Hillner (eds.), *Religion, Dynasty and Patronage in Early Christian Rome* (Cambridge, 2007), 225–261, at 225 n. 3 and 241. They date to 366–384, 400 / 2, 5th c., 428 / 30, 440 / 61, mid-5th c., before 440, 459 / 70, 461 / 8, 468 / 83, 401 / 17, 440 / 61.

18 For Gaul, see esp. Wood, "The Audience of Architecture". On the question of whether these were actually ever set up in buildings, see M.J. Roberts, *The Humblest Sparrow: the Poetry of Venantius Fortunatus* (Ann Arbor, MI, 2009), 61, and R. Favreau, "Fortunat et l'épigraphie", in *Venanzio Fortunato tra Italia e Francia* (Treviso, 1993), 161–173. We also know, from these same authors' collected letters, that church dedications were viewed as important ceremonies that could link far-flung individuals; see Wood, "The Audience of Architecture". For example, the introduction to the canons of the Council of *Arausicanum* in 529 states that the bishops had come to the town on the occasion of the dedication of the basilica which the *illustrissimus praefectus et patricius* Liberius had built: "Cum ad dedicationem basilicae, quam inlustrissimus praefectus et patricius filium noster Liberius in Arausica civitate fidilissima devotione construxit, Deo propitiante et ipso invitante convenissimus et de rebus, quae ad ecclesiasticam regulam pertinent, inter nos spiritalis fuissit oborta conlatio" (*MGH Concilia Aevi Merovingici*, 46).

19 Cf. A. Jones, *Social Mobility in Late Antique Gaul: Strategies and Opportunities for the Non-Elite* (Cambridge, 2009), esp. 31–32.

20 Some are founded by bishops—Patiens at Lyons and Perpetuus at Tours, see Sidonius Apollinaris, *Ep.* 2.10 and 4.18 (*MGH AA* 8, 33–35 and 68–70).

21 Sidonius Apollinaris *Ep.* 4.15 to Elaphius (MGH AA 8, 66–67), and Ep. 7.9.21 to Perpetuus (MGH AA 8, 116): "Hic vobis ecclesiam iuvenis miles, tenuis solus, adhuc filius familias et iam pater exstruxit". Both poems refer to the construction as the fulfillment of a vow, and this seems to be a common theme in fifth-century accounts of secular church-building; we might also think of Galla Placidia's church of San Giovannia Evangelista in Ravenna, as described by Agnellus (Agnellus, *LPR*, ch. 42).

22 See Roberts, *The Humblest Sparrow*, 61–71. Around 500, Avitus of Vienne refers to a church built by the *dux* Arigius (*Ep.* 50, *MGH AA* 6.2: 78), and to a monastic church built by King Sigismund of Burgundy (*Hom.* 25, *MGH AA* 6.2, 145–146). Ennodius of Pavia describes a baptistery built by his friend and cousin Armenius: Ennodius, #128 (*Carm.* 2.20, *MGH AA* 7, 134–135): "Conditor Armenius, supero qui dignus honore est, / Hic peperit fontem vivificantis aquae". Venantius Fortunatus was writing poems to commemorate secular as well as episcopal friends, and their construction activity: a basilica in honour of St. Martin rebuilt by Basilius *vir illustris* and his wife Baudegunde, and a basilica built by Duke Launebod of Toulouse and his wife Berethrude, see Fortunatus *Carm.* I.7 and II.8 (*MGH AA* 4.1, 11 and 36–37). There are also several poems in honour of Bishop Leontius of Bordeaux and his wife Placidina, but I have not counted them among the secular donors. Of all Fortunatus' poems that mention the construction of a church, there are twenty-eight for bishops, four for royal donors and two for non-royal secular donors.

23 Agnellus, *LPR* ch. 57: "Incohatio uero aedificationis ecclesiae parata est ab Iuliano".

24 Agnellus, *LPR* ch. 59: "Sed, sicut superius dixi, in tempore istius ecclesia beati Vitalis martiris a Iuliano argentario constructa est. [...] Expensas uero in praedicti martiris Vitalis ecclesia, sicut in elogio sanctae recordationis memoriae Iuliani fundatoris inuenimus,.xxvi. milia aureorum expensi sunt solidorum". Julian also donated to the church a marble reliquary, which still survives, with the inscription: "Julianus Argent(arius) servus vest(er) praecib(us) vest(ris) basi

(licam) a funda(mentis) perfec(it)". (*CIL* XI. 289; F.W. Deichmann, *Ravenna, Hauptstadt des spätantiken Abendlandes*, vol. 2, 2 [Wiesbaden, 1976], 4).

25 Agnellus, *LPR* ch. 63.

26 Agnellus, *LPR* ch. 77.

27 Agnellus, *LPR* chs. 57, 61, and 77.

28 I have suggested elsewhere that this church was a thank-offering for surviving the plague; see D.M. Deliyannis, *Ravenna in Late Antiquity* (Cambridge, 2010), 250–254.

29 See S.J.B. Barnish, "The Wealth of Iulianus Argentarius: late antique banking and the Mediterranean Economy", *Bzyantion*, 55 (1985), 5–38.

30 Agnellus, *LPR* ch. 98: "Additus his meritis felix Smaragdus in aeuum, / Cuius in his titulis participantur opes".

31 *CIL* XI.11; see L. Prati, ed. *Flumen aquaeductus: nuove scoperte archeologiche dagli scavi per l'acquedotto della Romagna* (Bologna, 1988), 29.

32 See D.M. Deliyannis, "Church-Building in Rhetoric and Reality in the 5th–7th Centuries", in C. Radtki, M. Danner and D. Boschung (eds.), *Politische Fragmentierung und kulturelle Kohärenz in der Spätantike* (Paderborn, 2015), 159–182; D. Janes, *God and Gold in Late Antiquity* (Cambridge, 1998); Roberts, *The Humblest Sparrow*; and *idem*, *The Jeweled Style: Poetry and Poetics in Late Antiquity* (Ithaca, 2010).

33 Wood, *The Proprietary Church*, 27.

34 A council held at Orange in 441 explicitly stated that churches had to be dedicated by the bishop in whose territory they lay; the Councils of Orleans (511) and Lérida (546) also have laws about who dedicates private churches and chooses priests for them. See Wood, *The Proprietary Church*, 15–16.

35 L. Pietri, "Évergétisme chrétien et fondations privées dans l'Italie de l'Antiquité tardive", in J.-M. Carrié and R. Lizzi Testa (eds.), *"Humana sapit". Études d'antiquité tardive offertes à Lellia Cracco Ruggini* (Turnhout, 2002), 253–263, provides a list of sixty-eight private foundations in Italy from the fourth to the sixth century, based mainly on papal letters. See also Wood, *The Proprietary Church*, 16 and Bowes, *Private Worship*, 223 and 291 n. 25.

36 Gregory of Tours, *Libri historiarum X*, II.17, II.20, and VI.20 (*MGH SS rer. Mer.* 1.1, 64–67 and 288–289).

37 See Hillner, "Families, Patronage". And it's not just Rome: Severinus of Noricum was buried in 488 in a church donated by the *clarissima* Barbaria, from Naples; Bowes, *Private Worship*, 217; Eugippius, *Vita Severini*, chs. 46 (*MGH AA* 1.2, 30).

38 Gregory of Tours, *Gloria martyrum*, 64 (*MGH SS rer. Mer.* 1,2, 81–82): Alcmina and Placidina.

39 *Le Liber pontificalis: texte, introduction et commentaire* (=*LP*), 2nd ed., ed. L. Duchesne, 3 vols (Paris, 1955–1957), I.46; trans. R. Davis, *The Book of Pontiffs ("Liber pontificalis")* (Liverpool, 2000), 105: "Hic beati Martini ecclesiam iuxta sanctum Silvestrem Palatini inlustris viri pecuniis fabricans et exornans, eo ipso instante dedicavit".

40 *Liber pontificalis*, ed. H. Geertman, "Le biografie del *Liber pontificalis* dal 311 al 535. Testo e commentario", in *idem* (ed.), *Hic fecit basilicam: studi sul Liber Pontificalis e gli edifici ecclesiastici di Roma da Silvestro a Silverio* (Leuven, 2004), 169–236, at 225: "basilicam sanctorum Silvestri et Martini a fundamento construxit iuxta Traianas, ubi et super altare tyburium argenteum fecit…" As I have noted (D.M. Deliyannis, "Ecclesius of Ravenna as Donor in Text and Image", in E. Gatti and S. Danielson (eds.), *Envisioning the Medieval Bishop* [Turnhout, 2014], 41–62), we see this also in the contemporary rise of the portrait of a bishop-donor in mosaics in Rome, Ravenna, and later Porec.

41 D.M. Deliyannis, "A Biblical Model for Serial Biography: the Roman *Liber Pontificalis* and the Books of Kings", *Révue Bénédictine*, 107 (1997), 15–23 and *idem*, "Church-Building in Rhetoric and Reality", 169–170.
42 See G. Kalas, "Architecture and Élite Identity in Late Antique Rome: Appropriating the Past at Sant'Andrea Catabarbara", *Papers of the British School at Rome*, 81 (2013), 279–302.
43 In the *Charta Cornutiana*, he lists himself as "Flavius Valila qui et Theodorius vir clarissimus et inlustris et comes et magister utriusque militiae" (*LP*, ed. Duchesne, I.cxlvi). This document is known from a twelfth-century copy, but is presumed to be original.
44 "ut obsequium nostrum possit propitiationem divinitatis mereri".
45 ILCV, 1785:Haec tibi mens Valilae devovit praedia ChristeCui testator opes detulit ipse suas.Simplicius qu(a)e papa sacris caelestibus aptansEfficit vere muneris esse tui.Et quod apostolici deesent limina nobisMartiris Andreae nomine composuit.Utitur haec heres titulis ecclesia iustisSuccedensq(ue) domo mystica iura locat.Plebs devota veni, perq(ue) haec commercia disceTerreno censu regna superna peti.Translation by Kalas, "Architecture and Élite Identity", 293.
46 There are other cases where both inscription and *Liber pontificalis* survive and do complement each other; for example, the virgin Demetrias is commemorated in an inscription (ILCV, 1765) from the church of St. Stephen on the Via Latina, as having given the church to Pope Leo, around 450; and in the *LP Vita Leonis*, this donation is also reported. See A. Kurdock, "*Demetrias ancilla dei*: Anicia Demetrias and the Problem of the Missing Patron", in Hillner and Cooper (eds.), *Religion, Dynasty and Patronage*, 190–224, at 223.
47 Paul the Deacon, *Historia Langobardorum* 6.1 (*MGH SS rer. Lang. et Ital.*, 164).
48 *Vita s. Desiderii ep. Cadurcensis*, 16–17 (*MGH SS rer. Mer.* 4, 574–576), even to the extent of listing estates bequeathed to the church of Cahors in Desiderius' will, ch. 34 (591). We see the same type of description in the late seventh-century *Vita Eligii ep. Noviomagensis* (Noyon) I.32, II.6–7, etc. (*MGH SS rer. Mer.* 4, 688–689 and 697–700).
49 *Vita Leudegarii episcopi et martyris*, ch. 2 (*MGH SS rer. Mer.* 5, 284–285).
50 *Passio Praejecti episcopi et martyris Arverni*, ch. 15 (*MGH SS rer. Mer.* 5, 234–235).
51 Desiderius of Cahors, *Ep.* I.11 (*MGH Epistolae* I, 199–200).
52 Desiderius of Cahors, *Ep.* II.13 (*MGH Epistolae* I, 210) says that King Dagobert had given a sum of 500 solidi from a villa to support the lights in a church at Metz.
53 Maya Maskarinec, *City of Saints: Rebuilding Rome in the Early Middle Ages* (Philadelphia, 2018), 94–95 and 181–182.
54 Hans Belting, "Eine Privatkapelle im frühmittelalterlichen Rom", *Dumbarton Oaks Papers* 41 (1987): 55–69; Natalia Tereiatnikov, "For whom is Theodotus praying? An interpretation of the program of the private chapel in S. Maria Antiqua", *Cahiers archéologiques. Fin de l'antiquité et Moyen Âge* 41 (1993), 37–46; Arno Rettner, "Dreimal Theodotus? Stifterbild und Grabstiftung in der Theodotus-Kapelle von Santa Maria Antiqua in Rom", in H.-R. Meier, C. Jäggi and P. Büttner (eds.), *Für irdischen Ruhm und himmlischen Lohn. Stifter und Auftraggeber in der mittelalterlichen Kunst* (Berlin, 1995), 31–46; and S. J. Lucey, "Art and Socio-Cultural Identity in Early Medieval Rome: The Patrons of Santa Maria Antiqua", in E. Ó Carragáin and C. L. Neuman de Vegvar (eds.), *Roma Felix: Formation and Reflections of Medieval Rome* (Aldershot, 2007), 139–158.
55 Maskarinec, *City of Saints*, 21–23, 94–95, and 228 n. 91. There are several of these, dating back to the seventh century, and most of them recounting donations by popes or clerics; see D. de Francesco, "Partizioni fondiarie e proprietà

ecclesiastiche nel territorio Romano tra VI e VIII secolo. Prospettive di ricerca alla luce dei dati epigrafici", *Mélanges de l'École française de Rome, Moyen Âge* 110 (1998), 29–77.

56 A reliquary from St. Maurice d'Agaune that mentions the priest Teuderic, Nordoalaus, and Rihlindis who oversaw its construction, and the artists Undiho and Ello, and on a late eighth-century reliquary for Agricola and Vitalis, an indication that Bishop Haddebert of Clermont made it with financial help from King Charles, Count Itier, and "other Christians who gave gold and gems for their souls". Cited in R. Favreau, "Commanditaire, auteur, artiste dans les inscriptions médiévales", in M. Zimmermann (ed.), *Auctor et Auctoritas. Invention et conformisme dans l'écriture médiévale. Actes du colloque tenu à l'Université de Versailles-Saint-Quentin-en-Yvelines (14–16 juin 1999)* (Paris, 2001), 37–59, at 37. Agaune inscription in *Corpus inscriptionum Medii Aevi Helvetiae*, ed. C. Jörg (Fribourg, 1977), vol. 1 no. 8, 89–91; Agricola / Vitalis inscription in *Corpus des inscriptions de la France médiévale*, vol. 18, eds. R. Favreau, J. Michaud, and B. Mora (Paris, 1995), 160–162.

57 *Vita s. Desiderii ep. Cadurcensis*, 54 (*MGH SS rer. Mer.* 4, 600–601).

58 Favreau, "Commanditaire", 48.

59 In addition to Wood, *The Proprietary Church*, see esp. P. Jobert, *La notion de donation: convergences, 630–750* (Paris, 1977) and E. Magnani, "Don aux églises et don d'églises dans le sud-est de la Gaule", in Bougard, La Rocca and Le Jan (eds.), *Sauver son âme*, 379–400.

60 Jobert, *La notion de donation*, 205–225. The relevant documents are papyri published in *Die nichtliterarischen lateinischen papyri Italiens aus der zeit 445–700*, ed. J.O. Tjader, 3 vols. (Lund, 1954–1982), nos. 16 (c. 600), 20 (c. 600), and 21 (625); the phrase used is *pro oblatione et remedio animae meae*.

61 J.M. Pardessus, ed., *Diplomata chartae, epistolae, leges aliaque instrumenta ad res Gallo- Francicas spectantia: Instrumenta ab anno 628 ad annum 751*, Volume 2 (Paris, 1849), no. 452, 255–258. See J. Barbier, "Testaments et pratique testamentaire dans le royaume franc (VIe-VIIIe siècle)", in Bougard, La Rocca and Le Jan (eds.), *Sauver son âme*, 7–79, at 47.

62 *Date eleemosinam, et ecce omnia munda sunt vobis*. See *Marculfi formularum* II.1–4 (*MGH Leges* 5, *Formulae Mer. et Kar. Aevi*, 70–77).

63 Cf. Magnani, "Don aux églises", 386–387.

64 *Marculfi formularum* II.1 (*MGH Leges*, *Formulae Mer. et Kar. Aevi*, 72): "in luminaribus ipsius oratorii vel alimonia ac substantiale victu, vestitu quoque, substantacione ipsorum pauperum…", trans. A. Rio, *The Formularies of Angers and Marcult: Two Merovingian Legal Handbooks* (Liverpool, 2008), 180.

65 *pro timore Dei et amore pauperum Christi*, e.g., *Marculfi formularum* II.4 (76), II.6 (78), II.17 (87).

66 Testament of Abbo 49 and 51: *pro animae nostrae remedio* (ed. / trans. in P.J. Geary, *Aristocracy In Provence: the Rhône Basin At the Dawn of the Carolingian Age.* [Philadelphia, 1985], 68–71); noted by Magnani, "Don aux églises".

67 No. 483, ed. Pardessus, *Diplomata chartae*, 291: "Dum quisque in praesenti saeculo conversari videtur, cogitare debet quatenus animae suae consolationem pro eleemosyna sanctorum locorum vel orationum subsidia hic adquirere possit dicente Domino: Date eleemosinam, et ecce omnia munda sunt vobis (*Luke* 11:41). Et iterum: Sicut aqua extinguit ignem, ita eleemosyna extinguit peccatum (cf. *Eccles.* 3:30). Quapropter ego Ansbertus, filius Willibaldi quondam, dono pro remedio animae meae, at pro retributione aeternae salutis".

68 *Formulae Salicae Merkelianae* (MGH *Leges, Formulae Mer. et Kar. Aevi*, 241).

69 *Codice diplomatico Longobardo*, ed. L. Schiaparelli, vol. 1–2 (Rome, 1929–1933), #31 (AD 723, *vendite que posseditis et date aelimosinis et avevitis tensaurum in*

celo), #34 (AD 724, *redemptione anime nostrae*), #35 (AD 724 *pro anima sua*), #7 (AD 685, *pro anima*), #14 (AD 710, *pro mea peccata*), #16 (AD 713–714, *pro mercidem et remedium anime mee*), #18 (AD 714, *pro anime nostre salute* and *pro remedio animarum parentum nostrorum et nostrarum*).

70 See a charter of donation by Aethelbert II of Kent, dating to 732, given *pro remedio tantum animae meae* (Sawyer 23); for other Anglo-Saxon charters using these phrases, see H.F. Forbes, *Heaven and Earth in Anglo-Saxon England: Theology and Society in an Age of Faith* (Farnham, 2013), 225–257.

71 Angenendt, "Missa specialis" and Paxton, *Christianizing Death*, 66–69.

72 P.J. Geary, *Phantoms of Remembrance: Memory and Oblivion At the End of the First Millennium* (Princeton, 1994).

73 A. Augenti, "Ravenna e Classe: archeologia di due città tra la tarda Antichità e l'alto Medioevo", in *idem* (ed.), *Le città italiane tra la tarda Antichità e l'alto Medioevo, Atti del Convegno (Ravenna, febbraio 2004)* (Florence, 2006), 185–217, at 191–193. The first reference to this church is by Agnellus, and archaeologically its remains dated to the eighth or ninth century. It has been proposed that it was built by Aistulf as a new palace-church, in the moment when he was planning to establish his court in Ravenna; and indeed there is no apparent reason that any later individual would build a church here. P. Porta, "Il centro del potere, il problema del palazzo dell'esarco", in A. Carile (ed.), *Storia di Ravenna* II.1 (Venice, 1991), 269–283, at 278–280, discusses previous interpretations of this building as a secular structure attached to the palace.

74 All of this is described in *LPR* ch. 119. Deichmann, *Ravenna, Hauptstadt*, 2.2, 349, notes that St. Paul stood until the thirteenth century; see *ibid.*, 374, for St. Theodore.

75 It should also be noted that poetic epitaphs were composed for the Lombard general Droctulf c. 600, and, according to Agnellus, for Bishops Marinianus (d. 606), Maurus (d. 671), Damianus (d. 708), and Felix (d. 725; his is not a poem) (*LPR* chs. 103, 114, 134, and 150). However, none of these mention patronage, except in a very general way.

76 S. Kostof, *The Orthodox Baptistery of Ravenna* (New Haven, 1965), 19–20 and 142; now found in the southwestern absidiole, the cross has incised on it the following inscription: "De donis Dei et S(an)c(t)e Marie Felex et Stefanus optulerunt temporibus D(om)n(o) Theodoro Apostolicum", usually assumed as referring to Archbishop Theodore, r. 677–91.

77 *Scriptorum veterum nova collectio e Vaticanis codicibus edita ab Angelo Maio,* vol. 5.5 (Vatican, 1831), 134: "Ad honorem d(omi)ni n(ostri) I(e)h(su) Xri(sti) et s(an) c(t)i Eleuchadii sub temp(ore) dom(ini) Valeri archiep(iscopi) ego Petru / s presb (iter) fecit".

78 *LPR* ch. 148.

79 About this, see D.E. Trout "Inscribing identity: the Latin epigraphic habit in late antiquity", in P. Rousseau (ed.), *A Companion to Late Antiquity* (Chichester / Malden, MA 2009), 170–186.

80 See, e.g., M. Kulikowski, *Late Roman Spain and Its Cities* (Baltimore, 2004), 34.

81 *LPR* ch. 92 (*Et litteris marmore exaratis epitaphium super corpus eius sic inuenies*); *CIL* XI. 305.

82 *LPR* chs. 103 (*Et est ibi epithaphium exaratum ita*), 114 (*Epitaphium uero desuper inuenies scriptum continentem ita*), 134 (*Epitaphium inuenies super sepulchrum eius continentem ita*), 150 (*Epitaphiumque ipsius inuenies abens continentes ita*), 153 (*Epitaphium inuenies super eum continentem ita*), and 163 (*Epitaphium super sepulchrum eius inuenietis exaratum*). The latter two are missing from the surviving *LPR* manuscripts, but from the way that Agnellus introduces them it seems clear that he had originally copied them into the text.

83 *LPR* ch. 116 (*Epitaphium ipsius deletum est*), 124 (*Epitaphium uero eius clare legere non potui*—although that is the epitaph of the wicked archbishop Theodore, so perhaps he simply didn't want to report it).
84 *LPR* ch. 115 (mosaic) and ch. 149 (a poem, *super ipsius regias invenies scriptum*).
85 As noted in *PL* 127, 95. See A. Mai *Scriptorum veterum nova collectio e vaticani codicibus*, vol. 5 (Rome, 1831), ch. 3, 209–236, and, for the Roman examples, see de Francesco, "Partizioni fondiarie".
86 Ed. Tjäder, respectively nos. 25, 20, 21, 22, 44, 18–19, 23, and 24; see Brown, *Gentlemen and Officers*, especially the prosopographical list at the end.
87 Ed. Tjäder, nos. 61, 20, and 21.
88 See Brown, *Gentlemen and Officers*, 192 and 183.

8 The exarchate, the empire, and the élites: some comparative remarks

Tom Brown's pioneering analysis of the evolution of the late Roman and early Byzantine elite in the Ravenna exarchate in *Gentlemen and Officers* set a high standard for research into the ways in which late Roman administrative and military arrangements interfaced with social and economic structures. It also suggested the possibility of significant parallels with the remaining lands of the empire in Sicily, the south Balkans and Anatolia.

Given a common legal, institutional and administrative framework across the empire as a starting point on the one hand, and bearing in mind the different regional characteristics concerned, I want to use the example of social development in the exarchate as a basis for comparing what happened during the course of the seventh century in Constantinople and Anatolia. The major problem with this approach is, clearly, the sources: we simply do not have for the eastern territories of the empire, apart from Egypt, the sort of detailed documentary data—in particular the papyri—that Tom was able to exploit for the exarchate. Instead, we have to rely on the somewhat problematic chronicle and historiographical writing, on indirect and oblique data in the letters of churchmen, on the chance survival of material relating to the way the imperial court and imperial justice worked—such as the accounts of the trial of pope Martin or Maximus the Confessor—and above all on the lead seals of officials, soldiers and administrators.

The key question is, therefore, can we track individual members of the élite in the east, and can we build up the sort of picture we have for Italy, and to some extent now for North Africa, for other regions, most especially for Anatolia?[1] In particular, what happens to these people in the period of major social and political change that begins in the period of the Arab Islamic raids and attacks from the 640s onwards? And is there a difference between the metropolitan area and the more distant provinces? Many members of the establishment appear to have survived the changes of the later seventh century because their property had been based largely in the metropolitan area, in and around the capital, or because such properties in the provinces had been preserved:[2] metropolitan members of the senate, a body which seems during the seventh century in particular to have taken an increasingly active role in government affairs and policy-making decisions, for example.[3] Yet paradoxically, across the second half of the seventh and into the eighth century the status of all but the highest grades (*hypatos*, *anthypatos*, *apo hypatōn*) associated with the senate was reduced—an indication of the declining importance of the order as such, and hence of the social élite that it had represented.[4] Metropolitan families did not entirely escape enemy depredations or internecine strife, but they were relatively unscathed compared with the loss of lands and property of those who hailed from the conquered provinces or those regions regularly subject to hostile military activity.[5] While there is no evidence relating to the fortunes of named individuals in this respect, we can profitably compare their fate with that of members of the Roman élite in the fifth-century west, such as Paulinus of Pella, for example, whose property in southern Gaul was destroyed by Visigothic federates in factional conflict with the Roman authorities and who was reduced to poverty thereafter.[6]

For the imperial capital there is some evidence for élite continuity. John Pitzigaudes was sent in 676/7 by Constantine IV to negotiate with the caliph Muʻawiya, and is described as "the *patrikios* John, surnamed Pitzigaudes, a man of ancient lineage in the state". What exactly "ancient lineage" means remains unclear, although it may suggest an old and established family, with roots perhaps going back into the sixth century. The term recurs for the early eighth century when the emperor Philippicus Bardanes is reported to have dined with "citizens of ancient lineage", suggesting some awareness of ancient (aristocratic) family traditions in Constantinople.[7] Theophanes notes the oppressive fiscal demands made during the reign of Justinian II upon highly placed persons, and of confiscations of land and property, and we occasionally glimpse individual members of the older élite in the sources.[8] Nikephoros, the father of the usurper Philippicus Bardanes, was a *patrikios*, and may possibly be identified with the *patrikios* and general of the same name who commanded an army under Constans II in 667;[9] the *patrikios* Justinian, father of the patriarch Germanus, was involved in the rebellion of Mizizius in Sicily in 668, and appears to have been a member of the established senatorial élite and very possibly related to the family of the emperor Justinian I;[10] and the *patrikios* and prefect of the city Troilus in the 650s–60s appears to have been a member of this same established élite group.[11]

The church was undoubtedly a safe haven for the older élite, especially in the metropolitan region, although it is impossible to follow the appearance of "new men" on account of the adoption of an appropriate Christian name by most of those who had progressed to senior ecclesiastical rank—bishop or beyond. Of the 135 signatories from the patriarchate of Constantinople at the final session of the council of 680, for example, or the 183 signatories at that of 691/2, only one appears to be "foreign"—the (probably) Frankish Segermas, bishop of Horkistos in Galatia II, at the council of 691/2.[12] The contraction and retrenchment of provincial municipal culture together with the concentration of resources (including educational resources) in

Constantinople meant that the church provided one of the most stable environments for the continued influence of the cultural inheritance of the traditional social élite. And as is well-recognised it is precisely in the realms of theological and dogmatic literature and the great variety of genres and sub-types it encompassed, that the emphasis is found after the middle of the seventh century and until well into the eighth.[13] Thus, in the context of the later seventh and early eighth centuries, it appears to have been the educated members of the old establishment who provided the church with the literacy, learning and cultural capital it needed to maintain this tradition, on the one hand, and who on the other provided the central administration and the court with the bureaucratic know-how and literacy to manage the state.[14]

Was this situation replicated in a provincial milieu? Who made up the new élite, and how new was it in fact? By the end of the seventh century I can identify four intersecting "pools" from which the individuals who made up the elite in the provinces were drawn. The most obvious is constituted by those who belonged to the "old" establishment already mentioned, individuals despatched from the centre to take up posts in the provinces, military, civil or ecclesiastical. They overlapped to some extent with a second group, those persons whose origin lay among the provincial élites in the eastern provinces that were lost from the 630s onwards.[15] How many wealthy or influential persons from Syria left for imperial territory cannot be known for want of evidence, but what data there are suggest that quite a few important persons from the Syrian provinces ended up at court or on imperial territory and survived by virtue of service within the imperial system. This was but one aspect of a wider movement. The flight of people from Greater Syria to Anatolia, Constantinople or beyond, to Italy and to Rome, is a recognised feature of the period, and included, for example, a substantial number of monks and nuns.[16] Among the best-known are certain popes and senior clergy of the second half of the seventh century: Theodore of Tarsus (archbishop of Canterbury 668–690),[17] for example, Sergius (687–701), born in Sicily, but whose Syrian father, Tiberios, hailed from Antioch;[18] John V (685–686), also from the region of Antioch;[19] Sisinnius (708);[20] Constantine (708–715);[21] and Gregory III (731–741).[22] Sergius and John V also had connections with the Syrian monastery of St Saba at Rome.[23] In the period 685–8 Antioch in Syria was again in imperial hands as the emperor Constantine IV exploited the situation within the Caliphate. Its subsequent loss probably instigated another wave of refugees.[24]

Others of clearly Syrian background appear in the imperial administration or in the eastern church: the patriarch Anastasius, appointed by Leo III after the abdication of Germanus in 730, was apparently of Syrian origin. He seems to have had no association with Rome, and may represent those who had arrived originally as refugees.[25] In the secular and administrative establishment of the empire other individuals stand out: George, "the Syrian", *patrikios* and general logothete in 711, held high office and in a post that required literacy and a good education, while Isoes, *patrikios* and count of the *Opsikion* in the year 718 bears a Syrian name (Ishō) and was probably the son of refugees of some status and influence.[26] He may be the same person as Isoes, *patrikios* and *kuaistor* (quaestor), represented on a seal of the same period (in light of the relative scarcity of this name in the Byzantine sources). The position of quaestor was one of the most important palatine offices and required a familiarity with the law and a high degree of literacy, so Isoes must have been a man of some education.[27] Both men reached the highest levels of the palatine system and their example suggests the ways in which elements of provincial élites could penetrate to the heart of the imperial system.

Members of the Armenian nobility had been prominent in the eastern Roman world for decades before the events of the seventh century, of course, especially in the military, and such men were frequently accompanied by their own personal armed retinues.[28] Their numbers increased in the course of the second half of the seventh century, an illustration of the tendency for the imperial government to rely on skilled senior men of "provincial" origin. Other non-Romans also played a role—Turkic, Slavic, Iranian and Semitic names begin to appear in greater numbers than hitherto in chronicles, histories and on lead seals.[29] The *patrikios* Sisinnius Rhendaci (u)s, a senior confidant of the emperor Artemius, bore a Slavic name and is representative of these high-ranking newcomers to the establishment,[30] while there were senior military commanders who had been transferred from duties (and homeland) in the western provinces to serve in the east, such as the general Florus—with an obviously western name—who, along with two other commanders, Cyprianus and Petronas, appeared in command of a victorious Roman force in Anatolia in 673. Such senior officers continued to be readily transferred from one front to another across the breadth of the empire as needs required.[31]

A third group that can be distinguished somewhat dimly in the sources consists of persons of higher status in provincial society, landowners with possessions in both town and country in Anatolia as well as elsewhere. Whether or not they had obtained senatorial rank, families of curial status made up the majority of landowners in their urban territories. They represented for the most part a well-established local élite, even if the financial independence of some could be threatened with absorption into the estates of bigger landowners in their locality.[32] Hardly anything is known of the provincial élite outside areas that are relatively well documented, such as Egypt or Italy, and we have even fewer sources to tell us about this group after the sixth century. Only in the case of the clergy, especially the episcopate, do we have some indication of their local importance and role in society.

But it is very probable that many of the important "new" families or individuals of uncertain background who come to dominate the army and civil administration of the empire from the later seventh century came from this context, relatively well-off families rooted in provincial administrative traditions, who had remained invisible in the sources of the preceding centuries.[33] I would suggest that the family of the later eighth-century patriarch Tarasius, born ca. 730–740 in Constantinople, may be an indicative case. Tarasius' paternal grandfather, Sisinnius, had been a *komes* of the *Exkoubita*,[34] his maternal grandfather was a *patrikios* also, and both sides of the family are reported to have come from a line of *patrikioi* largely associated with military positions. His father George became a *kuaistor*, one of the leading judicial officials in Constantinople, and his brother, also named Sisinnius, was a high-ranking military officer. The limited evidence indicates with little doubt that the family was originally from Isauria or the immediately neighbouring provinces, clearly of provincial origin, and clearly associated closely with the military, through which they were probably able to improve their fortunes.[35] In the mid-seventh century Theodore of Koloneia appears as a high-ranking military commander in the 650s, and later an important senior and influential figure at court. His epithet, "of Koloneia", indicates a provincial origin, possibly Armenian, although this is again by no means certain.[36] Daniel of Sinope, *patrikios* and prefect of Constantinople, despatched by the emperor Anastasius II on a diplomatic mission to Damascus in 714, may be of similar background.[37] Similarly representative may have been the future emperor Leo III, whose family was transferred from Syria to Thrace in the 680s. Leo prospered and achieved the rank of *spatharios*, from which position he was then able to advance his career at court and through active military and diplomatic service. The reliability of all the details of his story is questionable, but the outline of the tale certainly reflects a plausible and recognised means of advancing a career and the fortunes of a provincial family that had hitherto no direct association with the court and was of modest means.[38] By the same token, the *Life* of St. Philaretos, a Paphlagonian landowner born at the beginning of the eighth century, whose estates are described in the hagiography as being very extensive, may also be representative of such middling élite provincials. The *Life* itself, written in the 820s, is to a degree inventive and follows classical models. Yet the details of Philaretos' property and flocks may again be taken to reflect a recognisable reality for the times, and again reveals a little about the provincials at whose existence our other sources only hint.[39]

In the years after the early 640s, as more military units were established across the provinces of Anatolia than had hitherto been the case, many members of provincial élites would have found it convenient and profitable to associate themselves with the military, especially in regions most affected by warfare and the presence of soldiers. No doubt there were also regions where the process was much less developed. The process may well have been similar to that which evolved in the provinces of the western empire during the fifth century, or in later sixth- and seventh-century Italy. While there were important similarities, however, the similarities or parallels ought not to be pushed too far in light of the differences in time and place between these regions—late Roman Gaul, for example, was largely occupied either under treaty or by conquest by "barbarian" groups, whereas Anatolia, subjected to economic dislocation and warfare though it was, was never occupied.[40] Nevertheless, association with the military was a source of power, influence and access to the government at Constantinople, as well as a means of protecting local interests and promoting those of family, kin and clients.

The imprecision and absence of detail concerning most of the people mentioned in the sources makes it in most cases impossible to be definite about their background and career details, although we can discern the faint outline of a trend. The distinction between the composition of the three groups discussed thus far was certainly very blurred, but it seems that this is the best we can do with the limited evidence at our disposal, and the general picture fits the overall framework. But there is also a good deal of sigillographic evidence for provincial military careers for the period ca. 650–800 that indicates that individuals could rise, through a series of steps, from relatively humble positions such as *komes* to more elevated ranks such as those of *drouggarios* or *tourmarches*. Some of these can be shown to have continued to advance to even higher rank and status; a greater number probably moved only a relatively short distance in status over their lifetimes, although the lack of specificity makes it very difficult in most cases, although not all, to trace continuity across an individual's career. At the very least this body of material illustrates the fact that there was a substantial number of officers and officials in the non-metropolitan regions who almost certainly came from the middling to lower levels of the provincial elite.[41]

One element that may illustrate changes in the composition of the élite of the eastern empire across this period is the changing pattern of personal names of those who held high office or important provincial posts. It suggests that the origins of members of the senate in Constantinople and of the power élite, the people who actually ran the empire at Constantinople, began to change, especially from the middle decades of the seventh century. The state establishment and power élite had never been exclusive and it had always been possible for a social newcomer to be taken in during the later Roman period. In view of the dramatic geopolitical changes in the period ca. 640 on, and the focus on the Anatolian hinterland of Constantinople, it seems likely that it was now chiefly individuals from these territories who came to dominate the imperial establishment at court, and certainly in the provinces. While it is important to treat the material with caution, especially in evaluating the evidence of names and naming patterns, the number of non-Greek names of officials who appear in the sources is very striking from the 660s and after. This pattern suggests to me that there took place a shift in the cultural and social origins of key personnel in the imperial establishment at all levels. While many of these may well have belonged to refugee groups who had resettled within the empire north of the Taurus mountains, it is just as likely that just as many had their origins in the provinces of Anatolia.[42]

Although barely discernible in the sources, a fourth and final group can be made out, consisting of individuals of much humbler social origin, people who achieved higher social status and office through their joining the retinue of an important individual. One or two are mentioned in the narrative sources from time to time, and it may be that some of the hundreds of seals of imperial officials were issued by people such as this.[43] While certainly constrained structurally by the strong socio-economic divisions that existed, vertical mobility was not an unusual feature of eastern Roman society, and its potential was increased in a context where warfare and the military came to dominate.[44]

The nature of the changing élite in the core regions of the empire, dimly discernible though it is, does seem to differ in some respects from those in more distant regions, especially Italy and Africa. There it seems that there existed a relatively clear distinction between the "imperial" élite of high-ranking officers appointed largely from outside their province or region, and the remaining members of the military, predominantly local men commanding local units. While the situation that generated these developments was by no means the same in both regions, there appears in both cases to have been little overlap between these two groups. Individuals who can be identified as belonging to the imperial élite were moved or transferred from region to region and appointed in the course of their careers to posts in several very different commands or geographical situations, unlike those who remained at a local level. In these outer regions we find, therefore, a two-level system: the soldiers, along with the lower and middle-ranking officers or officials were drawn largely from local society, whereas higher-ranking persons belonged to the cosmopolitan, "imperial" class of functionaries. Movement from the level of provincial magnate or official into the senior ranks of the imperial service élite was limited, and even more so in respect of access to the imperial court itself.[45] Whether this really is a contrast between the core regions (Anatolia and the Balkans/Aegean) and the periphery (N. Africa, Italy and Sicily, although Sicily counts in many respects to the core) is, however, difficult to determine for the lack of precise data about more than the handful of examples noted already.

There remains thus a question of the degree to which any of the provincial cases for which we have some evidence—Italy in particular, but Egypt and N. Africa to a lesser extent also—can serve as models or at the least can offer useful parallels to what was going on in Anatolia. Undoubtedly Italy and the exarchate in particular seem to offer the closest parallel, the more so since they remained longest in relatively close touch with the Constantinopolitan establishment. This affected both the senior levels as well as the rank and file (where, for example, methods for maintaining and supplying the soldiers followed remarkably similar patterns for a while).[46] But there were significant divergences, most obviously in respect of the ways in which the elite within the exarchate evolved its own localised loyalties and values, especially when its relationship with Rome and the papacy was at issue. The papacy could offer the same sort of inducements in respect of social status as Constantinople, of course, and while the latter was by far the more influential, it did mean that there was a competitor, one that did not exist in the imperial heartlands in Anatolia, the Aegean or south Balkan region. Whereas the élite of the exarchate had two poles of authority and sources of status to which they could look, therefore, those in the central imperial lands had but one, at Constantinople. The consequences of this are only beginning to be drawn out, but one obvious result is that political loyalties in the exarchate were subject to a set of negotiable factors that did not exist in, for example, Anatolia, a factor that led to an élite in northern Italy that ultimately enjoyed a greater degree of autonomy and evolved a wider range of cultural and political identities.

The territorial reduction of the empire and the effective disappearance of cities as social and economic intermediaries between the provinces and Constantinople in the course of the later seventh century, together with the reconfiguration of important aspects of the state administration—military and fiscal—together played a significant role in the shift in emphasis in élite culture and in the composition of those who ran the east Roman state. From the middle years of the seventh century the imperial focus on the immediate hinterland of the capital, Anatolia, may have encouraged a further regionalisation or localisation of society and administration in the more distant regions. This is not to suggest that the empire ignored Italy or north Africa—indeed, as the political history of the years after 650 will readily demonstrate, strenuous efforts, within the limits of the constrained resources available to the government at Constantinople, were made to maintain imperial authority and control over these regions. But the evolution of new networks of power and patronage between capital and provinces, as well as within the provinces, was inevitable.

The emergence of a differently constituted and differently configured elite, so obvious in Italy in particular from the later sixth century, is discernible in the limited evidence for Anatolia and Constantinople. It was this élite, neither entirely new nor yet by any means unchanged, that formed one key element in the process of transformation that produced the medieval east Roman—the Byzantine—empire.

Notes

1 For N. Africa see J. Conant, *Staying Roman: Conquest and Identity in Africa and the Mediterranean, 439–700,* (Cambridge, 2012). The material presented here has to a great extent been incorporated into J. Haldon, *The empire that would not die: The paradox of eastern Roman survival, 640–74.0* (Cambridge, MA, 2016).

2 Detailed discussion: L. Brubaker and J.F. Haldon, *Byzantium in the iconoclast era, c. 680–850: A history,* (Cambridge, 2011), 584–606.

3 See, for example, for the reign of Constans II, the *sakellarios* Philagrius and the general Valentinus; later the *koubikoularios* Andreas and the general Theodore of Koloneia. See *PmbZ*, (R.-J. Lilie, C. Ludwig, T. Pratsch, I. Rochow et al.,

Prosopographie der mittelbyzantinischen Zeit. Erste Abteilung (641–867), 6 vols. (Berlin-New York, 1999–2002), #6124, #8545, #353 and #7312 respectively.

4 Detailed analysis: H.-G. Beck, *Senat und Volk von Konstantinopel. Probleme der byzantinischen Verfassungsgeschichte*, Sitzungsber. d. Bayer. Akad. d. Wiss., phil.-hist. Kl., Heft 6, 1966, (repr. in H. G. Beck, *Ideen und realitäten in Byzanz* [London 1972] XII); for a summary J. F. Haldon, *Byzantium in the seventh century: the transformation of a culture,* (Cambridge, 1997), 167–168.

5 Thus troops hostile to the government of Martina attacked the gardens and vineyards of Constantinopolitans on the Asian side of the Bosporus in 642. Nikephoros. §31. The degree to which persecution of certain members of the Constantinopolitan elite under Phocas had any impact is not clear.

6 See Paulinus, *Eucharisticus,* in H.G. Evelyn White, ed. and trans., *Ausonius,* (Cambridge MA 1921), ii: 295–351 and comments and discussion of P. R. L. Brown, *Through the eye of a needle: Wealth, the fall of Rome, and the making of Christianity in the west, 350–550 AD* (Princeton, 2012), 390–392.

7 Theophanes, *Chronographia*, ed. C. de Boor, 2 vols. (Leipzig, 1883, 1885), 383; Engl. trans. *The Chronicle of Theophanes Confessor*, trans. C. Mango and R. Scott (Oxford, 1997). 533.

8 *PBE* (*Prosopography of the Byzantine Empire 641–886*, ed. J.R. Martindale, online version (London, 2000)) Ioannes 3; *PmbZ*, #2707. For Justinian II's demands: Theophanes, 367 (trans. Mango-Scott, 513); Nikephoros, patriarch of Constantinople, *Short History,* Text, trans. and commentary by C. Mango (CFHB, ser. Washingtoniensis 13 = DOT 10), (Washington D.C., 1990), §39 (see *PBE* I, Theodotos 3; *PmbZ* #7904). Justinian II is associated in the Syriac historiography also with action directed against "the nobility and great men": Michael the Syrian, *La Chronique de Michel le Syrien, Patriarche Jacobite d'Antioche*, ed. et trad. J.B. Chabot, 4 vols. (Paris, 1899, 1901, 1905, 1924), ii, 473; see A. Palmer, *The seventh century in the West-Syrian Chronicles* (Liverpool, 1993): 206–207.

9 See *PmbZ* #6150, #5258 and #5254 (and the caution expressed by the editors regarding the problem of making such identifications too readily); *PBE* I, Philippikos 1, Nikephoros 1.

10 *PmbZ* #3557 and #2298. See also *PLRE* III: 529 (Germanus 5); *PBE*, Germanus 8, Mizizios 1, Justinian 3.

11 *PmbZ* #8524.

12 See *Acta Conciliorum Oecumenicorum* II, 2.1–2: *Concilium universale Constantinopolitanum tertium*, ed. R. Riedinger (Berlin, 1990–1992), II, ii. 2. 778–796; and *PmbZ* #6525. The total of bishops from all patriarchates at each council was 166 and 227 respectively, see also H. Ohme, *Das Concilium Quinisextum und seine Bischofsliste. Studien zum Konstantinopler Konzil von 692,* Arbeiten zur Kirchengeschichte 56, (Berlin-New York, 1990), 145–170.

13 A. Cameron, "New Themes and Styles in Greek Literature: seventh-eighth centuries", in A. Cameron and L. I. Conrad, eds., *The Byzantine and early Islamic Near East*, i: *problems in the literary source material* (Princeton, 1992), 81–105.

14 M. Kaplan, *Les hommes et la terre à Byzance du VIe au XIe siècles,* (Paris, 1992) 310–326; and "Les grands propriétaires de Cappadoce (VIe-XIe siècles)", in *Le aree omogenee della Civiltà rupestre nell'ambito dell'Impero bizantino: la Cappadocia* (Galatina, 1981), 125–158.

15 See Balādhurī, *Kitāb futūh al-Buldān. The origins of the Islamic State*, trans. P.K. Hitti, (London 1916/Beirut 1966), 231f., for example, who describes the local élite and their followers fleeing Barbalissos for imperial territory.

16 See H. Ditten, *Ethnische Verschiebungen zwischen der Balkanhalbinsel und*

Kleinasien vom Ende des 6. bis zur zweiten Hälfte des 9. Jahrhunderts (Berliner Byzantinische Arbeiten 59, (Berlin, 1993), 64 and n. 126.

17 *PBE* Theodoros 50; *PmbZ*, #7320.

18 *PBE* Sergios 30 and Tiberios 9; *PmbZ*, #6689.

19 *PBE* Ioannes 31, *PmbZ*, # 3414; for his father, Kyriakos, see *PBE* Kyriakos 6.

20 *PBE* Sisinnios 35, *PmbZ*, #6819.

21 *PBE* Konstantinos 136, *PmbZ*, #1170.

22 *PBE* Gregorios 7, *PmbZ*, #2523.

23 St Saba: J.-M. Sansterre, *Les moines grecs et orientaux à Rome aux époques Byzantine et carolingienne (milieu du VIe siècle-fin du IXe siècle)*, 2 vols. (Brussels, 1983); "Le monachisme byzantin à Rome", in *Bisanzio, Roma e l'Italia nell'alto medioevo*, Settimane di studio del centro italiano sull'alto medioevo, 34, (Spoleto, 1988), 701–746.

24 See R.-J. Lilie, *Die byzantinische Reaktion auf die Ausbreitung der Araber*, Misc. Byz. Monacensia 22, (Munich, 1976), 102, 106f. with n. 15; G. Rotter, *Die Ummayaden und der zweite Bürgerkrieg (680–692). Abh. für die Kunde des Morgenlandes,* 45, (1982), 179.

25 *PBE* Anastasios 2, *PmbZ*, #285.

26 *PBE* Georgios 3, *PmbZ*, #2105. See Theoph. 378.27 (trans. Mango-Scott, 528).; and *PBE* Isoes 1 and J. Nesbitt, N. Oikonomidès, *Catalogue of Byzantine seals at Dumbarton Oaks and in the Fogg Museum of Art, III: West, Northwest and Central Asia Minor and the Orient,* (Washington D.C., 1996), 39.30; *PmbZ*, #3518.

27 *PBE* Isoes 3; *PmbZ*,#3519 with references. There are only two other persons of this name known from the eighth and ninth centuries: see *PBE* Isoes 2, *PmbZ*, #3520 (a priest who attended Nicaea II in 787); and *PBE* Isoes 4, *PmbZ*, # 3522 (an imperial *mandator* of the ninth century). The *quaestor* was instrumental in framing imperial legislation and in managing judicial matters at court. See N. Oikonomidès, *Les listes de préséance byzantins des IXe-Xe siècles,* (Paris, 1972), 321–322; J. B. Bury, *The Imperial Administrative System in the Ninth Century, with a revised text of the Kletorologion of Philotheos* (British Academy Supplemental Papers, I. London, 1911), 73–77; *Ecloga, Das Gesetzbuch Leons III. und Konstantinos' V.*, ed L. Burgmann (Forschungen zur byzantinischen Rechtsgeschichte X, Frankfurt a. M. 1983), proem, 40ff., 102ff. See also A. Gkoutzioukostas, Ο θεσμός του κοιαίστωρα του ιερού παλατίου: Η γένεση, οι αρμοδιότητες και η εξέλιξή του, (Thessaloniki, 2001), 119ff.

28 N. Garsoïan, "The problem of Armenian integration into the Byzantine empire", in H. Ahrweiler and A. Laiou, eds., *Studies on the internal diaspora of the Byzantine empire,* (Washington DC, 1998), 61–66.

29 See J. F. Haldon, "The fate of the late Roman elite: extinction or assimilation?", in L. Conrad and J.F. Haldon, eds., *Elites old and new in the Byzantine and early Islamic Near East*. Papers of the VIth Workshop in Late Antiquity and Early Islam (Princeton, 2004), 214–215; P. Charanis, "The Armenians in the Byzantine empire", in *Byzantinoslavica,* 22 (1961), 196–240; "Ethnic changes in the Byzantine empire in the seventh century", *DOP* 13 (1959), 23–44; F. Winkelmann, *Quellenstudien zur herrschenden Klasse von Byzanz im 8. und 9. Jahrhundert*, Berliner Byzantinische Arbeiten 54, (Berlin, 1987) 203–207; S. Gero, "Armenians in Byzantium: some reconsiderations", *Journal of Armenian Studies* 2 (1985), 13–26; also H. Ditten, "Prominente Slawen und Bulgaren in byzantinischen Diensten (Ende des 7. Bis Anfang des 10. Jhdts"., in Köpstein, H. and F. Winkelmann, eds., *Studien zum 8. und 9. Jahrhundert in Byzanz* (Berliner Byzantinische Arbeiten 51, (Berlin, 1983), 95–11; *Ethnische Verschiebungen zwischen der Balkanhalbinsel,* 72–82; and J.-Cl. Cheynet "The Byzantine aristocracy

(8th–13th centuries)", in J.-Cl. Cheynet, *The Byzantine aristocracy and its military function* (Aldershot, 2006): I, 1–43: 12.

30 See esp. Ditten, "Prominente Slawen und Bulgaren", 104–109 (sources, literature and an etymology of the name); also Ph. Malingoudis, "Zur sozialen und ethnischen Assimilierung der Slawen in Byzanz: der Fall der Rhendakioi", *Annuaire de l'Université de Sofia "St. Kliment Ohridski"* 87/6, (1994), 13–20; *PmbZ* #6752.

31 See Theoph. 354. 11–13 (Mango-Scott 494); Theophilus of Edessa, *Chronicle*, R.G. Hoyland, *Theophilus of Edessa's Chronicle and the circulation of historical knowledge in Late Antiquity and early Islam,* (Liverpool, 2011), 167–168; *PmbZ*, #4173 (Kyprianos), #5909 (Petronas) and #6206 (Phloros).

32 See Haldon, *Byzantium in the seventh century,* 140–141; and esp. Kaplan, *Les hommes et la terre à Byzance,* 164–169 on emphyteutic leases; and 169ff. on the provincial landed élites and their characteristics.

33 Haldon, "The fate of the late Roman elite", 216–219, 229–231; Cheynet, "The Byzantine Aristocracy", 10, 21ff.

34 A post that was abolished or renamed (as *domestikos*) during the reign of Constantine V and at some point before 765: J. F. Haldon, *Byzantine Praetorians: an Administrative, Institutional and Social Survey of the Opsikion and Tagmata, c.580–900,* Poikila Byzantina 3, (Bonn, 1984), 228–235, 355.

35 *PmbZ* #7235 with references; *PBE I*, Tarasios 1; with Sisinnios 85, Tarasios 6, Georgios 122. Detailed discussion in Efthymiadis 1998: 6–11.

36 He was probably the same as the Theodore who acted for the emperor's brother as commander of military forces in Thrace in 656 (*PmbZ* #10698), and the Theodore mentioned as *komes* of the Opsikion in 680: *PmbZ* #7345. Theodore was instrumental in preventing the wife and children of Constans II from leaving Constantinople to join the emperor in Sicily, and later served Constantine IV in his negotiations and subsequent crushing of the rebellious Anatolikon soldiers in September 681: see *PmbZ* #7312; *PBE* I, Theodoros 3.

37 *PmbZ* #1218.

38 For full details: *PmbZ* #4242; *PBE* Leo 3; P. Speck, *Kaiser Leon III., die Geschichtswerke des Nikephoros und des Theophanes und der Liber Pontificalis*, Poikila Byzantina, 19–20, (Bonn, 2003). We know very little of the processes through which such transfers were carried out, nor whether they entailed grants of land from the state, the compulsory sale of property in the regions of origin, and so forth: see Ditten, *Ethnische Verschiebungen zwischen der Balkanhalbinsel und Kleinasien,* 158–161.

39 V. *Philareti,* L. Rydén, *The Life of St Philaretos the merciful written by his grandson Niketas. A critical edition with introduction, translation, notes and indices* (Acta Universitatis Upsaliensis. Studia Byzantina Upsaliensia 8. (Uppsala, 2002), 117. See *PmbZ* #6136 for literature and discussion with C. Ludwig, *Sonderformen byzantinischer Hagiographie und ihr literarisches Vorbild. Untersuchungen zu den Viten des Äsop, des Philaretos, des Symeon Salos und des Andreas Salos* (Berliner Byzantinistische Studien 3. (Berlin, 1997), 74–166.

40 See P. Brown, *Through the eye of a needle,* 392–400; D. Harrison, "The development of élites: from Roman bureaucrats to medieval warlords", in W. Pohl and M. Diesenberger, eds., *Integration und Herrschaft. Ethnische Identitäten und soziale Organisation in Frühmittelalter* (Vienna, 2002), 289–300; P. Brown, *Religion and society in the age of St. Augustine* (London, 1972), 233; and T. S. Brown, *Gentlemen and officers: Imperial administration and aristocratic power in Byzantine Italy, A.D. 554–800,* (Rome, 1984), 107–108.

41 The best analyses of this corpus of material remain F. Winkelmann, *Quellenstudien zur herrschenden Klasse*; and *Byzantinische Rang- und Ämterstruktur im 8. und 9.*

Jahrhundert, Berliner Byzantinische Arbeiten 53 (Berlin, 1985), together with the often detailed studies for individuals in *PmbZ*.

42 Haldon, *Byzantine Praetorians,* 211–216; cautionary comments on names and naming traditions: Brown, *Gentlemen and officers*, 67–68.

43 Such a person may have been the logothete of the general treasury, Theodotos, during the first reign of Justinian II, formerly a monk and hermit, implied somewhat obliquely by Theophanes to have been of humble origins: Theoph., 367 (trans. Mango–Scott, 513); Nikephoros, §39 (*PmbZ* #7904; *PBE* I, Theodotos 3).

44 Personal service for an individual powerful person was often the key to advancement, A. P. Kazhdan and M. McCormick, "The social world of the Byzantine court", in H. Maguire, ed., *Byzantine court culture from 829 to 1204,* (Washington D.C, 1997), 176–185, 189–195. The imperial *chartoularios* Paul, for example, Leo III's senior chancery official, was sent to Sicily in 717/718 to deal with the usurpation of Basil Onomagoulus and promoted directly to *patrikios* and *strategos* of Sicily: F. Dölger and A. Müller, *Regesten der Kaiserurkunden des oströmischen Reiches 565–1453* (Corpus der griechischen Urkunden des Mittelalters und der neueren Zeit, Reihe A, Abt. I. i–iv Munich–Berlin 1924–1965); ii, 2nd ed. ed. P. Wirth (Munich 1977); 2nd revised edn. A. Müller, i, 1–2 (Munich, 2003): #282; *PmbZ* #5815. Whether Paul came from this social background is not known, of course. For a general survey of stability and instability at court and in the imperial administrative establishment more widely in the later seventh to ninth centuries: Winkelmann, *Quellenstudien zur herrschenden Klasse,* 98–142.

45 Conant, *Staying Roman,* 196–241; Brown, *Gentlemen and officers*, 61–79. Before the conquest of Egypt in the early 640s there was another somewhat different pattern, in which both senior and junior officials and commanders were generally Egyptian, with a small number of high-ranking outsiders: B. Palme, "The imperial presence: government and army", in R. Bagnall, ed., *Egypt in the Byzantine world, 300–700,* (Cambridge, 2007), 244–270.

46 Haldon, *The empire that would not die*, 148–149; cf. Brown, *Gentlemen and officers,* 85–88.

9 Bishops and merchants: the economy of Ravenna at the beginning of the Middle Ages

Enrico Cirelli

Introduction

The end of the rule of the exarchate in 751 marks the beginning of a new phase for Ravenna, losing its real political power, but assuming a new "ideological" position as model of the Imperial power during the Middle Ages. In the last fifteen years the excavations conducted in Classe, one of the main Adriatic ports, give us a new quantitative perspective for the period that follows the fall of the western Roman empire. Ravenna and Classe played a fundamental role in the creation of a new economic system that laid the foundations for the following political assets. Despite the fall of the Exarchal administration, infrastructure and civic services were still guaranteed, probably by the Episcopal authority, in the same way that was happening in many other Italian cities from the north to Sicily, and the same was true especially with regard to the urban defences.[1] If we adhere to old-fashioned historical theories the final act of late antiquity is in fact during the seventh century with the Arab invasions. Certainly the idea that north-western Europe was cut off from the newly Islamic Mediterranean from the seventh century, thereby causing it to develop a dynamic economic focus within the Frankish realm of Charlemagne, has been comprehensively disproved not only by archaeology but also by a more inquisitive reading of contemporary documents, as recently demonstrated[2] (Figure 9.1).

Trade with North Africa

In fact Tunisia was one of the major partners for the economy of Late Roman Imperial territories by the beginning of the fifth century, with various differences. This is particularly evident for fine wares. African red slip wares was the most attested production in the first season of Classe excavations,[3] and more has been uncovered in each subsequent season, notably a full set of northern African Amphorae together with a thousand of central Tunisian lamps and hundreds of vessels Hayes form 85b, were found (Figure 9.2).[4] Two hundred *spatheia*, close to the Keay XXVIf form/Bonifay type 31, a bit smaller and with a longer and slender body.[5]

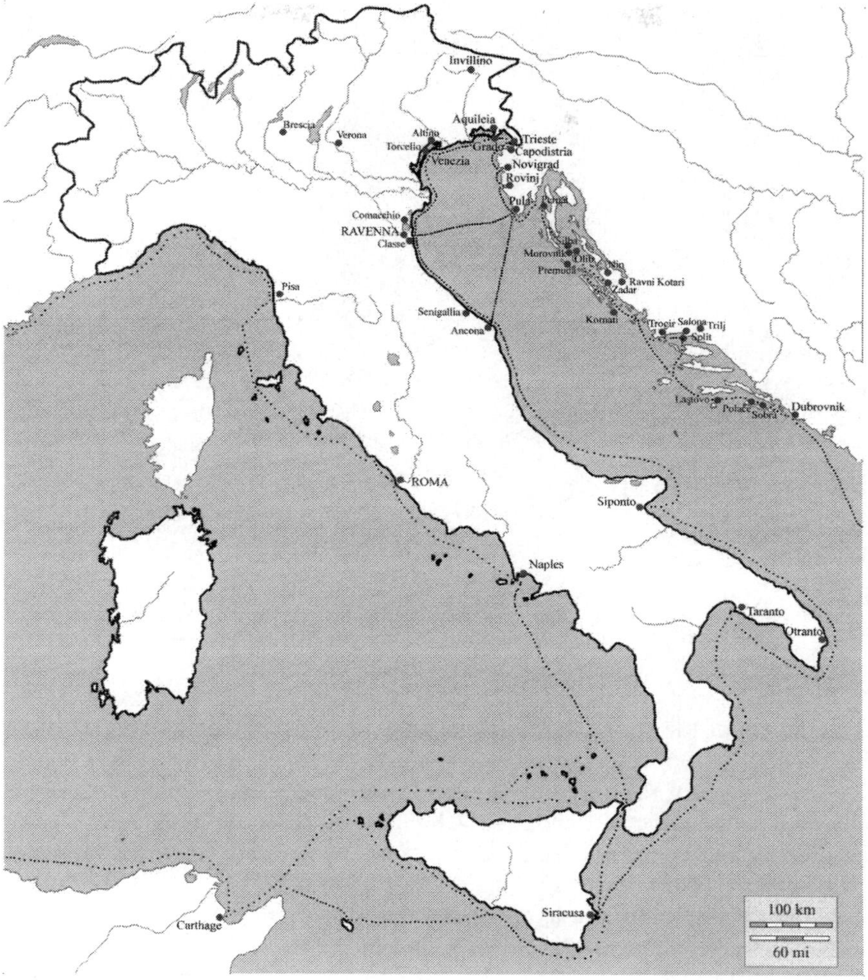

Figure 9.1 Trade routes and sites.

Inside the contexts analysed until now, northern African amphorae are well testified both before and after the Justinian conquest, with a small decrease overall in the number of *spatheia*, from 16.5% to 4.5%, also becoming smaller in size.

The number of big cylindrical amphorae, on the contrary, increases in percentage, even if the total amount is a bit smaller and despite the changing of typologies. Inside the settlement most of the late Roman African amphorae types were found, particularly the Keay VIIIb, filling nearly all of building no. 6 (Figure 9.3).

Figure 9.2 Central Tunisian sixth-century lamps and African Red Slip Ware bowls (Hayes 85B forms) from the site of Classe (Ravenna).

Tunisian amphorae are otherwise testified in all the different types of settlements of the whole Adriatic coastline, along the Marche and Abruzzo in central Italy and along the Dalmatian ports,[6] and in shipwrecks.[7] Ravenna was not the only terminal and other points of distribution crossed the sea, joining the Istrian and Dalmatian coasts with northern African products such as in the ship found close to Sobra,[8] Lastovo, Salona,[9] Morovnik, Olib (shipwreck A),[10] Silba (shipwreck A),[11] and Pula.[12] Northern African amphorae are also well testified in the north-east of Italy, in the late antique port of Aquileia[13] and in the sites of the Venice Lagoon such as Altino,[14] Torcello,[15] and through them they reached Verona,[16] Concordia,[17] Oderzo,[18] Treviso,[19] Caorle[20] and almost all the inland settlements, villas, castles and urban sites.[21]

Eastern commerce

It is important to emphasise the great number of eastern amphorae inside much more of the contexts analysed in the port area of Classe from the beginning of the fifth century. Inside this group the small quantity of LRA2, the Greek amphora, is astonishing, which may confirm the hypothesis that this container was mostly used to supply the Balkan and the army that defended the River Danube.[22] This container is also well distributed along

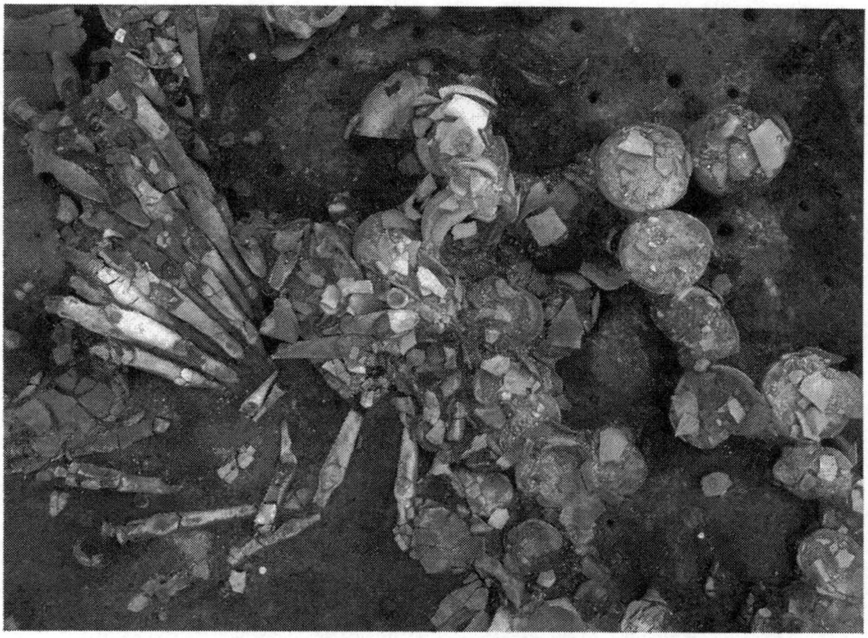

Figure 9.3 Tunisian amphorae in a beginning of the sixth-century warehouse from Classe.

the coastline of Albania and the eastern side of the Adriatic,[23] but becomes rare in the north if we leave out the fortified sites, as for instance Udine,[24] and Ibligo Invillino.[25] A second group of eastern containers is constituted by the Aegean LRA3. This small wine amphora was very widespread above all in Ravenna and inside its territory, with a peak at the end of the fifth century. In the second half of the sixth century LRA3 slowly decreases, probably replaced by other wine containers produced in the same region. Less successful was the contemporary Agora form M273, even with the many different Opait variants (about 1%),[26] in particular the variant produced in Samos. Its typological evolution, the Samos cistern type amphora, diffused from the second half of the sixth (at Argos inside contexts of AD 585) and overall during the seventh century, has the same success.[27] It is hard to say if this container is a mark of the favoured trade relationship between Constantinople and its territories in the western Mediterranean Sea. Despite its importance the number is not relevant in Adriatic contexts and its distribution is wide even in the hinterland. In Classe it reaches a value of about 1% in seventh-century contexts. It was also often used as a burial coffin for children, for instance in the one identified close to the timber houses that took place inside the ruins of the building no. 2 and close to building 14.[28]

A new form, probably produced in the northern Aegean islands (with an intense micaceous fabric), has been found above all inside contexts dated between the end of the fifth and the beginning of the sixth century. The major diffusion is attested in the area of Thessalonike and complete vessels are on show at the Museum of Byzantine Culture, coming from various excavations of its territory.[29] A good comparison for this type of amphora comes from the Palatine Hill in Rome, where these late Roman vessels have been identified and analysed by thin-section, revealing their eastern origin.[30]

Despite its wide diffusion in all the Mediterranean Sea and its distribution as far as Ireland, the LRA1 amphora is not the best represented eastern amphora in the Port Area of Classe. This globular container was produced in various centres: Cyprus,[31] Rhodes[32] and along the coasts of Seleucia and Cilicia (e.g., Elaiussa Sebaste).[33] In the contexts that we have studied until now, LRA1 are attested with all the typologies identified by Dominique Pieri.[34] After the Justinianic conquest of Ravenna this amphora and its goods grew considerably in quantity, from a value of 8% to 14% of the whole context. LRA1 was used mainly to transport wine, but thanks to some *tituli picti* read over the amphorae found in Classe,[35] we know that they might have also transported honey and other goods.[36] These inscriptions written on the amphorae are not constantly used and that could testify that usually the costumer would have easily identified the product, normally wine, and its quantity, without this sort of "label". The *tituli picti* identified over these Cilician amphorae are mainly written in Greek, but we have also examples of Latin and one case of Hebrew inscription.[37]

Otherwise the most common eastern amphorae in the fifth-century deposits at Classe is the LRA4, produced at Ashkelon and Gaza to export famous wine.[38] Archaeology testifies how the entire territory of Gaza was intensively converted to the production of wine from fourth century, a product exported and diffused all over the Mediterranean and as far as Cornwall.[39] LRA4 is attested in all the contexts, particularly between the end of the fifth and the beginning of the sixth century, when in some contexts it reaches more than the 40%, with a progressive decline in the second half of the sixth (17%). In the site of Classe the LRA 4B3, the late seventh-century small variant is also testified.[40] In San Severo and into the Basilica Petriana the eighth-century variant has also been identified,[41] produced at Ashkelon together with the eighth-century, bag-shaped amphora produced in Egypt. Rare but notable is also the presence of the late variant of the Form 9b in Cypriot red slip ware, dated to the mid-eighth century.[42]

In northern Italy Ravenna was the most important terminal for the distribution of this container, found in great quantity inside all the north Adriatic settlements in Italy and Istria,[43] compared to the rest of western Adriatic coastline but above all in comparison with the eastern coast, where LRA4 are uncommon.[44] Fewer quantities were also found of other

Palestinian amphorae as the LRA 5 and LRA6 (4–6%), identified in Classe and inside some of Ravenna's contexts.[45] The distribution in the Adriatic Sea is even more uncommon, but episodically testified within all the main sites.[46] Much rarer is another import from Palestine, the amphora Agora M334,[47] a carrot amphora produced in the territory of Acco, which reached Ravenna and its territory in particular during the fifth century.[48]

The Egyptian LRA7 wine amphora has been found in our contexts with a value of less than 1%. It has a wide regional circulation and outside Egypt, this container has been widely found only inside the Port of Carthage within contexts dated to the end of the sixth century. In the rest of the Mediterranean ports it is rare inside the most important cities excavated until now, for example Rome in the seventh century, Naples in the Tyrrhenian Sea, and Ravenna and Aquileia on the Adriatic coasts.[49] The same small quantity of an Egyptian or Nubian small ring-based container, characterised by a pink fabric is testified inside fifth-and sixth-century contexts at Classe. This amphora is really uncommon in other parts of Italy, where it has only been found, up to now, in Naples.[50]

Italic productions

The only amphora surely identified as an Italic production, within the fifth to seventh century contexts studied until now in Classe, is the famous Keay LII type.[51] This wine amphora, whose production area has been localised definitively in south Italy (Calabria and Sicily),[52] has been found with values of about 4% in all the contexts analysed. It should be connected with the many properties that the Archbishop had in southern Italy. This amphora was in any case widely diffused, in small quantities, within the Adriatic Sea, in fifth- to seventh-century contexts,[53] and also in the internal routes reached by Ravenna's redistribution, as for instance S. Maria *in Padovetere* (Comacchio).[54] Some eighth-century amphorae, identified in the later phases of the Portual area, might be associated with local production, but only mineralogical analysis will be able to confirm this hypothesis.

Dynamics and trend

The contexts that have been studied until now show in Adriatic sites some trends and dynamics of the commercial activities of this region, during its major period of increase. The quantity of amphorae exposed comes from the calculation of some of the most important contexts of the Port Area of Classe and might receive some updating in the following years. In a sample of 167 amphorae, eastern Mediterranean products are represented in about 85% of the amphorae, versus 18% of North African and 2% of the Italic products (mostly Sicily and Calabria). Even if we calculate the size of the amphorae, northern African products in this context do not go beyond the value of 25% of the whole ensemble of goods contained.

The most important consideration, which we get from this frame, is the general standing of the imports coming from the main production centres of the Mediterranean Sea between the beginning of the fifth and the mid-seventh century. We can also observe that in the second half of the sixth century, eastern amphorae notably increase in comparison with the Tunisian products. This is also attested by the rise of fine ware, such as Phocean red slip ware, especially the form Hayes 3.[55]

The eastern Mediterranean area after the mid-sixth century is dominant as far as Ravenna and Classe amphorae and goods supply are concerned. Eastern and western Mediterranean products travelled anyway together in the same ships, as for instance LRA1 and *spatheia* inside the shipwreck of Cavtat,[56] and all the trade was probably decentralised and conducted much more by private merchants or "companies" compared to previous centuries.[57]

After the Justinianic conquest, Carthage played a strategic role in the control of the western Mediterranean.[58] This pattern really changes in the first quarter of the seventh century, and has nothing to do with the Arab conquest, which only took place in Tunisia at the end of the same century.[59] This territory continued to supply the demand of the main urban, rural and fortified settlements in Italy, France and Spain.[60] If the trend is the same as the fifth and sixth centuries, the size is completely different. The number of importations drastically decreases and we should study the reason of this phenomenon, linked to the capability of North African land owners to generate surplus or simply due to the difficulties in finding good markets.

The collapse of the importation of goods is similar to the decrease of number of coins in this territory during the eighth century. The most significant downward curve can be seen already during the sixth century, but the decrease of specimens between the seventh and eighth centuries is especially impressive, decreasing as it does from 204 pieces to 11 coins only.[61] It is rather difficult, however, to accept the idea that the economy of this Mediterranean region moved on to a system of barter as suggested by some scholars. It might be easier to assume instead that these territories entered in a different economic system, based on agricultural exploitation with a partially autonomous regional distribution, and became independent from other commercial routes, as for instance the one that ran down from the Bavarian axis to reach Ljubljana and move to internal Croatia, where there is well attested evidence of Carolingian trade in swords and winged lances,[62] or Aquileia\Grado and the Venetian lagoons, descending the Adriatic following both coastal trajectories (Figure 9.4).

Ravenna and many other north Adriatic and Ionian cities were reached between the end of the seventh and the eighth century by globular amphorae, brought to the forefront by the discoveries of Comacchio[63] and Otranto.[64] These materials indicate that Ravenna and its territories were still integrated into extended trade networks, even if the quantities suggest a function of consumption of products and no longer one of redistribution.

Figure 9.4 New routes in eastern Adriatic and the Balkans.

These amphorae have mainly Aegean or other eastern fabrics, coming both from the Byzantine and from the Islamic world (Figure 9.5).[65]

On some specimens were found raw graffiti which indicate that the marketing of these products was carried out by merchants of Arab origin. The major product imported by then was probably wine, even if the quantities are significantly small. Their number tends to increase towards the Carolingian period, with the evidence of new types of amphorae, imported from the east, especially in the tenth century.

In early medieval written sources such as *descriptiones,* and in other charters dated between the eighth and tenth centuries, wine continued to be widely associated with the term "amphorae", although it is possible that this term indicated a unit of measure equal to about 26 litres, which, incidentally,

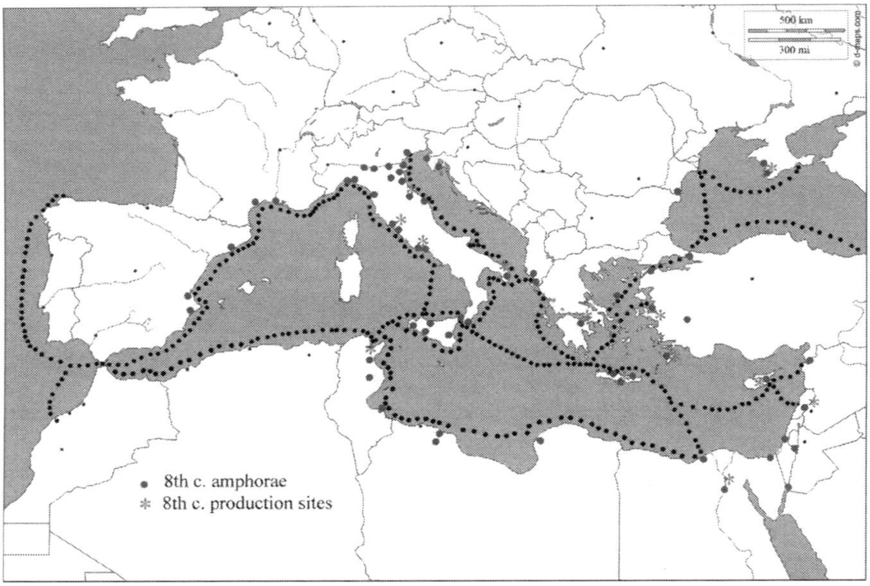

Figure 9.5 Eighth-century amphorae distributive map.

is the same amount that could fill the globular amphora found by now in various parts of the Italian peninsula.[66] The same trade routes also imported eighth-century domestic ware, such as Palestinians casseroles, Aegean cooking pots and jugs with filters.

Mediterranean trade, even if on a lower scale, was probably active along each side of the Adriatic coasts from Epirus, Illyria to Dalmatia, or from Apulia towards the north.[67] Until the end of the eighth century this "intimate sea", to use Predrag Matvejević's definition, remained under the control of Byzantium as did many Istrian towns, such as Trieste, Koper, Novigrad, Rovinj, Pula and Labin, and the territory within Motovun and Buzet.[68] The same happened in Dalmatia with the islands of Kvarner (Osor and Arbe), Krk, along the coast of Zadar, and in its hinterland where eighth-century Byzantine jewels have been found,[69] at Trogir and Ravni Kotar,[70] together with Aegean seventh-century wine amphorae, such as Samo's cistern type, visible in their museums but unfortunately still unpublished (Figure 9.6).

Split and Dubrovnik started to acquire new importance in this period, as fortifications and places of refuge from Slavic pressure, before being transformed into market places.[71] In some areas of the Dalmatian coast traces of the trade with the eastern Mediterranean were found, dating to the seventh and eighth centuries, in Polače-Mljet, Trilj, in the Krka river and to Cape Pernat (Cres), but with only a small quantity of imported pottery,[72] as

Figure 9.6 Seventh-century Samo's cistern type amphora from the Museum of Trogir.

for instance the two late seventh-century miniaturist *spatehia* and the contemporary late African slip ware found at Nin (Nona).[73] In places such as Lastovo, Kornati, Premuda items related to navigation with new, lighter and smaller, boats have also been found,[74] as recently suggested for other sites in the Mediterranean Sea.[75]

For this period we have evidence of many *negotiatores* in the written sources in Ravenna, some of these certainly *Venetici*,[76] and increasing overall by the end of the eighth century, demonstrating a predominant development of the merchants of the duchy compared to merchants of other regions of the Adriatic, although, the hegemony of these groups would only come to dominate the scene from the tenth century.[77] The trade of Ravenna with the Adriatic territories seems to have been limited to cheese, wool, hides, wine, oil, wax and slaves, as shown by the Venetian prohibition of AD 960 regarding the commerce of "brethren" with the Saracens, relevant to the markets of Venice, Istria, Dalmatia and southern Italy.[78] Contemporary with this change it has been observed that, during the eighth and ninth centuries, there is a renewed productive input, driven by Ravenna's Episcopal elite, possibly similar to that attempted by the Pope inside the territories of the duchy of Rome.[79] This new productive activity had been attested to by only scarce archaeological evidence, but finally some of them have begun to be underlined in recent surveys.[80] Small quantities of fine ceramics, as for instance glazed potteries, have been identified in archaeological surveys and excavations, as in other Adriatic regions.[81] Later glazed ware dated to the Carolingian period have been identified in Ravenna inside its new productive landscape, at Montaccio for instance, one of those directional settlements,[82] and in another rural site close to the Via Emilia, in Medicina.[83] This class of pottery is, however, very little attested,[84] indicating a high social status of the users, despite the difficulty of judging these dynamics by starting from ceramics.[85] Glazed vessels have been also found in new ninth-century houses with porches recently excavated at Ravenna, the same type of houses as those belonging to a now fairly well-known group of urban aristocratic housing, in S. Stefano *in fundamento regis,* over the ruins of the imperial palace, as happened to the old monuments in other Italian cities such as Brescia and Rome.[86] Other ceramic products with fine fabric and incised decoration, but without glazed over other painted surface, have been connected to this eighth- to tenth-century new horizon of manufacture. This ceramic is well testified inside Ravenna, for example, at the monastery of S. Severo,[87] in Decimano's territory,[88] and in Bassa Romagna,[89] mostly over end-of-the-ninth century site, and inside new "directional centres" in Ravenna's southern landscape.[90]

What has not been found so far on these sites are containers like those identified in Comacchio by Gelichi and Negrelli in their recent work, perhaps related to the transport of fish, that reached perhaps even settlements along the Middle Adriatic coast, have been identified on some sites in the central Adriatic region, in Senigallia for instance,[91] and in Istria.[92] The products of the atelier found close to the *Basilica Petriana* had at least a regional circulation, as shown by examples of the same type found on some sites of the western Romagna and inside River Lamone's valley, in small settlements, perhaps always new directional centres of population, or central places, rural settlements where we observe a polarization of older sparse sites, as has been suggested recently by Negrelli.[93] The first engine of this economic dynamism during this period, failing the weight of a strong centralised taxation, is the initiative of élites, and, primarily in the north Adriatic area, the archbishop of Ravenna plays a major role.[94] Its richness was funded by considerable real estate assets, mostly lands and buildings. Ravenna's Archbishop had also a treasure of precious objects of liturgical use, wide currency reserves, and its wealth did not differ substantially from that of a large secular owner. The landed property was owned in large part by the grant of land in long lease or level (from the eighth century onward).[95] After the mid-eighth century the archbishops had in fact attempted to build a territory, as did the Pope at the beginning of the same century, within the boundaries of the former exarchate, but in a more limited form, between the Adriatic and the Apennines, and between the Po and the Panaro.[96] The archbishops' properties were indeed much more extensive and included the territories still in Sicily, Istria, Pentapolis and Umbria, as recorded by Andrea Agnello in the *Liber Pontificalis,* and recently discussed by Salvatore Cosentino.[97] In the same period a wider central Adriatic market is reached by another product of great importance from northern Italy: the soapstone.[98] This class of material was produced in the Alps region and distributed inside the entire Italian peninsula, mostly during the early Middle Ages.[99] In the Ravenna area, this material has been found in huge quantities, especially on sites dating from between the eighth and the tenth centuries, inside the monastic complex of S. Severo at Classe, where thousands of vessels have been quantified, and it was extremely widespread along the Adriatic coast, following the same trajectories, and reaching for instance the ports of Senigallia,[100] Ancona, and the Marche's hinterland through intermediate markets.[101] Soapstone has been also found in large quantities (100 specimens) in rural areas of Ravenna territories inside central places,[102] and tenth-century castles.[103] The same fluvial routes, the Po River and its tributaries, and the same roads were also crossed by grindstones, going down from the Alps to the Archbishops lands, in the Carolingian Age as in the past.[104] Grindstone's fluvial trade is also testified during the early Middle Ages along the River Rhine, in continuity with the Roman fluvial trade route,[105] at Lüttingen and Salmorth in the hearth of the Frankish kingdom.[106] These basalt and tuff objects were mined in the Eifel mountains in Germany and directed to other market places taking off in the eighth and ninth centuries in the North Sea, as long distance trade goods,[107] demonstrating that not only relics, luxury items and precious metals were exported during this difficult period, at the origins of the European economy.

Perspectives

Archaeological evidence demonstrates how Ravenna undertook a political and ideological role as much as an economic predominance in the distribution of goods since the beginning of the fifth century. This role was carried out until the early Middle Ages, by the rising of the many north Adriatic emporiums, and the definitive affirmation of Venice in the Carolingian period.[108] Close to famous architectural and mosaic evidence, pottery data tells us that the city is fully inscribed within the Mediterranean economy and that it played a fundamental role in the last years of Roman society at the cusp of the early Medieval world.

The political change of the sixth century had an effect only on the quantity of goods rather than on the commercial vectors. The same happened in the Lombard Kingdom and in south Italy.[109] Different percentage representation among eastern and western productions, above all on the basis of amphora finds, show us the prevalence of eastern trade between fifth and seventh century on the Adriatic coast, with Ravenna as a focus centre of distribution.[110]

Despite this the city did not have a kindly territory for agricultural exploitation on account of the great number of marshes and the many rivers which crossed the city, although the choice of this site as an imperial see was a success in economic terms. The town was probably able to receive charges coming from North Africa and the eastern Mediterranean and played the fundamental role of economical intermediary with the countryside and the River Po Valley. Most of the many Ravenna ports were reached by primary goods coming from these river tracks, and every kind of foodstuff and luxury object, during the whole Late Roman period, before the Gothic war and after the Lombard conquest. In this period trade movements started to decrease in intensity and narrow because of an economical general flexure that ran over Byzantine towns, such as Rome, Naples and Ravenna as well as Lombard reign sites as Brescia, Verona, Milan and other northern Italians towns.[111] Ravenna's wheat supply included many different countries. Cassiodoro remembers wheat importations from the provinces of Istria and Liguria, which are loaded by military annona.[112] The bishop and the church had at their disposal Sicilian wheat, until the Aghlabid conquest of the island in ninth century and probably even later. However, we will not be able to obtain archaeological evidence of these goods, transported inside sacks or others perishable materials.

Important news comes from this archaeological excavation, where trade continuity, even with northern Africa during sixth and seventh century, in its numerical value, has been demonstrated. A certain volume of imports continued to reach the North Adriatic coast also during the eighth century, as recent studies demonstrate.[113] This trade was controlled since the abandonment of the most important warehouses of the port canal of Classe, inside one of the many other ports that are testified for Ravenna by written sources.[114]

Oil, wine and cereals reached Ravenna through two fundamental primary trade routes; the first one, coming from eastern Mediterranean, crossing the Aegean and Ionian Seas sailed along the coast of Dalmatia and docked at Ravenna, probably after Aquileia.[115]

A second route reached the city from the south and could have joint African and eastern ships landing at Syracuse and sailing along Adriatic coast, perhaps with mixed goods cargos coming from different countries (for instance Syrian wine and African oil, African red slip ware and Sicilian wheat, eastern amphorae and fine ware, African amphorae and ARS fine ware). The analysis of new closed contexts of other Adriatic ports revealed that in the same period the most important quantity of amphorae was imported from the eastern Mediterranean, above all from Greece and the Aegean islands and from Anatolian territories. Italic exports are rare between the sixth and eighth centuries; it is possible that this might be due to a lack of research.

The protagonists of this trade network vary over time. At first they were linked to the Imperial fiscal movement and gradually were managed by a new class of merchants, linked to ecclesiastical elites and to private bankers.[116] Adriatic bishops invested in commerce. They had a merchant fleet and taxation privileges over the trade goods (*teloneum, siliquaticum, laudaticum, cispiaticum*) as recently highlighted (Figure 9.7).[117] Political change and cultural choices completely transformed the system of trade, and gradually the economy of the entire region looked to new forms of exploitation of the ancient communication network.[118] This information, enriched with practical details of early medieval travel, the storms, fevers, delays, miracles and pirates, will give us a clearer view of the origins of this new society.

In a new century when Dublin or Helsinki have as good a claim to be the economic dynamos of Europe as Paris or the Rhineland (the Franco-German "axis" which created the European Union in the 1950s—choosing Charlemagne as its hero—now looks not a little tired), the historical meaning of "Europe" itself needs re-visiting. Even if we might be rightly sceptical about the "Roman economy" as a single normative historical construct, the European economy becomes surely an even more diffuse and varied concept. We need to continue disentangling what "an economy" can mean realistically in the pre-modern period, where new and old religions, pilgrimage, war, despotism, weather, trade, diplomacy, piracy, slavery and disease all add up to a complex brew of factors in growth and contraction, seen through the cloudy lens of over a hundred decades.

The early medieval Mediterranean, together with the Arab Middle East and the Viking north, were indeed alive with traffic and trade, and Charlemagne and his contemporaries looked south and east for their inspiration in powerful and fundamental ways.[119]

Figure 9.7 Imperial trade privilegia for Ravenna's archbishop represented in S. Apollinare in Classe's mosaic.

Notes

1 L. Arcifa, "La città nel Medioevo: sviluppo urbano e dominio territoriale", in *Catania: l'identità urbana dall'antichità al settecento*, edited by L. Scalisi, (Catania, 2009), 73–111.

2 M. McCormick, *Origins of the European Economy. Communications and Commerce AD 300–900,* (Cambridge, 2001); C. Wickham, *Framing the Early Middle Ages: Europe and the Mediterranean 400–800,* (Oxford, 2004).

3 A. Augenti *et al.* "Classe, Podere Chiavichetta: dati dalla campagna di scavo 2001", in in S. Gelichi C. Negrelli (eds.), *La circolazione delle ceramiche nell'Adriatico tra Tarda Antichità ed Altomedioevo, III Incontro di Studio Cer.Am.Is. Sulle ceramiche tardoantiche ed altomedievale (Venezia, 2004)*, (Mantova, 2007), 257–295.

4 A. Augenti, E. Cirelli, "Classe: un osservatorio privilegiato per il commercio della tarda Antichità", in G. Guiducci, S. Menchelli, M. Pasquinucci, S. Santoro (eds.), *LRCW3, Late Roman Coarse Wares, Cooking Wares and Amphorae in the Mediterranean. Archaeology and Archaeometry. Comparison Between Western and Eastern Mediterranean,* BAR Int. Ser. 2185, (Oxford, 2010), 605–615.

5 M. Bonifay, *Etudes sur la céramique romaine tardive d'Afrique,* BAR Int. Ser. 1301, (Oxford, 2004), 124–125, fig. 67; T. Ghalia, M. Bonifay, C. Capelli, "L'atelier de Sidi-Zahruni: mise en evidence d'une production d'amphores de l'Antiquité tardive sur le territoire de la cité de Neapolis (Nabeul, Tunisie)", in J.M. Gurt i Esparraguera, J. Buxeda, M.A. CauOntiveros (eds.), *LRCW1. Late Roman Coarse Wares, Cooking Wares and Amphorae in the Mediterranean, Archaeology and Archaeometry*, BAR Int. Ser. 1340, (Oxford, 2005), fig. 3, no. 2.

6 D. Vrsalović. *Istraživanje i zaštitapodmorskiharheološkihspomenika u S.R.*

Hrvatskoj, (Zagreb, 1974), 140, nn. 133–138; Z. Brusić, M. Jurišić, Ž. Krnčević, *Blago šibenskogpodmorja. Exibition Catalogue,* (Šibenik, 2001), 66–68; R. Auriemma and E. Quiri, "La circolazione delle anfore in Adriatico tra V e VIII sec. d.C.", in S. Gelichi C. Negrelli (eds.), *La circolazione delle ceramiche nell'Adriatico tra Tarda Antichità ed Altomedioevo, III Incontro di Studio Cer.Am.Is. Sulle ceramiche tardoantiche ed altomedievale (Venezia, 2004)*, (Mantova, 2007), 34–37.

7 V. Vidrih Perko, "Seaborne Trade Routes in the North East Adriatic and their Connection to the Hinterland in the late Antiquity", in G.P. Brogiolo, P. Delogu (eds.), *L'Adriatico dalla tarda Antichità all'età carolingia,* (Firenze, 2005), 49–77.

8 A. Kisić, "Nalaz potonulog trgovačkog broda s početka IV. Stoljeća u uvali Sobri na Mljetu/Archaeological finds from the sunken ship of the 4th century in the bay of Sobra", in *Anali Historiskog Institau Dubrovniku* 24–25 (1987), 7–31.

9 J. Jeličič-Radonič, "Nova istraživanjagradskihzidina Salone", in *Prilozi Povijesti Umjetnosti u Dalmaciji* 37 (1998), 26.

10 A. Parker, *Ancient Shipwrecks of the Mediterranean and the Roman Provinces,* (Oxford, 1992), 294, no. 760; 403–404, no. 1084.

11 A. Parker, 283, no. 721.

12 S. Gluščević, "Hidreoarcheološki Očevid u ukolici Pule", in *Obavijesti* 35\1 (2003), 102–106.

13 M. Bueno, M. Novello, V. Mantovani, "Progetto Aquileia: Casa delle Bestie Ferite Commercio e consumo ad Aquileia. Analisi delle anfore tardoantiche alla luce di alcuni contesti", in *Rei Cretariae Romanare Fautorum Acta* 42 (2012), 164–165.

14 F. Ferrarini, "Osservazioni su due tipologie di anfore della media età imperiale ad Altino", in *Quaderni di Archeologia del Veneto* 9 (1993), 163.

15 A. Toniolo, "Anfore dall'area lagunare", in S. Gelichi C. Negrelli (eds.), *La circolazione delle ceramiche nell'Adriatico tra Tarda Antichità ed Altomedioevo, III Incontro di Studio Cer.Am.Is. Sulle ceramiche tardoantiche ed altomedievale (Venezia, 2004)*, (Mantova, 2007), 96–98.

16 B. Bruno, "Ceramiche da alcuni contesti tardo antichi e altomedievali di Verona", in S. Gelichi C. Negrelli (eds.), *La circolazione delle ceramiche nell'Adriatico tra Tarda Antichità ed Altomedioevo, III Incontro di Studio Cer.Am.Is. Sulle ceramiche tardoantiche ed altomedievale (Venezia, 2004)*, (Mantova, 2007), 161, pl. 11.

17 E. Di Filippo Balestrazzi, "Concordia Sagittaria: quartiere nord-ovest. Relazione preliminare delle campagne 1982–1987", in *Quaderni di archeologia del Veneto* 4 (1988), 148–150; 175–176.

18 G.M. Sandrini, A. Saccocci, C. Rallo, "Cinque pozzi romani a Oderzo", in *Quaderni di archeologia del Veneto* 4 (1988), 67.

19 R. Auriemma and E. Quiri, "La circolazione delle anfore in Adriatico tra V e VIII sec. d.C.", in S. Gelichi C. Negrelli (eds.), *La circolazione delle ceramiche nell'Adriatico tra Tarda Antichità ed Altomedioevo, III Incontro di Studio Cer.Am.Is. Sulle ceramiche tardoantiche ed altomedievale (Venezia, 2004)*, (Mantova, 2007), 36.

20 M. Verzar Bass. *Scavi ad Aquileia. L'area ad est del Foro. Rapporto degli scavi 1989–1991,* (Roma, 1994), 434, no. 273.

21 G. Murialdo, "Alto-Adriatico e alto-Tirreno nel mondo mediterraneo: due mari a confronto tra VI e X secolo", in S. Gelichi C. Negrelli (eds.), *La circolazione delle ceramiche nell'Adriatico tra Tarda Antichità ed Altomedioevo, III Incontro di Studio Cer.Am.Is. Sulle ceramiche tardoantiche ed altomedievale (Venezia, 2004)*, (Mantova, 2007), 10.

22 O. Karagiorgou, "LR2: a container for the Military annona on the Danubian Border?", in S. Kingsley, M. Decker (eds.), *Economy and Exchange in the East Mediterranean during Late Antiquity, (*Oxford, 2001), 129, 146.

23 P. Reynolds, "Trade networks of the East, 3rd to 7th centuries: the view from Beirut (Lebanon) and Butrint (Albania) (fine wares, amphorae and kitchen wares)", in *LRCW3, Late Roman Coarse Wares, Cooking Wares and Amphorae in the Mediterranean. Archaeology and Archaeometry. Comparison Between Western and Eastern Mediterranean,* BAR Int. Ser. 2185, (Oxford, 2010), 95.

24 M. Buora, "Viabilità e insediamenti nell'antico Friuli. Un problema di continuità", in *La* Venetia *nell'area padano-danubiana. Le vie di comunicazione. Atti del Congresso Internazionale,* edited by G. Rosada (Padova, 1990), 52.

25 M. Mackensen, "Amphoren und Krüge", in V. Bierbrauer (ed.), *Hauskeramik, Invillino-Ibligo in Friaul I. Die römische Siedlung und das spätantik-frühmittelalterliche Castrum,* (München, 1987), 245–265, fig. 44, no. 8.

26 A. Opait, *Local and imported ceramics in the Roman province of Scythia (4th–6th centuries AD):aspects of economic life in the province of Scythia*, BAR Int. ser. 1274, (Oxford, 2004).

27 P. Arthur, "Eastern Mediterranean amphorae between 500 and 700: a view from Italy", in L. Saguì (ed.), *Ceramica in Italia; VI–VII secolo, Atti del Convegno in onore di John W. Hayes (Roma, 1995)*, (Firenze, 1998), 167.

28 E. Cirelli, D. Ferreri, "Catalogo", in A. Augenti, C. Bertelli, (eds.), *Felix Ravenna. La croce, la spada, la vela: l'alto Adriatico fra V e VI secolo.* Catalogo della Mostra (Ravenna, 2007). (Milano, 2007), 153, fig. VII.33; D. Ferreri, "Sepolture e riti funerari a Classe: una lunga prospettiva diacronica", in *Atti del V Congresso Nazionale di Archeologia Medievale (Foggia-Manfredonia, 2009)*, edited by G. Volpe and P. Favia, (Firenze, 2009), 459–464; D. Ferreri, "Spazi cimiteriali, pratiche funerarie e identità nella città di Classe", in *Archeologia Medievale* XXXVIII (2011), 53–68.

29 D. Papanikola Bakirtzi, "Ceramics in Late Antique Thessalonikē", in L. Salah Nasrallah, Ch. Bakirtzis, S.J. Friesen (eds.), *From Roman to Early Christian Thessalonikē. Studies in Religion and Archaeology*, (Boston, 2010), 274.

30 M. Casalini, M. Crespi. "Anfore tardoantiche di piccole dimensioni a fondo piatto dalle pendici nord orientali del Palatino. Nuovi dati alla luce di un riesame tipologico e petrografico", in *Rei Cretariae Romanae Fautores Acta* 41 (2010), 101–112.

31 D. Pieri, "Les centres de production d'amphores en Méditerranée orientale durant l'antiquité tardive: quelques remarques", in M. Bonifay, J.C. Tréglia (eds.), *LRCW2, Late Roman Coarse Wares, Cooking Wares and Amphorae in the Mediterranean. Archaeology and archaeometry,* 671–688. BAR Int. Ser. 1662, (Oxford, 2007), 611–625., 613–614.

32 J.Y. Empereur, M. Picon, "Les régions de production d'amphores impérial en Méditerranée orientale", in *Amphores romaines et histoire économique. Dix ans de recherché (Sienne 1986)*, (Roma, 1989), 236–243.

33 F. Burragato, M. Di Nezza, A.F. Ferrazzoli, M. Ricci, "Late Roman amphora types produced at Elaiussa Sebaste", in M. Bonifay, J.C. Tréglia (eds.), *LRCW2, Late Roman Coarse Wares, Cooking Wares and Amphorae in the Mediterranean. Archaeology and archaeometry,* BAR Int. Ser. 1662, (Oxford, 2007), 689–700; A.F. Ferrazzoli, M. Ricci, "Elaiussa Sebaste: produzioni e consumi di una città della Cilicia tra V e VII secolo", in M. Bonifay, J.C. Tréglia (eds.), *LRCW2, Late Roman Coarse Wares, Cooking Wares and Amphorae in the Mediterranean. Archaeology and archaeometry,*. BAR Int. Ser. 1662, (Oxford, 2007), 671–688.

34 D. Pieri, *Le commerce di vin oriental à l'époque byzantine (Ve–VIIe siècles). Le témoignage des amphores en Gaule,* (Beyrouth, 2005).

35 G. Fiaccadori, "I frammenti iscritti", in G. Bermond Montanari (ed.), *Ravenna e il porto di Classe. Venti anni di ricerche archeologiche a Ravenna e Classe*, (Imola, 1983), 238–241.

36 C. Panella, "Merci e scambi nel Mediterraneo tardoantico", in A. Carandini, L. Cracco Ruggini, A. Giardina (eds.), *Storia di Roma, vol. III. L'età tardoantica. II. I luoghi e le culture*, (Torino, 1993), 665–666; E. Cirelli, R. Lasi 2003, "Schede", in A. Augenti (ed.), Palatia—*Palazzi Imperiali tra Ravenna e Bisanzio.* Catalogo della mostra (Ravenna, 2002) (Ravenna, 2003), 59.

37 G. Lacerenza, "Le iscrizioni giudaiche in Italia dal I al VI secolo: tipologie, origine, distribuzione", in *I beni culturali ebraici in Italia: situazione attuale, problemi, prospettive e progetti per il futuro,* Atti del Convegno (Ravenna 2001), edited by M. Perani, (Ravenna, 2003), 71–92.

38 P. Reynolds, *Trades in the Western Mediterranean, A.D. 400–700: the ceramic evidence*. BAR Int. Ser. 604, (Oxford, 1995)., 71; P. Arthur, "Eastern Mediterranean amphorae between 500 and 700: a view from Italy", in L. Saguì (ed.), *Ceramica in Italia; VI–VII secolo, Atti del Convegno in onore di John W. Hayes (Roma, 1995)*, (Firenze, 1998), 162.

39 C.A.M. Glucker, *The city of Gaza in the Roman and Byzantine Periods*, BAR Int. Ser. 325, (Oxford 1987), 93–94.

40 D. Pieri, Les importations d'amphores orientales en Gaule méridionale durant l'Antiquité tardive et le Haut Moyen *Age*, in *Société Française d'étude de la céramique antique en Gaule*, Actes du Congrès d'Istres, (Marseille, 1998), 101–102.

41 B.M. Mancini, "Ceramica dalla basilica di San Severo: i rinvenimenti al di sotto della sala capitolare", in E. Cirelli, E. Giorgi, G. Lepore (eds.), *Economia e Territorio. L'Adriatico centrale tra tarda Antichità e alto Medioevo (IV–VIII sec.),* (Oxford, 2019), 155–161; M. Simonetti, "I materiali ceramici della basilica Petriana a Classe. Il contesto dell'abside", in E. Cirelli, F. Diosono, H. Patterson (eds.), *Le forme della crisi. Produzioni ceramiche e commercio nell'Italia centrale tra Romani e Longobardi (III–VIII secolo),* Atti del Convegno (Spoleto–Campiello sul Clutunno, 2012), (Bologna, 2015), 51.

42 P. Armstrong "Trade in the east Mediterranean in the 8th century", in *Byzantine Trade, 4th–12th Centuries. The Archaeology of Local, Regional and International Exchange. Papers of the Thirty-eighth Spring Symposium of Byzantine Studies, St John's College*, ed. by M.M. Mango, (Oxford, 2009), 160.

43 V. Vidrih Perko, *Amphorae of the Eastern Adriatic and its Northeastern Hinterland,* in S. Čače, A. Kurilić, F. Tassaux (eds.), *Les routes de l'Adriatique antique. Géographie et économiel Putovi Antičkog Jadrana. Geografija I Gospodarsto,* Actes de la Table ronde (Zadar, 2001), (Bordeaux-Zadar, 2006), 209–224.

44 R. Auriemma and E. Quiri, "La circolazione delle anfore in Adriatico tra V e VIII sec. d.C.", in S. Gelichi C. Negrelli (eds.), *La circolazione delle ceramiche nell'Adriatico tra Tarda Antichità ed Altomedioevo, III Incontro di Studio Cer.Am.Is. Sulle ceramiche tardoantiche ed altomedievale (Venezia, 2004)*, (Mantova, 2007), 46.

45 M.G. Maioli, "Strutture economico-commerciali e impianti produttivi nella Ravenna bizantina", in A. Carile (ed.), *Storia di Ravenna. Dall'età bizantina all'età ottoniana. II. 1. Territorio, economia e società*, (Venezia, 1991), 242, pl. 11, fig. 1.

46 P. Reynolds, *Hispania and the Roman Mediterranean, AD 100–700. Ceramics and Trade.* (London 2010.), 229.

47 H.S. Robinson, *The Athenian Agora, V, Pottery of the Roman Period. Chronology*, (Princeton, 1959).

48 M.L. Stoppioni Piccoli, "Le anfore", in G. Bermond Montanari (ed.), *Ravenna e il porto di Classe. Venti anni di ricerche archeologiche a Ravenna e Classe*, (Imola, 1983), 132, 139, nos. 8.14, 8.16; G. Piazzini, *Ravenna e il Levante. I ritrovamenti di Agorà M334 a Classe (RA)*, E. Cirelli, F. Diosono, H. Patterson (eds.), *Le forme della crisi. Produzioni ceramiche e commercio nell'Italia centrale tra Romani e Longobardi (III–VIII secolo)*, Atti del Convegno (Spoleto-Campiello sul Clutunno, 2012), (Bologna, 2015), 39–44.

49 L. Saguì, D. Manacorda, "L'esedra della Crypta Balbi e il monastero di S. Lorenzo in Pallacinis", in *Archeologia Laziale* 12\1 (1995), 121–134, fig. 4, no. 4.

50 P. Arthur, *Naples from Roman town to city-state: an archaeological perspective* (London, 2002), 150.

51 S. Keay, *Late Roman Amphorae in the Western Mediterranean. A Typology of Economic Study: the Catalan Evidence*, BAR Int. Ser. 196, (Oxford, 1984); P. Arthur, "Eastern Mediterranean amphorae between 500 and 700: a view from Italy", in L. Saguì (ed.), *Ceramica in Italia; VI–VII secolo, Atti del Convegno in onore di John W. Hayes (Roma, 1995)*, (Firenze, 1998), 134; E. Cirelli, D. Ferreri, "Catalogo", in A. Augenti, C. Bertelli, (eds.), *Felix Ravenna. La croce, la spada, la vela: l'alto Adriatico fra V e VI secolo.* Catalogo della Mostra (Ravenna, 2007). (Milano, 2007), 153, VII.34.

52 C. Capelli, "Il contributo delle analisi minero-petrografiche allo studio delle anfore Keay LII", in L. Saguì (ed.), *Ceramica in Italia; VI–VII secolo, Atti del Convegno in onore di John W. Hayes (Roma, 1995)*, (Firenze, 1998). 335–342.; F. Pacetti, "La questione delle Keay LII nell'ambito della produzione anforica in Italia", L. Saguì (ed.), *Ceramica in Italia; VI–VII secolo, Atti del Convegno in onore di John W. Hayes (Roma, 1995)*, (Firenze, 1998), 185–208.

53 R. Auriemma and E. Quiri, "La circolazione delle anfore in Adriatico tra V e VIII sec. d.C.", in S. Gelichi C. Negrelli (eds.), *La circolazione delle ceramiche nell'Adriatico tra Tarda Antichità ed Altomedioevo, III Incontro di Studio Cer.Am.Is. Sulle ceramiche tardoantiche ed altomedievale (Venezia, 2004)*, (Mantova, 2007), 50–51.

54 M. Cesarano, C. Corti, "Santa Maria in Pado Vetere and Po's Delta in the Light of new excavations (2014–2015)", in I. Borzić, E. Cirelli, K. Jelinčić, A. Konestra, I. Ožanić (eds.), *TRADE. Transformations of Adriatic Europe (2nd–9th c.)*, Proceedings of the International Conference (Zadar, 2016), fc.

55 J.W. Hayes, *Late Roman Pottery*, (London, 1972).

56 J. Mesić, "Podmorska zaštitna istrazivanja i rekognosciranja Odjela za zaštitu arheološke baštine u godini", in *Obavijesti* 32\2 (2000), 53–59.

57 M. Bonifay, *Etudes sur la céramique romaine tardive d'Afrique,* BAR Int. Ser. 1301, (Oxford, 2004).

58 G. Murialdo, "Alto-Adriatico e alto-Tirreno nel mondo mediterraneo: due mari a confronto tra VI e X secolo", in S. Gelichi C. Negrelli (eds.), *La circolazione delle ceramiche nell'Adriatico tra Tarda Antichità ed Altomedioevo, III Incontro di Studio Cer.Am.Is. Sulle ceramiche tardoantiche ed altomedievale (Venezia, 2004)*, (Mantova, 2007), 10.

59 T. MacMaster, "Not With a Bang? The Economics of Trade and the End of Byzantine North Africa", M. Lau, C. Franchi, and M. Di Rodi, eds. *Landscapes of Power* (Oxford, 2014), 73–91.

60 P. Reynolds, *Hispania and the Roman Mediterranean, AD 100–700. Ceramics and Trade.* (London 2010.), 130–131.

61 E. Baldi, *The coin evidence as a source for the history of Classe (Ravenna):*

excavations of the harbour area (2001–2005) and the Basilica of San Severo (2006–2010), BAR Int. Ser. 2736, (Oxford, 2015).

62 Ž. Tomičić, "Karolinško koplje iz varaždina – prinos poznavanju najranije prošlosti grada", in *Radovi Zavoda za znanstveni rad HAZU Varašdin* 24 (2013), 137–152.

63 C. Negrelli, "Towards a definition of early medieval pottery: amphorae and other vessels in the northern Adriatic between the 7th and the 8th centuries", in Gelichi, Hodges 2012—S. Gelichi, R. Hodges (ed.), *From one sea to another: trading places in the European and Mediterranean Early Middle Ages*, Proceedings of the International Conference (Comacchio, 2009), Seminari del Centro Interuniversitario per la Storia e l'Archeologia dell'Alto Medioevo, 3, (Turnhout, 2012), 415–438.

64 M. Leo Imperiale, "Anfore globulari dal Salento. Produzione e circolazione nell'Adriatico meridionale durante l'alto Medioevo", in *VII Congresso Nazionale di Archeologia Medievale*, Atti del Convegno (Lecce, 2015), edited by P. Arthur and M. Leo Imperiale, (Sesto Fiorentino, 2015), 426–431.

65 J. Vroom, *Early medieval pottery finds from recent excavations at Butrint, Albania*, in *Atti del IX Congresso Internazionale sulla Ceramica Medievale nel Mediterraneo (Venezia, 2009)*, (Firenze, 2012), 291.

66 G. Pasquali, "Alla ricerca dell'anfora perduta: recipienti e misure del vino dal tardo antico all'alto medioevo", in D. Balestracci, A. Barlucchi, F. Franceschi, P. Nanni, G. Piccinni, A. Zorzi, *Uominipaesaggistorie. Studi di storia medievale per Giovanni Cherubini*, (Siena, 2012), 459–466.

67 V. Vidrih Perko, "Seaborne Trade Routes in the North East Adriatic and their Connection to the Hinterland in the late Antiquity", in G.P. Brogiolo, P. Delogu (eds.), *L'Adriatico dalla tarda Antichità all'età carolingia*, (Firenze, 2005, 49–77.

68 M. Vicelja-Matijašić, "Byzantium and Istria: some aspects of byzantine presence in Istria", in *Acta Histriae* 13 (2005), 185–204.

69 N. Jakšić, "Il ruolo delle chiese rurali nella formazione del ducato croato medievale", in *Hortus Artium Medievalium* 14 (2008), 105–106.

70 D. Dzino, *Becoming Slav, Becoming Croat. Identify Transformations in Post-Roman and Early Medieval Dalmatia*, (Leiden, 2010), 155–175.

71 M. Jurković, "Some aspects of continuity and discontinuity between Late Antiquity and the Early Middle Ages in Dalmatia", in *Dalmatia, Predci i predšasnici, mitovi i utopije na Balkanu*, Proceedings of the Conference, (Blagoevgrad, 1997), 415–427; F. Curta, "A note on trade and trade centers in the eastern and northern Adriatic region between the eighth and the ninth century", in *Hortus Artium Medievalium* 16 (2010), 267–276.

72 M. Petrinec, "Metal Objects of Byzantine Origin in Medieval Graves from Croatia", in *Towards Rewriting? New Approaches to Byzantine Archaeology and Art*, Proceedings of the Symposium on Byzantine Art and Archaeology (Cracow, 2008), edited by P. Grotowski and S. Skrzyniarz, (Warsaw, 2010), 197–212.

73 *Spatheia* and *ARS* vessels are exposed in the city museum. For a catalogue see: I. Borzić, M. Čelhar, K. Gusar, M. Ilkić, M. Radović, D. Vujević, *Arheološka istraživanja okoliša crkve sv. Križa u Ninu. Katalog izložbe povodom 50. obljetnice Odjela za arheologiju Sveučilišta u Zadru*, Zadar 2013.

74 J. Ferluga, "Navigation et commerce dans l'Adriatique au VIIe et VIIIe siècles", in *Byzantinische Forschungen* 12 (1987), 49–51.

75 C. Beltrame, M. Bondioli, "A hypothesis on the development of Mediterranean ship construction from Antiquity to Late Middle Ages", in *Connected by the Sea. Proceedings of the 10th International Symposium on Boat and Ship*

Archaeology (Roskilde, 2003), edited by L. Blue, F. Hocker and A. Englert, (Oxford, 2006), 89–94.

76 T. Brown, *Gentlemen and Officers: Imperial Administration and Aristocratic Power in Byzantine Italy*, (Rome, 1984), 91.

77 S. Gelichi, "La storia di una nuova città: Venezia nell'alto Medioevo", in V. West-Harling (ed.), *Three empires, three cities: identity, material culture and legitimacy in Venice, Ravenna and Rome (750–1000)*, (Turnhout, 2015), 51–98.

78 J. Hoffmann, "Die östliche Adriaküste als Hauptnachschubbasis für der venezianischen Sklavenhandel bis zum Ausgang des elften Jahrhunderts", in *Vierteljahrschrift für Sozial und Wirtschaftsgeschichte* 55 (1968), 165–181.

79 G. Arnaldi, *Le origini dello stato della Chiesa*, (Roma, 1987), 111.

80 N. Mancassola, "Paesaggi tardoantichi e paesaggi altomedievali: alcuni contesti romagnoli a confronto", in E. Cirelli, E. Giorgi, G. Lepore (eds.), *Economia e Territorio. L'Adriatico centrale tra tarda Antichità e alto Medioevo (IV–VIII sec.)*, (Oxford, 2019), 245–252.

81 S Gelichi, "Tra Comacchio e Venezia. Economia, società e insediamenti nell'arco nordadriatico durante l'Alto Medioevo", in *Genti nel Delta da Spina a Comacchio, Uomini, Territorio e Culto dall'Antichità all'alto Medioevo*, Catalogo della mostra, edited by F. Berti, M. Bollini, S. Gelichi and J. Ortalli, (Ferrara, 2007), 365–386.

82 M. Librenti, "Primi dati relativi all'età medievale delle ricognizioni di superficie nel territorio delle Ville Unite", in *In agro decimano. Per un catalogo del patrimonio archeologico del territorio a sud di Ravenna*, edited by G. Montevecchi and P. Novara, (Ravenna, 2000), 214.

83 M. Librenti, "Ricognizione di superficie e insediamento medievale nella pianura emiliano romagnola: alcune considerazioni", in *Atti del II Congresso Nazionale di Archeologia Medievale*, edited by G.P. Brogiolo, (Firenze, 2000), 170–174.

84 G.P. Brogiolo, S. Gelichi, "La ceramica invetriata tardo-antica e medioevale nel nord Italia", in *La ceramica invetriata tardoantica e altomedievale in Italia*, edited by L. Paroli, (Firenze, *1992*), 30.

85 A. Molinari, "Fonti materiali, archeologia e storia economica del Medioevo: verso quali modelli interpretativi?", in F. Ammannati, *Dove va la Storia Economica?: metodi e prospettive, secc. XIII–XVIII*, (Firenze, 2011), 307–321.

86 A. Augenti, "A tale of two cities. Rome and Ravenna between 7th and 9th century AD", in *774. Ipotesi su una transizione*, edited by S. Gasparri, (Turnhout, 2008), 175–198.

87 E. Cirelli, E. Lo Mele, "Lacultura materiale di San Severo alla luce delle recenti ricerche", in P. Racagni (ed.), *La basilica ritrovata: i restauri dei mosaici di San Severo a Classe, Ravenna*, (Bologna, 2010), 39–54.

88 N. Mancassola, "Le forme del popolamento rurale nel territorio Decimano dalla caduta dell'Impero Romano all'anno Mille", in *Orme nei Campi. Archeologia a sud di Ravenna*, edited by M. Ficara and V. Manzelli, Firenze 2008, 89–103

89 M. Cavalazzi, M. Abballe, A. Benato, M. De Felicibus, "Archeologia dei paesaggi in Bassa Romagna. Il progetto 'Bassa Romandiola' (2009–2013)", in *Storiografia e Archeologia nella "Romandiola". Tradizione e nuove ricerche sul territorio, Atti del Convegno del Centro di Studi sulla Romandiola nord occidentale (Lugo, 2012)*, (Lugo, 2015), 129–172.

90 For the birth of new directional centers: N. Mancassola, "Le forme del popolamento rurale nel territorio Decimano dalla caduta dell'Impero Romano all'anno Mille", in *Orme nei Campi. Archeologia a sud di Ravenna*, edited by M. Ficara and V. Manzelli, Firenze 2008, 89–103.

91 E. Cirelli, G. Lepore, M. Silani, "Ceramiche e vita quotidiana a Senigallia tra

Medioevo ed età moderna: il caso di via Gherardi", in *Facta,* 7 (2013), 2015, 49, fig. 8.

92 In Koper\Capria, *Acroma depurata*'s small containers have been identified together with "undefined globular forms". See V. Vidrih Perko, *Amphorae of the Eastern Adriatic and its Northeastern Hinterland,* in S. Čače, A. Kurilić, F. Tassaux (eds.), *Les routes de l'Adriatique antique. Géographie et économie/ Putovi Antičkog Jadrana. Geografija I Gospodarsto,* Actes de la Table ronde (Zadar, 2001), (Bordeaux-Zadar, 2006), 219.

93 C. Negrelli, "Dalla tarda Antichità all'alto Medioevo (V–IX secolo)", in S. Gelichi, C. Negrelli (eds.), *A misura d'uomo. Archeologia del territorio cesenate e valutazione dei depositi,* (Firenze, 2008), 251.

94 S. Cosentino, "Ricchezza e investimento della chiesa di Ravenna tra la tarda antichità e l'alto medioevo", in S. Gelichi, R. Hodges (ed.), *From one sea to another: trading places in the European and Mediterranean Early Middle Ages,* Proceedings of the International Conference (Comacchio, 2009), Seminari del Centro Interuniversitario per la Storia e l'Archeologia dell'Alto Medioevo, 3, (Turnhout, 2012), 417–440.

95 S. Cosentino, "L'approvvigionamento annonario di Ravenna dal V all'VIII secolo: l'organizzazione e i riflessi socio-economici", in *Ravenna da capitale imperiale a capitale esarcale,* Atti CISAM XVII (Ravenna, 2004), (Spoleto, 2005), 431.

96 A. Carile, "La società ravennate dall'Esarcato agli Ottoni", in A. Carile (ed.), *Storia di Ravenna, II.2, Dall'età bizantina all'età ottoniana. Ecclesologia, cultura e arte,* (Venezia, 1992), 395.

97 S. Cosentino, "Ricchezza e investimento della chiesa di Ravenna tra la tarda antichità e l'alto medioevo", in S. Gelichi, R. Hodges (ed.), *From one sea to another: trading places in the European and Mediterranean Early Middle Ages,* Proceedings of the International Conference (Comacchio, 2009), Seminari del Centro Interuniversitario per la Storia e l'Archeologia dell'Alto Medioevo, 3, (Turnhout, 2012), 419.

98 R. Hodges, "Adriatic Sea Trade in an European perspective", in S. Gelichi, R. Hodges (ed.), *From one sea to another: trading places in the European and Mediterranean Early Middle Ages,* Proceedings of the International Conference (Comacchio, 2009), Seminari del Centro Interuniversitario per la Storia e l'Archeologia dell'Alto Medioevo, 3, (Turnhout, 2012), 207–234.

99 T. Mannoni, H.R. Pfeifer, V. Serneels, "Giacimenti e cave di pietra ollare nelle Alpi", in *La pietra ollare dalla preistoria all'età moderna,* Atti del Convegno (Como, 1982), (Como, 1987), 7–46.

100 M.T. Gatto, "Pietra ollare dalle Marche del Nord: ricostruzione delle antiche rotte commerciali nell'alto e medio Adriatico tra tarda Antichità e alto Medioevo", in I. Borzić, E. Cirelli, K. Jelinčić, A. Konestra, I. Ožanić (eds.), *TRADE. Transformations of Adriatic Europe (2nd–9th c.),* Proceedings of the International Conference (Zadar, 2016), fc.

101 E. Cirelli, G. Lepore, M. Silani, "La tavola di Duchi, Vescovi e Mercanti a Senigallia", in *Atti del Convegno Internazionale (Faenza, 2015),* (Firenze, 2016), 133, fig. 1.5.

102 M. Cavalazzi, M. Ficara, "Importazioni e cultura materiale in età tardoantica nell'Ager Decimanus", in E. Cirelli, F. Diosono, H. Patterson (eds.), *Le forme della crisi. Produzioni ceramiche e commercio nell'Italia centrale tra Romani e Longobardi (III–VIII secolo),* Atti del Convegno (Spoleto-Campiello sul Clutunno, 2012), (Bologna, 2015), 53–61.

103 E. Cirelli, D. Ferreri, "Vivere e morire nel castello di Rontana. Lo sfruttamento del gesso in un insediamento di fondazione medievale della vallata del Lamone",

in P. Lucci, S. Piastra, *I gessi di Brisighella e Rontana,* Memorie dell'Istituto Italiano di Speleologia, s. II, 28, (2015), 545–568.

104 M. Cortelazzo, "Le macine in cloritoscisto granatifero (pietra ollare) della Valle d'Aosta", in *Bullettin d'Etudes Preisthoriques et archeologiques alpines,* XXIV, Numéro special consacré aux Actes du XIIIe Colloque sur les Alpes dans l'Antiquité (Brusson, 2012), (Aosta, 2013), 89–124.

105 O. Williams Thorpe, *Provenance and Archaeology of Roman millstones from the Roman Mediterranean,* in *Journal of Archaeological Science* 15 (1988), 283.

106 D. Ellmers, *Frühmittelalterliche Handels-schiffahrt in die Mittel und Nordeuropa,* (Neumünster, 1972); F. Fenwick, *The Graveney Boat,* BAR Int. Ser. 53, (Oxford, 1978); C. Beltrame, G. Boetto, *Macine da relitti,* in *Archeologia Subacquea,* 2 (1997), 171.

107 M. Pohl, *Quern-stones and Tuff as Indicators of Medieval European Trade*, in *Papers from the Institute of Archaeology,* 20 (2010), 148–153.

108 S. Gelichi, C. Negrelli, D. Calaon, E. Grandi, "Comacchio tra IV e X secolo: territorio, abitato e infrastrutture", in *Atti del IV Congresso Nazionale di Archeologia Medievale (Abbazia di San Galgano, Chiusdino-Siena, 2006)*, edited by R. Francovich and M. Valenti, (Firenze, 2006), 121.

109 G.P. Brogiolo, S. Massa, B. Portulano, M. Vitali, "Associazioni ceramiche nei contesti della prima fase longobarda di Brescia-S. Giulia", in G.P. Brogiolo, S. Gelichi (eds.), *Le ceramiche altomedievali (fine VI–X secolo) in Italia settentrionale: produzione e commerci*, (Mantova, 1996), 15–32.

110 A. Augenti, E. Cirelli "From suburb to port: the rise (and fall) of Classe as a centre of trade and redistribution", in S. Keay (ed.), *Rome, Portus and the Mediterranean,* (London, 2012), 205–221.

111 T. Brown, N. Christie, "Was there a Byzantine model of settlement in Italy?", in *Mélanges de l'École Française de Rome. Moyen-Age*101\2 (1989), 377–399.

112 S. Cosentino, "L'approvvigionamento annonario di Ravenna dal V all'VIII secolo: l'organizzazione e i riflessi socio-economici", in *Ravenna da capitale imperiale a capitale esarcale*, Atti CISAM XVII (Ravenna, 2004), (Spoleto, 2005), 418–420.

113 S. Gelichi C. Negrelli, "Ceramica e circolazione delle merci nell'Adriatico tra VII e X secolo", in *Actas del VIII Congreso Internacional de Cerámica Medieval (Ciudad Real\Almagro, 2006)*, edited by J. Zozaya, M. Retuerce, M.A. Hervás, A. de Juan, (Ciudad Real, 2009), vol. I, 51.

114 Six ports are listed by Andrea Agnello, during Felix bishop's life. See:Agn., *L.P. Rav.,* 370.

115 E. Kislinger, "Dyrrhachion und die Küsten von Epirus und Dalmatien im Frühen Mittelalter—Beobacthungen zur Entwicklung der byzantinischen Oberhoheit", in *Millennium* 8 (2011), 330.

116 T. Brown, "L'aristocrazia di Ravenna da Giustiniano a Carlo Magno", in *Felix Ravenna*, vol. 131/132 (1986), 91–98.

117 S. Cosentino, "Constans II, Ravenna's Autocephaly and the Panel of the Privileges in St. Apollinare in Classe: A Reappraisal", in T.G. Kolias, K.G. Pitsakis, C. Synellis (eds.), *Aureus. Volume dedicated to Professor Evangelos K. Chrysos*, (Athens, 2014), 153–169.

118 T. Brown, "The transformation of the Roman Mediterranean 400–900", in *The Oxford Illustrated History of Medieval Europe*, (Oxford, 1988), 1–62.

119 T. Dickinson, D. Griffiths, *The Making of Kingdoms*, (Oxford, 1999).

Part III

Ravenna after the exarchate

10 *Renovatio*, continuity, innovation*

Ravenna's role in legitimation and collective memory (eighth to ninth centuries)

As a capital and symbol of Byzantine power, in the eighth century, Ravenna was central to the Lombard kings and popes in their struggle to co-opt Byzantine authority on the peninsula. But how did different groups, i.e., the popes, the Lombards, and the Ravennati themselves, perceive the city and its role in legitimating, or denying, their claims to authority and in the creation of their collective memory? This chapter will argue that while the Lombards in the eighth century resumed expansion, and thus taking Ravenna can be seen as a continuation of traditional territorial extension, it was based on new royal ideological claims of *renovatio* developed by King Liutprand and his successors. As a result, the city became a site of contention between the still developing but competing ideological claims of the popes and Lombard kings. Although elements of both positions were innovative, the Lombards stressed *renovatio,* and their role as Italy and the pope's defenders, while the popes emphasised continuity with the past, as representatives of St. Peter, despite new expanded claims of authority.

Although the popes stressed their links to St. Peter as the ultimate font of authority, they also laid claim to Romano-Byzantine imperial power. In the seventh and early eighth centuries, the popes maintained a presence on the Palatine hill, a place long associated with imperial authority. By the later eighth century, as part of the complex process of developing their ideological claims while seeking aid against the Lombards, the popes moved back to the Lateran, their traditional base. Part of the significance of places like Ravenna, and the Palatine, for the popes in the fraught decades of the mid-eighth century was to keep them out of the hands of groups like the Lombards in order to deny access to alternate narratives of legitimacy based on imperial authority. What that ultimately meant for places like Ravenna, and, perhaps for a short period of time, the Palatine, was that it was considered a place that had, in the past, been important. Indeed, from the mid-eighth century, both Lombards and Carolingians emphasised the physicality of the city of Ravenna for the assumption of imperial power. The Lombard king Aistulf situated himself in the palace structure upon conquering the city, while Charlemagne and his successors exported pieces of *spolia* from

Ravenna to the new capital at Aachen. By appropriating Ravenna as a site of imperial power and then dismantling and transferring its cultural heritage, the Carolingians via this *translatio* completed the idea of a glorious past Ravenna, necessarily contrasted with the current city at the end of the eighth century.

Finally, scholars have noted Ravenna's marginal place in ninth-century Italy, but have not considered the implications of the exclusion of contemporary Ravennati from the collective memory of the city constructed by dominant Carolingian and papal narratives. While the main source for ninth-century Ravenna, Agnellus' *Liber Pontificalis ecclesiae Ravennatis,* does show his *campanilismo,*[1] or local pride, it also demonstrates a desire to rewrite the Carolingian and papal narratives of Ravenna's history to claim continued relevance for the city and its ecclesiastical and military elite. Indeed, despite Ravenna's lack of centrality in the papal and Carolingian conceptions of imperial authority after 774, Ravenna and its archbishops complicated the negotiation of the relationship between the two because of its strategic, and therefore the archbishop's political, importance to the Carolingians.

In 568, soon after Justinian's death, the Lombards began to carve out a kingdom in the north of Italy. At the end of the sixth century, as part of their general defensive strategy and specifically to combat the invading Lombards, the Byzantines embarked upon an administrative reorganisation of the Italian peninsula. In addition to the systematic fortification of sites, the Byzantines placed power firmly in the hands of the military elite and divided the peninsula into regions either placed directly under the authority of the military governor of Italy, the exarch, or under the authority of a duke, who nevertheless was subject to the exarch.[2] As in Africa, the exarch was to be the head of the military and civil administration for Italy.[3]

Despite the exarch and the Lombard kings holding the highest authority in Byzantine and Lombard Italy, respectively, in practice, in the sixth and seventh centuries, regional leaders, mainly dukes, were largely autonomous,[4] although the Lombard kings used the concept of a united Italy to try and assert their authority over their newly conquered subjects and their own Lombard aristocracy.[5] In the last twenty years, research on sixth- through eighth-century Italy has, in fact, set out to deconstruct rulers' claims of authority, and has demonstrated the level of political fragmentation and limits of royal Lombard and imperial Byzantine power in this period.[6] By the end of the seventh century, the Byzantines focussed their resources on retaining their territories in the south of Italy, signalled by the creation of the theme of Sicily between 692 and 695 by Justinian II.[7] In the eighth century, although the Byzantines may have wanted to retain formal control over the exarchate, the territory centred on Ravenna, they could not spare the resources to defend it.[8] Therefore, it became an area over which Lombards, the papacy, and later the Franks tried to exercise their expansionist policies.[9]

Thus, with the exception of the extreme south of the peninsula, which retained both political and economic ties with Byzantium, despite the authority of the exarch, Byzantine Italy was ruled by the popes and dukes, who by the early eighth century were autonomous regional leaders and pursued their own political agendas, and thus the political situation should be understood above all as one of local interests.[10] At the same time, as elsewhere in Europe, bishops were gaining power, taking over imperial functions in many cases, especially in the case of the bishop of Rome, the pope, who from the seventh century were responsible for basically all building, including secular projects like maintaining the Aurelian Walls.[11] Promoting both of these trends, in 732 or 733, the Byzantine Emperor Leo III transferred the ecclesiastical provinces of southern Italy from Rome's control to the patriarch of Constantinople, further linking southern Italy to the Byzantine empire and leaving Rome as an autonomous duchy.[12]

It is important to acknowledge the limitations of the power of the popes, Lombard kings, and even the exarchs in the seventh and eighth centuries, and one of the bases of this chapter's argument is that the seventh and early eighth centuries was a period in which no one group had hegemonic control. Instead of emphasising the limits of power, however, this chapter will show that the lack of political and cultural hegemony, which included the ideas of what being Roman and Roman power meant, allowed for more social agency and experimentation. Although the Lombard kings, popes, and even archbishops of Ravenna focussed on different aspects of Roman authority in their developing ideological claims, it remained the standard for legitimation.

From the fifth century, the Honorian emperors, Odoacer, the Ostrogothic kings, and later the exarchs made Ravenna their seat of power in the fifth and sixth centuries to avoid, and at times deliberately counter, the entrenched power of the Roman senate and later the popes in Rome, the empire's traditional capital.[13] Ravenna's fifth- and sixth-century monumentalisation, which has been extensively studied, therefore bolstered its authority and lent it political legitimacy.[14] At the beginning of the fifth century, Galla Placidia and Honorius deliberately chose Ravenna as an imperial residence, and began a building program to turn Ravenna into a new, Christian, *sedes imperii.* In churches such as San Giovanni Evangelista, Galla Placidia and the Honorian emperors used imperial portraits to link the imperial family to Christ and orthodoxy, as well as to the eastern Roman emperors.[15] Subsequently, the archbishops of Ravenna in the later sixth and seventh centuries commissioned imperial imagery as part of a multi-faceted ideological program to raise the status of their see.[16] The sixth-century archbishops of Ravenna gained important imperial privileges, which elevated their status in the ecclesiastical hierarchy, and also began to create a lasting image of their see by establishing a historical foundation for its importance and by producing visual representations of its bishops together with Byzantine emperors, reinforcing the link between Ravenna and imperial favour.[17] This policy was continued and elaborated in the seventh century, and was one of the key factors that made Ravenna so attractive to the Lombard kings, and Lombard occupation of it dangerous to the popes, in the eighth century. Ravenna reached the height of its ecclesiastical importance in 666, when Emperor Constans II granted Ravenna a privilege of autocephaly, which gave the archbishop autonomy and allowed him to be consecrated by three of his suffragan bishops instead of having to go to Rome to be confirmed and consecrated by the pope.[18]

In 682, Constantine IV, as part of a larger effort to reconcile theological differences in the churches of the Byzantine empire, officially revoked the *Typus* of autocephaly and subordinated Ravenna to Rome once more, although the church of Ravenna gained important privileges and retained an elevated status in the west.[19] Although the grant of autocephaly was short-lived, its memory was fundamental to the ambitions of the eighth-century archbishops of Ravenna, who continued to consolidate their power in the exarchate by soliciting privileges from the Byzantine emperors and by appealing to secular rulers, whether the exarchs in disputes with their clergy, or the Lombards and Carolingians in their struggles with the popes.

From the seventh century, while Ravenna's archbishops were furthering their own ambitions, the Lombard kings were consolidating and expanding their control. Since the Lombard invasion the Lombard kings had relied on the support of northern bishops, who were often at odds with the papacy,[20] but from the end of the seventh century the church and the kings' role as its protector and promoter became increasingly important to the royal ideological program. Continuing crises in the Byzantine empire, and in Italy struggles between the Byzantine emperors and the popes, caused a search for the reasons behind Byzantine defeats, seen as divine punishments, and led to the questioning of individual emperors' ability to protect their people and enforce orthodoxy.[21] Thus, the Lombard kings formulated a new type of ideology to justify their rule, based on an idea of *renovatio,* or a renewal of the entire peninsula under the Catholic Lombard kings. King Cunipert began the royal program, calling the Synod of Pavia in 698 in concert with Pope Sergius at the Lombard capital to address the Three Chapters controversy.[22] It rapidly developed in the early eighth century during the reign of King Liutprand (r. 712–744) along with the resumption of Lombard territorial aspirations over the exarchate and Byzantine Italy generally, and reached its pinnacle under King Aistulf (749–755), who briefly conquered Ravenna in 751.

Drawing largely on Christian imperial ideology, the Lombard kings positioned themselves as protectors and promoters of the church as well as administrators of justice in ecclesiastical disputes. The development of royal ideology can be traced through subsequent additions to the Lombard Laws. In the prologue to the laws of the first year of his reign (712), Liutprand called himself a Catholic Christian prince, who through God's wisdom and inspiration promulgated the laws and judged wisely, and drew parallels between himself and King Solomon.[23] Liutprand called the Lombard nation happy and Catholic, as well as favoured by God in the prologue for 717, while in that of 721 he asserted that the Lombards were divinely chosen.[24]

In addition to making claims about the holy nature of the Lombard state and kingship in the prologues, beginning with the laws of the eleventh year (723) Liutprand began to issue laws which he stated were for the religious salvation of the kingdom, including laws drawn from canon law regarding sorcery, adultery, and marriage.[25] For example, laws 33 and 34 prohibit men from marrying their godmothers, goddaughters, or the widows of their cousins, and state that the pope in Rome had sent him a letter stating that such unions should not take place, but it was God's wish that Liutprand promulgate it.[26] In concert with a new attack on the exarchate, in 727 he issued another set of laws to position himself as the defender of orthodoxy in Italy. In addition to laws banning sorcery and calling for judges to seek out witches and sorcerers, in the prologue to his laws from that year he stated that, in defence of the Catholic law of the kingdom, all Lombards must be Catholic.[27]

Liutprand further portrayed himself as the protector of orthodoxy in inscriptions in the palace that he built for himself with marble and mosaic *spolia* from Rome at Cortoleona, *c.* 729. They describe the Byzantine emperor falling into a pit of schism, thus presenting the dichotomy between the schismatic emperor and Liutprand, the defender and promoter of the faith.[28] As in the laws, in the inscriptions Liutprand compared himself to the Old Testament King Solomon, stressing the king's role as a mediator between his subjects and the divine, alluding that the Catholic Lombards had taken up the mantle of the Chosen People from the Romans, who were being punished for their sins and the sins of their leader.[29] Liutprand's successor Aistulf further asserted that the Roman people had been given to him by God in the preface to the laws issued in 749, the first year of his rule, thereby explicitly claiming the remaining Byzantine territories.[30]

The increasing importance of Catholicism in Lombard royal ideology was independent of the pope, and of the ecclesiastical hierarchy in the Lombard kingdom. Unlike their Carolingian counterparts in the later eighth century, the Lombard kings followed the example of Roman and Byzantine emperors and did not receive ecclesiastical consecration; indeed, the church played no constitutional role in royal succession.[31] The conquest of Ravenna, an imperial capital rich in Christian imperial imagery, was a critical element in this ideological program, but Lombard ambitions led to conflict with the popes, who began to claim Ravenna and other former imperial territories for themselves as part of their Republic of St. Peter.

During the 720s and 730s the political situation in Italy was volatile, which resulted in various challenges to Byzantine imperial authority and the beginnings of papal and royal Lombard ideology that justified rule over Byzantine territory. In 723/4, because of discontent over Leo's heavy taxation, Pope Gregory II stopped sending taxes to Constantinople, a move which was viewed by the emperor as tantamount to rebellion.[32] In response, the exarch Paul gathered an army from Ravenna and the Pentapolis and marched to Rome to punish the pope.[33] In the end, he was stopped by the Romans along with the Lombards of Spoleto and the Lombard kingdom adjacent to the duchy of Rome, and had to return to Ravenna unsuccessful.[34] Initially the armies followed Paul to Rome, but soon after his failure, in 725/6, the military elite of the exarchate, the Pentapolis and the Veneto rebelled, each electing their own dukes. A battle ensued between imperial and papal factions in Ravenna during which the exarch Paul was killed.[35] The armies of Ravenna and the Veneto also sought to elect their own emperor, but Pope Gregory opposed the idea, since any emperor in Italy supported by the army could pose a threat to his autonomy.[36]

In 727, Liutprand marched again on the exarchate, a continuation and intensification of his previous policies. Taking advantage of the discord, earlier in his reign, Liutprand pushed into Byzantine territory. He seized the important city of Osimo in the Pentapolis, reducing the Pentapolis to the Adriatic coast and the road from Rimini to Rome, as well as several *castra* in Emilia.[37] The reception to Liutprand in the exarchate was mixed; while he had to conquer some cities, others greeted him as a liberator, preferring Lombard to Byzantine rule.[38]

After a brief period of peace in the early 730s, hostilities resumed, culminating in the brief Lombard conquest of Ravenna and another papal alliance with the southern dukes.[39] In 741, the new pope, Zacharias, sent an embassy to Liutprand regarding four cities in the duchy of Rome that Liutprand had captured in 739 in retaliation for Gregory III's alliance with the southern dukes.[40] In exchange for the return of the cities, Zacharias reversed the policy of his predecessors Gregory II and Gregory III and sent the Roman army to help Liutprand against the duke of Spoleto, Transamund.[41] However, after he had restored order in the duchies and bound them to the kingdom, Liutprand hesitated to return the four cities that he had promised to the papacy.[42] In response, Zacharias travelled to Terni to appeal to Liutprand personally.

Despite the divergent interests of the popes and the Lombard kings, Liutprand's claims for further Lombard expansion were based on his championing Catholicism. Zacharias knew that he could not rely on the Byzantines for aid against the Lombards, and in fact was the first pope not to seek papal confirmation from the emperor.[43] While his predecessor Gregory sought to weaken the Lombard kings through strategic alliances, Zacharias and his successor Stephen II tried a new tactic, and made personal appeals to both the Lombard and Frankish kings. This strategy proved highly effective, perhaps because the popes confronted the kings with the physical presence of the heir to St. Peter. Liutprand and Zacharias concluded a twenty-year peace between the Lombard kingdom and the duchy of Rome, and Liutprand formally gave over to St. Peter, and therefore the pope as his representative, the four cities seized from the duchy.[44] Additionally, he freed the captives he had taken from the various Byzantine provinces of Italy, delivering them to the pope, including captives from Ravenna—the consuls Leo, Sergius, Victor, and Agnellus.[45] As Tom Noble stresses, the pope acted as an independent head of state, ruler of the new Republic of St. Peter, instead of on the Byzantine emperor's behalf, and the *Liber Pontificalis*'s discussion of these events contains the first unambiguous description of the papal territory as *respublica*.[46] Although the terminology is innovative, one should not forget the insecure political position of the popes in the 740s. As they would after Aistulf's conquest of Ravenna in 751, it was at especially perilous moments that the popes made grander assertions, drawing on the traditional authority of St. Peter.

Indeed, after concluding this treaty with the pope in 741/2, Liutprand once again marched against the exarchate in 742/743, taking the *castrum* of Cesena, and apparently planned a siege and blockade of Ravenna itself.[47] Although Liutprand respected the authority of St. Peter, and therefore the pope, over the duchy of Rome as a whole, he felt that he could attack the exarchate with impunity. Both the archbishop of Ravenna, John, and the exarch Eutychius sent a letter to the pope begging him for aid against the Lombards.[48] In response, the pope sent the bishop of Mentana and *vicedominus*, Benedict, and the *primicerius notariorum* Ambrose as ambassadors with gifts to Liutprand, asking him to leave Ravenna and give back Cesena, which Liutprand refused to do.[49] Zacharias then decided to go and appeal to Liutprand himself.[50]

The journey of the pope from Rome to Lombard territory to come and beseech the Lombard king in his capital was a dramatic performance that Liutprand could not ignore. He eventually agreed to give back the territory that he had taken from the city of Ravenna and restored two-thirds of the territory of Cesena to the exarchate, stating that he already had agreed to restore the *castrum* but only after his envoys returned from Constantinople.[51] Liutprand's appeal to Constantinople shows that he, and his successors, were determined to treat the exarchate and the newly acknowledged Roman state as two separate entities, the first ruled by a secular ruler, and thus open to conquest, and the other under the spiritual protection of the pope, a distinction maintained by his successor Aistulf as well.[52] Doing so allowed Liutprand to position himself as the champion of the Catholic faith while still expanding territorially. The problem was that the papacy laid claim to the exarchate, depicting its inhabitants as part of its flock, and thus an attack on it was construed as an attack on St. Peter.[53]

After Liutprand's death, popes continued to make personal appeals to Lombard kings, turning the royal ideology of kings as defenders of the faith to their advantage. Pope Zacharias employed a similar strategy in 749 against King Ratchis (r. 744–749/756–757). Since he demanded in-person that Ratchis leave Perugia, a town on the military road that linked Rome and Ravenna, the king was forced to acquiesce.[54] Despite the potential for spies and information to pass with them, he could not limit pilgrims from travelling to Rome.[55] Ratchis' brother and successor, Aistulf (r. 749–756), had similar problems with Pope Stephen. After sending envoys to Aistulf in newly conquered Ravenna in 751 and realising that military aid against the Lombard that he had requested from the Byzantine emperor Constantine V was not forthcoming, in 753 Stephen II sent a secret message to Pepin through a pilgrim, asking that the Franks send an embassy to bring him to Francia.[56] In an attempt to avoid making concessions to the pope, when Stephen arrived at Pavia, Aistulf sent a message to him that he was only willing to discuss the duchy of Rome; territory acknowledged to be under the authority of St. Peter, neither Ravenna and the exarchate nor any other former Byzantine territories captured by the Lombards were up for discussion.[57] After entering Pavia and exchanging gifts with Aistulf, Stephen pursued the subject anyway, and John the *silentarius* gave the imperial letters to the king, but Aistulf would not be persuaded. The Frankish envoys then asked Aistulf to let Stephen go with them to Francia. Although Aistulf tried to persuade the pope not to go, he gave his permission, and thus in November 753 Stephen and the Frankish envoys departed Pavia.[58] Aistulf, like his predecessors Liutprand and Ratchis, was at a disadvantage in a face-to-face meeting with the pope. Although he refused to acknowledge that Ravenna too was under the protection of St. Peter, mainly by forbidding discussion of the issue, he could not stop Stephen from going to Francia, even though he was aware that the outcome would be potentially disastrous.

For Aistulf, it was paramount that Ravenna remained outside of papal control. In 751, he conquered the city, effectively ending Byzantine rule in most of Italy. Like Theodoric and the Ostrogoths in the late fifth and early sixth centuries,[59] in the eighth century Aistulf and the Lombards linked Rome and Ravenna as the ideological foundations for their claims to the empire. Upon seizing Ravenna, Aistulf took over the palace complex as his own,[60] thus positioning himself as the latest in the series of leaders who had laid claim to the right to rule Italy since 402, when Ravenna became the imperial residence of the western Roman emperor. The palace was erected at the end of the fourth or beginning of the fifth century for the last of the western Roman emperors, with the major work on the residential buildings completed by the mid-fifth century; it served as the base of the Roman emperors, the Ostrogothic kings and the exarchs, and finally Aistulf.[61] Thus, despite changes in the ruling group, the palace remained the seat of power throughout late antiquity for practical reasons, but also because it was already established as a proper centre of power in the minds of the citizens.[62]

The palace's importance as a locus of power was reflected in its imperial and royal imagery. In the palace, in the *triclinium* (dining hall) called *ad mare* there were mosaics of Theodoric standing between female personifications of Rome and Ravenna.[63] Although by the time Agnellus was writing in the ninth century the mosaics had been destroyed, Deliyannis argues that Agnellus' description is so detailed that either he had seen them earlier in his life or had known someone who had.[64] If so, they were likely still in the palace when Charlemagne came to Ravenna in 787 and 801,[65] and therefore we can assume that they were intact during the Lombard occupation of the city in the 750s.

In Ravenna, imperial imagery was not restricted to the palace. Throughout the city churches contained the portraits of emperors, including images in San Giovanni Evangelista from the fifth century, Sant'Apollinare Nuovo and San Vitale after the Gothic wars of the sixth century, and Sant'Apollinare in Classe in the seventh. These churches linked Christianity and imperial rule, and therefore underscored the Christian nature of the city and the centrality of Christianity in the late antique conceptions of rulership.[66] For the emperors and later the Lombards, although Christianity was central, they claimed a direct divine link, not mediated by the clergy;[67] the images in Ravenna reinforce this vision of rulership by emphasising the archbishop's connection to imperial power, not vice-versa.

Deliyannis notes how the city's monuments and mosaics would have struck a visitor such as Charlemagne in the 780s with a sense of imperial and regal magnificence,[68] and we can imagine that they must have had a similar impact on Aistulf and the Lombards thirty years earlier. When Aistulf entered the city of Ravenna in 751 and installed himself in the imperial palace, he was surrounded by regal splendour and symbolism, which he sought to use to his advantage in the creation of his vision of Lombard rulership. Possessing Ravenna meant more than territorial expansion and merely pushing the Byzantines out of Italy. It meant possessing a former Roman capital, which was integral to the pursuit of the eighth-century kings' vision for the kingdom. Aistulf was taking over a city whose monumentalisation had been "an important and successful component of a propaganda contest about authority in Italy",[69] a city that developed in opposition to traditional Roman authority. Showing his determination to stay permanently in Ravenna, Aistulf began building projects, including the rebuilding of the Basilica Petriana.[70] Additionally, he issued charters from the exarchal palace in Ravenna and began minting coins in the city.[71]

Aistulf's gold and bronze coins from Ravenna allowed him to illustrate and legitimate his overlordship of the formerly Byzantine exarchate, as did taking over the palace and issuing charters in it. These coins fused elements common to Byzantine coins, such as the portrayal of the ruler wearing the *paludamentum* and holding a *globus cruciger*, with distinctive Lombard attributes to create an image of a Lombard king of Italy who would be readily recognisable to all the inhabitants of his realm. At Ravenna Aistulf shifted from having St. Michael, the patron saint of his people and particularly of the monarchy, on the reverse, to putting a cross-potent modelled on contemporary Byzantine coinage on his tremisses; he may have been moved by practical reasons—perhaps an appeal to Byzantine interests in Ravenna, or perhaps because of the models and personnel available to mint in Ravenna—or may have been emphasising his connection with Byzantine imperial power. All of the coinage from Ravenna has similar, and striking, busts on the obverse which has led to scholarly debate because they are unlike other effigies on Lombard coinage.[72] Within the context of Aistulf's royal program, it is clear that the bust is meant to be recognisable as a Lombard king dressed in Byzantine imperial military dress, highlighting both his role as king of the Lombards and as a Byzantine ruler.[73] Thus in Ravenna itself, Aistulf stressed continuity with previous rulers, although his claim in his law to rule over the Romans, entrusted to him by God, further developed Liutprand's ideology of *renovatio.*[74]

By the 750s, when Aistulf was resident in the city, the popes were unambiguously claiming Ravenna, and other former Byzantine territories, as part of the Republic of St. Peter, despite Lombard rule.[75] In the 730s, the popes laid claim to the duchy of Rome as part of a new Republic of St. Peter, but they had not clearly included Ravenna in their territorial claims. As Lombard control of Ravenna and its imperial associations became increasingly likely, papal assertions of authority over it became stronger. After the 738 Lombard siege of Ravenna, Gregory appealed to Duke Ursus of Venice and Antonius of Grado to return Ravenna to the "holy republic" and to the Byzantine emperor Leo III.[76] Although Gregory did not explicitly claim Ravenna for the Republic of St. Peter in this letter, he saw its safety as his responsibility.

As part of the development in papal strategy and ideology, papal attitudes towards loci of imperial power in Rome, as well as towards Ravenna, shifted subtly in response to the threat posed by the Lombards and their desire for Frankish aid. Through the seventh century, Byzantine officials continued to occupy and maintain the Palatine and its palaces, which had previously been inhabited by Roman emperors, and where the exarchs, and presumably also emperors, stayed on their rare visits to Rome, such as Constans IIs in the 660s.[77] At the beginning of the eighth century, Pope John VII (r. 705–707) moved the main episcopal palace to the Palatine, presumably using the Domitianic palace, which was attached to the church of Santa Maria Antiqua by a large ramp. As with the imperial palace complex in Ravenna, the physical occupation of palaces linked the inhabitant with imperial predecessors. However, early in his reign Pope Zacharias (r. 741–752), moved the papal residence from the Palatine back to the Lateran and refurbished it, adding two *triclinia,* one decorated with painting, mosaics, marble, glass and metal, and the other with bronze railings and paintings, as well as a portico and a tower.[78]

Much like Pope Leo III would later do, Zacharias sought to build public spaces that were appropriately impressive for the ideological claims that he was making, despite his political weakness.[79] Although not physically resident on the Palatine, Zacharias, with the patronage of Theodotus, the uncle of the future Pope Hadrian, decorated a chapel in Santa Maria Antiqua, which contains his image, and Pope Paul (757–767) also added decorations to the east aisle of the church. Both of these programs were linked to John VIIs fresco cycle, which affirmed the papal position on Monothelitism, by the use of vela, painted textiles thought to represent the curtains used in Moses and Aaron's Old Covenant tabernacle, with the same pattern of X's and spades.[80] Both during John VIIs pontificate and later during Zacharias', Santa Maria Antiqua reaffirmed the orthodoxy of the popes in their theological struggles with the Byzantine emperors.[81] Paul also used terminology in his letters that linked the present city of Rome to the ancient empire and distanced the Byzantine empire from it. In discussing the social organisation of Rome, Paul also used the ancient phrase *senatus et populus,* while also consistently calling the Byzantines "Greeks".[82] From the mid-century, by focussing on the Lateran and their ties to St. Peter, while also keeping a presence on the Palatine, and thus a link to Roman imperial authority, the popes adjusted the way that they asserted their authority in light of their attempts to navigate a dangerous situation and seek Carolingian aid. According to Andrea Augenti, the popes left the Palatine when they no longer needed to be physically present for their self-legitimation.[83] Instead, the emphasis on the Lateran and St. Peter as "traditional" fonts of papal authority appear to be a conscious decision based on a weak and uncertain political position in the 740s and 750s, despite the innovations in their ideological claims. Afterwards, the hilltop of the Palatine remained, as far as we can tell archaeologically, abandoned, while in the ninth and tenth centuries on its slopes new, semi-rural settlement clusters began to form.[84]

When Pepin intervened military on behalf of the popes in 755, Aistulf was forced to cede Ravenna and other territory conquered from the Byzantines to the papacy. In the mid-eighth century, the physical occupation of Ravenna and its centres of power were central to the Lombard kings and popes as regional rulers in Italy, demonstrating the materiality of Ravenna as a source of authority. Therefore, Pope Stephen's possession of Ravenna, the only city to rival Rome as a centre of imperial power in Italy, marked the popes' victory over the Lombard kings as much as the papal pact with the militarily superior Carolingians. Soon after this defeat, Aistulf died. Although the Lombard kingdom lasted until Charlemagne conquered it in 774, and the last Lombard king, Desiderius, attempted to revive the power of the Lombard monarchy, the popes had a monopoly on sites of Roman imperial power, as well as the military aid of the Franks.

After the Carolingian intervention, Pope Stephen removed the archbishop of Ravenna, Sergius, because he took autonomous actions, which subverted the new regime of papal control in the exarchate.[85] Stephen envisioned direct papal rule in the exarchate, and sent the priest Phillipus and the duke Eustachius to take over ecclesiastical and secular administration of the exarchate for the papacy.[86] He also had Ravenna's local officials brought to and held in Rome.[87] However, after Stephen died, his successor Paul abandoned Stephen's attempt at direct papal rule and instead restored Sergius in order to gain support in the exarchate.[88] Sergius' support was instrumental because of the re-stabilisation of Lombard royal power. Although in 757 Desiderius had agreed to papal terms in order to win the

Lombard throne, by 758 he was following the anti-papal policies of his predecessors.[89] With the political situation rapidly deteriorating, Pope Paul needed active support in the exarchate, which he had been ruling directly. Therefore, he restored Sergius to the see in Ravenna, allowing him to exercise the powers previously granted by Stephen to Phillipus and Eustachius, and giving him jurisdiction in the exarchate akin to that previously exercised by the exarch, though now exercised in the name of the papal republic.[90] Through this grant, therefore, Sergius paradoxically gained from the pope much of what he had previously sought through an alliance with the Lombards, and the archbishops of Ravenna were able to complicate the relationship between the papacy and the Carolingians after the conquest of the Lombard kingdom in 774.[91]

Despite being in a weaker position than his predecessors, in 769 Desiderius tried to influence the appointment of the archbishop of Ravenna, who was essentially in charge of the city, much as he had done in Rome with a disputed papal election after Pope Paul's death two years earlier. Under papal rule, in the absence of an external Byzantine or Lombard threat to encourage cooperation, the military and clerical elites of Ravenna had begun to fight each other. The clerical elite had profited from the end of Byzantine power—in Ravenna the removal of the exarch had made the archbishop the most powerful civil authority—and the military elite at the end of the 760s tried to reassert itself. After Sergius' death, the archdeacon Leo was properly elected by the clergy, but Duke Maurice of Rimini, aided by Desiderius, had the *scrinarius* of Ravenna, the layman Michael, elected instead.[92] However, Desiderius did not appear to draw any long-term benefits from his aid.[93] Ultimately, Archbishop Leo would court the aid of the Carolingians, not the Lombards, to try and gain autonomy for his see. Despite his disinterest in an alliance with Desiderius, he also refused to accept papal authority.[94] In both Rome and Ravenna, there were tensions between local factions, who appealed to outside parties to defeat their rivals locally and were exploited by them because of their strategic importance. These cases illustrate how profoundly different Desiderius' position was from previous kings, as he recognised that the only way to exert authority in Rome or Ravenna was to have influence over the pope or archbishop, thus abandoning ambitions to physically rule Ravenna.[95]

Once the Carolingians conquered the Lombard kingdom and Charlemagne became emperor, the popes had to negotiate the relationship between their position and the Carolingian rulers. Pope Leo III constructed two *triclinia*, a new banqueting hall and audience chamber in his residence at the Lateran, public spaces designed to impress.[96] In the smaller, the Aula Leonina, he commissioned a mosaic of St. Peter, enthroned, with Pope Leo and Charlemagne kneeling below. In the image Pope Leo receives the *pallium* from Peter's right hand, while Peter hands Charlemagne a standard. As Caroline Goodson has argued, these mosaics and the rest of Leo's building program in the years around 800 show the pope's desire to define separate roles for the popes and the Carolingians; after Charlemagne's death Pope Paschal I (r. 817–824) set out to renegotiate the relationship between the popes and Carolingians by embarking on an extensive program of building and renovating churches, asserting and achieving authority and autonomy for the papacy through translating relics from outside of the walls into papal churches in Rome and setting the stational liturgy.[97] Although high-ranking visitors might see Leo's mosaics, papal building projects, as well as cultic practices and processions associated with and linking these churches, demonstrated papal prestige to most of the population.[98]

In sum, after 774, the development of papal ideology continued to be a constant negotiation with secular authorities on the peninsula. However, since Ravenna was no longer a seat of secular power, the popes focussed instead on whether their authority and rights were respected in the city. Despite the pope's political authority in the exarchate, at times they had difficulty enforcing their administrative control. Pope Leo III, who was unpopular in Ravenna, complained to Charlemagne that he could not enforce his rights over land associated with the *palatium* (palace) of Ravenna.[99] While Leo was trying to define the separate roles of the pope and emperor, issues in Ravenna complicated matters, particularly because Charlemagne realised how important the archbishop was politically, sending *missi* to supervise an archiepiscopal election in 788, to Hadrian's distress.[100] Noble has argued that Ravenna's government was a "double dyarchy", in which the king and pope divided rule of the city, while the archbishop and pope shared authority. The exarchate was clearly within the Republic of St. Peter, but, as Noble states, "in this one zone only the pope's authority was less than complete".[101] The archbishops' continued desire for autonomy from Rome and Ravenna's strategic value to the Carolingians led to a triangular relationship between Ravenna, Rome, and the Franks.[102] The archbishops of Ravenna petitioned the Carolingians for privileges, stressed their city's glories, and obstructed papal control in the exarchate during the reigns of Charlemagne and Louis the Pious.[103]

Although Ravenna remained a significant issue for the popes as long as the archbishops and Ravennati challenged their authority, its links with imperial power ceased to be significant to papal ideology; in fact, the papacy allowed the Carolingian to dismantle and relocate its monuments. Charlemagne, like the Lombards, linked Rome and Ravenna as fonts of imperial power. Instead of wanting to occupy it, however, Charlemagne exported marble columns from Ravenna (as well as Rome) for his palatine church at Aachen, and Pope Hadrian authorised him to take marble and mosaics from Ravenna's palace.[104] Charlemagne's use of *spolia* from Ravenna for his new capital at Aachen both underscored Ravenna's fundamental association with imperial authority, and its tangible nature, and signified the transfer of this power with the relocation of its monuments. Thus, Ravenna became a formerly important imperial place, that could be dismantled and have its authority transported, while as a preeminent archbishopric it was acknowledged as having a continued relevance, divorced from its status in the Roman/Byzantine Empire while remaining an "accessible replica" of Constantinople.[105]

Our main narrative source for Ravenna, Agnellus' *Liber Pontificalis ecclesiae Ravennatis* should be seen as a response to papal and Carolingian conceptions of Ravenna as a place that used to matter. Agnellus, a priest and member of Ravenna's aristocracy, composed the *LPR*, an archiepiscopal history, as a series of lectures given between 830 and 846.[106] Originally, the *LPR* probably contained twenty bishops' lives, although only eighteen have been preserved.[107] The *LPR* is a *gesta episcoporum,* a genre that was modelled on the Roman *Liber Pontificalis* and was produced only in Carolingian Europe.[108] The surviving examples of the genre were commissioned by the current bishops and thus culminated with a glowing account of his reign, but Agnellus had problems with George, and thus portrayed him in an extremely negative light.[109]

A main theme of the *LPR* is hostility towards Rome and the assertion of Ravenna's right to independence from it. Through the *LPR,* Agnellus seeks to elevate the status of the see of Ravenna to that of Rome, by making the legendary founder of the see, St. Apollinaris, into St. Peter's companion; the result is that Agnellus respects Rome's pre-eminence in the west while denying its right to control Ravenna.[110] Tom Brown has argued that the local pride shown by Agnellus in his text, through his discussions of both the clergy and the lay aristocracy, who were often tied by kinship and friendship, reflected a new type of local pride of the ninth century, or *campanilismo.* Nevertheless, Agnellus, writing in a period in which Ravenna had lost its political pre-eminence, was the first writer to present Ravenna as a late antique capital city, although there is evidence that Charlemagne and, as argued earlier, the eighth-century Lombard kings saw Ravenna as the Constantinople of the West.[111] Even though Agnellus' attitude towards the Roman past is ambiguous, he takes its continuity for granted, unlike the rupture between the Roman past and the Frankish present characteristic of Carolingian historians outside of Italy.[112] This perceived continuity was fundamental for demonstrating that Ravenna, with its monuments that Agnellus meticulously described, and the noble deeds of its citizens, including his ancestors, continued to matter because of its rich history. Despite his antipathy for certain archbishops, such as George, Agnellus' quintessential bad bishop who attempted to curry favour with Lothar at the expense of Ravenna's wealth and clergy, Agnellus and the archbishops sought to define Ravenna's place in an Italy. Although Ravenna was increasingly marginalised by popes and Carolingians, its remembered history, as well as its monuments, from imperial portraits in churches to the remains of the imperial palace, persisted in telling the story of a glorious past.

In conclusion, an analysis of the use of imperial authority by the archbishops of Ravenna, the Lombard kings, and the popes in light of the shifting and often uncertain political circumstances of the time shows the constant negotiation of power relations and gives insight into their dynamics. In the fraught political situation of the second quarter of the eighth century, there was a rapid development in both Lombard royal and papal ideologies. As the Lombards positioned themselves as protectors of orthodoxy and set their sights on Ravenna, a city whose monuments were erected to legitimise alternatives to the authority of Rome and which was heavily linked to Christian imperial authority, the popes claimed it for St. Peter, the ultimate font of Christian authority. Despite the constructed and negotiated nature of these ideologies, after the Carolingian conquest of Italy, the *translatio* of architectural elements and imperial authority from Ravenna to Aachen (as well as the creation of a dominant narrative that legitimated papal and Carolingian uses of the Roman past) marginalised Lombard and Ravennati social memory of their past visible in narrative sources such as Agnellus' *LPR.*

Notes

* I would like to thank the National Endowment of the Humanities and the Professional Staff Congress of CUNY for their generous financial support of this project. Additionally I would like to thank my dissertation director, Richard Gyug, for his supporting my work on Ravenna from start to finish, archaeologists Enrico Cirelli and Andrea Augenti for their generosity and collaboration, as well as Deborah Deliyannis and Tom Brown for their encouragement and insight.

1 T.S. Brown, "*Romanitas* and *Campanilismo*: Agnellus of Ravenna's View of the Past", in *The Inheritance of Historiography 350–900,* ed. Christopher Holdsworth and T.P. Wiseman (Exeter: University Publications, 1986), 107–114.

2 Enrico Zanini, *Le Italie Bizantine: Territorio, insediamenti ed economia nella provincia bizantina d'Italia (VI – VIII secolo)* (Bari: Edipuglia, 1998), 61; Noble, *The Republic of St. Peter*, 6.

3 However, Byzantine and papal sources stress continuity and make no distinction between the imperial government before and after Ostrogothic period, and thus refer to the Byzantine government as Roman. Nevertheless, historians typically use the term. "Byzantine Italy" for Roman areas after Justinian's reconquest of the peninsula in order to contrast the pre- and post-Ostrogothic periods, and to distinguish between the Byzantine government in general with the Romans of the city and duchy of Rome (cf. Chris Wickham, Framing the Early Middle Ages: Europe and the Mediterranean, 400–800 (Oxford: Oxford University Press, 2004, 33–37). In this chapter, "Roman" refers to the population of Italy which saw itself as such, and Byzantine to the east Roman/ Byzantine government.

4 Thomas F. X. Noble, *The Republic of St. Peter: The Birth of the Papal States 680–825* (Philadelphia: University of Pennsylvania Press, 1984), 6–9.

5 See Nicole Lopez-Jantzen, "Kings of All Italy? Overlooking Political and Cultural Boundaries in Lombard Italy". *Medieval Perspectives* 29 (2014): 75–92.

6 C.f. Zanini, *Le Italie Bizantine*, 21; Salvatore Cosentino, *Storia dell'Italia Bizantina (VI–XI secolo): da Giustiniano ai Normanni* (Bologna: Bononia University Press, 2008).

7 Zanini, *Le Italie Bizantine*, 21; Cosentino, *Storia dell'Italia Bizantina,* 94.

8 Brown, *Gentlemen and Officers,* 148–150.

9 Zanini, *Le Italie Bizantine*, 99; Noble, *Republic of St. Peter,* 43.

10 Zanini, *Le Italie Bizantine*, 70–1, 99–100; Cosentino, *Storia dell'Italia Bizantina*, 63, 239–241.

11 Caroline Goodson, *The Rome of Pope Paschal I: Papal Power, Urban Renovation, Church Building and Relic Translation, 817–824* (Cambridge, Cambridge University Press, 2014), 67.

12 Noble, *Republic of St. Peter,* 39–40; Vivien Prigent, "Les Empereurs Isauriens et la Confiscation des Patrimoines Pontificaux d'Italie du Sud", *Mélanges de l'École Français de Rome* 116.2 (2004), 565–578, 592–594. Prigent argues that Leo III made administrative and fiscal changes beginning perhaps even before 732/3, but the seizure of the papal patrimony in southern Italy did not occur until the 740s. As Paolo Delogu notes, although the popes participated in the administration of the city, they could not exercise secular government in their own right, even as stand-ins for Byzantine officials. Through the seventh century, representatives from the exarch in Ravenna administered the city with the support of the popes. See Delogu, "The Papacy, Rome and the Wider World", 199.

13 Deborah Deliyannis, *Ravenna in Late Antiquity* (Cambridge: Cambridge University Press, 2010), 3; Andrew Gillett, "Rome, Ravenna and the Last Western Emperors", *Papers of the British School at Rome* 69 (2001), 162–165. Andrew Gillett first put forth this contention regarding the Honorian emperors, while Deliyannis expanded it to include later groups.

14 Deliyannis, *Ravenna in Late Antiquity,* 3.

15 Deliyannis, *Ravenna in Late Antiquity,* 68–69; Piero Piccinini, "Immagini d'autorità a Ravenna", in *Storia di Ravenna: Dall'età Bizantina all'età Ottoniana, Ecclesiologia, Cultura e arte,* vol. 2.2, ed. Antonio Carile (Venice: Marsilio Editori, 1992), 32–33.

16 See Nicole Lopez-Jantzen, "From the Roman Empire to the Middle Ages: The Struggle for Ravenna in the Eighth Century", (PhD thesis, Fordham University, 2012), 129–169.

17 See Lopez-Jantzen, "From the Roman Empire to the Middle Ages", 140–155.

18 *RIS* 2.1, 146.

19 Agnellus, *LPR*, c. 124; *LP*, 82.4.

20 T. S. Brown, "Lombard Religious Policy in the Late Sixth and Seventh Centuries: The Roman Dimension", in *The Langobards before the Frankish Conquest: An Ethnographic Perspective*, ed. Giorgio Ausenda, Paolo Delogu and Chris Wickham (Woodbridge: Boydell Press, 2009), 295–296.

21 Leslie Brubaker and John Haldon, *Byzantium in the Iconoclast Era c. 680–850: A History* (Cambridge: Cambridge University Press, 2011), 29–32. For an overview of challenges facing the Byzantine Empire at the beginning of Leo IIIs reign, see ibid, 71–79.

22 Paolo Delogu, "Il regno longobardo", in *Longobardi e Bizantini,* ed. Paolo Delogu, André Guillou and Gherardo Ortalli (Turin: Utet, 1980), 115; Jörg Jarnut, *Storia dei Longobardi*, trans. Paolo Guglielmotti (Turin: Einaudi, 1995), 67.

23 *Liutprandi Leges,* in *Leges Langobardorum.* MGH, Leges 4, edited by Frederick Bluhme. Hanover, 1869, 107. See also Nicholas Everett, *Literacy in Lombard Italy, c. 568–774* (Cambridge: Cambridge University Press, 2003), 250.

24 *Liutprandi Leges,* 109, 116.

25 On marriage, see *Liutprandi Leges,* 33, 34.V. On adultery, see 34, 76, 95, and 140. Regarding sorcery, see 84, and 85.

26 *Liutprandi Leges*, 33, 34.

27 *Liutprandi Leges,* 141.

28 Reproduced in Everett, *Literacy in Lombard Italy,* 249.

29 Everett, *Literacy in Lombard Italy,* 250. In Italy, Pope Agatho (r. 678–681) and later hagiographers saw Byzantine military successes and failures as caused by the orthodoxy, or lack, of the emperors. See Brubaker and Haldon, *Byzantium in the Iconoclast Era,* 20.

30 *Ahistulfi Leges, Leges Langobardorum.* MGH, Leges 4, edited by Frederick Bluhme. Hanover, 1869, 195.

31 Paolo Delogu, "Kinship and the Shaping of the Lombard Body Politic", in *The Langobards before the Frankish Conquest: An Ethnographic Perspective,* ed. Giorgio Ausenda, Paolo Delogu and Chris Wickham (Woodbridge: Boydell Press, 2009), 269.

32 *LP,* 91.15–16; T. S. Brown, *Gentlemen and Officers: Imperial Administration and Aristocratic Power in Byzantine Italy A.D. 554–800* (Rome: British School at Rome, 1984), 114; Hallenbeck, *Pavia and Rome,* 21. Note that, just before, there was a plot against the pope in Rome. According to the *LP,* an imperial official, Basil, along with others, including a subdeacon, were plotting against the pope and sought the assent of the duke Marinus, who also held the Byzantine title of *spatharius.* Marinus gave his consent, but the plot was discovered and the organizers killed. Since Marinus could not remove the pope, the emperor sent another official to Rome, as duke, to do so. Paul appears to have sent men to Rome in order to help carry out the emperor's orders.

33 *LP,* 91.16; Noble, *The Republic of St. Peter,* 29.

34 *LP,* 91.16; Jarnut, *Storia dei Longobardi,* 88. Noble (*The Republic of St. Peter,* 29) argues that Paul had difficulty recruiting troops for this task.

35 John Haldon, *Byzantium in the Seventh Century: The Transformation of a Culture* (Cambridge: Cambridge University Press, 1990), 89; Noble, *The Republic of St. Peter,* 29–30; Brown, *Gentlemen and Officers,* 93; Jarnut, *Storia dei Longobardi,* 88. Haldon disagrees with Noble, Brown, and Jarnut over the motivation for the revolts. For Noble et al., the armies revolted as a consequence of the promulgation of iconoclasm in Italy, which they place in 725/6. Haldon argues, however, that the struggle between Rome and Constantinople and the subsequent revolt of 725/6 had nothing to do with Leo's iconoclastic policies of the 730s but instead were strictly over taxation.

36 *LP,* 91.17; Noble, *The Republic of St. Peter,* 32.

37 *LP,* 91.19; Melucco Vaccaro, *I longobardi in Italia,* 77; Noble, *The Republic of St. Peter,* 30; Cosentino, *Storia d'Italia Bizantina,* 242; Jarnut, *Storia dei Longobardi,* 88. Fasoli ("La Pentapoli fra il Papato e L'Impero", 59) states that Liutprand also temporarily took Ravenna at this point. However, it is more likely that the Lombards temporarily held Ravenna at some point in the 730s.

38 Noble, *The Republic of St. Peter,* 31.

39 Hostilities broke out over Bologna, which had been conquered by Liutprand in the 720s but had been re-taken by the Byzantines. Subsequently, Hildeprand, who had been elected co-ruler when Liutprand was ill in 735, and the duke of Vicenza, Paradeo, attacked and briefly conquered Ravenna before the Byzantines retook it. Note that the date of Ravenna's capture is highly contested. See Brown, *Gentlemen and Officers,* 92; Ottorino Bertolini, *Roma di fronte ai Longobardi* (Bologna: L. Cappelli, 1941), 457–458; Hallenbeck, *Pavia and Rome,* 32; Zanini, *Le Italie Bizantine,* 99; Jarnut, *Storia dei Longobardi,* 90–91; Cessi, "La Crisi dell'Esarcato Ravennate", 1685; Noble, *The Republic of St. Peter,* 41–42. The dating of this event is controversial. Several scholars, including Brown and Bertolini, place the event in 732. Similarly, Hallenbeck places it before 735, and Zanini states that it occurred between 731 and 734. Jarnut discusses it after the events of 732, stating that it occurred in the same

period, and subsequently discusses events of 739, leaving open the possibility of a date between 732 and 739. However, later Jarnut states that Liutprand attacked Ravenna again in 740, based on the letter Gregory wrote to Charles Martel (Jarnut, *Storia dei Longobardi,* 92). It is unclear whether he sees these as two separate attacks or one, but he does not mention the Venetians when discussing the latter. Based on the dating of Paul the Deacon and papal letters, Cessi states that it had to have occurred after 737, and Noble, after reviewing the debate, argues for the later date of 738.

40 *LP,* 93.4–5.

41 *LP,* 93.5.

42 *LP,* 93.6.

43 Noble *The Republic of St. Peter,* 49.

44 *LP,* 93.6--11; Noble, *The Republic of St. Peter,* 51–52. Those territories were Narni, some of the church's patrimony in the Sabina which the Spoletans had previously taken, as well as Osimo, Ancona, and Umana, located in the Pentapolis and the land around Sutri. Note that the recipient was St. Peter, not the duchy of Rome.

45 *LP,* 93.9.

46 *LP,* 93.11; Noble, *The Republic of St. Peter,* 52. For Delogu, the concept of a *respublica* separate from the empire could only come about after the Lombards conquered Ravenna in 751, and was therefore developed by Pope Stephen II (see Paolo Delogu, "The Papacy, Rome and the Wider World in the Seventh and Eighth Centuries", in *Early Medieval Rome and the Christian West*, edited by Julia Smith (Leiden: Brill, 2000), 214–215. Brubaker and Haldon's reassessment of the beginnings of iconoclasm also stress the positive relationship between the papacy and the emperors during the pontificate of Zacharias (r. 741–752) (Brubaker and Haldon, *Byzantium in the Iconoclast Era*, 86–89).

47 *LP,* 93.12; Noble, *The Republic of St. Peter,* 52–53.

48 *LP,* 93.12.

49 *LP,* 93.12.

50 *LP,* 93.12–13.

51 *LP,* 93.15. Noble (*The Republic of St. Peter,* 54) interprets the state referred to in the *Liber Pontificalis* as the papal state, thus arguing that this is the first piece of land that the papacy acquired in the exarchate. However, in the context of Liutprand's reply, the state must still refer to Byzantium and the exarchate.

52 See Noble, *The Republic of St. Peter,* 54–55. Noble focusses on the political aspects of these events, while this chapter argues that to Liutprand, the duchy of Rome was under St. Peter's protection in much the same way as Cluny later would be, whereas Ravenna and the exarchate were ruled by a separate secular power.

53 Noble, *The Republic of St. Peter,* 55.

54 *LP,* 93.23.

55 *Liber Pontificalis,* 93.23. See also Walter Pohl, "Frontiers in Lombard Italy: The Laws of Ratchis and Aistulf", in *The Transformation of Frontiers: From Late Antiquity to the Carolingians*, ed. Walter Pohl, Ian Wood and H. Reimitz (Boston: Brill, 2001), 140–141.

56 *LP,* 94.15–18; Noble, *The Republic of St. Peter,* 74–75.

57 *LP,* 94.21.

58 *LP*, 94.19–24; Noble, *The Republic of St. Peter*, 74–75.

59 Deborah Deliyannis, "Charlemagne's Silver Tables: The Ideology of an Imperial Capital", *Early Medieval Europe* 12:2 (2003), 167.

60 On July 4, 751 Aistulf issued a charter confirming privileges to the abbey of Farfa, "*in palatio*". The document is preserved in Fantuzzi V: 8, 203–204.

61 Enrico Cirelli, *Ravenna: archeologia di una città* (Florence: All'Insegna del Giglio, 2008), 78, 81–83, 88–92.
62 Andrea Augenti, "Ravenna e Classe: archeologia di due città tra tarda Antichità e l'alto Medioevo", in *Le città italiane tra la tarda Antichità e l'alto Medioevo. Atti del convegno (Ravenna, 26–28 febbraio 2004)*, ed. Andrea Augenti (Florence: All'Insegna del giglio, 2006), 187.
63 Agnellus, *LPR,* c. 94.
64 Deliyannis, "Charlemagne's Silver Tables", 167, n. 30.
65 Deliyannis, "Charlemagne's Silver Tables", 167, n. 30; Bryan Ward-Perkins, *From Classical Antiquity to the Middle Ages: Urban Public Building in Northern and Central Italy A.D. 300–850* (Oxford: Oxford University Press, 1984), 165. Ward-Perkins states that both the mosaics and the statue of Theodoric remained "untouched" until the early ninth century.
66 Deliyannis, *Ravenna in Late Antiquity,* 63.
67 See Lopez-Jantzen, "From the Roman Empire to the Middle Ages", 30–31, 186–195.
68 Deliyannis, "Charlemagne's Silver Tables", 173.
69 Deliyannis, *Ravenna in Late Antiquity*, 3.
70 Agnellus, *LPR, c.* 155; Wickham, *Early Medieval Italy*, 46.
71 One extant charter remains: Fantuzzi V: 8, in which Aistulf confirmed privileges given to the abbey of Farfa by Duke Lupo of Spoleto.
72 There are thirteen extant coins, of which five are gold and eight are bronze. For the image of Aistulf, see Ermanno Arslan, "Le Monete", in *I Longobardi,* ed. Gian Carlo Menis (Milan: Electa, 1990), 164; Ernesto Bernareggi, *Moneta Langobardorum*, trans. Paolo Visonà (Lugano: Cisalpino-Goliardica, 1989), 80–81; Philip Grierson and Mark Blackburn, *Medieval European Coinage: With a Catalogue of the Coins in the FitzWilliam Museum, Cambridge,* vol. 1: *The Early Middle Ages (5th–10th cs.)* (Cambridge: Cambridge University Press, 1986), 65. For Bernareggi, the realism and the similarities depicted in all of the coins are evidence for a true portrait of Aistulf, instead of representing an iconographic *topos*. Grierson acknowledges that it is tempting to see the figure as a true portrait because of the level of detail, but concludes that because there are similar effigies on Lombard crosses and the helmet piece of Agilulf, the image on the coins was probably a generalized depiction of a Lombard king.
73 See Lopez-Jantzen, "From the Roman Empire to the Middle Ages", 200–208 for an extensive discussion of these coins.
74 *Ahistulfi Leges*, 195.
75 Noble, *Republic of St. Peter,* 43; Delogu, "The Papacy, Rome and the Wider World", 214–215.
76 *Epistolae Langobardicae Collectae* 11.
77 Haldon, *Byzantium in the Seventh Century*, 59–60. In fact, epigraphic evidence shows that Pope John VIIs (r. 705–707) father was a *cura palatinii,* a Byzantine official who was in charge of the imperial palace on the Palatine. See ICUR, II, 442.
78 *LP,* 93.18. This work is no longer extant.
79 For Leo III, see John Mitchell, "The Power of Patronage and the Iconography of Quality in the Era of 774", in *774: Ipotesi su una transizione,* ed. Stefano Gasparri (Turnhout: Brepols, 2008), 281.
80 Stephen Lucey, "Palimpsest Reconsidered: Continuity and Change in the Decorative Programs at Santa Maria Antiqua", in *Santa Maria al Foro Romano Cento Anni dopo: Atti del Colloquio Internazionale, Roma 5–6 maggio 2000,*edited by John Osborne et al. (Rome: Campisano, 2004), 85, Gregor Kalas, personal communication.

81 Andrea Augenti, "The Palatine Hill from the Fifth to the Tenth Century", *Early Medieval Rome and the Christian West*, edited by Julia Smith (Leiden: Brill, 2000), 50–51; Per Jonas Nordhagen, "Constantinople on the Tiber", *Early Medieval Rome and the Christian West*, edited by Julia Smith (Leiden: Brill, 2000), 129–134. As Nordhagen argues, John retained the image of Pope Martin, who died in exile because of his refusal to accept Monothelitism, labelled Martin as a saint, and placed his own image alongside it, an example of the Byzantine practice of presenting politically contentious images for the purpose of imperial propaganda.

82 *Codex Carolinus* 13, 24, 30, 32; Delogu, "The Papacy, Rome and the Wider World", 215–216; Clemens Gantner, "The Label 'Greeks' in the Papal Diplomatic Repertoire in the Eighth Century", *Strategies of Identification: Ethnicity and Religion in Early Medieval Europe*, edited by Walter Pohl and Gerda Heydemann (Turnhout: Brepols, 2013), 325–328.

83 Augenti, "The Palatine Hill from the Fifth to the Tenth Century", 52–53.

84 Augenti, *Il Palatino nel Medioevo: Archeologia e Topografia secoli VI–XIII* (Rome: L'erma di Bretschneider, 1996), 61–79.

85 *Codex Carolinus* 49, 568; Ottorino Bertolini "Sergio arcivescovo di Ravenna (744–769) e i papi del suo tempo", *Studi Romagnoli,* 1 (1950)", 565–566.

86 *Codex Carolinus* 49, 569; discussed in depth in Ottorino Bertolini, "Le prime manifestazioni concrete del potere dei Papi nell'Esarcato di Ravenna (756–757)", in *Scritti scelti di storia medievale,* ed. O. Banti (Livorno, 1968), 595–612.

87 Agnellus, *LPR,c.* 159. Agnellus states that this was a result of their role in the plot against the pope. This event may, however, correspond to Fulrad's taking of hostages to Rome after the Second Peace of Pavia (see *LP,* 94.47).

88 Agnellus, *LPR,* c. 157; *Codex Carolinus* 14, 512; Bertolini, "Sergio arcivescovo di Ravenna", 574–575. Paul was consecrated May 29, 757. In a letter to Pepin in 758, Paul writes "Sergium vero archiepiscopum, iuxta id quod vestrae innotuit excellentiae, indesinenter inminemus, ut suae restituatur ecclesie", i.e., that Sergius would be restored to his see, but had not yet been. Bertolini argues that Sergius returned to Ravenna between the end of 758 and February 759, when Paul returned the monastery of S. Hilarius to Ravenna's jurisdiction.

89 Not only had he not given over the agreed-upon cities to the pope, but in March 758 he marched on Spoleto, deposing Duke Alboin and placing Spoleto directly under royal rule until he appointed Gisulf duke in 759. Regarding the cities, Paul wrote to Pepin in 758 (*Codex Carolinus* 14). The *LP* is very brief and skips over the important political events of Paul's papacy.

90 Agnellus, *LPR,c.* 159; Bertolini, "Sergio arcivescovo di Ravenna", 578.

91 Bertolini, "Sergio arcivescovo di Ravenna", 578.

92 *LP,* 96.25; *The Republic of St. Peter,* 119.

93 Noble, *The Republic of St. Peter,* 119–120.

94 *Codex Carolinus* 49, 53–55; *LP* 97.14–17; Deliyannis, *Ravenna in Late Antiquity,* 285. According to the *LP,* Pope Hadrian even sent envoys to Desiderius exhorting him to make sure that Archbishop Leo did not hurt Paul, whom he wanted exiled, not killed, for his role in a murder in Rome. Leo, however, had Paul tried and killed in Ravenna.

95 Noble, *Republic of St. Peter,* 113.

96 Mitchell, *The Power of Patronage,* 278, 281.

97 Goodson, *The Rome of Pope Paschal I,* 6–7, 14–17.

98 Goodson, 79.

99 Leo III, ep. 9 (MGH Epist. 3), 101.

100 *Codex Carolinus,* 85; T.S. Brown, "Louis the Pious and the Papacy: A Ravenna

Perspective", in *Charlemagne's Heir: New Perspectives on the Reign of Louis the Pious 814–840*, edited by Peter Godman and Roger Collins (Oxford: Oxford University Press, 1990), 301.

101 Noble, *Republic of St. Peter*, 172.

102 Brown, "Louis the Pious and the Papacy", 297.

103 For a detailed discussion, see Brown, "Louis the Pious and the Papacy", 300–307.

104 Deliyannis, *Ravenna in Late Antiquity,* 298.

105 Martinez Pizarro, *Writing Ravenna,* 17.

106 Deborah Deliyannis, Introduction to *The Book of Pontiffs of the Church of Ravenna* (Washington, D.C.: Catholic University of America Press, 2004), 9–13; Joaquín Martínez Pizarro, *Writing Ravenna: The Liber Pontificalis of Andreas Agnellus* (Ann Arbor: University of Michigan Press, 1995), 2. Note that the only information we have about Agnellus comes from passages within the *LPR;* there are no external references to him.

107 The lives of Valerio (788–802) and Petronace (817–835) are missing. See Antonio Carile, "Agnello Storico", in *Storia di Ravenna: Dall'età Bizantina all'età Ottoniana, Ecclesiologia, Cultura e arte,* vol. 2.2, ed. Antonio Carile (Venice: Marsilio Editori, 1992), 375.

108 Martinez Pizarro, *Writing Ravenna,* 33.

109 Agnellus states that after becoming archbishop, George deprived him of his monastery for a few years. See Agnellus, *LPR,* c. 136, and c. 171–175.

110 Brown, "*Romanitas* and *Campanilismo*", 109.

111 Martinez Pizarro, *Writing Ravenna,* 17; Deliyannis, "Charlemagne's Silver Tables", 173–177. Deliyannis argues that Charlemagne saw Ravenna as a Byzantine imperial capital, and therefore used Ravenna as a model for his new capital at Aachen to appropriate Byzantine imperial power in the west.

112 Brown, "*Romanitas* and *Campanilismo*", 109, 111.

11 Thomas Morosini, first Latin patriarch of Constantinople, and the Ravenna connection

In recent years Thomas Morosini, the future Latin patriarch of Constantinople, has been adopted by some historians as a son of Ravenna by virtue of his supposed residence there. The *Oxford Dictionary of Byzantium* has him studying in Ravenna, when he received the call to become Latin patriarch of Constantinople,[1] while Thomas Madden repeats what has become a common opinion that Morosini was the prior or even the abbot of the important monastery of S. Maria in Porto, just outside the walls of Ravenna.[2] This connection between the future patriarch of Constantinople and a monastery at Ravenna was first made in 1938 by L. Santifaller.[3] It was adopted more recently by G. Fedalto[4] and then by A. Carile,[5] who seized upon it as a way of explaining the presence of the scenes of the Fourth Crusade, which have been preserved in the church of S. Giovanni Evangelista at Ravenna. They were originally part of the floor of the nave laid down in 1213 under the direction of the then abbot of the monastery Guglielmo.[6] In recent years they have been treated as some sort of a memorial to Thomas Morosini, who died two years earlier in June or July 1211.[7] This has been accepted all too uncritically, because otherwise there is nothing of substance in the historical record to connect Ravenna to the Fourth Crusade and the conquest of Constantinople.[8]

The main source, which historians have used to justify placing the future Latin patriarch of Constantinople at the monastery of S. Maria in Porto at Ravenna, is the *Historia de bello Constantinopoli by* Paolo Ramusio (1532–1600), who was the son of the more famous Giovanbattista Ramusio, the author of *Navigationes*. His *Historia* was an updated version of Villehardouin's *Conquest of Constantinople*, done under official auspices. The acquisition in 1541 of a manuscript of Villehardouin's text by the Venetian emissary to the Emperor Charles V caused quite a stir at Venice because it underlined the heroic role played by Venetians in a great enterprise. The emissary Francesco Contarini gave the manuscript added significance by presenting it to the Council of Ten. The council first had it turned into Italian and then in 1556 commissioned a Latin version from Paolo Ramusio. This was completed in 1572, a year after the battle of Lepanto, which briefly gave the Venetian part in the conquest of

Constantinople in 1204 new relevance. It was a moment that was quickly over because the Italian version was not published until 1604[9] and a Latin version had to wait until 1609.[10] Paolo Ramusio made notable additions to Villehardouin's original text with the aim of adding lustre to the Venetian contribution to the conquest of Constantinople. The scholarship displayed won the approval of Edward Gibbon.[11] The editor of the first printed edition gives a list of the sources consulted by Ramusio. He made very good use of the Byzantine historians and of the Venetian chronicles. But none of these contain the information connecting Thomas Morosini to the monastery of S. Maria in Porto. Scrupulous historian that he was Ramusio inserts the word *dicitur*. In other words, he was relying on traditions, which are likely to have originated in the Morosini family, to which—being a Morosini on his mother's side[12]—the Doge Nicolò Contarini (1630–1631) may also have had access. In his edition of Marcantonio Sabellico's *Degli istorici degli cose veneziane i quali hanno scritto per pubblico decreto* he added the information that Thomas Morosini was a Camaldolese monk.[13] To be sure, he says nothing about him having any links with the monastery of S. Maria in Porto. However, connections—almost certainly erroneous—had long been made between that monastery and Peter Damian—one of the most famous early members of the Camaldolese order.

Surprisingly overlooked has been another account linking Thomas Morosini to S. Maria in Porto. At exactly the same time that Paolo Ramusio was compiling his history of the Fourth Crusade, Girolamo Rossi was writing his history of Ravenna, which has been the starting point for all subsequent study of the city's past. Concerning Archbishop Ubaldo of Ravenna (1208–1216), the historian tells us that he resigned office and donned the habit of a canon of S. Maria in Porto. What is more, he assures us that Ubaldo was not the only one to do this.[14] He claimed that Doge Pietro Ziani (1205–1229) and Thomas Morosini, patriarch of Constantinople (1205–1211), also resigned their offices before becoming canons of S. Maria in Porto.[15] It was long ago pointed out that Rossi was muddling Archbishop Ubaldo with Ubaldo, bishop of Gubbio, who was certainly associated with S. Maria in Porto.[16] Archbishop Ubaldo of Ravenna never resigned his office, but died outside Perugia on his return from the Fourth Lateran Council, which rules out the possibility that he ever became a member of the S. Maria in Porto community.[17] Pietro Ziani did indeed resign office in 1229 because of old age, but rather than joining the canons of S. Maria in Porto he became a Benedictine monk and entered the monastery of S. Giorgio Maggiore at Venice.[18] Just as erroneous will be the information given about Thomas Morosini, who died of a severe illness[19] at Thessalonica in 1211, but it confirms that some four hundred years after the death of Thomas Morosini there was a strong tradition, which linked him to the monastery of S. Maria in Porto. Can we put any trust in it? On the positive side, S. Maria in Porto had ties to Venice going back to the twelfth century. The church of S. Maria della Carità was founded in 1134 as a dependency of S. Maria in Porto at a time when its rule—the Regula Portuense—was at its most prestigious.[20] Paolo Ramusio's claim that the Ravenna house had a reputation as "a seminary of men distinguished by their sanctity" is not that wide of the mark. It did after all produce Alimanno, who was bishop of Senigallia from 1190–1193,[21] and St Aldebrando, who was famed for his preaching against the Patarenes. The latter is attested as a canon and subdeacon of S. Maria in Porto in 1199—in other words, exactly when Thomas Morosini was supposed to have been resident there. He went on to become provost of the cathedral of Rimini in 1222 and around 1230 bishop of Fossombrone in the Romagna. In the cathedral there is a portrait of him in the robes of a Portuense canon.[22]

If a Venetian—but not only a Venetian—decided at the end of the twelfth century to go into monastic retreat at Ravenna, then S. Maria in Porto was an obvious choice. But why did nobody before Paolo Ramusio and Girolamo Rossi pick up a tradition that Thomas entered this monastery and why is there no trace of him in the very full records, which survive for S. Maria in Porto? There is a justifiable suspicion, as with all traditions, that it was of more recent manufacture. The Venetian annexation of Ravenna in 1441 called out for the invention of traditions that might reconcile the people of Ravenna to Venetian rule. The long-standing link between S. Maria in Porto at Ravenna and S. Maria della Carità at Venice was something to build on. It was important for the Venetian authorities to put their stamp on S. Maria in Porto, because it had a central role to play in the communal life of Ravenna; housing, as it did, the image of the Madonna greca, which was not only the focus of a powerful confraternity, but also the palladium of the city.

Tradition took the miraculous discovery of the image back to the first Sunday after Easter (*Domenica in Albis*) in the year 1100, when the founder of S. Maria in Porto came across it washed up on the seashore. This tradition goes back to notices dated 21 December 1142 supposedly left by the third prior of S. Maria in Porto, Giovanni Bono, who is described as a Venetian.[23] They were transcribed by Girolamo Fabri in the mid-seventeenth century,[24] but a century and a half later Count Marco Fantuzzi was unable to see the document. He was told that parts of it had been overwritten by a later hand.[25] Be that as it may, the cult of the image of the Madonna greca centred on S. Maria in Porto continued to flourish into the fourteenth century. However, the exposed position of the monastery outside the walls of Ravenna left it prey to the endemic warfare of the later middle ages. By 1419 it resembled nothing so much as a "*stabulum animalium*".[26] The intervention of the lord of Ravenna Obizo da Polenta laid the foundations for a recovery,[27] which continued under the Venetians. An earnest of its new-found prosperity was the installation in 1481 of a new altar-piece (now in the Brera at Milan), which it commissioned from the Ferrarese artist Ercole de' Roberti.[28] There were also proposals for new conventual buildings to house the growing community, but to the dismay of the canons of

Santa Maria in Porto fuori the Venetian Council of Ten insisted that these should be built within the safety of the walls of Ravenna. It was a way of bringing the cult of the Madonna greca under closer supervision. It was left to the new prior Silvano to implement this contentious measure, which he did in 1503. He was a Venetian from the great family of Morosini and for good measure he was also prior of S. Maria della Carità at Venice.[29] It seems most likely that the move of the monastery under the direction of a Morosini within the walls of the city provided a perfect occasion for the elaboration of the story that a Morosini patriarch of Constantinople had Ravennate connections. It would have provided a way of boulstering the prior's prestige. There are bound to have been family traditions about Thomas Morosini, perhaps even ones linking him with S. Maria in Porto, but there is absolutely no reason to suppose that these identified him as prior of S. Maria in Porto, still less its abbot, since that position did not exist.

It is important to snuff out a modern insistence that at the time of his election to the patriarchal throne of Constantinople he was prior of S. Maria in Porto. This is a nigh impossibility, because a Gualdus is attested as prior of the monastery between February 1192 and June 1204,[30] while a successor Matthew was holding office by 4 June 1205.[31] That leaves a brief interval, in which Morosini could conceivably have been prior of S. Maria in Porto, but from January 1205 he was in frequent communication with Innocent III over his elevation to the patriarchate of Constantinople. If he had indeed been the prior of S. Maria in Porto, would the pope not have addressed him as such? After all, the fame of the monastery and its rule was not just limited to Ravenna. Innocent III remained content to refer to him as a papal subdeacon, which is one of the few hard facts all are agreed on about Thomas Morosini before his election to the throne of Constantinople. Reclusive monks were not a normal recruiting ground for papal subdeacons, who were selected above all for their practical abilities and social standing.[32] Nor does the disobliging portrait of Thomas Morosini drawn by Niketas Choniates—"fatter than a hog raised in a pit"—fit the mould of a monk, whose life has hitherto been subject to an ascetic regime. However, Choniates was intrigued by his dress, which must have been sufficiently different from the dress of other Latin prelates to be worth commenting upon. It fitted tightly around his waist, but was looser around the chest and gathered at the wrists.[33] This may well be a description of the habit worn by canons regular, but of the cathedral chapter of Padua rather than of the monastery of S. Maria in Porto.

For it has been known for more than two centuries that Thomas Morosini was a canon of the cathedral chapter of Padua,[34] or, as it was called at the time, the *canonica* of S. Maria, whence a possible confusion with the canons of S. Maria in Porto. Morosini is first attested as a canon of the cathedral chapter of Padua in 1196, though he was then engaged on purely family business. He was seeking to ensure the succession of his nephews Marino and Albertino to the fief that their father Giovanni Morosini had held from the papal monastery of

S. Maria della Vangadizza at Badia Polesine—some thirty miles from Padua.[35] If Giovanni Morosini, as seems almost certain, was the son of Doge Domenico Morosini,[36] then so was Tommaso Morosini, which would explain his career, given that the younger sons of the Venetian patriciate often went into the Church, where a glittering career might await them.[37] He is first attested in the 1180s as a member of the chapter of St Marks, Venice. He was then made a papal subdeacon by Pope Urban III (1185–1187), who tried to pressurise the chapter of Treviso cathedral into accepting him as a canon: an effort that was repeated by his successor Pope Clement III (1187–1189), which is testimony to the reluctance of the Treviso chapter to admit a Venetian to its number. The chances are that their resistance succeeded, because we next find Morosini as a canon of the cathedral chapter of Padua. Among its attractions were the opportunities it provided to widen his education. In 1196 he was away from Padua studying at Bologna and was contemplating studying somewhere else the next year. The temptation is to think that somewhere else might have been S. Maria in Porto at Ravenna, which, as the example of S. Aldebrando demonstrates, did offer an education but one that compared to Bologna was very basic, given that its rule emphasised not scholarship but good works.[38] In any case, Thomas Morosini was soon back at Padua taking an active role in the administration of the lands and rights belonging to the cathedral chapter. He was the *sindicus et procurator* of the chapter in its dispute with the hospital of S. Maria della Mandria in Padua. The case was of long standing and had been sent before Pope Innocent III, who delegated its hearing in March 1202 to Marco, bishop of Castello (Venice), and to the abbot of the Venetian monastery of S. Ilario. They duly heard it in February 1203 with Thomas Morosini representing the chapter. The case was decided in favour of the cathedral chapter.[39] Soon afterwards Thomas Morosini drops out of the records of the cathedral chapter at Padua. This has to be assessed in the light of the information provided by Innocent III in his letter to the Emperor Baldwin of 21 January 1205, where it is stated that the pope and his brethren were well acquainted with the elect of Constantinople because of "the long stay he had made earlier at the apostolic see". On the basis of this visit the pope formed the impression that "he was of noble family, of honest morals, circumspect in outlook and competently educated".[40] This visit could either have been made earlier in Innocent III's pontificate, but this is unlikely because it is known that representations at the papal curia on behalf of the chapter of Padua in the lawsuit over S. Maria della Mandria, which took up much of the early part of Innocent III's pontificate, were in the hands of another member of the chapter.[41] A date after February 1203 therefore seems the more likely. At some point in 1204 Morosini was back in Venice, because it was from there that the pope summoned him on learning in early January 1205 that he had been elected patriarch of Constantinople. As Innocent III made clear, he considered him a worthy candidate for the patriarchal throne of Constantinople. He had proved his practical abilities in his capacity as syndic and procurator of the cathedral chapter of Padua. That the Venetian canons of St Sophia chose Thomas as patriarch must have owed almost everything to the Doge Enrico Dandolo, who needless to say never consulted him, but the doge will have realised that—as indeed turned out to be the case[42]—here was a member of the Venetian patriciate, who would be acceptable to the pope as Latin patriarch of Constantinople. However, the pope felt that the election infringed the rights of the papacy and insisted that it be quashed, so that the appointment was entirely in papal hands, to which end he first ordained Thomas in quick succession to the diaconate (5 March 1205) and then to the priesthood (26 March 1205), before consecrating him patriarch (27 March 1205). These are details that might present problems about identifying him with the canon of the cathedral chapter of Padua. If, as a canon of a cathedral chapter, Morosini was already in major orders, there would have been no need for the pope to ordain him deacon and priest. However, though canons of cathedral chapters might well be ordained priests, they did not have to be, but could remain in minor orders as a reader or subdeacon, as seems to have been the case at Padua. In the documentation of Thomas Morosini's activities as a canon of Padua there is no indication that he had taken major orders, but remained a subdeacon. It goes without saying that, if he had been the prior of S. Maria in Porto, he would have been in major orders and his ordination by the pope would have been unnecessary.

We can therefore rule out the possibility that Thomas Morosini was ever prior of S. Maria in Porto. He is, after all, attested as a canon of the cathedral chapter of Padua to within a few months of being appointed patriarch of Constantinople. His administrative duties and his defence of the rights of the cathedral chapter provided an excellent preparation for the tasks that faced him as patriarch of Constantinople. Niketas Choniates has turned him into a figure of fun,[43] which has obscured the fact that Thomas was one of the most considerable figures in the early history of the Latin Empire of Constantinople. His early death in 1211 was almost as much a blow as the death of the Emperor Henry of Hainault five years later. Thomas Morosini succeeded in establishing the Latin Church as an ongoing concern. He took an active interest in the implantation of western monasticism in the Latin Empire of Constantinople by his donation of a Greek monastery to the abbey of St Silvester of Nonantola, just outside Modena. He accompanied it with a plea for the monks of Nonantola to colonise its new acquisition with suitable personnel.[44] His dogged battle with the Emperor Henry for the restitution of church lands did much to reverse the adverse settlement made in 1204 by the Partitio Romaniae.[45] In doing so he worked for the interests of the church rather than for Venice, as Thomas Madden has clearly recognised in a thumbnail sketch, which remains far and away the best assessment of Thomas Morosini.[46]

There are two more reasons why whether or not Thomas Morosini was a canon of S. Maria in Porto has no direct relevance to the scenes of the fourth crusade depicted on the mosaic pavement of S. Giovanni Evangelista at Ravenna. In the first place, the future patriarch of Constantinople did not go on the Fourth Crusade. What, therefore, would have been the point of including scenes of the conquest of Zadar and Constantinople, at which he was not present, if the mosaics were intended as his memorial? Secondly, the links between S. Maria in Porto and S. Giovanni Evangelista were looser than some scholars have wished us to believe. They insist that the former was dependency of the latter in order to provide a plausible connection between Morosini and S. Giovanni Evangelista, without which it is difficult to maintain that these scenes present a specifically Venetian version of the Fourth Crusade.[47] Providing grounds for a belief that S. Maria in Porto was a dependency of S. Giovanni Evangelista is a document of Pope Celestine III dated 19 April 1191. It takes the form of a papal confirmation of the concession made to the prior and community of S. Maria in Porto by the abbot and community of S. Giovanni Evangelista to the effect that the latter would make equal provision for S. Maria in Porto from the revenues of properties it had acquired.[48] This has, in fact, nothing to do with the latter being a dependency of the former. It refers to a grant made by the abbey of S. Giovanni Evangelista to S. Maria in Porto in April 1108 soon after its foundation. It contained a rather vague acknowledgement that it would apply to any later acquisitions.

The idea that Thomas Morosini was prior of S. Maria in Porto has to be ruled out, as does the notion that he had some connection to the Fourth Crusade cycle. Both propositions were encouraged by a conviction that Ravenna sent a contingent to the Fourth Crusade, just as it had to the Third Crusade, when one of its contingents was led by Gerard, archbishop of Ravenna and Adelardo Cattaneo, bishop of Verona. Gerard would die in 1189 or 1190 at the siege of Acre. Although Adelardo did not go on the Fourth Crusade, he provided hospitality to the Crusaders, who passed through Verona. It can hardly be a coincidence that on the Fourth Crusade there was a contingent of crusaders from Verona, who later attached themselves to Boniface of Montferrat. Did Ravenna follow suit? Did Archbishop Gerard leave behind a crusading tradition? There are reasons for believing that he was a Cistercian.[49] In his time, if not necessarily under his auspices, the monastery of S. Severo in Classe experienced considerable building activity.[50] It is not impossible that this was connected to its conversion into a Cistercian house, though this is normally dated to the mid-thirteenth century.[51] A Cistercian presence in Ravenna would not be without significance given the leading role that the order played in the preaching and organisation of the fourth crusade. There is another rather unexpected connection between Ravenna and the fourth crusade. When the archiepiscopal throne of Ravenna fell vacant in the summer of 1201, there was a majority among the Ravennate clergy, who supported the candidacy of Cardinal Soffredo, who was one of the papal legates responsible for organising the Fourth Crusade. However, Innocent III's approval of this choice was not forthcoming.[52] The Ravennate clergy had rather reluctantly to accept as their archbishop their second choice—Alberto Oseletti, bishop of Imola. The historian of Ravenna, Girolamo Rossi, endows the latter with a military temperament and puts him in command of a Venetian fleet against the Saracens, "for at that time", in his words, "Saladin was occupying almost all the cities previously held by the Christians". Rossi then goes on to provide an account of the third crusade. It is clear that he is muddling Alberto with his predecessor Gerard, who did participate in the Third Crusade, though this Rossi completely ignores.[53] A more elaborate version of Archbishop Alberto's crusading activities is provided by Serafino Pasolini, a seventeenth-century Ravennate antiquarian. In his narrative of the cult of the Madonna greca he has under the year 1205 the archbishop sailing off under the protection of "Maria Greca" from Ravenna. He was seeking the recovery of the Holy Sepulchre; having been appointed "commander of the Venetian fleet against the Saracens".[54] In another work, he gives the names of five leading figures from Ravenna, who had helped Cardinal Carsendino to recover Ravenna for the papacy. They then joined Archbishop Alberto who had been appointed "Capitan Generale dell'Armata" that the Venetians were sending against the Saracens. Later they entered the service of the Emperor Otto IV and finally they went to the aid of Azzo d'Este, lord of Ferrara.[55] The whole thing is a farrago. These leading figures from Ravenna have names that were far more distinguished in the seventeenth and eighteenth centuries than they were in the early thirteenth century.[56] *Pace* a historian of Ravenna as distinguished as A. Vasina[57] the notion that Archbishop Alberto participated in the Fourth Crusade seems to be a later invention.

The main reason why historians have been so happy to accept Thomas Morosini's connection with Ravenna is that it provides a plausible explanation of the presence in the Church of S. Giovanni Evangelista of a series of panels depicting the Fourth Crusade. They originally formed a pavement, which, a surviving inscription tells us, was laid down in 1213 under the auspices of Abbot Guglielmo. Its importance is considerable because it represents one of the earliest, if not the very earliest, accounts of the Fourth Crusade. It has to be said that it does not seem to have been greatly appreciated at Ravenna, because it was covered over half a century later and was only rediscovered during excavations carried out in 1763.[58] Ruling out any connection between Thomas Morosini and the Fourth Cusade cycle in the church of S. Giovanni Evangelista makes its existence more of a mystery than ever. It means that for the time being we shall have to abandon a favourite interpretation of this cycle as a specifically Venetian version of the history of the Fourth Crusade.[59] A major problem is that we know next to nothing about Abbot Guglielmo, who supervised the construction of the pavement.[60] Until we do we are left with the potentially more fruitful approach of the late Professor N. Kenaan—Kedar, who sought to understand the cycle as a whole. She saw it as a thanks-offering by a wife for the safe return of her husband from the Fourth Crusade.[61]

But this is not to argue that Thomas Morosini had no connection with Ravenna. One piece of contemporary evidence has been completely overlooked. Before despatching the papal notary Magister Maximus to Constantinople in August 1212 Innocent III provided him with a succinct report on the anarchy into which the church of Constantinople had descended since the death of Thomas Morosini a little over a year earlier. He dwelt on an incident which occurred the previous Christmas, when the Latin bishop of Brysis (*Vericensis*) abandoned his see and came to Constantinople, where he occupied the seat in St Sophia reserved for the patriarch. He did not stop there. He also made a distribution of patriarchal property. He even went so far as to seize the patriarchal seal, in order to authenticate letters, which he then despatched to Ravenna. These enabled him to lay hands on sums of money deposited there by Thomas Morosini.[62] If nothing else, it shows that Thomas Morosini banked at Ravenna, which suggests that there was some substance to the traditions linking him to Ravenna, later picked up by sixteenth-century antiquarians. The evidence of the papal letter is, however, not easy to interpret. Morosini was not the only prelate to bank at Ravenna to judge by what we know about Archbishop Rainer of Split, who took up office in 1175. He was a native of Tuscany and had previously been bishop of Cagli in the Marche, some hundred miles south of Ravenna. Not wishing to take his valuables with him on the sea voyage to Split, he deposited them with the monastery of S. Maria in Porto at Ravenna. Upon his murder in 1180 his successor sent to Ravenna to recover the property, which rightfully belonged to the church of Split.[63] This anecdote makes it more likely than not that Thomas Morosini also deposited sums of money with the canons of S. Maria in Porto. One can understand why an archbishop of Split might want to entrust the safekeeping of his valuables to this monastery. Ravenna was at least a point of embarkation for Dalmatia, but it was another matter for a Venetian, who became Latin patriarch of Constantinople. It suggests that he had had previous dealings with S. Maria in Porto. This does not mean, however, that he was ever its prior, which has to be ruled out for the reasons given above, but it did provide the basis for the elaboration of later traditions. What these previous dealings were must necessarily remain a matter of speculation. However, it should not be forgotten that Thomas Morosini's relations with both Venice and the Venetian colony in Constantinople deteriorated as his patriarchate progressed.[64] With this in mind depositing large sums of money in Venice might not have been the most sensible thing to do, while the action of the archbishop of Split opens up the possibility that Ravenna had a reputation as a safe haven for ecclesiastical wealth.

Notes

1 *Oxford Dictionary of Byzantium*, ed. A. Kazhdan (Oxford, 1991), III, sub Thomas Morosini.
2 T.F. Madden, "The Venetian Version of the Fourth Crusade: Memory and the Conquest of Constantinople in Medieval Venice", *Speculum*, 87(2012), 318.

3 L. Santifaller, *Beiträge zur Geschichte des Lateinischen Patriarchats von Konstantinopel (1204–1261) und der venezianischen Urkunde* (Weimar, 1938), 25.
4 G. Fedalto, *La Chiesa latina in Oriente* (Verona, 1973), I, 183.
5 A. Carile, *Per una storia dell'impero latino di Costantinopoli (1204–1261)*, 220; A. Carile, "Episodi della IV Crociata nel mosaico pavimentale di S. Giovanni Evangelista di Ravenna", *Corsi di Cultura sull' Arte Ravennate e Bizantina*, 23(1976), 109–130.
6 R. Farioli Campanati, *I mosaici pavimentali della chiesa di S. Giovanni Evangelista in* Ravenna (Ravenna, 1995); G. Morelli, *Il Medioevo dell'Abate Guglielmo: nei mosaici di San Giovanni Evangelista l'Europa cortese si* racconta (Ravenna, 2011); C. Fiori and E. Tozzola, *San Giovanni Evangelista a Ravenna: storia di una chiesa, di mosaici perduti e di mosaici ritrovati* (Ravenna, 2014), 58–60.
7 J.P. Migne, *Patrologia Latina* (Paris, 1841–1864), 216, no.xcvii, 459–460 (5 August 1211).
8 A notable exception is G. Tassinari, "San Giovanni Evangelista e i mosaici della quarta crociata: considerazioni araldiche", *Ravenna: studi e ricerche*, 24(2017), 23, n.8. I have to thank Tom Brown for calling my attention to this article.
9 Paolo Ramusio, *Della guerra di Costantinopoli per la restitutione de gl'imperatori Comneni fatta da' Sig. Venetiani et Francesi, l'anno MCCIV libri sei* (Venice: Domenico Nicolini, 1604).
10 Paolo Ramusio, *De bello Costantinopolitano et imperatoribus Comnenis per Gallos et Venetos restititutis historia* (Venice: Marcantonio Brogiolo, 1609).
11 E. Gibbon, *The History of the decline and fall of the Roman Empire*, ed. J.B. Bury (London, 1898), VI, 412, n. 120.
12 F.C. Lane, *Venice: a maritime republic* (Baltimore, 1973), 398.
13 F.S. Marchesa Dondi-Orologio, *Serie cronologico-istorica dei canonici di Padova* (Padua: Tipografio di Seminario, 1805), 118.
14 There is a historical basis to bishops resigning to become canons of S. Maria in Porto. In 1199 Enrico, bishop of Senigallia pledged his stole as part of his promise to become a canon of S. Maria in Porto, once he had resigned his bishopric: A. Polverari, *Regesti Senigallesi (secc. VII–XII)* (Senigallia, 1974), no. 362, 126.
15 G. Rossi (Rubeus), *HIstoriarum Ravennatum—Libri Decem* (Venice: Aldus, 1572), 280–281.
16 *Dizionario biografico degli Italiani*, ed. A.M. Ghisalberti (Rome, 1960–), sub Ubaldo, san.
17 G.L. Amadesi, *In Antistitum Ravennatum chronotaxim ab ejus Ecclesiae exordiis.... disquisitiones perpetuae* (Faenza: Josephus Antonius Archius, 1783), III, 36–41.
18 *Andreae Danduli Ducis Venetiarum Chronica per extensum descripta aa.46–1280*, ed. E. Pastorello [Rerum Italicarum Scriptores, XII/1 (Bologna, 1938), 291.23–25.
19 *Extrema aegritudine laborante*: Migne, *Patrologia latina*, 216, no. xcvii, 459.
20 Migne, *Patrologia latina*, 179, no. ccxi, 257.
21 *Regesti Senigalliensi*, xxviii, no. 363, 126.
22 *Dizionario Biografico degli Italiani*, sub Aldebrando, santo. Illustration in Raimond van Marle, *Development of the Italian Schools of Painting*, I (Hague, 1923), fig. 231.
23 M. Fantuzzi, *Monumenti Ravennati de' secoli di mezzo: per la maggiore parte inediti* (Venice: Francesco Andreoli, 1802–1805), II, no. LXIII, 122–124.
24 G. Fabri, *Effemeride sagra et istorica di Ravenna antica* (Ravenna: Stamperia camarale ed arcivescovale, 1675), 368.
25 G. Montanari, "Istituzioni ecclesiastiche e vita religiosa nella diocesi di Ravenna", in *Storia di Ravenna*, III (Venice, 1993), 291–292.

26 N. Widloecher, *La congregazione dei Canonici regolari lateranensi. Periodo di formazione (1402–1483)* (Gubbio, 1929), 59.
27 C. Egger, "Canonici regolari di Santa Maria in Porto", in *Dizionario degli istituti di perfezione,* II (Rome, 1973), 147–148.
28 J. Manca, *The Art of Ercole de'Roberti* (Cambridge, 1992), 38–45.
29 A. Tarlazzi, *Memorie Sagre di Ravenna* (Ravenna, 1852), 340–342.
30 Fantuzzi, *Monumenti*, II, 278; III, 292, 293.
31 Fantuzzi, *Monumenti*, II, 279.
32 Jochen Johrendt, "Der vierte Kreuzzug, das lateinische Kaiserreich und die päpstliche Kapelle unter Innocenz III", *Legati, delegati e l'impresa d'Oltremare (secoli XII–XIII) / Papal Legates, Delegates and the Crusades (12th–13th Century)*: Atti del Convegno internazionale di studi Milano, Università Cattolica del Sacro Cuore, 9–11 marzo 2011, eds. Maria-Pia Alberzoni and Paschal Montaubin (Turnhout, 2014), 51–114].
33 Niketas Choniates, *Historia*, ed. J-L. van Dieten [CFHB 11] (Berlin/New York, 1975), 623.70–79; 647.6–17.
34 F.S. Dondi dall'Orologico, *Serie cronologico-istorica dei canonici di Padova* (Padova: Tipografia del Seminario, 1805), 118.
35 A. Rigon, "<<*Si ad scolas iverit*>> Il canonico di Padova Tommaso Morosini, primo patriarca latino d"Oriente, in un inedito documento del 1196", *Quaderni per la storia dell' Università di Padova*, 33(2000), 1–8.
36 In 1195 a Giovanni Morosini was in command together with Ruggero Premarino of a Venetian fleet, which swept the Pisans out of the Adriatic, but the following year he was replaced by Giacomo Querini. His death in the mean time provides a possible explanation.
37 Enrico Dandolo, patriarch of Grado, is a good example: see T.F. Madden, *Enrico Dandolo and the Rise of Venice* (Baltimore, 2003), 19–38.
38 M.C. Miller, "Secular Clergy and religious life: Verona in the age of reform", in *Medieval Religion: New Approaches*, ed. C.H. Berman (New York/London, 2014), 167.
39 F.S. Marchesa Dondi dall'Orologio, *Dissertazioni sopra l'istoria ecclesiastica di Padova* (Padua: Tipografia del Seminario, 1802–1817), VII, 62–63.
40 *The Deeds of Pope Innocent III*, transl. J.M. Powell (Washington D.C., 2004), 176.
41 Augustinus: Dondi dall'Orologio, op.cit., VI, 185.
42 Tafel & Thomas I, no. cxxxv, 538–539: 30.iii.1205.
43 Niketas Choniates, 623.70–79; 647.6–17.
44 G. Tiraboschi, *Storia dell'augusta badia di S. Silvestro di Nonantola* (Mantua: Società tipografica, 1785), II, no. cdiii, 339–340.
45 Filip van Tricht, *The Latin* Renovatio *of Byzantium: the Empire of Constantinople (1204–1228)* (Leiden/Boston, 2011), 230, 308–317, 334–337.
46 Madden, *Enrico Dandolo,* 180–183.
47 *Pace* Madden, "The Venetian Version of the Fourth Crusade", 317–322.
48 Fantuzzi, *Monumenti Ravennati*, VI, no. XXVIII, 56; Migne, *Patrologia Latina*, 204, 867.
49 A.J. Andrea, *The Capture of Constantinople: the* "Hystoria Constantinopolitana" *of Gunther of Pairis* (Philadelphia, 1997), 34.
50 A. Augenti et al. "Il monastero di San Severo a Classe", in *VI Congresso Nazionale di Archeologia Medievale*, eds. F. Redi and A. Forgione (Florence, ca. 2012) 238–245.
51 József Laszlovszky, "The monastery of San Severo in Classe/Ravenna: Archaeological and Historical Data for the Transformation of a Late Antique Basilica during the Middle Ages", *Annual of Medieval Studies*, 13(2007), 201.

52 A. Potthast, *Regesta Pontificum Romanorum inde ab Anno Post Christum natum MCXCVIII ad Anno MCCCIV* (Berlin, 1874), I, p. 135, no. 1546.
53 G. Rossi, *Historiarum Ravennatum,* 276.
54 S. Pasolini, *Relatione breve e divota della Madonna Greca de' canonici portuensi di Ravenna* (Ravenna: Stampa camarile e arciepiscopale, 1676), 75–77.
55 S. Pasolini, *Huomini illustri di Ravenna antica et altri professori di lettera & armi* (Bologna: Pier-maria Monti, 1703), 115–116.
56 Antonio Saffi, Alessandro Giudice, Desdeo Carrari di Ubertino, Pietro Rasponi, Ridolfo Spreti di Araldo.
57 A. Vasina, *Le crociate nel mondo italiano* (Bologna/Padua, 1973), 34. But see now G. Tassinari, "San Giovanni Evangelista e i mosaici della quarta crociata: considerazioni araldiche", *Ravenna: studi e ricerche*, 24(2017), 25–29, who subjects these traditions to proper scrutiny.
58 Fiori and Tozzola, *S. Giovanni Evangelista*, 63–79.
59 T.F. Madden, "The Venetian Version of the Fourth Crusade: Memory and the Conquest of Constantinople in Medieval Venice", *Speculum*, 87(2012), 317–322; D.M. Perry, *Sacred Plunder: Venice and the Aftermath of the Fourth Crusade* (University Park PA, 2015), 54.
60 G. Morelli, *Il medioevo dell'Abate Guglielmo: nei mosaici di San Giovanni Evangelista l'Europa cortese si racconta* (Ravenna, 2011), 83–84.
61 R. Farioli Campanati and N. Kenaan-Kedar, *Le copie dei mosaici medievali di San Giovanni Evangelista* (Ravenna, 2001), 40–43; N. Kenaan-Kedar, "Pictorial and Sculptural Commemoration of Returning or Departing Crusaders", in *The Crusades and Visual Culture*, ed. E. Lepina, A.J. Morris, S.A. Throop, L.J. Whatley (Farnham/Burlington, 2015), 98–102. See now Michael Angold, "A papal Version of the Fourth Crusade; The Mosaics of San Giovanni Evangelista at Ravenna", *Speculum*, 94/4 (October 2019), 1–27.
62 Migne, *Patrologia Latina*, 216, clvi, 675–681.
63 Archdeacon Thomas of Split, *History of the Bishops of Salona and Split*: Latin Text by O. Peric; edited and translated by D. Karbic, M.M. Sokol, and J.R. Sweeney [Central European Medieval Texts, 4] (Budapest/New York, 2006), 120–121, 128–129.
64 R.L. Wolff, "Footnote to an incident of the Latin occupation of Constantinople: the Church and the Icon of the Hodegetria", *Traditio*, 6(1948), 319–328.

Part IV

Empire and elites

12 Dux to episcopus: From ruling cities to controlling sees in Byzantine Italy, 554–900

Introduction

In the twilight of the Roman world, it became relatively common for men engaged in traditional bureaucratic careers within the Roman administration to abandon their claims to purely secular authority through civic or imperial offices and become leaders of the church. The most prominent of these men included Ambrose of Milan, who in 374 left his post as *consularius* of Aemelia and Liguria, and was subsequently elevated to the position of Bishop of Milan, but there were many others. In the fourth century in the East a number of members of the *curiales* strove to obtain episcopal sees as a crowning achievement of their political ambitions (as much as a desire to avoid curial responsibilities), such as Eleusius of Cyzicus (d. ca. 393) and Iulius Eugenius in Laodiceia Combusta (ca. 320–340). In the fifth century in Gaul, Germanus (d. ca. 448) served as governor in Gaul before becoming bishop of Auxerre, while Sidonius Apollinaris (d. 489) became the Bishop of Auvergne after a career as a poet, senator, and ultimately urban prefect of Rome. The permeability between civic or imperial positions and episcopal office seen in this first wave was slowed only by church councils and legal decree in the sixth century, when Justinian prohibited "civil servants or *curiales* from access to the episcopate, unless they had already ruptured their ties to the world by entering the monastic order at a young age".[1]

In the early Middle Ages, this practice continued in various regions, fuelled by both external and internal pressures, including the growing responsibility for bishops over secular affairs and the patchwork application of church canon and imperial legislation. In the exarchate of Italy, with its fusion of military and civil offices in the wake of the Lombard migration into the peninsula, the pattern of movement from secular to episcopal offices, although nominally prohibited under the laws expounded by the emperor in Constantinople, still occurred in a number of prominent instances. In the major Byzantine cities in Italy from the end of the sixth century through the ninth century, a number of laymen holding administrative and military office "un-girded" the military belts of their positions to take up the clerical garb and rank as bishop or archbishop. Sometimes setting aside their wives, these men would occupy the episcopal sees of the central cities of the territory, Ravenna and Naples. The patterns of these shifts suggest the growing entrenchment of elites from the East as a hereditary or aristocratic elite, adopting both the pastoral and leadership roles within the church as the next phase of a career overseeing the administration and defense of the territory. The examples of archbishops Agnellus (557–570) and Sergius (744–769) in Ravenna, and Stephen II (767–800) and the clan of the Sergii in Naples beginning in the ninth century, attest to the varying nature of the practice and shed light on both how members of the secular elite took over archiepiscopal sees in Byzantine Italy, and the benefits and misfortunes brought to the churches they occupied.

Limits to episcopal office

In 513 while on a pilgrimage to Rome, Caesarius of Arles personally presented Pope Symmachus a letter in which he petitioned the pope to address some of the violations taking place in Gaul: the alienation of church property, the abduction and marriage of nuns, and the purchasing of episcopal office. All had been regulated by earlier church councils and decrees, but their practice still continued. Added to this group of clearly improper behaviours Caesarius raised a new issue and proposed a limitation and prohibition on the appointment of certain men to the status of priest or bishop:

> I likewise request that no layman who has exercised jurisdiction in public office or has governed provinces on behalf of any ruler be ordained a cleric or bishop unless he has for a long time lived the way of life prescribed by law and his life has been examined.[2]

Although in agreement, Pope Symmachus's response was somewhat reserved:

> As for laypersons, we decree that they should not be permitted to enter the priesthood easily. Times and ranks have been established for them by which they ought to aspire to this status. For whoever is promoted without due process easily inspires ill will, and without the appropriate experience he cannot be officially elected.[3]

While it is clear that rules were in place to deal with the problematic issue of those in political power taking episcopal power, it remained a frequent topic for councils. Caesarius himself was involved in three regional councils, Agde in 506, Epaone in 517, and Arles in 524, which specifically addressed the problems of clerical behaviour, including the inherent conflicts in the permeability of clerical and episcopal office for those of military and administrative backgrounds without proper oversight or review.[4]

Although moving from lay positions of authority to those of bishop could be problematic, Claudia Rapp has observed that, as early as the fourth century, episcopal service within the ranks of elite families was desired: "the fact that a candidate for the episcopate could point to a pedigree of ecclesiastical service among his relatives and ancestors must have been a source of pride and distinction for the individual, motivating him to uphold the family tradition. … Moreover, such a family background also contributed to a future bishop's qualifications for this ministry in the eyes of his contemporaries".[5] This explains why ten of the fifty-five bishops in Italy from 350 to 450 came from families with a clerical tradition, and in many instances having clerical ancestors remained one of the common qualities of bishops for some communities.

Following the elevated profile of the issue of episcopal offices held by former imperial and civic leaders, the prohibitions against movement between positions of purely secular authority and episcopal careers would be incorporated into Roman law, including in Justinian's legal projects of the 530s. In the imperial edict issued to the Patriarch Epiphanius and forwarded to the leaders of the Church, Justinian clearly stated the prohibitions and limitations to ordination for those who were formerly in civil or curial service unless they left at a young age.[6] Although time in a monastic community and the abandonment of wealth would allow for exceptions to be made, having progeny, legitimate or otherwise, would have created a permanent obstacle for obtaining the rank of bishop: "He may have neither children nor grandchildren, either those recognised by law or those rejected".[7]

Despite pleas of various church leaders and codification in imperial legislation, the connections between secular governance and episcopal rule remained muddled not only in the activities of those looking to further a political or administrative career by becoming a bishop, but in the language circulating in the highest levels of the church itself. At the end of the sixth century, Gregory the Great (pope from 590–604), in his *Liber regulae pastoralis* (designed to synthesise various traditions of thought on pastoral care into a cohesive philosophy of spiritual authority) comments obliquely on the possible problems for those who specifically seek the office of bishop for its institutional authority.[8] The problem for Gregory hinged on the language of 1 Timothy 3:1–7, which outlines the qualifications of a bishop, beginning with the statement that "Whoever aspires to the office of bishop desires a noble task".[9] Gregory explained that in the time of the apostles, those holding the office of bishop were often martyred, connecting the "noble task" to the position, but ended his analysis with the problems of his own age. A man might "seek the glory of honor rather than the ministry of good work, and is witness against himself that he does not desire the office of bishop" for the correct reasons.[10] That man further does not understand the sacred office, but desires authority for the subjugation of others and the praise it offers.

Although the template Gregory offers is abstract, it was a firm reminder of the important status of bishop at the dawn of the seventh century, and the necessity of the office to be distinct from secular positions of authority. It further underscores the desires of those who sought the episcopal see for the power of the office rather than its spiritual leadership. And despite both the pastoral and legal impediments to the office of bishop for those who had also managed the responsibilities of government, the barrier was effectively permeable for the right candidates.

Ruling "*as an exarch*" in Ravenna: from soldier to archbishop

The situation of the city of Ravenna was unique in Byzantine Italy. Although easterners made up only a small number of the city's residents, its position as the administrative centre of the exarchate reinforced its political proximity to Constantinople despite its real distance (and later genuine animosity to Byzantine rule).[11] Further still, the late Roman imperial monuments of the first half of the fifth century, and the royal palaces of the Ostrogothic kingdom of the early sixth century, were physical reminders of the city's august position as a centre of independent political power.[12] This fact was also reflected in the nature of the church in the city, which at many times sought to distance and differentiate itself from its northern rival, Milan, and the papacy in Rome, first in the adoptions of Roman and Milanese saints as its own, then through the controversy over the *pallium* in the sixth century, and later during its claims of imperially designated independence.[13] Although by the eighth century, the fate of the Church of Ravenna would remain closely intertwined with that of Rome, control of the see remained critical to control of the city and influence in the region. Following the arrival of the Ottonian emperors in the 950s, the eventual usurpation of the see as a position that was held by imperially appointed candidates at the very end of the tenth century attests to the importance the church of Ravenna still held.[14]

In Byzantine Italy, the first recorded instance of crossing the permeable barrier between administrative rule and the episcopal office occurred during the sixth century. The successor to Ravenna's first archbishop, Maximian, who had been appointed by Justinian in the wake of the conquest of the Gothic kingdom, was a man named Agnellus. He served as archbishop from 557 to 570 according to the account of his life in the *Liber pontificalis ecclesiae ravennatis*, the serial biographies of the bishops and archbishops composed in the middle of the ninth century by a cleric also named Agnellus and modelled on the *Liber pontificalis* of Rome.[15] The biography of the archbishop, written more than two centuries after his death, offers only scant details of his life outside of his episcopal career, yet it is nevertheless worth considering in light of his accomplishments.

According to the *Liber pontificalis* of Ravenna, "after the death of his wife, [Agnellus] relinquished his military belt (*cingulum militiae*, standing in for both military service and public life) and devoted and offered himself completely to God".[16] The biography continues its introduction on his religious career, as deacon under Ecclesius (who served as bishop from 522–532), and ending with a statement of Agnellus's attributes: "[He was] sprung from noble stock, wealthy in possessions, rich in animals, abounding in wealth".[17] Although noble stock would have been advantageous, the real as opposed to figurative wealth of the archbishop might have been a concern for the author of the biography and his audience, and perhaps the contemporaries of the archbishop.

Especially problematic would have been his surviving family members, who are addressed at length in the biography in the succeeding section:

> At the end of his life, when he was close to death, he left as his heir, after the death of her mother, his granddaughter, the daughter of his daughter, leaving her, when his death occurred, among other wealth five silver ornamental vessels for the table and many other things, since it is not our task to digress about diverse wealth. But it should be asked by us why this married man obtained such a noble see. As you know, the author of the apostles says the husband of one wife and who has children can be ordained a bishop, with true providence, and the canons confirm this. But let us return to the sequence and discuss women later.[18]

Unfortunately, after describing Agnellus's episcopal career, the biography ends without returning to the issue of the inheritance of his granddaughter. The moveable wealth of the silver vessels would not have been out of the ordinary as a valuable and notable part of her patrimony, likely described in a will to which the biographer had access (although most of the other surviving wills of the sixth and seventh centuries are concerned with the transmission of land and shares in larger estates).[19]

What is essential for the discussion here is the contextualisation of this problematic fact: Agnellus had a family, and especially an heir who would receive benefits on his death. To reconcile this, the biographer relied on the same passage in 1 Timothy that describes the attributes of a bishop, including the fact that he "is to be above reproach, married only once. ... He must manage his own family well and see that his children obey him, and he must do so in a manner worthy of full respect".[20] Despite the biographer's claim on Apostolic precedent, by the sixth century this custom ran counter to the legal statues of Justinian as well as the developing practice of clerical celibacy which had crept into the core traditions at the end of late antiquity likely connected to the responsibility for the preparation of the Eucharist or the importance of practiced asceticism; the practice of celibacy ultimately set the priests and bishops apart from the communities they helped oversee.[21]

Agnellus's status as a layman with a military career that ended in the 520s would have been an important asset for the unique core issue of his episcopal career: the reconciliation of Gothic churches in Ravenna.[22] His previous position and career also illustrates the close connection between imperial power and the growing responsibilities of the church (and the benefits the church derived from their relationships). Specific to the political context, his *vita* in the *Liber pontificalis* goes on at length about the various churches that had fallen into the possession of the church of Ravenna after legal degrees deprived the Arian Ostrogothic church of its existence, and the various means Agnellus took to rehabilitate and recondition them for contemporary catholic use.[23] The integration of these churches, and the Goths who still must have felt some draw towards them, would have seemed fitting to fall on a man who likely served in some capacity under the Gothic administration (at least during the lifetime of Theoderic, whose rule ended with his death in 526). This does not equate to an abandonment of Romanness (or at least Catholic-ness, as he was a deacon under bishop Ecclesius), but it alludes to his military service and perhaps suggests that he had familiarity with the Ostrogothic soldiers living in Ravenna.[24]

Although the *Liber Pontificalis* presents a wealth of information about the churches of Ravenna that had undergone some form of renewal under Agnellus's patronage, perhaps the most critical limitation of this short biography is that we do not know any further details as to what Agnellus's career may have been before the 520s, likely a factor of the author's leanings. It is likely that Angellus was a member of the military, or military bureaucracy, which in the middle of the sixth century had taken on administrative roles, and that according to the *Liber Pontificalis* he had wealth in both land and animals, and the ability to offer for his heirs substantial patrimony. However, the account leaves us with many questions: Given that he was the first of the bishops who was acknowledged for his prior lay career, how did Agnellus counter the proscriptions against bishops having heirs? How was he able to preserve such a substantial patrimony for his granddaughter? Were the limitations on becoming a bishop overlooked in his appointment or was his time as deacon sufficient? Despite these problems, the career of Agnellus marks the first nexus between the attainment of episcopal office after military and administrative service visible in newly Byzantine Italy.

Subsequently, in the main centres of Rome, Ravenna, and Naples, despite close relationships between local aristocracies and the church, the episcopal and papal offices would manage to avoid dominance by members of the former senatorial and current administrative elite. This situation would last through the middle of the eighth century, when Sergius rose to occupy the see of Ravenna.

According to the *Liber pontificalis* of Ravenna, the election of Sergius was fraught, the victim of internal strife between various Ravennate factions or divisions within the clergy which prevented him from immediately assuming his role after his papal consecration, although generally offered a positive perspective on his career. The description in the *Liber pontificalis* begins by commenting broadly on Sergius's visage, his ancestry (sprung from the most noble family), and the fact that he did not have a clerical background. The second sentence of the *vita* makes this clear: "He was a layman and had a wife. After he took up the rule of the church, he consecrated his wife Euphemia as a deaconess, and she remained in that condition".[25] Although he set her aside to fulfill his obligation of clerical and episcopal celibacy, his status as a layman of elite standing was one of his most noted features.

The fact that Sergius was also responsible for the city after the end of the exarchate was also mentioned in the *Liber pontificalis*. In this context, Sergius's pre-episcopal status of a layman (and that of his near contemporary, Stephen of Naples, discussed later) was used in an argument for the validity of the papacy of Constantine, who served as pope for the brief period from 5 July 767 through August of the following year. His elevation from layman to bishop of Rome was instigated by his brother Toto, the duke of Nepi, who had personally secured his election and claimed the title of Duke of Rome, and was challenged by various Roman factions in a case we will return to in the conclusion.[26]

Although the earlier Agnellus proved to be an effective archbishop and patron of the integrated ex-Gothic churches, the author of the *Liber pontificialis* was clear on Sergius's success, maneuvering between Rome and the Lombards (despite the predation of both), assigning him both the facets of political and religious power. After 751, his biographer claimed, "he had jurisdiction over the whole Pentapolis, from the borders of Persiceto up to Tuscany and the river Volano, he ruled everything like the exarch, just as now the Romans are accustomed to do".[27] Although the rest of the account of his episcopacy is lost in the surviving manuscripts, for Deborah Deliyannis it is clear that in the mind of his ninth-century biographer, "Sergius represents an ideal combination of ecclesiastical and secular authority to which the ninth-century bishops of Ravenna should aspire".[28] In both cases, Sergius and Agnellus do not simply seek the honor of the position (a situation feared by Gregory the Great), but according to their descriptions in the *Liber pontificalis* of Ravenna, they instead put to use their skills and connections in the service of the church and the city of Ravenna.[29]

From *dux* to *episcopus* and *episcopus* to *dux* in Naples

In 751, the Lombards began their occupation of Ravenna and the Pentapolis, acts which allowed for expansion of Sergius's role as archbishop.[30] They had made good on threats to seize territory under Roman control, an act that directly precipitated the arrival of the Franks in Northern Italy and decreased the area of direct Byzantine rule to portions of southern Italy. In the following century, Naples, a city with historically strong ties to both Constantinople and to Greek culture, would begin the long process of re-envisioning itself both as Italian and independent (to varying degrees). There were many aspects of this process: one involved the translation and rehabilitation of Greek hagiography in an Italian context; a second was the production of the serial biography of the bishops of the city in the same vein as the *Liber pontificalis* of Rome and Ravenna; a third was the slow development of ducal domination of the office of bishop.

These last two aspects are for the most part intertwined, as the history of Naples in the eighth and ninth century is primarily preserved in the serial biography, untitled in the middle ages but known in contemporary editions as the *Gesta episcoporum neapolitanorum*, or alternatively as the *Chronicon episcoporum sanctae neapolitanae ecclesiae*, the source which describes and celebrates the close collaboration between the *duces* who led the city and its bishops.[31] Surviving as an autograph, the *Gesta* was composed in three distinct sections: the first, by an anonymous author (assigned to the ninth century on paleographic grounds), covers the lives of the bishops to 763 and was formed by compiling information from earlier sources, primarily the *Liber pontificalis* of Rome. The work was continued by a Neapolitan hagiographer, translator and cleric, John the Deacon, up through 872; and on the final page of the codex concluded with an imperfect biography of the life of bishop Athanasius II by Peter the Subdeacon. In total, its aims were to not only provide an institutional history of the Neapolitan church but to position it positively between Rome and its other southern rivals.

The first secular ruler of the Neapolitans to obtain the position of bishop was Stephen II. Unlike the accounts from Ravenna, the *Gesta* of Naples explained at length how a layman who was serving as duke came to become bishop, and the process of rapid education needed for the transition from secular authority to sacred office. It reports that during the last year of the life of Bishop Paul (763–766), a plague swept through Naples taking the lives of many citizens, as well as most of the members of the clergy. Those who remained selected Stephen as bishop, although he had been serving as the *dux* of the city for twelve years; even before the collapse of the exarchate, Naples had fallen under the authority of the Byzantine governor in Sicily, and in taking up the title of *dux* in 755 he became the first "locally elected *dux*".[32]

After the crisis brought about by the plague and his selection as bishop, Stephen legitimised his new position by appointing his son Gregory as his successor as *dux* (so as not to hold the two simultaneously), receiving tonsure, and going to Rome to be consecrated by the recently installed pope Stephen III (while the position of *dux* may not have been hereditary at the outset, it would remain within the family for several generations). In addition to papal consecration, bishop Stephen II undertook a rapid clerical education: "thus he began to study divine matters as if he had been a little boy undergoing schooling".[33] Part of the success that Stephen found as bishop (or at least as presented in the *Gesta*) was in the patronage of various local churches and monasteries and the gifts of high value objects, but he also used the position to carefully ensure that his family would maintain control in Naples.

This is evidenced by Stephen II's nomination and support of his son-in-law Theophylact after the death of his own son and *dux* Gregory. Luigi Berto has argued even Stephen's acceptance of the episcopal see was primarily political, and that his "decision to become bishop was dictated by the desire to ensure that the control of power in Naples remained firmly in the hands of his family, and [his appointment of Theophylact] shows that he continued to exert a certain influence on Neapolitan politics".[34] Nevertheless, despite the cooption of the episcopal see as a means to control both the church's property and the succession of dukes, the church as an institution also benefited, not only in enhanced stability but also in the fact it became the almost singular focus of religious patronage.

Although with Stephen II's death in 800 the episcopacy would go to an individual outside of his family, it was not outside of its influence. Stephen II's successor was a layman, Paul, chosen by his son-in-law Theophylact, an act that would further solidify the coordination between dukes and bishops in Naples. Although the downfall of Theophylact would end the nascent formation of a dynasty, one descendent of Stephen II would continue to remain central to the rule of the city through the early ninth century despite interlopers in the position of both bishop and duke: the son of Stephen II, also Stephen, would serve as *dux* from 821 until his assassination in 832. While a long-lasting dynasty did not evolve from this family, Stephen II's accession to the episcopal see paved the way for his successor Sergius. Although Sergius came from neighbouring Cumae, his descendants would control Naples directly for another two and a half centuries, and within a generation mark the point when the position of *dux* and that of *episcopus* were held simultaneously.

The story of Sergius, narrated primarily though the *Gesta* of the bishops of Naples, in many ways parallels that of Stephen. While originally from the neighbouring community of Cumae, he was supported by the Neapolitans to be *dux* in 839, and his success in dealing both with a crisis within the episcopacy and the ongoing problems with the Lombard duchy of Benevento allowed him a great degree of local control.[35] Rather than taking the position of bishop himself as his predecessor Stephan II had done, Sergius placed one of his sons, a young deacon named Athanasius, on the episcopal see after the death of John IV in 849. In the following year, he appointed his eldest son Gregory as heir and co-ruler.

To help qualify his elevation at the tender age of twenty, the *Gesta* highlights Athanasius's education before being bishop, that "he remained under tutors and writers, so as he might be given instruction in every catholic institution being unaware of worldly business".[36] Following his consecration by pope Leo IV, his early episcopacy was equally lauded:

> After being enthroned [as bishop], he began to bestow extravagantly the abundance of doctrine that he learned in during his childhood. He established schools for lectors and singers; he instituted schools of

> literature for some of those starting instruction; he brought others together in the scribal office, as the provident shepherd might protect his flock with a pen, insofar as he required nothing, he might exhibit his consideration for the Lord, as it is heard: "The Holy Church will flourish in your days, redeeming the blood of Christ".[37]

In addition to his administration, the *Gesta* highlighted at great length the resources used to renovate the major ecclesiastical monuments of the city, and his establishment of a monastery connected to one of Naples' most important saints, Januarius.

This arrangement of first father as *dux* and son as bishop changed in 864, when Athanasius's brother Gregory became the sole *dux*. This arrangement continued to significantly benefit the Church of Naples through gifts, patronage, and most importantly stability. While this remained a period of extensive regional conflict, often connected to the appearance Aghlabid raiders originally based in North Africa and other mercenaries forces, as well as between the various independent principalities, the internal political situation of Naples remained relatively peaceful.[38]

The internal calm would be ruptured in 870 after the death of the *dux* Gregory. His son, Sergius, likely threatened by the autonomy of his uncle Athanasius, had him along with his other relatives imprisoned. This precipitated a larger regional conflict involving Benevento, Amalfi, and ultimately the emperor Louis II, during which time Athanasius was effectively exiled, first to Sorrento and later to Rome.[39] Although he would eventually gain the assistance of the emperor and had the support of pope Hadrian II, Athanasius would die in exile in 872 and unlike his predecessors he would be buried outside of Naples, in the monastery of Saint Benedict in Montecassino. With the end of his episcopal reign, the second section of the *Gesta* of the bishops of Naples comes to an end, although a much fuller account of Athanasius's life appeared shortly afterward as an independent *vita*, and the return of his remains to Naples would establish him as one of the city's central patron saints.[40]

The final page of the *Gesta* begins the episcopacy of Athanasius II (876–898), the ultimate successor and nephew of the first bishop Athanasius and brother of the reigning *dux* Sergius. The author of this short final section, who identified himself in the manuscript as Peter the Subdeacon, begins by introducing Athanasius II's family legacy and his papal confirmation: "He was consecrated in the church of the holy martyr Nazarius, located in place called Canzia, in the territory of Capua, by the pope John VIII".[41] The specificity of the location outside of Naples suggests that the relationship between Athanasius and his brother Sergius was already strained, and furthermore the *Gesta* suggests a strong association between the pope and his bishop. Unfortunately, this section of the text ends suddenly and does not address the later developments of the bishop's career.

Athanasius II would come to hold not only the position of bishop but also that of *dux*. The adoption of both roles was recounted in the contemporary account of Erchempert, a monk from Montecassino, in his *Historia Langobardorum Beneventanorum degentium*. He suggested that because of his continued reliance and engagement with the Aghlabids, the reigning *dux* Sergius I was ultimately deposed, blinded, and sent to Rome by Athanasius II (his brother), who according to the chronicler "appointed himself as leader in his place".[42] This Athanasius took his new role as *dux* seriously: rather than reject the Aghlabids, he reaffirmed the treaties with them as they then lashed out against Benevento, Spoleto, and Rome, and plundered significant sites in their territories including the monastery of San Vincenzo al Volturno in 881, a factor which would ultimately lead to the excommunication by John VIII of the entire community of Naples.

By joining together the positions of both bishop and *dux*, Athanasius II was able to successfully protect Naples and its interests during a period that saw growing regional violence. Much of it was at the hands of raiders under contract with or supported by the Neapolitans, who sought to protect the city through a first-strike doctrine. Nevertheless, under Athanasius II the policies were always flexible, and although Naples had allowed (and likely encouraged) Muslim raiders to establish a base at the mouth of the Garigliano River, in 915 they also took part in the military campaign to dislodge them.[43] The flexibility in external policies reflected flexibilities in internal policies as well; as already noted, since late antiquity canon and statue strongly prohibited holding an episcopal see while simultaneously serving as military commander. Contemporary writers, who were rather more concerned with their duplicitous diplomacy, never raised the issue. Nor were there complaints about the institutionalisation of hereditary rule by the Sergi clan or their monopoly on the office of bishop.

What could account for the acceptance of the Neapolitans of such centralised authority in one family, first with that of Stephen and later with that of the decedents of Sergius, who ruled the city (with only a short intermission) until its absorption by the Normans in 1137? In looking at the formation of other dynastic families, Patricia Skinner noted that the instability and violence in Naples in the eighth century had a lasting effect: "Perhaps a reason for the family's dominance can be found in the history of Naples prior to 840, which is best characterised as bloody, with incessant coups and assassinations. The desire for peace and stability must have played a strong part in the people's choice and continued support of the count of Cuma [Sergius] and his family as their rulers".[44] By the death of Athanasius II in 898, nearly 60 years after the accession of his grandfather as *dux*, his family would continue to directly occupy the office of *dux* and coopt and control the occupants of the episcopal see of Naples until the twelfth century.

Conclusions and connections

These examples from Byzantine Ravenna and Naples offer keys to understanding one way in which local elites could co-opt the position of bishop as a means to enhance their own authority but also as a necessity in the defense their communities. In other regions, the process looked quite different. For example, although there was some survival of Roman patterns of life in Merovingian Gaul, it had been long politically removed from the policies of the Byzantine emperors in Constantinople and even those of Rome. There, the arguments of pope Gregory may not have resounded loudly.

This is apparent in the career of Gregory's near contemporary and the progenitor of the Carolingian line, Arnulf of Metz (bishop 613–628, d. 640). His life and career were preserved in a Merovingian *vita* and elaborated and extrapolated in a section based on the *vita* in the *Liber de episcopis Mettensibus* of Paul the Deacon, a serial biography of the bishops of Metz composed under the patronage of Angilram, bishop of Metz and advisor to Charlemagne more than a century later.[45]

Both the *Vita* and the *Liber* of Paul the Deacon agree on the benchmarks and chronology of Arnulf's career. He was a noble Frank who was educated and trained to assist in the administration of the Frankish kingdom of Austrasia under King Theudebert II. He married an unnamed girl "from a famous and most noble family" and with her had two sons, identified only in the *Liber* as Chlodulf and Ansegisel, the latter of whom was identified as the great-great-grandfather of Charlemagne by Paul the Deacon in the extensive genealogy he offers of Arnulf's decedents.[46]

Arnulf proved an apt advisor and administrator on behalf of Theudebert, and according to the *Liber* served as the mayor of the palace (although in connection to his leadership of the Church of God). The *Vita*, on the other hand, offers a short vignette on his elevation to the episcopacy:

> As it happened, when the city of Metz was in need of a bishop, with a single voice the people demanded Arnulf, the *domesticus* [responsible for royal estates] and the royal advisor, be bishop. While he wept and being compelled, because it was the will of God, he took over the city and its rule, and immediately began to wear the episcopal miter, as he wished to uphold responsibly the willingness to serve and the primacy of the royal court.[47]

This account affirms two important aspects of Arnulf's election. First, he did not desire the position or receive it after years of royal service, but was appointed by popular acclamation, and even more importantly, he still continued to operate in his position within the courts of Theudebert, Chlothar, and later that of Degobert.[48] What is also remarkable about Arnulf's career as bishop, in addition to maintaining his role with the Frankish kings, was his voluntary retirement from the position as bishop of Metz, replaced by an equally holy Goericus Abbo. This allowed Arnulf to spend his remaining years as an eremitic recluse with his companion Romaricus, a period unmentioned in Paul the Deacon's *Liber*.

While the majority of the *Vita* of Arnulf is dedicated primarily to the miracles he performed, and the account of his episcopacy in the *Liber de episcopis Mettensibus* is focussed on his role as the progenitor of the Carolingian dynasty, neither address the conflict between serving as mayor of the palace for a Frankish king and as bishop of one of the kingdom's more important cities. Under Roman law and church canon, Arnulf's position in the Merovinigan administration, the time he would have had to dedicate to secular matters, his children, and later his abandonment of the episcopacy in favour of a monastic lifestyle would all have been significant violations, and yet both texts about his life celebrate all of these aspects. Despite the concern expressed by Caesarius in the first half of the sixth century, the career of Arnulf exemplified the "secular" nature of the role of most Merovingian bishops, whose hagiography merges the political and the spiritual in a manner alien to Gregory the Great's *Liber Regulae Pastoralis*, ultimately laying the groundwork for bishops who were also political and military leaders within the late Merovingian and Carolingian realm.[49] This evolution was relatively uniform in Gaul, but as we have seen in the case of Italy, men who cross from military leadership into episcopal positions did so at the confluence of regional instabilities and larger political conflict.

These examples, from Byzantine Italy along with that of Arnulf, suggest that the transition from layman to bishop was possible but relied on the acquiescence and support of the community. Without it, any of the many issues of legitimacy could be raised. This was this case of the papal pretender Constantine II, who held the see of St. Peter for just over a year in 767–768. Constantine's case is complicated by the only surviving source, the *Liber pontificalis* of Rome, which does not offer him a discreet biography but introduces his brief tenure within the biography of his successor, Stephen III, and is clearly biased against the former's legitimacy.

On the death of Pope Paul in 767, Toto, the duke of Nepi sought to obtain a political hold on the city of Rome through the appointment of his own candidate as pope.[50] Although he had promised Paul to not interfere, after Paul's death Toto entered the city, claimed the title of duke, and had his brother, Constantine, who was a layman, ordained and then immediately consecrated as pope. This was radical enough for Rome, the first instance where "the military aristocracy acted specifically as a result of the certain knowledge that the papal office was the highest one" in the Roman territory, but followed on similar contemporary co-options of episcopal sees in Ravenna and Naples.[51]

The difference in Rome, however, was that much of the population did not approve of the election, which was described as essentially a coup. To counter this, the leaders of the papal bureaucracy, Christophorus the *primicerius* and his son Sergius, sought and received unlikely aid from the Lombard king Desiderius; together with the majority of the local elites who had rejected the legitimacy of the newly enthroned pope and duke, a force entered the city, killing Toto in battle and imprisoning Constantine. After a day of confusion, Stephan III was elected and subsequently confirmed as pope.

This did not end the conflict with the imprisoned former pope Constantine. He was first exiled, and then blinded, but Stephan III decided that a council should be called to deal with the improper election of Constantine and the issue of the consecration of laymen to the papal see in general. Taking place the year later, the now-blind Constantine was recalled and questioned about his legitimacy. During this process, although he had acknowledged that he had been a layman, he argued that he claim to the papacy was not novel. As recorded in the *Liber pontificalis*, his claim was that he was not breaking tradition "since Sergius archbishop of Ravenna had been made an archbishop when still a layman, and Stephen bishop of Naples had also been a layman when he was unexpectedly consecrated bishop".[52]

The council thought otherwise, and raised the objections which had existed since Late Antiquity: "the sacred canons were brought forward and clearly scrutinised, and a decision was pronounced by this sacerdotal council under interdict and anathema: no layman should ever presume to be promoted to the sacred honour of the pontificate, nor even anyone in orders, unless he had risen through the separate grades and had been made cardinal deacon or priest".[53] Although Constantine's brief occupation of the papal see was deemed illegitimate, he nevertheless held the office with some acquiescence from the local community. His reign came to an ignominious end not only because he had been elevated without the proper career, but also because the political tides turned against his family and he never fully gained the support of the church and the bureaucrats he himself was said to lead. And yet, while Constantine's conversion from layman to bishop failed, the evidence in Ravenna and Naples would indicate that in other political contexts the barrier between a lay career and episcopal position was permeable as long as the arrangement was beneficial to the church and the community.

Notes

1 Claudia Rapp, *Holy Bishops in Late Antiquity: The Nature of Christian Leadership in an Age of Transition* (Berkeley: University of California Press, 2005), 205; see also 196–199. The lengthy list of prohibitions and restrictions for bishops was capitulated in an edict from Justinian to the Patriarch Epiphanius, and codified as Nov. Just. 6.1 (535).

2 Caesarius of Arles, *Ep.* 7b.3. "Illud etiam pari supplication deposcimus, ut de laica conversatione, qui in singulis iudicium officiis meruerunt, aut certe rexerunt subaliqua potestate provincias, nisi multo ante tempore praemissa conversatione legitima et vita examinata, nullus aut clericus aut episcopus ordinetur". *Sancti Caesarii Episcopi Arelatensis Opera omnia. Vol. 2: Opera varia*, ed. Germain Morin (Bruges: Maretioli, 1942), 12. Translation from *Caesarius of Arles: Life Testament, Letters*, trans. William E. Klingshirn, Translated Texts for Historians 19 (Liverpool: Liverpool University Press, 1994), 90.

3 Symmachus, *Ep.* 15.3. "De laicis personis decernimus, ne facile ad sacerdotium permittantur accedere, de quibus et tempora et gradus constituti sunt, per quos ad hanc dignitatem debeant adspirare: quia quicumque sine instituto promovetur, non facile caret offensa, et sine experiment non potest quis electionis obinere sententiam". *Epistolae Romanorum pontificum genuinae et quae ad eos scriptae sunt a S. Hilaro usque ad Pelagium II*, ed. Andreas Thiel (Braunsberg: Peter, 1868), 724. Translation after *Caesarius of Arles: Life Testament, Letters*, 92. On the reception of this rescript, see Detlev Jasper and Horst Furhmann, *Papal Letters in the Early Middle Ages*, History of Medieval Canon Law (Washington, D.C.: Catholica University of America Press, 2001), 68–69.

4 On Caesarius's role in leading these councils, see William E. Klingshirn, *Caesarius of Arles: The Making of a Christian Community in Late Antique Gaul* (Cambridge: Cambridge University Press, 1994), 97–104; 37–45.

5 Rapp, *Holy Bishops in Late Antiquity: The Nature of Christian Leadership in an Age of Transition*, 191.

6 Nov. Jus. 6.1.1. "Et neque ex officiali aut ex curiali veniat fortuna, nisi tamen ex novella aetate".

7 Nov. Jus. 6.1.4. "Neque filios aut nepotes habens neque cognitos legi neque illi odibiles".

8 George E. Demacopoulos, "Gregory's Model of Spiritual Direction in the *Liber Regulae Pastoralis*", in *A Companion to Gregory the Great*, ed. Bronwen Neil and Matthew Dal Santo, Brill's Companions to the Christian Tradition, Vol. 47 (Leiden: Brill, 2013).

9 1 Timothy 3:1. "εἴ τις ἐπισκοπῆς ὀρέγεται, καλοῦ ἔργου ἐπιθυμεῖ".

10 Greg. Mag. *Liber Regulae Pastoralis* 1.8. "Ipse ergo sibi testis est, quia episcopatum non appetit, qui non per hunc boni operis ministerium, sed honoris gloriam quaerit".

11 Thomas S. Brown, *Gentlemen and Officers: Imperial Administration and Aristocratic Power in Byzantine Italy A.D. 554–800* (Rome: British School at Rome, 1984), 64–69.

12 The lasting legacy of these monuments, and their reflection on Ravenna's once illustrious past, were core to the city's identity from the eighth century onward. In particular, the *Liber Ponificalis* of Agnellus of the ninth century and the hagiographic output of the tenth sought to reconcile the situation of the city's medieval position with its past: see Deborah Mauskopf Deliyannis, *Ravenna in Late Antiquity* (Cambridge: Cambridge University Press, 2010), 295–299; Thomas S. Brown, "*Romanitas* and *Campanilismo*: Agnellus of Ravenna's View of the Past", in *The Inheritance of Historiography, 350–900*, ed. C. Holdsworth (Exeter: University Publication, 1986); Edward M. Schoolman, *Rediscovering Sainthood in Italy: Hagiography and the Late Antique Past in Medieval Ravenna*, The New Middle Ages (New York: Palgrave, 2016).

13 Adam Serfass, "Unraveling the *Pallium* Dispute between Gregory the Great and John of Ravenna", in *Dressing Judeans and Christians in Antiquity*, ed. Kristi Upson-Saia, Carly Daniel-Hughes, and Alicia J. Batten (Farnham: Ashgate, 2014); Augusto Simonini, *Autocefalia ed Esarcato in Italia* (Ravenna: Longo, 1969).

14 Still valuable on the archbishops of Ravenna in the Ottonian period is Giulio Buzzi, "Ricerche per la storia di Ravenna e di Roma dell' 850 al 1118", *Archivio della reale società Romana di storia patria* 38 (1915).

15 Agnellus of Ravenna, *Liber Pontificalis Ecclesiae Ravennatis*, CCCM 199 (Turnhout: Brepols, 2006). (Hereafter *LPER*). On the literary composition of the text, see Joaquín Martínez Pizarro, *Writing Ravenna: The Liber Pontificalis of Andreas Agnellus* (Ann Arbor: University of Michigan Press, 1995).

16 *LPER* 84. "...sed post amissiam coniugem, relictum militae cingulum, se totum Deo obtulit atque donavit". Translation after *Agnellus of Ravenna: The Book of Pontiffs of the Church of Ravenna*, trans. Deborah Mauskopf Deliyannis (Washington, D.C.: The Catholic University of America Press, 2004), 198. In the ninth century, the *cingulum miliae* came to serve as a sign of participation in public life rather than military service, and its deprivation could serve as part of penance. See Karl Leyser, "Early medieval canon law and the beginnings of knighthood" in *Institutionen, Kultur und Gesellschaft im Mittelalter: Festschrift für Josef Fleckenstein zu seinem 65. Geburtstag* ed. Lutz Fenske, Werner Rösener, and Thomas Zotz (Sigmaringen: Thorbecke, 1984). Republished in Karl Leyser, *Communications and Power in Medieval Europe, 1: The Carolingian and Ottonian Centuries* (London: Hambledon Press, 1994).

17 *LPER* 84. "Ex nobili ortus prole, diues in possessionibus, animalibus locuples, abundas opibus".

18 LPER 84. "Hic ad finem uitae, cum circa uicinam esset mortem, neptam suam, filiam filiae suae, post funus matris heredem reliquit, quam inter ceteras diuitias quinque ornamenta mensae uasculorum argent ea relinquens et multa alia, quia nobis perdiuersas discurrcre opus non est diuitias, mors interuenit. Sed quaercndum nobis est, cur iste coniugatus talem egregiam optinuit sedem. Si int elligatis auctorem apostolum dicentem unius uxoris uirum et filios habentem episscopus ordinari, recta prouid entia, cum et hoc canones praecipiant. Sed reddeamus ad ordinem et de mulieribus postea disputemus". Trans. Deliyannis, 198.

19 This is one of a number of instances where the author Agnellus had direct access to an archival document. On these sources in the *Liber pontificalis* of Ravenna, see Deliyannis's introduction to Agnellus of Ravenna, *Liber Pontificalis Ecclesiae Ravennatis*, 47–49.

20 1 Timothy 3:2–4. "δεῖ οὖν τὸν ἐπίσκοπον ἀνεπίλημπτον εἶναι, μιᾶς γυναικὸς ἄνδρα... τοῦ ἰδίου οἴκου καλῶς προϊστάμενον, τέκνα ἔχοντα ἐν ὑποταγῇ μετὰ πάσης σεμνότητος".

21 David G. Hunter, *Marriage, Celibacy and Heresy in Ancient Christianity: The Jovinianist Controversy*, Oxford Early Christian Studies (Oxford; New York: Oxford University Press, 2007); Roger Gryson, *Les origines du célibat ecclésiastique du premier au septième siècle* (Gembloux: Duculot, 1970); David G. Hunter, "Clerical Celibacy and the Veiling of Virgins: New Boundaries in Late Ancient Christianity", in *The Limits of Anicent Christianity: Essay on Late Antique Thought and Culture in Honor of R. A. Markus*, ed. William Klingshirn and Mark Vessey (Ann Arbor: University of Michigan Press, 1999).

22 Deliyannis, *Ravenna in Late Antiquity*, 144–146. On the status of the Arian church in Ravenna, see Thomas S. Brown, "The Role of Arianism in Ostrogothic Italy: The Evidence from Ravenna", in *The Ostrogoths from the Migration Period to the Sixth Century: An Ethnographic Perspective*, ed. Frederico Marazzi and S. J. B. Barnish (Woodbridge: Boydell, 2007).

23 The relationship between the archbishops of Ravenna and the imperial government was by nature close, and the church benefited financially from their long-term relationship. See Thomas S. Brown, "The Church of Ravenna and the Imperial Administration in the Seventh Century", *English Historical Review* 94 (1979).

24 The issue of "Ostrogothic-ness" as a type of genuine identity has been deeply affected by the work of Patrick Amory, who suggests that the label is not one strictly of ethnic identity but one that is bound by occupation, status, and other affinities and was mutable based on contexts. In the case of the opening of the military, Amory notes: "In Theoderic's later years, and under his immediate successors, the military and civilian populations were no longer distinguishable in

Italy. People from Italian families were active at the highest levels of the military; people combined military and civilian positions". Patrick Amory, *People and Identity in Ostrogothic Italy: 489–554* (Cambridge: Cambridge University Press, 1997), 152.

25 *LPER* 154. "Iste laicus fuit et sponsam habuit. Quam, post regimen ecclesiae suscepit, eam Euphimiam sponsam suam diaconissam consecrauit, et in eodem habitu perman sit". Trans. Deliyannis, 278.

26 Thomas S. Brown, *Gentlemen and Officers* (British School at Rome, 1984), 205–220; Thomas F. X. Noble, *The Republic of St. Peter: The Birth of the Papal State: 680–825* (Philadelphia: University of Pennsylvania Press, 1984), 112–116.

27 *LPER* 159. "Igitur iudicauit iste a finibus Persiceti totum Pentapolim et usque ad Tusciam et usque ad amnem Walani, ueluti exarchus sic omnia dispon ebat, ut soliti sunt modo Romani facere". Translation Deliyannis, 284.

28 Deborah M. Deliyannis, "The *Liber pontificalis* of the Church of Ravenna and its relation with its Roman model", in *Liber, Gesta, histoire: Ecrire l'histoire des évêques et des papes, de l'Antiquité au XXIe siècle*, ed. François Bougard and Michel Sot (Turnhout: Brepols, 2009), 289.

29 According to the *Liber pontificalis* of Rome, after the death of Archbishop Sergius, the duke of Rimini Maurice would seize Ravenna with the help of a layman and *scrinarius* named Michael, who wished to be confirmed as archbishop in place of a certain archdeacon Leo who had the support of the populace and the church. Michael and Maurice were ultimately unsuccessful, and Leo, who had been sent to Rome, returned to serve as archbishop.

30 On the Lombard treatment of Ravenna during middle of the eighth century, see Nicole Lopez-Jantzen, "From Roman Empire to the Middle Ages: The Struggle for Ravenna in the Eighth Century" (Fordham University, 2012).

31 *Gesta episcoporum neapolitanorum*, ed. G. Waitz, MGH SS rer Lang., 398–435, (hereafter *GEN*). On this history of this text and the authorship of the second half which covers the eighth and ninth century and its creation, see Domenico Mallardo, "Giovanni Diacono Napoletano: La Continuazione del 'Liber Pontificalis'", *Rivista di Storia della Chiesa in Italia* 4 (1950); H. Achelis, *Die Bischofchronik von Neapel (von Johannes Diaconus u.a.)* (Leipzig: S. Hirzel, 1930); Thomas Granier, "La difficile genèse de l'*Histoire des évêques de Naples* (milieu du ixe-début du xe siècle): le *scriptorium* et la famille des évêques", in *Liber, Gesta, histoire. Écrire l'histoire des évèques et des papes, de l'Antiquité au XXI*, ed. François Bougard and Michel Sot (Turnhout: Brepols, 2009). Although *dux* seemed to have been the official title as it appears in the seals of the ninth century, the author of the *Gesta* applies a number of others (including *consul* and *magister militum*) interchangeably. On the development of the position of *dux*, see: Francesco Borri, "Duces e magistri militum nell'Italia esarcale (VI–VIII secolo)", *Reti Medievali Rivista* 6, no. 2 (2005).

32 Thomas S. Brown, "Byzantine Italy, c. 680–c. 876", in *The New Cambridge Medieval History, vol. 2: c. 700–c. 900*, ed. Rosamond McKitterick (Cambridge: Cambridge University Press, 1995), 341–343. On the history of Naples in this period, see also Barbara M. Kreutz, *Before the Normans: Southern Italy in the Ninth and Tenth Centuries* (Philadelphia: University of Pennsylvania, 1991).

33 *GEN* 42. "sic de divinis coepit studere rebus, acsi puerulus in eis fuisset educatus".

34 Luigi Andrea Berto, "Utilius est vertatem proferre". A Difficult Memory to Manage: Narrating the Relationships between Bishops and Dukes in Early Medieval Naples, *Viator* 39 (2008): 60.

35 When Sergius became *dux*, there were two bishops: Tiberius, who had been deposed and imprisoned by the *dux* Bonus (832–834) in favor of John IV, a popular deacon (*GEN* 55–56). Sergius let John serve until his death in 841.

36 *GEN* 63. "sub tutoribus et auctoribus mansit, quatenus, negotii secularis ignarus, omni institutione catholica imbueretur".

37 *GEN* 63. "Inthronizatus ergo, ubertatem doctrinae, quam in pueritia suxerat, coepit affluenter impertiri. Ordinavit autem lectorum et cantorum scolas; nonnullos instituit gramatica inbuendos; alios colligavit ad scribendi officium, ut sic pastor providus caulas sui gregis muniret, quatenus nullius indigens, Domino suam praesentaret speculationem atque verissime audiret: 'Floret sancta ecclesia in diebus tuis redempta sanguine Christi'".

38 Part of the internal stability was the Neapolitan reliance on Aghlabids in various military ventures, an association that was intermittent but further strained Naple's relationships with Benevento and Rome. Kreutz, *Before the Normans: Southern Italy in the Ninth and Tenth Centuries.*

39 The event is described at length in *GEN* 65. Louis II's involvement in southern Italy would ultimately lead to his capture and detention by the duke of Benevento; see Thomas Granier, "La captivité de l'empereur Louis II à Bénévent (13 août–17 septembre 871) dans les sources des IXe–Xe siècles", in *Faire l'événement au Moyen Âge*, ed. Claude Carozzi and Huguette Taviani-Carozzi (Aix-en-Provenece: Publications de l'Université de Provence, 2007).

40 Antonio Vuolo, *Vita et translatio s. Athanasii neapolitani episcopi (BHL 735 e 737) sec. XI* (Rome: Istituto Storico Italiano per il Medioevo, 2001). This was part of larger Neapolitan efforts to recast their hagiography in the ninth and tenth century: Thomas Granier, "Transformations de l'église et écriture hagiographique à Naples autour de l'An Mil", in *Année Mille, An Mil*, ed. Claude Carozzi and Huguette Taviani-Carozzi (Aix-en-Provence: 2002; reprint, *Reti Medievali*). More generally, see: Thomas Granier, "L'hagiographie napolitaine du haut Moyen Âge: contexte, corpus et enjeux", *Bulletin du CRISMA* 2 (2001).

41 *GEN* 66. "Consecratus est autem in ecclesia beati Nazarii martyris, sita in loco qui dicitur Canzia, territorio Capuano, a Iohannę octabo papa".

42 Erchempert *Historia* 39. "in loco illius se ipsum principem instituit". *MGH S Lang.*, 231–264 (Hannover, 1878). On the events surrounding these conflicts, see: Thomas Granier, "Napolitains et Lombards aux VIIIe-XIe siècles. De la guerre des peuples à la guerre des saints en Italie du Sud", *Mélanges de l'Ecole française de Rome. Moyen-Age, Temps modernes* 108 (1996).

43 Jean-Marie Martin, *Guerre, accords et frontières en Italie méridionale pendant le haut moyen âge* (Rome: École française de Rome, 2005), 62–82.

44 Patricia Skinner, *Family Power in Southern Italy: The Duchy of Gaeta and Its Neighbours, 850–1139* (Cambridge: Cambridge University Press, 1995), 85. This observation is also made by Berto, "'Utilius est vertatem proferre". A Difficult Memory to Manage: Narrating the Relationships between Bishops and Dukes in Early Medieval Naples", 51.

45 The *Vita Sancti Arnulfi* (BHL 689–692) and its most prominent variants were edited by Bruno Krusch appear in *MGH SRM* 2, 426–446 (Hannover, 1888). A new edition and translation of the *Liber* has appeared in Paul the Deacon, *Liber de apiscopis Mettensibus*, trans. Damien Kempf, Dallas Medieval Texts and Translations 19 (Paris: Peeters, 2013).

46 *Vita Sancti Arnulfi* 5, 433 "inclitam et nobilissimam gente puellam". This text is also reflected in Paul the Deacon, *Liber de apiscopis Mettensibus*, 73.

47 *Vita Sancti Arnulfi* 7, 434–435. "ut urbs Metensium praesule indigeret. Tunc una vox populorum Arnulfum domesticum adque consiliarium regis dignum esse episcopum adclamavit. Ille autem lacrimans et conpulsus, quia Deo ita placitum fuit, urbem at gubernandum suscepit, sicque deinceps episcopales gestans infulas, ut eciam domesticatus sollicitudine adque primatum palacii hacsi nollens teneret".

48 In the seventh century, many Frankish royal officials, especially those who held the position of *domesticus* or *referendarius* (acting frequently as royal judges, tax collectors), became bishops later in their careers. Paul Fouracre and Richard A. Gerberding, *Late Merovingian France: History and Hagiography, 640–720* (Manchester: Manchester University Press, 1996), 140; Silvia Cantelli Berarducci, "Elezioni e consacrazioni episcopali nella Gallia merovingia del sec. VI", *Archivio Storico Italiano* 172 (2014): 71–72.

49 On the shifting nature of episcopal power in the Late Merovingian world and its effects on hagiography, see the introduction to Fouracre and Gerberding, *Late Merovingian France: History and Hagiography, 640–720*, 48–51.

50 On this episode, see Noble, *The Republic of St. Peter: The Birth of the Papal State: 680–825*, 112–117.

51 Noble, *The Republic of St. Peter: The Birth of the Papal State: 680–825*, 113.

52 *LP* Stephanus III 19. "Sergius archiepiscopus Ravennantium laicus existens archiepiscopus effectus est, et Stephanus episcopus Neapolitanae civita is et ipse laicus repente episcopus consecratus est". Translation after Davis 97.

53 *LP* Stephanus III 20. "Tunc adlatis sacratissirnis canonibus iisque liquido perscrutatis, prolata est sententia ab eodem sacerdotale concilio sub anathematis interdictu, nullus umquam praesurni laicorum neque ex alio ordine, nisi per distinctos gradus ascendens diaconus aut presbiter cardinalis factus fuerit, ad sacrurn pontificatus honorem promoveri". Trans. Davis, 98.

13 The Duke of Istria, the Roman past, and the Frankish present*

Introducing the Plea of Rižana, Tom Brown commented on the irony that such richness stemmed from a backwater province in the Carolingian Age.[1] Brown was of course right; Istria is a very obscure region for the entire early Middle Ages, which at the same time produced the single most informative evidence for the study of imperial Italy, and this fifty years after the Lombard conquest of Ravenna. The thick darkness, however, thins out already few decades before the composition of the charter and, from the second quarter of the eighth century, we are able to finally cast some light on the region. It is the period of the Frankish conquest and a time of important and deep changes in the social and economic fabric of the province. Due to this conjuncture, the Frankish takeover of Istria has already attracted the attention of historians, with several valuable works published on the topic.[2]

There is however an aspect, which in my opinion could benefit from some more scrutiny. The first mention of a Frankish authority over Istria originates from a letter written in 791. In the epistle, we are told that an anonymous *dux de Histria* did well (*benefecit*) during the wars against the Avars in the east.[3] The immediate interpretation would have been that the duke showed peculiar valour in the battlefield, and that this was the reason why Charles commented on his actions. Indeed, we know that those who governed for the Frankish authorities were warriors often involved in battles, which sometimes cost them their lives.[4] The *dux de Histria* must have been a fighter too, but I think that Charlemagne's commentary on the new captain's conduct, once understood in the proper context, could offer us more, enriching our knowledge of the Carolingian conquest.

Istria, a centuries-old province of the Roman empire, was a new acquisition for the Franks, as already mentioned. In a letter dated between 776 and 780, Pope Hadrian (772–795) lamented the defiant attitude of its inhabitants. Backed up by the Greeks, the local aristocracies had blinded bishop Maurice, perhaps of the seat of Novigrad (*Civitas Nova*), who was collecting the *pensiones beati Petri* in the region.[5] Horrified by the brutality of the torment imposed to Maurice, pope Hadrian demanded the intervention of Marcarius, the duke of Friuli.[6] Hitting hard on bishops could have been an imperial policy of the age: ecclesiasts apparently acted as forbearers of the Carolingian expansion triggering the local authorities' retaliation.[7] In the neighbouring regions of Istria, Duke Maurice of Venice ordered patriarch John of Grado killed, perhaps due to his closeness to the Franks.[8] The blinding of Maurice suggests that in the late 70s of the eighth century, the Istrians still acted as subjects of the Roman empire: in a few months they would fight for the Franks instead. The *dux de Histria* seems to have played an important role in this transition.

Charlemagne extended his authority to the Adriatic peninsula in the aftermath of Maurice's punishment, but the nature of its conquest remains unclear. Probably, Charles took the region meeting no resistance. In different times and circumstances, Alsace and Bavaria had also been brought under Carolingian control rather peacefully.[9] Closer to Istria, Ravenna and the Romagna may have similarly gone over to the Franks without a fight. The exact moment of Charlemagne's takeover is also a matter of debate. Narrating his master's great achievements, Einhard mentioned Istria alongside the conquests in central and south-eastern Europe, but he did not date the event.[10] The acquisition of the region could have been led by Marcarius in the immediate aftermath of Maurice's mutilation; later on, as retaliation for the imperials breaking the truce with the 788 attack to Calabria; or even sometime in between.

The mention of a *dux de Histria* stems from the only surviving personal letter of Charlemagne's. The king wrote the epistle to queen Fastrada from the Frankish encampment at the boarders of the empire, during the wars against the Avars.[11] In the first part, Charles told his wife the salient moments of the battle versus the heathens. In his account, while the bulk of the Frankish army remained with him on the banks of the river Ennes (*Anisa*), the Italian *scara* entered Pannonia at the end of August, crushing the Avars in the field and successively conquering the Hring (in the text called *uualum*).[12] King Pippin (781–810), at the time little more than a child, led the expedition from the Lombard kingdom. The *Annales Laureshamenses* narrated that the boy king crossed Illyricum into Pannonia in order to reach the hearth of Avaric power, moving therefore close to Istria.[13] The duke of the region may have joined Pippin at this point of the campaign. He was an envoy of him, who had Charlemagne informed on the campaign: it was according to his source (*ut dictum est nobis*) that the king was able to tell his wife that the duke of Istria did well (*benefecit*) together with his men (*ill. cum suis hominibus*). Charlemagne described thereafter the general penitence that his followers and he had performed at their camp on the Ennes.[14] Concluding his letter, the king asked his wife to join the litanies if her health allowed, together with some of her close *fideles*.[15]

The letter survives in the *formulae* of Saint-Denis, a collection that historians have dated to various moments of the ninth century, where the most famous document is the epistle of Cathulf to Charlemagne.[16] The text is somehow a foreign body in the collection and different explanations have been proposed for its inclusion in the formulary book. Thirty years ago,

Michael McCormick maintained that the letter survived because of the liturgical description it contained. Once the guidelines for fighting the pagans became particularly precious, as was the case when west Frankia faced the northmen's raids in ninth century, a Saint-Denis copyist thought that the text could have become of some use.[17] Alternatives explanations are of course possible and, in her impressive study of the *collectio*, Johanna Story explained the presence of this letter due to the bonds between abbot Fardulf of Saint-Denis and Fastrada.[18] Through these divergences, historians generally agree that this letter, so precious to us, did not owe its survival to its intrinsic historical interest.[19]

Because of its function as a *formula*, the copyist omitted the names and the function of the captains that Charlemagne enlisted in the Italian *scara* of Pippin. Therefore, we can only read of the given bishop, duke, and counts (*fuerunt ille episcopus, ill. dux, ill. et ill. comites*), without knowing their identity or exact role.[20] Even the young king's name is missing (*dilecti filii nostril ill. nomine ill.*). The *dux de Histria* closes the brief catalogue. Although as anonymous as the others, he is the only ranking aristocrat whose domain is remembered. The reason for this is a matter of opinion: in mine, the mention of the *ducatus* on Istria survived because of the king's commentary on the duke's actions. The *benefecit*—that he did well—may have captured the attention of the copyist, who decided to write down the office too.

That the armies of recently conquered regions joined the *scarae* of Charlemagne in further military activities beyond the frontiers, as the Istrians did, seems to have been the general rule rather than the exception. Even the hardest of Charlemagne's enemies joined the Frankish armies soon after capitulating in order to bring war to further regions. In the *Annales regni Francorum*, we read that the Saxons west of the Elbe fought the ones on the opposite bank, which the Royal Annalist called *Transalbiani*.[21]

Like Saxony, Friuli and other boarder regions, Istria became a territory on the open Carolingian frontier in the east, one of the period's hottest political spots. The Istrian armed forces, thereafter, became necessary for the wars in Pannonia.[22] We know that King Pippin led armies of Lombards, Bavarians and Alemanni a few years after the foundation of his vast kingdom.[23] The 796 campaign against the Avars had among its captains a certain Vojnomir, *quedam Sclavus*, who may have stemmed from the elites of the newly conquered territories east of Friuli or Bavaria.[24] Aristocracies may have been willing to follow the king in his wars of expansion. Indeed, joining the "war-trail" (Airlie) of the Franks was not only duty, but also an incredibly remunerative enterprise and one of the easiest ways to create trust between masters and conquered. From a top down perspective, war was one of the sounder ways to co-opt local elites; while from a bottom-up one, it remained the best social ladders at disposal. Living on the edges of the Frankish kingdoms in a moment of expansion toward the east, the lord *de Histria* was probably obliged to serve as a token for his brand new position, but he may have blessed the great chances that conflict opened in front of him for plunder, glory and visibility.[25]

Being a centuries-long frontier province, Istria was a highly militarised region.[26] In the Plea of Rižana its westernmost fringe, the ancient *civitas* of Trieste, was recorded as *numerus Tergestinus*, a possible hint of its role and identity, being the *numerus* of a Roman military unit.[27] The town rose at the borders of the Lombard kingdom and it was perhaps mostly the Lombards that the Istrians had battled for decades. Gregory the Great and Paul the Deacon (probably relying on Secundus of Trento) did narrate conflict between the Istrians and their eastern neighbours, Slavs and Avars, however no witness recorded the Istrian soldiers campaigning in the east, reaching Illyricum or Pannonia.[28] The *dux de Histria*, therefore, must have been responsible for the prompt rising of an army apt to new tasks, as suggested by Stefan Esders.[29] I may add that he must have adopted rapid and harsh measures to enrol Istrian *milites* in the retinue of the Frankish king of Italy; we can easily imagine them as draconian in nature.

The duke's identity is a matter of opinion. Ernst Dümmler tentatively identified the anonymous lord of Istria with John, who was present thirteen years later at the Plea of Rižana.[30] There is no positive evidence for that, but the idea is appealing and has been followed by many scholars. A cluster of evidence and few speculations could corroborate this suggestion. In the first instance, the name John: although a Roman and Christian Classic (perhaps the most common late antique name), becomes rather rare among the lay aristocracies of the post-Roman west. In the whole history of the Kingdom of Italy between the Carolingian and the Ottonian conquest, Eduard Hlawitschka found only three occurrences.[31] Conversely, the name was omnipresent in the neighbouring regions of imperial background, like Ravenna, Venice, Naples and, indeed, Istria, where military men were given names taken from the late antique repertoire.[32] Other than John of Istria, one of the two remaining officers with this name enlisted by Hlawitschka was the late eighth-century *dux de Persiceta*, a region at edges of the exarchate, like Istria strongly influenced by the eastern empire.[33] This aspect, together with John's deep knowledge of the Istrian society and landscape, and the possible nature of the Carolingian takeover of the region, led some historians, Harald Krahwinkler among them, to suggest that the duke was a local highborn.[34] If this suggestion is grounded and John was an Istrian aristocrat it is highly possible that he was the first man that Charlemagne raised to the duchy of Istria. We know that after conquering Italy, the Franks tried to leave the regional structures of power untouched, raising local men to power or confirming the former aristocrats in order to rely on officers able to master the specifics of a given territory. Only in a second moment did men much closer to the Carolingians take power into their hands.[35] Strong comparison stems from other provinces of Roman heritage: around 802, Obelerius from Metamaucum gained the *ducatus* on the Venetian lagoons, apparently with Frankish support.[36] Also in the aforementioned Zadar, Charlemagne confirmed the duchy to a certain Paul, who may well have been a local aristocrat.[37] The same was true in the most rebellious of the neighbouring regions: we are not sure if Hrotgaud was already duke of Friuli under king Desiderius (756–774), but historians agree that, even if Charlemagne appointed him to his office, he must have been a Lombard and perhaps a native of the region.[38] It was also the case of his fellow dukes Gaidus and Stabilinus, who revolted with him in 776.[39] After Hrodgaud's rebellion, downfall and death, Marcarius and Eric succeeded him. We are not sure on Marcarius' origin, but Eric stemmed from a powerful Alemannian family.[40] In Istria, we could suspect a similar pattern. From the *Translatio sanguinis Domini* we know that John's successor, a certain Hunfried, had previously governed Chur and was a man of northern descent.[41] Thereafter, John may have been the first Frankish duke of the province and the man mentioned in the 791 letter.

Appointing John must have been a problematic decision. Hrodgaud's revolt had clearly showed the difficulties in managing conquered Italy.[42] Istria was no exception and in 799 the inhabitants of Tarsatica, a town on the easternmost fringes of the peninsula, ambushed and killed Eric of Friuli, the hero of the Avaric wars.[43] In this troublesome province and difficult moment, the Franks may have elected the duke for reasons unfathomable to us. Charles probably had a limited range of choices and John may have the best candidate. After all, "Charlemagne had to work with what he was given", as Stuart Airlie frankly put it.[44] The new duke may have been part of a group of aristocrats who opposed the empire, a supporter of the Roman church in Istria, a hard and handsome warrior or even the last master of soldiers (*magister militum*) of imperial Istria. He surely knew his region and the means to enforce Carolingian authority in there, as his successes in the war suggested. Moreover, if he was the same John of the Plea of Rižana, the groans of the Istrians could only confirm his local expertise and ability to extract resources. It was a convenient solution but also a dangerous one. As Duke Hrodgaud did, local aristocrats were able to ride discontent and drive dissent. Keeping an eye on the new duke may have become necessary.

From these tense years, which saw the first east Roman action in Italy for some time, we can gain an insight of how the co-optation of these suspicious new aristocrats may have worked in practice. In 788 an imperial army disembarked in southern Italy to be promptly faced by the Lombards of Benevento and Spoleto under the aegis of Charlemagne.[45] In this tense moment, many shadows could have troubled the king. In the first instance, Carolingian writers claimed that the imperial army was very big.[46] More disturbing was that, among the many patricians leading the imperial troops, there was also Adelchis, the son of Desiderius and the last king of the Lombards. On the other side Duke Grimoald (788–806) led the men of Benevento. The duke was, from a Frankish perspective, a treacherous ally, as most of the Italians were. Before submitting to the Franks, he had fought king Pippin in many occasions.[47] He had the name of a Lombard king loaded with dangerous symbolic capital. His father and predecessor Arechis II (757–787), who gave Grimoald his name, was a subject of king Desiderius, who had married Adalperga, the king' daughter and Adelichis' sister.[48] Arechis had also shared suspicious relationships with the east Romans: the pope even claimed that the old duke had his hair and beard trimmed according to the Greek fashion and was ready to offer Italy to the lords of Constantinople.[49] In such a situation Charlemagne may have wanted a direct witness he could trust in order to proof the loyalty of his new (and shifty) subjects in Benevento. The royal annalist recorded that the king sent a certain *missus* Winigis together with few Franks in order to see what was going on and inform the king.[50] This may have a relative common practice: men on the field must have informed the highest Carolingians on the working of things.[51] In one among the many actions of the 791 Avar campaign, we read of some Franks (*quibusdam Francis*) who accompanied the Saxons and a larger army of Frisians, which moved with the king.[52] Did they have the same role as Winigis did? This necessity to overlook and report the actions of their newly gained subject and alleys could also explain the rather puzzling opening of the 796 entry where the Royal Annalist introduced the previously mentioned Vojnomir.[53] In the narrative, we could read that duke Eric gave a part of his army to the reclusive Vojnomir, but this would have been almost an unicum. On the contrary, we could also interpret the passage suggesting that, in this campaign, the war's burden was mostly sustained by Vojnomir's army and that the duke of Friuli mostly sent emissaries of his in order to watch his actions in Pannonia. Afterwards, the Royal Annalist recorded of the immense richness of the Avar rulers and how it reached Charlemagne's court. More outspoken is the Reviser, who narrated that in 798 a certain *missus* Eburis commanded the left wing (*cornus*) of the Obodrite army led by duke Thrasco against the Saxon Nordliudi, in a clash beyond the Elbe.[54] The Frank was on the field, leading (and supervising?) the Obodrites and making sure that Charlemagne received hostages, just as the men of Eric assured that the Avaric treasure arrived in Aachen.

Similar mistrust must have accompanied the elusive John and his rise to the Istrian duchy. Being an officer of imperial background in the last decades of the eighth century may have been a magnet for suspicion. In these years, which proceeded and followed the Frankish conquest of Italy of 774, relationships with the empire were strained. Lombards and east Romans were in fact the victims of a vicious denigrating campaign, which left clues in the *Codex Carolinus* and the *Liber pontificalis*.[55] The popes often complained with alarmed tones that the Greeks, together with the Lombards, planned to overthrow the Frankish rule, restore the previous order and take brutal retaliation on the papacy, and we saw that in 788 the empire finally made a move against the Franks in Italy.[56] Still in the middle of the ninth century, the rumour that the aristocracies of Rome were ready to submit once more to Constantinople and ask for a master of soldiers ruling them, was credible enough to force Louis II (844–875) to swiftly return to Rome.[57]

John was eventually able to dissipate this cloud of suspicion. In the Plea of Rižana the local elites complained how the duke was eager to demonstrate his closeness to the Frankish ruler at their expenses.[58] This complaint may have had long story rooting in the wars against Avars and in the role that the *dux de Histria* plaid in them.[59] We know that unlike the leading aristocrats, many who lived on the boarder of the empire, as the Istrians did, were unenthusiastic or even hostile when military campaigns began due to its high costs and danger of reprisals.[60] John, on the other hand, used war to gain visibility and trust from the new masters. He was able to collect tribute for the Franks in money, kind and, most importantly, horses.[61] This is a clue of the measures that the duke must have taken to rapidly raise an army to campaign in the east, because horses, a fundamental gear for war, must have become even more precious in the aftermath of the equine plague of 791.[62] After his first campaign with the Carolingians, John may have joined the war of 796, which I mentioned previously, or the one again led by Pippin of Italy in the same year, but the initial steps toward this circle of trust were already taken in 791. King Pippin and his closest friends involved in the war in the east may have known that the Istrians soldiers could have been deceitful allies. They had for centuries joined with the much-despised Greeks and, only few years before, they brutally retaliated against bishop Maurice, mercilessly blinding him. However, looking at these recently acquired subjects during the successful campaigns against the Avars, the king realised that they could be trusted. Charlemagne heard about this, and informed his wife that the new duke that many were observing had behaved well: perhaps against every expectation, he "did well [*benefecit*]" after all.

Notes

* This chapter was financed by the FWF Project 24823, The Transformation of Roman Dalmatia. I wish to thank Helmut Reimitz, Katharina von Winckler and Bernhard Zeller for help and suggestions.

1 T.S. Brown, "Byzantine Italy, *c.* 680–876", in *The New Cambridge Medieval History II: 700 c.–900 c.*, ed. R. McKitterick (Cambridge, 1995), 320–348, at 338: *It is all the more ironic that the most informative document on the society of Byzantine Italy survives from this obscure region and from the period immediately after imperial rule.* The Plea of Rižana is edited in … *in loco qui dicitur Riziano….: Zbor v Rižani pri Kopru leta 804 / Die Versammlung in Rižana / Risano bei Koper / Capodistria im Jahre 804*, ed. H. Krahwinkler, Knjižnica Annales, 40 (Koper, 2004). Literature on the topic is now vast: the latest contribution is J.R. Davis, *Charlemagne's Practice of Empire* (Cambridge, 2015), 102–104, with plenty of references.

2 Notably: P. Štih, "Istria at the Onset of the Frankish Rule, or the Impact of the Global Politics on the Regional and Local Conditions", in Idem, *The Middle Ages between the Eastern Alps and the Northern Adriatic, East Central and Eastern Europe in the Middle Ages450–1450*, 11 (Leiden and Boston, 2010), 212–229; L. Margetić, "Sul passaggio del potere sull'Istria da Bisanzio ai Franchi", *Acta Histriae*, 2 (1994), 15–24.

3 *Epistolae variorum Carolo Magno regnante scriptae* 20, ed. E. Dümmler, MGH Epp., 4 (Berlin, 1895), 493–567, at 528–529. On the Frankish *ducatus Histriae* see:

S. Esders, "Spätantike und frühmittelalterliche Dukate: Überlegungen zum Problem historischer Kontinuität und Diskontinuität", in *Die Anfänge Bayerns: Von Raetien und Noricum zur frühmittelalterlichen Baiovaria*, ed. H. Fehr and I. Heitmeier, Bayerische Landesgeschichte und europäische Regional-geschichte, 1 (Ottilien, 2012), 425–465, at 433–438.

4 S. Airlie, "The Aristocracy: Captains and Kings", in *Charlemagne: Empire and Society*, ed. J. Story (Manchester, 2005), 90–102, at 94.

5 *Codex Carolinus* 63, ed. W. Gundlach, MGH Epp., 3 (Berlin, 1892), 459–657, at 590. Maurice was identified with the bishop of Novigrad thanks to a fragmentary inscription found there: M. Jurković, "Il ciborio di Novigrad (Cittanova d'Istria)", *Hortus Artium Medievalium*, 1 (1995), 141–149.

6 On Marcarius: E. Hlawitschka, *Franken, Alemannen, Bayern und Burgunder in Oberitalien (774–962)*, Forschungen zur oberrheinischen Landesgeschichte, 8 (Freiburg/Bresgau, 1960), 235; H. Krahwinkler, *Friaul im Frühmittelalter: Geschichte einer Region vom Ende des fünften bis zum Ende des zehnten Jahrhunderts* Veröffentlichungen des Instituts für österreichische Geschichtsforschung, 30 (Vienna, 1992), 144–145.

7 I explored this in F. Borri, "L'Adriatico tra Bizantini, Longobardi e Franchi. Dalla conquista di Ravenna alla pace di Aquisgrana (751–812)", *Bullettino dell'Istituto storico italiano per il Medio Evo*, 112 (2010), 1–56, at 13–14. See also: I. Basić, "New Evidence for the Re-Establishment of the Adriatic Dioceses in the Late Eighth Century", in *Imperial spheres and the Adriatic: Byzantium, the Carolingians and the Treaty of Aachen (812)*, ed. M. Ančić, J. Shepard, and T; Vedriš (London, 2018), 261–287.

8 John the Deacon, *Istoria Veneticorum* II, 22, ed. L.A. Berto, Storici italiani dal Cinquecento al Millecinquecento ad uso delle scuole, 2 (Bologna, 1999) p. 106. On Maurice: L.A. Berto, *In Search of the First Venetians: Proposopography of Early Medieval Venice*, Studies in the Early Middle Ages, 41 (Turnhout, 2014) 313.

9 On Bavaria: G. Bührer-Thierry, "De la fin du duché au début de l'empire: dix ans de transitions en Bavière à la lumieère des chartes (788–799)", in *774: Ipotesi su una trasizione*, ed. S. Gasparri, Seminari del Centro interuniversitario per la storia e l'archeologia dell'alto Medioevo, 1 (Turnhout, 2008), 27–39, at 27. On Alsace: H. Hummer, *Politics and Power in Early Medieval Europe: Alsace and the Frankish Realm, 600–1000* (Cambridge, 2005), 57.

10 Einhardi, *Vita Karoli Magni* 15, ed. G. Waitz, MGH, SS rer. Germ., [25] (Hannover and Leipzig, 1911), 18: *post quam utramque Pannoniam et adpositam in altera Danubii ripa Daciam, Histriam quoque et Liburniam atque Dalmaciam.*

11 On the wars against the Avars: W. Pohl, *Die Awarenkriege Karls des Großen 788–803*, Militärhistorische Schriftenreihe, 61 (Vienna, 1988); F. Bowlus, *Franks, Moravians and Magyars: The Struggle for the Middle Danube 788–907* (Philadelphia / Pn, 1995), 46–60.

12 *Epistolae variorum* 20, ed. Dümmler, 528.

13 *Annales Laureshamenses* 791, ed. H. Pertz, MGH SS, 1 (Hanover, 1826), 22–39, at 34: *Pippinus filius eius de Italia transmisit, ipse introivit in Illyricum et inde in Pannonia*. See the geographical considerations in: P. Štih, "On the Eastern Border of Italy in the Early Middle Ages", in Idem, *The Middle Ages*, 190–211, at 192–193.

14 It is recorded also in *Annales regni Francorum* 791, ed. F. Kurze, MGH SS rer. Ger., [6] (Hanover, 1895), 88. On this: D.S. Bachrach, *Religion and the Conduct of War, c. 300–c. 1215* (Woodbridge, 2003), 39–40; H. Reimitz, "Conversion and Control: The Establishment of Liturgical Frontiers in Carolingian Pannonia", in: *The Transformation of Frontiers from Late Antiquity to the Carolingians*, ed. W.

Pohl, I. Wood, and H. Reimitz, The Transformation of the Roman World, 10 (Boston, Leiden, and Cologne, 2000), 189–208, at 198–199.

15 *Epistolae variorum* 20, ed. Dümmler, 529.

16 *Collectio s. Dionysii* 25, ed. K. Zeumer, MGH Formulae Merowingici et Karolini aevi (Hanover, 1886), 510–511. Cathulf's letter is edited in *Epistolae variorum* 7, ed. Dümmler, 501–504. On the collection: J. Story, "Cathwulf, Kingship, and the Royal Abbey of Saint-Denis", *Speculum* 74 (1999), 1–21, at 11–21; A. Rio, *Legal Practice and the Written Word in the Early Middle Ages: Frankish Formulae, c. 500–1000* (Cambridge, 2011), 141–144. On the range of dating: see W. Levison, "Das Formularbuch von Saint-Denis", *Neues Archiv*, 41 (1919), 283–304.

17 M. McCormick, "The Liturgy of War in the Early Middle Ages: Crisis, Litanies, and the Carolingian Monarchy", *Viator*, 15 (1984), 1–23, at 14; followed by W. Pohl, "Liturgie di guerra nei regni altomedievali", *Rivista di Storia del Cristianesimo*, 5 (2008), 29–44, at 29.

18 Story, "Cathwulf", 18–19; but see also: M. Garrison, "Letters to a King and Biblical exempla: The Examples of Cathuulf and Clemens Peregrinus", *Early Medieval Europe*, 7 (1998), 305–328, at 319.

19 This, on the other hand, seems to be the opinion of R. McKitterick, *Charlemagne: The Formation of a European Identity* (Cambridge, 2008), 43–46, who suggested the collection to be a dossier of material valuable for the writing of history.

20 *Epistolae variorum* 20, ed. Dümmler, 528.

21 *Annales regni Francoum* 804, ed. Kurze, 118.

22 See the consideration, pertinent to the Austrasian kingdom, of R. Collins, Theodebert I, "Rex Magnus Francorum", in: *Ideal and reality in Frankish and Anglo-Saxon society: Studies presented to J.M. Wallace-Hadrill*, ed. P. Wormald, D. Bullough, and R. Collins (Oxford, 1983), 7–33.

23 H. Wolfram, *Grenzen und Räume: Geschichte Österreichs vor seiner Entstehung*, Österreichische Geschichte 1 (Wien, 1995), 158.

24 *Annales regni Francorum* 796, ed. Kurze, 98. On Vojnomir: W. Pohl, *Die Awaren: Ein Steppenvolk im Mitteleuropa*, 2nd ed. (Munich, 2002), 319; Krahwinkler, *Friaul*, 150.

25 M. Innes, "Charlemagne's Government", in *Charlemagne*, 71–89, at 74. Moreover on the economic gains: T. Reuter, "Plunder and Tribute in the Carolingian Empire", in Idem, *Medieval Polities and Modern Mentalities*, ed. J.L. Nelson (Cambridge, 2006), 231–250, at 236; together with J.L. Nelson, "Introduction", in Eadem, *The Frankish World, 750–900* (London, 1996), xiii–xxxi, at xxviii–xxix.

26 G. Ravegnani, "L'Istria bizantina: le istituzioni militari ai confini dell'esarcato ravennate", *Acta Histriae*, 7 (1999), 77–84.

27 *Placitum Risani*, ed. Krahwinkler, 72.

28 Gregory the Great, *Registrum Epistolarum* IX, 154, ed. D. Nogbert, CCSL 140-A, 2 vols (Turnhout, 1982), II, 710; Paul the Deacon, *Historia Langobardorum* IV, 24, MGH SS rer. Lang. (Hanover, 1878), 12–186, at 125.

29 Esders, "Spätantike und frühmittelalterlichen Dukaten", 436.

30 MGH Epp., 4, 528.

31 Hlawitschka, *Franken*, 210–212, who, however, believed Istrian John to be a Frank.

32 S. Cosentino, "Antroponimia, politica e società nell'esarcato in età bizantina e post-bizantina,' in *L'héritage byzantin en Italie* (VIIIe–XII^e^siè*cle) II: Les cadres juridiques et sociaux et les institutions publiques*, ed. J.-M. Martin, A. Peters Custot, and V. Prigent, Collection de l'École française de Rome, 461 (Rome, 2010), 279–295. See also the proposopography in T.S. Brown, *Officers and*

Gentlemen: Imperial Administration and Aristocratic Power in Byzantine Italy A.D. 554–800 (London, 1984), 250–282.

33 I. Santos Salazar, "Castrum Persiceta: Potere e territorio in uno spazio di frontiera dal secolo VI al IX", *Reti Medievali: Rivista* 7 (2006), 1–20, at 7.

34 Krahwinkler, *Friaul*, 211–215; moreover: Esders, "Spätantike und frühmittelalterlichen Dukaten", 435–436.

35 Gasparri, *Italia longobarda*, 130–132; Idem, "Il passaggio dai Franchi ai Longobardi", in *Il futuro dei Longobardi: L'Italia e la costruzione dell'Europa di Carlo Magno; Saggi*, ed. C. Bertelli and G.P. Brogiolo (Milan, 2000), 25–43. Moreover: G. Tabacco, "L'avvento dei Carolingi nel regno dei Longobardi", in *Il regno dei Longobardi in Italia*, ed. S. Gasparri, Istituzioni e società, 4 (Spoleto, 2004), 443–479; K. Brunner, *Oppositionelle Gruppen im Karolingerreich*, Veröffentlichungen des Instituts für österreichische Geschichtsforschung, 25 (Vienna, Cologne, and Graz, 1979), 43; Hlawitschka, *Franken*, 25–30.

36 Berto, *In Search of the First Venetians*, 315–317.

37 *Annales regno Francorum* 806, ed. Kurze, 120.

38 Hrotgaud was raised by Charlemagne: *Annales regni Francorum* 776, ed. Kurze, 43; he was already in charge at the moment of the Carolingian takeover: Andreas of Bergamo, *Historia* 4, MGH SS rer. Lang. (Hannover, 1878), 220–230, at 224. On Hrotgaud: S. Gasparri, *I duchi longobardi*, Studi storici, 109 (Rome, 1978), 71–72; and Idem, *Italia longobarda*, 125, who convincingly suggests that Hrodgaud was duke since the time of Desiderius. Moreover: Hlawitschka, *Franken*, 199; Krahwinkler, *Friaul*, 126–134.

39 On Gaidus: Gasparri, *I duchi*, 56; Hlawitschka, *Franken*, 182. Stabilinus, Gasparri, *I duchi*, 61–62; Hlawitschka, *Franken*, 269.

40 On Eric: Hlawitschka, *Franken*, 176–177; Krahwinkler, *Friaul*, 143–157. Moreover: J.B. Ross, "Two Neglected Paladins of Charlemagne: Erich of Friuli and Gerold of Bavaria", *Speculum* 20 (1945), 212–235. Hlawitschka, *Franken*, 235, thought that Marcarius: *in den Gebieten nördlich oder nordwestlich der Alpen beheimatet gewesen sein.*

41 *Translatio sanguinis Domini* 3–5; 15–16, ed. T. Klüppel, *Die Reichenauer Heiligblut-Reliquie*, Reichenauer Texte und Bilder, 1 (Stuttgart, 1999), 28–31; 40. Hlawitschka, *Franken*, 206–207. Moreover: R. Kaiser, *Churrätien im frühen Mittelalter: Ende 5. bis Mitte 10. Jahrhundert* (Basel, 2008), 60–61.

42 Davies, *Charlemagne's Practice*, 136–137.

43 *Annales regni Francorum* 799, ed. Kurze, 108: *Ericus dux Foroiulensis post tot prospere gestas res iuxta Tharsaticam Liburniae civitatem insidiis oppidanorum oppressus est.* Einhard, *Vita Karoli Magni* 12, ed. Waitz, 16. On this: Krahwinkler, *Friaul*, 151–158; S. Gasparri, "Istituzioni e poteri nel territorio friulano in età longobarda e carolingia", in *Paolo Diacono e il Friuli altomedievale, secc. VI–X*, Atti del XIV Congresso internazionale di studi sull'alto Medioevo (Spoleto, 2001), 105–128, at 121.

44 Airlie, "The Aristocracy", 94.

45 On the 788-imperial expedition: O. Bertolini, "Carlomagno e Benevento", in *Karl der Große: Lebenswerk und Nachleben I*, ed. H. Beumann (Düsseldorf, 1965), 609–671, at 637–655. Now see also: S. Gasparri, *Desiderio*, Profili (Rome, forthcoming).

46 Alcuin, *Epistolae* 7, ed. E. Dümmler, MGH Epp., 4 (Berlin, 1895), 1–481, at 32.

47 Bertolini, "Carlomagno e Benevento", 666.

48 On Arechis II: Gasparri, *I duchi*, 98–100.

49 *Codex Carolinus* 83, ed. Gundlach, 616–619.

50 *Annales regni Francorum* 788, ed. Kurze, 82: *et fuit missus Wineghisus una cum paucis Francis, ut praevideret eorum omnia, quae gessissent.*

51 T. Živković, "The Origin of the Royal Frankish Annalist's Information about the Serbs in Dalmatia", in *Spomenica akademika Sime Ćirkovića*, ed. S. Rudić, Zbornik radova (Istorijski institut u Beogradu), 25 (Beograd, 2011), 381–398.

52 *Annales regni Francorum* 791, ed. Kurze, 88: *Saxones autem cum quibusdam Francis et maxime plurima Frisonum.*

53 *Annales regni Francorum* 796, ed. Kurze, 98: *Heiricus dux Foroiulensis missis hominibus suis cum Wonomyro Sclavo in Pannonias hringum gentis Avarorum longis retro temporibus quietum, civili bello fatigatis inter se principibus, spoliavit,—chagan sive iuguro intestina clade addictis et a suis occisis—thesaurum priscorum regum multa seculorum prolixitate collectum domno regi Carolo ad Aquis palatium misit.*

54 *Annales regni Francorum [q.d. Einhardi]* 798, ed. Kurze, 105: *legatus regis Eburis nomine, qui in eodem proelio fuit et in Abodritorum acie dextrum cornu tenuit.* Živković, "The Origin", 386.

55 Gasparri, *Italia longobarda*, 146–160.

56 *Codex Carolinus* 57, ed. Gundlach, 582–583.

57 *Liber pontificalis* 105, cx–cxii, ed. L. Duchesne, *Le "Liber Pontificalis:" Texte, introduction et commentaire*, Bibliothèque des Écoles françaises d'Athènes et de Rome, 2 (Paris, 1886–1892), II: 134.

58 *Placitum Risani*, ed. Krahwinkler, 74–78.

59 Esders, "Spätantike und frühmittelalterliche Dukaten", 443–446.

60 *Karoli capitula Italica* 3, MGH Cap. I (Hanover, 1883), n. 101, 208. On this Reuter, "Plunder and Tribute", 243–244.

61 *Placitum Risani*, ed. Krahwinkler, 78.

62 On this: C. Gillmor, "The 791 Equine Epidemic and its Impact on Charlemagne's Army", *Journal of Medieval Military History*, 3 (2005), 23–45; T. Newfield, "A Great Carolingian Panzootic: The Probable Extent, Diagnosis and Impact of an Early Ninth-Century Cattle Pestilence", *Argos*, 46 (2012), 200–210.

14 Hegemony, elitedom and ethnicity

"Armenians" in imperial Bari, *c.*874–1071

Nicholas S.M. Matheou

Introduction*

According to the late eleventh-century historian William of Apulia, in 1016 a band of Norman mercenaries ascended the summit of Monte Gargano on pilgrimage to the shrine of St. Michael,[1] when they happened upon a stranger:

> There they saw a man clothed in the Greek manner by the name of Melus, and were amazed at the exile's strange costume which they had never seen before, with his head wrapped around in a turban. When they saw him they asked who he was and whence he had come. He replied he was a Langobard by birth and a noble citizen of Bari (*Langobardum natu civemque fuisse ingenuum Bari*), forced from his fatherland (*patriis*) by the ferocity of the Greeks.[2]

Melus, rendered "Meles" in Greek sources, first appears in 1009 when he and a relative named Dattus rebelled against the east Roman governor-general, the *katepanō*, taking Bari, Ascoli and Troia, before being defeated by a new *katepanō* in 1011 and fleeing to the prince of Salerno.[3] Then in 1016, as a result of the meeting narrativised by William, Normans joined with Meles, invading the east Roman province or theme of Longobardia and suffering a heavy defeat near Cannae in 1017.[4] Meles' rebellion represents Bari's elitedom, the *archontes*, coming into a new period of political action, and in proclaiming himself the first *dux Apuliae* he perhaps sought to follow the examples of Naples, Gaeta and Amalfi, not to say Venice.[5] After the defeat he fled north to spend the remainder of his days as titular duke at the court of the western emperor, his son raised a hostage in Constantinople with the eastern emperor.

There are no details on his background or heritage, but Meles' identification as "a Langobard by birth and a noble citizen of Bari" resonates with other sources. The eleventh-century Barese chronicler Lupus *protospatharius* notes how "in the year 1010 Langobardia rebelled from the emperor by the work of *dux* Melus",[6] whilst the late eleventh/early twelfth century chronicler of Monte Cassino, Leo Marsicanus, names him "Melus … first and most famous of the citizens of Bari and indeed of the whole of Apulia, a most vigorous and most prudent man (*Melus … Barensium civium immo totius Apuliae primus ac clarior erat, strenuissimus plane ac prudentissimus vir*)".[7] Likewise the late eleventh-century east Roman historian, Ioannes Skylitzes, describes "A magnate (*dynastēs*) among the inhabitants (*epoikoi*) of Bari named Meles [who] incited the people in Longobardia to take up arms against the Romans".[8] Thus each historian explicitly constructs Meles as a representative of Longobardia/Apulia and a prominent citizen of Bari. Yet Meles' name is not Latinate or Lombard but Armenian, "Mleh",[9] and Dattus also appears to have an Armenian name, "T'adēos". William also draws attention to his "Greek dress", describing a common elite costume found across the south-central and eastern Mediterranean.[10] So how did an actor with an Armenian name, and dressed in characteristically "Greek" clothes, come to take political action as a noble citizen of Bari, and to be remembered as a patriotic Longobard of Apulia?

This is the question explored in this chapter. It looks at the evidence for identified Armenians in east Roman Bari, and analyses their integration into local elitedom. Through this analysis it becomes possible to deduce dynamics of elite formation in the city, and the construction of politically salient identifications in response to the conditions of imperial hegemony. The theme of Longobardia's late ninth-century establishment, and the subsequent development of a provincial social system, provides a singular case study for the interaction of cities and elites in the Italian peninsula with the eastern Roman Empire. Although the Italian provinces are often claimed to be atypical, often without explanation, Bari's unique evidence permits close analysis of elite practices in a provincial city and thematic capital.[11] The presence of identified Armenian actors provides the analytical entry point for investigating these practices.

In the most astute study to date Nina Garsoïan elucidated the many different forms of east Roman Armenianness,[12] with the ethnic category able to cover often sharply differing actors and cultural stuff. This purposefully vague term refers to the basically arbitrary bits of custom, dress, language, "material culture" and so on that get associated with a given ethnic category in a given time and place, and is intended to emphasise the non-predetermined quality of what "stuff" gets endowed with symbolic value. There have been studies of "Armenians" in east Roman Italy, but these leave the category unproblematised, so that pan-imperial elites appear alongside regional actors in undifferentiated analysis, collating evidence with the assumption that it represents one ethnic phenomenon.[13] Thus this chapter provides an initial case study that points to a more comprehensive assessment of different forms of east Roman Armenianness. It analyses whether "being Armenian" affected elites' integration into and consequent reshaping of Bari's social system, and what this in turn reveals about imperial rule's constitutive role in the urban space. The first section lays out the evidence for Armenians in east Roman Italy and Bari, developing a critical framework that situates these actors in social dynamics, and the second broadens the scope to a social-historical analysis of elites in Bari. Finally the conclusion brings these two strands together in a critical understanding of Barese elitedom's transformation under imperial rule.

Situating "Armenians" in imperial Bari

There is no need to connect Barese actors to the inconclusive evidence for identified Armenians settling in imperial Italy and Sicily between the mid-sixth and mid-ninth centuries, since the late ninth-century east Roman revival provides the strongest conditions for actors entering the south.[14] Between the loss of Ravenna in 751 and the 860s imperial holdings on the Italian mainland had been reduced to a few heel and toeholds protecting Sicilian sea routes, but during the island's protracted ninth-century loss, southern Italy became more important.[15] During and after various campaigns between 869 and 892 the imperial centre explicitly sought to create hegemonic space, making large sections of Apulia legible for domination and exploitation.[16] Skylitzes notes that Basileios I (*r.* 867–886) rebuilt and repopulated the city of Iontos as Kallipolis with settlers from Herakleia on the Pontos,[17] and the mid-tenth century *Life of Basileios* records his relocation of three thousand slaves from the Peloponnese: "settling them in freedom by imperial decree as a colony (*apoikia*) in the theme of Longobardia".[18] Settlement can also be inferred from chronicle accounts mentioning Paulician units on Nikephoros Phokas the Elder's successful 885 campaign,[19] with eleventh-century sources confirming the later existence of militarised heterodox communities.[20] The Phokas family itself descended from identified Armenians, and particularly at this early date many members may have continued to identify with some form. In fact one chronicle variant of this same section explicitly claims that Phokas "settled Armenians" in the conquered cities.[21]

This is the only direct evidence for Armenian settlement in the late-ninth century, but the names of a significant number of contemporary officials make them likely to have identified as such.[22] A certain Gregorios, the common Armenian Grigor, is found in Otranto in 873 and Bari in 876, while Mousoulikes (Mušełik) is first found as *stratelates* of Kephalonia in the 880 conquest of Taranto, and then as governor-general or *strategos* of Sicily in 881/882. Taranto's conqueror was a certain Leon Apostyppes, whose name (Levon/Łevond),[23] surname "Abustub", and sons' names David and Vardas, indicate Armenian connections. Importantly the names of three of the first four *strategoi* of Longobardia make it highly probable that they were identified as Armenians. First is Symbatikios (Smbatik) (890–892), supreme western commander and *strategos* of almost all the western themes, who in 890 conquered Benevento. This conquest did not last but was nevertheless crucial in the theme of Longobardia's formalisation, with the city probably intended as thematic capital.[24] Indeed, the theme's earliest dated mention is Symbatikios' 892 grant of privileges to the monastery of Monte Cassino, where he specifies the monks' freedom from the depredations of "Greek, Lombard and Armenian officials".[25] Importantly this phrase is repeated by the *strategos* Georgios (892–894) in his 892 privileges for the monastery of S. Vincenzo al Volturno. Georgios may also have had an Armenian connection like his successor Varsakios [Vałaršak] (894–899), who was Mousoulikes' predecessor as Sicilian *strategos* in 880/881.[26]

So the monastic charters demonstrate that identified Armenians were prominent in the theme of Longobardia's late ninth-century foundation, with the names of high-level officials providing further indicative clues. Indeed, the paucity of source survival and chronicle coverage suggests that a greater number of Armenian incomers from different elite strata should be imagined—notably *De Ceremoniis*, a mid-tenth-century work compiling diverse imperial documents, records thirty-six Armenians on a 935 campaign to Longobardia.[27] Unfortunately it is impossible to demonstrate direct connections between identified Armenians resident in Bari and members of the pan-imperial title- and office-holding elite, who often stayed in Italy for only a short period.[28] But it is possible to imagine associated, lower-strata Armenophone elites entering and subsequently settling in similar socio-economic status to other Grecophone incomers and local Latinate elites. The imperial centre may have been directly involved or these actors could have been followers brought to the south by high-level officials—and of course not only identified Armenians—that formed local relationships which encouraged them to stay.[29] High-ranking officials and well-off magnates also had unfree dependents, with the best evidence for east Roman manumission practices coming from southern Italian documents. Notably this consists both of protocols specifying formulae and the freed slave's status—"whether you are of the Russian *genos*, or the Skythian, Hagarene, or Ismaelite, I free you from the present day to be free in all ways and a citizen, a Roman"[30]—and attestations in documents, one bilingual eleventh-century will proclaiming a certain Pitzoulos "*eleutheros, panteleutheros kai politēs Romaiōn…; …liber, omnino liber et civis Romanus* (*sic*)".[31] In addition to citizenship freedmen were granted land and moveable property,[32] much as Basileios I's aforementioned colony, providing the means to reproduce a status at least higher than the majority of agrarian subalterns.

So there were doubtless many, varied routes by which identified Armenians entered east Roman Longobardia,[33] but settling followers and freedmen of pan-imperial elites is one model to make sense of the rich evidence—some 200 documents—for Bari and surrounding region in the tenth and eleventh centuries. One early example is the name Garzanitis/Charsianitis, first appearing in two documents of the 960s.[34] This is first attested as the surname of a mid-ninth-century Anatolian *strategos*, Charzanites, and resonates strongly with the Armenian-descended Morocharzanioi found in mid-ninth-century Constantinople.[35] Most strikingly, in the *Life of Basileios* it is specified that Nikephoros Phokas in

885–886 brought "some choice units from among the Charsianites and Cappadocians".[36] It thus appears as strong evidence for an Armenian-associated surname from the ninth-century pan-imperial elite, and/or a regional name of settled troops, becoming a given name in east Roman Longobardia, appearing again in documents of 999, 1002 and 1039.[37] Notably this is not an isolated case,[38] with Meles naming his son Argyros, the surname of a mid-tenth-century *strategos* of Longobardia and Calabria, and by way of comparison the Armenian surname of a *katepanō* of Italia 1008–1010, "Kourkouas", is attested in a 1054 inscription from Otranto and as the name of a prominent notary in mid-eleventh-century Taranto.[39] Nevertheless, although it confirms the model's plausibility, there is no reason to assume that these Garzanitis/Charzianitis had any personal connection to Armenianness.

The first indication of local actors reproducing Armenian cultural stuff appears in a document of 977 witnessed by a certain Cricorus, "Grigor" tellingly rendered in western Armenian pronunciation.[40] Thereafter a clutch of Barese documents reveal a notable presence of identified Armenian actors. The earliest from 990 records a land dispute concerning the cleric Caloiohannes, heir to three plots of land in the plain of Ceglie bought by his father "Dumnellus of the city of Bari" from "Vartisky the Armenian", wife of "Corki the Armenian" and daughter of a certain "Moses Pascike".[41] But after Dumnellus' death the cleric Mele, "son of Simagonus the presbyter and Armenian", seized one of the plots, with Mele's son Iohannes selling part of this in turn to Cricorus "son of Achan the Armenian". Now Caloiohannes was demanding his rights and appointing a certain "Sepus the Armenian" as overseer. This document records the resolution, "made and mediated by Cricorus son of Petrus the Armenian", and witnessed by five people, a certain Leon in Greek, Andreas, Falcus and Iohannes in Latin, and Husep in Armenian. Thus it records six local figures explicitly identified as Armenians and a further six identifiable by association, name and even language, leaving only a third of the eighteen named actors. The names are of particular interest, with western Armenian pronunciations of Georgi (Corki), Grigor and Sebeos (Sepus), while Vartisky appears a rendering of Vardọuhi and Achan of Išxan.[42] Similarly Simagonus would appear to be Šemavon, while Mele is Mleh, and Husep the unchanged Armenian version of Joseph. The appearance of Moses Pascike is also notable, with his undoubtedly Armenian surname perhaps indicating a higher socioeconomic position.[43]

In 1001 another Mele, "son of Cotuneus", is found in the Cretacio district with his wife Gemma selling eight plots of land to Magelgardus son of Sassonus for a specified amount of imperial coinage.[44] Here there are no ethnic identifications, but at this date the name is still associated with identified Armenians. A different "Mleh" rendered "Mel" is found in Ceglie in a document of 1003, a certain Calomaria's son from a previous marriage.[45] Calomaria sought her and her daughter Balsama's rights from her soon-to-be separated second husband, Caloiohannes the cleric, perhaps the very same as that of 990. The significant presence in Ceglie is confirmed in another document of 1005, recording the sale of a house by the married couple "Eustratius son of Petrus" and "Sanda of Bari" to "Auria daughter of Cumsfride" for ten *solidi*.[46] Sanda's father had bought the property from a certain "Petros son of Muscellica (Mušełik)" and "his wife Iemma". These names strongly indicate spoken Armenian, with pronounced forms of Museł in the diminutive, Emma, and Peter, which appears in Latin as "Petros" and is declined as *Petrosi*.[47] The property also abutted that of "Amatus son of Muscelius (Mušeł)", whose grandchildren Maius, Ursus and Lupus lived there.

Most importantly, the document refers to "the church of Saint George [which] had been constructed by Moses the Armenian cleric", a still extant building with strikingly Caucasian architectural features known into the modern day as S. Giorgio "of the Armenians".[48] The year 1005 forms the *terminus ante quem* for the church's foundation, and another document of 1011 implies that it was built not much earlier than the late tenth century.[49] Here Archontissa, "daughter of Armodoctus of Taranto" and "widow of Moses the Armenian cleric", came to an agreement with her stepson Andreas over rights to part of her husband's former property. Andreas, a child from Moses' former marriage, had denied her the stipulated inheritance of twelve *solidi*, and the moveable and immoveable properties of her *morgengabe*, a wedding gift granted according to Lombard law. The document recounts Moses' extensive property in detail, revealing easily enough wealth for church building,[50] and positions it with reference to the land owned by others in the area, including that of "Mele [Mleh] son of Fasan" and "Amatus son of Muscelus [Mušeł]",[51] as well as some situated "in front of *our church* of Saint George (*ecclesia nostra Sancti Georgii*)".[52] This identifies her deceased husband as the church's founder, and alongside the document of 990 points to a notable Armenian clerical presence, with three different identified clerics alongside an ecclesiastical foundation. Significantly a certain Mele the priest is also found witnessing two documents in Conversano in 1009,[53] and in 1015 Mele son of Maio, cleric, abbot and rector of the church of S. Gregorio Armeno, gave all his properties to his relative "Simeon (Šimovn) son of Andreas of Bari".[54] This is the *terminus ante quem* for S. Gregorio's foundation, built in the courtyard of the *katepanō*'s buildings, and the perimeter walls' funerary inscriptions bear Armenian-associated names such as "Melipezzis" and "Meliciacca".[55]

Hence there is strong evidence for identified Armenian and Armenian-associated actors in and around Bari *c.* 977–1020, the exact same period as Meles' lifespan and rebellion. Indeed, the name Mele is incredibly common, appearing twenty-two times between 990 and 1031, with some fifty further appearances between 1031 and 1126.[56] The early eleventh-century *Life of St. Neilos of Rossano* also reveals expectation of contact with identified Armenian actors, when the saint returns from Longobardia to his hometown in Calabria, and children throw stones at him saying: "'Hey, you Bulgarian monk!' while some others called him a Frank, and others an Armenian".[57] Although presented as exoticised Others to emphasise Neilos' strange dress, these three ethnonyms are not random but refer to ethnic categories present and recognised in the region.[58] Thus the *Life* reveals Armenians imagined as part of east Roman Italy's ethnic makeup, and perhaps particularly that of Longobardia as opposed to Calabria.[59]

Nevertheless, despite strong evidence for the reproduction of cultural stuff, after 1011 there are no actors identified as "the Armenian" in documents. One of those miraculously healed by St. Nicholas' relics in 1087 is referred to as "Armenius", perhaps in this instance a given name rather than an ethnic category but even so strongly indicating the prominence of locally identified actors.[60] But it remains that no later document specifically identifies any actor, so that the reproduction of Armenian cultural stuff like language must be postulated through proxy information such as names, presenting significant methodological problems. Names are useful indicators of sociocultural reproduction, especially when their written forms provide phonetic clues, but they are far from one-to-one indicators for ethnic belonging. The remarkable prominence of "Mele" from the late tenth and early eleventh centuries on is an indication of prominent Armenian-associated actors, but the exact manner of the name's diffusion is impossible to track, and after around 1030 it may indicate Meles' own historic prominence in local elites' symbolic universe. And even if "Armenian" names were used to demonstrate ethnic identifications, the ethnonym's absence in documentation suggests that this was irrelevant at the level of sociopolitical action. Onomastics' generational aspect is paramount: a mid-eleventh-century Barese named Mele suggests a symbolic association, but the values are now lost and ethnic identification cannot be assumed. "Amatus son of Muscelius" has an Armenian-named father but a Lombard name, like his three grandchildren Maius, Ursus and Lupus, who remained networked with identified Armenians in the same district around S. Giorgio. Clearly Maius, Ursus and Lupus could have reproduced a hereditary Armenian sense of self despite their "Lombard" names, and alongside any predominant Longobard identification, but it is impossible to know.

Bearing this in mind, it is still important that distinctively Armenian-sounding names recur across the eleventh and into the early twelfth centuries, suggesting the reproduction of at least some language use. A document of 1028 refers to Michael son of "Sepus the priest",[61] another of 1031 records the land of "Davit son of Chrusafus",[62] and variations on K'urt/K'urtik appear in 1044, 1052, 1060 and 1086.[63] One document of 1078 is witnessed by Krikorios *protōspatharios*, judge of Italia, another Krikorios witnesses in 1099,[64] while Dattus appears in 1041, 1052, 1093 and 1127.[65] Of course many of these attestations post-date Robert Guiscard's 1071 conquest, but as demonstrated later this does not form a significant dividing line in Barese elitedom's makeup or self-articulation. In fact many of the clearest indications of spoken Armenian come from this later period. Diminutive forms of Peter, "Petrak", appear thirteen times between 1073 and 1120, with one figure in 1091 referred to as "Petracca" in Latin but signing his name "Petros" in Greek, confirming that in this instance at least it is the diminutive form and not a fixed local variant.[66] Another document of 1093 has a certain "Ieorgi" selling landed properties to "Petrus son of Maraldus", placing "Melias son of Petracce", *tourmarchos* of Bari, as the sale's overseer and witness to the contract.[67] Here Melias is the more common Greek rendering of Mleh, and the plaintiff's name apparently represents a mixed Armeno-Greek pronunciation of Georgi.[68] There are also names such as Iohannacius (Hovhannak) and Sergius (Sargis) that, albeit less conclusive, appear in several contexts associated with other "Armenian" named actors, such as Sergius son of Iohannacius in 1086,[69] Iohannacius son of Sergius in 1098—perhaps the same family's next generation[70]—and a certain Sergius found witnessing with Melia in 1067.[71] Finally, by way of comparison, two funerary inscriptions from Soleto reveal an Asotes (Ašot) and Arsakes (Aršak) in the late eleventh and early twelfth centuries, and Kortikes is common in contemporary Taranto, appearing alongside a certain *Armenus* as a monastic villein in 1114.[72]

Taken together Husep's use of Armenian in official documentation alongside Armenian-pronounced names indicate moderate language use and the reproduction of some cultural stuff—as late as 1210 in Cretacie a certain "Garganus (Gurgēn) son of Corticius" bought property from "Bella daughter of Meliciacce [Mlitseak]", witnessed by a certain Petracce.[73] In sum, therefore, the evidence represents a strong demonstration of "Armenian" involvement and settlement in the late ninth and tenth centuries, and resident "Armenian" actors in Bari and Longobardia from the late tenth, across the eleventh, and into the twelfth centuries. But it also presents a complex picture irreducible to an image of bounded ethnoreligious communities. "Armenian" actors and their descendants are continuously networked with "Lombards" and "Greeks", and as much as no ethnic identification distinguishes between them after 1011, neither is there a strong pattern of "Armenian" names clustering together. There are a handful of significant cases, but it is not consistent, just as often single "Armenian" names appear in otherwise entirely "Lombard" associations, and identified actors visibly take on local sociocultural forms. Likewise identified Lombard families begin taking Greek names from the late tenth century, with "Caloiohannes son of Dumnellus of the city of Bari" in 990 and Mele "son of Caloiohannes of Bari" in 1077 aptly demonstrating the lack of distinct ethnocultural onomastics.

The recurrence of "Armenian" names is therefore evidence of settled actors' material-symbolic integration into the locale through marriage and other structured relationships, not a singular "Armenian community".[74] Moreover this cannot be seen as the simple story of a monolithic "ethnic group" arriving into a static population, "losing" their identity and "becoming" Lombard through "assimilation". Such perspectives naturalise "being Armenian" and "being Lombard" as fundamentally opposed ontological conditions, erasing the dynamism in the local population, the transformative effects of incoming actors and the diverse historical reproduction of cultural stuff. Talk of an "Armenian community" conjures moreover the essentialist image of an internally homogeneous, externally bounded entity. This points to the methodological problem termed "groupism" by the sociologist Rogers Brubaker: when ethnic categories like "Armenian" are met in sources, human actors identify as such, or ethnocultural forms are identified, this is taken to represent an objective and self-reproducing "ethnic group".[75] Reducing the endless gradations and variations of the sociocultural world to a multichrome mosaic of monochrome ethnic blocs, groupism masks the specific situations and contingencies of a given actor's identification, instead concocting teleologies from the presumed characteristics of assumed groups.

So how can "Armenian" actors be situated in social dynamics? The key is to focus investigation at the micro-level of actor-to-actor association, identifying the structural integration of cultural stuff into the social system through everyday practices, and the manner of its reproduction thereafter. Rather than "assimilation", it is necessary to distinguish the structural imperatives in Bari's social system that guided elites to identify and politically organise on particular bases. In imagining these micro-level associations, Actor-Network Theory provides useful premises and terminology, seeing both human and non-human actors performing together in assemblages termed "actor-networks".[76] These are not fixed social units, but material-symbolic clusters of associated human and non-human/non-human actors that require regular performance in everyday practices. Hence there are no "Barese Armenians" prior to a set of actors—officials, priests, landowners, clothing, jewellery, church buildings and so on—performing together as an actor-network, actively relating the different elements together. Through rhythmical performances in everyday practices, associated actors are identified in particular ways and endowed with value, defining thereby the cultural stuff instrumentalised in a given actor's sense of self—the valorised bits of language, dress, custom and so on fetishised as the putative group's defining characteristics, in contemporary common-sense their "culture".[77] As Bruno Latour notes, "Groups are not silent things, but rather the *provisional product* of a constant uproar made by the millions of contradictory voices about what is a group and who pertains to what".[78] Thus actor-networks are always on the cusp of dissipating, requiring relations to be rhythmically performed or they will dissolve, in Latour's words: "no group, only group formation".[79] So rather than actors "being Armenian" and remaining so in stable, self-reproducing communities, the ethnic category is made relevant through its concrete realisation in a particular actor-network's performance.

But micro-level associations do not have limitless possibilities. Instead they operate in practically determinate conditions created by the social system's infrastructural ecological and property relations. They are also dialectically limited by hegemonic discourses and the apparatuses of institutions, organisations and practices in which these discourses are anchored—in Bari the pre-existing dominant forms of Lombardness, and the civic institutions that intersect with ecclesiastical and, from the late ninth century, imperial apparatuses.[80] These determinate conditions can be characterised as "social structures", not rigid boundaries equally and absolutely constraining for all actors, but systemic biases effective in practical moments: differential patterns, constraints and opportunities for action that vary by actor and according to the other actors involved.[81] Agency in turn depends on the capacity for dialectical variation within determinate limits, creating a dynamic that can be termed a "structured process", recognising both a given structure's differentiated effects and the capacity for variation, with action both reinforcing and reconstituting the structure in the moment when it is effective.[82] In the dialectical interplay between infrastructural ecology and property relations, micro-level associations, hegemonic discourses and institutional apparatuses, it is possible to identify the dynamics that produce a more-or-less coherent hegemony over the social system's taxonomy and symbolic universe—a generalised and generally dominant consensus over the values, associations and practical outcomes of elite identification as Lombard, Armenian, Greek or Roman.[83]

So it is possible to imagine the arrival of identified Armenians into east Roman Bari and Longobardia associated with pan-imperial elites serving in state apparatuses. They had been identified in actor-networks performed through sociocultural forms of language, dress, worship and everyday practice valorised in their previous social system—whether this was elsewhere in the empire or Caucasia itself—and for some undeterminable time they continued to be identified as Armenians. In the new situation, however, different conditions prevail, and the same human and non-human actors began to associate in different ways. Onomastics shift to reflect structured relationships developed in the new locale, as well as symbolic association with the pan-imperial elite and hegemonic sociocultural forms—notably the name Byzantius is common in tenth- and eleventh-century Bari but unknown elsewhere in the empire, surely a demonstration of symbolic association with the imperial hegemon.[84] The appearance of these new relational practices alongside the reproduction of cultural stuff indicates that there were no structural constraints excluding identified Armenians from Barese elitedom—indeed, local elites may have seen identified Armenians and Greeks as bearers of Roman imperialness and sought to emulate them. It also, however, indicates that there was no value attached to reproducing Armenian cultural stuff as such, and so there are no meaningful intra-elite ethnic boundaries where names marked distinct groupness. A lack of value explains why no later eleventh-century actors are identified as "the Armenian" in official documents, unlike those of the later tenth and earlier eleventh century. Despite the fact that later actors reproduced Armenian cultural stuff, formed networks in the same locales mediated by the same non-human actors, and reproduced elite status through hereditary ownership of the same land, there were no structural imperatives to "be Armenian". The *Armenius* of 1087 in Bari and the *Armenus* of 1114 in Taranto indicate that there were situations in which Armenianness was instantiated, but these performed moments did not operate in a rhythmical manner among Barese elites to reproduce a salient identification with distinguishing, symbolically valuable cultural stuff.

Hegemony, elitedom and ethnicity

The question then becomes simple: why was incoming actors' cultural stuff not reproduced alongside a salient ethnic identification, creating the appearance and sometimes reality of a distinct "community", as happened with Armenian settlers in contemporary Macedonia and Cappadocia?[85] Answers lie in the practical conditions of Barese elitedom and the structural imperatives to valorise one ethnic category over another. As parts of hegemonic ideologies, ethnic discourses are anchored in hegemonic apparatuses: assemblages, institutions and nexuses of political-economic organisation composed by everyday practices and reproduced over time and space into social structures: in the case of Bari, urban-civic institutions and ecclesiastical and imperial apparatuses.[86] Ethnic discourses anchored in hegemonic apparatuses are inscribed in rituals governed by everyday practices, and reproduced in the everyday life of an actor seeming to autonomously choose according to subjective belief. In Louis Althusser's terminology hegemonic apparatuses "interpellate" human actors in their "hailing" or "calling upon" them as, for instance, always-already "being Armenian", with human actors guided towards this identification through structural imperative.[87] Whereas ethnicity seems a subjective sense emerging "from within", human actors are in fact moved by the practices of a complex hegemonic system, choosing, for example, to "be Longobard" rather than "be Armenian". Yet hegemonic apparatuses are not totalitarian machines, however complex the system remains open and varies in effects according to particular situation, so that actors retain "bottom-up" agency to dynamically shape their interpellations for horizontal political action, according to the dialectally determined structural limits outlined earlier—a process discernible in Meles' revolt.

The church is the clearest institutional apparatus framing the lived experience of Barese Armenians. S. Giorgio's eleventh-century history reveals identified Armenian actors networked around a church built for themselves, presumably using some form of Armenian rite. This is certainly the case in the period of identified Armenian ecclesiastics *c.* 990–1011, and since several other Barese clerics appear with Armenian names and the foundation is later known as "of the Armenians",[88] it could easily have continued throughout the eleventh century at least. But even so these churches were undoubtedly recognised as canonical by their Greek and Latin rite neighbours. There is no reason to assume that "Archontissa daughter of Armodoctus of Taranto",[89] widow of "Moses the Armenian cleric", was raised in the Armenian rite, but she married an Armenian priest without appreciable consequence, referring to S. Giorgio as "our church". Most persuasively in 1059 S. Giorgio is within the pope's patriarchal purview, with Nicholas II's confirmation of tax exemptions revealing its subjugation to other local foundations of lay piety, the churches of S. Maria and S. Salvatore built by a certain Maria Lignitus.[90] Finally Archbishop Helias of Bari—grandchild of a former abbot of S. Giorgio[91]—took over the church and its properties in two sales of the 1090s, one in 1091 from a certain "Passarus son of Theodorus", witnessed by "Stephanitzios son of Meles" and Petros/Petracce, and another in 1099 from Meliciacca (Mlitseak),[92] "son of Bizantius of the city of Bari".

So Longobardia's Armenian churches were part of the same ecclesiastical apparatus as their Latin and Greek neighbours, elite actors' private foundations to serve limited networks ultimately under the pope's patriarchal authority. Despite instances of competition and individual prejudice, the Latin and Greek rites of Longobardia were mutually tolerant and institutionally intertwined under both pope and empire. The imperial centre intervened in Latin episcopal elections, and sought to counterbalance papal influence by creating autocephalous bishoprics. There are also hints that attitudes were hardening for some by the later eleventh century,[93] but at no point was there hegemonic consensus that Latin and Greek Christians were mutually heretical or schismatic. Indeed the various *strategoi* and *katepanōs* of southern Italy patronised and founded churches, monasteries and even cities under papal protection, and in 1033 the *katepanō* issued a bilingual document confirming Petrus the cleric's bequest of all his properties to the church of S. Eustrazio located in Bari's imperial court (*edificata est intus in ipsa curte imperiali de iamdicta civitate Vari*).[94] This closeness is demonstrated by a Calabrian Greek's election as antipope in 1008, and whilst the imperial centre on occasion pushed the Greek rite, tension was sporadic and networked interaction the rule.

In this ecclesiastical apparatus, therefore, it was difficult for systemic biases excluding Armenian actors to develop and create imperatives to valorise a peculiarly Armenian religiosity. For this reason Barese Armenians need not be seen as arriving with any clearly defined pro- or anti-Chalcedonian position.[95] Rather, it is possible that settled actors had previously associated with the independent Armenian ecclesiastical apparatus but, in their new situation, integrated their foundations into the Barese and ultimately therefore the papal apparatus. This possibility is confirmed by a mid-tenth-century Armenian prince's visit to the pope, returning to the east with relics, as well as a letter of 1080 in which Pope Gregory VII asks Bishop Roffredus of Benevento to investigate a certain Macharus, an Armenian resident of Frigento.[96] The pope had received a letter from the Armenian patriarch informing him of Macharus' conviction for heresy, and was pursuing the matter. Gregory thus accepts the Armenian patriarch as a legitimate authority in heretical matters, although he did also enquire about rumoured oddities in Armenian practice. Nevertheless this suggests that Armenian incomers could associate with the independent Armenian Church in the east but also that of Rome in the west. Archbishop Helias, with his common Armenian name and descent from an abbot of S. Giorgio, may also indicate that descendants of integrated Armenian churchmen became prominent in Bari's ecclesiastical hierarchy.[97] Despite the presence of an Armenian rite, therefore, its institutionalisation in Bari's ecclesiastical apparatus contributed to the lack of bounded ethnoconfessional identifications.

Alongside the church, indeed, intertwined with it, the most important hegemonic apparatus framing Barese elites' lived experience is the empire itself. A ninth-century northern Lombard commented on those under imperial sovereignty referring to their lord as *dominatio* rather than *dominus*, the empire not the emperor, revealing the state system perceived as a unitary totality, an objectified thing with practical force.[98] This reification is the outcome of a rhythmical accumulation of moments of apparent imperial presence, situational performances in which actors representing the empire materialised its power in the world. Notably these moments become a *topos* in southern Italian hagiography, encounters between saints and various imperial officials from *strategoi* and *katepanōs* to local fortress commanders, with a variety of positive and negative outcomes.[99] This variety reflects the real variability of interaction with imperial representatives, irreducible to a single positive or negative characterisation, and aggregating into a set of lived conditions in which the empire was regularly experienced by southern Italian elites. This was certainly the case in Bari, where the imperial system materialised in the city's everyday life as administrative centre of both the theme of Longobardia and the catepanate of Italia, not least through the presence of the professional military regiments, the *tagmata*.[100] The empire profoundly reshaped the urban space, particularly after the building of the large fortified *praitorion* in the city centre for the *katepanō*'s administration (*c.* 1010–1016).[101] This was constructed in response to Meles' revolt, but also reflects a general trend of high officials investing in the city's built environment.[102] These buildings' physical presence and inclusion as non-human actors in Barese actor-networks, like the moments of interaction with human actors, (re)produced a strong sense of imperial presence in the city, forming a provincial urban space out of that which had existed prior to the Roman takeover of 874.

But Barese elites did not merely experience the empire in the urban space, they lived and (re)produced it. Although the highest echelons of the military and fiscal-administrative apparatus were appointed from the pan-imperial elite, beneath this level the overwhelming majority were locals.[103] Hence the highest officials were demonstrably present through the imperial system's capacity to centripetally and centrifugally circulate human and non-human actors, while the rest of Longobardia's imperial apparatuses functioned through long-established and newly settled elites—a significant number of which were lower-strata elites brought in through imperial apparatuses and *tagmata*, such as the Smaragdus, *protospatharius* and *topotērētēs* of the Scholai found ratifying a document in 992.[104] Official functions were granted alongside honorific titles with both carrying annual salaries in gold coinage, no doubt a significant source of the imperial monetisation of Barese social relations in the tenth century.[105] This combined system of salaried titles and offices was central to the empire's political-economic reproduction across its territory, so that at least until *c.* 1080 anyone who might be considered part of the "east Roman aristocracy" was a paid up member of state apparatuses.[106] The system created a self-reinforcing structured process of imperial reification through the integration of provincial exploitation and domination. Hence the imperial centre's strategies to co-opt varied elites, at least in certain times and places, created the impression of quasi-total state control, since each of these—from pan-imperials to local magnates and more humble urban or regional actors—reproduced imperial ideology in a transmuted form that inscribed their own position therein. Thus one inscription from Brindisi *c.* 975–1025 records Lupus *protospatharius*, "illustrious and pious in his acts of beneficence", paying for the city's refortification on behalf of the "magnificent and benign emperors", asserting his local pre-eminence at the same time as instantiating imperial ideology.[107] Of course, this process worked in tandem with the threat of violence latent or realised in each rhythmical moment of integration, eloquently demonstrated by the dominant presence of imperial regiments.

Such strategies are seen already in the 890s when a certain Godinis is found as imperial *protōspatharios*, an actor who must have already been a prominent magnate, having the wherewithal to rent and administer all the properties of the important monastery of S. Vincenzo al Volturno. A generation later seven of the nine witnesses in a 917 document from Conversano bear the title *imperialis spatharius candidatus*, including the adjudicating official, the judge Liusprando, and by the mid-tenth century the majority of judges in Apulian coastal cities bear imperial titles.[108] Even Latin bishops and abbots preferred imperial officials and dignitaries as *advocatores*,[109] many having themselves been secular elites with titles and offices prior to their western-style elections. Titles were also material rewards for loyalty, with Sergius and Theophylactus of Bari receiving the title of *protōspatharios* in 982 after handing the city to the *katepanō* following a brief revolt.[110] This comes in a period of intense and murderous competition among Longobardia's elitedom, mysteriously recorded in the annals of Bari and often including the titles and offices of those involved.[111] The exact circumstances surrounding these entries are lost, although some wider significance is proposed in the conclusion, but for the moment it is important that a clear majority of elites involved had imperial titles and/or offices, with members of the *tagmata* particularly prominent.[112]

Imperial apparatuses also created structural imperatives to integrate through intervention in land ownership. Land is the central means of production in both tax- and lordship-based regimes of accumulation,[113] and it is notable that the best evidence for Armenian actors are legal disputes over landed property. This integrative process again worked in dialectical interplay between the macro and the micro: appointed *strategoi* and *katepanōs* controlled and interfered with landed property in their provinces, and local magnates like Godinis orchestrated and ratified their control of land through imperially sanctioned legal-juridical processes. An instructive example is the Barese judge Byzantius, who remained a "faithful and true servant to our powerful and holy emperors [against] the rebel Maniakes (1043) and later against the Franks", and was rewarded by the *katepanō* with the village of Fogliano in 1046.[114] Byzantius now had total control, free from public taxation and interference from any "officials of the province", with the right to attract more settlers and attach agricultural lands to Fogliano and a nearby claimed-to-be deserted village,[115] as well as power of jurisdiction in all but capital charges. This clearly shows the matrix of material factors involved in a given elite's instantiation and reproduction of hegemonic ideology, with Byzantius contributing to imperial reification even as he gains wide remit to act as a relatively autonomous magnate, even a lord.

Like the ecclesiastical apparatus, therefore, imperial apparatuses did not create structural imperatives that encouraged incoming actors to form bounded ethnoreligious groupness—again unlike in contemporary Cappadocia.[116] Symbatikios' 891 grant refers to "Greek, Lombard and Armenian officials" without hierarchical distinction, and later administration seems no different. Instead Greek, Armenian and Latinate speaking elites associated alike through the imperial system, and undoubtedly many of their actions had no specific sanction within pan-imperial ideology. Nevertheless, the structural imperatives to integrate created by the imperial apparatus meant that, over the tenth century, Bari's varied elites increasingly exercised exploitative domination with, within and through the imperial system, contributing thereby to its reification in the locale. No doubt the empire "looked" and "felt" different in Longobardia as opposed to other regions, but this heterogeneity in practice does not change its capacity to be lived, experienced and reified in each provincial situation. Each institutional apparatus, urban-civic, ecclesiastical and imperial, intersected in the everyday practices of Barese elites, self-evident in two documents of the early 1070s. In the first of 1071, witnessed by Angelus the imperial judge, Nikolaus the cleric, and Mel the notary, the priest Basilius and his wife Gayta wished to give their privately built church to Rusando the priest and his son Bisantio the deacon, but due to Norman invasions (*iniqui normanni*) they instead put the land in the care of Mel son of Caloiohannis, *demonosios* of Bari—a civic official and "powerful person (*hominem potentem*)" able to care for the property in such times.[117] In another of 1073 the monk Iohannes received the church of S. Nicolo del Monte for his lifetime from Angelus the deacon, choosing Mele the *protomagistros* as an *advocator*, and presenting the document to Sifandus, *imperialis protospatharius* and judge of Italia. As John Haldon notes: "One of the most important points to bear in mind is the close identity between the institutional and systemic evolution of the state and its systems or apparatuses, and the individuals and groups from whom they were recruited or who comprised them, and whose local and vested interests determined to a large extent how such arrangements actually functioned in practical terms".[118]

But the imperial system did play a constitutive role in the reproduction of ethnicity, not by privileging one ethnic category over another, but by constructing Longobardia as a coherent space, its populace as a coherent people and Bari's elitedom as a coherent political-economic unit. In 921 the patriarch Nikolaos Mystikos wrote a letter to the "priests, archpriests, *archontes* and general body of the people in Longobardia", and the Venetian–east Roman treaty of 992 specified that Venetian ships cannot carry the goods of "Longobards of the city of Bari".[119] These are indicative of the multiplicity of moments in which imperial and ecclesiastical apparatuses constructed a singular community in the region, tying a shared Longobardness to socio-economic relations and political-economic organisation: in these instances diplomacy and the Barese elites' participation in commercial exchange.[120] Such moments reached into the everyday of elite actors, such as Romuald, *prosopo* of Longobardia and *imperialis protospatharius* of the Chrysotriklinos, found ratifying a document in 954, or Archbishop Byzantius of Bari's reference *c.* 1025–1030 to the recently desolated churches of the "cities of Italia, and indeed Apulia (*Italie immo Apulie civitatum*)".[121] Thus, through the rhythmical accumulation of performed moments in which "being Longobard" discursively framed a given actor's interaction with intersecting institutional apparatuses, this appellation became constitutive of local elites' self-situation. Importantly, this structured process encompassed not only local elites already identified as Lombard but also Greek- and Armenian-speaking incomers, who might otherwise have formed bounded identifications that explicitly Othered local actors. Instead, however, institutional apparatuses interpellated varied elites as Longobards in common, and this everyday lived experience in turn encouraged Barese elitedom to inscribe their actions in imperial ideology as such. Consequently not only did the *archontes* reproduce hegemonic ideology in transmuted form, but they were in turn subjected—formed into subjects—through ethnic interpellation by imperial apparatuses operating within the locale's hegemonic consensus, regardless of a given actor's heritage or mother tongue.

In the hegemonic conditions created by imperial and ecclesiastical apparatuses, therefore, Bari's diverse elites were encouraged to form horizontal solidarities and articulate common groupness. From pre-existing constructions of Lombardness a new kind of Longobardness was (re)produced as the ethnic frame in which elite actors situated their antagonisms, apparently transcending any internal distinctions based on language or rite.[122] This is clear from the fact that hierarchies of power relations in Bari did not form around ethnic differentiations within local elitedom. Late tenth- and early eleventh-century documents identify Armenian actors without legal distinction, revealing them owning, exploiting and exchanging property as well as forming local solidarities. In Vartiski and Corki's dispute with Caloiohannes—two identified Armenians and a Greek-named actor with a Lombard-named father—the case is arbitrated by an Armenian and witnessed by Greek, Armenian and Latinate speakers. The only constitutive ethnic feature is the Lombard common law through which the dispute is negotiated, applied to all parties without distinction. Such situations rhythmically repeated over time and space would encourage actors to identify with the Lombard tradition, not to the exclusion of an Armenian, Greek or Roman sense of self, but as the basis for political action. Thus when Fogliano was granted to the judge Bizantius as an imperially sanctioned lordship, his descendants held it in inheritance "according to the law of the Longobards (κατὰ τὸν νῶμων [*sic*] τὸν Λογγιβαρδδ[ικὸν])".[123]

The lack of an ethnic power hierarchy in Bari reflects the lack of structural imperatives to create a closed, nativist Lombard identification. Instead elites of varied background identified with a locally (re)produced Longobardness, regardless of particular heritage and associated cultural stuff. Barese elitedom's position between pan-imperial apparatuses above and subalterns below meant that they formed horizontal solidarities, networks that became the basis for corporate political action. Identifying as Longobard may even have helped to gain the spontaneous consent of exploited subalterns, especially considering the whole villages owned and exchanged by identified Armenians. Regardless, Bari's sociopolitical networks were formalised in legal-juridical processes based on local iterations of Lombard common law, legitimised by their civic integration into imperial and ecclesiastical apparatuses, and formed by local elites often bearing imperial or ecclesiastical titles and offices. One example has already been seen in Mele the priest's gift of a *morgengabe* to his wife Archontissa, a wedding gift including moveable and unmoveable properties to be the wife's possessions within the marriage and retained by her on widowhood—referred to in one document of 901 as "the nuptial rite of our Longobard people (*nuptiarum secundum ritus gentis nostre langobardorum*)".[124] Here an Armenian priest forms a structured relationship with a member of the local elite, fittingly named *archontissa*,[125] ritually performing this relationship through Lombard common law. Through the performance of structured exchanges within a Lombard frame, elite actors of varied background like Mele and Archontissa were materially and symbolically integrated into the locale as Longobards.

In addition to the *morgengabe* these structured relationships were practised through another form of ritual gift exchange, the *launegilt*, alongside common legal transactions such as wills. They included both small, moveable objects such as clothing, jewellery and furnishings, and immoveable properties such as arable land, vineyards and buildings. They played, therefore, a fundamental role in the regulation of socioeconomic relations and valorisation processes, with smaller objects evidencing Barese elitedom's integration into the interregional systems of exchange implied by the Venetian–east Roman treaty.[126] In one document of 1054 a certain Mele *magistros* gave his daughter Specia eight silk head-scarves or mantles, specifying three for everyday use and including one in "Grecisco" style.[127] Thus an actor with an Armenian name and imperial title gifted objects that became identified "Greek" actors in performed actor-networks, symbolically valorised through exchange and experience in the everyday.[128] In such manner non-human actors helped to (re)produce elite connection to the locale and to integrate incomers into sociopolitical networks, thereby endowing their cultural stuff with local value.[129]

Through repeat performances of actor-networks mediated by the same non-human actors and cultural stuff, what appears a highly heterogeneous sociocultural space would be perceived as a unity in the symbolic universe of Barese elitedom. Tehmina Goskar has demonstrated Longobardia's "shared culture of objects", interregionally exchanged goods found across the central and eastern Mediterranean endowed with particular value through intraregional structured exchange.[130] Goskar also notes the now-lost significations contained in costume and appearances, seen with Neilos' dress above as well as Skylitzes' comments that the citizens of Kallipolis, descended from those ninth-century settlers, "even today have the same customs, dress, and civic *mores* as the Romans".[131] This does not mean that they "retained" some monolithic east Roman identity, but that the social system in Kallipolis facilitated the reproduction of particular constructs across the entire period, integrating them into the locale. Michael McCormick also emphasises the importance of a locally identified naming stock, visibly demonstrated in the recurrent names found among eleventh-century Barese elites, which are both extraordinarily heterogeneous in origin and remarkably homogeneous in use.[132] This interplay of hetero- and homogeneity reflects the structured processes of elite integration, with the valorising mediation of varied actors and cultural stuff reproduced through sociopolitical networks formalised by Lombard common law—by the twelfth century referred to simply as "Barese custom".[133] Thus families of mixed Lombard, Greek and Armenian names, worshipping in different rites but practicing Lombard law, while serving in imperial and papal apparatuses dressed in east Roman fashions, could identify as Longobards and be perceived as exemplary Barese *archontes*.[134]

One final example demonstrates these structured processes clearly, a Barese document of 1028 rare for being a dedicated *morgengabe* rather than integrated into a marriage contract.[135] It contains a striking miniature of Mel, master blacksmith (*magister ferrarius*), presenting the charter to Alfarana—perhaps an Alpheranites, a prominent Barese family—dressed in the garments and jewellery gifted in the document. Even more striking is the document's wording in Mel's own voice: "This is the morning-gift (*morgengabe*). I transfer to you a quarter part of all my stable and moveable inheritance. ... Of vines and vineyards, lands and territories, fields and woods. ... Of gold and silver, copper and iron ... of silk, linen and woollen cloths, of wooden and glass vessels and all other household goods".[136] Hence Mel portrays the exchange as an active performance depicted in the moment of handing the document to Alfarana, herself dressed in the full finery of the bequest, thereby endowing all the objects with value and transforming them into actors in turn. Mel is clear, moreover, about the socioeconomic relations involved in the gift: moveable and unmoveable property, agricultural lands, mineral wealth, perishable goods, and so on. The document thus provides a vignette of the structured processes through which incoming actors integrated into local elitedom, contributing thereby to the transformation of Bari's social system, and the (re)production of a new kind of Longobardness.

The formation of an urban polity

So this is the transformation that produced Meles with whom this chapter began, evident in the violent elite competition of the late tenth and early eleventh centuries. As noted this is revealed in a series of mysterious chronicle entries recording the murderous interactions of various actors, with one titled official even killed by "the people of Bari" in 987. Notably many of these actors have non-Lombard names as well as imperial offices and titles, often specifically identified with tagmatic regiments like the *exkoubitai*.[137] The period coincides with intense Arab raids across southern Italy, causing mass emigration from the Kalabrian theme and significant disruption elsewhere.[138] The *tagmata*'s continuous presence in Longobardia suggests that the region was better protected, but the density of troops and high-ranking officers, many of whom settled, apparently contributed to elite fractiousness.[139] Hence the integration of new actors into Barese elitedom engendered struggles over the means to reproduce elite status. Incomers did not form a bloc against local elites as "insiders" versus "outsiders", but conflicts accumulated through antagonistic moments caused by piecemeal settlement. The exact constellation of factors would be different in each moment, but it is easy to imagine how the wealth available through inter- and intraregional exchange, land ownership and imperial and ecclesiastical apparatuses created opportunities for violent struggle.

Thus Meles personifies Barese elitedom in his varied background and dress but strong Longobard identification, and represents the culmination of antagonistic processes through which emerged a more coherent if highly fractious elitedom able to take corporate political action. Through socioeconomic relations, imperial interpellation and horizontal sociopolitical interaction experienced in a Longobard ethnic frame, Barese elites developed a level of relative coherence. Meles is claimed to act on behalf of the citizens of Bari, the Longobards of Longobardia, rebelling to gain some form of autonomous rule. Thus the structured processes in imperial Bari reconstituted existing relations into a provincial social system with the city as political centre, and an ethnic phenomenon in the form of an urban citizenry in their native land. This ethnic phenomenon was possible because of the wealth of pre-existing Lombard discourses and constructs: the eleventh-century chronicler Lupus *protospatharius* notes that the year 916 marked "three hundred and fifty years since the Langobards entered Italy under their king Alboin", in 966 that 400 years had passed, and 517 in 1083.[140] These entries indicate ethnic narratives in east Roman Longobardia that identified Barese Longobards with the "original" sixth-century Lombards.[141] Yet even so particularities are articulated, with Lupus notably contrasting "Lombardia" in western imperial northern Italy with "Langobardia" in the east Roman south.[142] This distinction is reflected in William of Apulia's use of *Lombardi* for northern Italians but *Langobardi* for Apulians, a usage also present in twelfth-century sources.[143] It is surely not coincidental that this nomenclature mirrors the east Roman theme and Greek terminology. Thus the same ethnic category's differentiated patterns of reproduction in north and south were recognised by contemporaries. This points to the ultimate story which Meles and the "Armenians" of imperial Bari allow us to tell: the formation of an urban elitedom that (re)produced an ethnic phenomenon with "typical" hallmarks, citizens representing a historic people in their historic land—with that land even objectified and endowed with agency, as when Lupus notes that "Langobardia rebelled from the emperor by the work of *dux* Melus".

So, despite the latent potentials in pre-existing discourses and constructs, this ethnic phenomenon is not testament to the assimilatory strength of Lombardness in Apulia and Bari, but the dynamics of elite interaction under east Roman hegemony. Barese Longobardness is the product of a particular time and place encompassing actors of widely varying backgrounds, and there is no *a priori* reason why incomers should have "assimilated" rather than Othering locals and being Othered themselves in turn. Meles appears in 1009 a generation after the first attested "Mele the Armenian presbyter" in 990,[144] but is claimed to be "Langobard by birth". Whether this is "true" or not is unimportant, this is how William saw fit to depict him as a representative of Barese elitedom—indeed, the writer's "accurate" description of his dress may reflect a desire to establish affinity with this Barese-Longobard hero.[145] Meles' son Argyros received an education to enter the pan-imperial elite in Constantinople, but returned to his father's Norman and Longobard loyalties in 1029, being elected *princeps et dux Italiae* in 1042 and rebelling against the Romans. He soon switched sides, however, serving in state apparatuses in Constantinople and Paphlagonia, before returning to become the first local to hold the highest imperial office as *magistros vestes* and *doux* of Italia, Kalabria and Sicily. Argyros' ability to rebel and claim an even more august title than his father indicates that Barese elitedom had become a political constituency, and his appointment reflects imperial recognition of this fact.

This political coherence is seen in William of Apulia's description of Bari's desperate defence against Robert Guiscard in 1071, likely resulting in the one-off tribute tax three years later. But this conquest is not the end of the story. Under Guiscard's successors the Apulian cities continued to harbour intense sociopolitical action, and in the face of ducal opposition Grimoald Alpheranites was elected Bari's ruler in 1121, first governing as *dominator* and later as *princeps*. As noted the Alpheranites were a prominent Barese family, with the earliest attested members found in the personal staff of the *katepanō* Basileios Boiannes in 1019, the *protōspatharios* Iohannes and his brother the *topotērētēs* Byzantius. Thereafter members of the family are found with imperial titles participating in urban elite life, one document of 1065 records the dowry agreement between Alfarana, daughter of Iohannes, and Russo, son of Amorusus.[146] The exceptional wealth involved marked the union between a daughter of the Alpheranites and the son of a prominent clerical family, with each item given a monetary value and witnessed by a *kommerkiarios*, the imperial official concerned with custom duty and other commercial taxes.[147] The Alpheranites are therefore a paradigmatic example of Barese elitedom's transformation under imperial rule: elite actors associated with state apparatuses settled in similar socioeconomic status to local elites, reproducing this status through structured relationships with longer-based actors in imperially sanctioned ritual exchanges.[148]

The full transformation of Barese elitedom is thus personified in Grimoald Alpheranites' election: a descendent of east Roman functionaries with an emphatically Lombard name issuing imperially modelled documents on the city's behalf. The period of autonomous rule hence forms a fitting conclusion to Meles' story, demonstrating clearly the emergence of a polity in Bari's urban space. The structural efficacy of imperial integration for elites' horizontal political action is seen in the appearance of offices and dignities long after the end of east Roman rule—twelfth-century documents even mention those held by ancestors, and several between 1071 and 1119 are dated by imperial regnal years. Finally Bari's maturation as a sovereign space is seen in Roger II's elevation of his son Tancred as prince after its 1132 conquest, thereby recognising the city as a distinct political unit, and its elitedom as a distinct political constituency.

Notes

* This chapter is a welcome opportunity to return to regions and questions I first explored as an undergraduate with Tom Brown. I must as ever thank my dearest comrades, Ilya Afanasyev and Lorenzo Bondioli, for their mutual aid (co-) writing this paper, as well as Phil Booth, and Mathew Kinloch for their incisive comments and criticisms.

1 The oldest shrine to Saint Michael on the European continent, today in Foggia province, northern Puglia.

2 William of Apulia, *La Geste de Robert Guiscard*, (ed.) M. Mathieu (Palermo, 1961), bk. I.

3 V. von Falkenhausen, "Between Two Empires: Byzantine Italy in the Reign of Basil II", in P. Magdalino (ed.), *Byzantium in the Year 1000* (Leiden, 2003), 153–155; & eadem, "A Provincial Aristocracy: The Byzantine Provinces in Southern Italy (9th–11th Century)", in M. Angold (ed.), *The Byzantine Aristocracy IX to XIII Centuries* (Oxford, 1984), 224.

4 Both Longobardia and Langobardia are found in both Latin and Greek sources, Longobardia has been chosen here simply because it scans better with the more common English "Lombard/Lombardy".

5 As Vera von Falkenhausen has noted, Meles' title suggests less an attempt to mimic the Lombard princes of Benevento, Capua or Salerno, than to achieve a similar status to the "dukes" of Naples, Gaeta, Amalfi and, notably, Venice, as cities with maritime interests "of" but not "in" the empire of New Rome; see von Falkenhausen, "Between Two Empires", 147. Tehmina Goskar has demonstrated the strong connections between Apulia, particularly Bari, and Venice, see: Goskar, *Objects, People and Exchange: Material Culture in Medieval Southern Italy c.600–c.1200* (Doctoral thesis University of Southampton, 2009), 119–138.

6 Lupus Protospatharius, *Antiche cronache di Terra di Bari* (eds.) G. Cioffari and R. Lupoli Tateo (Bari, 1991).

7 *Chronica monasterii Casinensis*, ed. H. Hoffmann, MGH Scriptores 34 (Hanover, 1980) II, 37, 237.

8 *Ioannis Scylitzae Synopsis Historiarum*, I. Thurn (ed.) (Berlin, 1973) 348; translation adapted from John Wortley (trans.), *John Skylitzes. A Synopsis of Byzantine History 811–1057* (Cambridge, 2010), 330.

9 There is the chance that his name is drawn from Ismael as some chronicle variants record, but considering the prominence in Bari of variations on Mleh this option is much more probable.

10 Goskar, *Objects, People and Exchange*, 127–133.

11 "Typical" tends to refer to those areas of Asia Minor that remained under east Roman rule from antiquity and became the first themes, Italy is far less atypical when compared with the regions newly conquered in the later ninth to eleventh centuries; see Leonora Neville, *Authority in Byzantine Provincial Society 950–1100* (Cambridge, 2004), 2–3.

12 N. Garsoïan, "The Problem of Armenian Integration into the Byzantine Empire", in H. Ahrweiler & A. Laiou (eds.), *Studies on the Internal Diaspora of the Byzantine Empire* (Cambridge Massachusetts, 1998) 68.

13 For two recent such articles, see G. Strano, "Alcune notazioni sulla presenze armena nell'Italia meridionale in età bizantina", in G. De Sensi Sestito (ed.), *La Calabria nel Mediterraneo. Flussi di persone, idee e risorse* (Soveria Mannelli, 2013), 189–202; & G. Dédéyan, "Le stratège Symbatikios et la colonisation Arménienne dans le theme de Longobardie", in *Ravenna da Capitale Imperiale a Capitale Esarcale* (Spoleto, 2005), 461—493.

14 There is plenty of evidence for particular actors, and suggestive clues for settlers in Ravenna, but nothing tangible or connectable to particular communities. Particularly in Sicily there may have been networks that reproduced forms of Armenianness, fleeing to southern Italy in the ninth century with their better documented Greek-speaking compatriots, but the evidence is simply lacking, see Strano, "Alcune notazioni".

15 See: V. Prigent, "Notes sur l'évolution de l'administration byzantine en Adriatique (VIIIe–IXe siècle)", dans *Mélanges de l'École française de Rome. Moyen Âge*, 120/2, 2008, 393–417.

16 On hegemonic space, there termed "state space", see J. C. Scott, *The Art of Not Being Governed: An Anarchist History of Upland South-East Asia* (Yale, 2009), 40–63.

17 Modern Gallipoli; interestingly this interpolated passage only appears in one manuscript of the twelfth century, see Skylitzes, 151 & 146; M. McCormick, "The Imperial Edge: Italo-Byzantine Identity, Movement and Integration, A.D. 650–950", in Ahrweiler & Garsoïan, *Internal Diaspora*, 18–19.

18 *Chronographiae quae Theophanis continuati nomine fertur liber quo vita Basilii imparatoris amplectur*, I Ševčenko (ed.) (Berlin, 2011), 263.

19 H. Grégoire, "La Carrière du premier Nicéphore Phocas", Προσφορά εις Σίλπωνα Π. Κυριακίδην. Ελληνικά, Παράρτημα 4, Athènes, 1953, pp. 232–254; see also McCormick, "Imperial Edge", 34–35.

20 J. Hamilton, B. Hamilton & Y. Stoyanov (ed. & trans.), *Christian Dualist Heresies in the Byzantine World c.650-c.1450* (Manchester, 1998), 139–140.

21 A continuator to the late ninth-century Georgios Monachos explicitly mentions Nikephoros the Elder having "a number of Armenians" with him when he conquers Taranto, Bari, Reggio, Trapea and Amantea, and that he established them there, see Strano, "Alcune Notazioni", 194–195; see also: *vita Basilii*, 245–247.

22 Dédéyan, "Le stratège Symbatikios", 482–485.

23 This reconstruction, as well as those following, are plausible suggestions of Armenian originals based on Latin and/or Greek renderings.

24 This is the argument in Vera von Falkenhausen, *La dominazione bizantina nell'Italia meridionale dal IX all'XI secolo* (Bari, 1978). Constantine Zuckerman has recently disputed von Falkenhausen's dating through Longobardia's absence in the Kleterologion of Philotheos, dated to 899. Zuckerman discards the mention of Longobardia among Symbatikios' commands (*Symbatikios imperialis prothospatharius et stratigos Macedonie, Tracie, Cephalonie atque Longibardie*), arguing that at this stage it was simply part of the theme of Cephalonia. But the charter, as an official imperial document, is harder evidence than the Kletorologion, which might have not included Longobardia because of the theme's institutional instability in its early stages—the capital, Benevento, had only recently been lost to Lombards in 895. Indeed, the Kleterologion still presents a problem for Zuckerman, since the name of this putative command, "Kephalonia and Longobardia", is not found in the text. See C. Zuckerman, "Squabbling Protospatharioi and Other Administrative Issues from the First Half of the Tenth Century", *Revue des études byzantines* 72 (2014), 193–233, at 206–209.

25 Von Falkenhausen, *Dominazione*, 178.

26 All these figures, their possible connections, and some later more spuriously "Armenian" figures, can be found in Dédéyan, "Le stratège Symbatikios", 482–485.

27 These come as cavalry "from the Senate (από βουλής) with the engineers (μαγγανάριοι)", see: A. Moffat (ed. and trans.), *The Book of Ceremonies* (Canberra, 2012), vol. II, 661; & C. Zuckerman, "Squabbling Protospatharioi".

28 See, for example, Grégoire, "La Carrière".

29 Von Falkenhausen, "A Provincial Aristocracy: The Byzantine Provinces in Southern Italy (9th–11th Century)", in M. Angold (ed.), *The Byzantine Aristocracy: IX to XIII Centuries* (Oxford, 1984), 213.

30 G. Ferrari, "Formulari Notarili Inediti dell'Età Bizantina", *Bullettino dell' Instituto Storico Italiano* 33 (1913), no. 38.

31 *Codice Diplomatico Barese* [*CDB*], vol. 5, *Le pergamene di S. Nicola di Bari: periodo normanno (1075–1184)*, F. Nitto di Vito (ed.) (Bari, 1900–1982), no. 46; there is also the appearance of a certain "Stefanus son of Mel, who is a slave" in the late eleventh and early twelfth centuries: *CDB*, vol. 5, no. 10; *CDB*, vol. 5,

no. 54; *CDB*, vol. 5, framm. 11; as well as "Ivanus the freedman" in *CDB*, *Le pergamene della Cattedrael di Terlizzi* vol. 3, no. 20.

32 As seen, for example, in a will from the eastern provinces: Speros Vryonis, Jr., "The Will of a Provincial Magnate, Eustathius Boilas", *Dumbarton Oaks Papers*, Vol. 11 (1957), 263–277.

33 At the same time, however, countless other routes, models and points of entry should be imagined for the movement of elites in imperial space, resulting, for example, in the appearance of a certain Iouditta-Judith, a Lombard of Calabria, as a wealthy landowner in eleventh-century Ephesos, see: Gregory the Cellarer, *Life of St. Lazarus of Mt. Galesion: An Eleventh-Century Pillar Saint*, (trans.) Richard P.H. Greenfield (Washington D.C., 2000), 119.

34 *CDB*, *Le pergamene del Duomo di Bari (952–1264)* vol. 1, G. Nitto de Rossi & F. Nitti di Vito (eds.) (Trani, 1897–1899), no. 4; *Codice Diplomatico Pugliese* [*CDP*], *Le Pergamene di Conversano* vol. 20, G. Coniglio (ed.) (Bari, 1975), no. 23.

35 J. S. Codoñer, *The Emperor Theophilos and the East, 819–842* (Oxford, 2014), 79–80.

36 *Vita Basilii*, 245.

37 *CDP*, vol. 20, no. 30; *Prosopographie der mittelbyzantinischen Zeit Online. Berlin-Brandenburgische Akademie der Wissenschaften. Nach Vorarbeiten F. Winkelmanns erstellt*. (2013). Berlin, Boston: De Gruyter. Retrieved 21 Nov. 2017, from https://www.degruyter.com/view/db/pmbz, #21235; *CDB*, vol. 4, no. 27.

38 In addition to these instances there is a "Trachanioti" found in two documents of *CDB*, *Le pergamene di Barletta* vol. 8, F. Nitti di Vito (ed.) (Bari, 1912), no. 17, and a "Maniaki" found in *CDB*, vol. 5, no. 1.

39 It is worth noting that in addition to the four "Mlehs" in the 1075 tax document there are also two figures named "Argirus"; von Falkenhausen, *Dominazione*, 171, & 181, & in chapter 18 of this volume.

40 *CDB*, vol. 1, no. 5.

41 *CDB*, vol. 4, no. 4.

42 A certain "Boccus son of Achan of Bari" also appears in Ceglie in *CDB*, vol. 4, no. 12, suggesting the nominative form *Achan*, and by way of comparison a certain Iskhanakios [Išxanak] appears in a Tarentine document of 1033, see chapter 18 of this volume.

43 Whilst his surname is of certain Armenian origin, its exact derivation is not clear.

44 *CDB*, vol. 1, no. 8; Gemma here may be a rendering of the spoken Armenian "Iemma".

45 *CDB*, vol. 4, no. 8.

46 *CDB*, vol. 4, no. 9.

47 This is of course the same as the Greek version of the name, but in context and considering the unique declination it is very likely to be a rendering of the Armenian, notably Eustratius is called son of Petr*us*, indicating that Petros is a purposeful rendering.

48 This is seen in the basic architectural structure, a classic domed hall of the type found across ninth- to eleventh-century Caucasia—including both "Armenian" and "Georgian" regions—as well as the decorative features, including typical horseshoe arches and a *gavit'* style narthex.

49 *CDB*, vol. 4, no. 11; Armadoctus is an extremely odd name not attested anywhere else, and so perhaps of non-Latinate, Lombard or Greek origin, but unfortunately nothing can be suggested without serious issue. The closest Armenian name is Aramadukht or Vahramadukht, but both of these would be female, meaning "daughter of Aram/Vahram". It is possible to imagine that an

honorific name referring to Archontissa's father was mistaken as her father's name, but this can only be a suggestion.

50 In *CDB*, vol. 5, no. 1 there is also mention of a "house and bathhouse of Moses" associated near to S. Giorgio.

51 Surely the same Amatus mentioned in the 1005 document.

52 Emphasis added.

53 *CDP*, vol. 20, nos. 32 & 33; notably the names "Gregorio" and "Kyrcori" also appear in these documents, both inconclusive in themselves but still indicators of possible Armenian associations.

54 *CDB*, vol. 4, no. 13.

55 A brief history of the church in the eleventh century, solely based on surviving documents and including references to the inscriptions, can be found at http://www.basilicasannicola.it/ (accessed 01/06/2017).

56 *CDB*, vol. 4, no.4; *CDB*, vol. 4, no. 5; *CDB*, vol. 4, framm. 3; *CDB*, vol. 1, no. 8; *CDP*, vol. 20, nos. 32 & 33; *CDB*, vol. 4, no. 11; *CDP*, vol. 20, no. 34; *CDB*, vol. 4, no. 13; *CDB*, vol. 8, no. 4; *CDB*, vol. 4, no. 15; *CDB*, vol. 4, no. 16; *CDB*, vol. 4, no. 17; *CDB*, vol. 1, no. 14; *CDB*, vol. 1, no. 15; *CDB*, vol. 4, no. 18; *CDB*, vol. 4, no. 19; *CDB*, vol. 1, no. 16; *CDB*, vol. 1, no. 17 *CDB*, vol. 4, no. 20.

57 A. Rocchi (trans.), *Vita di San Nilo Abate* (Rome, 1904), 62–63; see also: Goskar, *Objects, People and Exchange*, 110–111.

58 Franks would include most people north of the Alps, including, for example, Normans, while for Bulgars see Cristina Torre, "Gli Slavi nella Calabria bizantina", in De Sensi Sestito (ed.), *La Calabria nel Mediterraneo*, 203–222.

59 Von Falkenhausen, "Between Two Empires", 160–161.

60 J. McGinley and H. Mursurillo (trans.), "An anonymous Greek account of the transfer of the Body of Saint Nicholas from Myra in Lycia to Bari in Italy", *Bolletino di S. Nicola*, N. 10, *Studi e testi*, (October 1980), 3–17. By way of comparison a certain *Armenus* appears alongside a *Curticis* as villeins of the Tarantine monastery of S. Pietro Imperiale in 1114, see chapter 18 of this volume.

61 *CDB*, vol. 1, no. 18; another Sepe appears witnessing a document in 1103, *CDB*, vol. 5, no. 33.

62 *CDB*, vol. 4, no. 20.

63 *CDB*, vol. 3, no. 6; *CDP*, vol. 20, no. 40; *CDB*, vol. 4, n.39; *CDB*, vol. 5, no. 6.

64 *CDB*, vol. 5, no. 3; *CDB*, vol. 5, no. 28.

65 *CDB*, vol. 3, no. 5; *CDP*, vol. 20, no. 40; *CDB*, vol. 5, no. 35; *CDB*, vol. 3, no. 28; *CDB*, vol. 5, no. 74; von Falkenhausen, 125, & 134.

66 Important also in this regard is the fact that Greek names appear in diminutive form in the documents, such as *CDB*, vol. 5, no. 16.

67 *CDB*, vol. 5, no. 17.

68 It appears in the nominative as "Ieorgi", so this appears to be the only way of reconciling the oddity, and Iemma is certainly used in the other document to represent a "Ye" sound.

69 *CDB*, vol. 5, no. 6.

70 *CDB*, vol. 5, no. 26.

71 *CDB*, vol. 5, framm. 11.

72 A. Jacob, "Vaste en Terre d'Otrante et ses Inscription", *Aevum*, May 1, (1997), 252; & in chapter 18 of this volume.

73 *CDB*, vol. 6, no. 78.

74 For example the practice of "brother-making" or *adelphopoieia*, see: Claudia Rapp, *Brother-Making in Late Antiquity and Byzantium: Monks, Laymen and Christian Ritual* (Oxford, 2015).

75 R. Brubaker, *Ethnicity Without Groups* (Cambridge Mass., 2004), 7–27.

76 B. Latour, *Reassembling the Social* (Oxford, 2005), 21–156.

77 For "cultural stuff" see: F. Barthes, *Ethnic Groups and Boundaries*, (Boston, 1969), 9–38; for everyday practices-based theory of identification, value production and fetishization see: D. Graeber, *Towards an Anthropological Theory of Value* (New York, 2001), 49–89.
78 Emphasis added; Latour, *Reassembling*, 31.
79 Latour, *Reassembling*, 27–42.
80 These must have been in existence before the imperial takeover, especially as imperial forces were actively invited in by citizens in 874, see: von Falkenhausen, *Dominazione*, 20–21.
81 B. Jessop, "Interpretive Sociology and the Dialectic of Structure and Agency", *Theory, Culture & Society* 1996, vol. 13(1), 119–128; Graeber, *Value*, 60–63.
82 Cf. E. M. Wood's comments on class as a "structured process": *Democracy Against Capitalism* (Cambridge, 1996), 76–107.
83 This approach has been significantly re-worked from that presented in A. Wimmer, *Ethnic Boundary Making* (Oxford, 2013).
84 The aforementioned Melicciacca in 1099 is "son of Bizantius of the city of Bari", see note 92.
85 See Garsoïan, "Armenian Integration", & S. Peter Cowe, "Armenian Immigration to the Sebastia Region, Tenth-Eleventh Centuries", in Richard Hovannisian (ed.), *Armenian Sebastia/Sivas and Lesser Armenia* (Costa Mesa C. A., 2004), 111–136; & N. S. M. Matheou, "Armenians in East Roman Cappadocia, *c.* 900–1071: Settlement, the State Apparatus, and the Reproduction of Ethnicity", (*forthcoming*). There is also the question of the lack of identified "Greeks" and/or "Romans".
86 Much of this framework and model is adapted from: Wimmer, *Boundary*; & L. Althusser, *On the Reproduction of Capitalism* (London & New York, 2014), 70–207.
87 For a critical view of interpellation see J. Rehmann, *Theories of Ideology* (Leiden, 2013), 147–178.
88 One papal document from 1059 refers to a certain "Abbot Mele", see: *CDB*, vol. 4, no. 38.
89 As noted, this is an odd name that may suggest some Caucasian origin, but without any further identification there is no reason to assume this, see note 40.
90 *CDB*, vol. 1, no. 24; likewise S. Gregorio Armeno, if it had been an Armenian foundation, is in the hands of the Adralisto family by *c.* 1040, see note 55.
91 "Nikeforius, relative of Helias the abbot, grandson of Maraldus the abbot of St. George", *CDB*, vol. 5, no. 1.
92 Both versions appear in the document, and it's apparently a local variant diminutive of Mleh, perhaps combining Greek and Armenian forms.
93 Von Falkenhausen, "Between Two Empires", 155–158.
94 This would appear to refer to the *katepanō*'s buildings, rebuilt in the 1010s, see: *CDB*, vol. 4, no. 21.
95 Indeed, pro and anti Chalcedonian positions are not even fixed in Caucasia itself in the same period, see Garsoïan, "Armenian Integration", 104–109.
96 See the online Prosopography of the Byzantine World: http://db.pbw.kcl.ac.uk/pbw2011/entity/person/162203.
97 And of course this is made more likely by the noted prominence of churchmen with Armenian names, including the main notary of the cathedral *c.* 1040–1080, "Mel".
98 McCormick, "Imperial Edge", 23.
99 Ranging from official spiritual and financial support, to threats and Divine judgement against the official in question, see von Falkenhausen, "Provincial Aristocracy", 211–212.
100 Archontes in Bari in general write much better than their colleagues in other towns; return to what Vera says about Bari as a provincial capital in her article on the subject.

101 Two later historians, William of Apulia and Hugo Falcandus, describe the august built environment of Bari in the aftermath of two attacks, one of Robert Guiscard in 1071, the other of William II of Sicily in 1155, see: William of Apulia, bk. II: "There was no city in Apulia which exceeded the opulence of Bari. He besieged it, wealthy and strongly-defended, that by overcoming the rulers of so great a city he might therefore terrify and subject the lesser towns, for of all the cities along the Apulian coast Bari was the greatest", and Hugo Falcandus, *The History of the Tyrants of Sicily by "Hugo Falcandus" 1154–1169*, G. A. Loud and T. Wiedemann (trans.) (Manchester, 1998), 74: "the most powerful city in Apulia, celebrated by fame and immensely rich, proud in its noble citizens and remarkable in the architecture of its buildings, now lies transformed into piles of rubble".

102 The best surviving evidence for this trend are pious foundations by *strategoi* and *katepanos*, associated not so much with the founder's person or family but his role as governor-general, as Vera von Falkenhausen has noted "not so much a private as an official character; they were linked not so much with the person or the family of the founder as with the latter's office as governor". See von Falkenhausen, "Provincial Aristocracy", 211–214.

103 Von Falkenhausen, "Provincial Aristocracy".

104 *CDP*, vol. 20, no. 27.

105 Seen, for example, in *CDP*, vol. 20, no. 11.

106 L. Neville, *Authority in Byzantine Provincial Society* (Cambridge, 2004), 39–65.

107 Edward A. Freeman, *Sketches from the Subject and Neighbour Lands of Venice* (1880), section 17.

108 *CDP*, vol. 20, no. 7; von Falkenhausen, "Provincial Aristocracy".

109 *CDB*, vol. 1, no. 28.

110 As were members of the Chryselioi family who handed Dyrrachion over in 1005.

111 These include Pasaarus *protospatharios*' death in 973; Porphyrius *protospatharios* murder of Bishop Andreas of Oretanum in 978; Sergius *protospatharios* death at the hands of "the people of Bari" in 987; Ioannes Ammiropoulos *patrikios*' arrival in 989 and murder of Leo Cannatus, Nicolaus the judge, and Porphyrius; Petrus the *exubitis*' murder in 990; and Marco Theodorus the *excubitus*' death in 997; see Lupus Protospatharius.

112 Indeed, throughout the late tenth and early eleventh centuries, when the imperial centre could not focus on southern Italy and the region suffered from intense Sicilian Arab raids, Bari had a continuous imperial presence of titled elites and officials associated with the military, fiscal-legal, and administrative apparatuses, particularly the *tagmata*.

113 On these questions in relation to the eastern Roman empire, see J. Haldon, *The State and the Tributary Mode of Production* (London & New York, 1993); J. Banaji, *Theory as History: Essays on Modes of Production and Exploitation* (Leiden, 2010); & V. Prigent "The Mobilisation of Fiscal Resources in the Byzantine Empire (Eighth to Eleventh Centuries)", in John Hudson & Ana Rodriguez (eds.), *Diverging Paths? The Shapes of Power and Institutions in Medieval Christendom and Islam* (Leiden, 2014), 182–229.

114 *CDB*, vol. 4, no. 32.

115 Of course, claiming a place is deserted forms an ideological claim for its enclosure and appropriation, establishing private property and overriding any forms of commoning that may exist there.

116 I am preparing a forthcoming study on this topic.

117 *CDB*, vol. 4, no. 44.

118 J. Haldon, "Res publica Byzantina? State Formation and Issues of Identity in Medieval East Rome", *Byzantine and Modern Greek Studies*, vol. 40, issue 1 (April, 2016), 12.

119 Von Falkenhausen, "Provincial Aristocracy", 143–144, & 157.
120 See, for example, in the letters of Nikolaos Mystikos, no. 75 noting that Basileios I "subjugated Longibardia"; no. 82 referring to Pandulph, prince of Benevento's request to be made strategos of "all Longobardia"; and no. 85 "To the priests, archpriests, *archontes* and the general body of the people of Longibardia": R. J. H. Jenkins & L. G. Westerink (eds. & trans.), *Nicholas I Patriarch of Constantinople. Letters* (Washington D. C., 1974).
121 *CDP*, vol. 20, no. 12; *CDB*, vol. 8, no. 8.
122 Both William of Apulia in the late eleventh century and Hugo Falcandus in the mid-twelfth explicitly distinguish between *Lombardi*/*Lambardi* in northern Italy and *Longobardi*/*Langobardi* in the south, a discovery I first made doing my undergraduate dissertation with Tom Brown, see William of Apulia, bk. I; & Hugo Falcandus, 121, note 105.
123 *CDB*, vol. 4, no. 32.
124 *CDP*, vol. 20, no. 3.
125 This is the female version of *archon*, the general Greek term for elites.
126 Seven percent of the documents in Bari record the movement of objects, as opposed to the roughly one percent from elsewhere in the south, and Apulian marriage contracts were especially object rich, see: Goskar, *Objects, People and Exchange*, 314.
127 Ibidem., 143; *CDP*, vol. 20, no. 42.
128 Goskar, *Objects, People and Exchange*, 146–147.
129 Ibidem., 285–286.
130 Ibidem., 109; see also Graeber, *Value*, 91–116.
131 For a brilliant discussion of clothing and identifications see: Goskar, *Objects, People and Exchange*, 193–194.
132 McCormick, "Imperial Edge", 18–19.
133 Goskar, *Objects, People and Exchange*, 309–310.
134 McCormick, "Imperial Edge", 19–21; Goskar, *Objects, People and Exchange*, 111.
135 *CDB*, vol. 1, no. 14; the same actors seem to appear in: *CDB*, vol. 1, nos. 16 & 17.
136 A *morgengabe* was written in similar style in Trani in 965, perhaps indicating a local tradition, see Goskar, *Objects, People and Exchange*, 314.
137 For the *exkoubitai* see: *Oxford Dictionary of Byzantium*, vol. 1, 646–647.
138 Von Falkenhausen, "Between Two Empires".
139 Ibidem.
140 Lupus Protospatharius.
141 On the importance of such narratives for identity see: M. R. Somers, "The Narrative Constitution of Identity: A Relational and Network Approach", *Theory and Society*, vol. 23, no. 5 (October, 1994), 605–649.
142 Lupus Protospatharius, 1082.
143 See note 122.
144 Von Falkenhausen, "Between Two Empires", 175–176; "Provincial Aristocracy", 224.
145 Goskar, *Objects, People and Exchange*, 132–133: "The purpose of William's description of Melo may not therefore be an illustration of difference between Normans and southern Italians (Apulians), but framed differently, perhaps a statement of affinity between the author and the figure of Melo and the people he represented. William's instinct for description lay in these visual and tangible aspects of Melo's culture. There was no contradiction in his expression as a Barese-Lombard hero, possibly Armenian name and his Greek dress. These were the signifiers that were the reality of cultural exchange in southern Italy at this time".
146 Goskar, *Objects, People and Exchange*, 313; *CDB*, vol. 4, no. 36.
147 Goskar, *Objects, People and Exchange*, 311.
148 Ibidem, 305–306.

Part V

Elites and cities

15 What was wrong with bishops in sixth-century southern Italy?

It seems a very long time since many of the people here at Tom's Fest met up for the inaugural Medieval Italy research day at the University of Birmingham in the late 1980s, and it is a privilege to have been asked to mark Tom's distinguished career in early medieval Italian history since then. Since one of his more recent articles has dealt with a turn to religious policy,[1] I thought I'd investigate a phenomenon that only made it into a brief footnote in my study of Amalfi,[2] the problem of bishops not doing their jobs properly. I hope that what follows will offer an entry point into the Dos and Don'ts of being a bishop in Byzantine southern Italy, as well as a flavour of how bishops interacted (or didn't) with their urban environment.

We can start by asking: what did a model bishop look like? It is tempting to turn to later evidence, the compilations of (papal)/episcopal lives from Rome and Ravenna,[3] which are mainly notable for their idealisation of their pastors (although Agnellus's vicious portrait of Bishop George of Ravenna at the end of the *LPR* is useful as a "what not to do").[4] Put simply, these texts suggest that a good bishop remained in his city and defended it to the best of his ability; was preferably well-born (an ancient pedigree was desirable but not essential) yet humble; did not dissipate his church's wealth, but used it both to glorify God and the saints through building works (preferably, but not essentially, richly decorated); and supported the weak and vulnerable through charitable acts and actively defending them in cases of oppression. A good bishop was also concerned for the moral well-being of both his clergy and flock, and in the uneasy centuries of post-Roman transition, heresy was always a threat.[5] The role of bishop was undeniably a political as well as a pastoral one, but the trick was not to become *too* entangled in secular affairs (unless they were to the benefit of the bishop's own family). How then did the bishops of southern Italy measure up to such ideals?

The source I'll be using is a familiar one, the letters of Pope Gregory I.[6] From the very first letter in the published edition of Gregory's collection, dated September 590 and appointing Peter the Subdeacon as rector over all the bishoprics in Sicily (I.1), to nearly the last, his berating of Leo, bishop of Catania in March 604 for the latter's neglect of the goings-on at the monastery of St Vitus on Mount Etna (XIV.16), the letters provide important clues as to the ongoing duties and obligations of the southern Italian and Sicilian episcopate. Although many of the qualities expressed might quite reasonably be expected of bishops wherever they were (and comparative models of episcopal probity are, of course, available from contemporary Francia in the extensive accounts of another Gregory, the bishop of Tours),[7] the smooth running of the southern Italian and Sicilian episcopate was, arguably, particularly important to the papacy. The Roman church, after all, held substantial landed properties in early medieval southern Italy and Sicily, from which the popes derived much revenue, and relations between the local bishops and local *rectores* of the patrimony needed to be cordial if resources were to be distributed appropriately.[8]

At the same time, however, as the letter to Leo demonstrates, Gregory was often provoked to write by the failings of bishops: if things *were* going smoothly, after all, there would probably be far less need to write and so far less letters for the historian to peruse. Gregory in fact himself expresses precisely this sentiment in a letter to the exarch of Ravenna, Romanus, in February 591:

> Even if no reason at all were to crop up for writing to your Excellency, yet we with paternal love would be worried about the condition of your health, making us keen to learn through the frequent exchange of messengers what we desire to hear from you. (I.32)[9]

The letter then goes on to more substantive business—social niceties or not, every letter had a purpose.[10] We might compare the complaints and demands in Gregory's letters with those written by the senator Cassiodorus for his Gothic masters earlier in the century, which also point up failings in their recipients.[11] Yet the act of letter-writing was not simply a mechanistic tool to give out orders: it also expressed a desire to maintain a practice that marked out the sender and recipient as members of a literate, still-Roman elite: those "social niceties" were a core part of that practice of signalling.[12] Keeping the highly constructed nature of the letters themselves in mind, therefore, I want in this chapter to explore the dynamics of how potential or actual failure was perceived and presented in Gregory's letters, and see whether the recurring themes within this category tell us anything about the wider social picture in the south in this period.

Absence

One thing that clearly was "wrong" was the fact that some bishops struggled to have a flock to minister to at all, and some sees lacked staff to minister to the flock. From the early 540s, the entire Byzantine empire had been devastated by a plague that had still not entirely run its course by the end of the century, and extended westwards as far as Britain.[13] (In this context, Gregory's letter to Romanus enquiring after his health takes on an added edge.) Paul the Deacon's much later account of the social dislocation that the plague caused in northern Italy in the 560s is well known,[14] and the effects of the disease were clearly felt in the south as well. In October 590, writing to Bacauda, the bishop of Formia in southern Lazio, Gregory recognises the lack of clergy and people (*tam clerus quam plebis destitutam*) in nearby Minturno and agrees to Bacauda's plan to link the church of Minturno to Formia (I.8). In July 591, a letter to Felix, bishop of Siponto in northern Apulia, reveals the same problem of lack of clergy at Canosa ["Canusium"], and orders him to appoint two priests (I.51). In September 595, the "deserted nature of the place and the shortage of people (*loci desertio…imminutio personarum*)" in Carinae (Sicily) led to it being joined to Reggio di Calabria under Boniface rather than a new bishop being appointed to succeed the [unnamed] and deceased incumbent (VI.9).[15] Not just the population, but also their pastors, are likely to have died in the pandemic: John of Squillace (II.32) was ordered in July 592 to minister also to the "destitute (*destituta*)" church of Cotrone in Calabria until the latter replaced its deceased bishop. In the same month Felix, the bishop of Agropoli, was charged with visiting and caring for three other neighbouring churches (II.35).

Whilst we would expect the pope to take an interest in episcopal appointments—and indeed see him actively intervening in local matters, for example at Syracuse in July 595 (V.54) and Locri in 597–598 (VII.38 and IX.76)—the cluster of appointments in the south in this relatively short period (the evidence base, after all, extends only a decade and a half) speaks of major disruption. Work on the later Black Death of the fourteenth century has recognised the impact that large-scale epidemics had not only on the population at large but also on the provision of pastoral care: priests, after all, were extremely vulnerable to infection if part of their job was to provide comfort and last rites for the deceased and their families.[16] A somewhat unnoticed detail of Paul's account, after all, apparently has *lay-people* constrained to bury their dead relatives, and dying themselves in the process without a funeral, a clear measure of social disruption (although part and parcel of Paul's overarching desire to convey the extremity of the situation): no priests are mentioned at all.

A variation on the theme of vacant sees and population fall is the case of Pimenius, bishop of Amalfi, who was in 596 "not content to reside in his church, but wanders abroad through various places (*in ecclesia sua residere non esse contentum, sed foris per loca diversa vagare*)". Worse, others were following his example. Anthemius the subdeacon, Gregory's representative and manager of estates in Campania, was charged to correct Pimenius or to consult with Gregory about confining him to a monastery (VI.23). The question is why Pimenius felt the need to wander. Did he not have a congregation at Amalfi? One might legitimately ask just how many people actually lived there at this early date, given that it did not have Roman origins, was inaccessible and had a distinct lack of natural resources, but it is striking that this letter, like so many others in the collection, simply addresses the problem at hand—absenteeism—rather than enquiring as to its reasons.

As well as the plague, however, there was the issue of insecurity caused by war to deal with in the Italian South at this time. The Lombards had controlled much of Campania since 572 and attacked Naples in 581 and Montecassino ten years later.[17] One wonders against this background whether Pimenius was in fact a "defector" of sorts. If he is indeed the same "Primen" who appears as bishop of Nocera (hardly a metropolis itself, IX.45) two years later—and given how unusual his name is the occurrence of two men in such close proximity would be huge coincidence—then he would have moved from an area under Byzantine control to one conquered by the Lombards. It would be a highly unusual move: the real disruption of the Lombard attacks, at least in Gregory's letters, might be better represented in the flight of clergy *from* their incursions. Maximian, bishop of Syracuse in Sicily, for example, was asked to send back clergy who had fled from the diocese of Formia on the mainland (IV.42, August 594). Cyprian, the deacon and defender of Sicily, was asked in October 593 to track down the church valuables that priests fleeing from the Lombards on the Italian mainland had brought with them to Sicily (IV.15). Sometimes, however, it was bishops themselves who were accused of removals, as in the case of Bishop Severinus of Myrie who had fled to Squillace (V.9).

As well as flight from the Lombards, the clergy and people of a see might be depleted still further by being taken captive: the ransoming of hostages features frequently in the letters as an act of charity. A letter of April 596, for example, reveals that Lombard incursions were still causing "calamity (*calamitatis*)" and "affliction (*afflictio*)", not least by leaving many hostages in need of ransoming: Gregory therefore sent Anthemius, his subdeacon in Campania, funds to assist with this (VI.32), though he is somewhat ambivalent about church valuables being sold to raise the money for ransoms.[18]

Heresy and unbelief

Another issue dogging the Pope was the danger of Arian and other schismatics.[19] The Arian heresy, of course, had a long history in Italy before it appears in the Register, and it was persistent—the Ostrogoths had been Arians, and early Lombard rulers were too.[20] Gregory writes to Bishop Demetrius of Naples in December 590 addressing the problem of a certain Stephen, who had returned to the Catholic faith after a period of "doubts over this matter (*pro huius re dubietate*)", but who had been part of a group in Naples whom Demetrius is urged to try to bring back into the Catholic communion (I.14). The two issues of depopulation and schism come together in Gregory's letter to all Italian bishops dated January 591, where he links the Arian schism with the "grim pestilence which is threatening everywhere (*ubique gravis mortalitas imminet*)", and attributes the plague to the anger of God over the Arian heresy (I.17). Arians were not the only problem: the bishop of Tyndari in Sicily, Eutychius, is congratulated for his efforts against the heretical "Angelii" in August 593 (III.59); Manicheans are mentioned in Sicily in October 594 (V.7); and Bishop Agnellus of Terracina was taken to task for not preventing tree worshippers in his diocese in April 598 (VIII.19).

Zeal against unbelievers could be taken too far, however. In March 591 Gregory had written to Agnellus's predecessor as Bishop of Terracina, Peter, instructing him to desist from moving the town's Jewish community on from their traditional meeting places: "we want them to be allowed to gather together as their custom was, at that place which they obtained for their meetings with your consent…(*volumus…locum quem, sicut praediximus, cum tua conscientia quo congregentur adepti sunt, eos sicut mos fuit ibidem liceat convenire*)" (I.34). Tension continued, however, and Bishops Bacauda of Formia and Agnellus of Fondi ["Fundi"] were appointed to investigate (II.45, 591/2). Peter's death may have resolved the issue, and in the meantime Agnellus's see was overrun by the Lombards: his move to Terracina in November 592 was, it seems, an ideal outcome (III.13 and 14). Whilst Jews were not allowed to actively proselytise, their right to worship unmolested was a central plank of Gregory's papacy, and he reinforced this in a letter to Victor, bishop of Palermo, in June 598 (VIII.25).[21] Victor had earlier been accused by Gregory of only "pretending (*dissimulat*)" to take care of his flock (V.4)—perhaps this warning had stirred him up a little too far.

(Im)morality and corruption

Assuming your bishop stayed in his appointed see, there was no guarantee that he would do his job properly, if the letters are anything to go by. Bishop Severinus was not the only one to misbehave: Bishop Demetrius of Naples was deposed by September 591, accused of corruption and "involved in so many and such business dealings (*tantis et talibus negotiis inventus est involutus*)" and evil-doing (II.3) that Gregory felt compelled to eject him. Naples, as we shall see, was a particularly turbulent city when it came to appointing bishops, and the caretaker appointed to visit the see until a replacement for Demetrius was found clearly did not get on with the Neapolitans.

Failure to establish a relationship of trust with the local clergy and laypeople of the see seems to have been a common problem. Bishops in Gregory's letters seem to have been quite vulnerable to accusations of misdemeanours, suggesting that they sometimes fell foul of strongly entrenched local interests. A "wicked rumour (*sinister rumor*)" circulated about the behaviour of Bishop Leo of Catania, but was investigated and dismissed in July of 592 (II.29). Leo faced another challenge from his own clergy in November 597 relating to the division of church income (VIII.7). We learn the following year that the clergy of Catania were in the habit of wearing ostentatious kid-leather boots (*calciatis campagis*)—permitted to the clergy of Messina by an earlier pope—but whose spread to Catania was troubling to Gregory in a letter to Bishop John of Syracuse in June 598 (VIII.27). Gregory informs John of a further complaint against Leo in October 598 (IX.32). As we have just seen, however, the bishop of Catania was still holding on to his somewhat precarious position in 604. Other bishops, such as Gregory, bishop of Agrigento, came under suspicion in November 592 (III.12). Peter the subdeacon of Campania is ordered to investigate the ill-feeling between Festus, bishop of Capua, and his flock in May 593 (III.34). Complaints against Bishop Boniface of Reggio by his own clergy were referred to five other bishops (Paulinus, bishop of Taurum, Proculus, bishop of Nicotera, Palumbus, bishop of Cosenza, Venerius, bishop of Vibona and Marcian, bishop of Locri) in April 599 (IX.135).

High-legged kid leather boots were not the only sign of ostentation out of control in the far south. Boniface, bishop of Reggio di Calabria, whom we have just met as the subject of complaints in 599, had already drawn a rebuke from Gregory because his charitable works were somewhat undermined by Boniface's self-publicity (III.4). A letter to Bishop Felix of Messina in July 591, similarly, discouraged him from sending the pope expensive presents and planning to come to Rome (I.64)—extravagance and absenteeism wrapped up into one. Instead, the bishop was encouraged to support new, local church foundations (II.6).

The church's property was central to another of Gregory's concerns, particularly the fact that some bishops kept concubines and fathered children who made claims to inherit it.[22] Andrew the bishop of Taranto ["Tarentum"] was found to have had a concubine and suspended in June 593 (additional misdemeanours are added in the letter of suspension, III.44). Bishop John of Gallipoli was charged with imposing the punishment and investigating the case (III.45). But the enforced separation of married subdeacons from their wives threw up some problems of supporting the women that bishops also had to deal with (IV.34), and the offspring of bishops, such as Euplus, the son of Eusanius of Agrigento (presumably a replacement for Gregory, mentioned earlier), caused more discussion of how to separate church property (to which Euplus was not entitled) from the personal property of his mother (to which he was) (IV.36).[23]

The confusion between personal and church property also concerned Gregory when he referred to the wills of Bishop Theodore of Lilybaeum in February 595 (V.23; the bishopric was filled by Decius: VI.13, September 595), and Bishop Importunus of Atella in May 599 (IX.143). Bishop Felix of Siponto comes under suspicion in June 593, when Gregory ordered him to inventory the lands of the Sipontine church and berated him for the behaviour of his grandson/nephew (*nepos*) accused of rape (III.41 and 42). Not only bishops faced rumour and accusation of sexual impropriety. A cleric in

Naples, Peter, was accused by some boys of "tempting them to sin (*de temptationem sceleris*)", and summarily forbidden from approaching the altar without an investigation being carried out (IX.70; subdeacon Anthemius of Campania is also asked to investigate, IX.69).

Local politics: Naples

We have already seen that bishops might struggle to establish themselves in a city, and this exposes something of the patterns of urban life in the south at this time. Failure to establish oneself might suggest that only part of the city's population supported a particular candidate, whether or not he had a pre-existing connection to the city, and the losers amongst clergy and laity might subsequently work quite hard to destabilise a bishop before he even got going. Moreover, the bishop's traditional role of protector was difficult to carry out effectively against the background of war, insecurity and disease that prevailed in this period.

Episcopal elections, the letters confirm, were a particular moment of tension.[24] Peter, bishop of Otranto, was made visitor of Brindisi, Lecce and Gallipoli in November of 595, and charged with getting the people in those towns to "remove partisanship and with one and the same consensus to look for priests to be put in charge of them (*ut remoto studio uno eodemque consensu tales sibi praeficiendos expetant sacerdotes*)" (VI.21). Almost exactly the same formulaic language occurs in a letter to Bishop Agnellus of Terracina, instructing him to help the residents of Formia elect a successor to Bacauda (VII.16), and to Fortunatus of Naples regarding the see of Misenum in December 598 (IX.81 and 82).[25]

But Fortunatus's own path to the see of Naples had hardly been smooth. The disgraced Demetrius was temporarily replaced in December 591 by the somewhat reluctant Paul, bishop of Nepi as visitor (II.8, II.9, II.14, II.23), and the latter clearly had a turbulent relationship with the Neapolitans (III.2). We might suggest here that having an external figure in temporary charge, rather like the later practice of having a foreign *podestà* in the Italian city-states, was prone to shine a light on internal practices (corruption? appropriation of resources? nepotism?) that the inhabitants would far rather remain in the shadows. In December 592 we learn that Gregory had tried without success to install his subdeacon, Florentius, to the bishopric of Naples: Florentius had in fact "fled from the city itself, miserably avoiding his ordination (*refugiens civitatem ipsam ordinationem suam lacrimabiliter evitasset*)" (III.15). What did he know that dissuaded him from the move? We are not told—but Bishop Paul, far away from his home in Nepi, had clearly not kept his dissatisfaction with his situation a secret. His relationship with the Neapolitans had completely broken down, and Gregory asked Peter the subdeacon to convene a meeting of the clergy in May 593 to resolve the issue of appointing a new leader. Paul, meanwhile, was to be compensated handsomely for his stint as visiting bishop (III.35, a payment of 100 *solidi* and a small orphan boy as his servant). By August 593 Fortunatus was installed at Naples as bishop (III.58), and initially seems to have had a much better relationship with his flock (III.60, V.50).

Gregory's letters dealing with Naples reveal the complexity of Neapolitan society (e.g., I.48, I.53, I.63, I.66, IV.31, VI.29, VII.1, IX.36 and IX.105). Fortunatus often worked alongside Gregory's subdeacon for Campania, Anthemius (VII.20), who like him was charged with dealing with destitute clergy and nuns (I.23) and supporting the poor and destitute (I.37, I.57, VI.37, IX.85: though several of the poor women listed here are allocated huge sums of money and addressed as "Domina"). Fortunatus, meanwhile, was reminded to defend his own clergy from being taken to court by laymen in the city (VI.11, September 595). Both instructions are revealing, suggesting that the powerful Neapolitan aristocracy claimed something of a hold over clerical matters and ecclesiastical resources.[26] In addition, the city was a magnet for refugees from Lombard incursions (I.48). The bishop was also charged with supporting clergy from nearby towns such as Venafro that had been captured by the Lombards.

The tendency for factionalism in Naples, however, broke out again in October/November 598, and Fortunatus was again instructed to try to bring the parties to a conclusion (IX.47). By November/December 598, however, Fortunatus was obviously embroiled in a lengthy dispute of his own with the Neapolitan aristocracy, whom Gregory appears to support in a letter to the bishop (IX.77), as well as facing complaints from abbots in the city (IX.172). Fortunatus also attracted criticism from Gregory for not preventing a nunnery in the city being used as a barracks for soldiers (IX.208, July 599). Had he essentially picked the wrong side to support in 598 and lost control of sections of the city? It seems so. His lack of care for local monasteries is further indicted in April 600 (X.9), but his death soon afterwards exposed the cracks in Neapolitan politics, as Gregory rejected both candidates put forward to succeed him (X.19). A letter of January 601 reveals Fortunatus's successor to be one Paschasius (XI.19), who is subsequently ordered to distribute alms to the poor and not-so-poor "honorable but hard-up (*honestis ac egenis*)" of the city (XI.22). The bottom line, it seems, mattered: the "honorable" were to be kept on-side by repeated promises of material support.

Naples was, of course, the largest and most diverse community in the south at this time, precociously urbanised, populous and relatively wealthy, drawing in individuals and communities from neighbouring and distant locations.[27] Some clues as to why being the city's bishop was so difficult are contained in Gregory's letters to southern Italian laypeople, including women such as the patrician Clementina of Naples (I.11, IX.86), whose servants were implicated in a plot against Bishop Paul during his caretaking of the see (III.1, September 592). She was also clearly used to intervening in episcopal elections: Gregory writes to her in March 600 that she should not be upset at the appointment of Amandus to the bishopric of Sorrento (X.6), taking him away from Naples (X.7). (The timing here might be crucial: the month before Fortunatus died, was Clementina lining up a preferred candidate for the larger episcopate?) Taken together with the evidence for church resources being directed toward honourable people, and the difficulties of finding someone to serve as its bishop, it is clear that Naples represented a real challenge to anyone appointed to be its pastor.

None of this drama, predictably enough, makes it into the main source for the Neapolitan episcopate in the early Middle Ages, the *Gesta Episcoporum Neapolitanorum*, compiled in the ninth century, and modelled squarely on its Roman and Ravennate precursors. Demetrius's episcopate of three years, and Fortunatus's of seven, are perfunctorily dealt with in single lines, and the big news during the episcopate of the former is in fact the tremendous flood at Rome and Gregory's own election as pope.[28] The *Gesta*'s purpose, amply illuminated by Thomas Granier, was to "demonstrate the continuity, the legitimacy and the glory of the Neapolitan episcopal line", enhanced by the sanctity of some of its members and bolstering the ambitions of the ducal family, rather than dwell on episodes of conflict already centuries old.[29] After all, the factionalism of the sixth century was by no means dead in the ninth, and hagiography—the *Gesta*, like the other *libri* from Rome and Ravenna, was surely this rather than history—provided a way to smooth out periods of political tension by emphasising what united Neapolitans, rather than divided them.[30]

What we do not know from Gregory's letters or related chronicles, in many of these cases, is what happened next—there are very few reiterations of the same orders about the same matter, suggesting that Gregory's demands were met. But the repeated letters to some bishops reveal that even if one matter was closed, there was always room for improvement. People complained to the pope about their bishops it seems, and even a nasty rumour was sufficient to provoke enquiry.

Against this background of many difficulties, however, regular business such as the transfer and interment of saints' relics were still being arranged (e.g., I.52, July 591—an order to the bishop of Sorrento, John, to allow the interment of St Agatha's relics on the island of Capri; III.19), and church dedications being ordered (I.54). A general letter to the bishops of Sorrento, Terracina, Portus, Naples, Nocera, Ostia and Formia in October 598 charged them all with building churches to house relics (IX.45).[31] In addition, Gregory's own *Dialogues* set up many of the ideals of episcopal life with which this chapter started: the humility of Constantius, bishop of Aquino, and the bravery of his successors Andreas and Jovinus, facing up to war and famine which left the city without a pastor after the death of Jovinus (III.8); the chastity of Andrew, the bishop of Fondi ("Funda"), evicting a nun who had lived with him chastely from before his elevation to bishop, thereby protecting his reputation and hers (III.7); and the miracle-working of bishops from some of the very same cities that later attracted attention in his letters, for example the aged and blind Sabinus of Canosa (III.5).[32]

Conclusion

Gregory, as bishop of Rome and as pope, was a hard act to follow, but the standards he set—and indeed his own life—went on to be used as a model for future pontiffs, not least in the ninth century that saw such a flourishing of hagiography in southern Italy as elsewhere.[33] Christopher Hanlon has recently discussed how Gregory employed the triad of "ordo", "auctoritas" and "potestas"—order, authority and power—to shape his administration of the papal patrimony.[34] This ethos is clearly visible in the letters, but his plan was disrupted by the surrounding crises of the late sixth century. Working from just his letters perhaps magnifies the air of disaster, but more than anything else they bear witness to a perfect storm of difficulties that made being a bishop in the south in this decade and a half a particularly demanding job: negotiating vested local interests (particularly if you were not from the same community—though it was possibly even worse if you were); supporting refugees from war; picking up the threads of pastoral care in communities devastated by plague; and confronting (or not) heretical beliefs. On top of this, bishops with families had to negotiate the tricky balance of supporting partners and children that they were not even supposed to have, but that in the "Byzantine context"[35] had previously been a tolerated, perhaps even regular, part of clerical life. Moreover, the number of episcopal vacancies in this period suggests that many bishops had to carry on with more than one full-time workload, "visiting" being something of a euphemism for filling the shoes of more than one person. It is hardly any surprise that some chose to go missing like Pimenius, and that others were "following his example (*eius exemplum sequentes*)": what was really wrong with bishops in the south at the end of the sixth century was the task they were expected to fulfill—even if Gregory only wrote to them repeatedly when he was displeased, his letters speak volumes about the demands placed on the episcopate: they were fire-fighting in exceptional circumstances whilst dealing with a leader whose mantra was "must do more", "must do better" and "don't expect more resources". It is little wonder that some turned their backs on such a challenging environment.

Notes

1 T. S. Brown, "Lombard religious policy in the late sixth and early seventh centuries: the Roman dimension", in *The Langobards before the Frankish Conquest: an Ethnographic Perspective*, ed. Giorgio Ausenda and Paolo Delogu (Woodbridge: Boydell, 2009), 289–308.
2 Patricia Skinner, *Medieval Amalfi and its Diaspora* (Oxford: OUP, 2013).
3 *Liber Pontificalis: Texte, introduction et commentaire*, 2 vols (Paris, 1886–1892); English translation of the lives to 715 in *The Book of the Popes (Liber Pontificalis)*, tr. R. Davis (revised edition, Liverpool, 2000); followed by *The Lives of the Eighth-Century Popes*, tr. R. Davis (Liverpool, 1992) and *The Lives of the Ninth-Century Popes AD 817–891*, tr. R. Davis (Liverpool, 1995). Ravenna: *Agnelli Ravennatis Liber Pontificalis Ecclesie Ravennatis*, ed. D. Deliyannis (CCM

199, Turnhout, 2006); English translation *Agnellus of Ravenna: The Book of Pontiffs of the Church of Ravenna*, tr. D. Deliyannis (Washington, 2004). The literature on these two texts is extensive, but pertinent to the present discussion is Emanuele Pazza, "La Sicilia e i papi nell'alto medioevo: spigolature dal *Liber Pontificalis*", *Annali della Facoltà di Scienze della formazione (Catania)*, 14 (2015), 97–105 http://ojs.unict.it/ojs/index.php/annali-sdf/article/view/193/186 [accessed 22 May 2016], which discusses a further dimension in the lives of bishops, their conflicted loyalties to Rome and Byzantium; and Claire Sotinel's collected essays, *Church and Society in Late Antique Italy and Beyond* (Aldershot: Variorum, 2010).

4 And see Ann Moffatt, "Sixth-century Ravenna from the perspective of Abbot Agnellus", in *The Sixth Century: End or Beginning?* ed. Pauline Allen and Elizabeth Jeffreys (Brisbane, 1996), 236–246.

5 Robert McEachnie, "A history of heretics past: the sermons of Chromatius of Aquileia, 388–407", *Church History*, 83 (2014), 273–296; *Arianism: Roman Heresy and Barbarian Creed*, ed. Guido Berndt and Roland Steinacher (Aldershot: Ashgate, 2014).

6 *S. Gregorii Magni registrum epistolarum*, ed. D. Norberg, 2 vols (CC Series Latina 140 and 140a, Turnhout: Brepols 1982). All translations from *The Letters of Gregory the Great*, tr. John R. C. Martyn, 3 vols (1—Books 1–4; 2—Books 5–9; 3—Books 10–14) (Toronto: PIMS, 2004): the numeration of letters in this volume varies slightly from the Norberg edition. See also *Gregorio Magno e le origini dell'Europa: Atti del convegno internazionale, Firenze, 13–17 maggio 2006*, ed. C. Leonardi (Firenze: All'Insegna del Giglio, 2014).

7 Kalani L. Craig, "Bishops and balancing acts: divine and human agency in Gregory of Tours's vision of episcopal authority", in *Envisioning the Bishop: Images and the Episcopacy in the Middle Ages*, ed. Sigrid Danielson and Evan Gatti (Turnhout: Brepols, 2014), 63–90.

8 Explored in *Sicilia e Italia suburbicaria tra IV e VII secolo: Atti del convegno di studi (Catania, 24–27 ottobre, 1989)*, ed. S. Pricoco, F. Rizzo Nervo and T. Sardella (Soveria Mannelli [CZ]: Rubbettino, 1991). The following centuries would see this resource diminished: Vivien Prigent, "Les empereurs isauriens et la confiscation des patrimoines pontificaux d'Italie du sud", *MEFRM*, 116 (2004), 557–594.

9 *Scribendi ad excellentiam vestram si causa omnino suppeteret, nos tamen esse oportet caritate paterna de vestrae salutis incolomitate sollicitos, ut, quod de vobis audire cupimus, internuntiorum frequentia cognoscamus.*

10 Richard M. Pollard, "A cooperative correspondence: the letters of Gregory the Great", in *A Companion to Gregory the Great*, ed. Bronwen Neil and Matthew Dal Santo (Leiden: Brill, 2013), 291–314.

11 The *Variae* of Cassiodorus are online at The Latin Library http://www.thelatinlibrary.com/cassiodorus.html [accessed 22 May 2016]. English translations include: *Cassiodorus: Variae*, tr. S. J. B. Barnish (Liverpool: Liverpool UP, 1992); *The Letters of Cassiodorus*, tr. Thomas Hodgkin (London: Henry Frowde, 1886), online at Project Gutenberg http://www.gutenberg.org/files/18590/18590-h/18590-h.htm#CONTENTS [accessed 22 May 2016].

12 On this see Adam Schor, "Becoming bishop in the letters of Basil and Synesius: tracing patterns of social signaling across two full epistolary collections", *Journal of Late Antiquity*, 7.2 (2014), 298–328. The entire issue of the journal is dedicated to late antique letter writing.

13 On the "Justinianic plague", Peter Sarris, "The Justinianic plague: origins and effects", *Continuity and Change*, 17 (2002), 169–182; O. J. Benedictow, "The Justinianic plague pandemic: progress and problems", *Early Science and*

Medicine, 14 (2009), 543–548; Dionysius Stathakopoulos, *Famine and Pestilence in the Late Roman and Early Byzantine Empire* (Aldershot: Ashgate, 2003); *id.*, "The Justinianic plague revisited", *Byzantine and Modern Greek Studies*, 24 (2000), 256–276, reprinted in *The Formation of Classical Islam 1: Late Antiquity on the Eve of Islam*, ed. A. Cameron (Farnham: Ashgate, 2013), 87–108; Nancy Benovitz, "The Justinianic plague: evidence from the dated Greek epitaphs of Byzantine Palestine and Arabia", *Journal of Roman Archaeology*, 27 (2014), 487–498.

14 *Pauli Diaconi Historia Langobardorum*, II.4, ed. L. Bethmann and Georg Waitz, *MGH Scriptores Rerum Langobardorum*, (Hannover: Hahn, 1878), 45–187, at 74.

15 This unusual move, linking an island see to one on the mainland, is discussed by Jeffrey Richards, *Consul of God: the Life and Times of Gregory the Great* (Abingdon and New York: Routledge, 1980), 10–11.

16 E.g. R. A. Davies, "The effect of the Black Death on the parish priests of the medieval diocese of Coventry and Lichfield", *Historical Research*, 62 (1989), 85–90.

17 Mariano dell'Omo, "A proposito dell'esilio romano dei monaci cassinesi dopo la distruzione longobarda di Montecassino", in *Montecassino: Dall prima alla seconda distruzione*, ed. D. Faustino Avagliano (Montecassino, 1987), 485–512.

18 He was less impressed with Fortunatus bishop of Fano's request to sell church plate to raise ransoms (VII.13, November 596), or the sale of vessels from Italy in Sicily (VIII.26). In other cases, however, Gregory allowed church assets to be used, as in a case at Messina in July 597 under Bishop Donus (VII.35). Bishop Felix of Siponto is also charged with delaying helping those who had ransomed themselves from captivity (IV.17).

19 Emanuela Prinzivalli, "Gregorio Magno e le eresie", in *Gregorio Magno*, ed. Leonardi, 101–112.

20 Ostrogoths: T. S. Brown, "The role of Arianism in Ostrogothic Italy: the evidence from Ravenna", in *The Ostrogoths: from the Migration Period to the 6th Century*, ed. S. J. Barnish and F. Marazzi (Woodbridge: Boydell, 2007), 417–426. Lombards: Marilynn Dunn, "Lombard religiosities reconsidered: "Arianism", syncretism and the transition to Catholic Christianity", in *Heresy and the Making of European Culture*, ed. A. Roach and J. Simpson (Farnham: Ashgate, 2013), 89–112; Piero Majocchi, "'Arrianorum abolevit heresem': the Lombards and the ghost of Arianism", in *Arianism*, ed. Berndt and Steinacher, 231–238.

21 See, on this, Bruno Judic, "Grégoire le grand et les juifs: pratique juridique et enjeux theologiques", and David M. Freidenreich, "Jews, pagans and heretics in early medieval canon law", both in *Jews in Early Christian Law: Byzantium and the Latin West, 6th to 11th Centuries*, ed. John Tolan and Nicholas de Lange (Turnhout: Brepols, 2014), 95–118 and 73–94 respectively.

22 Again, not just a concern in Italy: Brian Brennan, "*Episcopae*: bishops' wives viewed in sixth-century Gaul", *Church History*, 54 (1985), 311–323. As Giorgio Otranto points out, however, the presence of female partners in the Byzantine South may also have shaded into actual liturgical functions: "Note sul sacerdozio femminile nell'antichità in margine a una testimonianza di Gelasio I", *Vetera Christianorum*, 19 (1982), 341–360, translated in full into English by Mary Ann Rossi, "Priesthood, precedent, and prejudice: on recovering the women priests of early Christianity", *Journal of Feminist Studies in Religion*, 7 (1991), 73–94, at 86–87.

23 In November 594 a visitor was appointed to the Agrigento diocese (Peter, bishop of Triocala) (V.12).

24 J. A. Eidenschink, *The Election of Bishops in the Letters of Gregory the Great* (Washington DC, 1946) remains the only monograph-length study; see also Peter

van Nuffelen, "Episcopal succession in Sicily during the 6th century AD", in *Zwischen Ideal und Wirklichkeit: Herrschaft auf Sizilien von der Antike bis zum Spätmittelalter*, ed. D. Engels, L. Geis and M. Kleu (Wiesbaden: Franz Steiner, 2010), 189–200; *Episcopal Elections in Late Antiquity*, ed. Johan Leemans (Berlin: de Gruyter, 2011) and, for an example of how bishops interfered in the election of others, Maurizio Tagliaferri, "L'arcivescovo Mariniano di Ravenna e l'elezione di Massimo di Salona", in *La chiesa metropolitana ravennate e i suoi rapporti con la costa adriatica orientale*, ed. M. Tagliaferri (Imola: University Press Bologna, 2005), 75–82.

25 Urban factionalism, highlighted by Tom Brown in his "Urban violence in early medieval Italy: the cases of Rome and Ravenna", in *Violence and Society in the Early Medieval West*, ed. Guy Halsall (Woodbridge: Boydell, 1998), 76–89, has received much more attention in an eastern, Byzantine context, e.g., Michael Whitby, "Factions, bishops, violence and urban decline", in *Die Stadt in der Spätantike: Niedergang oder Wandel*, ed. C. Witschel and J.-U. Krause (Munich, 2006), 441–462; Umberto Roberto, "The circus factions and the death of the tyrant: John of Antioch on the fate of the emperor Phocas", in *Byzanz: das Römerreich in Mittelalter*, 3 vols, ed. Falko Daim and Jörg Drauschke (Mainz/Regensburg, 2010), I, 55–77.

26 The delicate political balance extended beyond the time of Gregory of course: L. A. Berto, "'Utilius est veritatem proferre'. A difficult memory to manage: narrating the relationships between bishops and dukes in early medieval Naples", *Viator,* 39 (2008), 49–63.

27 Although there is little charter evidence this early, Naples' economic life has been illuminated by archaeological investigation: Paul Arthur, *Naples: from Roman Town to City-State* (London: British School at Rome, 2002) and *id.*, "Naples: a case of urban survival in the early Middle Ages", *MEFRM*, 103 (1991), 759–784; to which should now be added *Napoli, la città e il mare: Piazza Bovio tra romani e bizantini*, ed. Daniela Giampaola (Milan: Electa, 2010).

28 *Gesta Episcoporum Neapolitanorum*, part I, 22, ed. G. Waitz, in *MGH SSRLI* (Hanover, 1878), 413–414.

29 Thomas Granier, "L'hagiographie napolitaine du haut Moyen Âge: context, corpus et enjeux", *Bulletin du CRISIMA*, 2 (2001), 13–40, consulted online at http://www.rmoa.unina.it/1097/1/RM-Granier-Hagiographie.pdf [accessed 20/11/17]. Granier has written extensively on the city's early medieval religious life, in particular "Lieux de mémoire, lieux de culte à Naples aux Ve-Xe siècles", in *Faire mémoire: Souvenir et commémoration au Moyen Âge*, ed. C. Carozzi and H. Taviani-Carozzi (Aix-en-Provence: Université de Provence, 1999), 63–101.

30 Berto, "Utilius"; Thomas Granier, "La difficile genèse de l'Histoire des évêques de Naples (milieu du IXe-début du Xe siècle: le scriptorium et la famille des évêques", in *Liber, Gesta, Histoire. Actes du colloque international*, ed. François Bougard and Michel Sot (Turnhout, 2009), 265–282.

31 Contextualising such orders: Giorgio Otranto, "Cristianizzazione del territorio, comunità locali e culti fino a Gregorio Magno tra sviluppi spontanei e spinte centralizzatrici", in *Chiese locali e chiese regionali nell'alto medioevo: Settimane di studio del CISAM*, 61, 2 vols (Spoleto: CISAM, 2014), I, 51–112. On the issue of what Gregory thought saints were meant to *do*, see Matthew Dal Santo, *Debating the Saints' Cults in the Age of Gregory the Great* (Oxford: Oxford University Press, 2012).

32 *Grégoire le Grand, Dialogues*, ed. A. de Vögué, 3 vols (Sources Chrétiens, 251, 260, 265, Paris, 1978–80), II, 284–6, 278–84 and 272–4 respectively; Gregory the Great, *Dialogues*: adapted English translation at Tertullian.org [accessed 20/12/18].

33 Giorgia Vocino, "Bishops in the mirror: from self-representation to episcopal model. The case of the eloquent bishops, Ambrose of Milan and Gregory the Great", in *Religious Franks: Religion and Power in the Frankish Kingdoms. Studies in Honour of Mayke de Jong*, ed. Rob Meens *et al.* (Manchester, 2016), 331–349, pre-print version at http://epub.oeaw.ac.at/0xc1aa5576%200x0039071b.pdf [accessed 20/12/18].
34 Christopher Hanlon, "Gregory the Great and Sicily: an example of continuity and change in the late sixth century", in *The Bishop of Rome in Late Antiquity*, ed. Geoffrey D. Dunn (Farnham, 2016), 197–215, at 198.
35 Otranto "Note", quoted in Rossi, "Priesthood", 85.

16 Before the Venetians? Evidence for slave trading out of Italy, 489–751[1]

Thomas J. MacMaster

Not long after I had first arrived at the University of Edinburgh in September 2010, Tom Brown mentioned an article that had a provocative take (and a terrible title): "New Light on the Dark Ages" as well as Michael McCormick's much longer book, *The Origins of the European Economy*.[2] I read these on his suggestion with great attention as McCormick seemed to make a compelling case that the export of humans was one of the keys for the emergence of Venice as a commercial power in the later eighth century and that that slave trade played a crucial role in the development of the European economy itself. Certainly, it was a novel argument and, over the next few months and then years, we picked some of those ideas apart while finding many of them not completely wrong.

Of course, I am far from the only person to have responded as both those scholars who see slavery and the slave trade as significant in the medieval world and those who see it as economically marginal have found much to critique in McCormick's work. Some, like Daniel Melleno and Matthew Delvaux, have taken McCormick's arguments on the importance of the slave trade as a given and explicitly extended them northwards into other circuits of trade.[3] Other readers, though, have placed important limitations on McCormick's ideas. While Joachim Henning has argued that McCormick is mistaken on the idea of western European involvement in supplying European slaves to the Arab market,[4] David Wyatt argues that McCormick's basic hypotheses externalises the demand for slaves (and hence the economic rationale for slave raiding) as something outside of western Europe.[5] More recently, Alice Rio has emphasised the unimportance of the Carolingian state to any significant long-distance slave trade as well as the relatively minor role of slavery within those core territories.[6]

Most of these critiques and expansions though look at the period after 750. So, perhaps, it might be worth adding two further refinements. Both, it should be emphasised at the outset, are somewhat speculative and, like McCormick's own piece itself, are handicapped by a very limited number of written sources and by archaeological data that can, in most cases, only be considered ambiguous at best.

McCormick's argument that a Venetian-dominated slave trade in the mid-eighth century was something new emerging virtually from nothing may not be as strong as it initially seemed. It presupposes both a general dearth of Mediterranean slave trading in the previous century and the non-involvement of Italy in what little trade there was. This would appear to be a rather weak argument in light of both some unfortunately fragmentary evidence from Italy itself, particularly from the sixth century, and the large-scale movements eastward of slaves from Africa in the seventh and eighth centuries.

Life in Italy in the four centuries between Theodosius's death and Charlemagne's conquest saw a great deal of human misery and the repeated breakdown of order. Capture of both soldiers and civilians during wars and invasions were, of course, a normal experience in the period. As central authority crumbled in the sixth century, it seems likely that slave raiding and the movement of captives played a not insignificant role in the steady increase in disorder. Those processes in themselves would have contributed to the further decline of both urban and rural life.

Even in the apparent tranquil respite of Ostrogothic-ruled Italy, though, Italians were themselves entering slavery even without warfare. Poverty had driven parents to sell their own children throughout the Roman era. Though it had been clearly illegal under Roman law for Roman citizens to sell their children in the second century,[7] in the fourth, Constantine had legalised it.[8] Mothers were expressly forbidden from selling their children as slaves; it remained a paternal prerogative.[9] Even then, it seems to have been something only done in difficult times; a law issued in 451 stated that freeborn children sold into slavery by their parents as result of famine were to have their freedom restored while, if the children had been sold to barbarians or shipped overseas, a fine of six ounces of gold was to be levied instead.[10]

While a prohibition in written law does not mean something did not happen, selling one's own children seems to have been seen in those years as a mark of desperation. Yet, by the early sixth century, it had become normalised in at least some areas and not seen as something worth condemning. In a letter written on behalf of King Athalaric (526–534), Cassiodorus describes a fair at Marcellianum, a suburb of the town of Consilinum in Lucania (near the modern Sala Consilina), noting among its attractions:

> There stand ready boys and girls, with the attractions that belong to their respective sexes and ages, whom not captivity but freedom sets a price upon. These are with good reason sold by their parents, since they themselves gain by their very servitude. For one cannot doubt that they are benefited even as slaves, by being transferred from the toil of the fields to the service of cities.[11]

That Cassiodorus, a high official writing on behalf of a king, seems to regard the sale of children as not merely normal but commendable shows that, in Gothic Italy at any rate, the sale of children by their parents was legal and merely part of the local colour. Presumably, these rural to urban movements of slaves were not limited to Lucania and would have been more widely practiced than evidenced.[12]

One would be hard-pressed to imagine that, if sales of formerly free children were commonplace in the reign of Athalaric, there would have been some sudden diminution of enslavements during the long, drawn-out struggle between the Ostrogoths and the armies of Justinian. Though it seems not to have been a topic of interest to Procopius, even in *De Bello* we receive a few impressions of some level of slave taking by the advancing Roman armies, as when Hildiger enslaves convalescent Goths he encountered as he advanced in Picenum.[13] Procopius places a speech into the mouth of Wittigis in which he states:

> When I reflect upon the fate of the Vandals and the end of Gelimer, the thoughts which come to my mind are of no ordinary kind; nay, I seem to see the Goths and their children reduced to slavery, your wives ministering in the most shameful of all ways to the most hateful of men, and myself and the granddaughter of Theoderic led wherever it suits the pleasure of those who are now our enemies; and I would have you also enter this battle fearing lest this fate befall us.[14]

Other evidence would also suggest that this sort of fate could be expected for Gothic women. While praising Belisarius's marital fidelity, he informs us of the vast number of beautiful Gothic and Vandal women the General owned yet largely ignored,[15] suggesting that quite large numbers of explicitly civilian Ostrogoths were enslaved during the fall of their kingdom. Later, Procopius alludes to Totila taking the possessions of Italians but leaving them their persons as though it were unusual.[16]

It appears undeniable that widespread devastation occurred across much of the Italian countryside during the Gothic Wars. The population of Italy, which had already been in general decline, seems to have fallen considerably at this time. There appears to have been a long delay before many areas returned to the level of population and of cultivation that they had known prior to the war, let alone to the levels found before the fifth century. In the surviving accounts, though, neither side seems to have pursued a deliberate policy of wreckage; both, of course, hoped to enjoy the benefits of a prosperous Italy post-war. Yet, large areas of Italy appear to have suffered catastrophic collapse.

A contributory factor might be that large numbers of Italians (both Goths and Romans) found themselves enslaved by soldiers on both sides and sold outside the peninsula and that the sale of Italians helped finance the war itself. Slavery itself seems to have been understood to be a normal outcome of warfare. As described by St. Isidore, "Slavery is called from saving. Among the ancients, they called 'slaves' them that were saved from death in war".[17] In the following century, as in many other times and places,[18] slave-taking played a considerable role in long-lasting conflict.[19] It seems not unreasonable to suggest that it, while not the primary purpose of either side during this war or the later conflicts involving the Lombards, would have played a role in shaping the nature of warfare and its impact on Italian society.

The war years were, of course, the period of the "Plague of Justinian" and the Plague is often thought to have had an enormous impact on the population of Italy and of the Mediterranean world at this time.[20] Despite the implications of some of the written sources, the material evidence does not unambiguously show signs of a notable population decline in the most urbanised and densely populated regions of the eastern Mediterranean (where it ought to have killed the most) in the decades after 542.[21] Instead, some cities appear to have been expanding and prosperous in the second half of the sixth century, while in much of the Levant, there is no significant decline in urban life until the middle of the eighth century.[22] Indeed, the latest research pushes the minimalist argument regarding the sixth-century pandemic and its impact.[23] If these findings are accepted and the plague was far less deadly than later plagues (for any of various reasons; a different prevalence of pre-existing conditions between the sixth and fourteenth centuries or other dynamics might serve as explanation), Italy's falling population needs better explanation. Similarly, if the minimalist position is wrong, a question might be posed as to why, in the aftermath of the plague, populations rebounded in some of the regions faster than normal demographics should have allowed.

In either case, the movement of significant numbers of people out of Italy, whether as willing refugees or as unwilling captives, could help to explain why Italy in the sixth century seems to have had far greater demographic decline than many other regions of the Roman world.[24] The appearance of relative demographic stability or even growth further east might also be explicable. The importation of workers into the Middle East that is known from the seventh and eighth century goes some length to explain the lack of perceptible decline in many places[25] and even appears to be something that had begun considerably earlier with large-scale population transfers from Armenia and the Persian Empire into Roman territory (including slaves as well as those who were expected to provide military service) in the time of Maurice.[26] It would be surprising if similar patterns were not already being followed in sixth-century Italy.

Whether or not a trade in Italians as slaves existed before or during the Gothic War, the invasion of the Lombards saw regular slave taking and the export of Italians as slaves. The best way to understand early medieval Italy, it has been suggested by a certain wise man,[27] is to simply read Gregory the Great's *Registrum epistularum* in their entirety; the evidence found in them would seem to make this point. The topic of slavery regularly crops up in Gregory's writings and, whether he is discussing proper discipline for paganising slaves,[28] planning the English mission,[29] or using slavery as a metaphor for his own position,[30] it clearly is something frequently present in his thoughts.

Due, perhaps, to its very ubiquity, however, Gregory rarely gives us details about the lives of slaves, the practice of slavery, or the slave trade. Sometimes, though, an intriguing detail might be mentioned. In one letter sent to the Emperor Maurice, Gregory recalls the lack of defenses against the Duchy of Spoleto. He mentions in passing that:

> After this, a heavier blow came with the arrival of Agilulf, so that, with my own eyes I saw Romans bound like dogs with ropes around their necks who were being led to Francia to be sold.[31]

Gregory, speaking apparently as an eyewitness, addresses a modern objection to the idea of an early medieval slave trade. Iron chains and collars are barely known from the archaeology of the period and, it has been suggested, that they have not been found in the archaeological record, there must not have been a slave trade on anything but a minute scale.[32] If, instead, ropes are the normal means of binding captives on the march, the lack of material evidence becomes far less problematic. Certainly, in a generally impoverished period, ropes would be far easier to obtain than iron chains and markedly less expensive.

He also shows in this letter how the continuing raiding of the Lombards was not merely destructive of the physical plant of the imperial exarchate or painful due to the killing of Romans. It would also have entailed the removal of portions of the most productive members of society; presuming similarities to other times and places, those most likely to have been removed would be young women and men, impacting the surviving communities for years to come.

Similarly, fear of slave raids might change the daily lives of rural communities. Dispersed populations might move into the apparent safety of walled cities that still possessed imperial garrisons or they might relocate to the shelter of more easily defended sites like Amalfi and Venice. Where neither was an easy option, a sense of impermanence might develop. Rather than causing demographic decline by the direct removal of people, persistent slave-raiding could easily have the same effect through an increased sense of insecurity in rural areas; this would lead to the abandonment of outlying fields and even entire settlements alongside shifts towards an increase in pastoralism. Combined with the removal of some of those in their highest years of fertility and agricultural productivity, population decline could have accelerated. A shift in settlement patterns in areas like Tuscany around the time of the Lombard invasion towards more defensible sites might be linked to these factors.[33]

This is reflected in other letters of the Pope; Gregory informed the Bishop of Messina that it was permissible under canon law to sell church utensils to redeem captives taken by the Lombards,[34] and he instructed John, the Bishop of Ravenna, to send Abbot Claudius to Fano to purchase any free men he found held there as slaves and to ransom any captives after attacks by the same Duke of Spoleto.[35]

What would have happened to those taken captive would not have all been of one piece. Some, as we have seen, were soon ransomed by church leaders or their own relatives and soon returned home. Some would have found themselves enslaved permanently within Italy. At one time, it was a commonplace that the bulk of the Roman population living under Lombard rule were either enslaved or turned into some shadowy group of unfree people like the *aldii;* that, though, seems rather unlikely at present (no matter how we define slavery).[36]

It should also not escape notice that, in the letter to Maurice, Gregory actually tells us something of the ultimate fate of these captive Italians; they are being taken to Francia, presumably to be sold. While he doesn't tell us whether they would be walked over the Alps or carried there by coastal shipping, it does suggest that the movement of slaves out of Italy was not unknown at the time; that he makes the assumption that they will be sold abroad is in itself telling. In other sources, southern Gaul (and in particular Marseille) appears as a destination for slaves and captives from Britain,[37] Italy,[38] and even beyond.[39]

Of course, the best-known story involving Pope Gregory and slavery does not come from his letters. Rather, it is in Bede's *Ecclesiastical History* where he relates (as something he knows only from oral tradition) the encounter between Gregory and the group of young Angle slaves in the Roman market that would inspire the future Pope to send a mission to the English.[40] Whether or not Gregory ever actually had the reported conversation, the idea of English slaves being sold in Rome did not surprise Bede, those he had heard this from, or his intended audience in the early eighth century. The presentation implies that everything about the story is perfectly normal; the only oddity is that this group of slaves had come from the far-off realm of Deira.

It was only a few decades after Bede wrote that another anecdote about a Roman slave market appears. In this one, found in the *Liber Pontificalis*, we find the very first appearance of Venetians as slave merchants. They have come to Rome to buy slaves in Rome. They only draw down the ire of Pope Zacharias for their intention of selling them to Muslims in Africa.[41]

While Rome figures in these incidents as a place where slaves are sold, it seems more a matter of being a convenient meeting place for merchants with their human cargoes and potential buyers rather than a home for either large-scale slave raiding or slave trading. In later ages, or so McCormick's book would suggest, Venice provided that space. Before its emergence, though, what other place might have served such a function?

The most obvious choice would be the city of Ravenna and its satellites. There, more than almost anywhere else in the western Mediterranean, maritime contact with the east was sustained throughout these centuries and, with it, an economy integrated into wider systems of exchange.[42] While much of that contact was through governmental channels, it persisted just as Ravenna endured as a city even while others declined. From the beginning of the fifth century, it was usually the primary seat of military and political power in Italy. As such, it would have been the logical destination for any captives resulting from warfare by the last western Emperors, Odoacer, or Theodoric. During the later stages of the Gothic War and throughout the nearly two-century-long struggle with the Lombards, Ravenna again was the seat of military power.

Prisoners taken by soldiers from there who were not ransomed (probably the vast majority) would have naturally ended up in the city or its environs. Some, of course, would go on to freedom and manumissions, and are represented among the surviving texts from Ravenna.[43] Many of those who did not quickly regain their freedom are likely to have found themselves as slaves within the exarchate.

The upper classes of the entire exarchate possessed large estates worked by slaves, even if not on the scale of earlier times, while domestic labour was provided by slaves in even more middling homes.[44] The Ravennan elite, of course, was no exception and, as shown by Tom Brown, it seems reasonable to presume that slaves provided much of the workforce on their properties, whether as labourers, tenants, or in other roles.[45]

Domestic labour and slavery is not especially a controversial connection; it is perhaps the most easily demonstrated in most societies where slavery has existed. Similarly, few would argue that a woman who had been purchased to provide domestic labour was not a slave. That domestic slavery existed throughout this period has seldom, if ever, been contested.

More frequently questioned, though, is the role of slavery in agriculture. Slaves—named as *serui*—appear in texts from sixth- and seventh-century Italy that show them working on land owned by those who own them. They appear to have been held as chattel but they still may not be "slaves" in the sense that we might imagine. The *Edictum Rothari* refers to *serui massarii*;[46] they appear to have lived in their own homes and tilled fields for themselves, paying some type of rent to their owners. As they held higher wergild than other slaves in that law code[47] and may themselves possess slaves of their own,[48] it is hard to picture them as being completely dependent, unlike the *serui rustici* (field slaves)[49] and *serui ministeriales* (household slaves)[50] that appear in the same laws. These *serui massarii* might be imagined then as something more like serfs; as tenants and slaves, they seem, in our usual modes of thought, to be neither quite one or the other.

While the origins of unfree tenants as a group is intensely problematic from a historiographic perspective, for the present purposes a better question is whether their number would have been reinforced from those captured in war and raiding. It seems reasonable to think that the answer would be something like "seldom" but that is at best a guess. More likely, though, enslaved captives would have found themselves in those other categories of household and field slaves working not as tenant farmers but directly in either the homes or the unleased fields of their owners. Those slaves might be supervised by still other, more privileged slaves. This is the sort of scenario Agnellus appears to be referencing in his account of John III (606–625).[51]

Indirect evidence is also possible. It was at one time argued that evidence of manumission suggested a dying out of slavery, the general correlation appears to be between high rates of manumission and large numbers of people entering into slavery as freed slaves were more easily replaced.[52] That there were at least some manumission of people like Bilesarius, Sisivera, and Secundus happening in Ravenna[53] implies that slaves were widely available under the Exarchs, even if direct evidence is lacking.

But did those officers support their genteel life by actually selling some of their captives onwards? While there is no explicit evidence for against, it would seem altogether likely that at least some of the ships leaving from Classe for the south and east carried the occasional human cargo. Under the emperors from Justinian to Heraclius, their destinations would have been over a wide area and, unfortunately, relatively hard to trace. Some of the goods shipped in return would undoubtedly be among those that have left archaeological traces but, again, it is impossible to determine which of those came for other reasons. Without explicit written evidence, slave trades can be nearly impossible to trace.

It might be possible, though, to find some suggestive evidence that, after the Empire had lost Syria, Egypt, and, eventually, North Africa to the Arabs, the Ravennati, like the later Venetians, maintained trading relationships with some of those areas. Enrico Cirelli has reported the discovery of amphorae in Classe that appear to date from the last century of the Exarchate.[54] These appear to have been produced in the Levant but what is particularly arresting about them is that they have some of the earliest Arabic epigraphic remains found in Europe. Dating as they do prior to the general adoption of Arabic by non-Muslims in coastal Syria and Palestine, it seems plausible that, prior to their arrival at their final resting place, they had passed through Muslim hands. The ships that brought them are unlikely to have originated in Roman-ruled ports or to have returned to such. Rather, these (and many less easily identifiable or ephemeral objects) are likely to have been brought by merchants either visiting from or returning to the now-Muslim ruled parts of the Mediterranean.

Ravenna and Classe, of course, are not the only places that were the sites of significant exchange in their region. Just a short distance away, Comacchio seems to have developed as a place relatively free from Roman law as the older towns' harbours silted up during the seventh century.[55] As a liminal site between the exarchate and the Lombard kingdom, it would have been an ideal place for the sale of unransomed captives of the Lombards to merchants based within the Roman empire or even further afield. This might, perhaps, have been one of the destinations of the sorts of prisoners Gregory the Great had observed, if they were to be exported out of Italy. Of course, it should be borne in mind that Comacchio, while significant in the scope of its geographic connections, was by no means a large place in itself, something that can be seen as indicative of the rather underdeveloped state of the Lombard economy.[56]

The militarised elites of both the Lombard states and the remaining Roman enclaves preyed aggressively upon civilian populations in enemy territories. Neither group developed mass-slaveholding economies; the very nature of their societies probably precluded it. Both also continued to import luxury goods from abroad, even if in much smaller amounts than had been known in earlier periods. Both seem to have found these captives to be a worthwhile product to exchange for other commodities even as they kept some portion for their own uses. Ravenna and its satellite ports would have been the centre of these longer-distance slave-trading networks in northern and eastern Italy.

These networks, of course, would have been relatively small scale and subsidiary to other economic activities. Even if insignificant, they were active well before the middle of the eighth century and might even stretch back at least to the fifth century. After the first decades of the seventh century, though, the evidence for continued exports from Italy itself becomes significantly less common than what it had been in the previous century. This might be due to no more complicated of a reason than the chance survival of evidence or to the lowered level of warfare in the peninsula. A third possibility is that, during the crises of the reign of Heraclius, both maritime trade and east Mediterranean demand for slaves may have been negatively impacted and, when demand returned, a vast new reservoir of slaves had appeared in North Africa from the middle of the century onwards.[57] Similarly, the general disorder and continuing decline of an already depressed Italian economy is unlikely to have encouraged otherwise unknown trade.

The new pattern does, however, seems to have broken down in its turn in the middle of the eighth century, a break that was recognised by McCormick. What exactly that was that drove the shift is, I believe, not as simple as the end of the plague cycle of the previous two centuries or even the slowing of Muslim expansion as he has suggested.[58]

There had been significant change in the slave trade within the Islamic empire in the middle of the eighth century. In North Africa, treaties had been imposed on many Berber communities when they were first defeated by the invading Arab forces that stipulated both conversion to Islam and that the converts would be obligated to provide human as tribute to the new rulers. The scale of this seems to have been massive and,[59] by the end of the seventh century, North Africa figures almost exclusively in Arabic accounts as a place for the export of labour with even religious scholars sent there depicted as exporting slaves to the eastern lands.[60] North Africans were also playing a key role in the gathering of slaves for shipment eastwards, whether brought northwards across the Sahara or southwards from raids on the Christian lands to the north,[61] patterns that would remain strong in the 'Abbasid era.[62]

The tributes of slaves imposed in the conquest were seen as especially onerous by newly converted Muslims, particularly those communities unable to meet their obligations by raiding Christian and pagan populations within the Maghreb or in trading across the Sahara and forced to give over their own members. The renewed enforcement of slave tributes by 'Ubayd Allāh ibn al-Habhab in 739 sparked growing discord among African Muslims.[63] In Tangier, an attempt to enslave a fifth of the Muslim population of the city itself sparked the Berber rising that would lead to the creation of the first Muslim state outside the control of the Caliphate as the rebels embraced Islam in its Kharijite form, asserting that the authorities were not upholding the religion.[64]

The Berber revolt meant that the easy tribute of slaves from North Africa had declined, if not quite disappeared. When al-Mansūr became Caliph in 754, the governor of Ifrīqīya refused to send the customary tribute of slaves as part of his oath of loyalty, explaining that, as Ifrīqīya was now completely Muslim, slaves could no longer be exacted from it.[65] Two years later, the de facto independence of al-'Andalus under the Umayyad ʿAbd al-Raḥman ibn Muʿāwiyah similarly deprived rulers in Qayrawān and the eastern capitals of tribute in the form of Spanish captives.

These political changes may have been as significant as the general cessation of military expansion and the end of the plague cycles in the revival of a commercial slave trade in the early 'Abbasid era. Regardless of what had caused the increase in demand for slaves on the Islamic side of the Mediterranean, McCormick has demonstrated that there was an apparent uptick in evidence for an export of humans from Italy in the middle of the eighth century with some number of identifiably Muslim merchants coming to Italy to purchase slaves.

More or less simultaneously, it seems, Italian merchants began again crossing the Mediterranean, taking with them their own cargoes of slaves. Whether this was an expansion of an already established trade or a restoration of it is not entirely clear and probably never will be. The volume of slaves exported from Italy in the years between 489 and 751, it is probably safe to say, was never as high as it would soon become. However, it seems likely that this trade had a long "prehistory" before the Venetians became the dominant middlemen. It should be remembered that, until the middle of the ninth century, it would appear that most of the slaves sold by Italian merchants originated within Italy itself; only after 840 do they seem to have begun to rely increasingly on sources of slaves along the Dalmatian coast or brought southwards over the Alps.

Amalfi[66] and Venice[67] appear to emerge as significant participants in Mediterranean trade and Venice became the major trading centre in the upper Adriatic in the middle of the eighth century. Neither city possessed a great natural harbour; both had been established by refugees on marginal sites that would not have drawn visitors to them in earlier times. Instead, the Amalfitans and Venetians built their own boats and took their products to the buyers rather than waiting for ships that might never come. That difference between a passive and an active trade proved crucial in giving them the responsibility for the eventual revival of European trade as Michael McCormick has shown and seems inarguable. That humans were, at the very least, one of the products that they carried and sold also seems inarguable. Based on present evidence, though, it cannot be clearly stated that slaves were the most vital of products for them.

Indeed, McCormick's argument that the emergence of Venice as a trading centre was in direct response to a surge in demand for slaves within the Caliphate after the end of recurring plagues seems rather unlikely. Though that may have been a contributory factor, the increased demand for slaves imported into the Islamic empire seems to have been driven by the collapse of the slave-tribute system in North Africa. This increase in demand coincided with a simultaneous change within Italy that, perhaps, played a more significant role in the change of trading patterns.

The final conquest of Ravenna by the Lombards under Aistulf in 751 might have been more significant for the rise of Venice than any other event. Ravenna's role as the primary face of imperial interests in Italy disappeared as did its easy connections to the remainder of the empire. Its satellites could no longer function as ports on the edges of two different societies; they could no longer prosper as the places of not-always licit exchange. Those roles shifted northwards to Venice, a self-governing even if nominally still imperial toehold. If so, then Venice merely took the place of Ravenna and its satellites as a place for buying slaves; to whatever extent we imagine that trade as being (whether merely incidental or as a significant system of exchange), it would have been one that was continuous, with only a change in venue. What did change, though, was that, in its new home, the Venetians themselves, unlike the Ravennati, went out seeking new markets rather than waiting for others to come to them. That, while more pedestrian than other theories, is the crucial change. Changes in demand for slaves in the east, while giving opportunity for the Venetians, was not the primary factor.

Notes

1 This chapter is directly inspired by a great many conversations with T. S. Brown over the course of the past eight years. When I was working under him on a doctoral dissertation on the early medieval slave trade, other scholars would regularly ask why I spoke so little of Italy. This chapter is, at least in part, an answer to that. During the time I was his student (something I continue to think of myself as), not only did I learn immense amounts regarding the world of the first millennium and how to ask the questions to which I wanted to find answers, but I also learned a perhaps greater amount about how to be a scholar and a human being directly from him. Thanks also to Michael McCormick who read over and commented on an earlier version of this chapter and was exceedingly generous and helpful (if not outright enthusiastic) to a junior scholar suggesting he might have been in error.

2 M. McCormick, "New Light on the 'Dark Ages", *Past & Present,* 17–54; *Origins of the European Economy: Communications and Commerce, AD 300–900,* (Cambridge, 2001).

3 See D. Melleno, *Before They Were Vikings: Scandinavia and the Franks up to the death of Louis the Pious,* (Unpublished PhD Dissertation, University of California-Berkeley, 2014) with its partial goal of extending the discussion begun

by McCormick into the North Sea and Baltic as well as M. Delvaux, *Unwilling Journey: Human Trafficking in the Viking World, ca. 700–950 CE* (forthcoming).

4 J. Henning, "Slavery or Freedom? The causes of early medieval Europe's economic advancement", *Early Medieval Europe,* 12:3 (2003), 269–277: Henning argues that whatever west Europeans ended up as slaves in Muslim lands were much more likely to be the victims of Muslim and Byzantine pirates than of European merchants.

5 D. Wyatt, *Slaves and Warriors in Medieval Britain and Ireland: 800–1200,* (Leiden, 2009), 20–23.

6 A. Rio, *Slavery After Rome,* (Oxford, 2017), 24–28.

7 *Codex Iustinianus,* P. Krueger, ed., (Berlin, 1906), 7.16.1.

8 *CJ,* 4.43.2. The expansion of Roman citizenship appears to have made the former ban increasingly problematic.

9 *CJ,* 2.4.26.

10 *Novellae* Valentinian III, 33.1 in *Codex Theodosiani Libri XVI cum Constitutionibus Sirmondianis et Leges Novellae ad Theodosianum Pertinentes*, T. Mommsen and P. Meyer, eds., 3 vols., (Berlin, 1962).

11 Cassiodorus, *Variae,* 8.33.4: *praesto sunt pueri ac puellae diuerso sexu atque aetate conspicui, quos non fecit captiuitas esse sub pretio, sed libertas: hos merito parentes uendunt, quoniam de ipsa famulatione proficiunt. Dubium quippe non est seruos posse meliorari, qui de labore agrorum ad urbana seruitia transferuntur.*

12 It might be objected that the *Edictum Theoderici* explicitly legislated that children were not to be punished for the error of their parents and that the parents had the right to reclaim their children (Edictum Theoderici, 94). Whether or not Cassiodorus was aware of that, of course, depends on which Theoderic is presumed to have been involved in the legislative process. S. W. Lafferty, *Law and Society in the Age of Theoderic the Great: A Study of the Edictum Theoderici,* (Cambridge, 2013), 159–160, sees it as an Ostrogothic law code (which Cassiodorus would have had a hand in composing) and finds them as mutually supportive.

13 Procopius, *De Bello,* 6.18.1 (in Procopius, *Complete Works*, H B Dewing, ed. and trans., 7 vols., (Cambridge, MA, 1913–1928).

14 Procopius, *De Bello,* 5.29.8; trans. Dewing, vol. 3, 137–139 (original: Ἐννοοῦντά με δὲ τό τε Βανδίλων πάθος καὶ τὸ τοῦ Γελίμερος τέλος οὐδὲν εἰσέρχεται μέτριον, ἀλλὰ Γότθους μὲν ὁρᾶν μοι δοκῶ ξὺν τοῖς παισὶ δεδουλωμένους, γυναῖκας δὲ ὑμετέρας ἀνδράσιν ἐχθίστοις τὰ πάντων αἴσχιστα ὑπηρετούσας, ἐμαυτὸν δὲ ἀγόμενον καὶ τὴν τῆς Θευδερίχου θυγατρὸς παῖδα ὅπη ποτὲ τοὺς νῦν πολεμίους ἀρέσκει· ταῦτα βουλοίμην ἂν καὶ ὑμᾶς ὅπως μὴ προσπέσωσι δείσαντας ἐς μάχην τήνδε καθίστασθαι.)

15 Procopius, *De Bello*, 7.1.12.

16 Procopius, 7.31.24.

17 Isidore, *Etymologiae*, 5.27.32: Seruitus a seruando uocata. Apud antiquos enim qui in bello a morte seruabantur, serui uocabantur.

18 For the Romans, see the remarks by W. V. Harris, "Towards a Study of the Roman Slave Trade", *Memoirs of the American Academy in Rome*, Vol. 36, The Seaborne Commerce of Ancient Rome: Studies in Archaeology and History (1980), 121–123; the major role of the northern barbarians in supplying slaves to the Empire has been noted by N. Lenski, "Captivity, Slavery, and Cultural Exchange between Rome and the Germans from the First to the Seventh Century CE", in C. M. Cameron, ed., *Invisible Citizens: Captives and their consequences,* (Salt Lake City, 2008), 82–85 while the same author discusses similar dynamics along the eastern frontier (N. E. Lenski, "Captivity and Slavery among the Saracens in Late Antiquity (ca. 250–630 CE)", *Antiquité Tardive,* 19 (2011), 237–266). These activities all presume low-level and endemic warfare as a natural

source for slaves. Similar dynamics are observable in West Africa during the height of the Atlantic slave trade; both external and civil wars within the Kingdom of Kongo were fueled by the sale of captives (see L. M. Heywood, "Slavery and Its Transformation in the Kingdom of Kongo: 1491–1800", *Journal of African History,* 50:1 (2009), 1–22, and J. Thornton, "Demography and History in the Kingdom of Kongo, 1550–1750", *Journal of African History,* 18:4 (1977), 507–530.

19 See T. J. MacMaster, "Not With a Bang? The Economics of Trade and the End of Byzantine North Africa", M. Lau, C. Franchi, and M. Di Rodi, eds., *Landscapes of Power* (Oxford, 2014), 73–91.

20 J. C. Russell, "That Earlier Plague", *Demography.* 5:1, (1968), 181–183.

21 J. Durliat, "La Peste du VIe Siècle: Pour un Nouvel Examinen des Sources Byzantins", in Zech, ed., *Hommes et Richesses dans l'Empire Byzantin: 1, IVe–VIIe Siècles,* (Paris, 1989), 107–119. See n.23.

22 C. Foss, "Syria in Transition, A. D. 550–750: An Archaeological Approach", *DOP,* 51 (1997), 260.

23 L. Mordechai and M. Eisenberg, "Rejecting Catastrophe: The Case of the Justinianic Plague", *Past & Present*, 244:1 (2019), 3–50; L. Mordechai, M. Eisenberg, T. P. Newfield, A. Izdebski, J. E. Kay, and H. Poinar, "The Justinianic Plague: An inconsequential pandemic?" *Proceedings of the National Academy of the Sciences,* 116:51, (December 17, 2019), 25546–25554.

24 The same explanation posed here might also be an explanation for significant declines in sub-Roman populations in lowland Britain and the upper Balkans during the same era. However, this is, again, quite speculative.

25 M. Morony, "'For Whom Does the Writer Write?' The First Bubonic Plague Pandemic According to Syriac Sources", in L. K. Little, ed., *Plague and the End of Antiquity,* (Cambridge, 2007), 85. See L. Mordechai and M. Eisenberg, "Rejecting Catastrophe: The Case of the Justinianic Plague", particularly at 26 for a summary of current research on this point.

26 Evagrius Scholasticus, *Historia Ecclesiastica,* J. Bidez and L. Parmentier, eds., G. Sabbah, A. J. Festugière, and B. Grillet, trans., *Histoire Ecclésiastique,* 2 vols., (Paris, 2011–2014), 5.19; Sebeos, *Patmut'iwn Sebeosi,* T. Greenwood, trans., *The Armenian History Attributed to Sebeos,* (Liverpool, 1999), 86–87; Theophylact Simocatta, *Historiae,* C. de Boor and P. Wirth, eds., (Stuttgart, 1972), 3.15.15; Theophanes, *Chronographia,* C. de Boor, ed., (Bonn, 1839), 253–258.

27 T. S. Brown.

28 Gregory the Great, *Registrum Epistulae,* P. Ewald and L. Hartmann, eds., *MGH, Epistularum, I–II, Gregorii I Papae Registri,* (Berlin, 1881–1899), 9.205.

29 Gregory the Great, *Registrum Epistulae,* 6.10.

30 Servus servorum dei.

31 Gregory the Great, *Registrum Epistulae* 5.36: *post hoc plaga grauior fuit aduentus Agilulfi, ita ut oculis meis cernerem Romanos more canum in collis funibus ligatos, qui ad Franciam ducebantur uenales.*

32 See J. Henning, "Strong Rulers—Weak Economy? Rome, the Carolingians and the Archaeology of Slavery in the First Millennium AD", in Jennifer Davis & Michael McCormick (Eds*), The Long Morning of Medieval Europe. New Directions in Early Medieval Studies* (Aldershot: 2008) 38–45.

33 R. Francovich and R. Hodges, *Villa to Village,* (London, 2003), 67.

34 Gregory the Great, *Registrum Epistulae,* 7.35.

35 Gregory the Great, *Registrum Epistulae* 2.38.

36 Found in many Lombard laws (*Edictum Rothari,* 28, 76–102, 126–127, 129, 205, 208, 210, 216–219, 235, 244, 258, 376–377; *Leges Grimwaldi,* 1; *Leges Liutprandi,* 60, 66, 68–9, 78, 87, 97, 106, 111, 120–121, 124–126, 132, 139–40, 142–143, 147;

Leges Ratchis, 7), T. Hodgkin (*Italy and Her Invaders*, vol. vi [Oxford, 1896], 586 ff.) considered them to be the majority of the former Roman population; beyond that they were neither fully free nor fully enslaved, little can be said with certainty about their origins.

37 Gregory the Great, *Registrum Epistulae* 6.10.

38 Paul the Deacon, *Historia Langobardorum,* L. C. Bethmann and G. Waitz, eds., *MGH, Scriptores Rerum Langobardicum et Italicarum, saec. VI–IX,* (Hannover, 1878), 12–187, 5.1.

39 Venantius Honorius Clementianus Fortunatus, *Vita Sancti Germani Urbis Parisiacae Episcopi,* B. Krusch, ed., *MGH, SRM, VII, Passiones vitaeque sanctorum aevi Merovingici (V), (*Hannover, 1920), 372–418, 72; Dado of Rouen, *Vita Eligii Episcopi Noviomagensis,* B. Krusch, ed., *MGH, SRM, IV, Passione. Vitaeque Sanctorum Aevi Merovingici,* (Hannover, 1902), 663–741, 1.10.

40 Bede, *Historia Ecclesiastica Gentis Anglorum,* J. E. King, ed. and trans., *Baedae Opera Historica,* (Cambridge, MA, 1930), 2.1

41 *Liber Pontificalis,* L. Duchesne, ed. and trans, *Le Liber Pontificalis,* 3 vols., (Paris, 1955–1957), 1.433.

42 R. Francovich and R. Hodges, *Villa to Village,* (London, 2003), 51.

43 Brown, 204.

44 See J. Banaji, *Exploring the Economy of Late Antiquity: selected essays,* (Cambridge, 2016), 157–167.

45 T. S. Brown, *Gentlemen and Officers: Imperial Administration and Aristocratic Power in Byzantine Italy,* (Rome, 1984), 202–204.

46 *Edictum Rothari,* 132, 134, 137, 234, 352.

47 *Edictum Rothari,* 132.

48 *Edictum Rothari,* 134.

49 *Edictum Rothari,* 103–127, 134, 279–280, 378.

50 *Edictum Rothari,* 76–102, 126–127, 130–131, 376.

51 Agnellus, *Liber Pontificalis ecclesiae Ravennatis,* 104.

52 See, especially, O. Patterson, *Slavery and Social Death,* (Cambridge, MA, 1990), 209–239, and "Three Notes of Freedom: The Nature and Consequences of Manumission", in R. Brana-Shute and R. J. Sparks, eds., *Paths to Freedom: Manumission in the Atlantic World,* (Columbia, 2009), 16–30.

53 Tjäder, P. Ital 9, 12. See Brown, *Officers and Gentlemen,* 203.

54 E. Cirelli in this volume.

55 M. McCormick, "Comparing and connecting: Comacchio and the early medieval trading towns", in S. Gelichi and R. Hodges, eds., *From one sea to another. Trading places in the European and Mediterranean Early Middle ages: Proceedings of the International Conference, Comacchio 27th–29th March 2009* (Turnhout, 2012), 477–502; see also S. Gelichi, D. Calaon, E. Grandi, and C. Negrelli, "The history of a forgotten town: Comacchio and its archaeology", in the same volume, 169–207.

56 R. Hodges, *Dark Age Economics: A new audit,* (London, 2012), 110.

57 See T. J. MacMaster, *The Transformative Impact of the Slave Trade on the Roman World, 580–720,* (Unpublished PhD Thesis, University of Edinburgh, 2016), 229–263.

58 McCormick, "New Light on the 'Dark Ages'", 42–43.

59 See T. J. MacMaster, "Not With a Bang? The Economics of Trade and the End of Byzantine North Africa", M. Lau, C. Franchi, and M. Di Rodi, eds., *Landscapes of Power* (Oxford, 2014), 73–91.

60 Abu al-Abbas Ahmad ibn Muḥammad ibn Idhāri al-Marrākushi, *Kitāb al-Bayān al-Mughrib fī Ākhbār Mulūk al-Andalus wa'l-Maghrib*, I. Abbās, ed., (Beirut, 1983) 38.

61 Ibn Idhāri, 64, 70; raids on Sicily, Sardinia, and Gaul resulted in large numbers of captives.

62 During and after the Berber revolt, the Kharijite Ibāḍiyya would become dominant in the movement of slaves from the Bilād al-Sūdān, across the desert, and onwards to the core lands of the east (see E. Savage, *A Gateway to Hell, a Gateway to Paradise: The North African Response to the Arab Conquest,* (Princeton, 1997), 67–87). In addition to men used for labour, enslaved Berber and sub-Saharan African women would be sought after in ʻAbbasid Iraq (See al-Mukhtār ibn ʻAbdūn Yuhannā Ibn Buṭlān, *Risāla fī Shirā' ar-Raqīq wa-Taqlīb al-'Abīd,* A. Harun, ed., *Nawādir al-Makhṭūṭāt,* 5:15, 1954, 337–340, with its celebrated discussion of the attributes of various nationalities of slave women).

63 Abu Ja'far Muḥammad ibn Jarīr al-Tabari, *Tārīkh al-Rusul wa al-Mulūk*, M. J. de Goeje, ed., 15 vols. (Leiden, 1879–1901), 2.815–6; Ali ʻIzz al-Dīn Abu al-Hassan Ibn al-Athīr al-Matbaʻah al-Azhariyah, *al-Kāmil fī al-Tārīkh,* ed. C. J. Tornberg, 13 vols., (Leiden, 1851–1876), 3.92.

64 ʻAbd al-Rahman ibn Abdallah Ibn ʻAbd al-Ḥakam, *Futūh Misr,* C. C. Torrey, ed., *The History of the Conquest of Egypt, North Africa and Spain known as the Futūh Misr of Ibn ʻAbd al-Hakam,* (New Haven, 1922), 123.

65 Ibn Idhāri, 73.

66 A. O. Citarella, "Patterns in Medieval Trade: The Commerce of Amalfi before the Crusades", *Journal of Economic History,* 28:4, (Dec. 1968), 536.

67 McCormick, "New Light on the 'Dark Ages'", 39.

17 Urban life in Lombard Italy: Genoa and Milan compared

Ross Balzaretti

This chapter is a contribution to the ongoing debate about what constituted "the city" in Lombard-period Italy, a debate to which Tom Brown has made such a distinguished contribution with his work on Ravenna and latterly the Lombards.[1] Taking as a starting point the possible connection between Genoa and Milan posited by Paul the Deacon in his account of the flight of Bishop Honoratus from inland Milan to coastal Genoa in the face of the Lombard invasion of 3 September 569 (*Historia Langobardorum* II 25), this chapter uses a comparative methodology to make a contribution to the history of urbanisation in Lombard Italy.[2] "Lombard Italy" is a problematic phrase as gender, ethnic and political identities are all hard to pin down, even from archaeological evidence.[3] Moreover, the Lombard state was weak especially by comparison with contemporary Byzantium,[4] particularly in the first extremely unstable decades from Alboin to Agilulf (d. 616), which saw the definitive end of any functioning system of taxation.[5] Very large and complex settlements such as late imperial Milan (capital of the empire between 286 and 402 when it moved to Ravenna) need stability,[6] as provided by income from taxes, to be able to thrive and therefore the late sixth-century north Italian world of ethnic, political and military conflict, where the state had few resources, ought not on the face of it to have been one where cities could be supported. Many archaeologists have argued exactly that: Lombard Italy was essentially a rural society, of low population and its cities were merely places of the imagination.[7] Others, usually historians, have argued that it was an urbanised society but that its urban centres were poor.[8]

It will be argued here that comparison shows clearly that Milan remained a settlement of a different order to Genoa throughout the sixth to eighth centuries (when Genoa was ostensibly "Byzantine" and Milan "Lombard").[9] While the comparison is not perfect because Milan is better evidenced than Genoa, notably in the eighth century, the comparative process remains worthwhile because, first, direct comparison between cities is rare in Italian historiography which has often been dominated by local civic patriotism,[10] and second, comparing Genoa and Milan raises interesting questions about how the Lombard "state" may have operated at the regional level rather than at the supra-regional level of the kingdom.[11] Milan as former capital of an empire and not merely its own region (*Regio XI*) was different to Genoa, merely the central place of *Regio IX* (Liguria), a province within that empire albeit one substantially larger than the modern region.[12] As adjacent regions however, economic connections between them were of course to be expected, and the recent archaeology of the circulation of ceramics and soapstone has provided some evidence in support of that.[13] Milan is closer to the Mediterranean than to the Adriatic, making it possible that exchange between the inland areas and the western Mediterranean coast took place in late Antiquity as it did with the Po delta area.[14] Does this mean that Genoese and Milanese inhabitants had a residual sense of regional identity to sustain them in a world shattered by the arrival of Lombard armies in the 560s? Or did those violent political events fracture any such identity to the point where economic exchange at a regional level completely ceased? In part the answer to this depends on the degree to which northern Italy was meaningfully ruled by an effective Lombard state, which could be debated more than it is.[15] The culprit is Paul the Deacon's seductive master narrative in the *HL* with its extended sequence of seemingly effective Lombard rulers, particularly Agilulf, Grimoald and Liutprand.[16] Yet, although Lombard rulers and the aristocracy which supported them were relatively poor by both Byzantine and Frankish standards, there is evidence that they did live in cities or what they thought were cities.[17] This in turn means that subtle blending of political and economic life at urban sites was the key to their continued existence.[18]

Comparing Genoa and Milan also implies comparison between Byzantine and Lombard Italy which there is insufficient space to undertake here. It should be noted that Ravenna, Rome and Naples are all far better evidenced than Genoa, making it hard to situate the latter as a Byzantine city in any meaningful sense.[19] Any direct comparison between Ravenna and either Genoa or Milan has to remain implicit as neither place has anything approaching the depth of documentary evidence for the sixth and seventh centuries, notably the papyri, which made a book like *Gentlemen and Officers* possible.[20] While a few Lombard cities, notably Brescia, are better evidenced than Milan in that time period, the difference between them is far less great, making it possible to see Milan as a Lombard city alongside others.[21]

Establishing the connection

The *Barrington Atlas*, the definitive mapping of the ancient Greek and Roman worlds published nearly two decades ago, shows clearly that *Mediolanum* (Milan) was at the centre of a largely centuriated agricultural hinterland and was a place that was well connected via an extensive road network to neighbouring towns and cities. One of these connections was to *Genua* (Genoa), on the Mediterranean coast. It was possible to travel from Milan on the road directly south via *Ticinum* (Pavia) to *Clastidium*

(Casteggio), and then take the *Postumia* to Genoa, via the Polcevera valley.[22] Although the section between Pavia and Casteggio is less well documented than is ideal, it is in fact the only logical route between the two cities.[23] For this reason it was probably the route taken by Bishop Honoratus of Milan when he fled his city for Genoa to escape Alboin's invasion in September 568, an event which linked Milan and Genoa at the outset of the Lombard period.

The flight of Honoratus is, however, problematically documented for there is no strictly contemporary evidence, either for the bishop himself or his supposed escape to Genoa. The most influential "evidence" is from Paul the Deacon, writing his *HL* at the end of the eighth century, who reported that:

> Alboin, igitur Liguriam introiens, indictione ingrediente tertia, tertio Nonas Septembris, sub temporibus Honorati archiepiscopi Mediolanium ingressus est. Dehinc universas Liguriae civitates, praeter has quae in litore maris sunt positae, cepit. Honoratus vero archiepiscopus Mediolanium deserens, ad Genuensem urbem confugit.[24]

> Alboin, having then entered Liguria, entered Milan at the start of the third indiction, on the third day of September, at the time of Archbishop Honoratus. From then on he took all the *civitates* of Liguria, except those which are sited on the sea shore. Indeed, Archbishop Honoratus abandoning Milan fled to the city of Genoa.[25]

This passage is endlessly quoted by historians and archaeologists, especially of Genoa,[26] but its veracity is questionable because Paul's account was written two centuries after the event and uncorroborated in any other source.[27] It has to be taken on trust, despite his unusual reference to an exact date and the possibility that Paul may have learnt about Honoratus from a now lost early Milanese episcopal list or relied on the also now lost work of Secundus of Trent, a not entirely credible view given that neither text exists today.[28]

The episcopal "exile", which supposedly began in 568, ended when King Rothari conquered Genoa and other coastal settlements in the 640s. Rothari's conquest, like the flight of Honoratus, is not documented in strictly contemporary sources.[29] Fredegar writing in the 660s—so much closer in time to these events than Paul was to Honoratus—stated that Rothari reduced the coastal *civitates* to villages (*vici*) as part of his conquest of the region:

> Chrotharius cum exercito Genaua maretema, Albingano, Varicotti, Saona, Ubitergio at Lune civitates litore mares de imperio auferens vastat, rumpit, incendio concremans; populum derepit, spoliat et captivitate condemnat. Murus civitatebus supscriptis usque ad

> fundamento distruens, vicus has civitates nomenare praecepit.[30]
>
> Rothari went with his army and took from the Empire the coastal cities of Genoa, Albenga, Varigotti, Savona, Oderzo [in Friuli...] and Luni. He ravaged and destroyed them and left them in flames; and the inhabitants, stripped of their belongings, were seized and condemned to servitude. He ordered that these cities should be known as villages in future; and he razed their walls to the ground.[31]

These five places were the principal late Roman settlements on the coast so it is probably significant that Genoa is listed first implying a centralised function as capital of the area in his eyes. The other sites, listed west to east, have each been investigated by archaeologists so Fredegar's statements about fires and demolition can in fact be tested, and research at Albenga, Varigotti, Savona and Luni has indeed found evidence of burning in the seventh century (and been attributed to the Lombard attacks by excavators). It has also shown that those settlements *survived* the "conquest", which challenges the veracity of Fredegar's record,[32] questioning whether the Mediterranean coast did indeed become part of the Lombard kingdom in the 640s.[33] There is currently no archaeological evidence of the violent attack at Genoa or indeed of seventh-century walls.[34]

Lombard urbanism: archaeological evidence from Genoa and Milan

At this point it is worth reflecting on what the recent archaeology of Genoa and Milan in the first century or so of Lombard rule in Italy might tell us about life there.[35] Lombard-period Milan is reasonably well-known archaeologically, although a thorough synthesis is still lacking.[36] Genoa, less so.[37] Piera Melli's survey of the latter constructs an argument which combines archaeological with historical evidence, some of the latter of dubious worth. She stresses the difficulties of excavating in a living city where nevertheless an impressive 120 archaeological interventions were carried out between 2000 and 2015.[38] Archaeologically, there is clear evidence of continued occupation in the late sixth century. A *domus* in the centre of the old Roman town (Piazza Matteotti) was reconfigured at some point in the sixth century using *spolia* and still in use into the seventh century.[39] Thirty-three human burials within the walls have been dated to this period.[40] The port, Melli argues, continued to function as the evidence of imported pottery demonstrates, including storage jars for olive oil and fish sauce (Keay 26 type) and fine tables wares from Tunisia, the coastal areas of Palestine and Egypt and more rarely wine containers from the Balearic islands (Keay 79). Ceramics from the Lombard-occupied areas, including the Aosta valley and eastern Po plain have also been found, demonstrating exchange with inland areas.[41] As much of this pottery was found at residential sites, Melli argues that it demonstrates continued urban living, something also evident at via Mattoni Rossi in the seventh century by the importation of sand and earth to create gardens, similar to many sites in other towns at this time.[42] A sizeable rubbish dump at the Scuole Pie site containing much Mediterranean pottery and similar sites on the slopes of the Castello hill suggest continued residential use in this area in the sixth and seventh centuries.[43] Although elite residences have not been found, Melli argues (correctly) that is due to lack of evidence and does not indicate urban collapse. Regarding church buildings there is some evidence for the sixth-century phases underneath the current cathedral of San Lorenzo, which some think was built for the exiled Milanese bishops who succeeded Honoratus. There is no archaeological evidence for the early phases of any of the other churches of supposedly Milanese origins.[44] A rescue excavation at Santa Sabina in 2006 discovered early medieval walling and 23 graves nearby, probably of sixth-century date.[45] In the extra-mural area nearest to the coast (Porta della Vacca, via del Campo and vico del Campo), more pottery, wooden remains and food waste of sixth-/seventh-century date has been found, suggesting to Melli both residence here and portside activities.[46] A tile with a crude Greek name ("Rodon") was found in Piazza Santa Sabina,[47] as well as a Greek funerary inscription for the solider Magnus who died in 590, both raising the possibility of direct links with the eastern Mediterranean in this period. Evidence for some continued occupation into the eighth century has been found at Mattoni Rossi, the slopes of Castello and the cloister of San Lorenzo.[48] It is therefore plausible to see sixth- and seventh-century Genoa as an urban society which had links with the outside world, including parts of the Lombard polity.

Milan by contrast was part of the Lombard polity from an early stage and its archaeology supports that. Caterina Giostra's recent survey, which sets Milan in a comparative context with Brescia, Bergamo, Turin and elsewhere, provides a good comparison with Melli's thoughts on Genoa. Giostra argues that evidence of Lombard elites, which written sources place at Milan, can be found archaeologically at several sites in the north-western part of the city around the old Roman palace and adjacent circus. An unpublished excavation (carried out in 2013) in via Illica (outside the Roman wall near the Castello Sforzesco) revealed a sunken hut with a nearby burial and a small pottery flask which has been identified as "Lombard".[49] It is connected by Giostra with King Agilulf's activities at the old Roman *palatium* site nearby (he issued a charter from there. Another recent nearby excavation (at via Gorani and Sant Maria alla Porta) has turned up Lombard pottery, in turn linked by Giostra with the supposed foundation in the eighth century of the church of San Giorgio al Palazzo by Bishop Natalis. Near the circus, where the king's son Adaloald was acclaimed in 602 in a ceremony redolent of Byzantine court practice (see later), at the church of San Pietro *in vinea* (in via Vigna) a gold pendant cross was documented by seventeenth-century antiquarians. These finds suggest to Giostra the re-use of late antique buildings in the Lombard period, which were "ruralised" at that time. Directly north of the city at San Simpliciano a famous tile has survived with an inscription proclaiming that Agilulf and Adaloald restored the site of that basilica. Most likely in the same period a man called Marchebaldus was buried near Saint Ambrose's grave in the basilica of Sant'Ambrogio with a gold seal ring, full military equipment and a gold pectoral cross with an image of a *tremissis* of Emperor Heraclius stamped on it. A little later in the seventh century the finely worked funerary stone of Aldo, its quality suggestive of his elite status, found at the church (now demolished) of San Giovanni in Conca proclaimed his Catholicism against the nasty Arians, i.e., Kings Arioald and Rothari who moved the capital to Pavia.[50] The expensively produced sculptural decoration of the church of Santa Maria d'Aurona, probably founded by King Liutprand's sister in the early eighth century, completes Giostra's survey. Milan was clearly materially as well as politically Lombard, with good evidence for elite occupation. Genoa was clearly not part of the Lombard polity in this way, indeed there is some good evidence for Greek residents in the late sixth century and it did not become so even after Rothari's conquest, but people who lived there do seem to have interacted with the Lombards to the north at least in material terms, through importing pottery and soapstone.[51]

Urban political elites

For reasons of space, the rest of this chapter focusses on the activities of urban political elites in both cities, understanding that they had a significant influence on economic life as already suggested. The written evidence is patchy but the letters of Pope Gregory the Great document quite well the Milanese bishops of his time, who resided exclusively at Genoa, usefully evidencing both Milan and Genoa within the same texts.[52] It is conventionally stated that the bishops of Milan remained at Genoa until King Rothari conquered Genoa around 643, a few years after which bishop John "the Good" returned to Milan. As with Honoratus, the contemporary evidence for John is poor.[53] But the situation was more complex as Gregory's letters reveal that some clergy willingly remained in Milan, living under Lombard rather than Byzantine rule, for reasons of religious doctrine as well as political affiliation (the "Three Chapters" dispute) meaning that the Lombard invasion ruptured the Milanese church at least into two factions.[54] Gregory revealed relatively little about non-ecclesiastics and after Gregory's death information about interactions between the two cities is certainly much poorer until, in the case of Milan, the early eighth century when the evidence of charters proves more helpful as it reveals that the political and economic activities of Lombard aristocratic elites extended beyond individual cities.[55]

It would seem the bishops dominated "politics" in Milan rather than kings although this may merely reflect the ecclesiastical bias of the few surviving records. It is unclear exactly when a Lombard king first took control of Milan despite the seemingly transparent statement reported in a late version of the Lombard origin legend that "Then (i.e., during the initial invasion of Italy) the citizens of Pavia and the metropolis of Milan together with all the remaining cities of Italy, since they were empty as had been preordained by God, surrendered themselves to King Alboin".[56] The arrival of Alboin and his soldiers and the subsequent departure of Bishop Honoratus for Genoa in September 569 profoundly redefined existing ecclesiastical relationships both within Milan and between Milan and Genoa as before that the Genoese bishop had been a distant suffragan of the Milanese metropolitan. Paul the Deacon did not elaborate any further about Honoratus who was not mentioned in any of Gregory's letters. However, Gregory's missive to the sub-deacon John in April 593 reported that "many of the inhabitants of Milan have settled there [Genoa], forced by barbaric savagery".[57] John was instructed to visit these people in Genoa to help secure the appointment of Constantius as successor to Laurence as archbishop of Milan.[58] Genoa at this moment was still technically part of the Byzantine Empire (viz. the solider Magnus evidenced in 590 who was probably part of a local garrison) although the practical extent of its direct links with the east is hard to gauge. Genoa was certainly defendable as still-functioning forts (*castra*) at Perti in the west and (probably) Filattiera in the east formed part of the defensive *limes*.[59] Honoratus therefore made a rational decision to go to Genoa to escape contamination by anti-Catholic Lombard rule in Milan. Many Genoese historians have additionally stated that Honoratus (and the Milanese elite presumed to have accompanied him but not mentioned in Paul's account) founded the church of Sant'Ambrogio (the quintessential Milanese saint) just north of the cathedral of San Lorenzo even though this church definitely does not have an archaeologically confirmed sixth-century phase.[60] Pavoni developed that point arguing that the Milanese church acquired a landed patrimony in eastern Liguria during this period of "exile" but as the only documentation is later medieval in date this remains unproven and unprovable.[61]

The significance attributed by Genoese historians to the arrival of Honoratus in their city has not been replicated by Milanese historians' views of Alboin. They have focussed instead on what they see as the barbaric interruption in the glorious Roman history of the city initiated by the Lombard conquest even though the first decades of Lombard rule at Milan are not reliably evidenced.[62] Gregory's letters illuminate the political actions of bishops Laurence II (573–592/3), Constantius (593–600) and Deusdedit (600–603) the immediate successors of Honoratus, but unfortunately, Gregory's opinion of the church of Milan constitutes "the view from Rome" and it has to be treated with trepidation. His hints that some clergy had in fact remained in Milan when the bishops left must mean that some Milanese clerics compromised with the incoming "barbaric" Lombards despite their "savagery". This compromise was, like the flight of Honoratus, a rational response in the circumstances rather than the sinful act of treason insinuated by Gregory, for example in *Dialogues* 4.55 a cautionary tale of the "extremely dissolute" Valentine "defender of the church of Milan" who died while visiting Genoa. This man was buried in the Genoese church of San Siro only for two devils to drag out his body as punishment for his mortal sins. Gregory's rather obvious moral point that sinfulness gets its just reward obscures the fact that he was in this story also attacking those Milanese clergy who had remained even though Agilulf was now Milan's ruler.[63] Bishop Laurence II fared better with Gregory for he ended the schismatic position of the Milanese church by re-joining the Roman communion in 573, although not without reservation. His death seems to have divided the Milanese church over who should succeed him. Gregory wrote to a Milanese cleric called Magnus to say that he thought that Bishop Laurence had wrongly excommunicated him, hinting at factionalism within the local church at this point. Constantius who eventually succeeded Laurence seems to have been on good terms with Gregory but the latter's advice that he should discipline his clergy again indicates dissent. Gregory was markedly cooler to his successor Deusdedit who had "set out for Genoa" after his election from among the Milanese clergy suggesting that he normally resided in Milan, and was perfectly free and able travel from there to the Ligurian coast. Deusdedit and other clerics who had remained in Lombard Milan were regarded as "collaborators" by Gregory, a position which it was easier to adopt in far-distant Rome.

Gregory's death on 12 March 604 returned both the Milanese see and Genoa to their customary obscurity. He did not note who succeeded Deusdedit, who probably had died in 603. The traditional candidate is Asterius but he is not securely documented until 629 so it is possible that there was a period of vacancy or even another disputed election. It was Bede who noted that Bishop Asterius "of Genoa" (*episcopus genuensis*) had consecrated Birinus as first bishop of the West Saxons in 629 (probably the year after Queen Theodelinda, Agilulf's widow died).[64] Bede's attribution "of Genoa" rather than "of Milan" may imply continuing strife in the latter, which is plausible since Columbanus when he visited Agilulf and Theodelinda at Milan did not mention the local bishop in his letter to Pope Boniface IV about the "Three Chapters" which he drafted at the king's request probably in 613. Jonas of Bobbio in his life of the saint explained that Columbanus stayed in Milan for the purpose of stamping out the Arian heresy with the "cauterization" of Scripture and that he even wrote a tract (*libellus florenti scientia*) against Arians.[65] The fact that Columbanus ended up founding a monastery completely outside the archdiocese at Bobbio is both a clear indication of the weakness of Asterius, who seems to have been unable to stop him, and also that the local clergy did not welcome the feisty Irish monk in Milan itself.

Agilulf was the first king of the Lombards with a securely documented connection to Milan as he seems to have made the city his principal residence.[66] He received both Hunnish and Frankish ambassadors there and issued *de Mediolanio in palatio* his famous grant to Columbanus in support of the foundation of a monastic community at Bobbio.[67] Agilulf and Theodelinda had a summer palace at Monza, where their son Adaloald was born and adjacent to which the queen had built and lavishly endowed a church dedicated to Saint John the Baptist, at least according to Paul the Deacon.[68] In a ceremony in the old circus, a stone's throw from the ancient basilica of Sant'Ambrogio, he engineered the succession of his son Adaloald to the kingship in a late example of the old Roman *adventus*.[69] This took place in the presence of ambassadors from the Frankish king Theudebert who had promised his daughter to Adaloald in marriage.[70] After Agilulf died in 616 his son did manage to continue to rule in Milan with his mother Theodelinda: "Agilulf died at Milan, and his son Adaloald took up the administration of royal power with his mother Theodelinda and ruled with his mother for ten years".[71] Theodelinda died *c.* 628. The succeeding kings Arioald (d. 636) and Rothari (d. 652) appear not to have lived in Milan. A subsequent period of royal rule from Milan took place in 661 when Perctarit was based there while his brother and rival Godepert was established in neighbouring Pavia, which was by then established as the accepted capital of the kingdom.[72] These events suggest that Milan was effectively the royal capital of the Lombard kingdom between 591 and 628. Its bishops remained in Genoa for the entirety of those years, in a sort of uneasy standoff. Arioald and Rothari may have been Arians which would certainly have complicated any choice of bishop and a possible return to Milan.[73]

Tom Brown stated in 1984 that as result of Rothari's campaign Byzantine Genoa lost its "administrative functions and its economic links with other regions".[74] This view is supported with some archaeological evidence as North African pottery stopped arriving in the region in the mid-seventh century and it was not replaced by distinctively Lombard pottery with the exception of a single intriguing find of early seventh-century "Lombard pottery" at Perti.[75] The absence of documentary evidence for Genoa at this time makes it impossible to know what politics was like there in the mid-seventh century. Given that Rothari's motivations for issuing his Edict in November 643 are unknown, it is a possibility that it was issued as part the process of the political assimilation of formerly Byzantine territory within the expanding Lombard polity in order to clarify Lombard legal custom for new "Lombards" in Genoa and its region.[76] Although Roman practice was incorporated within the Edict it nevertheless was a distinctive political act—the first written code of law for Lombards—which posed a direct challenge to Byzantine traditions of law-making and rulership in the Italian peninsula, which would still have pertained in Genoa at this date.

Given the almost total lack of written evidence for Genoa before the Carolingian conquest it can be reasonably stated that the political histories of Genoa and Milan significantly diverged in the Lombard period.[77] Either side of the year 700 two Milanese archbishops—Mansuetus and Benedict—unsuccessfully engaged in jurisdictional disputes with the bishops of Pavia and from then on the latter became the Lombard capital. The *Versum de Mediolano Civitate* (probably written around 739) during the pontificate of Theodore, the (probable) brother of King Liutprand, harked back nostalgically through Roman-tinted spectacles to an earlier age of Milan's political centrality.[78] After Liutprand's demise in 744 royal interests shifted decisively eastwards to Friuli, the homeland of Ratchis and Aistulf and then to Brescia, the focus for Desiderius and his wife Ansa. Milan only became important again during Charlemagne's reign, a king for whom Genoa was also on the radar.[79]

Of the later Lombard kings, the best evidenced is probably Liutprand (who ruled 712–744). He has a single documented connection to Genoa, interestingly once again reported only by Bede who noted (in his "Greater Chronicle" and *Martyrology*) that Liutprand translated the relics of Saint Augustine from Sardinia to Pavia via Genoa.[80] The veracity of this is hard to prove in the absence of other early evidence, although it was picked up by later writers including Jacopo da Varagine in his *Golden Legend* (written in the 1260s). Local tradition stated that the body rested for a night at Savignone, midway up the Polcevera valley (the Genoa-Milan route, see earlier in this chapter). More associations between Liutprand and Milan are reported in some texts, once again not contemporary with the events recorded. If a short "biography" found on folio 358 of an early eleventh-century manuscript now at Gotha (Forschungsbibliothek I 84, perhaps written at Fulda) can be trusted Liutprand may have been born at Milan:

> Primum omnium LEGES ADDIDIT ET ADIVNXIT SED AMPLIFICAVIT Domnus Liutprand, rex Langobardorum, ortu et natione Mediolanum metropoli Italiae, Magnus ac summus gubernator populi atque patriae, Regnavit atque gubernavit populum communem Italiae annos triginta et unum et menses septem, et dormivit in pace cum patribus suis.[81]

> First of all HE ADDED TO AND EXPANDED THE LAWS, the Lord Liutprand, king of the Lombards, by origin and by birth from Milan the metropolis of Italy, the great and most high governor of the people and country, who ruled and governed the common people of Italy for thirty one years and seven months, and he rests in peace with his ancestors (my translation).

Although mostly derived from Paul the Deacon's verdict on Liutprand (in *HL* VI) the Gotha manuscript presents this text as a continuation of the prologue to Liutprand's legislation.[82] Paul did not in fact say that Liutprand was "by birth from Milan, the metropolis of Italy" and that information is unique to this manuscript. The Gotha book, a well-known miscellany of

Carolingian legal texts, preserves an interesting version of the Lombard laws (f. 339ra–376rb) from Rothari through to Aistulf. The text of Liutprand's laws comprises the prologue followed by the brief *vita*, then an index of Liutprand's laws, then between years seven and ten the text known as the *Memoratorium de mercedibus commacinorum*, followed by the rest of the laws. Some pages earlier in the book on folios 336–338 is the text of the so-called *Historia Langobardorum Codicis Gothani*, a distinctive version of the Lombard *origo* ("origin-legend"),[83] which ends with a section praising the "great king Pippin", son of Charlemagne. As the last fact mentioned is Pippin's conquest of Corsica from the Arabs in 807 and the text ends in the present tense, it is presumed that this version was written before 810 when Pippin died and, according to the *Annales Laurissenses Minores*—the so-called Lorsch Chronicle, was buried in Milan.[84]

As already seen an earlier section of the "Codex Gothanus" (Chapter 5 in the MGH edition) describes how Alboin's invasion of Italy included his subjugation of Pavia and the *metropolis* of Milan. The use of *metropolis* links Liutprand's biography with this version of the *Origo* in the same manuscript (Gotha, I 84). In Modena, Biblioteca Capitolare, O.I.2 (dated *c.* 991) there is another variant of the text which adds a section listing the Lombard kings and their Carolingian successors up to and including Charlemagne.[85] But this version was probably compiled by someone hostile to the Carolingians as it reports that King Aistulf "was persecuted by the king of the Franks". Some reputable authorities state that Aistulf was crowned in Milan in July 749, possibly in the basilica of Sant'Ambrogio, although there is no contemporary evidence for this.[86] Between *c.* 660 and *c.* 810 therefore Perctarit, Liutprand, Aistulf and Pippin were linked in various ways to Milan, to add to the example of Agilulf, his son Adaloald and his mother Theodelinda, already discussed. Only Liutprand had any link with Genoa.

Epilogue: Milan and Genoa diverge

In the course of the eighth century written sources suggest that the two places moved apart with Milan becoming a more complex settlement with a more developed hinterland in part because of the presence there of kings and aristocrats whose actions are evidenced in historical narratives, charters and the *Versum*.[87] That complexity does not appear to have happened in Genoa until at least the tenth century, as where charters survive there only from 916.[88] The handful surviving from the Lombard period for Milan and its region mostly relate to Campione on the eastern shore of Lake Lugano (*c.* 50 km north of Milan) and were preserved when the monastery of Sant'Ambrogio acquired properties early in the ninth century which had been owned Toto of Campione.[89] The first two charters (dated 725 and 735) record purchases of servants by Toto, and the remainder (dated between 748 and 810) reveal that Toto and his family built a small church in Campione dedicated to Saint Zeno and endowed it with property which included an olive grove. Toto had other property in neighbouring villages for which Campione probably functioned as a central place for produce. The relation of Campione to Milan is a good example of what Horden and Purcell meant by "a complex set of short distances and definite places" for the simple set up at Campione became complex when Toto bequeathed the lands and its workforce to the archbishop of Milan in 777. At that point and by that action his workers and surviving family entered into a new relation with a much larger central place which although further away was still physically and psychologically "near". It is probably not coincidental that the first three of these charters are nearly contemporaneous with the *Versum de Mediolano Civitate*, which, given its celebratory tone, was surely written in Milan, or perhaps by a homesick Milanese.[90] It is in 24 stanzas (72 lines) which praise the monumental buildings of the city notably the impressive fifth-century basilica of San Lorenzo and its many saints, bolstering Milan's established political centrality with a strongly Christian message.[91] Stanzas 8 and 9 make this clear:

> This is the queen of cities and mother of this country,
> Rightly called by the name *metropolis*,
> Praised by the nations of all ages.[92]
>
> The dignity of its power is constant,
> and to it travel the bishops of Italy,
> to be instructed in the correct ways of the synodal canons.[93]

Its final stanzas (18 and 19) deal with contemporaries of the author, Liutprand and his brother:

> The Lombards hold the sceptre of power there,
> Liutprand the pious king with the merit of sainthood,
> to whom Christ has given such grace and sanctity.[94]

The following stanza (19) continues:

> The great bishop Theodore ornamented the whole city,
> happily born of royal seed,
> the people in their love compelled him to the episcopate.[95]

Most of the 24 verses focus on the saints that protected the city: Ambrose, Nazarius, Victor, Laurence, Vincent, Eustorgius, Nabor, Felicity, Valeria, Protasius, Gervasius and Eufemia, each of which had a church. Toto of Campione's will of 777 provided that four of these churches—San Nazaro, San Vittore *ad corpus*, San Lorenzo and Sant'Ambrogio—were to benefit from the gift of an annual oil render (sourced from olives grown at Campione).[96] To this potent mix the gift by Toto of his church dedicated to Saint Zeno added another saint, which complicated the existing religious geography of the Milanese church. It is probable that like San Zeno on a small scale the communities at San Nazaro, San Vittore and San Lorenzo, as Sant'Ambrogio itself, received lay patronage at this period on a larger scale which has gone unrecorded. This combination of charters and praise poem is of course unusual and their contemporaneous production may mark out Milan as an exceptional Lombard city with a powerful sacred identity, which may have been in large part due to Liutprand's presence in the city. There is certainly nothing comparable from Genoa in this period.

Also without Genoese parallel (until the later tenth century) is the foundation of a Benedictine community dedicated to Ambrose adjacent to the fourth-century basilica recorded in several controversial eighth-century charters which report a series of gifts, as was a common pattern for monastic foundations at this time. The sequence began in 742—not long after the *Versum*—when Liutprand was still king of the Lombards and his brother Theodore probably still archbishop of Milan.[97] The aristocrat Theopert (*vir magnificus*) gave his inherited house and land (mixed arable and woodland) near Milan to Aunemund, deacon and custodian acting on behalf of the Sant'Ambrogio basilica.[98] Aunemund leased the property back to Theopert for his lifetime, with the proviso that should Theopert at a later point wish to live at a *cellula* near the basilica he had to return the land. A fabricated charter dated 784 suggests that Theopert had become a cleric, was living at the *cellula* and at that point giving his property in perpetuity with full ownership rights to the abbot and monastery on his death.[99] Further gifts of property west of Milan followed. On 20 August 765 Ursus son of Theodulf (*vir devotus*) gave an arable field in "Torriglas" to Ambrosius, custodian of the *oratorium beati Ambrosii* nearby.[100] Ursus made his gift in perpetuity and the custodians were allowed to do with it as they wished according "to holy law".[101] In return Ursus was to have masses said and lights lit for his soul and those of his parents.[102] The deed was witnessed by five men, including a moneyer. Little is known about the benefactors themselves, although lay gift-giving to old-established urban churches was happening all over the north of Italy and elsewhere in the eighth century.[103] Within the immediate vicinity of Milan ancient and prestigious foundations in and around Monza and in Lodi received far larger gifts at the same time as Sant'Ambrogio.[104] In Milan itself, besides Sant'Ambrogio, it is possible that Santa Maria d'Aurona and the Monastero Maggiore—two nunneries which acquired extensive lands in a later period—may have been founded and endowed at this time.[105]

Political narratives tend to present a short-term view of historical development. Horden and Purcell in their exceptional book *The Corrupting Sea* make a very strong case for the long view of historical development based on ecological and economic analysis. In a section on "dispersed hinterlands" they argued that "Just as the site of a town should be re-conceived as a number of overlapping ecologies, so should its hinterland be thought of as a complex set of short distances and definite places".[106] This perspective undermines the traditional view that "real" cities—especially "exceptional" ones like Milan—could only be supported by extended networks of long-distance trade facilitated by political elites, such as that suggested by the remarkable excavations at Comacchio in the Po delta.[107] In this perspective economic interaction between Milan and Genoa over the long term is a more important issue than the short-term activities of kings and bishops. At the current state of archaeological knowledge, the economies of Milan and Genoa seem to have been distinct, with Milan focussed on Po Valley exchange and Genoa on Mediterranean exchange, but there are hints of connections between them (as seen earlier) and more may become apparent once excavations of the port are published in full. It has been argued here that comparing the political histories of these two places suggests an equally complex picture. Political interaction between Milan and Genoa can be definitely observed during the latter decades of the sixth century thanks to the survival of the letters of Gregory the Great. The Lombard conquest of Milan may indeed have developed links between the two cities by forcing Milan's bishop to migrate to Genoa. After Gregory died in 604, written documentation largely disappears until the second decade of the eighth century when the survival of a few charters and, a few years later, a poem in praise of Milan may mean that Milan at that point was transforming into a very different type of settlement to Genoa. The survival of this clutch of text of itself suggests as much. Milan, more like its old late Roman self, soon dominated its hinterland in ways which only occurred in Genoa several centuries later, if indeed they ever did.

Notes

1 T. S. Brown, *Gentlemen and Officers: Imperial administration and aristocratic power in Byzantine Italy A.D. 554–800* (London 1984), based on his doctoral thesis undertaken at Nottingham, "Social structure and the hierarchy of officialdom in Byzantine Italy, 554–800 A.D.", unpublished doctoral thesis, University of Nottingham, 1975; Byzantine Italy, *c.* 680–*c.* 876, in *The New Cambridge Medieval History*, vol. 2, ed. by R. McKitterick (Cambridge, 1995), 349–380; "Gibbon, Hodgkin, and the Invaders of Italy", in *Edward Gibbon and Empire*, ed. by R. McKitterick and R. Quinault (Cambridge, 1997), 137–161; "Urban violence in early medieval Italy: the cases of Rome and Ravenna", in *Violence and Society in the Early Medieval West*, ed. by G. Halsall (Woodbridge, 1998), 76–89; "Lombard religious policy in the late sixth and seventh centuries: the Roman dimension", in *The Langobards before the Frankish conquest. An ethnographic perspective*, ed. by G. Ausenda, P. Delogu and C. Wickham (Woodbridge, 2009), 289–299. I would like to thank Tom for his friendship, support and wise advice over so many years.

2 B. Ward-Perkins, "The Lombard city and the urban economy", in *The Langobards before the Frankish conquest*, ed. by Ausenda, Delogu and Wickham, 95–106 summarises recent debates about Lombard urbanism. C. Wickham, *Framing the Early Middle Ages. Europe and the Mediterranean, 400–800* (Oxford, 2005), 644–656 surveys urbanism across the Italian peninsula. C. Wickham, *The Inheritance of Rome. A History of Europe from 400 to 1000* (London, 2009), 143 for Lombard cities (e.g., Verona, Milan) being less significant than Byzantine ones (notably Rome, Naples and Ravenna). More broadly, N. Christie, *From Constantine to Charlemagne. An Archaeology of Italy AD 300–800* (Aldershot, 2006), 277–279; A. Augenti, ed., *Le città italiane tra la tarda antichità e l'alto medioevo* (Firenze, Giglio, 2006) and M. Valenti, "Le città del centro-nord", *Longobardi. Un popolo che cambia la storia* (Milan, 2017), ed. by G.P. Brogiolo, F. Marazzi and C. Giostra (Milan, 2017), 128–133.

3 Splendidly discussed by Giulia Vollono, "Constructing Identity in Lombard Italy", PhD thesis 2017, University of Sheffield.

4 A. Louth, "The Eastern empire in the Sixth Century" and "The Byzantine empire in the seventh century", in *The New Cambridge Medieval History*, vol. 1, ed. by P. Fouracre (Cambridge, 2005), 93–117 and 291–316; J. Moorhead, "The Byzantines in the West in the Sixth Century", in *The New Cambridge Medieval History*, vol. 1, 118–139; E. Zanini, *Le Italie bizantine: territorio, insediamento ed economia nella provincia bizantina d'Italia (VI–VIII secolo)* (Bar, 1998).

5 Wickham, *Framing*, 58.

6 A. Pizzi, ed., *Milano capitale dell'impero romano. 286–402 d.c.* (Milan, 1990).

7 For example, G. P. Brogiolo and S. Gelichi, *La città nell'altomedioevo italiano. Archeologia e storia* (Bari, 1998), 122–145.

8 C. Wickham, "Aristocratic Power in Eighth-Century Lombard Italy", in *After Rome's Fall. Narrators and Sources of Early Medieval History*, ed. by A. C. Murray (Toronto, 1998), 160.

9 For an earlier attempt at comparison in a later period, see R. Balzaretti, "Chestnuts in Charters: Evidence for Specialised Production in Tenth-Century Genoa and Milan", in *Italy and Early Medieval Europe: Papers for Chris Wickham*, ed. by R. Balzaretti, J. S. Barrow, and P. Skinner (Oxford, 2018), 356–371. Cf. B. Ward-Perkins, "Old and New Rome Compared: The Rise of Constantinople", in *Two Romes: Rome and Constantinople in Late Antiquity*, ed. by L. Grig and G. Kelly (Oxford, 2012), 53–80, where the evidence-base is obviously hugely greater.

10 There are many studies of particular towns but most are framed without much in the way of comparative context. For Genoa, e.g., R. Pavoni, *Liguria medievale. Da provincia romana a stato regionale* (Genoa, 1992), 82–148; for Milan, e.g., G. Tabacco, "Milano nell'età longobarda", in *Milano e i Milanesi prima del mille*, X Congresso internazionale di studi sull'alto medioevo (Spoleto, 1986), 19–43.

11 M. Whittow, "How much trade was local, regional and inter-regional? A comparative perspective on the late Antique economy", in *Local Economies? Production and Exchange of Inland Regions in Late Antiquity*, ed. by L. Lavan (Leiden, 2013), 133–165.

12 R. Balzaretti, *Dark Age Liguria. Regional Identity and Local Power, c. 400–1020* (London, 2013), 4.

13 Melli, *Genaua, Kainua, Genoa, Ianua. Genova. Le molte vite di una città portuale dal Neolitico al VII secolo d.c.* (Genoa, 2017), p. 260.

14 C. Negrelli, "Produzione, circolazione e consume tra VI–IX secolo dal territorio del Padovetere a Comacchio", in *Genti del Delta da spina a Comacchio: Uomini, territorio e culto dall'antichità all'alto Medioevo* (Comacchio: Corbo Edit.,

2007), 437–472, e.g., fig. 20, 461; C. Negrelli, "Dal VI all'VII secolo continuità e rotture nella circolazione dei manufatti ceramici tra Romagna e Delta Padana", in *Le forme della crisi: Produzioni ceramiche e commerce nell'Italia centrale tra Romani e Longobardi (III–VIII sec. d.C)*, ed. by E. Cirelli, F. Diosono, and H. Patterson (Bologna: Ante Quem, 2015), 139–49, fig. 1, 139; S. Gelichi, "Societies at the Edge: New Cities in the Adriatic Sea during the Early Middle Ages (8th–9th Centuries)", in *New Directions in Early Medieval European Archaeology*, ed. by S. Gelichi and R. Hodges (Turnhout, 2015), 285–300, fig. 3, 293. A. Alberti, "Produzione e commercializzazione della pietra ollare in Italia settentrionale", in *I Congresso Nazionale di Archeologia Medievale: Auditorium del Centro studi della Cassa di risparmio di Pisa (ex Benedettine), Pisa, 29–31 maggio 1997*, ed. by S. Gelichi (Firenze, 2000), 335–339.

15 P. Delogu, "Kingship and the shaping of the Lombard body politic", in *The Langobards before the Frankish conquest,* ed. by Ausenda, Delogu and Wickham, 251–274.

16 W. Goffart, *The Narrators of Barbarian History (A.D. 500–800). Jordanes, Gregory of Tours, Bede and Paul the Deacon* (Notre Dame, 1988); C. Heath, *The Narrative Worlds of Paul the Deacon. Between Empires and Identities in Lombard Italy* (Amsterdam, 2017); S. Ghosh, *Writing the Barbarian Past. Studies in Early Medieval Historical Narrative* (Leiden and Boston, 2016).

17 C. Frugoni, *A Distant City. Images of Urban Experience in the Medieval World* (Princeton, 1991), 54–57.

18 P. Horden and N. Purcell, *The Corrupting Sea. A Study of Mediterranean History* (Oxford, 2000), 89–122; Wickham, *Framing*, 728–741; R. Hodges, *Dark Age Economics. A New Audit* (London, 2012), 1–18.

19 Brown, *Gentlemen and Officers*; R. Krautheimer; *Rome: Profile of a City, 312–1308* (Princeton, 1980); P. Arthur, *Naples from Roman town to city-state: an archaeological perspective* (London, 2002).

20 J. O. Tjäder, ed., *Die nichtliterarischen lateinischen Papyri Italiens aus der Zeit 445–700*, 3 vols (Lund, 1955–1982).

21 G. P. Brogiolo, *Brescia altomedievale: Urbanistica ed edilizia dal IV al IX secolo* (Mantua, 1993) and G. P. Brogiolo, ed., *Dalle* domus *alla corte regia. S. Giulia di Brescia. Gli scavi dal 1980 al 1992* (Florence, 2005).

22 R. J. A. Talbert, ed., *The Barrington Atlas of the Greek and Roman World* (Princeton, 2000), Map 39 *Mediolanum*; P. Tozzi, "Caratteristiche e problemi della viabilità del settore meridionale del territorio di *Mediolanum*", in *Milano e i Milanesi prima del mille (VIII–X secolo): Atti del X congresso internazionale di Studi sull'alto medioevo* (Spoleto, 1986), 59–84 at 75.

23 M. Pearce and P. Tozzi, "Map 39 *Mediolanum*", in *The Barrington Atlas of the Greek and Roman World: Directory*, ed. by R. J. A. Talbert, vol. I (Princeton, 2000), 573–586 state (at 573) that "for much of the map our knowledge is surprisingly scant".

24 *HL* II 25, ed. Waitz, 86.

25 Translated by Foulke, *History of the Longobards* (Pennsylvania, 1907), 79 (with minor modification). L. Capo, ed. and Ital. trans., *Paolo Diacono, Storia dei Longobardi* (Milan, 1992), 104–107, 449 (commentary).

26 Most recently Melli, *Genaua*, 250 "a group of senior clergy and noblemen guided by the metropolitan Honoratus, to which was added the bishop of Acqui, Sedaldo, fled to Genoa". The author of the *Acta Sanctorum*, Febr. 2, 1st edn, 163–167, writing in the 1660s and quoting this passage by Paul, was already deeply sceptical.

27 J.-C. Picard, *Le Souvenir des Évêques. Sépultures, listes épiscopales et culte des évêques en Italie du Nord des origins at X^{e}siècle* (Rome, 1988), 73, 741. The name

of the bishop in Genoa when Honoratus arrived is unknown as is the impact of his arrival on the local church: V. Polonio, "Tra universalismo e localismo: costruzione di un sistema (569–1321)", *Atti della Società Ligure di Storia Patria*, 39 (2009), p. 77.

28 W. Pohl, "Paulus Diaconus und die 'Historia Langobardorum': Text und Tradition", in *Historiographie im frühen Mittelalter*, ed. by A. Scharer and G. Scheibelreiter (Vienna, 1994), 375–406.

29 Pavoni, *Liguria medievale*, 103; N. Christie, "Byzantine Liguria: an imperial province against the Longobards, AD 568–643", *Papers of the British School at Rome*, 58 (1990), 229–271; A. Musarra, *Genova e il mare nel Medioevo* (Bologna, 2015), 15 and "Genova e il mare nell'Alto Medioevo: una rilettura delle fonti", *Bullettino dell'Istituto Storico Italiano per il Medio Evo*, 119 (2017), 113.

30 Fredegar IV, 71.

31 English translation by J. Wallace-Hadrill, *Fourth Book of the Chronicle of Fredegar with its continuations* (Oxford, 1960), 59–60, with minor modification.

32 Balzaretti, *Dark Age Liguria*, 45–53.

33 Wickham, *Framing*, 712.

34 Melli, *Genaua*, 272.

35 For reasons of space I have relied here on two recent surveys: C. Giostra, "I longobardi e le città: forme materiali e scelte culturali", *Hortus Artium Medievalium*, 20 (2014), 48–62 (Milan at 54–55) and Melli, *Genaua*, 250–273 and Melli, ed., *Genova dalle origini all'anno mille*, 202–239 (Genoa).

36 Recent archaeology is treated at some length in my forthcoming *The Lands of Saint Ambrose: Monks and Society in Early Medieval Milan* (Turnhout, 2019), Chapter 3 "Roman Milan Transformed".

37 The publication of material from excavations in the port and elsewhere is awaited (Melli, *Genaua*, 282). Excellent more specialist surveys include F. Benente, "Dark Age Liguria: analisi di dati editi e problem aperti per una riflessione sul popolamento della Liguria orientale tra tarda Romanità e alto Medioevo", *Archeologia Medievale*, 44 (2017), 193–218; G. Murialdo, "La Liguria altomedievale: il periodo longobardo e franco (metà VII-IX secolo) tra enfasi storiografica ed evidenza archeologica", *Ligures*, 10 (2012), 5–44; P. Tedesco, "La Liguria tardoantica e altomedievale: una nota di storia economica", *Rivista Storica Italiana*, 129.3 (2017), 1094–1105.

38 Melli, *Genaua*, 16.

39 Melli, *Genaua*, 253–254.

40 Melli, *Genaua*, 257–258.

41 Melli, *Genaua*, 258–260; Melli, *Genova dalle origini*, 209–212.

42 Melli, Genaua, 261. For a positive interpretation of urban gardens, with which I agree, see C. Goodson, "Garden Cities in Medieval Italy", in *Italy and Early Medieval Europe*, ed. by Balzaretti, Barrow and Skinner, 345.

43 Melli, Genaua, 262.

44 Melli, *Genaua*, 266.

45 Melli, *Genaua*, 266–267, 282. It remains unpublished.

46 Melli, *Genaua*, 267.

47 Melli, *Genaua*, 268, Fig. 135.

48 Melli, *Genaua*, 273.

49 Giostra, "I longobardi", 54.

50 Giostra, "I longobardi", 55.

51 Melli, *Genaua*, 260.

52 D. Norberg, ed., *S. Gregorii Magni Registrum epistularum*, CCL 140, 140A. 2 vols (Turnhout, Brepols, 1982), abbrev. as *Regr.*; trans. by J. R. C. Martyn, *The Letters of Gregory the Great*, 3 vols (Toronto, 2004).

53 Picard, *Le Souvenir des Évêques*, 81–83.

54 C. Sotinel, "The Three Chapters and the transformations of Italy", in *The Crisis of the* Oikoumene. *The Three Chapters and the Failed Quest for Unity in the Sixth-Century Mediterranean*, ed. by C. Chazelle and C. Cubitt (Turnhout, 2007), 111.

55 Wickham, "Aristocratic power in eighth-century Lombard Italy".

56 The so-called *Historia Langobardorum Codicis Gothani*, ch. 6, preserved in Gotha, Forschungsbibliothek, Memb. I 84, an early eleventh-century manuscript associated with Mainz or Fulda. This can be taken as a compressed version of Paul's *HL* II 25–26, although significantly Paul never termed Milan a metropolis.

57 Gregory, *Regr*. 3.30, trans. Martin, 255.

58 The election is thoroughly discussed by R. A. Markus, *Gregory the Great and his world* (Cambridge, 1997), 140–142.

59 Balzaretti, *Dark Age Liguria*, 54–55. Both the subject of through excavation.

60 Balzaretti, *Dark Age Liguria*, 84–85. Melli's account (*Genaua*, pp. 253–254) relies on twelfth-century documents.

61 Pavoni, *Liguria medievale*, 104, 146 and 148.

62 C. La Rocca, "Milano longobarda", in *Milano antica a medievale*, *Storia illustrata di Milano*, ed. by F. Della Peruta, vol. 1 (Milan, 1992), 161–180.

63 Brown, "Lombard religious policy in the late sixth and seventh centuries".

64 Bede, *Historia ecclesiastica*, III 7. Melli, *Genaua*, 255. Bede of course was writing a century after the event. Asterius was buried at San Siro in Genoa (Picard, *Le Souvenir des Évêques*, 76).

65 Jonas of Bobbio, *Life of Columbanus and his disciples*, I 30, trans. O'Hara and Wood, 166–167. The tract does not survive.

66 Agilulf was probably elected as king in May 591: O. Bertolini, "Agilulfo, re dei Longobardi", *Dizionario Biografico degli Italiani,* 1 (1960).

67 *HL* IV 12 (Huns), ed. Waitz 121; Brühl, *CDL* III (24 July 613), 7, trans. O'Hara and Wood, 309–310. This is the oldest surviving text of a Lombard royal diploma although it is preserved only in manuscripts of mid-ninth century or later date.

68 *HL* IV 21–22, 25, 27, ed. Waitz, 123–125.

69 M. McCormick, *Eternal Victory: triumphal rulership in late antiquity, Byzantium and the early medieval West* (Cambridge, 1986), 292–295. Remains of the circus can still be seen at the church of San Maurizio (the old Monastero Maggiore) and in adjacent streets (via Morigi, via Vigna and via Circo): P. M. De Marchi, "Milano e le testimonianze altomedievali del monastero Maggiore. Il riutilizzo della torre del civico romano", *Quaderni del Chiostro del Monastero Maggiore di Milano*, 1 (2004), 48–50.

70 *HL* IV 30, ed. Waitz, 127. Agilulf was effectively in a relationship of clientship to the Frankish kings Guntram and Childebert as the various references made by Fredegar to payments of gold show: *The Fourth Book of the Chronicle of Fredegar*, Ch. 45, ed. Wallace-Hadrill, 37–39 discussed by I. N. Wood, *The Merovingian Kingdoms 450–751* (London, 1994), 164–169.

71 *Prosperi continuatio Havniensis*, ed., T. Mommsen, *MGH AA* IX (Berlin, 1891), 339, Engl. trans. by S. Muhlberger, "The Copenhagen continuation of Prosper: a translation", *Florilegium* 6 (1984), 94.

72 W. Pohl, "Memory, identity and power in Lombard Italy", in *The Uses of the Past in the Early Middle Ages*, ed. by Y. Hen and M. Innes (Cambridge, 2000), 9–28.

73 Brown, "Lombard religious policy", 294.

74 *Gentlemen and Officers*, 14.

75 T. Mannoni and G. Murialdo, eds., *S. Antonino: un insediamento fortificato nella Liguria bizantina* (Bordighera, 2001), 356–359; Balzaretti, *Dark Age Liguria*, 53, 75–76.

76 This could be implied by Rothari's statement in his prologue that he hopes everyone "will willingly set himself against his enemies and defend himself and his homeland".

77 S. Macchiavello and A. Rovere, "The Written Sources", in *A Companion to Medieval Genoa*, ed. by C. E. Beneš (Leiden, 2018), 27–48.

78 The arguments are rehearsed by R. Cassanelli, "Il complesso monastico di S. Maria d'Aurona. Architettura e liturgia a Milano tra età longobardo e carolingia", *Hortus Artium Medievalium*, 23 (2017), 118 who concludes that this sibling relationship is plausible.

79 Balzaretti, *Dark Age Liguria*, 97–100; Balzaretti, "Early Medieval Genoa", in Beneš, *Companion to Medieval Genoa*, 81–82; P. Guglielmotti, "Genova and Liguria", in Beneš, *Companion to Medieval Genoa*, 52; A. Musarra, *Genova e il mare nel Medioevo* (Bologna, 2015), 15–17 and "Genova e il mare", 117.

80 J. T. Hallenback, *The Transferal of the Relics of St. Augustine of Hippo from Sardinia to Pavia in the Early Middle Ages* (Lewiston, NY, 2000), 9–11.

81 *MGH Scriptores rerum langobardicarum et italicarum saec. VI–IX*, ed. G. Waitz (Berlin, 1878), 11. Manuscript digitized at: https://archive.thulb.uni-jena.de/ufb/rsc/viewer/ufb_derivate_00010754/Memb-I-00084_0358r.tif (accessed 02.08.18).

82 H. Mordek, *Bibliotheca capitularium regun Francorum manuscripta. Überlieferung und Traditionszusammenhang der fränkischen Herrschererlasse* (Munich, 1995), 141.

83 *MGH Scriptores rerum Langobardicarum*, ed. Waitz, 7–11.

84 The *Annales Lauriss Min*, p. 121 (*Pippinus rex Italiae obiit; sepultus est Mediolanum* (only in BAV Pal. Lat. 243) and *Chronicon Vedast*, *MGH SS*, 13, p. 707 (*Rex Italiae Pippinus, Karoli Magni filius, obiit 8. Id. Iulii, Mediolanum sepelitur*) say he was buried at Milan (J. Nelson, "Carolingian Royal Funerals" in *Rituals of Power. From Late Antiquity to the Early Middle Ages*, ed. by F. C. W. J. Theuws abd J. Nelson (Leiden, 2000), 160–116). The origin of these texts is not firmly established, but neither is a strictly contemporary notice although each was probably written in the latter part of the ninth century: R. McKitterick, *History and Memory in the Carolingian World* (Cambridge, 2004), 35–36 and Picard, *Le Souvenir des Évêques*, 94.

85 Mordek, *Bibliotheca capitularium*, 256.

86 J. Jarnut, *Storia dei longobardi* (Turin, 1995), 110.

87 See Balzaretti, *Lands of Saint Ambrose*, Chapter 10.

88 Balzaretti, *Dark Age Liguria*, 104–107; Balzaretti, "Early medieval Genoa", 76–80.

89 S. Gasparri and C. La Rocca, eds., *Carte di famiglia. Strategie, rappresentazione e memoria del gruppo familiare di Totone di Campione (721–877)* (Rome, 2005); R. Balzaretti, "Monasteries, towns and the countryside: reciprocal relationships in the archdiocese of Milan, 614–814", in *Towns and Their Territories: Between Late Antiquity and the Early Middle* Ages, ed. by G.P. Brogiolo, N. Gauthier and N Christie (Leiden, 2000), 244–248 and Balzaretti, *Lands of Saint Ambrose*, Chapter 6.

90 Pighi, *Versus de Verona/Versum de Mediolano Civitate* (Bologna, 1960), 89–91 (diplomatic transcription), 145–147 (edition), 147–148 (Italian translation). This text is preserved in a single manuscript (Verona, Biblioteca Capitolare XC (85), f. 25–27), a ninth-century collection of poetry perhaps written around 870, possibly at Verona or elsewhere in northern Italy. Who wrote the poem is unknown but it is generally thought to have been composed in the latter years of the Lombard King Liutprand's reign, *c.* 739–740.

91 B. Ward-Perkins, *From Classical Antiquity to the Middle Ages. Urban Public Building in Northern and Central Italy AD 300–850* (Oxford, 1984), 224–229. My translation draws on an unpublished version by Professor Ward-Perkins.
92 Hec est urbium regina mater atque patrie/Que precipuo vocatur nomine metropolis/Quam conlaudant universi nationes seculi.
93 Ingens permanet ipsius dignitatis potencia/Ad quam cuncti venientes presules Ausonie/Iuxta normam instruuntur sinodali canone.
94 Sceptrum inde Langobardi principalem optinent/Liutprandum pium regem meritis almificum/Cui tantum sancitatis Christus dedit graciam.
95 Totam urbem presul magnus ornavit Theodorus/veniens benigne natus de regali germine/quem ad sedem raptum traxit pro amore populus.
96 P. Fouracre, "Eternal Light and Earthly Needs: Practical Aspects of the Development of Frankish Immunities", in *Property and Power in the Early Middle Ages*, ed. by W. Davies and P. Fouracre (Cambridge, 1995), 53–81 and his "'FraZming' and Lighting: Another Angle on Transition", in *Italy and Early Medieval Europe: Papers for Chris Wickham*, ed. by R. Balzaretti, J. S. Barrow, and P. Skinner (Oxford, 2018), 305–314.
97 Picard, *Le Souvenir des Évêques*, 85–87 suggested that Theodore II was surrounded in "un halo de mystère romantique" (p. 85) because of his supposed royal connections. Late medieval documents regarded him as the brother of Aurona, Liutprand's sister. He was apparently buried at the monastery of Santa Maria "d'Aurona", founded by his sister (P. Dianzani, *Santa Maria d'Aurona. Fase altomedievale* [Florence, 1989], 9–11).
98 Alfio Rosario Natale, ed., *Il Museo Diplomatico dell'Archivio di Stato di Milano*, vol. I, pts 1 and 2 (Milan, 1970), doc. 11, unauthenticated twelfth-century copy. Abbreviated *MD*.
99 *MD* 28 copied onto the same parchment sheet as the 742 charter.
100 *MD* 17.
101 A formula found also in *MD* 23. Ten years before in 755 Aistulf, the previous king, had issued a law (*Aistulfi* 12) reminding people that gifts made to holy places for the sake of the soul could not be revoked and their provisions had to be respected.
102 Fouracre, "Eternal light and earthly needs", 68–78 who points out (p. 74) that lighting clauses were very rare in eighth-century Frankish charters.
103 Wickham, *Early Medieval Italy*, 43; Balzaretti, "Cities, emporia and monasteries", 225–228; Wickham, "Aristocratic Power in Eighth-Century Lombard Italy".
104 L. Schiaparelli, ed., *Codice diplomatico longobardo*, vol. 1, docs 82 (Monza), 231 (Monza, to the church founded by Queen Theodelinda (Paul the Deacon, *HL* IV 21), 155 (Lodi) and 218 (Lodi/Brescia).
105 Cassanelli, "Il complesso monastico di S. Maria d'Aurona" and E. Occhipinti, "Appunti per la storia del Monastero Maggiore di Milan in età medioevale: Il problema della origini e la configurazione giuridico-patrimoniale", *Studi di Storia e Diplomatica di Milano,* 2 (1977), 47–96.
106 Horden and Purcell, *Corrupting Sea*, 121.
107 S. Gelichi, "Comacchio: A Liminal Community in a Nodal Point during the Early Middle Ages", in *Venice and its Neighbors from the 8th to 11th Century*, ed. by S. Gelichi and S. Gasparri (Leiden, 2018), 142–167.

18 A dance to the music of time: Greeks and Latins in Medieval Taranto*

Vera von Falkenhausen

According to Strabo (VI, 1, 2), together with Naples and Reggio Calabria Taranto was one of the towns of the *Magna Graecia* where in his period Greek culture still persisted:

> νυνὶ δὲ πλὴν Τάραντος καὶ Ῥηγίου καὶ Νεαπόλεως ἐκβεβαρβαρῶσθαι συμβέβηκεν ἅπαντα καὶ τὰ μὲν Λευκανοὺς καὶ Βρεττίους κατέχειν, τὰ δὲ Καμπάνους, καὶ τούτους λόγῳ, τὸ δ᾽ ἀληθὲς Ῥωμαίους.[1]

This paragraph has often been discussed,[2] especially since the evidence of the survival of Greek culture is not homogeneous in the three towns: in contrast to Naples and Reggio, in Taranto only a few Greek inscriptions of the Roman period have survived,[3] among them two Jewish epitaphs of the fourth/fifth century.[4] Many Greek personal names appear however in Latin inscriptions.[5] But Greek did not entirely disappear in the town, and in the following pages I shall try to describe the coexistence of Greek and Latin language and secular and religious institutions in medieval Taranto.

Around 680, the Lombards occupied the town, and, in 743, a bishop of Taranto with the Lombard name *Aufredus* attended a papal council in Rome.[6] Some Latin documents, written in Taranto during the first quarter of the ninth century, have survived in the archive of Montecassino in the original or as copies in the *Registrum Petri Diaconi.*[7] Lombard officials, as for instance *sculdais* and *gastaldi*,[8] and many Lombard personal names, like Roderisius, Arnipertus, Rudilpertus, Rodegarius and others, are mentioned in these documents.[9] The name of a Latin notary, active in Taranto in the early ninth century, however, was Procopius.[10] Jewish funeral inscriptions of the eighth/ninth century are in Latin and Hebrew.[11] In about 840, Arabs occupied the city, using the harbour as a base for commerce and raids.[12]

According to *Theophanes Continuatus* Taranto was recovered by the Byzantine army in 880.[13] A few years later, presumably in 886, the commander-in-chief in Italy, the *patricius* George, tried to transfer the local bishopric from the ecclesiastical jurisdiction of Rome to the patriarchate of Constantinople,[14] whilst apparently neither he himself nor the Byzantine government made any effort to remove the dioceses of central and northern Apulia from the jurisdiction of the Roman Church. The reason for George's initiative might have been that an important part of the town's population and clergy was Greek. In fact, several Greek-Latin lead seals of a bishop called Romanos, dated to the seventh century, with a bilingual legend have been preserved: *Θεοτόκε βοήθει Ῥωμανοῦ/episcopi Tranti*,[15] although it is not entirely certain that they really belonged to a bishop of Taranto. On the other hand, I cannot find any other episcopal see which might be taken into consideration.[16]

By its geographical location, Taranto was situated between the culturally Lombard territories of central Apulia, and the more Hellenised area of the Salento, and the two neighbouring southern dioceses, Otranto and Gallipoli, belonged to the patriarchate of Constantinople. In around 830 at Otranto, the main seaport which connected southern Italy with Greece and the Byzantine capital, there was a Greek iconoclastic bishop,[17] and since then this diocese—later archdiocese—was and remained Greek until the Norman conquest in the second half of the eleventh century.[18] During the last decades of the ninth century, probably, after the Byzantine recovery of Apulia and Calabria, the Greek bishopric of Gallipoli was created as a suffragan of the Greek metropolitan see of Nikopolis/Santa Severina in Calabria.[19] As for Taranto, however, the attempt of the Byzantine *patricius* failed; the diocese remained under the ecclesiastical jurisdiction of Rome. All known bishops (later archbishops) of the Byzantine and post-Byzantine period were Latin,[20] as was the clergy of the cathedral.[21]

During the tenth century, Taranto was several times attacked by the Arabs, and conquered and destroyed probably in August 927 or 928.[22] The Muslim conquest must have been a major disaster: according to Lupus Protospatharius: *"perempti sunt omnes viriliter pugnando, reliqui vero deportati sunt in Africam"*,[23] and the anonymous author of the Kitab al-'Uyun states that 6000 *'ilj*, which is a rude term for infidels, were killed and mentions an enormous booty of slaves, gold and precious objects.[24] In about 965, however, the fortifications of Taranto were rebuilt. An elaborate Greek inscription celebrates the reconstruction by the emperor Nikephoros II and by another Nikephoros, called the "wall-builder" (τοιχοποιός) and "architect" (ἀρχιτέκτων), who probably can be identified with Nikephoros Hexakionites, then the Byzantine governor of southern Italy.[25] Maybe Taranto was partly repopulated in that period, for in the tenth and eleventh centuries Armenian names appear in the local documentation: there were the *prōtopapas* (πρωτοπαπᾶς) and *taboularios* (ταβουλάριος) Kourtikes,[26] and quite a number of people called Kourkouas.[27] In fact, after the Byzantine conquest, Armenian veterans had been settled in various parts of Byzantine southern Italy.[28]

Until the Norman conquest in the late 1060s Taranto was a provincial town of, apparently, moderate importance in the Byzantine *thema* of Langobardia, later katepanate of Italia:[29] the capital of the province and residence of the governor (*strategos, katepanō* or *doux*) was Bari, and the seaport of Taranto—once the most important harbour of the *Magna Graecia*—had lost some of its importance already in Roman times.[30] In 663, the fleet of the emperor Constans II arrived in Taranto during his Italian campaign,[31] but after the Byzantine recovery of the town and its hinterland in 880, the port is rarely mentioned,[32] since, as already said, the main harbour connecting the southern Italian provinces with Constantinople and the eastern provinces of the empire was Otranto.[33] Unlike Bari few high-ranking Byzantine civil servants or officers are mentioned in the Tarantine documents: only one *patrikios* and three *prōtospatharioi*.[34]

After a gap of almost 150 years the extant archival documentation of the town starts in the seventies of the tenth century, the oldest document being an *hypomnēma* (ὑπόμνημα) of the katepan Michael of 975, who confirms to the local monastery of St Peter (S. Pietro Imperiale) two charters (δικαιώματα καὶ ὑπονμήματα) of his predecessors Constantine, *prōtospatharios* of the Chrysotriklinos and *stratēgos* of Longobardia (πρωτοσπαθάριος ἐπὶ τοῦ χρυσοτρικλίνου καὶ στρατηγὸς Λαγουβαρδίας, before 969) and Michael Abidelas, *patrikios* and *katepanō* of Italia (πατρίκιος καὶ κατεπάνω Ἰταλίας, after 970 and before 975), concerning the donation of some houses close to the monastery.[35] A Latin sentence, again in favour of St Peter, concerning an olive grove was issued in 970 at Massafra, a settlement about 15 km north-west of Taranto, by three *gastaldi:* Triphilis and John, who sign in Greek, and Lupus who signs in Latin.[36] Moreover, for the Byzantine and Norman periods there has been preserved a consistent number of Greek and Latin private and public documents which, in my view, provide an interesting insight into the linguistic and more generally cultural situation of the town.

Located at the border area between culturally Lombard-Latin central Apulia and the Hellenised Salento, according to the extant documentation, the population of Taranto was divided: some used the Latin and others the Greek language, some lived under Lombard, others under Byzantine law,[37] some followed the Greek religious rite, others the Latin. The situation did not change after the Norman conquest. Since in the Salento no archival documentation of the Byzantine period has survived, whilst for the same time Taranto is well documented, in my view the town is an interesting example of multuculturalism in Byzantine and Norman southern Italy.

In contrast to other cities in Byzantine Italy, in Taranto Greek and Latin coexisted as literary languages: the Latin documents were written by members of the clergy of the archiepiscopal church, while the Greek ones were normally issued by clerics and secular notaries of the town, who sometimes had the title of *taboularios*. In some cases the notarial profession seems to have been hereditary in the same family.[38] The quality of language, script and layout of the Greek documents of Taranto is particularly elegant and attests to the excellent notarial training of the local notaries[39]; thanks to their competence they were even hired in other towns. In 1187 a document in Oriolo Calabro (prov. Cosenza) was written by the *grammatikos* (γραμματικός) Philip of Taranto.[40] According to an hypothesis of Santo Lucà even some Greek manuscripts, as for instance the *cod. Paris. gr.* 1624, *cod. Valic.* C 34, and *cod. Crypt. A. α* XI + *A. α.* XIII, might have been written in Taranto.[41]

During the Byzantine and Norman period, however, many more Greek than Latin documents were issued in Taranto. According to Jean-Marie Martin "*seul le hasard est responsable du fait que la documentation tarentine soit majoritairement grecque*",[42] but I cannot subscribe to this judgement: in fact "*le hasard*" must have favoured many different institutions, for the extant Greek documents once belonged to various archives: of the monasteries S. Pietro Imperiale, Ss. Elia e Anastasio di Carbone, S. Pietro dell'Isola Grande, S. Andrea dell'Isola Piccola and S. Vito del Pizzo, and to the archive of the Cathedral. Moreover 23 Greek documents issued in Taranto have been reused as palimpsests in two manuscripts of Grottaferrata, *cod. Crypt.* A.α. XI—A.α. XIII and *cod. Crypt.* E.α. VIII.[43] These latter documents often are scarcely legible, but can be identified as Tarantine by the script and the names of the scribes. For the Byzantine period I know of only two Latin documents issued in the city—one of them a charter of the archbishop—[44] and of 19 in Greek,[45] not counting the Greek charters of the Byzantine *katepanōs* and other high officials for recipients in Taranto.[46] For the Norman and early Hohenstaufen periods—the last Greek private document known to me being of 1228[47]—the proportion of private documents in Latin and Greek is 3 to 40,[48] and of public and administrative charters 4 to 5.[49] When in Taranto, even Bohemond I and his son, Bohemond II, sometimes used Greek for their charters,[50] and so did the royal katepan, Goffredus of Oria in 1143.[51] All the charters of the archbishops are in Latin,[52] but occasionally even the Latin clergy use Greek for their documents, as for instance the Latin monk Ursenando, abbot of the monastery of St Philip and Nicholas, who in 1029 sold a vineyard,[53] and the archdeacon John, who exchanged some landed property with the abbot of the monastery of S. Pietro Imperiale (1061).[54] Latin charters of the archbishops were sometimes signed by witnesses in Greek,[55] and the document of Vitalios, son of Eugene, a Greek donor, who in 1177 made an important donation to the archbishop to thank him for permission to build a memorial for his parents in the cemetery of the cathedral, just next to the central apse, is written in Greek.[56] Apparently the same was true for many people who lived under Lombard law, for in some Greek documents the women are represented by their *antistatōr* (ἀντιστάτωρ),[57] a term which seems to be the translation of *mundualdus*.[58] In his Greek testament (1086) the monk Genesios mentions that he left a vineyard to a friend διὰ ῥάβδου,[59] again a translation of the Lombard *per fustem tradere*.

It seems that members of the upper class especially used Greek: for the Byzantine period I know of 18 Greek signatures of persons who either themselves or and their fathers held a Byzantine office or honorary title, and only one in Latin.[60] In Bari, the capital of the katepanate of Italia, where the presence of Byzantine civil servants and officers is most obvious, for the same category the proportion is 56 Latin to 19 Greek signatures.[61] Even after the Norman conquest in 1104 a donation by a Norman widow Muriel to S. Pietro Imperiale, since 1080 a dependence of Montecassino, is signed by Στέφα(νος) (πρωτο)σπαθ(ά)ρ(ιος) ηπατ(ος) ο Οφυλος (Stephanos Ophylos *prōtospatharios hypatos*).[62]

The Greek or Latin cultural identity of the citizens, however, did not necessarily imply their political attitude for or against the Byzantine government. The supporters (συμμύσται) of a rebellion against the imperial authorities fomented by the archbishop of Taranto during the period of the Norman conquest, mentioned in a document of 1054, had Greek names: the brothers Eustathios and Leo Katanankes, the priest Bisantios of St Akyndinos and Basil Chrysochoos.[63]

Regarding the local anthroponymy, as in other towns of Byzantine Apulia, Greek, Latin and Lombard names were used by all communities without ethnic or cultural distinction: there is a Latin deacan called *Niciforo*[64] and a Greek *kathēgoumenos* called Οὗρσος (Ursus),[65] but during the Byzantine and Norman period Greek names apparently prevailed. In this context, however, I want to mention a strange phenomenon in the onomastics of Taranto, which does not appear in other parts of ex-Byzantine southern Italy: in the Norman period the *termini* of Byzantine honorary titles and military or administrative professions become personal names: in 1084 appears for instance *Stratelates* (Στρατηλάτης), son of John,[66] in 1142 Geoffrey, son of *Stratelates*,[67] and *Komes kortes* (Κόμης κόρτης), son of Daniel,[68] and in 1155 *Spatharios* (Σπαθάριος), son of Guido.[69] A Latin charter of 1138 is signed by *Krites* (Κριτής), son of Theophylaktos, who, as emerges from a comparison of his signatures, probably can be identified with *Iudex Tarentinus* or Κριτὴς Ταραντινός, *magister justiciarius* of the *regalis magna curia* in the years from 1159 to 1171.[70] He was a judge, but his personal name was *Krites*, or "judge".[71] This name is even used in Taranto in Latin transcription as *Criti filius Leonis Archontisse.*[72]

Although, as already said, the archbishop and the clergy of the cathedral remained Latin, there were several Greek churches and monasteries in Taranto and in its neighbourhood. In many cases, however, it is not possible to decide whether a church or a monastery mentioned in a document was Greek or Latin. The monastery of St Benedict, founded some time before 1028 by the abbot Leucius, close to the city walls at the *Porta Terranea,* and the monastery of St Mark, which in 1071 belonged to the Benedictine abbey in Bari,[73] were certainly Latin,[74] whilst S. Pietro Imperiale, a *basilikon monastērion* (βασιλικὸν μοναστήριον), that is a monastery directly dependent on the emperor, who could give it as *charistikion* to whomever he wanted,[75] was Greek,[76] and so was St Bartholomew, a church which in 1049 belonged to the family of a former Byzantine official, the *chartoularios* (χαρτουλάριος) and *topotērētēs* (τοποτηρητής) Nikephoros;[77] in the Norman period it became a *metochion* of the Greek monastery of St Elias and St Anastasius of Carbone in Basilicata.[78] The church of St Memnon, probably situated outside the walls of Taranto,[79] which became a dependency of S. Pietro Imperiale,[80] seems to have been Greek as well. André Jacob has published fragments of a Greek liturgical *diptychon* inscribed on terracotta, which were found in a cave close to Taranto, and are dated to the first half of the eleventh century.[81]

There were also many deacons, priests and monks who signed local documents in Greek. For the Byzantine period I know of 23 Greek signatures of at least 20 different priests or clerics, among them a *basilikos klērikos* (βασιλικὸς κληρικός),[82] that is, an honorary cleric of the church called Νέα in the imperial palace of Constantinople.[83] Moreover there were the priest Basil, who in the years 1029–1040 wrote several private Greek documents in the town,[84] and an archimandrite,[85] and in 1035 Theodosios abbot of S. Pietro Imperiale was contemporarily the *exarchos* (ἔξαρχος) of the imperial monasteries of the area.[86] Head of the Greek religious community was the *prōtopapas* (πρωτοπαπᾶς), who as in other Byzantine or ex-Byzantine towns in southern Italy,[87] sometimes acted as *taboularios* (ταβουλάριος).[88] In some documents of Taranto, however, issued during the 1040s a certain *Kinnamos Episkopos* (Κίνναμος Ἐπίσκοπος) appears, as heir and owner (κληρονόμος, δεσπόζων) of the church St Memnon in the neighbourhood of Taranto.[89] According to a hypothesis of Jean-Marie Martin, based entirely on homonymy, he was a *chorepiscopus*, who had been transferred to Taranto from his former see in Olevano sul Tusciano (Campania),[90] but it is more likely that in this case *Episkopos* is a surname otherwise known in Taranto and elsewhere in southern Italy.[91] In fact there is no element at all which could indicate that *Cennamus*, bishop of Olevano, mentioned in a Latin charter of Waimar III, prince of Salerno (July 1010), was Greek, since the name is commonly used among the Lombard population of the principality of Salerno,[92] whereas *Kinnamos Episkopos* of Taranto is never addressed with any of the honourable epithets due to a bishop, such as "most pious" (εὐσεβέστατος), "most beloved of God" (θεοφιλέστατος) or "most honourable" (τιμιώτατος); moreover, the name of his diocese is never mentioned in the documents. Thus in my view, *Cennamus episcopus* of Olevano sul Tusciano was not Greek, and *Kinnamos Episkopos* of Taranto was not a bishop, but seems to have been just the owner of the church.[93]

After the Norman conquest some of the Greek and Latin churches and monasteries of Taranto were given to the major Benedictine abbeys in southern Italy: S. Pietro Imperiale to Montecassino, St Benedict to the Ss. Trinità di Cava and S. Oronzo to S. Lorenzo at Aversa,[94] but many Greek monasteries survived in the town and its periphery, and the Greek religious rite continued to be cherished and celebrated. In the second half of the twelfth century the church of St George, belonged to the Norman official *Judex Tarentinus* or Κριτὴς Ταραντινός, who at the end of his life became a monk in the Greek monastery of S. Salvatore *de Lingua Phari* at Messina, and in his testament appointed his nephews *ephoroi* (ἔφοροι) of his church in Taranto.[95] We do not know whether St George had been founded by *Judex Tarentinus* himself or by his ancestors.[96] In the Norman and Hohenstaufen periods there are mentioned the Greek monasteries S. Pietro dell'Isola Grande,[97] S. Andrea sull'Isola Piccola,[98] S. Vito del Pizzo[99] and S. Maria di Ceserano.[100] In 1169 archbishop Giraldus dedicated the church of S. Maria di Galeso close to Taranto, founded by the baron and *logothetes* Richard of Taranto, a church which was to become a Cistercian abbey, *presentibus Ioannicio Magne Insule, Cosmate Parve Insule et Luca Sancti Viti abbatibus et universo clero Tarenti.*[101] Apparently the three Greek abbots were among the most prominent religious figures in the town. The Greek epitaphs of two nuns, who died in 1135 and 1152, respectively, are still preserved in the Archeological Museum of Taranto;[102] as before there are many Greek signatures of priests, clerics and sons of priests,[103] and Greek priests were appointed as *taboularioi* (ταβουλάριοι): the priests George, son of Nicholas, and Gentilios, son of Nicholas, are attested in that position in the years 1128/1129[104] and 1217 to 1228.[105]

The coexistence of Latin and Greek in the town created the cultural background for Norman high civil servants such as *Judex Tarentinus* or Κριτὴς Ταραντινός, the aforementioned *magister justiciarius* of the *regalis magna curia* (1159 to 1171), who issued Latin judgements that he signed in Greek. He was sent by the Norman king in an embassy to Constantinople, and at the end of his life became a monk in the Greek monastery of S. Salvatore *de Lingua Phari* in Messina, where he left in deposit his important Greek library of theological and juridical books.[106] The *Miracula* of Saint Cataldus, patron saint of Taranto, mention the *miles egregius de Taranto, dominus Bedengarius* [...] *eloquentissimus jurisque peritus* who was ordered by the king to come to Palermo *ad transferendum quoddam de Graeco in Latinum volumen.*[107]

This linguistic evidence explains the statement of the Jewish traveller Benjamin of Tudela, who visited the town in the 60s of the twelfth century, that the habitants of Taranto were Greek.[107] In fact, the head of the important Jewish community in Taranto, which according to the local tradition descended from the prisoners of war, who had been abducted from Jerusalem to Italy by the Emperor Titus in 70/71,[108] is called *protos* (πρῶτος) *Iudaice Tarenti.*[108]

As has already been said, the last known private document in Greek was issued in Taranto in November 1228 by the priest Gentilios, son of Nicolas, *basilikos taboularios* of Taranto (βασιλικὸς ταβουλάριος Ταράντου),[109] active since 1217.[110] In fact, during the first half of the thirteenth century Greek begins to dwindle in all the major towns of the kingdom of Sicily, where during the twelfth century this language had been normally used for private documents, as for instance in Reggio, Messina and Palermo.[111] There are various reasons for this linguistic change during the reign of Frederick II: 1) after the foundation of the kingdom of Sicily by Roger II the Greek speaking population was a minority compared to Latin speakers; thus the public administration became more and more Latinised; 2) especially after the Latin conquest of Constantinople in 1204 the Greek speaking population lived in a cultural diaspora; 3) in the Hohenstaufen period public administration was progressively run by officials with university degrees,[112] and Latin was the teaching language in the universities. Therefore the Greek upper class and intellectual élite became increasingly Latinised. Nevertheless in Taranto as in the major Sicilian towns Greek did not entirely disappear: some Latin documents of 1232 and 1237 were signed by a Greek judge, Stephanitzes the judge, son of Basil the notary (Στεφανίτζης κριτὴς υἱὸς Βασιλείου νοταρίου),[113] who was still active in 1249,[114] and during the same period the *magister* Petrakka, the notary and *groikos* (Greek) *taboularios* (Πετράκκα ὁ νοτάριος καὶ γροῖκος ταβουλάριος), translated a Greek charter of Roger II for the abbot of S. Elia e S. Anastasio of Carbone into Latin. His translation was signed by the same judge Stephanitzes son of the notary Basil.[115] Finally, if the royal notary Roger of Otranto at the end of the twelfth century writes in Greek his *stichoi eristikoi* (στίχοι ἐριστικοί) about the contrast between Otranto and Taranto,[116] there must have been somebody in Taranto to understand the text. In the second half of the thirteenth century it might have become more difficult to get a proper Greek education in the town. André Jacob has published an epigram about two young men from Taranto, both called John, who apparently went to continue their studies in southern Salento, where the Greek language and tradition survived through the late Middle Ages.[117]

A *protopapa Grecus* is still mentioned in 1249,[118] and during the thirteenth century Nicholas, a priest from Taranto, wrote a Greek treatise in defence of the Greek liturgy for marriage and Easter.[119] Greek monasteries survived as well. According to the *Rationes decimarum* of 1310 *monasterium S. Viti de Piczo* and *monasterium S. Andree et Petri de Insula Parva* were the most wealthy monasteries in the province of Taranto.[120] Both monasteries, always described as *ordinis s. Basilii,* are often mentioned in pontifical documents of the fourteenth and fifteenth centuries.[121] Moreover, up to the sixteenth century the monks of the Greek monastery of S. Vito del Pizzo, close to Taranto, continued to write notes in Greek on the margins of a liturgical Greek manuscript (*cod. Paris. Gr.* 1624).[122] Even the modern dialect of Taranto still preserves many Graecisms, indicating the historical and social depth of interaction between this part of the Italian peninsula and the Greek-speaking East Roman world.[123]

Appendix

Greek and Latin documents issued in Taranto from the Byzantine recovery in 880 to 1228

I. The Greek documents

I, a: Private documents

1. 981, April: donation (ἀφιέρωσις) to the monastery of St Peter (S. Pietro Imperiale), written by Gregory by order of Kortikes *protopapas* and *taboularios*. All the witnesses sign in Greek; among them there are the priests Constantine and John, the cleric Areskes and Stephen, son of the priest John (Trinchera, *Syllabus,* no. 8, pp. 6 f.; photograph in: von Falkenhausen, Amelotti, *Notariato e documento,* fig. I; Danella, *Privilegi sovrani,* fig. I; D'Agostino, Degni, *Cultura grafica,* fig. VII a).
2. 984, January: agreement (συμβίβασις): Nicholas Mansouris und his son in law give up their rights to one half of a fish pond (βιβάριον) in favour of Simon, abbot of the monastery of St Peter (S. Pietro Imperiale); written by Kortikes πρωτοπαπᾶς and ταβουλάριος. All the witnesses sign in Greek; among them there are the priests Eusthatios, Leo and Constantine, the cleric Kalokyros and George ἐκ προσώπου of Taranto (Trinchera, *Syllabus,* no. 9, pp. 7–9; photograph in: von Falkenhausen, Amelotti, *Notariato e documento,* fig. II; D'Agostino, Degni, *Cultura grafica,* fig. VII b).
3. 1029, April: sale (πρᾶσις) of a vineyard at Montefrese by the monk Ursenandus, abbot of the monastery St Philip and Nicholas, who writes his name in Latin, to John, son of Peter and Gemma; written by the priest Basil. All the witnesses sign in Greek; among them there are John κόμης κόρτης, Nicholas, son of the τοποτηρητής Pantaleon, and Kosmas, son of the κλεισουριάρχης Nicholas (Trinchera, *Syllabus,* no. 22, pp. 23 f.; photograph in: D'Agostino, Degni, *Cultura grafica,* fig. VIII).
4. 1032, July: donation (χαρτίον) of a piece of land by Oursos Benenatos to his freedwoman Maria; written by the priest Basil. Four witnesses sign in Greek, among them there is Achanys son of the cleric Asechanys; the deacon Nicephorus signs in Latin (Trinchera, *Syllabus,* no. 24, pp. 26 f.).
5. 1033, February: sale (πρᾶσις) of two vineyards at S. Angelo di Rascla by Leo, son of κόμης Ischanakios, to the Jew Theophylaktos, called Chimarias, written by the priest Basil. All the witnesses sign in Greek; among them there are the κόμης Ischanakes, the τουρμάρχης John and Nicholas, son of Nicholas from Taormina (Trinchera, *Syllabus,* no. 26, pp. 29–31).
6. 1035, August: emphyteusis (ἀσφάλεια) made by Theodosios, ἔξαρχος of the imperial monasteries and abbot of St Peter (S. Pietro Imperiale), of a vineyard to Grisantus, son of Athanasius, who writes his name in Latin; written by the notary Nicholas. All the witnesses sign in Greek, among them there is the son of the τουρμάρχης Anastasios (Trinchera, *Syllabus,* no. 30, pp. 35 f.).

7. 1039, January: sale (πρᾶσις) of land at S. Angelo di Rascla, by Leo, son of count Ischanakios, to the Jew Theophylaktos, called Chimarias, written by the priest Basil. All the witnesses sign in Greek, among them there are Leo, son of the τουρμάρχης John Tyrannos, and the priest Nicholas (Trinchera, *Syllabus,* no. 31, pp. 36–38).
8. 1040, April: donation (προσένεξις, πρᾶσις) of two pieces of land by Leo, son of count Ischanakios, to the church of St Memnon and to its heir and owner (κληρονόμος) Kinnamos, because they want to be buried close to the church; written by the priest Basil. All the witnesses sign in Greek; among them there are Leo, son of a τουρμάρχης John Tyrannos, and the priest Kalokyros (Trinchera, *Syllabus,* no. 32, pp. 38 f.).
9. 1042, July: sale (διάπρασις) of a piece of land close to the church of St Memnon by Mary, widow of the priest Falco, to Kinnamos; written by the notary John. All the witnesses sign in Greek, among them there is Stephen τουρμάρχης (Trinchera, *Syllabus,* no. 33, pp. 40 f.).
10. 1043, November: assurance (ἀσφάλεια). Sardo, son of Chrysanthos, promises Bartholomew, abbot of S. Pietro Imperiale, and his successors, to give them, when he dies, a document of donation; written by John Kourkouas. Four witnesses sign in Greek, among them there are the τουρμάρχαι Leo and Neophytos, whilst the *turmarcha* Michael Fileni signs in Latin (Trinchera, *Syllabus,* no. 27, pp. 31 f. The date 1033 given by the editor is erroneous).
11. 1045, April: donation (ἀφιέρωσις) of two pieces of land to the church of St Memnon and its owner (δεσπόζων) Kinnamos Ἐπίσκοπος by George, son of the late *domestikos* Constantine, and his sister Mary, who want to be buried within the enclosure of the church; written by John Kourkouas. All the witnesses sign in Greek, among them there are the priests Bisantios and Theodore (Trinchera, *Syllabus,* no. 34, pp. 41 f.; photograph in: von Falkenhausen, Amelotti, *Notariato e documento,* fig. IV; D'Agostino, Degni, *Cultura grafica,* fig. V).
12. 1047, April: exchange (ἀνταλλαγωγή). Martin, son in law of the *domestikos* Constantine, und his wife Donata, give some land close to the church of St Memnon to Kinnamos Ἐπίσκοπος, who has granted them a tomb; written by John Kourkouas. All the witnesses sign in Greek, among them there are the priests Bisantios and Tarasios, and Theophanes, the son of the archpriest Leo (Trinchera, *Syllabus,* no. 35, pp. 42 f.; photograph in: Danella, *Privilegi sovrani,* fig. V).
13. 1049, March: testament (τελευτεία θέλεσις) of Gemma, widow of Nikephoros χαρτουλάριος and τοποτηρητής, who leaves part of her property to her nephews and to the church of St Bartholomew which belongs to the family, written by John Kourkouas. All the witnesses sign in Greek; among them there are the priests Leo and Theophanes, son of the κόμης John, and the notary Genesios (Robinson, *History and Cartulary,* no. IV-53, pp. 150–157).

14. 1049, November: sale (ἔγγραφον τῆς πράσεως). The monk and abbot Phantinos resells to Kinnamos Ἐπίσκοπος part of some houses, for the price of four *nomismata* and three books: written by John Kourkouas. All the witnesses sign in Greek; among them there are the priest Bisantios and Theophanes, son of the archpriest Leo (Trinchera, *Syllabus,* no. 36, pp. 44 f.).
15. 1052, May: donation (ἔγγραφον τῆς ἀφιερώσεως), Oursos, son of Gregory, procurator of the late Kalos, who has been buried close to the church of St Peter (S. Pietro Imperiale), gives a piece of land to the abbot Bartholomew; written by John Kourkouas. All the witnesses, the priests, Leo, Peter and Leo, sign in Greek (Trinchera, *Syllabus,* no. 39, pp. 48 f.).
16. 1054, April: sale (πρᾶσις). Selitta and her relatives sell two vineyards to Bartholomew, abbot of St Peter (S. Pietro Imperiale) for a *nomisma skyphaton;* written by John Kourkouas. All the witnesses sign in Greek: the priests Theodore and John, the cleric Romanos, Michael, son of the deacon Stephen and John βασιλικὸς κληρικός (Trinchera, *Syllabus,* no. 41, pp. 51 f.).
17. 1057/1058: the text is illegible; written by Andrew ὁ τοῦ ἀρχιμανδρίτου (*cod. Crypt.* A.α. XI—A.α. XIII, foll. 146r, 151v, Crisci, *I palinsesti di Grottaferrata,* 65, who did not read the name of the notary).
18. 1061, February: exchange (ἀνταλλαγωγή): John archdeacon of the Cathedral, who writes his name in metrical Latin, exchanges land with Oursos abbot of S. Pietro Imperiale; written by Andrew ὁ τοῦ ἀρχιμανδρίτου. Among the witnesses there are the priest Eustasius, the deacons John and George, the subdeacon Papassy, and the *levita* Peter, who sign in Latin, whilst Anastasios, son of the τουρμάρχης Leo Lybakes, Oursos, son of the priest Gregory, and Theophylaktos sign in Greek (Trinchera, *Syllabus,* no. 45, pp. 58 f.).
19. 1067, February: donation of a vineyard to John, husband of the cousin of the issuer of the document; written by Andrew ὁ τοῦ ἀρχιμανδρίτου (*cod. Crypt.* A.α. XI—A.α. XIII, foll. 144r, 141v, Crisci, *I palinsesti di Grottaferrata,* 65, who did not read the name of the notary).
20. 1075, September: testament (διάταξις) of Genesios, son of Falco, who wants to become monk in the church of St Bartholomew. He frees his slave Lucia, and leaves his properties situated in Martzanellon, Broume, Bari, Paterno, Sala, Roustikiliano, Mesikouron, Palbetzanon and Lamakanikia, to his relatives, his godson, the daughter of his slave, and to the church of St Bartholomew; written by Andrew ὁ τοῦ ἀρχιμανδρίτου. The five witnesses sign in Greek (Robinson, *History and Cartulary,* II, 1, no. X-59, pp. 179–183).
21. 1084, February: agreement (τῆς συμβιβάσεως ἔγγραφον) between Stratelates, son of John, son of the late ἐκ προσώπου Nicholas, and the πατρίκιος Nicholas,[124] about the construction of an olive-press; written by Pankallos, son of John Kourkouas. Four witnesses sign in

Greek, among them there are Magiourellos πρωτοσπαθάριος and Trachaniotes ταγματοφύλαξ, whilst *Leo Iohannis Episcopi* signs in Latin (Trinchera, *Syllabus,* no. 48, pp. 62 f.; photograph in: von Falkenhausen, Amelotti, *Notariato e documento,* fig. V; D'Agostino, Degni, *Cultura grafica,* fig. VI).

22. 1084, February: the text is almost illegible, but it might be a marriage contract between the son of the late Luke and Saida; written by Pankallos, son of John Kourkouas (*cod. Crypt.* A.α. XI—A.α. XIII, foll. 142r, 143v, Crisci, *I palinsesti di Grottaferrata,* 65, who did not read the name of the notary).
23. 1086, January: testament (ἐσχάτη ἐπιταγή) of the monk Genesios, son of Falco: he leaves part of his property to Pankallos, son of John Kourkouas, to his *synteknos* Oursos and to his daughter Anna; the rest should be sold for the benefit of his soul; written by Pankallos, son of John Kourkouas. All the witnesses sign in Greek; among them there are the priests Theophylaktos and Oursos (Robinson, *History and Cartulary,* no. XII-61, 190–194; photograph in: G. Breccia, *Scritture greche,* fig. 1 b).
24. 1089, February: donation (ἔγγραφον τῆς ἀφιερώσεως) of a cave close to the gate τοῦ Ἑταιρειώτου by Hyakinthe, daughter of the late Pamphilos, to the church of S. Pietro Imperiale, where she wants to be buried, and to its ἔφορος and prior John written by Andrew ὁ τοῦ ἀρχιμανδρίτου. All the witnesses sign in Greek; among them there is the priest Nicholas Leontitzes, (Trinchera, *Syllabus,* no. 51, pp. 67 f.),
25. 1113, January: donation (τῆς ἀφιέρώσεως ἔγγραφον) of a piece of land in the village of Misikouron by Leo, son of Constantine to the monastery of S. Pietro dell'Isola Grande and the abbot John; written by Kalos son of Domnando. The three witnesses sign in Greek; among them there is the priest Anastasios (Magistrale [ed.], *Le pergamene*, no. 3, pp. 10–12, with a photograph).
26. 1116, August: contract of emphyteusis (ἔγγραφον) between Bernard *prepositus* of S. Pietro Imperiale, who writes his name in Latin, together with his substitute (ἀντιστάτωρ) and John, son of Bisantios, concerning two vineyards at Aquara, which belong to the monastery. John has to cultivate both vineyards and has to deliver every year six *lagenia* of wine to S. Pietro; in reward he receives one of the vineyards, but the monastery has the right of preemption. If he gives up cultivation, the vineyard returns to the monastery; written by Kalos, son of Domnando. The three witnesses sign in Greek; among them there is Basil, son of a priest Peter (Trinchera, *Syllabus,* no. 79, pp. 103 f.; photograph in: Danella, *Privilegi sovrani,* fig. VI).
27. 1119, February: text illegible; written by Kalos, son of Domnando (*cod. Crypt.* E. α. VIII, foll. 117v, 122r, Crisci, *I palinsesti di Grottaferrata,* 180),
28. 1123 February: donation (τῆς δωρεᾶς ἔγγραφον): Peter and Griphos, sons of Theodore, give two vineyards to the sisters Alfarana e Rosa.

Previously, in a lawsuit with the nun of the church of St Bartholomew,[125] the father of the two sisters had given two equal-sized vineyards to the church; written by Kalos, son of Domnando. Three witnesses sign in Greek, the cleric Robert signs in Latin (Robinson, *History and Cartulary,* ii, 1, no. XXV-72, pp. 243–245; photograph in: Breccia, *Scritture greche*, fig. 2 a).

29. date illegible: donation (δωρεά) by Bisantios, his sister Maria and Kalokyros, written by Kalos, son of Domnando (*cod. Crypt.* E. α. VIII, foll. 140v, 147r, Crisci, *I palinsesti di Grottaferrata,* 180).
30. 1128/1129: donation (τῆς δωρεᾶς ἔγγραφον) by Philardos and some relatives; written by the priest George, son of Nicholas, ταβουλάριος Ταράντου (*cod. Crypt.* E. α. VIII, foll. 151v, 152r, Crisci, *I palinsesti di Grottaferrata,* 181).
31. 1131, January: assurance (ἀσφάλεια). Sikenolfus, brother of the physician Pandolfus, promises Bernard, the prior of S. Pietro Imperiale, to give every year on the feast of the Hypapante (Purification) one *nomisma,* for the garden close to the church of St Memnon, given to him by the monastery; written by the *protopapas* Kalos, son of Domnando. The three witnesses sign in Greek; among them there is the priest Kalos (Trinchera, *Syllabus,* no. 109, p. 144).
32. 1137/1138: texte illegible: written by the *protopapas* Kalos, son of Domnando (*cod. Crypt.* E. α. VIII, foll. 154r, 149v, Crisci, *I palinsesti di Grottaferrata,* 180).
33. 1143, September: assurance (ἀσφαλιστικὸν ἔγγραφον). Nicholas, son of Hyakinthella, promises to John, the bursar of S. Pietro Imperiale, to give every year on Palm Sunday a measure of incense to the monastery, according to the contract about the cultivation of a piece of land in between the vineyards of Nicholas and the monastery, made with John's predecessor Anthony; written by Kourkouas, son of John. Two witnesses sign in Greek, whilst Nicholas, son of Melis, signs in Latin (Trinchera, *Syllabus,* no. 135, pp. 178 f.).
34. 1145, September: assurance (τῆς ἀσφαλείας ἔγγραφον). Theodore, son of Peter Kaprios, and his brother Stephen promise Hilarion, abbot of S. Elia e S. Anastasio of Carbone, to give 25 measures of wine for a vineyard, which belongs to the monastery, but had been planted by their father; written by Kourkouas, son of John. All the four witnesses sign in Greek; among them there are Sere, son of the τοποτηρητής Nicholas, and Leo, son of the priest Niketas (Robinson, *History and Cartulary,* II, 2, no. XL-88, pp. 47–50),
35. 1145 September: assurance (τῆς ἀσφαλείας ἔγγραφον). Griphos, son of Theodore Ankinellos, and Remedia, his sister-in-law make a contract with Hilarion, abbot of S. Elia e S. Anastasio di Carbone. They had cultivated a tract of land that belonged to the church of S. Bartolomeo, *metochion* of Carbone, which they were commanded to return to the owner. Now they agree to deliver every year in November to the

monastery four *kannatai* of oil; written by Kourkouas, son of John. All the four witnesses sign in Greek; among them there is Sere, son of the τοποτηρητής Nicholas (*ibid.,* no. XLa-89, pp. 51–53).

36. 1145 November: sale (πρᾶσις). John, prior of S. Pietro Imperiale, and his substitute Berengarius, both writing their names in Latin, sell four vineyards to Theophylaktos, son of the *magister* Nicholas, physician of the king, for the price of 60 *doukati.* Theophylaktos promises to deliver every year at the feast of St Peter's eight measures of wax. If the vineyards are not cultivated, they return to the monastery; written by Kourkouas, son of John. Two witnesses sign in Greek, Nicholas, son of Melis, signs in Latin (Trinchera, *Syllabus,* no. 140, pp. 186 f., photograph in: Danella, *Privilegi sovrani,* fig. VII).
37. 1150, March: donation (τῆς δωρεᾶς ἔγγραφον), written by Oursos, son of the priest Anastasios, ταβουλάριος Ταράντου (*cod. Crypt.* E. α. VIII, foll. 142v, 145r, Crisci, *I palinsesti di Grottaferrata,* pp. 180 f.).
38. 1151, October: sale (τῆς πράσεως ἔγγραφον). Mathew sells his μέρος for the price of 30 *doukati* to Sarakinos, son of Stephen; written by John, son of Leo, ταβουλάριος Ταράντου (*cod. Crypt.* E. α. VIII, foll. 125v, 130r, Crisci, *I palinsesti di Grottaferrata,* p. 180).
39. 1155, November: exchange (τῆς ἀναλλαγωγῆς ἔγγραφον). Spatharios, son of Guido, and his wife Emma exchange immobile property with Hyakinthos, brother of Spatharios: they give part of a house built on the city wall, and receive a vineyard and a field at Mourovetere; written by John, son of Leo, ταβουλάριος Ταράντου. Two witnesses sign in Greek, *Corsicus frater Bisarionis,* signs in Latin (Robinson, *History and Cartulary,* II, no. XLIV-93, pp. 65–67).
40. 1157, April: sale (πρᾶσις). Irene sells her part of a *moursion* (deep ditch) to Luke, abbot of the monastery of S. Andrea dell'Isola Piccola for the price of 10 new *doukati*; written by Oursos, son of the priest Anastasios, ταβουλάριος Ταράντου. Two witnesses sign in Greek, among them there is Constantine, son of the priest Nicholas, Grisogoanen, son of Theophilus, signs in Latin (Magistrale [ed.], *Le pergamene*, no. 7, pp. 23–25, with a photograph).
41. 1163 June: marriage contract (γαμικοῦ συμφώνου ἔγγραφον) written by Stephanitzes, son of Peter, ταβουλάριος Ταράντου (*cod. Crypt.* E. α. VIII, foll. 127v, 128r, Crisci, *I palinsesti di Grottaferrata,* 180).
42. 1168, July: marriage contract (γαμικοῦ συμφώνου ἔγγραφον) written by Stephanitzes, son of Peter, ταβουλάριος Ταράντου (*cod. Crypt.* E. α. VIII, foll. 118v, 121r, Crisci, *I palinsesti di Grottaferrata,* 180).
43. 1169/1170: exchange (τῆς ἀναλλαγῆς ἔγγραφον) written by Stephanitzes, son of Peter, ταβουλάριος Ταράντου (*cod. Crypt.* E. α. VIII, foll. 150v, 153r, Crisci, *I palinsesti di Grottaferrata,* 181).
44. 1171: assurance (τῆς ἀσφαλείας ἔγγραφον). Basil, son-in-law of Albabera, promises the hieromonk Dionysios to give every year at Christmas one litre of incense to the church of St Bartholomew,

metochion of the monastery of S. Elia e S. Anastasio of Carbone, for a house and a ruin he had bought from the church with the permission of the archimandrite of Carbone, Bartholomew; written by Stephanitzes, son of Peter, ταβουλάριος Ταράντου. The three witnesses sign in Greek (Robinson, *History and Cartulary,* II, 2, no. XLIX-95, 81–83; photograph in: Breccia, *Scritture greche,* tav. 3 a).

45. 1173, May: donation or sale by Joannikios, son of Petrakka Ritzos, his wife Argentia, and Nicholas, the *antistator* of Argentia; written by Stephanitzes, son of Peter, ταβουλάριος Ταράντου (*cod. Crypt.* E. α. VIII, foll. 134v, 137r, Crisci, *I palinsesti di Grottaferrata,* 180).
46. 1175, January: marriage contract (γαμικοῦ συμφώνου ἔγγραφον); there are mentioned textiles of cotton and silk, jewels and a field, for which is to be payed a *douleia* (contribution) in oil; written by Stephanitzes, son of Peter, ταβουλάριος Ταράντου. One of eight witnesses signs in Latin, the others in Greek (*cod. Crypt.* E. α. VIII, foll. 103v, 106r, 104v, 105r, Crisci, *I palinsesti di Grottaferrata,* 179 f.).
47. 1175, December: testament (ἐσχάτη καὶ τελευταία διάταξις) of Tarantina, daughter of John Kinnamos, sister of Piskopissa and widow of Theophylaktos, who leaves her property to relatives and to the monastery of Sta. Anna, where she wants to be buried, to the clergy of the Cathedral, to the nunnery St John, to the church of St Quiricus τῶν μαρμάρων and to the Holy Sepulchre at Jerusalem; written by Stephanitzes, son of Peter, ταβουλάριος Ταράντου. Four witnesses, among them Pankallos, son of the priest Maiouris, sign in Greek, whilst *Alexander Constantini de Iaspido filius* signs in Latin (Magistrale [ed.], *Le pergamene*, no. 9, pp. 31–34, with a photograph).
48. 1177, April: donation (ἔγγραφον τῆς δωρεᾶς) of property in the village of Kastinnion to archbishop Basil of Taranto by Vitalios, son of Eugene, who wants to build a funeral monument for his parents in the cemetery of the cathedral; written by Stephanitzes, son of Peter, ταβουλάριος Ταράντου. Two witnesses sign in Greek, whilst *W. Salvaticus* signs in Latin (Trinchera, *Syllabus,* no. 189, pp. 248 f.).
49. 1177, April: sale (τῆς πράσεως ἔγγραφον). Gemma, daughter of John Roufoulos and widow of Roger of Gallipoli, and her son John, who write their names in Latin, sell to the hieromonk Dionysios of the church S. Bartolomeo, *metochion* of the monastery of S. Elia e S. Anastasio di Carbone, a ruin close to the beach of the Mare Piccolo and the *Porta Ebraica*, for the price of three ounces of gold; written by Stephanitzes, son of Peter, ταβουλάριος Ταράντου. The three witnesses sign in Greek (Robinson, *History and Cartulary,* II, 2, no. LII-97, pp. 92–95).
50. 1161/1162 or 1176/1177: loan. Leo, son of Andrew, had made a loan to the issuer of the document, who had left a small house as security; written by Stephanitzes, son of Peter, ταβουλάριος Ταράντου (*cod. Crypt.* E. α. VIII, foll. 108v, 115r, Crisci, *I palinsesti di Grottaferrata,* 180).

51. date illegible, but ca. 1163–1177, February: sale of a vineyard (τῆς πράσεως ἔγγραφον) by Alexander, son of Leo Groppos, his wife and her *antistator,* to William; written by Stephanitzes, son of Peter, ταβουλάριος Ταράντου (*cod. Crypt.* E. α. VIII, foll. 136r, 135v, Crisci, *I palinsesti di Grottaferrata,* 180).
52. date and text illegible, written by Pankallos, son of Maiouros, ταβουλλάριος Ταράντου, (*cod. Crypt.* E. α. VIII, ff. 114r, 109v; Crisci, *I palinsesti di Grottaferrata,* 180). A witness of that name signs a document of december 1175 (Magistrale [ed.], *Le pergamene*, no. 9, pp. 31–34, with a photograph).
53. 1182, May: donation (τῆς καθαρας δωρεᾶς ἔγγραφον): Gemma, daughter of John Roufoulos and widow of Roger of Gallipoli, gives an olive tree to the church of S. Bartolomeo, *metochion* of the monastery of S. Elia e S. Anastasio of Carbone written by Kourkouas, son of John the judge. Gemma's son John signs in Latin, the three witnesses in Greek (Robinson, *History and Cartulary,* II, 2, no. LIV-99, 101–103; photograph in: Breccia, *Scritture greche*, tav. 3 b).),
54. 1193, 22 February: donation (τῆς ἀφιερώσεως ἔγγραφον). The priest Andrew gives himself, his books and four ounces of Sicilian tarì to the monastery of S. Elia e S. Anastasio of Carbone and the archimandrite Hilarion. If his wife allows him to become a monk, or if she dies before him, he wants to serve the monastery in the *metochion* of St Bartholomew; written by Constantine, son of Nicholas, ταβουλάριος Ταράντου. All the witnesses sign in Greek; among them there are the notary Agapetos, son of Nikephoros, τῆς Ταράντης ταβουλάριος and the priest Andrew, son of the notary Leo (R. Cotroneo, *Pergamene greche del secolo XIII,* Rivista storica calabrese 10 [1902] 40–42. The document is lost, and the edition is not reliable),
55. 1198, April: exchange (τῆς ἀναλλαγῆς ἔγγραφον) of houses between Poulita, daughter of the captain Maraldus, and the hieromonk Athanasios, bursar of the church St Bartholomew, *metochion* of the monastery of S. Elia e S. Anastasio di Carbone. Poulita gives a house close to the church and receives, with the permission of the archimandrite of Carbone, a house close to the beach of the Mare Piccolo and the *Porta Ebraica*; written by Agapetos, son of Nikephoros, ταβουλάριος Ταράντου. The three witnesses—among them the *Alexander iudex Taranti*—sign in Latin (Robinson, *History and Cartulary,* II, 2, no. LXIV-102, pp. 133–136).
56. 1200 (?), September: the text is illegible; written by Agapetos, son of Nikephoros, ταβουλάριος Ταράντου (*cod. Crypt.* E. α. VIII, foll. 141v, 146r, Crisci, *I palinsesti di Grottaferrata,* 180).
57. 1217, February: contract of lease (τῆς ἀσφαλείας ἔγγραφον). Samaro, son of Euphemios, declares that he has received a vineyard from Philip, prior of the monastery of S. Pietro imperiale. He agrees to cultivate it and deliver every year at Palm Sunday a measure of wax. If he does not

cultivate it, the vineyard returns to the monastery; written by the priest Gentilios, son of Nicholas, ταβουλάριος Ταράντου. Two witnesses, *Aripertus filius Leonis* and *Leo filius Goffredi* sign in Latin, Oursileon, son of Nicholas, signs in Greek (Trinchera, *Syllabus,* no. 269, p. 370)

58. 1217, August: contract of lease (τῆς ἀσφαλείας ἔγγραφον) of a vineyard between Philip, prior of the monastery of S. Pietro imperiale, and William Topoteretes, who has to deliver to the monastery, every year at the feast of the Hypopante (Purification) a litre of wax; written by the priest Gentilios, son of Nicholas, ταβουλάριος Ταράντου. Two witnesses sign in Greek, and *Jordanus filius Johannis Blatti,* in Latin (Trinchera, *Syllabus,* no. 270, p. 371).
59. 1221, May: exchange (ἀφιέρωσις καὶ ἀντικαταλλαγή). Basil, son of the notary John, gives to Nikodemos, abbot of the monastery S. Vito del Pizzo, a piece of land with olive trees, and receives 40 *tomoli* of grain; written by the priest Gentilios, son of Nicholas, ταβουλάριος Ταράντου, and signed by the κριτής Walter in Greek and by *Riccardus Buccarellus iudex Taranti* in Latin, and by a Greek and a Latin witness (von Falkenhausen, *Un inedito documento,* 17 f.),
60. 1228, November: emphyteusis (τῆς ἀσφαλείας ἔγγραφον). John, son of the physician Constantine, receives from Oursenandus, prior of S. Pietro Imperiale, four pieces of land to plant as a vineyard; written by the priest Gentilios, son of Nicholas, βασικλικὸς ταβουλάριος Ταράντου. All three witnesses sign in Latin: *Leo Sire Guirrisi filius, Iaspidus filius iudicis Alexandri, Paganus Malignus* (Trinchera, *Syllabus,* no. 281, 387 f.; photograph in: Danella, *Privilegi sovrani,* fig. VIII).

There are five more palimpsest documents from Taranto, which I have not yet been able to read (*cod. Crypt.* E. α. VIII, foll. 102v, 107r, foll. 138r, 133v, foll. 114r, 109v, foll. 120r, 119v, foll. 116v, 123r, foll. 124v, 131r, Crisci, *I palinsesti di Grottaferrata,* 180).

I, b: Documents of Byzantine officials and Norman authorities

1. 975, May: ὑπόμνημα with a lead seal. Michael *anthypatos patrikios* and *katepano* of Italia confirms to the monks of the monastery S. Pietro the charters (δικαιώματα καὶ ὑπομνήματα) of his predecessors Constantine imperial *protospatharios epi tou chrysotriklinou* and *strategos* of Langobaridia, and Michael Abidelas *patrikios* and *katepano* of Italia, concerning the possession of some houses close to the monastery, which had been illegally occupied by Oursoleon and John, *oikogenes* of the nun Kandida (Trinchera, *Syllabus,* no. 7, pp. 5 f.).
2. 999, November: σιγίλλιον, with a lead seal. Gregory Tarchaneiotes imperial *protospatharius* and *katepanō* of Italia gives the monastery of S. Pietro with all its property (villeins, fish-farms and three boats) in *charistikion* to the *spatharokandidatos* Christopher Bochomakes, who in the service of the emperor had fought against the Arabs, for the lifetime

of Christopher himself and his son, the monk Theophilos. Gregory promises to write to the emperor, who should issue a *chrysoboullos logos* to conferm the transaction (Trinchera, *Syllabus,* no. 10, p. 9).

3. Ind. 10, November (probably 1026): sentence (ἔγγραφον) with a lead seal. When Leo *spatharokandidatos, asekretes* and judge of Longobardia and Calabria was in Taranto, Bartholomew, abbot of the monastery of S. Pietro, complained to him about the family of the late *koubikleisios,* who had occupied a field of the monastery close to the Mare Piccolo at Mourovetere. The abbot showed the document of donation to the monastery, whilst the κόμης κόρτης Eudokimos, son of the κουβικλείσιος, could not present any document. Thus the judge decides to give the property back to the monastery (Trinchera, *Syllabus,* no. 21, pp. 22 f.).
4. 1054, June: σιγίλλιον, with a lead seal. Argyros *magistros, vestes,* and *doux* of Italia, Calabria, Sicily and Paphlagonia, son of Meles, makes a donation to Genesios ἐπὶ τῆς μεγάλης of Taranto, who had defended the cause of the emperor during a rebellion by the archbishop of Taranto and his fellow rebels, Eustathios Katanankes, his brother Leo, the priest Bisantios of St Akyndinos, and Basil Chrysochoos, who had driven him out of the town, confiscated his property and burned his houses. Thus Argyros gives him the property of Basil (Robinson, *History and Cartulary,* II, 1, no. V-109, pp. 158–162; photograph in: Breccia, *Scritture greche,* fig. I, a).
5. 1087, October: σιγίλλιον, with a wax seal of Bohemond I: John, prior of the monastery of S. Pietro Imperiale had required Bohemond I, son of the duke (Robert Guiscard), when he was in Taranto, to confirm a donation given to the monastery by Leo, son of David. There were vineyards, a cave close to the monastery of St John the Baptist, an uncultivated field and olive trees. Bohemond confirms the donation (Trinchera, *Syllabus,* no. 50, pp. 65 f.).
6. 1125, October: σιγίλλιον with a lead seal of Bohemond II: the heirs of Oursos Traballos, John Rouphos and Archontitzes, had turned to Bohemond II, saying that part of the property of Genesios, son of Akoses, belonged to them by heredity and a Latin document they no longer possess. The archbishop-elect, William, replies that the property belongs to the monastery of St Bartholomew in Taranto. Bohemond establishes a court with his constable Guido Kapriolos, his *pinchernus* Raoul, and Girardus Mansellus. Since the archbishop-elect did not appear at the court, the property is assigned to the heirs of Oursos Traballos and John Rouphos; written by Michael, notary of Bohemond II, and signed in Latin by Bohemond and Guido Kapriolos (Robinson, *History and Cartulary,* II, 1, no. XXVII-76, pp. 252–256; photograph in: Breccia, *Scritture greche*, tav. 2 b.).
7. 1126, Jannuary: σιγίλλιον of Bohemond II in favour of abbot Neilos of St Elias and St Anastasius of Carbone. The mother of Bohemond, the

late Constance, had decided to rebuild the monastery of S. Bartolomeo and establish a nunnery there. Following a suggestion of the then archbishop of Taranto, Rinaldus, she chose Aloisia as abbess. After a while, however, Aloisia decided to move to Jerusalem. Thus, with the agreement of the clergy of the cathedral, the archdeacon John and the *primicerius* Bernardus, Bohemond gives the monastery to abbot Neilos of the monastery of S. Elia e S. Anastasio di Carbone, in the presence of Walter, archbishop of Bari, Peter, archbishop of Otranto, Bagelardus, archbishop of Brindisi, and others; written by Michael notary of Bohemond II. (Robinson, *History and Cartulary,* II, 1, no. XXVIII-77, pp. 257–261).[126]

8. 1142, October: ὑπόμνημα of Goffredus of Oria, *katepanō* of Taranto, in favour of Hilarion, abbot of Carbone, who had appealed to the royal court against Theodore, son of Peter Kaprios, and his brother Romanos, who had leased some vineyards at Martzanellon close to the church of St Martin, which the monk Genesios had given to St Bartholomew, *metochion* of Carbone. For these vineyards the lease-holders had to deliver every year 50 measures of wine to the monastery, as indicated in the document. But very often the wine has not been delivered. Theodore asks for a delay, but two of the assessors, Archontitzes and Samaros, his sons-in-law, confirm the argument of the abbot. Thus Goffredus in the presence of Sere, son of the *topoteretes* Nicholas, Krites, son of Theophylaktos and ten others, decides that the vineyards should be returned to the monastery. The katepan signs in Latin and six witnesses in Greek: Sere, son of the τοποτηρητής Nicholas, Kostas, notary of the castle of Taranto, Nicholas, son of Bisantios, Komes Kortes, son of Daniel, Roger, son of Pantaleon (son) of Godinos, Leo, son of John (Robinson, *History and Cartulary,* II, 2, no. XXXVI-84, pp. 24–29).
9. 1219, October: sentence of the judge Hugh καπριλλίγγος in a legal dispute between the abbot of St Maurus at Gallipoli and Sergios. The latter is sentenced to pay every year at the feast of St Maurus half an ounce; written by the notary George, son of the judge Peter, ταβουλλάριος Τερέντου (Trinchera, *Syllabus,* App. I, no. 14, p. 529).[127]

II. The Latin documents of Taranto

II, a: Private documents

1. 1004: *cartula morgincaput*, wedding contract according to Lombard law between John, son of Fuscemarus, and Argentia, daughter of the late Peter, both inhabitants of Taranto: written by *Dominicus archidiaconus et notarius.* Only one Latin signature is legible (Leccisotti, *La pergamene,* no. 2, pp. 12 f.).
2. 1083, March: *chartula:* Triphilius, abbot of S. Maria di Ginosa, declares that archbishop Albertus and the episcopal clergy had given him the

church of Sts Philip and Nicholas. He promises to give every year at Christmas and Easter five *cannatae* of oil for the illumination of the church, and to provide a servant and a horse for the archbishop's imminent journey to Rome. The monks and clerics of St Philip and Nicholas together with the other clergy of Taranto have to be present at the archbishopric at the festivities of Christmas, Easter and the Ascension of the Virgin; written by the priest Michael, *notarius sancti episcopii,* and signed in Latin by Triphilius, the *prepositus* and a monk of his monastery, and by the two *advocatores,* and by six witnesses in Greek, among them two priests, a cleric and a σπαθαροκανδιδάτος (Magistrale [ed.], *Le pergamene,* no. 1, pp. 3–6).

3. 1104, February: *oblacio:* Muriel, widow of the late Gunduinus, and her son Petronus give the cleric Milius and his brother Basil with all their property to the monastery of S. Pietro Imperiale and the prior John; written by the priest Michael, *sacri episcopii Tarenti notarius.* Signed in Latin by two *milites,* the judge Nannonius, and Rainus *senescalcus,* and in Greek by Stephen πρωτοσπαθάριος and ὕπατος. The structure of the document follows the formula of private Greek documents (Gattola, *Historia,* I, p. 272).
4. 1138, June: *carta,* Henry *de Ponte* and his wife Azzulina, daughter of the *miles* Francus, offer themselves and some landed property at Massafra to the monastery of St Peter *Insule Tarentine;* written by the priest Petracca *sancte Tarentine ecclesie notarius,* and signed in Latin by archbishop Philip, and another witness, and in Greek by two witnesses. The structure of the document follows the formula of private Greek documents (Magistrale [ed.], *Le pergamene,* no. 6, pp. 19–22).

II, b: Documents of the archbishops

1. 1028, January: *scriptum concessionis:* archbishop Dionysius consecrates the church of Sts Benedict, John the Evangelist, Luke, Nicolaus and Leucius, close to the *porta Terranea,* and allows the founder, abbot Aleucius, to establish a monastery; written by the priest Angelus, *notarius de predicto Episcopio,* signed in Latin by the Archbishop, seven priests, two deacons and two subdeacons, and in Greek by the τουρμάρχαι John and Constantine, and by Adralestos and Theophylaktos, nephews or grandsons of the πρωτοσπαθάριος John (Guerrieri, *I possedimenti,* 188–191).
2. 1094/1095, march: *concessio:* archbishop Albertus gives to the clergy of the episcopal church dedicated to the Virgin Mary half of the *decimae* entitled to the Church and half of the donations given by the faithful; written by the priest Michael, *notarius et sancti episcopii primicerius,* and signed in Latin by the archbishop (Magistrale [ed.], *Le pergamene,* no. 2, pp. 7–9).
3. 1169, February: *privilegium:* archbishop Giraldus consecrates Margaret, the abbess elect of the monastery St Agatha, once living in the church of

St Peter, *que dicitur de presbitero Theogaristo,* and now in the church of St Simon. Written by the priest Nicholas, *sancti Tarentine ecclesie archidiaconus et notarius,* and signed in Latin by the Archbishop, the *cantor* and the *thesaurarius* of the Church, and four canons (Magistrale [ed.], no. 8, pp. 26–30).

4. 1187, August: *pagina:* archbishop Gervasius consecrates Luke, who had been promoted prior of the monastery of S. Maria de Ceresano by his predecessor archbishop Basil, abbot of the same monastery, which is organised according to the *regula sancti Basilii;* written by Sellictus, son of Salvo, *sancte ecclesie Tarentine notarius,* and signed in Latin by the archbishop, the *cantor,* the archdeacon and seven canons (Magistrale [ed.], no. 10, pp. 35–38).
5. 1193, October: *privilegium:* in the presence of John *de Butrunio iustitiarius et castellanus Tarenti,* Sarolus *prothoiudex,* Papaleo and Alexander, *regales iudices Tarenti* archbishop Gervasius returns to the canons of his Church the *decimae* given to them by his predecessor Basil; written by Sellictus *de Salvo de Taranto, sancte matris ecclesie Tarentine notarius,* and signed in Latin by the *iustitiarius* John *de Butrunio,* Sarolus *prothoiudex Tarenti,* Alexander *regius iudex Tarenti,* and four other witnesses, and in Greek by Leo, son of Constantine, κριτὴς Ταράντης and two other witnesses (Magistrale [ed.], no. 10, pp. 39–45; V. Campanella [ed.], *Le pergamene dell'Archivio arcivescovile di Taranto [1193–1373],* [Codice diplomatico Pugliese XXXIX], Bari 2018, no. 1, pp. 3–5).
6. 1197, October: *concessio,* Archbishop Angelus gives the church of S. Maria de Ceresano to the monastery of S. Vito de Pizzo and the abbot Gregory; written by Sellictus, son of Salvo, *sancte ecclesie Tarentine notarius,* and signed in Latin by the Archbishop, the *cantor,* the *thesaurarius,* and six canons (Magistrale [ed.], *Le pergamene,* no. 12, pp. 46–48).
7. 1208, June: *duo scripta consimilia:* before archbishop Berardus, the chapter and the judges Sarolus *regius prothoiudex Tarenti,* Raho *regius Tarentinorum iudex* and Leo *iudex Taranti*, son of the *iudex* Samatus a legal case is discussed between Polita, daughter of the *salinarius* Maurus, and her brother Theodore, about the heredity of a part of the salt flats which belong to the Church of Taranto. The final sentence is in favour of Theodore; written by Nicolaus, priest and canon of Taranto, and signed in Latin by the archbishop, five canons, and the three judges (*ibid.,* no. 13, pp. 49–54).
8. 1215, October: *concessionis et confirmationis pagina:* archbishop Gualterius confirms to Nicodemus, abbot of S. Vito de Pizzo, the concessions of his predecessors Angelus and Berardus, who had given to the monastery the church of S. Maria di Ceserano; written by the priest Paul, *notarius* of the archbishop, and signed by the archbishop, the *cantor,* the archdeacon and six canons (*ibid.,* no. 14, pp. 55–57).

II, c: Documents of Norman and early Hohenstaufen authorities

1. 1072, March: *cartula:* Petronus count of Taranto gives the church of St George to the monastery of St Benedict at Taranto. Petronus and three other witnesses sign in Latin, and one witness in Greek (S. Leone, G. Vitolo [eds.], *Codex diplomaticus Cavensis*, IX, Badia di Cava 1984, no. 125, pp. 368 f.).
2. 1090, August 19th: *confirmationis carta:* Bohemond, son of Robert Guiscard, confirms to the abbey of Montecassino the possession of the monastery of S. Pietri Imperiale in Taranto; written by Godescalcus *presbyter et monachus, eo tempore legatus apostolice sedis.* All the witnesses sign in Latin (Gattola, *Accessiones,* I, 205 f.; *Registrum Petri Diaconi,* III, no. 515, pp. 1410 f.).[128]
3. 1137, November: *scriptum:* the *iustitiarii* Roger of Bisignano, Roger of Barletta and Roger de Brahalla, sent to Taranto by the king to discuss a legal dispute about the property of a young villein between Peter, prior of S. Pietro Imperiale, and Guarinus *de Bella Aqua.* The *iustitiarii* decide in favour of the monastery; written by Guido, *magnifici regis domini nostri Rogerii notarius,* and signed by the three *iustitiarii* (Gattola, *Accessiones,* I, 254).
4. 1222, November: *scriptum:* before Henry *de Morra, magne imperialis curie magister iustitiarius,* and Simon *de Tocco eiusdem magne imperialis curie iudex* a legal dispute is discussed between Romanus, archimandrite of the monastery of S. Elia di Carbone, and the notary Roger, about a house close to the church of St Bartholomew. The sentence is in favour of the archimandrite; written by Paganus *nobilis de Rubo, eiusdem magne imperialis curie in iustitiaratu notarius,* and signed by the two judges (W. Holtzmann, *Papst-, Kaiser- und Normannenurkunden aus Unteritalien,* Quellen und Forschungen aus italienischen Archiven und Bibliotheken 36 (1956), no. 14, pp. 80 f.).

Notes

* Many thanks to Julian Gardner who greatly improved the English of this chapter.

1 But today all parts of it, except Taras, Rhegium and Neapolis, have become completely barbarized, and some parts have been taken and are held by the Leucani and the Brettii, and others by the Campani—that is, nominally by the Campani but in truth by the Romans, since the Campani themselves have become Romans.

2 G. Maddoli, *Il racconto di Strabone,* in: *Tramonto della Magna Grecia. Atti del XLIV Convegno di studi sulla Magna Grecia* (Taranto, 24–28 settembre 2004), (Taranto, 2005), 51–76; P. Poccetti, *Il declino (o i presunti declini) della Magna Grecia: aspetti della fenomenologia linguistica,* in: *ibid.*, 77–159.

3 *Iscrizioni greche d'Italia. Puglia,* eds. F. Ferrandini Troisi, (Rome, 2015), 85–136; Poccetti, *Il declino,* 108–111.

4 C. Colafemmina, *Gli Ebrei a Taranto. Fonti documentarie,* Bari 2005 (Società di storia patria per la Puglia. Documenti e monografie, 52), no. 3, 28 (in Greek), no. 4, 29 f. (in Greek and Hebrew).

5 A. M. Lombardo, *Nomi, cognomi e sopranomi grecanici nella Taranto romana,* Cenacolo, n. s. 11 (1999) 71—84; G. D'Angela, *Taranto: le epigrafi della necropoli romana di Piazza d'Armi, ibid.,* 7–84; V. Lomento, *Le iscrizioni latine della necropoli del Regio Arsenale di Taranto,* Archivio storico pugliese 57 (2004) 156–162.

6 V. Farella, *La chiesa di Taranto nell'alto Medioevo,* in: *La Chiesa di Taranto,* I. *Dalle origini all'avvento dei Normanni,* (ed.) C. D. Fonseca, (galatina, 1977), 65 f.

7 A. Gallo, *Il più antico documento originale dell'archivio di Montecassino,* Bullettino dell'Istituto storico italiano 45 (1929) 159–164; *Registrum Petri Diaconi. (Montecassino, Archvio dell'Abbazia, Reg. 3*), eds. J.-M. Martin, P. Chastang, L. Feller, G. Orofina, A. Thomas, M. Villani, Rome 2015 (Fonti per la storia dell'Italia meridionale. Antiquitates, 45), II, no. 191, 567 f., no. 194, 572 f., no. 305, 915, III, no. 396, 1126 f.

8 *Registrum Petri Diaconi,* II, no. 305, 915, III, no. 396, 1126 f. Taranto as *gastaldatum.*

9 *Ibid.,* II, no. 191, 567 f., no. 194, 572 f.,

10 *Ibid.,* II, no. 194, 572 f. (795 o 810), no. 305, 915 (807), III, no. 396, 1126 f. (809).

11 Colafemmina, *Gli Ebrei a Taranto,* nos. 6–19, 20–41.

12 J. Ackermann, *Das "Itinerarium Bernardi Monachi". Edition—Übersetzung—Kommentar,* Hannover 2010 (Monumenta Germaniae Historica. Studien und Texte, 51), ch. 4 f., 117; T. Leccisotti, *Le pergamene latine di Taranto nell'archivio di Montecassino*, Archivio storico pugliese 14 (1961), 11 f.; F. Gabrieli, *Taranto araba,* Cenacolo 4 (1974) 3–8; C. D'Angela, *Il porto nell'Alto Medioevo*, in Id., *Taranto medievale* (Taranto, 2002), Società di storia patria per la Puglia. Sezione di Taranto. Quaderni di Storia—Archeologia—Arte, 59–61; M. Di Branco, *915. La battaglia del Garigliano. Cristiani e musulmani nell'Italia medievale* (Bologna, 2019) 29 f., 37 f., 81–83, 108–111.

13 *Chronographiae quae Theophanis continuati nomine fertur Liber quo Vita Basilii imperatoris amplectur,* (ed.) I. Ševčenko, (Berlin-Boston 2011), (Corpus fontium historiae Byzantinae, 42), ch. 66, 230.

14 *MGH, Epistolae* VII, ep. 18, 343; *Italia Pontificia* IX. *Samnium—Apulia—Lucania,* (ed.) W. Holtzmann, (Berlin, 1962), 437; V. von Falkenhausen, *I Bizantini in Italia,* in: *I Bizantini in Italia,* (Milan, 1982), 53, 128.

15 V. Laurent, *Le corpus des sceaux de l'empire byzantin,* V, 1: *L'Église*, (Paris, 1963), no. 926, pp. 733 f.; G. Zacos, A. Veglery, *Byzantine Lead Seals,* I, 2, (Basel, 1972), no. 2340, 1281–1282, (who suggest the reading of the name as Ζώηλος); *Catalogue of Byzantine seals at Dumbarton Oaks and in the Fogg Museum of Art,* I. *Italy, North Balkans, North of the Black Sea,* (eds.) J. Nesbitt, N. Oikonomides, (Washington, D. C., 1991), I, no. 11. 1, 38 f.

16 C. D'Angela, *In margine al Convegno Magna Grecia bizantina e tradizione Classica,* in: Id., *Taranto medievale* cit., 45–47.

17 *Ignatius Diakonos und die Vita des hl. Gregorios Dekapolites,* (ed.) G. Makris, (Stuttgart—Leipzig, 1997), (Byzantinisches Archiv 17), 96–98; C. Mango, *On Re-Reading the Life of St Gregory the Decapolite,* Βυζαντινά 13 (1985), 637 f.

18 *Italia Pontificia* IX cit., 408 f.

19 *Ibid.,* 428. For the institution of the metropolitan see of Nikopolis/Santa Severina: V. Prigent, *Les évêchés byzantins de la Calabre septentrionale*, Mélanges de l'École Française de Rome. Moyen Âge 114, 2 (2002), 931–953.

20 *Italia Pontificia* IX, 435–438. Some archbishops have Greek names as for instance Dionysius, attested between 1008 and 1028 (A. Merodio, *Istoria Tarentina*, ed. C. D. Fonseca, [Taranto, 2000], 228 f.; F. F. Guerrieri, *Possedimenti temporali e spirituali dei Benedettini di Cava nelle Puglie,* I: *Terra d'Otranto,* [Trani, 1900], 191), or Basilius attested in the years 1177–1179 (F.

Trinchera, *Syllabus Graecarum membranarum,* [Naples, 1865], no. 189, 248 f.; J.-M. Martin, *La Pouille du* VIe au XIIe siècle, École Française de Rome 1993 [Collection de l' École Française de Rome—179, 589]. They may have had a mixed Latin-Greek background, and may have been bilingual.

21 A Latin document of archbishop Dionysius (1028) is signed by 11 clerics in Latin and by four Byzantine officials in Greek: Guerrieri, *Possedimenti,* 191. In 1004, the archdeacon and notary Dominicus writes a Latin marriage contract: Leccisotti, *Le pergamene latine,* 12. In 1061 a Greek document, issued by John, *archidiaconus et grammaticus* is signed by five Latin clerics and three secular Greek witnesses: Trinchera, *Syllabus,* no. 45, 58 f. Latin signatures of canons of Taranto: F. Magistrale (ed.), *Le pergamene dell'Archivio arcivescovile di Taranto,* I-II (1083–1258), (Galatina, 1999), no. 8, 26–30, no. 10, 35–37, no. 12, 46 f., no. 13, 49–53 *et passim.*

22 The various Latin, Greek and Arabic sources do not agree in dating of the Muslim conquest and destruction of Taranto. They indicate dates between 925 and 929, but apparently the year 927/928 is most likely: E. Leuthold jr., *Tesoretto di monete bizantine dei secoli IX e X nel Museo Nazionale di Taranto,* Rivista italiana di numismatica, ser. IV, 58 (1956), 31–35; V. von Falkenhausen, *Taranto in epoca bizantina,* Studi medievali, s. III, 9 (1968) 137; Schreiner, *Die byzantinischen Kleinchroniken,* I (Corpus fontium historiae Byzantinae XII, 1), (Vienna, 1975), 337.

23 Lupus Protospatarius (Monumenta Germaniae Historica, Scriptores V), 53.

24 Anonymous, *Kitāb al-ʿuyūn wa-l-ḥadāʾiq fī aḫbār al-ḥaqāʾiq. Chronique anonyme. Tome IV 256/8730–350/961*, (ed.) O. Saïdi, (Damascus, 1972), I, 244, paragraph 443. Many thanks to Jeremy Johns, who translated the paragraph.

25 A. Jacob, *La réconstruction de Tarente par les Byzantins aux IX^eet X^esiècles. À propos de deux inscriptions perdues,* Quellen und Forschungen aus italienischen Archiven und Bibliotheken 68 (1988) 9–19; V. von Falkenhausen, *La dominazione bizantina nell'Italia meridionale dal IX all'XI secolo,* (Bari, 1978), 84.

26 Trinchera, *Syllabus*, nos. 8 f., 6–9.

27 *Ibid.*, no. 27, 31 f., nos. 34–36, 41–45, no. 39, 48 f., no. 41, 51 f.; G. Robinson, *History and Cartulary of the Greek Monastery of. St Elias and St Anastasius of Carbone,* (Rome, 1929), (Orientalia Christiana Analecta, 15, 2), II, 1, no. IV–53, 150–157, no. XII-61, 190–194; E. Crisci, *I palinsesti di Grottaferrata. Studio codicologico e paleografico,* I, (Naples, 1990), 65.

28 H. Grégoire, *La carrière du premier Nicéphore Phokas,* in *Προσφορὰ εις Στ. Κυριακίδην ἐπι τῇ εικοσιπενταετηρίδι τῆς καθηγεσίας αὐτοῦ (1926–1951),* (Thessaloniki, 1953), 251 f.; von Falkenhausen, *I Bizantini in Italia,* 93 f., 132; G. Dédéyan, *Le stratège Symbatikios et la colonisation arménienne dans le thème de Longobardie,* in: *Ravenna da capitale imperiale a capitale esarcale. Atti del XVII Congresso internazionale di studio sull'alto medioevo (Ravenna, 6–12 giugno 2004)*, (Spoleto, 2005), I, 470–493.—Even among the villeins belonging to the Tarantine monastery of S. Pietro Imperiale in 1114 there was an *Armenus* and another called *Curticis*: E. Gattola, *Ad historiam abbatiae Cassinensis accessiones* I, (Venice 1734), 231 f.; *Registrum Petri Diaconi,* III, no. 576, 1566 f. See also Nicholas S.M. Matheou's chapter in the present volume.

29 von Falkenhausen, *Taranto in epoca bizantina,* 133–166.

30 E. Lippolis, *L'antichità classica,* in *Il porto di Taranto tra passato e presente* (Atti del Convegno, Taranto, 28 ottobre 1997), (Taranto, 1998), 9–24.

31 P. Corsi, *La spedizione italiana di Costante II, (*Bologna, 1983), 116 f.

32 von Falkenhausen, *Taranto in epoca bizantina,* 146.

33 Ead., *Tra Occidente e Oriente: Otranto in epoca bizantina*, in *Otranto nel Medioevo tra Bisanzio e l'Occidente*, (ed.) H. Houben, (Galatina, 2007), 13–60.

34 Trinchera, *Syllabus*, no. 48, 62 f.; Guerrieri, *Possedimenti*, 188–191; E. Gattola, *Historia Abbatiae Casinensis per saeculorum seriem distributa*, I, (Venice, 1733), 272.
35 Trinchera, *Syllabus*, no. 7, 5 f.; von Falkenhausen, *La dominazione bizantina*, 85 f., 182 f.
36 F. Carabellese, *L'Apulia e il suo comune nell'alto Medioevo* (Documenti e Monografie, 7), (Bari, 1905), 451 f. On the verso of the document there is a short description of the contents in Greek: η παραδοσις των ελεων τ(ῆς) Μεσαφρ(ας).
37 Leccisotti, *Le pergamene*, no. 2, 12–13 (a marriage contract according to the Lomard law); Guerrieri, *Possedimenti*, 190 (a charter of archbishop Dionysius of 1028, who dedicates the church of St Benedict in Taranto, defending the institution against any intrusion, saying: "*Nam, si ego qui supra archiepiscopus, vel cuncti mei posteriori et successores tivi predicto abbati, vel ad uos successores et cunctos vestros ordinatos, omnia in supradictorum lege Graecorum vel Langobardorum quaerendam istam concessionem irritam, vel scriptum istum reprobum facere et aliquam contrarietatem de omnia praedicti vobis facere praesumpserimus, … obligo et omnes posteros meos successores componere tibi vel ad tuos successores poena pro fatigium centum solidos*").
38 V. von Falkenhausen, M. Amelotti, *Notariato e documento nell'Italia meridionale greca (X-XV secolo)*, in: *Per una storia del notariato meridionale* (Studi storici sul notariato italiano, VI), (Roma, 1982), 28 f.
39 *Ibid.*, figg. II, IV, V; G. Breccia, *Scritture greche di età bizantina e normanna nelle pergamene del monastero di S. Elia di Carbone*, Archivio storico per la Calabria e la Lucania 64 (1997) 45–54, figg. 1°–3b; P. Danella, *Privilegi sovrani e documenti in lingua greca a Montecassino: un confronto*, in: *Documenti medievali greci e latini. Studi comparativi.* Atti del seminario di Erice (23–29 ottobre 1995), eds. G. De Gregorio, O. Kresten, (Spoleto, 1998), figg. V-VIII; Magistrale (ed.), *Le pergamene*, 153, 163, 169; S. Lucà, *Scritture e libri in Terra d'Otranto fra XI e XII secolo*, in: *Bizantini, Longobardi e Arabi in Puglia nell'Alto Medioevo.* Atti del XX Congresso internazionale di studio nell'alto medioevo (Savelletri di Fasano [BR], 3–6 novembre 2011), (Spoleto, 2012), 503–506; M. D'Agostino, P. Degni, *Cultura grafica nei documenti greci della Puglia nell'Alto Medioevo, ibid.*, 584–589, figs. V–VIII.
40 Trinchera, *Syllabus*, no. 222, 290 f.: χειρὶ Φιλίππου Ταραντινοῦ καὶ γραμματικοῦ.
41 Lucà, *Scritture e libri*, 506 f.
42 Martin, *La Pouille du VIe au XIIe*, 512.
43 See the appendix of this article and Crisci, *I palinsesti di Grottaferrata*, 65, 179–181.
44 Guerrieri, *Possedimenti*, 188–191; Leccisotti, *Le pergamene*, no. 2, 12–13. See Appendix of this article, II, a, 1, II, b, 1.
45 Trinchera, *Syllabus*, nos. 8–9, 6–9, no. 22, 23 f., no. 24, 26 f., nos. 26–27, 29–32, nos. 30–36, 35–45, no. 39, 48 f., no. 41, 51 f., no. 45, 58 f.; Robinson, *History and Cartulary*, II, 1, no. IV–53, 150–157; palinsests in: Cod. Crypt. A. α. XI and A. α. XIII, fols. 146r and 151v, and 144r and 141v, mentioned, but not read by Crisci, *I palinsesti di Grottaferrata*, 65. See Appendix, I, a, 1–19.
46 Trinchera, *Syllabus*, no. 7, 5–6, no. 10, 9, no. 21, 22–23; Robinson, *History and Cartulary*, II, 1, no. V–109, 158–162. Appendix I, b, 1–4.
47 Trinchera, *Syllabus* no. 281, 387 s. Photograph in: Danella, *Privilegi sovrani*, tav. VIII.
48 Appendix II, a, 1–4, I, a, 20–60.
49 Appendix II, c, 1–4, I, b, 5–9.
50 Trinchera, *Syllabus*, no. 50, 65 f.; Robinson, *History and Cartulary*, II, 1, no. XXVII-76, 252–256, no. XXVIII-77, 257–261.

51 G. Robinson, *History and Cartulary of the Greek monastery of St Elias and St Anastasius of Carbone*, II, 2, (Orientalia Christiana, XIX, 1), (Rome 1930), no. XXXVI–84, 24–29.
52 Appendix II, b, 2–8.
53 Trinchera, *Syllabus,* no. 22, 23 f. All witnesses sign in Greek.
54 *Ibid.*, no. 45, 58 f.; *Abbazia di Montecassino. I regesti dell'Archivio,* vol. VI (Aula II: Capsule XVIII-XXVII), (ed.) T. Leccisotti (Roma, 1971) (Ministero dell'Interno. Pubblicazioni degli Archivi di Stato, LXXIV), Tav. I. John himself uses a metrical Latin signature. A. Peters-Custot, *Les Grecs de l'Italie méridionale post-byzantine. Une acculturation en douceur,* École Française de Rome 2009 (Collection de l' École Française de Rome—420), 72, does not explain why she thinks he was Greek.
55 Guerrieri, *Possedimenti,* 191; Magistrale (ed.), *Le pergamene*, no. 11, 44 f.
56 Trinchera, *Syllabus,* no. 189, 248 f.
57 Crisci, *I palinsesti di Grottaferrata*, 180.
58 G. Ferrari dalle Spade, *Infiltrazioni occidentali nel diritto greco-italico della Monarchia normanna,* Rivista di storia del diritto italiano 12 (1939) 36 f. Similar cases are known from Gallipoli, where husbands or sons appear as the ἀντιστάτωρες of their wives or mothers: Trinchera, *Syllabus,* App. I, no. 6, 518 f. (1181), no. 8, 520 f. (1195), no. 11, 524–526 (ca. 1203), no. 12, 526 f. (1203), no. 15, 530 f. (1227) and ibid., no. 336, 506 f. (1331).
59 Robinson, *History and Cartulary,* II, i, no. XII—61, 192.
60 Greek: Appendix, nos. 2, 3, 4–10, 13, 18; Latin: Appendix, no. 10.
61 von Falkenhausen, *La dominazione,* 173.
62 E. Gattola, *Historia Abbatiae Casinensis per saeculorum seriem distributa,* I, (Venice, 1733), 272. The signature has not been read by the editor.
63 Robinson, *History and Cartulary,* II, 1, no. V–109, 160–162.
64 Trinchera, *Syllabus,* no. 24, 27.
65 *Ibid.*, no. 45, 58.
66 Trinchera, *Syllabus,* no. 48, 62 f.
67 Robinson, *History and Cartulary,* II, 2, no. XXXVI–84, 24–29.
68 Robinson's integration [Γοδινη] κομις κόρτης is not correct.
69 *Ibid.*, no. XLIV–93, 65–67.
70 Magistrale (ed.), *Le pergamene,* no. 6, 19–21, fig. 6.
71 E. Jamison, *Judex Tarentinus. The career of* Judex Tarentinus magne curie magister justiciarius *and the emergence of the Sicilian regalis magna curia under William I and the regency of Margaret of Navarre, 1156–1172,* Proceedings of the British Academy 53 (1967), 291 f.; reprint in: Ead., *Studies on the History of Medieval Sicily and South Italy,* (eds.) D. Clementi, Th. Kölzer, (Aalen, 1992), 468–470.
72 Magistrale (ed.), *Le pergamene,* no. 11, 39–45.
73 *Codice diplomatico Barese,* IV, (ed.) F. Nitti di Vito (Bari 1900), no. 45, 90.
74 V. Farella, *Il monastero di San Benedetto nel contesto urbanistico di Taranto medieovale*, in *L'esperienza monastica benedettina e la Puglia,* (ed.) C. F. Fonseca, (Galatina, 1984), II, 333–343, tav. XLI-XLVI; *Monasticon Italiae,* III. *Puglia e Basilicata,* (eds.) G. Lunardi, H. Houben, G. Spinelli, (Cesena, 1986), no. 297, 101.
75 J. Thomas, *Your Sword, Our Shield: The Imperial Monastery in Byzantine Civilization,* in: *Church and Society: Orthodox Christian Perspectives, Past Experiences, and Modern Challenges. Studies in Honor of Rev. Dr. D. J. Constantelos,* (ed.) G. Liacopulos, (Boston, 2007), 27–44.
76 von Falkenhausen, *Taranto in epoca bizantina,* 158, 160; *Monasticon Italiae,* III, no. 311, 104 f.

77 Robinson, *History and Cartulary,* II, 1, no. IV–53, 150–154.
78 Ead, *History and Cartulary,* II, 2 no. XXXVI-84, 24–29; *Monasticon Italiae,* III, no. 296, 100–101.
79 C. D'Angela, *Taranto medievale,* (Taranto, 2002), (Società di storia patria per la Puglia—Sezione di Taranto. Quaderni di Storia—Archeologia—Arte, 12), 177.
80 All known documents concerning St Memnon belonged to the archive of S. Pietro Imperiale.
81 A. Jacob, *Deux fragments de diptyches liturgiques byzantins sur ostraka découverts dans la grotte Leukaspide près de Tarente,* La Parola del Passato (2012) 216–233.
82 Robinson, *History and Cartulary,* no. IV–53, 150–157; Trinchera, *Syllabus,* nos. 8–9, 6–9, no. 31, 38 f., nos. 34–36, 41–45, no. 39, 48 f., no. 41, 51 f. (βασιλικὸς κληρικός).
83 R. Janin, A. A., *La géographie ecclésiastique de l'Empire byzantin,* I. *Le siège de Constantinople et le Patriarcat oecuménique,* tome III. *Les églises et les monastères,* (Paris, 1969), 361–364.
84 Trinchera, *Syllabus,* no. 22, 23 f., no. 24, 26 f., no. 26, 29–31, no. 32, 38 f.
85 In the years between 1057/1058 and 1089 Andrew ὁ τοῦ ἀρχιμανδρίτου, that is nephew or descendant of an archimandrite, wrote several private documents in Taranto: Crisci, *I palinsesti di Grottaferrata,* 65; Robinson, *History and Cartulary,* II, 1, no. X–59, 179–183, Trinchera, *Syllabus,* no. 45, 58 f., no. 51, 67 f.
86 Trinchera, *Syllabus,* no. 30, 35 f. His title has not been read correctly by the editor.
87 V. von Falkenhausen, *La tecnica dei notai italo-greci,* in *La cultura scientifica e tecnica nell'Italia meridionale bizantina*, Atti della sesta Giornata di studi bizantini (Arcavacata di Rende, 8–9 febbraio 2000), (ed.) F. Burgarella, A. M. Ieraci Bio, (Soveria Mannelli, 2006), 18–20.
88 Trinchera, *Syllabus,* nos. 8–9, 6–9, no. 109, 144; Crisci, *I palinsesti di Grottaferrata*, 180.
89 Trinchera, *Syllabus*, nos. 32–36, 38–45.
90 J.-M. Martin, *Κίνναμος ἐπίσκοπος—Cennamus episcopus. Aus avant-postes de l'héllenisme sud-italien vers l'an Mil*, Rivista di studi bizantini e neoellenici, n.s. 27 (1990) 89–99; Id, *Évêchés et monstères "grecs" en Italie méridionale au Moyen Âge (VIIe-XIII^{e}siècles),* Revue Mabillon, n.s. 27 (2016) 14.
91 Trinchera, *Syllabus,* no. 48, 63; Magistrale (ed.), *Le pergamene,* no. 1, 6, no. 9, 32; G. Caracausi, *Dizionario onomastico della Sicilia,* I, (Palermo, 1993), (Lessici siciliani, 7), 561.
92 V. von Falkenhausen, *Cennamus episcopus—Κινναμος ἐπισκοπος. Ein chorepiscopus zwischen Olevano al Tusciano und Tarent?* in: (eds.) M. Stuiber/M. Spadaccini, *Bausteine zur deutschen und italienischen Geschichte. Festschrift zum 70. Geburtstag von Horst Enzensberger* (Schriften aus der Fakultät Geistes- und Kulturwissenschaften der Otto-Friedrich-Universität Bamberg, 18), (Bamberg, 2014), 145 f.
93 *Ibid.,* 143–154.
94 von Falkenhausen, *Taranto in epoca bizantina,* 142.
95 E. Aar, *Gli studi storici in Terra d'Otranto*, Archivio storico italiano, s. IV, 9 (1882) 253.
96 According to the seventeenth-century scholar Ambrogio Merodio, *Istoria Tarentina*, 228 f.: the archbishop of Taranto Dionysius, attested during the years from 1008 to 1028, "donò la chiesa di S. Giorgio martire a Pantaleone ed Anastasio nell'anno quarto del suo arcivescovado (1011). Era detta chiesa, come si legge nella scrittura di detta donazione, dentro la città vicina alle mura del

Mare Grande, della quale si è perduta la memoria per le mutazioni giornaliere delle fabbriche".

97 Magistrale (ed.), *Le pergamene*, no. 3, 10–12; *Monasticon Italiae,* III, no. 309, 104.

98 Magistrale (ed.), *Le pergamene*, no. 7, 23–22; *Monasticon Italiae,* III, no. 310, 104.

99 V. Farella, *Note sul monastero italo-greco di S. Vito del Pizzo,* Cenacolo 4 (1974) 31 f.

100 Magistrale (ed.), *Le pergamene*, no. 10, 35–38, no. 12, 46–48.

101 The text of the inscription has been published by E. Jamison, *La carriera del logotheta Riccardo di Taranto,* Archivio storico pugliese 5 (1952) 185–187.

102 C. D'Angelo, *Due stele bizantine nel Museo Nazionale di Taranto,* Byzantion 48 (1978) 386, 389; A. Guillou, *Recueil des inscriptions grecques médiévales d'Italie,* École Française de Rome 1996 (École Française de Rome—222), nos. 176 f., 184 f.

103 Robinson, *History and Chartulary*, II, 1, no. XII-61, 190–194; Trinchera, *Syllabus*, no. 51, 67 f., no. 109, 144; Magistrale (ed.), *Le pergamene,* no, 1, 6, no. 3, 12, no. 7, 25, no. 9, 34.

104 Crisci, *I palinsesti,* 181.

105 Trinchera, *Syllabus,* nos. 269 f., 370 f.; no. 281, 387 f.; V. von Falkenhausen, *Un inedito documento greco del monastero di S. Vito del Pizzo (Taranto),* Cenacolo, n. s. 7 (1995), 17 f.

106 Jamison, *Judex Tarentinus,* 289–344, reprint, 467–522; According to the Byzantine tradition monks normally chose a monastic name with the same initial as their secular name. Κριτὴς Ταραντινός chose the name Κλήμης (Clement): Aar, *Gli studi storici in Terra d'Otranto*, 252–257.

107 *Acta Sanctorum,* Maii II, c. 24, 572; V. von Falkenhausen, *Un inedito documento*, 14.

107 M. N. Adler, *The Itinerary of Benjamin of Tudela,* (London, 1907), 9; Colafemmina, *Gli Ebrei a Taranto,* no. 29, 48.

108 R. Bonfil, (ed.), The Chronicle of Ahima'az (Leiden, 2009) (Studies in Jewish History and Culture, eds. H. Tirosh-Samuelson and G. Veltri, 22), 234; Colafemmina, *Gli Ebrei a Taranto*, 7f.

108 Magistrale (ed.), *Le pergamene,* no. 22, 76.

109 Trinchera, *Syllabus* cit., no. 281, 387 f., a photograph in Danella, *Privilegi sovrani*, tav. VIII.

110 Trinchera, *Syllabus* cit., nos. 269f., 370 f.; von Falkenhausen, *Un inedito documento greco*, 17 f.

111 V. von Falkenhausen, *I Greci in Calabria fra XIII e XIV secolo*, in *Petrarca e il mondo greco*, I: Atti del Convegno internazionale di Studi (Reggio Calabria, 26–30 novembre 2001), (Messina 2007) [= *Quaderni petrarcheschi* 12–13 (2002–2003)], 21–50; ead., *La presenza dei Greci nella Sicilia normanna. L'apporto della documentazione archivistica in lingua greca*, in *Byzantino-Sicula, IV:* Atti del I Congresso internazionale di archeologia della Sicilia bizantina, (ed.) R.M. Carra Bonacasa, Palermo 2002 (Istituto Siciliano di Studi Bizantini e Neoellenici. Quaderni, 15), 65–73; ead., *Die griechischen Gemeinden in Messina und Palermo (11. bis 13. Jahrhundert),* in *Urban Dynamics and Transcultural Communication in Medieval Sicily,* (eds.) T. Jäckh, M. Kirsch, (Mittelmeerstudien 17), (Paderborn 2017), 27–66; M. re, *La sottoscrizione del Vat. gr. 2294 (ff. 68–106): Il copista Matteo sacerdote e la chiesa di S. Giorgio de Balatis (Palermo, 1260/1261)*, Rivista di studi bizantini e neoellenici, n. s. 42 (2005), 163–201.

112 N. Kamp, *Die sizilianischen Verwaltungsreformen Kaiser Friedrichs II. als Problem der Sozialgeschichte,* Quellen und Forschungen aus italienischen Archiven und Bibliotheken 62 (1982) 129–131.

113 Magistrale (ed.), *Le pergamene,* no. 18, 67–69, fig. 19; O. V. Sapio, *Le pergamene di Taranto del secolo XIII,* Cenacolo, n. s. 9 (XXI), 1997, 48—51.

114 Magistrale (ed.), *Le pergamene,* no, 28, 106.
115 Rome, Archivio Doria Pamphili, fondo S. Elia di Carbone, no. 2.
116 C. O. Zuretti, *ΙΤΑΛΟΕΛΛΕΝΙΚΑ,* in *Centenario della nascita di Michele Amari,* I, (Palermo, 1910), 173–183; S. G. Mercati, *Note critiche al "Contrasto fra Taranto e Otranto" di Ruggero d'Otranto,* rivista degli Studi Orientali 9 (1921) 38–47, reprint in: Id., *Collectanea Byzantina,* II, (Bari, 1970), 347–357. Roger of Otranto was a fervent admirer of the admiral Eugenios of Palermo: *Eugenii Panormitani Versus Iambici,* (ed.) M. Gigante, (Palermo, 1964), (Istituto Siciliano di studi bizantini e neoellenici, Testi 10), 12–14.
117 A. Jacob, *Les annales du monastère de San Vito del Pizzo, près de Tarente, d'après les notes marginales du Parisinus Gr. 1624*, Rivista di studi bizantini e neoellenici, n. s. 30 (1993), 126–133.
118 Magistrale (ed.), *Le pergamene,* no. 28, 106 f.
119 F. Quaranta, *In difesa dei matrimoni greci e del mattutino pasquale. Un testo inedito del XIII secolo*, Studi sull'Oriente Cristiano 5, 2 (2001) 91–117.
120 D. Vendola, *Rationes decimarum Italiae nei secoli XIII e XIV,* (Vatican City, 1939), (Studi e Testi 84), nos. 1684 f., 130.
121 A. L. Tăutu, *Pontificia Commissio ad redigendum codicem iuris canonici orientalis. Fontes,* s. III, vol. VII, tom. II: *Acta Ioannis XXII (1317–1334),* (Vatican City, 1952), no. 94, 186 f. (1327); *ibidem,* vol. X. *Acta Innocentii P. VI (1352–1362),* Rome 1961, no. 16, 30–32 (1353), no. 50, 92–94 (1354), no. 94, 176 f. (1356); ibidem, vol. XI. *Acta Urbani V (1362–1370),* no. 157, 258 f. (1369); vol. XII. *Acta Gregorii XI (1370–1378),* Rome 1966, no. 9, 22–24 (1371), no. 88, 170–172 (1373), no. 160, 308–310, no. 214, 419 f. (1376); ibidem. vol. XIII, tom. I. *Acta Urbani VI (1378–1389), Bonifacii IX (1389–1404), Innocentii VII (1404–1406) et Gregorii XII (1406–1415),* Rome 1970, no. 87, 175 f. (1400); ibidem, vol. XIII, vol. II. *Acta pseudopontificum Clementis VII (1378–1394), Benedicti XIII (1394–1417), Alexandri V (1409–1410) e Johannis XXIII (1409–1415),* Rome 1971, nos. 47 f., 65–67 (1384), nos. 56 f., 72–75 (1386–1387), no. 65, 87–89 (1387); ibidem, vol. XIV. *Acta Martini P. P. V (1417–1431),* Rome 1980, no. 58, 141 f., no. 513, 1247 f.; ibidem, vol. XV. *Acta Eugenii P. P. IV (1431–1447),* Rome 1990, no. 309, 176; H. Hoberg, *Taxae pro communibus servitiis ex libris obligationum ab anno 1295 usque ad annum 1455 confectis,* (Vatican City, 1949), Studi e testi 144, 307, 336.
122 Jacob, *Les annales du monastère de San Vito del Pizzo*, 135–145.
123 G. Alessio, *Etimologie tarantine*, Archivio storico pugliese 4, 2 (1951) 85–96.
124 The signature of *Nikolaus Dei misericordia imperialis patrikius* can be found on a document of doubtful authenticity, issued at Mottola (25 km north-west from Taranto) in 1081: *Codex diplomaticus Cavensis* XI, 1081–1085, (eds.) C. Carlone, L. Morinelli, G. Vitolo (Battipaglia, 2015), no. 8, 25.
125 The nun must have been Aloisia, chosen as abbess by Constance, widow of Bohemund I: Robinson, *History and Cartulary,* II, 1, no. XXVIII–77, pp 257–261.
126 V. von Falkenhausen, Constantia *oppure* Constantinopoli*? Sui presunti viaggi in Oriente della vedova di Bohemondo I,* in Σύνδεσμος. *Studi in onore di Rosario Anastasi,* II, (Catania, 1994), 153–167.
127 The document, which does not exist any longer, apparently was in a very bad state, when it was published by Trinchera.
128 Constance, the widow of Bohemond I, and mother of Bohmond II has issued several Latin charters about property in Taranto, but normally without the indication of the *data topica.* Thus, in this context, I have not taken them into consideration. Her *donatio* to the archbishop of Bari (1117), issued *in Tarentino palatio* is a false patent (*Codice diplomatico barese,* V, [ed.] F. Nitti di Vito [Bari, 1902], no. 64, 111 f.).

The study of empire and cities in the early medieval Mediterranean

Personal reflections and conclusions[1]

In the summer of 1966 a school friend and I visited Italy for the first time, before starting my studies at the University of Edinburgh. This was no cultural grand tour but a beach holiday in Rimini. However it kindled in me an immediate and enduring love for the country, although at first this was centred on sun, food and wine. Soon, however, we tired of the packed beaches and the flashy hotels and bars that lined the Lungomare, and decided to go on day trips elsewhere. One was to Florence, which I remember being a long coach ride away, very hot and very crowded. Much more pleasant was an excursion to a nearby town of which I then knew little, despite Momigliano's famous remark about it being key to understanding Italian history.[2] The town was Ravenna, dominated at that time by a depressed industrial zone, redolent more of Antonioni's film *il deserto rosso* and Louise MacNeice's "bad smell mixed with glory",[3] rather than the prosperous tourist magnet which it is today. I had no idea then what a role this small city would come to play in my life, but I do recall sharing the reaction of Byron, Wilde and so many other visitors—wonder and delight at the remarkable churches and their dazzling mosaics.

At school I had concentrated on Latin, Greek and ancient history, but a perhaps naïve embrace of the "modernising" idealism of the time, epitomised by Harold Wilson's "white heat of technology", induced me to choose for my degree supposedly more "relevant" subjects, first Economics and then Politics and Modern History. However my first year European History course, if not exactly Plato to NATO, covered the period 800 to 1945 and my tutor's enthusiasm for the Middle Ages caused me to rethink my plans. Soon, thanks to the flexibility of the Edinburgh degree and the encouragement of a remarkable band of medieval historians, I had become a fully fledged medievalist. This interest took a new turn in my Honours years when I signed up for a course offered by a new arrival, Donald Nicol, a specialist in what was then an exotic and little known field, Byzantine studies. Donald's brilliant teaching and passionate love for his subject opened my eyes to a new and exciting world and inspired a lifelong interest in Constantinople and the Eastern Mediterranean. When I decided to proceed to postgraduate work, I did not want to be compartmentalised in a narrow area and kept being drawn back to my earlier interest in the classical world and its legacy. Fascinated by periods of transition and the process of interaction between cultures, I became curious about how relations with the East developed after the eclipse of Roman power in the West. It was at this point that I remembered Ravenna, which struck me as a meeting point between ancient and medieval, and between East and West. To my surprise and delight I discovered that what seemed to be an obvious topic had received little scholarly attention, especially among English language historians.

I did not wish to study this from a narrowly Byzantine perspective and so I decided to pursue my doctoral research under the supervision of Donald Bullough at the University of Nottingham, whom I knew to have a wide-ranging interest not only in Italy but also in Europe and the Mediterranean throughout the early Middle Ages. I was fortunate at Nottingham to have the benefit of his meticulous scholarship, and also to enjoy the friendship and help of some remarkable ancient and medieval historians, including Edward Thompson, Bernard Hamilton and, latterly, Robert Markus. At Donald's insistence, I then went off to pursue research in Italy, basing myself in two remarkable institutions, the Collegio Ghislieri of the University of Pavia and the British School at Rome. After two years of research in Italy, however, I became aware that I was losing sight of my original interest, the Byzantine dimension, and was fortunate enough to be awarded a junior fellowship at what has justly been described as a scholars' paradise, the Centre for Byzantine Studies at Dumbarton Oaks, Washington, D.C. My thesis and my overall scholarly development benefited enormously from access to its wonderful library and interaction with some brilliant, mostly young, Byzantinists.

After receiving my doctorate, I held a number of teaching posts in Scotland before taking up a research fellowship at the University of Birmingham. Once again I found myself in an extremely stimulating academic environment, with a remarkable array of Western medieval historians balanced by the recently established Centre for Byzantine Studies, headed by its dynamic founder, Anthony Bryer. I then spent two and a half years teaching medieval studies at the Australian National University in Canberra, where the experience of teaching a broad range of medieval subjects to very enthusiastic students gave me a greater understanding of the wider world, and placed my research in context.

Finally I was fortunate enough to return to Edinburgh to take up a lectureship in medieval history in 1980 and I continued to pursue teaching and research in that most agreeable of cities until my retirement in 2016. One of the many reasons I was happy to stay at Edinburgh for so long was the presence of many convivial and supportive colleagues. One in particular, Michael Angold, was rash enough to agree to put on joint courses, and helped maintain and encourage my love for and knowledge of Byzantium. I am delighted to have his typically illuminating contribution to this volume.

The point of this self-indulgent review of my academic journey is to point out how fortunate I have been in many respects. I secured posts in a series of pleasant and stimulating academic environments, and I met friends and colleagues who have encouraged me to develop my interests and ideas. As a result I have tried to make a humble contribution to the promotion of late Roman and early medieval studies, an area of scholarship which we can now in retrospect see to have enjoyed a golden age over the last fifty or so years. This can best be explained by examining some of the concerns that have preoccupied me and the progress that has been made.

Firstly, when I commenced my PhD research historians of early medieval Europe were a rarity both in Britain and the US. In the UK considerable attention was devoted to the Anglo-Saxon and Celtic worlds, but the number of full-time specialists devoted to Western continental Europe was effectively confined to three, Donald Bullough, my own supervisor, at Nottingham, Michael Wallace-Hadrill at Oxford and Walter Ullmann at Cambridge. Today, the situation has radically improved for the better. To take two reflections of this, most leading universities have at least one historian of early medieval Europe and at that great showcase of medieval studies in Britain, the Leeds International Medieval Congress, there are now dozens of lively sessions devoted to early medieval Europe. There are many reasons for this dramatic expansion, but I would like to single out two. One was a *generatio mirabilis* of young scholars who researched and completed their PhD on various European topics in the late 60s and early 70s, largely but not exclusively at Oxford, and partly under the inspiration of Peter Brown. Figures such as Roger Collins, Edward James, Rosamond McKitterick, Jinty Nelson, Chris Wickham and Ian Wood, all produced outstanding work and obtained lecturing posts in UK universities.[4] The work, advice and friendship of these remarkable scholars have been an immense help and inspiration to me over the years. Secondly, there was no specialist periodical devoted to the field in 1970,[5] but now a considerable number include articles on the field, and a prominent and influential role is played by the flourishing journal *Early Medieval Europe.* This I helped found on 28 November 1990 and I was honoured to serve as its coordinating editor for several years.[6]

Another problem in the first half of the twentieth century was a sharp dichotomy in scholarly approaches to ancient and medieval history. Classicists often approached the Late Roman Empire from the perspective of the Roman republic and early empire as a period of political decline and cultural decay, while medievalists preoccupied with legal and administrative history tended to concentrate on the well-documented periods of the central and later Middle Ages and only sallied occasionally into the so-called Dark Ages. However this unhealthy and artificial division has broken down for a number of reasons. There was a belated appreciation of the work of Henri Pirenne, in which he argued that Roman institutions survived long after the traditional period of the empire's "fall", the fifth-century Germanic invasions.[7] At the same time ancient historians paid increased attention to the late antique period and came to see it in more positive terms. The author who achieved most in this regard was of course Peter Brown, who argued especially in his *The World of Late Antiquity* that the late Roman world was one of great creativity, especially in the cultural and religious spheres.[8] There followed an explosion of late antique and early medieval studies, with a trend to see the transition from the ancient to the medieval world in the West in more gradual, smooth and largely peaceful terms.[9] The apogee of this new positive approach was seen in the lavish *Transformation of the Roman World* project involving numerous scholars from various European countries and the US, which was undertaken by the European Science Foundation in the 1990s and 2000s.[10] Although this upbeat approach has had its critics,[11] the ESF project did result in the publication of a large number of scholarly volumes from 1997 onwards, continuing with Brill's present *Series on the Early Middle Ages*, and has undoubtedly stimulated even more work in the field. Another factor has been a broadening of the chronological and geographical boundaries of the field to include Iran and the Arab world as well as Byzantium and the West, and to cover a wide period from the second century to the eighth century and beyond. This approach, which was first advocated in Peter Brown's 1971 volume, has given rise to the widespread use of the concept of "the Long Late Antiquity", a notion particularly suited to Ravenna's high degree of continuity.[12]

Another dichotomy, perhaps less central to the themes of this book, which concerned me and which persisted for decades in early medieval studies, was that between insular and continental history. All too often historians of the Anglo-Saxon and "Celtic" worlds have shown surprisingly little interest in links with mainland Europe or in the closely comparable societies there, and conversely European scholars have paid insufficient attention to comparative approaches with the richly documented societies of the British Isles. To some extent this divide has lessened in recent years and I would like to give credit to the approach taken by various friends, including Eamonn O Carragain, Edward James, Alan Thacker and the late Patrick Wormald.[13] I tried to tackle this issue by launching a group in Edinburgh the 1990s called EMERGE (Early Medieval Europe Research Group) which was aimed at bringing together continental and insular early medievalists by holding seminars and conferences.[14] The close links of the British Isles with the continent, and particularly Rome, are obvious in many spheres, most notably perhaps in pilgrim activities, the careers of archbishops such as Theodore and Wilfrid, and the influence of Mediterranean styles on insular art, especially manuscripts and sculpture. I have hunted diligently throughout my career for analogous examples of ties between North Britain and the Exarchate of Ravenna, but with very limited results. I can however point to a *monasterium Sancti Petri Scottorum* in the area of Forlì, recorded in a lease of 899, a *diaconia S. Maria Scottorum* in an undated lease from before the late tenth century and a monasterium dedicated to *S. Petrus Scottorum* in Ravenna itself recorded in 1049.[15]

Yet another problem for many years was the division between Byzantinists and Western medieval historians. The former maintained a defensive position, isolating themselves from Western developments while the latter displayed little interest in or knowledge of the Eastern Mediterranean. This situation has however radically improved over recent decades, with many Byzantine historians having positions in general History departments and having also to teach Western history, while many Western medievalists have reached out to study and even teach the Byzantine East. Instead of two distinct societies historians tend now to see Eastern and Western Christendom as "sibling" cultures and as distinguished a Byzantinist as Angeliki Laiou could conclude: "some tantalizing patterns of similarity emerge. Most historians today would agree that in some important ways the development of East and West was, indeed, parallel".[16]

Despite this more open and positive outlook, the progress made in the study of relations between East and West has I think been mixed. Some fields have received extensive attention including, not unexpectedly, diplomatic relations,[17] and the issue of ideological rivalry, especially following the creation of a separate Western empire with the coronation of Charlemagne in Rome in 800—the famous *Zweikaiserproblem* of German scholarship.[18] In recent years much of the emphasis has been on economic relations. This subject was of course central to the thesis of Henri Pirenne arguing for a break in Mediterranean unity following the Arab invasions and a supposed collapse of long-distance trade. Pirenne's ideas gave rise to spirited debate for several decades, but by the late twentieth century much of the steam had gone out of the controversy. Early in the present century however two remarkable books appeared, both of which put forward views radically different from those of Pirenne. In *The Corrupting Sea* (2000) Peregrine Horden and Nicholas Purcell argued for local connectivity, i.e., a relatively consistent level of low-level trade throughout Mediterranean history, while Mike McCormick, in his *Origins of the European Economy* (2001), provided abundant evidence for continuing communication throughout the seventh, eighth and ninth centuries and suggested that long-distance trade, handled especially by the Venetians, helped "kick-start" the European economy in the Carolingian period. These were followed by the publication of an equally monumental work on the role of the Mediterranean in the European economy by Chris Wickham in 2005.[19] These works and the reaction they provoked, together with burgeoning archaeological activity in Italy and to a lesser extent the Byzantine and Islamic areas, have resulted in a much fuller and more nuanced picture of the complex economic relations which existed in the Mediterranean throughout the early medieval period.[20]

Other fields of East-West relations have arguably fared less well. For a long time, the Roman populations of Western Europe or of the Eastern Empire failed to attract the detailed study of changing ethnic and cultural identities, of the sort that has produced major insights into the Germanic elites who dominated the post-Roman kingdoms of the West. This imbalance has however shifted with some important recent studies.[21] The sphere of religious relations is more complex. There have been numerous studies of the many conflicts between East and West, but the approach has often been narrowly theological and ecclesiastical.[22] More recently studies of religious controversies such as monophysitism, monotheletism and iconoclasm have pointed to their wider political, cultural and ideological effects, and indeed their contribution to broader tensions and the weakening of a united Christian Oikoumene.[23]

In term of political and cultural relations between the Byzantine world and specific areas of imperial Italy, we have to take a case-by-case approach, not least because local interests and attitudes (*campanilismo*, to use one of my favourite terms) were always strong. But we also have to face a serious historiographical problem: the relative neglect of the Romano-Byzantine element in early medieval Italy. Two exceptional cities, Rome and Venice, have always been accorded attention, because of their exceptional importance in the religious and economic spheres respectively. But for a long time Ravenna and the other cities in the orbit of the eastern empire received scant attention from scholars. The few Byzantinists who turned their gaze westward saw "Byzantine" Italy as a largely Hellenised province where eastern officials and troops were dominant—the line taken in the important, indeed ground-breaking, work of Charles Diehl, published in 1888.[24] Italian scholars, conscious of their country's domination by external powers up to 1860, mostly bought into this view of the imperial territories as "colonial" possessions occupied by a foreign state, and concentrated their attention on the Lombard areas of the peninsula, which were somewhat paradoxically seen as more "Italian".[25] Only gradually has there been a shift away from this portrayal of Ravenna and the Exarchate as an "alien" anomaly and proper emphasis on the area as a distinct but essentially Roman enclave, which had a dynamic character and development of its own.[26]

Gradually however this neglect and misunderstanding has been corrected. If we take the case of Ravenna, for example, the city had, for obvious reasons attracted the interest of first-rate historians of art and architecture, such as Giuseppe Bovini and F.W. Deichmann. Local Italian historians, many from the University of Bologna, made strenuous efforts to give the city the city the historical attention it deserved.[27] Extensive excavations in the area have been undertaken by archaeologists such as Andrea Augenti and Sauro Gelichi, including highly revealing work on the harbour site of Classe.[28] Much of the innovative research on early medieval Ravenna was the subject of two conferences in recent years, a major one held in Ravenna in 2004,[29] and a workshop in London in 2013.[30] To some extent there has been analogous progress in the study of other areas of imperial Italy. To tackle the problem of the political, economic and cultural relations of these areas with Byzantium, and of the related issue of their cities' continuity in terms of institutions, fabric and identity, we have, I think, to act as trufflehunters rather than parachutists, to use the famous distinction made by Emmanuel Le Roy Ladurie.[31]

At this point it is helpful to consider the rich pickings to be found in the present volume. The wide range of places and topics discussed not only cover many of my own interests but also offer case studies of the two key developments which Bryan Ward-Perkins identifies in his masterly introduction—the fluctuations in the power and influence of Byzantium over Italy and the change in imperial cities from a "typically 'Roman' structure" to "a world that was characteristically medieval".

The first section, on sources and historiography, fits in well with my own efforts to explore the wide range of evidence available and base my conclusions solidly on it. Two chapters deal primarily with the Ostrogothic period, a major interest of mine. My friend Cristina La Rocca has kindly offered an interesting chapter that has come out of her important work on Cassiodorus' *Variae*. This demonstrates that a letter often associated with Ravenna in fact refers to Salona in the strategically important province of Dalmatia and reflects an attempt to reinforce the loyalty of the cities to the Ostrogothic regime. A special word has to be said in praise of Brian Croke's excellent study on Procopius' *Gothic War*. I particularly enjoyed this chapter, firstly because it confirms the wonderful evidence which Procopius offers on sixth-century Italy (which historians besotted with the Lombard invasions have tended to ignore), and also because it confirms the remarkable ignorance of Greek *Hochkultur* literature in the Middle Ages even in the areas with close links to Constantinople. Finally it provides a wonderful case study of the reception of Byzantine texts during the Renaissance, including its use by Flavio Biondo, a Romagnol historian greatly admired by my first great teacher Denys Hay, and by myself. In a typically learned investigation another good friend, Roger Collins, uses a little known seventh-century letter collection from Visigothic Spain, which includes royal missives to a Byzantine patrician and to a Lombard king as a source for early medieval diplomacy, another interest of mine. The fourth chapter, by Edoardo Fabbro, reminds us that we cannot study imperial Italy without an awareness of its main external enemy, the Lombards. Here detailed knowledge of Paul the Deacon's *Historia Langobardorum* is used to reconstruct a coherent view of the Byzantines as hostile and unreliable, which was influential both during the history of the Lombard kingdom but also during Charlemagne's campaigns against Benevento.

The second section deals with an area central to Byzantine Italy and to my own research, the Exarchate of Ravenna. It starts with an illuminating chapter on perhaps the most important early exarch of Ravenna, Smaragdus, in which my colleague Jim Crow uses both historical and archaeological evidence to trace his long and active career in both East and West, something that I would have liked to do more fully in *Gentlemen and Officers*. Some of the arguments in the same volume are then, to my relief, confirmed in a wonderfully detailed chapter by Alessandro Bazzocchi, which uses a wealth of epigraphic and archival material to reconstruct the society of Byzantine Ravenna. Another friend who has produced as much good work on Ravenna as any scholar outside Italy, Deborah Mauskopf Deliyannis, then offers a nuanced and interesting chapter which places changing patterns of church building among Ravenna donors in a wider context of early medieval patronage. An old friend from my days at Birmingham, John Haldon, follows with an excellent comparative survey of elites and administration in the Byzantine East, pointing to similar developments and also differences from the better documented Exarchate. Then another close friend, Enrico Cirelli, uses the wealth of archaeological material unearthed in recent years to demonstrate how extensive Ravenna's trade was through the fifth and sixth centuries, and also how this continued on a reduced scale with different commodities during the period of archiepiscopal rule after 751.

That theme leads smoothly into the next section, on Ravenna after the Exarchate, a subject in which I have become increasingly interested. I was very pleased to find Nicole Jantzen-Lopez explore the tangled history of the decades following the end of exarchal rule when first the Lombards and later the popes and Carolingians competed with the archbishops, both for political power and for claims to the ideological inheritance of the empire. We then fast forward to the thirteenth century, when Ravenna remained more of a political and cultural force than is often recognised, as Dante's decision to go into exile there demonstrates. In an informed and closely argued chapter, my long-term colleague and friend Michael Angold shows that Thomas Morisini, Latin patriarch of Constantinople, was not a native of Ravenna as is generally thought and that the famous floor mosaics of San Giovanni Evangelista depicting the Fourth Crusade cannot be used as evidence for this. He may however have had financial dealings with the city.

The fourth section broadens the volume's horizons by considering elite activities in a wider European perspective. Since I have always stressed the role of the church in "Byzantine" Italy, I greatly enjoyed Edward Schoolman's incisive account of the increasing power of bishops over cities, including the remarkable case of Naples, where some bishops bore the title of *dux*, as well as the better-known examples of Rome and Ravenna. Francesco Borri then takes us across the Adriatic to a Byzantine province conquered by the Franks, Istria, and skilfully uses an important document, the *Plea of Rižana* of 804, not just to reconstruct local society, as I attempted to do in *Gentlemen and Officers*, but also to explain the wider context of the Frankish takeover of the peninsula. We then turn to an issue which has modern resonance and as well as being one of my preoccupations, the relations of Eastern immigrants with local communities. My former student Nicholas Matheou traces in fascinating detail the important role of an ethnic group that had already been prominent in earlier Ravenna, the Armenians, in imperial Apulia from the ninth to the eleventh centuries.

The final section concentrates on the institution that, exceptionally for early medieval Europe, remained relatively flourishing and distinctive in

Italy, the city. A friend of many years, Trish Skinner, paints a lively picture of the problems and temptations faced by South Italian bishops as a result of their temporal role in cities, and reminded me how of how valuable (and underused) the extensive corpus of Pope Gregory the Great's letters are as a source for such issues. Ransoming captives was a major episcopal activity, but it is clear from the careful study of Thomas MacMaster that other captives in Italy were unfortunate enough to be sold as slaves, well before the Venetians became prominent as slave traders from the late eighth century on. I find it depressing but perhaps not surprising that some of "my" gentlemen and officers may well have indulged in such a sordid trade. Another good friend, Ross Balzaretti, brings in the cities of Lombard Italy, whose development had both parallels with and differences from those of imperial Italy. His thought-provoking comparative study of Milan and Genoa (a Byzantine city until conquered by Rothari in the 640s) brings out the problems of evidence, the long-term resilience of many Lombard cities such as Milan, and the importance of ties with the hinterland, often overlooked because of an over-emphasis on trade. The section closes on a high note with a brilliant study by one of my dearest friends in Rome, Vera von Falkenhausen, on the southern city of Taranto. There, to a much greater extent than other cities such as Bari, Greek language and culture remained predominant through the period of imperial rule, and persisted as late as the thirteenth century.

Most, but not all, of these chapters grew out of contributions made by friends to two events, a conference held in Edinburgh to mark my (semi-) retirement in May 2015, *Viva La Differenza? Italian Towns in the Early Middle Ages, 500–1100*, and two wonderful sessions at the Leeds International Medieval Congress in July 2016. I would like to record my gratitude to those who organised and participated in these splendid occasions, both of which I found immensely flattering and enjoyable, as well as those who contributed separately. I am particularly pleased by the presence of scholars from diverse backgrounds; as far as I can work out, three continents are represented and every age decade from twenties (Nik Matheou) to eighties (Vera von Falkenhausen). The variety and quality of the contributions clearly demonstrate the vibrant health of scholarship on the areas of Italian history which interest me. I was particularly struck by the solid evidential base on which all the papers are based. Without being narrowly positivistic, I have always been attracted by the sheer weight of sources surviving from Ravenna and other parts of imperial Italy, and I have been concerned sometimes by the unduly speculative or theoretical approaches to some other areas of early medieval history, based on inadequate knowledge of the sources or even on non-existent evidence. There is certainly no room for complacency; some aspects of history, such as gender relations, have so far received surprisingly little attention in studies of imperial Italy,[32] and I worry that a prevailing climate of insularity and narrow anti-intellectual populism, in the UK and elsewhere, may restrict in future the great results which a scholarly and cosmopolitan approach to historical enquiry has achieved over the last half-century. To quote the Jeffersonian warning which one of my favourite historians, Marc Bloch, uttered as a resistance fighter in 1943: "Le peuple qui se sera libéré lui-même et par l'effort commun de tous ne pourra garder sa liberté que par la vigilance continue de tous".[33]

However I have no wish to conclude my survey of chapters which have given me great pleasure on a pessimistic note. Instead I shall end by expressing my gratitude to the editors of this volume, Nik Matheou and Tom MacMaster, both former students of mine. The energy and patience they have displayed in bringing this volume to fruition far outweigh any pedagogical help or encouragement I was ever able to give them as a teacher. I echo the words of the nineteenth-century eccentric Charles Caleb Colton: "No metaphysician ever felt the deficiency of language so much as the grateful".[34]

Notes

1 This is intended as a brief survey of various trends in early medieval historiography, related to my own development as a scholar. There is space only to mention a few of the colleagues, friends and students who inspired, influenced and helped me over five decades. I am delighted that many others have contributed to this volume, but there are more, too numerous to list, whom I wish to thank for their help, inspiration and friendship.

2 "When I want to understand Italian history I catch a train and go to Ravenna". A. Momigliano, "Cassiodorus and Italian Culture of his Time", *Proceedings of the British Academy* 41 (1955), 207–245, reprinted in *Studies in Historiography* (New York 1966), 207.

3 L. MacNeice, "Ravenna" in *Collected Poems* (London, 2002), 527. The poem was written in 1961, three years before Antonioni's film was released.

4 All obtained their doctorates between 1967 and 1976.

5 Note however that *Frühmittelalterliche Studien* was founded in 1967 and *Anglo-Saxon England* in 1972.

6 A date engraved on my memory because it coincided with the resignation of Margaret Thatcher as prime minister, an event which those present considered a good omen.

7 Especially his *Mahomet et Charlemagne*, published posthumously in 1937.

8 P. Brown, *The World of Late Antiquity, AD 150–750* (London, 1971).

9 For a useful survey of this, together with discussion of future challenges and possibilities, see M. Humphries, "Late Antiquity and World History. Challenging Conventional Narratives and Analyses", *Studies in Late Antiquity*, 1 (2017), 8–37.

10 For an early outline of the project, I. Wood, "Report: The European Science Foundation's Programme on the Transformation of the Roman World and Emergence of Early Medieval Europe." *Early Medieval Europe*, 6 (1997), 217–227.

11 Most notably B. Ward-Perkins, *The Fall of Rome and the End of Civilization* (Oxford, 2005).

12 See the discussion in A. Marcone, "A Long Late Antiquity? Considerations on a Controversial Periodization", *Journal of Late Antiquity*, 1, i (2008), 4–19, together with other articles in the *Journal of Late Antiquity*, I, i (2008).

13 Particularly worth singling out is much of the work of I. Wood, and *Britain in the First Millennium*, by another Frankish specialist, E. James.

14 The group eventually had to be wound up for reasons of finance and logistics. Being a very informal group launched before the Internet was common, it has left little in the way of a web footprint. However its final meeting, held in March 2017, was a great success, thanks especially to a splendid paper given by R. Collins.

15 R. Benericetti, ed., *Le carte ravennati dei secoli ottavo e nono* (Faenza, 2006), 152, no. 57; E. Baldaretti and A. Polverari, eds., *Codice Bavaro. Codex Traditionum Ecclesiae Ravennatis* (Ancona, 1983), 69 no. 110; E. Cirelli, *Ravenna. Archeologia di una città* (Borgo S. Lorenzo, 2008), 244, no. 204.

16 D.J. Geanakoplos, *Interaction of the "Sibling" Byzantine and Western Cultures in the Middle Ages and Italian Renaissance, 330–1600* (New Haven, 1976); A. Laiou, "Byzantium and the West", in A. Laiou and H. Maguire, eds., *Byzantium: A World Civilization* (Washington, D.C., 1992), 61–79.

17 Here I must pay tribute to the work of my friend J. Shepard, such as S. Franklin and J. Shepard, eds., *Byzantine Diplomacy: Papers of the Twenty-fourth Spring Symposium of Byzantine Studies, Cambridge March 1990* (Aldershot, 1992), which he co-edited, and his "Trouble-shooters and men-on-the-spot: the emperor's dealings with outsiders", *Settimane di Studio della Fondazione Centro Italiano di Studi sull' alto Medieovo*, lviii (Spoleto, 2011), 691–723. Note T.C. Lounghis, *Les ambassades byzantines en Occident, depuis la fondation des Etats barbares jusqu'aux Croisades (407–1096)* (Athens, 1980) and "East Roman Diplomacy towards Frankish States and relevant medieval theoretical approaches", *Settimane di Studio della Fondazione Centro Italiano di Studi sull' alto Medieovo,* lviii (Spoleto, 2011), 781–799.

18 The subject of a well-known book by W. Ohnsorge, *Das Zweikaiserproblem im früheren Mittelalter* (Hildesheim, 1947).

19 C. Wickham, *Framing the Middle Ages: Europe and the Mediterranean 400–800* (Oxford, 2005); N. Purcell and P. Horden, *The Corrupting Sea: A Study of Mediterranean History* (Oxford, 2000).

20 See the useful survey by another friend, S. T. Loseby, "Post-Roman Economies" in W. Scheidel, ed., *The Cambridge Companion to the Roman Economy* (Cambridge, 2012), 344–360.

21 C. Gantner and W. Pohl, eds., *Visions of Community in the Post-Roman World: The West, Byzantium and the Islamic World, 300–1100* (Aldershot, 2012); W. Pohl and G. Heydemann, eds., *Post-Roman Transitions: Christian and Barbarian Identities in the Early Medieval West* (Turnhout, 2013); I. Stouraitis, "Roman identity in Byzantium: a critical approach", *Byzantinishe Zeitschrift*, 107 (2014), 175–220.

22 A typical but useful study is H. Chadwick, *East and West: The Making of a Rift in the Church: From Apostolic Times until the Council of Florence* (Oxford, 2003).

23 The recent work in this field is too extensive to list here, but I would single out the work of P. Booth, K. Cubitt, M. Jankowiak, R. Price, and, for Iconoclasm, J. Haldon. On the implications for the West (a subject on which I hope to do more work) see the useful pointers in S. Esders, "'Great security prevailed in both East and West' The Merovingian kingdoms and the 6th Ecumenical Council (680/81)" in S. Esders, Y. Fox, Y. Hen, and L. Sarti, eds., *East and West in the Early Middle Ages: The Merovingian kingdoms in Mediterranean perspective* (forthcoming).

24 C. Diehl, *Etudes sur l'administration byzantine de l'Exarchat de Ravenna (568–754)* (Paris, 1888). A broadly similar approach was taken by the equally valuable work of L.M. Hartmann, *Untersuchungen zur Geschichte der byzantinischen Verwaltung in Italien (540–750)* (Leipzig. 1889), published one year later.

25 S. Cosentino, "La percezione dell storia bizantina nella medievistica italiana tra

ottocento e secondo dopoguerra", *Studi Medievali*, s.iii, 39 (1998), 889–909; G. Arnaldi, *Italy and its Invaders* (Cambridge, Mass, 2009), ch. 3.

26 As late as 1969, A. Guillou could portray the Exarchate as a not untypical regional province of the Byzantine Empire: *Régionalisme et indépendance dans l'empire byzantin au VIIe siècle: l'exemple de l'Exarchat et de la Pentapole d'Italie* (Rome, 1969). I attempted to correct this view in my *Gentlemen and Officers, Imperial Administration and Aristocratic Power in Byzantine Italy, 554–800* (London, 1984). Since then the Ecole française de Rome has published a series of informative conferences on *L'héritage byzantin en ltalie*. The most recent of these is J-M. Martin, A. Peters-Custot and V. Prigent, eds., *L'héritage byzantin en ltalie (VIIIe–XIIe siècle). Habitat et structure agraire* (Rome, 2017).

27 In addition to local journals such as *Felix Ravenna* and *Studi Romagnoli* much excellent work appeared in the various volumes of the *Storia di Ravenna* published in the 1990s. Particularly prominent was Augusto Vasina (1929–2016), who was honoured with a *Festschrift* which appeared in 2004: T. Lazzari, L. Macanzoni, and R. Rinaldi, eds., *La norma e la memoria. Studi per Augusto Vasina* (Rome, 2004).

28 See the references in E. Cirelli's paper earlier.

29 Published as *Ravenna da capitale imperiale a capitale* esarcale. 17th Congresso internazionale di studi sull'alto Medioevo (Spoleto, 2006).

30 Published, with numerous additional papers, as J. Herrin and J. Nelson, eds., *Ravenna. Its role in earlier medieval change and exchange* (London, 2016).

31 H. Swift, "The paratrooping truffler", *Times Higher Education,* no. 1353 (October 8th, 1998), 17.

32 There are however promising indications of new work, e.g., M. Betti, "Incestuous marriages in late Carolingian Ravenna", *Early Medieval Europe*, 23 (2015), 457–477.

33 M. Bloch, *Les Cahiers politiques,* organe clandestin du C. G. E. (Comité général d'études de la Résistance), n° 2, juillet 1943, <Réponse d'un historien>. Published in *L'Etrange Defaite* (Paris, 1946), 9.

34 C.C. Colton, *Lacon: or Many things in few words addressed to those who think* (London, 1822), 216. It goes without saying that my heartfelt gratitude also goes to my family, my wife Elizabeth, my son Alexander and my daughter Leonora, and indeed my brother Mike, for putting up with my obsession with Italy and Byzantium over the years and helping to keep me (relatively) sane and sensible.

Tom Brown Bibliography

This does not include book reviews and items published in newspapers and magazines.

1975 1975. *Social Structure and the Hierarchy of Officialdom in Byzantine Italy, 554–800 A.D* (Ph.D. thesis, University of Nottingham)

1975. 'Byzantine Malta: A Discussion of the Sources', in A.T. Luttrell, ed., *Medieval Malta, Studies on Malta before the Knights* (London), pp. 71–87.

1978. 'Cities of Heraclius', (with A. Bryer and D. Winfield), *Byzantine and Modern Greek Studies*, iv, pp. 15–38.

1978. 'Settlement and Military Policy in Byzantine Italy', in H. Blake et al., *Papers in Italian Archaeology, I, The Lancaster Seminar* (BAR Supp. Ser. 41, Oxford), II, pp. 323–338.

1979 1979. 'Imperial Administration and the Church of Ravenna in the Seventh Century', *English Historical Review*, XCIV, pp. 1–28.

1983 1983. 'La Chiesa di Ravenna durante il regno di Giustiniano', *Corso di Cultura sull' Arte Ravennate e Bizantina*, XXX, pp. 266–290.

1984 1984. *Gentlemen and Officers. Aristocratic Society and Imperial Authority in Byzantine Italy, 554–800 A.D.* (British School at Rome, London).

1985. 'Transformation and Continuity in Byzantine Italy: Society and Administration ca. 550–650', in V. Vavřínek, ed., *From Late Rome to Early Byzantium: Proceedings of the Byzantinological Symposium of the 16th Eirene Conference* (Prague), pp. 55–59.

1986 1986. 'Melting-pot or Salad Bowl? Assimilation of Immigrants in the Byzantine Cities of Italy', *17th International Byzantine Congress. Abstracts of Short Papers* (Washington), pp. 46–47.

1986. '*Romanitas* and *Campanilismo*: Agnellus of Ravenna's View of the Past', in C. Holdsworth and P. Wiseman, eds., *The Inheritance of Historiography* (Exeter), pp. 107–114.

1986 1986. 'The Aristocracy of Ravenna from Justinian to Charlemagne', *Corso di Cultura sull' Arte Ravennate e Bizantina*, XXXIII, pp. 135–149.

1986 1986. Published in Italian as 'L'aristocrazia di Ravenna da Giustiniano a Carlo Magno', *Felix Ravenna*, 131/2, pp. 91–98.

1988 1988. 'The Background of Byzantine Relations with Italy', *Byzantium and the West, c. 850–c. 1200. Proceedings of the XVIIIth Spring Symposium of Byzantine Studies* (Amsterdam) (=*Byzantinische Forschungen*, XIII), pp. 27–45.

1988 1988. 'The Interplay between Roman and Byzantine Traditions in the

Exarchate of Ravenna', in *XXXIV Settimana di Studio del Centro Italiano di Studi sull' Alto Medioevo* (Spoleto), pp. 128–167.

1988. 'Transformation of the Roman Mediterranean 400–900 A.D.', in G. Holmes, ed., *The Oxford Illustrated History of Medieval Europe* (Oxford), pp. 1–61.

1989 1989. 'New Introduction and Bibliography to Revised Edition of M. Bloch,' *Feudal Society* (London), pp. xi–xxi and 482–485.

1989. (With N.J. Christie) 'Was There a Byzantine Model of Settlement in Italy?', M*élanges de l'Ecole française de* Rome. *Môyen Age*, 101, pp. 377–399.

1990. 'Louis the Pious and the Papacy: A Ravenna Perspective,' in P. Godman and R. Collins, eds., *Charlemagne's Heir. New Perspectives on the Reign of Louis the Pious (814–840)* (Oxford), pp. 297–307.

1991. 'Ebrei e orientali a Ravenna', in A. Carile, ed., *Storia di Ravenna,* II, pt. i (Ravenna), pp. 135–149.

1991. 'Seven Dictionary Entries (Six Short, One Lengthy [on Ravenna]),' in A. Kazhdan, ed., *The Oxford Dictionary of Byzantium* (Oxford).

1992 1992. 'Editorial' (as Coordinating Editor),' *Early Medieval Europe*, I, pp. 1–2.

1992. 'The Political Use of the Past in Norman Sicily', in P. Magdalino, ed., *The Perception of the Past in the Twelfth Century* (London), pp. 191–210.

1993 1993. 'Ecclesio, santo', in *Dizionario Biografico degli Italiani*, vol. 42 (Rome).

1993 1993. 'Eleutherio (7. Sec.)', in *Dizionario Biografico degli Italiani*, vol. 42 (Rome).

1993 1993. 'Epiphanio, santo', in *Dizionario Biografico degli Italiani*, vol. 42 (Rome).

1993 1993. 'Eutichio', in *Dizionario Biografico degli Italiani*, vol. 42 (Rome).

1993. 'Ethnic Independence and Cultural Deference: The Attitude of the Lombard Principalities to Byzantium c. 876–1077', in V. Vavřínek, ed., *Byzantium and her Neighbours from the mid-9th till the 12th Century* (Prague), pp. 5–12.

1993. 'Everyday Life in Ravenna Under Theoderic: An Example of His 'Tolerance' and 'Prosperity'?', in *Teoderico il Grande e i Goti d'Italia. Atti del XIII Congresso Internazionale di Studi sull'Alto Medioevo*(Spoleto), pp. 77–99.

1993. 'History as Myth: Medieval Perceptions of Venice's Roman and Byzantine Past', in R. Beaton and C. Roueché, eds., *The Making of Byzantine History. Studies Dedicated to Donald M. Nicol* (Aldershot), pp. 145–157.

1994. 'Appunti sui monasteri dell'Italia meridionale: piazzaforti carolingi, emporia, centri culturali ovvero foci di identità etnica', in R. Francoviche, G. Noyé, eds., *La Storia dell' Alto Medioevo Italiano (VI–X secolo) alla luce dell' archeologia* (Florence), pp. 130–133.

1995. 'Byzantine Italy, 680–876'. in R. McKitterick, ed., *New Cambridge Medieval History*, vol. II (Cambridge), pp. 320–349.

1995. 'Justinian II and Ravenna', in R. Dostalova and V. Konzal, eds., *STEPHANOS. Studia Byzantina ac Slavica Vladimiro Vavřínek ad annum sexagesimum quintum dedicata* (Prague), pp. 29–36.

1996. 'Gibbon, Hodgkin and the Invaders of Italy', in R. Quinault and R. McKitterick, eds., *Gibbon and Empire* (Cambridge), pp. 137–161.

1998. 'Urban Violence in Early Medieval Italy: The Cases of Rome and Ravenna', in G. Halsall, ed., *Violence and Society in the Early Medieval West* (Woodbridge), pp. 76–89.

2007. 'The Role of Arianism in Ostrogothic Italy: The Evidence from Ravenna', in S. Barnish and F. Marazzi, eds., *The Ostrogoths from the Migration Period to the Sixth Century An Ethnographic Perspective* (Woodbridge), pp. 417–426.

2008. 'Byzantine Italy, 680–876', in J. Shepard, ed., *The Cambridge History of the Byzantine Empire, c.500–1492* (Cambridge), pp. 433–464 (a revised version of 'Byzantine Italy' cited for 1995).

2009. 'Lombard Religious Policy in the Late Sixth and Seventh Centuries: The Roman Dimension', in G. Ausenda, P. Delogu, and C. Wickham, eds., *The Longobards Before the Frankish Conquest: An Ethnographic Perspective* (Woodbridge), pp. 289–308.

2016. 'Culture and Society in Ottonian Ravenna: Imperial Renewal or New Beginnings?'. in J. Herrin and J.L. Nelson, eds., *Ravenna and its Role in Earlier Medieval Change and Exchange* (London), pp. 335–344.

2020. '680 (?) and All That. A Problematic Turning Point in the History of Early Medieval Italy', in I. Barbera, F. Borri, and A. Pazienza, eds., *I Longobardi a Venezia. Scritti per Stefano Gasparri* (Turnhout), pp. 261–271.

Forthcoming. 'The "Political" Use of Saints in Early Medieval Ravenna', in P. Kershaw and S. DiGregorio, eds., *Cities, Saints and Communities in Early Medieval Europe. Essays in Honour of Alan Thacker* (Turnhout).

Forthcoming. 'A Byzantine Cuckoo in the Frankish Nest? The Exarchate of Ravenna and the Kingdom of Italy in the Long Ninth Century', in C. Gantner, ed., *After Charlemagne. Carolingian Italy and Its Rulers* (Cambridge).

Forthcoming. 'Ravenna: Constantinople of the West?', in S. Tougher and D. Smyth, eds., *Constantinople: Queen of Cities. Festschrift for Paul Magdalino* (Abingdon).

Forthcoming. 'Ravenna and Other Early Rivals of Venice: Comparative Urban and Economic Development in the Upper Adriatic c. 751–1050', in M. Skoblar, ed., *The Adriatic Between Venice and Byzantium c.700–1453*, British School at Athens Studies in Greek Antiquity 2 (Cambridge).

Index

Note: *Italicized* page numbers refer to figures, **bold** page numbers refer to tables